REJECTING RETRIBUTIVISM

Within the criminal justice system, one of the most prominent justifications for legal punishment is retributivism. The retributive justification of legal punishment maintains that wrongdoers are morally responsible for their actions and deserve to be punished in proportion to their wrongdoing. This book argues against retributivism and develops a viable alternative that is both ethically defensible and practical. Introducing six distinct reasons for rejecting retributivism, Gregg D. Caruso contends that it is unclear that agents possess the kind of free will and moral responsibility needed to justify this view of punishment. While a number of alternatives to retributivism exist – including consequentialist deterrence, educational, and communicative theories – they have ethical problems of their own. Moving beyond existing theories, Caruso presents a new non-retributive approach called the public health-quarantine model. In stark contrast to retributivism, the public health-quarantine model provides a more human, holistic, and effective approach to dealing with criminal behavior.

Gregg D. Caruso is Professor of Philosophy at SUNY Corning and Honorary Professor of Philosophy at Macquarie University. He is also the Co-Director of the Justice Without Retribution Network (JWRN) at the University of Aberdeen School of Law. His research interests include free will, agency, and responsibility, as well as philosophy of mind, cognitive science, neuroethics, moral psychology, criminal law, punishment, and public policy. His books include *Just Deserts: Debating Free Will* (with Daniel C. Dennett, 2021), *Free Will and Consciousness: A Determinist Account of the Illusion of Free Will* (2012), *Exploring the Illusion of Free Will and Moral Responsibility* (2013), *Science and Religion: 5 Questions* (2014), *Neuroexistentialism: Meaning, Morals, and Purpose in the Age of Neuroscience* (co-edited with Owen Flanagan), and *Free Will Skepticism in Law and Society* (co-edited with Elizabeth Shaw and Derk Pereboom).

LAW AND THE COGNITIVE SCIENCES

Law and the Cognitive Sciences publishes book monographs exploring connections between law and the cognitive sciences. The books will be of interest to academics, students, and practitioners, and in particular to the scholars in the fields of legal theory, philosophy of law, psychology of law, the theory of law and artificial intelligence, general theory of private and criminal law, and evidence.

General Editors

Bartosz Brozek, *Jagiellonian University*
Jaap Hage, *University of Maastricht*
Francis X. Shen, *University of Minnesota Law School*
Nicole A. Vincent, *University of Technology Sydney*

Rejecting Retributivism

FREE WILL, PUNISHMENT, AND CRIMINAL JUSTICE

GREGG D. CARUSO
State University of New York Corning

CAMBRIDGE
UNIVERSITY PRESS

University Printing House, Cambridge CB2 8BS, United Kingdom

One Liberty Plaza, 20th Floor, New York, NY 10006, USA

477 Williamstown Road, Port Melbourne, VIC 3207, Australia

314–321, 3rd Floor, Plot 3, Splendor Forum, Jasola District Centre, New Delhi – 110025, India

79 Anson Road, #06–04/06, Singapore 079906

Cambridge University Press is part of the University of Cambridge.

It furthers the University's mission by disseminating knowledge in the pursuit of education, learning, and research at the highest international levels of excellence.

www.cambridge.org
Information on this title: www.cambridge.org/9781108484701
DOI: 10.1017/9781108689304

© Gregg D. Caruso 2021

This publication is in copyright. Subject to statutory exception and to the provisions of relevant collective licensing agreements, no reproduction of any part may take place without the written permission of Cambridge University Press.

First published 2021

A catalogue record for this publication is available from the British Library.

Library of Congress Cataloging-in-Publication Data
NAMES: Caruso, Gregg D., author.
TITLE: Rejecting retributivism : free will, punishment, and criminal justice / Gregg D. Caruso, State University of New York Corning Humanities and Social Sciences.
DESCRIPTION: Cambridge, United Kingdom ; New York, NY : Cambridge University Press, 2021. | Series: Law and the cognitive sciences | Includes bibliographical references and index.
IDENTIFIERS: LCCN 2020046886 | ISBN 9781108484701 (hardback) | ISBN 9781108723480 (paperback) | ISBN 9781108689304 (ebook)
SUBJECTS: LCSH: Lex talionis. | Punishment – Philosophy. | Criminal justice, Administration of – Philosophy. | Free will and determinism – Philosophy.
CLASSIFICATION: LCC K5103 .C369 2021 | DDC 345/.077301–dc23
LC record available at https://lccn.loc.gov/2020046886

ISBN 978-1-108-48470-1 Hardback

Cambridge University Press has no responsibility for the persistence or accuracy of URLs for external or third-party internet websites referred to in this publication and does not guarantee that any content on such websites is, or will remain, accurate or appropriate.

In memory of
Louis and Dolores Caruso
For
Elaini and Maya

Contents

Acknowledgments		*page* viii
1	Free Will, Legal Punishment, and Retributivism	1
2	Free Will Skepticism: Hard Incompatibilism and Hard Luck	35
3	The Epistemic Argument against Retributivism	109
4	Additional Reasons for Rejecting Retributivism	128
5	Consequentialist, Educational, and Mixed Theories of Punishment	156
6	The Public Health–Quarantine Model I: A Nonretributive Approach to Criminal Behavior	184
7	The Public Health–Quarantine Model II: The Social Determinants of Health and Criminal Behavior	229
8	The Public Health–Quarantine Model III: Human Dignity, Victims' Rights, Rehabilitation, and Preemptive Incapacitation	270
9	The Public Health–Quarantine Model IV: Funishment, Deterrence, Evidentiary Standards, and Indefinite Detention	297
References		329
Index		384

Acknowledgments

The majority of this book was written during a sabbatical from SUNY Corning at the School of Law at the University of Aberdeen in Scotland during the fall semester of 2019. I would like to thank Elizabeth Shaw and Greg Gordon, as well as members of the law school and philosophy department at the University of Aberdeen, for their warm welcome and for providing me with the support and facilities needed to research and write this book. The book benefited greatly from my numerous conversations with Elizabeth Shaw as well as my head-clearing walks in the Scottish countryside and highlands. I would also like to thank Dan and Joy Shaw, John and Margaret Callender, Nigel Dower, Patricia Clarke, J. R. Cameron, Gerard Hough, Beth Lord, Federico Luzzi, Luca Moretti, Stephan Torre, and Dasha Shapovalova for making my stay in Aberdeen a pleasant one.

Because this book builds on previous work, and because it has been a long time in the making, it has benefited enormously from the feedback and comments of numerous people. While I cannot thank them all here, I am especially indebted to the following people for their valuable input over the years: Derk Pereboom, Bruce Waller, Neil Levy, Farah Focquaert, Elizabeth Shaw, Stephen Morris, Michael Corrado, Benjamin Vilhauer, Saul Smilansky, Manuel Vargas, Robert Kane, John Martin Fischer, Eddy Nahmias, Stephen J. Morse, Sofia Jeppsson, Justin Caouette, Katrina Sifferd, Nicole Vincent, John Lemos, Oisin Deery, Ish Haji, Tom Clarke, Joe Campbell, Grace Campbell, Owen Flanagan, Victor Tadros, Paul Russell, Erin Kelly, Michael McKenna, Gunnar Björnsson, Dana Nelkin, Thomas Nadelhoffer, Marueen Sie, David Shoemaker, Joseph Margulies, Jennifer Chandler, Daniel Dennett, Rob Talisse, Rick Repetti, Bana Bashour, John Callender, Brian Earp, Jim Everett, Azim Shariff, Walter Sinnott-Armstrong, Adrian Raine, Marcus Arvan, Paul Bloom, Taylor Cyr, Patrick Todd, Constantine Sandis, Thomas Douglas, John Tasioulas, Allan McCay, Jeanette Kennett, Richard Menary, Bryce Huebner, Ragina Rini, Kevin Timpe, Matthew Kramer, Chris Surprenant, Christian Coseru, Wesley Buckwalter, Al Mele, Andrei Buckareff, Cory Clarke, Roman Altshuler, Brandon Warmke, Richard Double, David Rosenthal, Rik Peels,

Bob Hartman, Fritz McDonald, Robyn Repko Waller, Justin Capes, Per Milam, Leigh Vicens, Josh Weisberg, Ophelia Deroy, Travis Timmerman, Nomy Arpaly, Mark Balaguer, Michael Brent, Melissa Snater, Marianne McAllister, Andrea Glenn, Mario De Caro, Thom Books, Mich Ciurria, Josh May, Ken Levy, Helen Steward, Tamler Sommers, David Cummiskey, Matt Stichter, Ben Abelson, Paul Davies, Shaun Nichols, Stephen Kershnar, Alan White, Christian List, Barry Smith, Kristin Mickelson, Paul Noordhof, Michael Robinson, Daniel Speak, Philip Swenson, Ryan Lake, Neal Tognazzini, and Craig Agule.

I would also like to thank the audiences at talks at the following colleges for their helpful questions and comments on themes from the book: the University of Oxford, the University of Cambridge, King's College London, the University of Aberdeen, York University, Gothenburg University, Umea University, the University of Sydney, Macquarie University, Ludwig Maximilian University of Munich, Shandong University, Ghent University, the University of Calgary, Cornell University, Coe College, and the University of Edinburgh.

Chapter 2, while primarily new, includes some previous published material drawn from *Free Will and Consciousness: A Determinist Account of the Illusion of Free Will*, Lanham, MD: Lexington Books (2012); "Skepticism about moral responsibility," *Stanford Encyclopedia of Philosophy* (2018); and "A defense of the luck pincer: Why luck (still) undermines free will and moral responsibility," *Journal of Information Ethics* 28(1): 51–72 (2019). Chapter 3 includes material drawn from "Justice without retribution: An epistemic argument against retributive criminal punishment," *Neuroethics* 13(1): 13–28 (2020). Chapter 6 builds on material first introduced in "Free will skepticism and criminal behavior: A public health–quarantine model," *Southwest Philosophical Review* 32(1): 25–48 (2016). Chapter 8 includes some replies that first appeared in "Hard-incompatibilist existentialism: Neuroscience, punishment, and meaning in life" (coauthored with Derk Pereboom) in Gregg D. Caruso and Owen Flanagan (eds.), *Neuroexistentialism: Meaning, Morals, and Purpose in the Age of Neuroscience*, New York: Oxford University Press (2018).

1

Free Will, Legal Punishment, and Retributivism

Within the criminal justice system one of the most prominent justifications for legal punishment, both historically and currently, is *retributivism*. The retributive justification of legal punishment maintains that, absent any excusing conditions, wrongdoers are morally responsible for their actions and *deserve* to be punished in proportion to their wrongdoing. Unlike theories of punishment that aim at deterrence, rehabilitation, or incapacitation, retributivism grounds punishment in the *blameworthiness* and *desert* of offenders. It holds that punishing wrongdoers is intrinsically good. For the retributivist, wrongdoers deserve a punitive response proportional to their wrongdoing, even if their punishment serves no further purpose. This means that the retributivist position is not reducible to consequentialist considerations nor in justifying punishment does it appeal to wider goods such as the safety of society or the moral improvement of those being punished.

The dual aims of this book are to argue against retributivism and to develop and defend a viable nonretributive alternative for addressing criminal behavior that is both ethically defensible and practically workable. In the first half of the book, I argue that there are several powerful reasons for rejecting retributivism, not the least of which is that it is unclear that agents possess the kind of free will and moral responsibility needed to justify it. I also consider a number of alternatives to retributivism, including consequentialist deterrence theories, educational theories, and communicative theories, and argue that they have ethical problems of their own. In the second half of the book, I then develop and defend a novel nonretributive approach, which I call the "public health–quarantine model." The model draws on the public health framework and prioritizes prevention and social justice. I argue that it not only offers a stark contrast to retributivism, it also provides a more human, holistic, and effective approach to dealing with criminal behavior, one that is superior to both retributivism and other leading nonretributive alternatives.

1.1 FREE WILL AND THE CRIMINAL LAW

Since the issue of free will features centrally in the discussion to follow, it is important that I begin by defining what I mean by "free will." I maintain that the variety of free will that has been of central philosophical and practical importance in the historical debate is the sort required for moral responsibility in a particular but pervasive sense. This sense of moral responsibility is typically set apart by the notion of *basic desert* and is defined in terms of the control in action needed for an agent to be truly deserving of blame and praise, punishment and reward. As Derk Pereboom defines it:

> For an agent to be morally responsible for an action in this sense is for it to be hers in such a way that she would deserve to be blamed if she understood that it was morally wrong, and she would deserve to be praised if she understood that it was morally exemplary. The desert at issue here is *basic* in the sense that the agent would deserve to be blamed or praised just because she has performed the action, given an understanding of its moral status, and not, for example, merely by virtue of consequentialist or contractualist considerations. (2014: 2)

Understood this way, free will is a kind of power or ability an agent must possess in order to justify certain kinds of desert-based judgments, attitudes, or treatments – such as resentment, indignation, moral anger, and retributive punishment – in response to decisions or actions that the agent performed or failed to perform. These reactions would be justified on purely backward-looking grounds – that is what makes them *basic* – and would not appeal to consequentialist or forward-looking considerations, such as future protection, future reconciliation, or future moral formation (see Pereboom 2001, 2014; Levy 2011; Caruso and Morris 2017).

There are several distinct advantages to defining free will in this way. First, it provides a neutral definition that virtually all parties can agree to. Unlike some other definitions, it does not beg the question or exclude from the outset various conceptions of free will that are available for disputing parties to adopt. Second, by defining free will in terms of moral responsibility, this definition captures the practical importance of the debate. As Manuel Vargas writes:

> One advantage of making explicit an understanding of free will as linked to responsibility, is that it anchors philosophical concerns in something comparatively concrete and undeniably important to our lives. This is not a sense of free will whose only implication is whether it fits with a given philosopher's particular speculative metaphysics. It is not a sense of free will that is arbitrarily attached to a particular religious framework. Instead, it is a notion of free will that understands its significance in light of the role or function it plays in widespread and recognized forms of life. (2013b: 180)

Third, this definition fits with our everyday understanding of these conceptions. There is, for instance, growing evidence not only that ordinary people view free will and moral responsibility as intimately tied together but also that it is precisely the desire to blame, punish, and uphold moral responsibility that motivates belief in free will (see, e.g., Clark et al. 2014; Shariff et al. 2014; Feldman et al. 2016; Clark et al. 2018; Clark, Winegard, and Baumeister 2019; Everett et al. 2018). People, for instance, attribute more free will to performers of morally bad actions than morally good actions and morally neutral actions (Feldman et al. 2016; Clark et al. 2018; Everett et al. 2018), and pondering over morally bad actions leads people to increase their belief in free will of all humankind (Clark et al. 2014). They also appear to understand responsibility for actions and consequences first and foremost in the sense defined earlier (Cushman 2008). For instance, empirical findings from Shariff et al. (2014) and others support the hypothesis that free will beliefs, at least among ordinary people, positively predict retributive and backward-looking attitudes (see also Carlsmith and Darley 2008).

Lastly, rejecting this understanding of free will makes it difficult to understand the nature of the substantive disputes that are driving the free will debate. It is important, for instance, to distinguish between *consequentialist-based* and *desert-based* approaches to blame and punishment (see, e.g., Caruso and Morris 2017; Morris 2018; Dennett and Caruso 2021). Consequentialist-based approaches are forward-looking in the sense that agents are considered proper targets of reprobation or punishment for immoral actions on the grounds that such treatment will, say, prevent the agent or other agents from performing that type of action in the future. *Desert-based responsibility*, on the other hand, is considered to be backward-looking and retributivist in the sense that any punitive attitudes or treatments that are deemed appropriate responses to moral or legal offenses are warranted simply by virtue of the action/decision itself, irrespective of whatever good or bad results might follow from the punitive responses. By defining free will as the control in action required for basic desert moral responsibility, we are able to make sense of this distinction and sharpen one of the key questions in the free will debate: Do agents have the control in action (i.e., the free will) needed to justify various desert-based judgments, attitudes, or treatments such as resentment, indignation, moral anger, and retributive punishment? Since those who doubt or deny the existence of free will can adopt consequentialist and forward-looking approaches to blame and punishment, this cannot be what the substantive debate is about (see Caruso and Morris 2017). Hence, whatever else the free will debate is about, it must also be about basic desert moral responsibility.

One of the key claims of this book is that the issue of free will is relevant to the criminal law for at least two main reasons. First, the criminal law is founded on the idea that persons can be held morally responsible for their actions because they have freely chosen them. The US Supreme Court, for instance, has asserted:

> A "universal and persistent" foundation stone in our system of law, and particularly in our approach to punishment, sentencing, and incarceration, is the "belief in freedom of the human will and a consequent ability and duty of the normal individual to choose between good and evil."[1]

[1] *United States* v. *Grayson*, 438 U.S. 41 at 52 (1978), quoting *Morissette* v. *United States*, 342 U.S. 246, 250 (1952).

Indeed, the US courts have observed that "[t]he whole presupposition of the criminal law is that most people, most of the time, have free will within broad limits"[2] and that "the law has been guided by a robust common sense which assumes the freedom of the will as a working hypothesis in the solution of its problems."[3] The US Supreme Court, in fact, has gone so far as to suggest that "a deterministic view of human conduct ... is inconsistent with the underlying precepts of our criminal justice system."[4] While this last claim is controversial, since some legal scholars claim that the criminal law only requires compatibilist free will (see Morse 2010, 2013, 2018), one thing is clear: If human beings lack the control in action, that is, the free will, required for basic desert moral responsibility, then our current conception of the criminal law will need to be revised.

As the legal historian Thomas Andrew Green has observed,

> criminal law has been affected by the problem [of free will] at every level: the definition of criminal offenses, the assessment of responsibility, including the practices we have adopted to reach such an assessment; and the way we deal with those found guilty, both in the formal sense of the institutions of punishment or treatment and in the informal sense of social views regarding the guilty (2014: 2–3).

The UK House of Lords has held that "the criminal law generally assumes the existence of free will .... [I]nformed adults of sound mind are treated as autonomous beings able to make their own decisions how they will act."[5] The problem, however, is that the criminal law's appeal to free will is founded more on preference and convenience than fact. As Herbert Packer explains:

> The idea of free will in relation to conduct is not, in the legal system, a statement of fact, but rather a value preference having very little to do with the metaphysics of determinism or free will .... Very simply, the law treats man's conduct as autonomous and willed, not because it is, but because it is desirable to proceed as if it were. (1968: 74–75)

Matthew Jones further writes, "While most areas of law carry free will as a base assumption, criminal law relies on it to an even greater degree because it provides a philosophical basis for individual punishment" (2003: 1035). This brings me to my second point.

Free will is also relevant to the criminal law because of the important role it plays, historically and currently, in one of the most prominent justifications of legal punishment: *retributivism*. The retributive justification of punishment maintains

---

[2] *Smith v. Amontrout*, 865 F.2d 1502, 1506 (8th Cir. 1988).
[3] *Steward Machine Co. v. Davis*, 301 U.S. 548. 590 (1937).
[4] *United States v. Grayson*, 438 U.S. 41 at 52 (1978). See also *Bethea v. United States*, 365 A.2d 64, 83 n.39 (D.C. 1976), which asserts: "[T]he notion that a person's conduct is a simple function of extrinsic forces and circumstances over which he has no control is an unacceptable contradiction of the concept of free will, which is the *sin qua non* of our criminal justice system."
[5] *R v. Kennedy*, No. 2 (2007), A.C. 269, at 275.

that wrongdoers *deserve* the imposition of a penalty solely for the backward-looking reason that they have knowingly done wrong. Michael S. Moore, a leading retributivist, highlights this purely backward-looking nature of retributivist justification when he writes:

> [R]etributivism is the view that we ought to punish offenders because, and only because, they deserve to be punished. Punishment is justified, for a retributivist, solely by the fact that those receiving it deserve it. Punishment may deter future crime, incapacitate dangerous persons, educate citizens in the behaviour required for a civilized society, reinforce social cohesion, prevent vigilante behaviour, make victims of crime feel better, or satisfy the vengeful desires of citizens who are not themselves crime victims. Yet for the retributivist these are a happy surplus that punishment produces and form no part of what makes punishment just: for a retributivist, deserving offenders should be punished even if the punishment produces none of these other, surplus goof effects. (1997: 153; see also 1987, 1993)

This backward-looking focus on desert is a central feature of most pure retributive accounts of punishment (see, e.g., Kant 1790; von Hirsch 1976, 1981, 2007, 2017; Husak 2000; Kershnar 2000, 2001; Berman 2008, 2011, 2013, 2016; Walen 2014).[6] And it is important to emphasize that the desert invoked in retributivism (in the classical or strict sense) is *basic* in the sense that it is not in turn grounded in forward-looking reasons such as securing the safety of society or the moral improvement of criminals. Thus, for the retributivist, the claim that persons are morally responsible for their actions in the *basic desert* sense is crucial to the state's justification for giving them their *just deserts* in the form of punishment for violations of the state's laws. Retributivists typically also hold, in addition, that just punishments must be *proportional to wrongdoing*. Both the justificatory thesis and the proportionality requirement for punishments are reflected in Mitchell Berman's statement of retributivism: "A person who unjustifiably and inexcusably causes or risks harm to others or to significant social interests deserves to suffer for that choice, and he deserves to suffer in proportion to the extent to which his regard or concern for others falls short of what is properly demanded of him" (2008: 269).

In the US criminal justice system, the retributivist justification of legal punishment and the attendant proportionality requirement are widely embraced. In fact, a number of sentencing guidelines in the United States have adopted the retributivist conception of desert as their core principle,[7] and it is increasingly given deference in the "Purposes" section of state criminal codes,[8] where it can be the

---

[6] In Chapter 5, I will examine so-called mixed accounts of punishment, like R. A. Duff's (2001), that combine both forward- and backward-looking features. For the moment, though, I will focus on unmixed or pure retributive accounts.

[7] E.g., 204 Pa. Code Sect. 303.11 (2005); see also (Tonry 2004).

[8] E.g., Cal. Penal Code Sect. 1170(a)(1) (West 1985): "The legislature finds and declares that the purpose of imprisonment for crime is punishment."

guiding principle in the interpretation and application of the code's provisions.[9] Indeed, the American Law Institute recently revised the Model Penal Code so as to set desert as the official dominant principle for sentencing.[10] And courts have identified desert as the guiding principle in a variety of contexts,[11] as with the Supreme Court's enthroning of retributivism as the "primary justification for the death penalty"[12] (Robinson 2008: 145–146). Additional examples can be found in legislation, judicial decisions, sentencing guidelines, and criminal codes in England, Wales, Scotland, Australia, Canada, New Zealand, and Israel (see, e.g., Dingwall 2008; von Hirsch 2017).

For instance, in 2003 the UK Parliament established a Sentencing Guidelines Council consisting of senior judges, legal scholars, and criminologists to provide explicit guidance for sentencing decisions. The following year, the body promulgated an "overarching principle" relying substantially on conceptions of desert (see von Hirsch 2017: fn.9; Sentencing Guideline Council 2004; and Ashworth 2015: Chapter 4). This norm provides that a sentencing court is "required to pass a sentence that is commensurate with the seriousness of the offence," with the offence seriousness to be determined by two main parameters: "the *culpability* of the offender and the *harm* caused or risked being caused by the offence" (2004: s. 1.4; see also von Hirsch 2017: fn.9). Israel also recently adopted a desert-oriented sentencing statue, one that "articulates a retributive guiding philosophy for sentencing and contains a series of provisions related to various aspects of sentencing" (Roberts and Gazal-Ayal 2013: 457). For instance, its Sentencing Act of 2012 stipulates that "[t]he guiding principle in sentencing is proportionality between the seriousness of the offence committed by the offender and the degree of his culpability, and the type and severity of his punishment" (s. 40b). By viewing proportionality to the offender's culpability as the "guiding" principle in criminal sentencing, this provision aligns the statute with sentencing laws in other jurisdictions such as New Zealand and Canada. For example, the Canadian Criminal Code designates proportionality as "the fundamental purpose of sentencing" and states that "[a] sentence must be proportionate to the gravity of the offence and the degree of responsibility of the offender" (2006: s. 718.1). The New Zealand Sentencing Act similarly affirms the importance of proportionality in sentencing (2002: s. 8(a); see also Roberts and Gazal-Ayal 2013: fn.12). And in Australia, one example of judicial attention to the retributive justification of punishment in the context of a sentencing decision can be found in the following comments from Chief Justice Spigelman in a case relating to the torture and murder of a seven-month old child: "[T]he sense of outrage in

---

[9] E.g., Model Penal Code Sect. 1.02(2) (Official Draft 1962).
[10] American Law Institute, Model Penal Code Sect. 1.02(2) adopted May 24, 2017.
[11] See, e.g., the US cases *Spaziano v. Florida*, 468 U.S. 447, 462 (1984); *Gregg v. Georgia*, 428 U.S. 153, 183–184 (1976); Cotton (2000).
[12] *Spaziano v. Florida*, 468 U.S. at 461.

the community in such a case is so strong that the element of retribution must play a prominent part in the exercise of sentencing discretion" (R v. *Hoerler*, 2014, NSWCCA 184).

Consider, for instance, the recent revisions made by the American Law Institute as part of a fifteen-year project to revise the Model Penal Code, first introduced in 1962. The Model Penal Code is one of the most important developments in American law, and perhaps the most important influence on American criminal law. Conceived as a way to standardize and organize the often fragmentary criminal codes enacted by the states, the Model Penal Code has influenced a large majority of states to change their laws. While the Model Penal Code is not law and has no binding effect, it has been the model for many states' criminal codes and has been extremely influential on state and local lawmakers.

The Purposes provision of the revised code, now set in place by the vote of May 24, 2017, states:

§ 1.02(2). **Purposes; Principles of Construction.**
(2) The general purposes of the provisions on sentencing, applicable to all official actors in the sentencing system, are:
  (a) in decisions affecting the sentencing of individual offenders:
    (i) to render sentences in all cases within a range of severity proportionate to the gravity of offenses, the harms done to crimevictims, and the blameworthiness of offenders;
    (ii) when reasonably feasible, to achieve offender rehabilitation, general deterrence, incapacitation of dangerous offenders, restoration of crime victims and communities, and reintegration of offenders into the law-abiding community, provided these goals are pursued within the boundaries of proportionality in subsection (a)(i); and
    (iii) to render sentences no more severe than necessary to achieve the applicable purposes in subsections (a)(i) and (a)(ii).[13]

It is the inclusion of (2)(a)(i) that taints the entire Model Penal Code and sets retributivism as the official dominant principle for sentencing. While (2)(a)(ii) and (2)(a)(iii) are not retributive in nature, they are secondary to the subsection setting the "blameworthiness of offenders" as the primary justification for criminal sentencing. Note, first, that retributivism is to guide sentencing "in all cases," while rehabilitation, deterrence, incapacitation, and restorative justice are only to be pursued "when reasonably feasible." Second, the provision clearly states that (2)(a)(i) trumps (2)(a)(ii) in that the forward-looking, nonretributive approaches cited in (a)(ii) are only to be pursued "within the boundaries of proportionality in

---

[13] The revised Model Penal Code is available at: https://robinainstitute.umn.edu/sites/robinainstitute.umn.edu/files/mpcs_proposed_final_draft.pdf.

subsection (a)(i)." This amounts to saying that retributive proportional punishment cannot be overridden for forward-looking reasons.

The revised Purposes section therefore rests upon the theory of *limited retributivism*, setting a maximum and minimum for all sentencing based upon deontological and retributive principles, and allowing for forward-looking, nonretributive options only "when reasonably feasible" and "within the boundaries of proportionality." This is unfortunate, I contend, for at least two reasons. First, by setting desert as the official dominant principle for sentencing, the Model Penal Code, along with a number of state sentencing guidelines, has assumed that "most people, most of the time, have free will within broad limits." This assumption is highly questionable and has been the subject of one of the greatest debates in the history of philosophy. It should not be taken for granted. In fact, *free will skepticism* takes seriously the possibility that human beings are never morally responsible in the basic desert sense. Some skeptics defend the moderate claim that in any particular case in which we may be tempted to judge that an agent is morally responsible in the basic desert sense, we lack the epistemic warrant to do so (e.g., Rosen 2004). Others go further and deny that free will and basic desert moral responsibility are even possible (e.g., Strawson 1986, 1994). My own view, and the view I defend in the following chapter, is that our best philosophical and scientific theories about the world indicate that what we do and the way we are is ultimately the result of factors beyond our control, and because of this we are never morally responsible for our actions in the basic desert sense.

Setting desert as the official dominant principle for sentencing is unfortunate for a second reason as well. As trial judge Michael H. Marcus writes:

> The revision has essentially abandoned any solution other than guidelines to the problem of un-prioritized sentencing purposes, eschewing responsibility for improvement of the public safety performance of sentencing, and settling for whatever guidelines can bring us to moderate mass incarceration and sentencing disparity. Indeed, it is only by proposing guidelines, sentencing commissions, and related appellate review that the revision has any claim to improvement as compared with the [previous] Model Penal Code. Through the various drafts of the revision, it is apparent that the [American Law Institute] believes that programs and alternatives are appropriate for only a small "layer" of crimes .... Because the revision has yielded all to the continued archaic dominance of just deserts – retributivism however named – and because it evades responsibility for public safety, its only promise is that of guidelines. That promise is anemic indeed. (2007: 74–75)

I agree with Judge Marcus that, independent of worries over free will, the move toward retributivism will likely not reduce crime or increase public safety. Focused as it is on just deserts and the blameworthiness of offenders, it makes no effort at addressing the causal determinants of crime or rehabilitating and reintegrating offenders back into society. On the other hand, the public health approach developed in this book maintains that the criminal justice system should be focused on prevention, rehabilitation, and reintegration. It aims to replace the current *reactive* approach to criminal behavior with a *preventive* approach. I contend that it is indeed unfortunate that the American Law Institute has decided to continue the "archaic dominance" of just deserts and retributivism. When judges and attorneys assume that legal punishment is all (or primarily) about the blameworthiness of offenders and giving them their just deserts, they become blind to the fact that public safety, fairness, and the well-being of society are better served by adopting a more holistic approach focused on prevention, addressing social injustices that give rise to crime, and rehabilitation.

1.2 RETRIBUTIVISM AND PUNISHMENT

Depending on how retributivists view the relationship between desert and punishment, we can identify three different varieties of the view – *weak*, *moderate*, and *strong*.[14] *Weak retributivism* maintains that negative desert, which is what the criminal law is concerned with when it holds wrongdoers accountable,[15] is merely necessary but not sufficient for punishment. That is, weak retributivism maintains that while desert is a necessary condition for punishment, it is not enough on its own to justify punishment – other conditions must also be met. As Alec Walen describes it, weak retributivism is the view that "wrongdoers forfeit their right not to suffer proportional punishment, but that the positive reasons for punishment must appeal to some other goods that punishment achieves, such as deterrence or incapacitation" (2014). Wrongdoing, on this view, is merely a necessary condition for punishment: "The desert of the wrongdoer provides neither a sufficient condition for nor even a positive reason to punish" (Walen 2014; see also Mabbott 1939; Quinton 1954).

Moderate retributivism, on the other hand, maintains that negative desert is necessary and sufficient for punishment but that desert does not mandate punishment or provide an obligation to punish in all circumstances – that is, there may be other goods that outweigh punishing the deserving or giving them their just deserts (Robinson and Cahill 2006). Leo Zaibert, while eschewing the

---

[14] See, e.g., Alexander, Ferzan, and Morse (2009: 7–10), Walen (2014).
[15] *Negative desert* can be contrasted with *positive desert*, which has to do with an agent deserving praise or reward for good actions. It's important to note that there is another conception of "negative desert" that is widespread in the literature. This latter notion refers to the negative component of the retributivist thesis. As Walen examples, "Retributivism ... involves both positive and negative desert claims. The positive desert claim holds that wrongdoers morally deserve punishment for their wrongful acts." On the other hand, "[t]his positive desert claim is complemented by a negative one: Those who have done no wrong may not be punished. This prohibits both punishing those not guilty of wrongdoing (who deserve no punishment), and punishing the guilty more than they deserve (i.e., inflicting disproportional punishment)" (2014, s. 3.1). Having two different notions of negative desert can potentially be confusing, but I will try my best to make clear which conception is at play in different contexts.

taxonomy offered here, defends a kind of moderate retributivism when he argues:

> There are many reasons why sometimes refraining from punishing a deserving wrongdoer is more valuable than punishing him – even if one believes that there is [intrinsic] value in inflicting deserved punishment. Perhaps the most conspicuous cases are those in which the refraining is related to resource-allocation and opportunity costs ... To acknowledge the existence of these cases is not to thereby *deny* the value of deserved punishment: it is simply to recognize that this value, like any value, can be – and often is – lesser than other values. (2018: 20)

Mitchell Berman also defends a form of moderate retributivism, which he calls "modest retributivism" (2016), since he maintains that negative desert grounds a justified reason to punish, but not a duty. For moderate retributivists, negative desert is sufficient to justify punishment but other values and considerations may outweigh inflicting the deserved punishment.

Lastly, *strong retributivism* maintains that desert is necessary and sufficient for punishment but it also grounds a *duty* to punish wrongdoers. Immanuel Kant is perhaps the most famous representative of this latter view, since he famously argued that the death penalty was not only deserved but also obligatory in cases of murder:

> [W]hoever has committed murder, must *die*. There is, in this case, no juridical substitute or surrogate, that can be given or taken for the satisfaction of justice. There is no *Likeness* or proportion between Life, however painful, and Death; and therefore there is no Equality between the crime of Murder and the retaliation of it but what is judicially accomplished by the execution of the Criminal. Even if a civil society resolved to dissolve itself with the consent of all its members – as might be supposed in the case of a people inhabiting an island resolving to separate and scatter themselves throughout the whole world – the last murderer lying in prison ought to be executed before the resolution was carried out. This ought to be done in order that every one may realize the desert of his deeds, and that blood-guiltiness may not remain upon the people; for otherwise they might all be regarded as participators in the murder as a public violation of justice. (1790: Part II: 6)

Of course, not all retributivists support the death penalty – in fact, many contemporary retributivists do not – but here Kant seems to be embodying the strong retributivist view that we are not only justified in giving offenders their just deserts by punishing them, we have a duty to do so. Michael S. Moore also defends a form of strong retributivism and argues, like Kant, that society has a duty to punish culpable offenders:

> We are justified in punishing because and only because offenders deserve it. Moral responsibility ("desert") in such a view is not only necessary for justified punishment, it is also sufficient. Such sufficiency of justification gives society more than merely a right to punish culpable offenders. It does this, making it not unfair to

punish them, but retributivism justifies more than this. For a retributivist, the moral responsibility of an offender also gives society the *duty* to punish. Retributivism, in other words, is truly a theory of justice such that, if it is true, we have an obligation to set up institutions so that retribution is achieved. (1997: 91)

Strong retributivists therefore defend two distinct claims: (1) that negative desert is sufficient to justify punishing wrongdoers on the grounds that they deserve it and (2) that we have a duty to do so. Moderate retributivists, on the other hand, seek only to defend the first claim.

In what follows, I will limit my discussion to moderate and strong varieties of retributivism and leave weak retributivism aside – although I will briefly return to the weak retributivist thesis in Chapter 4. I will do so because, first, most leading retributivists defend one of these stronger forms of retributivism and it is my desire to address the dominant view, not a subordinate view held by few – see, for example, Moore (1997, 1987, 1993), Kershnar (2000, 2001), Husak (2000), Berman (2008, 2011), von Hirsch (1976, 2007, 2017), Alexander (2013), Alexander, Ferzan, and Morse (2009). Second, weak retributivism is considered by many retributivists to be "too weak to guide the criminal law" and as amounting to nothing more than "desert-free consequentialism side constrained by negative desert" (Alexander, Ferzan, and Morse 2009: 7). In fact, some theorists simply define retributivism in a way that excludes *weak retributivism* from consideration altogether. David Boonin, for example, defines retributivism as the claim that "committing an offense in the past is *sufficient* to justify punishment now, whether or not this will produce any beneficial consequences in the future" (2008: 86; emphasis added). Retributivist Mitchell Berman maintains that the "core retributivist thesis" is that

> [t]he goodness or rightness of satisfying a wrongdoer's negative desert morally justifies [i.e., is sufficient for] the infliction of criminal punishment, without regard for any further good consequences that might be realized as a contingent result of satisfying the wrongdoer's desert. (2016)

And Alec Walen in his *Stanford Encyclopedia of Philosophy* entry on "Retributive Justice" (2014) defines retributivism as committed to the following three principles: (1) that those who commit certain kinds of wrongful acts, paradigmatically serious crimes, morally deserve a proportionate punishment; (2) that it is intrinsically morally good – good without reference to any other goods that might arise – if some legitimate punisher gives them the punishment they deserve; and (3) that it is morally impermissible to intentionally punish the innocent or to inflict disproportionately large punishments on wrongdoers.

Lastly, the weight the criminal law gives desert and the way retributivism is practically implemented in the law (especially in the United States) indicate that the desert of offenders is typically seen as sufficient for punishment. The revised Model Penal Code makes this point rather clear. For these reasons, I will take as my target the claim that the desert of offenders provides sufficient grounds for punishment and that we are therefore justified in sometimes punishing wrongdoers for no purpose other than to see the guilty get what they deserve. Since this core claim is held in common among all moderate and strong varieties of retributivism, I will henceforth drop the moderate/strong distinction and focus instead on this shared feature.

I will also be limiting my investigation to the question of *legal punishment*. Punishment, we can say, is the intentional imposition of an unpleasant penalty or deprivation for perceived wrongdoing upon a group or individual, typically meted out by an authority. Everyday examples include a parent taking away their teenager's cellphone privileges for a week for bad behavior and a university expelling a student for plagiarism. Legal punishment is a specific sort of punishment; it is the intentional imposition of a penalty for conduct that is represented, either truly or falsely, as a violation of a law of the state, where the imposition of that penalty is sanctioned by the state's authority. More precisely, we can say that

> *[l]egal punishment* consists in one person's deliberately harming another on behalf of the state in a way that is intended to constitute a fitting response to some offense and to give expression to the state's disapproval of that offense. (Zimmerman 2011; see also Boonin 2008; Walen 2014)

This is Michael Zimmerman's (2011) definition and it is the one I will adopt herein since I think it best captures the key features of legal punishment. According to this definition, Person A legally punishes Person B if and only if A acts on behalf of the state in such a way that (1) he harms the punishee – this could include imposing an unpleasant penalty or deprivation; (2) this harm is *intended* by the state; (3) this harm is believed by the state to be *fitting* – in particular, fitting to the fact, perhaps in conjunction with some other facts, that the punishee is associated with some legal offense; (4) he thereby expresses the state's disapproval both of the offense and of the offender; and (5) he thereby acts in some legal official capacity (see Zimmerman 2011: 20). Note that the first three conditions set out what we may call the core requirements of punishment: intended harm that is (believed to be) fitting. The latter two conditions are unique to the legal context – that is, legal punishment is distinct from interpersonal punishment or punishment carried out by an angry mob since it is sanctioned by the state, expresses the state's disapproval, and is guided by a system of criminal laws concerned with punishment of individuals who are believed to have committed crimes.

It is important to stress that *intended harm* is a necessary condition of punishment. As Leo Zaibert correctly notes, "[W]hatever else punishment seeks to do, it seeks to make wrongdoers suffer (by somehow diminishing their well-being or by visiting upon them something they do not want)" (2018: 1). He goes on to write:

> To punish ... is to (try to) inflict suffering (or pain or misery or a bad thing, etc.) on someone as a response to her wrongdoing. Punishment without trying to inflict suffering is like gifting an object without intending to transfer any right over the thing gifted or like feeding someone without intending to give her some nourishment. (Zaibert 2018: 7)

The renowned legal philosopher H. L. A. Hart stresses this point in his definition of punishment, which he maintains "must involve pain or other consequences normally considered unpleasant" (2008: 4). Wittgenstein concurs, finding it perfectly "clear," that just as "reward must be something pleasant," punishment must be "something unpleasant" (1961: 78e; see also Tasioulas 2006; Boonin 2008; Zimmerman 2011; Zaibert 2018). The kind of harm, suffering, or harsh treatment meted out by the state in cases of legal punishment need not involve physical pain, but it must be unpleasant or diminish (at least temporarily) the well-being of offenders.

It must also be the case that the state (or someone acting on its behalf) deliberately intends the harm, since unintended harms do not constitute punishment. If I trip and knock over an elderly person, causing them harm, I do not thereby punish them. Punishment requires *intentional* harm. As Walen writes:

> For an act to count as punishment, it must ... [f]irst ... impose some sort of cost or hardship on, or at the very least withdraw a benefit that would otherwise be enjoyed by, the person being punished. Second, the punisher must do so intentionally, not as an accident, and not as a side-effect of pursuing some other end. (2014, s. 2.1)

Zimmerman concurs with this second requirement and writes, "[N]o accidental harming can qualify as punishment; if you punish someone, then the harm that you cause is something that you intended to cause" (2011: 7–8). He goes on to argue:

> This being the case, it might be thought that, although no accidental harm counts as punishment, perhaps the harm that punishment involves needn't be intended either, as long as it is foreseen. But I think that a little reflection shows that that can't be right. We often knowingly cause harm without intending to do so. Indeed, the harm that we knowingly cause might be just the same kind of harm as that caused by punishment but, unless we intend to cause it, we cannot be said to be engaged in punishment. Compare incarceration with quarantine, for example. The extent to which one's liberty is restricted may be the same in either case, but only the former qualifies as punishment, for only in the former case is the harm caused by the restriction to liberty intended. In the latter case, the harm is foreseen but it is not intended – although the restriction itself is of course intended, for otherwise it could not be classified as a case of quarantine at all. (2011: 9–10)

The comparison between punishment and quarantine will play an important role in the discussion to follow, but Zimmerman is absolutely correct that quarantine is not a form of punishment since it does not intentionally seek to cause harm. Punishment, on the other hand, requires that the harms caused be intended.

The question under discussion in this book, then, is whether *retributive legal punishment* is ever justified. That is, does retributivism as a theory of legal punishment withstand scrutiny? In particular, is state-sanctioned intentional imposition of harms (e.g., penalties and sanctions) for violating the state's laws ever basically deserved?

One reason to think that no human agents ever basically deserve legal punishment, as retributivism presupposes, is that we lack the control in action, that is, the free will, required for moral responsibility in the *basic desert* sense. Free will skeptics maintain that since what we do and the way we are is ultimately the result of factors beyond our control, we are never morally responsible for our actions in the basic desert sense. Free will skepticism therefore presents a serious challenge to retributivism: If we never basically deserve blame just because we have knowingly done wrong, neither do we ever basically deserve punishment just because we have knowingly done wrong. And this would remain true whether or not the criminal law assumes libertarian free will, since free will skepticism also denies that compatibilism preserves the kind of free will and moral responsibility needed to justify retributive legal punishment.

Free will skepticism, one might object, allows for non-basically deserved blaming and praising – for example, blaming that invokes desert grounded in consequentialist (e.g., Daniel Dennett 1984; Manuel Vargas 2013a) or contractualist (e.g., Ben Vilhauer 2013a, 2013b) considerations. For instance, according to one type of *revisionary* account, our practice of holding agents morally responsible in a desert sense should be retained, not because we are in fact morally responsible in this sense, but because doing so would have the best consequences relative to alternative practices. Daniel Dennett (1984) advocates a version of this position, as does Manuel Vargas (2013a). But punishment justified in this way would not be genuinely retributivist, since its ultimate justification would be consequentialist, and this is incompatible with retributivism as it has traditionally been understood. Dennett, himself, admits as much in my recent debate with him in *Just Deserts: Debating Free Will* (Dennett and Caruso 2021), where he makes clear that his consequentialist defense of the "system of desert" rejects retributivism. Furthermore, it is unclear that retributivism actually has the consequentialist value some think – this too is an assumption I will challenge in subsequent chapters.

My own reasons for favoring free will skepticism will be spelled out in detail in the following chapter. As we will see, they feature distinct arguments that target three rival views, *event-causal libertarianism*, *agent-causal libertarianism*, and *compatibilism*, and then claim that the skeptical position is the only defensible position that remains standing.[16] I maintain that the sort of free will required for basic desert moral responsibility is incompatible with both causal determination by factors

---

[16] See Chapter 2 for definitions. But in short, *libertarian* theories of free will reject the thesis of causal determinism and defend an indeterminist conception of free will in order to save what they maintain are necessary conditions for free will – the *ability to do otherwise* in exactly the same set of conditions

beyond the agent's control and with the kind of indeterminacy in action required by the most plausible versions of libertarianism. For this reason, I follow Pereboom in labeling my view *hard incompatibilism*, since it maintains that free will is incompatible with both determinism and indeterminism (Pereboom 2001, 2014; Pereboom and Caruso 2018). I also present a second, independent argument for skepticism that maintains that regardless of the causal structure of the universe, free will and basic desert moral responsibility are incompatible with the pervasiveness of *luck*. This argument is intended not only as an objection to event-causal libertarianism but extends to compatibilism as well. At the heart of the argument is the following dilemma, which Neil Levy (2011) calls the *luck pincer*: Either actions are subject to *present luck* (luck around the time of action), or they are subject to *constitutive luck* (luck in who one is and what character traits and predispositions one has), or both. Either way, luck undermines moral responsibility since it undermines responsibility-level control.

But even if one is not convinced by the arguments against the sort of free will required for basic desert, I argue that there remains a second strong *Epistemic Argument* against causing harm on retributivist grounds that is sufficient for the rejection of retributive legal punishment. This is because the burden of proof lies on those who want to intentionally inflict harm on others to provide good justification for such harm (see Vilhauer 2009a, 2012, 2015; Shaw 2014; Corrado 2017; Caruso 2020). This means that retributivists who want to justify legal punishment on the assumption that agents are free and moral responsible (and hence *justly deserve* to suffer for the wrongs they have done) must justify that assumption in a way that meets a high epistemic standard of proof since the harms caused in the case of legal punishment are often quite severe. It is not enough to simply point to the mere possibility that agents possess libertarian or compatibilist free will. Nor is it enough to say that the skeptical arguments against free will and basic desert moral responsibility fail to be conclusive. Rather, a positive and convincing case must be made that agents are in fact morally responsible in the basic desert sense, since it is the backward-looking desert of agents that retributivists take to justify the harm caused by legal punishment. This Epistemic Argument against retributive legal punishment is developed and defended in Chapter 3, but I can briefly summarize it here as follows:[17]

---

and/or the idea that we remain, in some important sense, the *ultimate source/originator* of action. *Compatibilism*, on the other hand, defends a conception of free will that aims to reconcile free will with causal determinism – the thesis that every event or action, including human action, is the inevitable result of antecedent circumstances in accordance with the laws of nature.

[17] The basic idea behind the Epistemic Argument was first introduced by Pereboom in *Living Without Free Will* (2001: 161). Benjamin Vilhauer then developed the argument in detail in a series of papers (2009a, 2012, 2015). I presented my own version of it in Caruso (2020). Others who have also defended versions of the Epistemic Argument include Double (2002), Shaw (2014), Corrado (2017), and Jeppsson (2020).

(1) Legal punishment intentionally inflicts harms on individuals and the justification for such harms must meet a high epistemic standard. If it is significantly probable that one's justification for harming another is unsound, then, prima facie, that behavior is seriously wrong.
(2) The retributivist justification for legal punishment assumes that agents are morally responsible in the basic desert sense and hence justly deserve to suffer for the wrongs they have done in a backward-looking, non-consequentialist sense (appropriately qualified and under the constraint of proportionality).
(3) If the justification for the assumption that agents are morally responsible in the basic desert sense and hence justly deserve to suffer for the wrongs they have done does not meet the high epistemic standard specified in (1), then retributive legal punishment is prima facie seriously wrong.
(4) The justification for the claim that agents are morally responsible in the basic desert sense provided by both libertarians and compatibilists faces powerful and unresolved objections and as a result falls far short of the high epistemic bar needed to justify such harms.
(5) Hence, retributive legal punishment is unjustified and the harms it causes are prima facie seriously wrong.

In developing the Epistemic Argument, I examine the leading extant accounts of basic desert moral responsibility and argue that they all fail to satisfy the high epistemic standard needed to justify retributive legal punishment – a standard, I contend, that is both reasonable and defensible. I therefore conclude that the Epistemic Argument provides sufficient reason for rejecting retributivism.

In addition to free will skepticism and the Epistemic Argument, I also provide several additional arguments against retributivism in Chapter 4. First, I argue that, even if the requisite capacity for control is in place and basic desert could be secured, there are good pragmatic reasons for rejecting retributivism. This is because retributive justice has "limited effectiveness in promoting important social goals such as rehabilitation and reforming offenders" (Shaw 2019a). Second, I argue that it is philosophically problematic to impart to the state the function of intentionally harming wrongdoers in accordance with desert since it is not at all clear that the state is capable of properly tracking the desert and blameworthiness of individuals in any reliable way. This is because criminal law is not properly designed to account for all the various factors that affect blameworthiness, and as a result the moral criteria of blameworthiness is often misaligned with the legal criteria of guilt (Kelly 2018). While a retributivist could argue that this second objection is more indicative of our broken criminal justice system, not retributivism per se, I argue that there are in principle reasons to doubt that the criminal justice system could ever properly align the legal criteria of guilt with the moral criteria of blameworthiness.

This is because, third, for the state to be able to justly distribute legal punishment in accordance with desert, it needs to be in the proper epistemic position to know what an agent basically deserves, but since the state is (almost) never in the proper epistemic position to know what an agent basically deserves, it follows that the state is not able to justly distribute legal punishment in accordance with desert. In Chapter 4, I label this the *Poor Epistemic Position Argument* (or PEPA) so as to distinguish it from the Epistemic Argument outlined earlier. I argue that it is practically impossible for the state to punish in accordance with desert, *without this leading to injustice*, since, due to the state's epistemic limitations, some people will inevitably end up getting more punishment than they deserve (and some less) judged on the retributivists own grounds. Lastly, I argue that even if retributivism could overcome all these various difficulties, there remains the additional problem that how the state goes about judging the gravity of wrong done, on the one hand, and what counts as proportional punishment for that wrong, on the other, is wide open to subjective and cultural biases and prejudices, and as a result, the principle of proportionality in *actual practice* does not provide the kind of protections against abuse it promises.

In the end, I conclude that there are at least six powerful reasons for rejecting retributivism: (1) the truth of free will skepticism (or what we can call the *Skeptical Argument*); (2) the *Epistemic Argument*; (3) the *Limited Effectiveness Argument* – that is, practical concerns over the limited effectiveness of retributive justice in promoting important social goals; (4) the *Misalignment Argument*, which argues that the criminal law is not properly designed to account for all the various factors that affect blameworthiness, and as a result the moral criteria of blameworthiness is often misaligned with the legal criteria of guilt; (5) the *Poor Epistemic Position Argument* (or PEPA); and (6) the *Indeterminacy in Judgment Argument*, which argues that judgments of gravity and proportionality are indeterminate, ambiguous, and too easily influenced by cultural biases and prejudices to guarantee respect for persons and prevent cruel and inhumane punishment.

Consider, for instance, the fact that the US criminal justice system widely embraces the retributivist justification of legal punishment and the proportionality requirement, yet this has not prevented the mass incarceration of its citizens nor has it been sufficient to protect against disproportionate punishment. While I am not suggesting that these problems are due solely to retributivism – since there is good reason to think that "three strikes" laws, mandatory minimums, and other policies responsible for mass incarceration were also motivated by the desire for deterrence[18] – my point is simply that commitment to limited retributivism has not *prevented* these abuses. As witnessed by the codes, provisions, and rulings cited earlier, it is clear that the retributivist justification of legal punishment and the attendant proportionality requirement are widely embraced in the United States (see fns.5–10). Yet, with only 4.5 percent of the world's population, the United States imprisons 25 percent of the world's prisoners – far more than any other nation in the world.

---

[18] This is partly why I also reject consequentialist deterrence theories of punishment (see Chapter 5).

The US imprisons roughly 700 prisoners for every 100,000 people,[19] whereas Scandinavian countries such as Sweden, Finland, and Norway hover around 60 per 100,000.[20] And not only does the United States imprison at a much higher rate, it also imprisons in notoriously harsh conditions.

American prisons are often cruel places, using a number of harsh forms of punishment including extended solitary confinement. The watchdog organization Solitary Watch estimates that 80,000 to 100,000 people in the United States are currently in some form of solitary confinement.[21] These prisoners are isolated in windowless, soundproof cubicles for 23 to 24 hours each day, sometimes for decades. Such excessively punitive punishment not only causes severe suffering and serious psychological problems, it does nothing to rehabilitate prisoners nor does it reduce the rate of recidivism. In fact, the United States has one of the highest rates of recidivism in the world, with a recent report by the Bureau of Justice Statistics (2018) finding an estimated 68 percent of released prisoners being rearrested within three years of release, 79 percent within six years, and 83 percent within nine years.[22] Norway, by contrast, has the world's lowest recidivism rate at 20 percent (Kristoffersen 2010; Encartele Inc. 2018). One of the big differences is that the Norwegian systems aim at rehabilitation and reintegration and prepare inmates for life after incarceration by providing them with educational opportunities and work training. It also encourages guards to cultivate friendships with the inmates, for inmates to interact with each other, and for inmates to exercise maximal autonomy. Treating inmates humanely helps them develop the interpersonal skills needed to successfully reintegrate back into society. US prisons, on the other hand, tend to isolate inmates and control every aspect of their lives – for example, when they eat and sleep, what they do, where they go, etc. This can instill a kind of learned helplessness that makes it extremely difficult for individuals to readjust to life on the outside.

Sentences in the United States also tend to be more punitive than other countries. Even controlling for crime rates and population size, the United States hands down longer sentences, spends more money on prisons, and executes more of its citizens than every other advanced industrial democracy (Farrell and Clark 2004; Blumstein, Tonry, and Van Ness 2005; Enns 2006: 3; Cowen 2010; Amnesty International 2012). A combination of three strikes laws and other legislation has also led to a disproportionate number of US prisoners serving life without the chance of parole.

[19] According to the Prison Policy Initiative, in 2018 the number was 698 per 100,000 (see: www.prisonpolicy.org/global/2018.html).
[20] According to the latest numbers, Norway imprisons 63 per 100,000, Sweden 59, Finland 51, and Denmark 63. See International Centre for Prison Studies, "World Prison Brief": www.prisonstudies.org/sites/default/files/resources/downloads/wppl_12.pdf.
[21] See also the Vera Institute report on "Solitary Confinement: Common Misconceptions and Emerging Safe Alternative" (2015). Available at: www.vera.org/downloads/publications/solitary-confinement-misconceptions-safe-alternatives-report_1.pdf.
[22] The report is available here: www.bjs.gov/content/pub/pdf/18upr9yfup0514.pdf.

In fact, the proportion of individuals serving life without parole in the United States is approximately 180 *times* greater than England (Enns 2016: 3). A recent report by the Sentencing Project (2017) found that there were 161,957 people serving life sentences, or one of every nine people in prison. An additional 44,311 individuals are serving "virtual life" sentence, yielding a total population of life and virtual life sentences at 206,268 – or one of every seven people in prison. The pool of people serving life sentences has more than quadrupled since 1984. Furthermore, nearly half (48.3 percent) of life and virtual life-sentenced individuals are African American, equal to one in five black prisoners overall. More than 17,000 individuals with life without parole or virtual life sentences have been convicted of nonviolent crimes. The United States incarcerates people for life at a rate of 50 per 100,000, roughly equivalent to the entire incarceration rates of the Scandinavian nations of Denmark, Finland, and Sweden (The Sentencing Project 2017).

Of course, there are many reasonable retributivists who acknowledge that we imprison far too many people, in far too harsh conditions. The problem, however, is that retributivism remains committed to the core belief that criminals *deserve* to be punished and suffer for the harms they have caused. This retributive impulse in *actual practice* (rather than in pure theory) often leads to practices and policies that try to make life in prison as unpleasant as possible. It also fuels the desire to continue to punish individuals even after they have been released. Consider voter disenfranchisement. In the 2016 US Presidential election, an estimated 6.1 million Americans were barred from participating due to felony convictions, with an estimated 3.1 million of those disenfranchised due to state laws that restrict voting rights even after the completion of sentences. Such voter disenfranchisement policies can only be justified on the assumption (correct or not) that it is *deserved*, since denying the vote to ex-offenders accomplishes little of forward-looking value. As Supreme Court Justice Thurgood Marshall so eloquently put it:

> It is doubtful ... whether the state can demonstrate either a compelling or rational policy interest in denying former felons the right to vote. [Ex-offenders] have fully paid their debt to society. They are as much affected by the actions of government as any other citizen, and have as much of a right to participate in government decision-making. Furthermore, the denial of a right to vote to such persons is a hindrance to the efforts of society to rehabilitate former felons and covert them into law-abiding and productive citizens.[23]

Since retributivists care little about rehabilitation and other forward-looking goods, the only rationale they need appeal to is giving wrongdoers their just deserts.[24]

---

[23] *Richardson v. Ramirez*, 418 U.S. at 78; Marshall J. dissenting

[24] Other potential policy interests defenders of voter disenfranchisement can point to include: (1) protecting against voter fraud or other election offenses, (2) prevention of harmful changes to the law, and (3) protection of the "purity" of the ballot box. But there are severe problems with each of these putative interests (see Human Rights Watch, Sentencing Project: www.hrw.org/legacy/reports98/vote/usvot980-03.htm).

Unfortunately, this desire for retribution, in actual practice, often overrides any theoretical commitments to proportionality and respecting human dignity.

1.3 THE PUBLIC HEALTH–QUARANTINE MODEL

If we reject retributivism, either because we come to doubt or deny the existence of free will or for other reasons, what are we left with? Many worry that without the justification of retributivism and the putative protection afforded by the principle of proportionality, we would be unable to successfully deal with criminal behavior. But traditionally, in addition to pure retributivism there have been a number of other common justifications of legal punishment, including consequentialist deterrence theories, moral education theories, and a variety of expressive, communicative, and mixed theories of punishment. While I will argue in Chapter 5 that these other approaches face significant moral concerns of their own – or, in the case of mixed theories, retain certain retributive components that are unjustified – the second half of the book will develop and defend what I contend is an ethically defensible and practically workable alternative to retributive legal punishment, one that is consistent with free will skepticism and preferable to these other nonretributive alternatives. I call it the *public health–quarantine model*. As we will see, the model not only provides a justification for the incapacitation of dangerous criminals consistent with free will skepticism, it also provides a broader and more comprehensive approach to criminal behavior generally since it draws on the public health framework and prioritizes prevention and social justice.

The core idea of the model is that the right to harm in self-defense and defense of others justifies incapacitating the criminally dangerous with the minimum harm required for adequate protection. Yet the model does not justify the sort of criminal punishment whose legitimacy is most dubious, such as death or confinement in the most common kinds of prisons in our society. In fact, the model is completely nonpunitive since it does not satisfy the definition of punishment introduced earlier. It also requires special attention to the well-being and dignity of criminals that would change much of current policy. Perhaps most importantly, the model also develops a public health approach that prioritizes prevention and social justice and aims at identifying and taking action on the social determinants of health and criminal behavior (see Chapters 6–8).

The model begins with Derk Pereboom's quarantine analogy, which draws on a comparison between treatment of dangerous criminals and treatment of carriers of dangerous diseases (see Pereboom 2001, 2013, 2014; Caruso 2016, 2017; Pereboom and Caruso 2018; Caruso and Pereboom 2020). In its simplest form, it can be stated as follows: (1) Free will skepticism maintains that criminals are not morally responsible for their actions in the basic desert sense; (2) plainly, many carriers of dangerous diseases are not responsible in this or in any other sense for having contracted these diseases; (3) yet we generally agree that it is sometimes permissible to quarantine them, and the justification for doing so is the right to self-protection and the prevention of harm to others; (4) for similar reasons, even if a dangerous criminal is not morally responsible for his crimes in the basic desert sense (perhaps because no one is ever in this way morally responsible) it could be as legitimate to preventatively detain him as to quarantine the nonresponsible carrier of a serious communicable disease (see Pereboom 2001, 2014).

The first thing to note about the theory is that although one might justify quarantine (in the case of disease) and incapacitation (in the case of dangerous criminals) on purely utilitarian or consequentialist grounds, Pereboom and I resist this strategy (see Pereboom and Caruso 2018; Caruso and Pereboom 2020). Instead, we maintain that incapacitation of the seriously dangerous is justified on the ground of the right to harm in self-defense and defense of others. That we have this right has broad appeal, much broader than utilitarianism or consequentialism has. In addition, this makes the view more resilient to a number of objections and provides a more resilient proposal for justifying criminal sanctions than other nonretributive options (see, e.g., Pereboom and Caruso 2018). One advantage it has, say, over consequentialist deterrence theories is that it has more restrictions placed on it with regard to using people merely as a means. For instance, as it is illegitimate to treat carriers of a disease more harmfully than is necessary to neutralize the danger they pose, treating those with violent criminal tendencies more harshly than is required to protect society will be illegitimate as well. In fact, the model requires that we adopt the *principle of least infringement*, which holds that the least restrictive measures should be taken to protect public health and safety. This ensures that criminal sanctions will be proportionate to the danger posed by an individual, and any sanctions that exceed this upper bound will be unjustified.

Second, the quarantine model places several constraints on the treatment of criminals (Pereboom 2001, 2014). First, as less dangerous diseases justify only preventative measures less restrictive than quarantine, so less dangerous criminal tendencies justify only more moderate restraints (Pereboom 2014: 156). We do not, for instance, quarantine people for the common cold even though it has the potential to cause you some harm. Rather, we restrict the use of quarantine to a narrowly prescribed set of cases. Analogously, on this model the use of incapacitation should be limited to only those cases where offenders are a serious threat to public safety and no less restrictive measures were available. In fact, for certain minor crimes perhaps only some degree of monitoring could be defended. Secondly, the incapacitation account that results from this analogy demands a degree of concern for the rehabilitation and well-being of the criminal that would alter much of current practice. Just as fairness recommends that we seek to cure the diseased we quarantine, so fairness would counsel that we attempt to rehabilitate the criminals we detain (Pereboom 2014: 156). Rehabilitation and reintegration would therefore replace punishment as the focus of the criminal justice system. Lastly, if a criminal cannot be rehabilitated and our safety requires his indefinite confinement, this account provides no justification for making his life more miserable than would be required to guard against the danger he poses (Pereboom 2014: 156).

In addition to these restrictions on harsh and unnecessary treatment, the model also advocates for a broader approach to criminal behavior that moves beyond the narrow focus on sanctions. As we will see, I situate the quarantine analogy within the broader justificatory framework of *public health ethics*. Public health ethics not only justifies quarantining carriers of infectious diseases on the grounds that it is necessary to protect public health, it also requires that we take active steps to *prevent* such outbreaks from occurring in the first place. Quarantine is only needed when the public health system fails in its primary function. Since no system is perfect, quarantine will likely be needed for the foreseeable future, but it should *not* be the primary means of dealing with public health. The analogous claim holds for incapacitation. Taking a public health approach to criminal behavior would allow us to justify the incapacitation of dangerous criminals when needed, but it would also make prevention a *primary function* of the criminal justice system. So instead of myopically focusing on punishment, the public health–quarantine model shifts the focus to identifying and addressing the systemic causes of crime, such as poverty, low social economic status, systematic disadvantage, mental illness, homelessness, educational inequity, exposure to abuse and violence, poor environmental health, and addiction (see Chapter 7).

Since the *social determinants of health* and the *social determinants of criminal behavior* are broadly similar, or so I will argue, the best way to protect public health and safety is to adopt a public health approach for identifying and taking action on these shared social determinants. Such an approach requires investigating how social inequities and systemic injustices affect health outcomes and criminal behavior, how poverty affects health and incarceration rates, how offenders often have preexisting medical conditions including mental health issues, how homelessness and education affect health and safety outcomes, how environmental health is important to both public health and safety, how involvement in the criminal justice system itself can lead to or worsen health and cognitive problems, and how a public health approach can be successfully applied within the criminal justice system (see Chapter 7). I contend that just as it is important to identify and take action on the social determinants of health if we want to improve health outcomes, it is equally important to identify and address the social determinants of criminal behavior.

Furthermore, the public health framework sees *social justice* as a foundational cornerstone to public health and safety (see Powers and Faden 2006). In public health ethics, a failure on the part of public health institutions to ensure the social conditions necessary to achieve a sufficient level of health is considered a grave injustice. An important task of public health ethics, then, is to identify which inequalities in health are the most egregious and thus which should be given the highest priority in public health policy and practice. The public health approach to criminal behavior likewise maintains that a core moral function of the criminal justice system is to identify and remedy social and economic inequalities responsible for crime. Just as public health is negatively affected by poverty, racism, and systematic inequality, so too is public safety. This broader approach to criminal justice therefore places issues of social justice at the forefront. It sees racism, sexism, poverty, and systemic disadvantage as serious threats to public safety and it prioritizes the reduction of such inequalities.

The core of the public health–quarantine model, then, is that the right to harm in self-defense and defense of others justifies incapacitating the criminally dangerous with the minimum harm required for adequate protection. The resulting account would not justify the sort of criminal punishment whose legitimacy is most dubious, such as death or confinement in the most common kinds of prisons in our society. The model also specifies attention to the well-being of criminals, which would change much of current policy. Furthermore, the public health component of the theory prioritizes prevention and social justice and aims at identifying and taking action on the social determinants of health and criminal behavior. This combined approach to dealing with criminal behavior, I maintain, is sufficient for dealing with dangerous criminals, leads to a more humane and effective social policy, and is actually preferable to the harsh and often excessive forms of punishment that typically come with retributivism.

1.4 IMPLICATIONS

Adopting the public health–quarantine model will, of course, have significant implications for our institutions of criminal justice and law. Since legal punishment seeks to make wrongdoers suffer and requires the intentional imposition of a penalty for conduct that is represented as a violation of a law of the state, and since the public health–quarantine model does not involve punishment in this way, it offers a nonpunitive alternative to treatment of criminals. When we quarantine an individual with a communicable disease in order to protect people, we are not intentionally seeking to harm or impose a penalty on them. The same is true when we incapacitate the criminally dangerous in order to protect society. The right of self-defense and prevention of harm to others justifies the limiting or restricting of liberty, but it does not constitute punishment as standardly understood. This is important for several reasons. First, the model demands that we view individuals holistically and that we adopt a preventive approach – one that understands that individuals are embedded in social systems, that criminal behavior is often the result of social determinants, and that prevention is always preferable to incapacitation. Second, after a criminal offense has occurred, courts would need to work with mental health experts, drug treatment professionals, and social service agencies to seek alternatives to incarceration. Lastly, for those who must be incapacitated, they would need to be housed in nonpunitive environments designed with the purpose of rehabilitation and reintegration in mind. Since most prisons in the United States, United Kingdom, and Australia are inhospitable and unpleasant places designed for punitive purposes, we would need to redesign them so that the physical environments and spaces we incapacitate people in better serve the goal of rehabilitation and reintegration (see Chapters 7 and 8 for details).

With regard to sentencing, voter disenfranchisement, and three strikes laws, the public health–quarantine model would require radical changes to our current, often excessively punitive, system. For one, felony voter disenfranchisement policies would be ended, since they serve no forward-looking benefit and are ultimately "a hindrance to the efforts of society to rehabilitate former felons and covert them into law-abiding and productive citizens." The sentence of life without parole would also be removed as an option, since it precludes from the outset the possibility of rehabilitation, violates the principle of least infringement, discourages the state from working to improve the well-being of offenders since they are seen as "lost causes," and prevents the reassessment of individual cases as circumstances change. While this may sound like a radical proposal, it is not a novel one. Portugal was the first country to abolish life imprisonment in 1884 and since then several other countries have followed suit, including Norway, Spain, Canada, Bosnia, Brazil, and Croatia. The maximum sentence one can get in Norway, for instance, is twenty-one years, and this is true even for murder. The Norwegian penal code does allow, however, for detention to be extended by five years at a time if the offender is still considered dangerous after serving their original sentence. While this may effectively allow for a life term if an offender cannot be rehabilitated and is deemed a serious continued threat to society, it has the benefit of requiring continued reevaluation and assessment. And unlike the United States, where one out of every nine people in prison is serving a life sentence, very few people in Norway ever serve more than a year. The average sentence in Norway is around eight months, more than 60 percent of prison sentences are up to three months, and almost 90 percent are less than a year.

The public health–quarantine model would similarly require incapacitation be kept to an absolute minimum and life without parole be eliminated as an option. A recent study by the Brennan Center for Justice found that 39 percent of the US prison population (roughly 576,000 people) is behind bars with little public safety rationale (Austin et al. 2016). They found that many offenders should not have been sent to prison in the first place. According to the report, up to 25 percent of prisoners (364,000 people), almost all nonviolent, lower-level offenders, would be better served by alternatives to incarceration such as treatment, community service, and probation. Another 14 percent (212,000 people) have already served long sentences and can be safely set free with little or no risk to public safety. Releasing these individuals would significantly and safely cut our prison population by more than a half million *and* save $20 billion annually – enough to employ 327,000 school teachers, 360,000 probation officers, or 270,000 new police officers. If these numbers are correct, adopting the public health–quarantine model would significantly aid in reducing mass incarceration since it would end life without parole and seek alternatives to incapacitation for offenders who pose little to no risk to public safety.

Three strikes laws would likewise need to be reversed since they prevent individual cases from being judged on their own terms, which would be needed if we are to accurately assess the threat an individual poses to society moving forward. Not all felonies are equal. And the fact that one person has committed three strikes does not mean they represent the same threat to society as another. Furthermore, three strikes laws often run afoul of principle of least infringement. Consider the following example:

> On November 4, 1995, Leandro Andrade walked into a Southern California Kmart. Andrade – who had several past criminal convictions – was about to commit a crime that would lead to a prison sentence of twenty-five years to life. Two weeks later, still a free man, Andrade struck again. This time, the target was a Kmart just three miles to the west of his previous crime. His plan was identical and would result in another sentence of twenty-five years to life. In two weeks, Andrade had attempted to steal nine VHS tapes: *The Fox and the Hound, The Pebble and the Penguin, Snow White, Batman Forever, Free Willy 2. Little Women, The Santa Clause,* and *Cinderella*. The total cost of the movies was $153.54. The actual cost to Andrade was fifty years to life. (Enns 2016: 1)

Under California's three strikes laws at the time, two counts of petty theft with a prior conviction carried consecutive sentences of twenty-five years to life. And while you might think this an extreme example, it is not:

> In 2010, 32,392 individuals were imprisoned in California [alone] with their second strike. Another 8,764 were incarcerated with their third strike. Of the second strikers, 833 were for petty theft. And like Andrade ..., an additional 341 individuals faced a potential life sentence for stealing items valued at $950 or less. (Enns 2016: 2)

On the public health–quarantine model, sentences like this would be in violation of the principle of least infringement since Leandro Andrade's acts of petty theft do not constitute a serious threat to society, at least not on their own, and should therefore be dealt with by other, less restrictive means.

These are only a few examples of the kinds of implications the public health–quarantine model would have, but hopefully they provide a sense of the wide-ranging nature of the reforms that would be required. Other implications will be discussed in subsequent chapters.

1.5 COMMON MISCONCEPTIONS

Since one of the main goals of this book is to develop and defend the public health–quarantine model, I would like to address a few potential misconceptions at the outset. Critics sometimes fear that my proposal will place offenders outside the moral community or flatten out important distinctions, treating the different capacities of agents as irrelevant and/or treating all offenders as if they were incompetent or mentally ill. For instance, retributivist C. S. Lewis (1953) famously argued that if retributivism were abandoned in favor of harm prevention, responsible offenders would be objectified and would no longer be protected by considerations of justice. According to Lewis:

> The Humanitarian theory removed from Punishment the concept of Desert. But the concept of Desert is the only connecting link between punishment and justice ... There is no sense in talking about a "just deterrent" or a "just cure." We demand of a deterrent not whether it is just but whether it will deter. We demand of a cure not whether it is just but whether it succeeds. Thus when we cease to consider what the criminal deserves and consider only what will cure him or deter others, we have tacitly removed him from the sphere of justice altogether; instead of a person, a subject of rights, we now have a mere object, a patient, a "case." (1953: 225)

In recent years, similar concerns have been echoed by Morse (2018), Smilansky (2011),and Dennett (2011, Dennett and Caruso 2020). Sometimes the concern is put in terms of P. F. Strawson's (1962) famous distinction between the *reactive* and *objective* attitudes. Strawson maintained that our justification for claims of blameworthiness and praiseworthiness is grounded in the system of human reactive attitudes, such as moral resentment, indignation, guilt, and gratitude. Strawson contends that because our moral responsibility practices are grounded in this way, if we were to abandon the notion of moral responsibility, we would be forced to adopt the cold and calculating objective attitude toward others, a stance that relinquishes the reactive attitudes. According to Strawson and his followers, the denial of all moral responsibility is unacceptable, self-defeating, and/or impossible, since to permanently excuse everyone would entail that "nobody knows what he's doing or that everybody's behavior is unintelligible in terms of conscious purposes or that everybody lives in a world of delusion or that nobody has a moral sense" (1962: 74).

While I take these concerns seriously and acknowledge that earlier versions of what Lewis (1953) calls the "humanitarian" approach may have been guilty of them, I also maintain that they are misguided when applied to the public health–quarantine model I defend. First, it is important to recognize that neither Pereboom nor I set out our position in a strict consequentialist theoretical context. Rather, we justify incapacitation on the ground of the right to self-defense and defense of others. That right does not extend to people who are nonthreats. The aim of protection is justified by a right with clear bounds and not by a consequentialist theory on which the bounds are unclear. It would therefore be wrong, according to our model, to incapacitate someone who is innocent since they are not a serious threat to society (Pereboom and Caruso 2018; see also Chapter 8). The principle of least infringement would also prohibit legal sanctions that exceed what is needed to protect public health and safety. As a result, it would oppose using individuals simply as a means to deter others by ratcheting up various punitive responses to crime, as was the case with three strikes laws and mandatory minimums. The public health–quarantine model therefore has distinct advantages over consequentialist theories of punishment. Furthermore, Victor Tadros (2011) has persuasively argued that "the objection against using someone merely as a means is best characterized as an objection against *'manipulative use'* – where someone is used in order to promote some further, independent goal. In contrast, harming someone to *eliminate* a threat they pose is much easier to justify, based on the right to self-defense" (Shaw 2019a: 101). Assuming, for the moment, that Tadros's distinction between eliminating harm and manipulative use is valid, concerns over treating individuals merely as means to an end, or as objects to be used, would appear to apply more to consequentialist theories of punishment than to the public health–quarantine model.

Second, neither free will skepticism nor the public health–quarantine model implies that the difference between agents who are reasons-responsive and those who are not is irrelevant to how we should treat offenders. On the contrary, free will skeptics typically claim that this difference is crucial for determining the right response to crime (Pereboom and Caruso 2018; Focquart et al. 2020). On the public health–quarantine model, the question of whether an offender is reasons-responsive is relevant for at least two reasons. First, it is important in assessing what kind of threat an individual poses moving forward and whether incapacitation is required. An offender suffering from a serious mental illness, for instance, differs in significant ways from one who is fully reasons-responsive. These differences will be relevant to determining what minimum restrictions are required for adequate protection. Second, if the capacities of reasons-responsiveness are in place, forms of treatment that take rationality and self-governance into account are appropriate. On the other hand, those who suffer from impairments of rationality and self-governance would need to be treated differently and in ways that aim to restore these capacities when possible. Understanding the variety of causes that lead to impairment of these capacities would also be crucial to determining effective policy for recidivism reduction and rehabilitation (Focquart et al. 2019). Hence, free will skepticism and the public health–quarantine model acknowledge the importance of reasons-responsiveness, self-governance, and differences in degrees of autonomy. But rather than see these as relevant for assigning blameworthiness and basic desert moral responsibility, they instead view them as important (in fact, essential) to determining the appropriate course of action moving forward.

Third, while it is true that in justifying incapacitation the public health–quarantine model appeals to an analogy with quarantine, it is also important to recognize that what is analogous here is the *justification* of incapacitation and quarantine – that is, both appeal to the right of self-defense and prevention of harm to others. The model does not require us to view wrongdoers as "ill" or "diseased." While some people who commit criminal acts do so because of mental illness or incompetency, many others do not. These distinctions matter exactly for the reasons just stated. Furthermore, I strongly want to resist what Bruce Waller (2006, 2011) calls "excuse-extensionism" – the idea that the denial of moral responsibility only makes sense on the basis of characteristics that make one incompetent (and thus excused) as a moral being (2011: 219). As Waller explains:

> [I]f we start from the assumption of the moral responsibility system (assumptions that are so common and deep that they are difficult to escape), then the denial of moral responsibility is absurd and self-defeating. But the universal denial of moral responsibility does *not* start from the assumption that under normal circumstances we are morally responsible, and it does *not* proceed from that starting point to enlarge and extend the range of excuses to cover everyone (so that *everyone* is profoundly flawed). That is indeed a path to absurdity. Rather, those who reject moral responsibility reject the basic system which starts from the assumption that all minimally competent persons (all who reach the plateau level) are morally responsible. For those who deny moral responsibility, it is never fair to treat anyone as morally responsible, no matter how reasonable, competent, self-efficacious, strong-willed, and clear-sighted that person may be. (2015: 103)

Since skeptics who globally challenge the moral responsibility system do not accept the rules of that system,[25] it would be wrong to interpret them as claiming that "nobody knows what he's doing or that everybody's behavior is unintelligible in terms of conscious purposes or that everybody lives in a world of delusion or that nobody has a moral sense" (Strawson 1962: 74). Instead, global skeptics maintain that our ordinary moral responsibility practices are unjustified *even when agents are competent and reasons-responsive.*

Fourth, rejecting basic desert moral responsibility does not require one to adopt what Strawson calls the objective attitude toward wrongdoers. As Pereboom and I have elsewhere argued:

> Strawson may be right to contend that adopting the objective attitude would seriously hinder our personal relationships (for a contrary perspective, see Sommers 2007). However, a case can be made that it would be wrong to claim that this stance would be appropriate if determinism did pose a genuine threat to the reactive attitudes (Pereboom 1995, 2001, 2014). While, for instance, kinds of moral anger such as resentment and indignation might be undercut if free will skepticism were true, these attitudes may be suboptimal relative to alternative attitudes available to us, such as moral concern, disappointment, sorrow, and moral resolve. The proposal is that the attitudes that we would want to retain either are not undermined by a skeptical conviction because they do not have presuppositions that conflict with this view, or else they have alternatives that are not under threat. And what remains does not amount to Strawson's objectivity of attitude and is sufficient to sustain the personal relationships we value. (Pereboom and Caruso 2018: 201)

---

[25] See, e.g., Waller (2011, 2015), Pereboom (2001, 2014), Levy (2011), G. Strawson (1986, 1994), and Caruso (2012, 2013, 2018, 2019).

According to *optimistic skeptics*, like myself, life without belief in free will and basic desert moral responsibility would not be as destructive as Strawson and Lewis contend.[26] Instead, prospects of finding meaning in life and sustaining good interpersonal relationships would not be threatened (see Pereboom 2001, 2014; Waller 1989, 2011, 2014; Caruso 2013, 2018, 2019). And although retributivism and sever punishment, such as the death penalty, would be ruled out, incapacitation and rehabilitation programs would still be justified.[27]

Lastly, critics are simply mistaken when they assume that adopting the skeptical perspective means abandoning all discourse about justice, rights, and respect for persons.

In the second half of the book, I argue that free will skepticism and the public health–quarantine model are perfectly consistent with respect for persons as well as various nondesertist theories of justice. In particular, I defend a *capabilities approach* to social justice and argue that not only is it consistent with free will skepticism, it can also serve as the moral foundation for my public health framework (Chapter 6). Appealing to work by Stephen Darwall (1992) and Benjamin Vilhauer (2013a, 2013b), I also argue that respect for persons and other safeguards against manipulative use can be made consistent with free will skepticism and can be incorporated into the public health–quarantine model (see Chapters 6 and 8; see also Shaw 2019a). For instance, the public health–quarantine model incorporates several important safeguards, including the *conflict resolution principle*, the *principle of least infringement*, the *principle of normality*, and the *prohibition of manipulative use*. There is no reason to think, then, that adopting the public health–quarantine model would require treating individuals as objects. Quite the opposite. I contend that, contra retributivists, we should resist narrowly conceiving of respect for persons in terms of giving wrongdoers their just deserts. Instead, respecting human dignity demands, at a minimum, that the capabilities and well-being of wrongdoers be taken into consideration, that we avoid punishments that dehumanize and disenfranchise individuals, and that we do everything we can to rehabilitate and reintegrate offenders back into the community. The public health–quarantine model does a better job at respecting human dignity in this sense than does retributivism (see Chapter 8).

---

[26] By "optimistic skeptics" I mean those who are optimistic about the implications of adopting the skeptical perspective (e.g., Pereboom 2001, 2014; Waller 1989, 1990, 2007, 2011, 2015; Nadelhoffer 2011; Levy 2011, 2015, 2016; Caruso 2013, 2018, 2019; Shaw 2019a, 2019b; Vilhauer 2009b, 2012, 2013a, 2013b; Morris 2018).

[27] Other free will skeptics who defend either incapacitation accounts or forward-looking consequentialist accounts include Pereboom (2001, 2013, 2014), Jones (2003), Vilhauer (2009b, 2013a, 2013b), Levy (2012), Corrado (2013), Chiesa (2011), Caruso (2016, 2017, 2020), Pereboom and Caruso (2018), Shaw (2014, 2019a, 2019b), Focquaert, Glenn, and Raine (2013, 2018), and Focquaert (2019). See also Shaw, Pereboom, and Caruso (2019).

1.6 BELIEF IN FREE WILL REMAINS AN OBSTACLE

I would like to close this chapter with some final thoughts on why the issue of free will should not be overlooked in discussions of criminal justice. It has been suggested to me, by friend and foe alike, that if my ultimate goal is criminal justice reform and the rejection of retributive practices and policies, I should work directly toward that goal and leave the contentious issue of free will aside. While I acknowledge that this may be a better rhetorically strategy, since getting people to question the existence of free will is no easy task, I resist it for two main reasons. First, I am a philosopher and am committed to the truth wherever it leads me. While this might sound high-minded, I have worked on the problem of free will for many years and am convinced that free will skepticism is the only reasonable position to adopt. This is not to say, of course, that the skeptical perspective is not consistent with other conceptions of responsibility – for example, causal responsibility, "take charge" responsibility, attributability, answerability, etc. (see Caruso 2018). Nor is it to deny that there remain good reasons for incapacitating dangerous criminals and engaging in forms of moral protest in the face of bad behavior (see Pereboom 2014, 2020). Rather, it is to insist that to hold people *truly deserving* of blame and praise, punishment, and reward would be to hold them responsible for the results of the morally arbitrary or what is ultimately beyond their control, which is fundamentally unfair and unjust. Given that I am convinced of the skeptical perspective, it would be utterly disingenuous of me to set the issue of free will aside or simply ignore it.

Second, and more to the point, to achieve meaningful and lasting criminal justice reform, I believe it is important to challenge the assumptions of free will and basic desert moral responsibility (cf. Fischborn 2018). There is growing evidence that free will beliefs are motivated by the desire to punish others and to justify holding them morally responsible (Clark et al. 2014; Clark, Baumeister, and Ditto 2017; Clark Winegard, and Sharrif 2019). Researchers have also found that free will beliefs correlate with increased punitiveness (Carey and Paulhus 2013; Nadelhoffer and Tocchetto 2013; Shariff et al. 2014). Leaving the concept of free will unchallenged increases the likelihood that our practices and policies will remain focused on individual responsibility and punitive responses to wrongdoing. This, in turn, will stand in the way of adopting the kind of public health alternative I recommend, which shifts public policy, funding, and focus to prevention, rehabilitation, and addressing the social determinants of criminal behavior.

Recent empirical work in social psychology indicates that how we assign responsibility is correlated with prior judgments of what counts as being morally bad, which are in turn dependent upon other larger social and cultural factors (see Hardcastle 2019). Take, for example, psychologist Mark Alicke's *culpable control model* of blame. It proposes that our desire to blame someone intrudes on our assessments of that person's ability to control his or her thoughts or behavior. As Valerie Hardcastle describes:

> Deciding that someone is responsible for an act, which is taken to be the conclusion of a judgment, is actually part of our psychological process of assessing blame. If we start with a spontaneous negative reaction, then that can lead to our hypothesizing that the source of the action is blameworthy as well as to an active desire to blame that source. This desire, in turn, skews our interpretations of the available evidence such that it supports our blame hypothesis. We highlight evidence that indicates negligence, recklessness, impure motives, or a faulty character, and we ignore evidence that suggests otherwise. In other words, instead of dispassionately judging whether someone is responsible, we validate our spontaneous reaction of blameworthiness. (2018: 320)

Data, in fact, suggest that we often exaggerate a person's actual or potential control over an event to justify our blame judgment and we will even change the threshold of how much control is required for a blame judgment (Neimeth and Sosis 1973; Eften 1974; Sosis 1974; Lerner et al. 1976; Lerner and Miller 1978; Schlenker 1980; Snyder et al. 1983; Alicke 1994, 2000, 2008; Alicke et al. 2008; Alicke Rose and Bloom 2008; Lagnado and Channon 2008; Clark et al. 2014; Everett et al. 2018).

Additional studies by Cory Clark and her colleagues (2014) have shown that a key factor promoting belief in free will is a fundamental desire to blame and hold others morally responsible for their wrongful behaviors. Across five studies they found evidence that greater belief in free will is due to heightened punitive motivations. In one study, an ostensibly real classroom cheating incident led to increased free will beliefs, presumably due to heightened punitive motivations. In a second study, they found that the prevalence of immoral behavior, as measured by crime and homicide rates, predicted free will belief on a country level. Additional studies by Clark, Baumesiter, and Ditto (2017) also demonstrate that free will beliefs are motivated by a desire to punish others and to justify holding them morally responsible. These findings have been replicated and confirmed in meta-analyses (Clark, Winegard, and Shariff 2019). There is good reason to think, then, that our desire to blame and hold others morally responsible comes first and *drives* our belief in free will, rather than the other way around.

Researchers have also found that our judgment on whether an action was done on purpose or not is influenced by our moral evaluation of the outcome of certain actions – that is, whether we morally like or dislike it (Nadelhoffer 2006). And we seem to have an asymmetric understanding of the moral nature of our own actions and those of others, such that we judge our own actions and motivations as more moral than those of the average person (Epley and Dunning 2000). As Maureen Sie describes:

> In cases of other people acting in morally wrong ways we tend to explain those wrongdoings in terms of the agent's lack of virtue or morally bad character traits. We

focus on those elements that allow us to blame agents for their moral wrongdoings. On the other hand, in cases where we ourselves act in morally reprehensible ways we tend to focus on exceptional elements of our situation, emphasizing the lack of room to do otherwise. (2013: 283)

Additional findings indicate that believing more strongly in free will is correlated with increased punitiveness (Carey and Paulhus 2013; Nadelhoffer and Tocchetto 2013; Shariff et al. 2014), and that weakening free will beliefs, either in general or by offering evidence of an individual's diminished decisional capacity, leads to less punitiveness (Pizarro, Uhlmann, and Salovey 2003; Monterosso, Royzman, and Schwartz 2005; Aspinwall, Brown, and Tabery 2012; Shariff et al. 2014).

For instance, Shariff et al. (2014) hypothesized that if free will beliefs support attributions of moral responsibility, then reducing these beliefs should make people less retributive in their attitudes about punishment. In a series of four studies they tested this prediction and found support for it. In Study 1 they found that people with weaker free will beliefs endorsed less retributive attitudes regarding punishment of criminals, yet their consequentialist attitudes were unaffected. Study 1 therefore supports the hypothesis that free will beliefs positively predict punitive attitudes, and in particular retributive attitudes, yet it also suggests that "the motivation to punish in order to benefit society (consequentialist punishment) may remain intact, even while the need for blame and desire for retribution are forgone" (2014: 7). Study 2 found that experimentally diminishing free will belief through anti-free-will arguments diminished retributive punishment, suggesting a causal relationship (2014: 6). Studies 3 and 4 further found that exposure to stories and findings from neuroscience implying a mechanistic basis for human action similarly produced a reduction in retributivism.

If these empirical findings are any indication, the concepts of free will and basic desert moral responsibility appear intimately connected with increased punitiveness and the desire to blame. Additional work also reveals that belief in free will is correlated with a number of other potentially harmful beliefs, desires, and emotions – including Just World Belief, Right Wing Authoritarianism, and increased Religiosity (Carey and Paulhus 2013; Nadelhoffer and Tocchetto 2013; for overview see Caruso 2019). By abandoning these beliefs, we can look more clearly at the causes and more deeply into the systems that shape individuals and their behavior, and this will allow us to adopt more humane and effective practices and policies. I propose that what we need is a radical paradigm shift in how we view criminal behavior.

It is quite common both in criminal law and everyday attitudes to portray criminal behavior as a failure of moral character and a matter of individual responsible. The retributive justification of legal punishment assumes, for instance, that, absent any excusing conditions, wrongdoers are morally responsible for their actions and *deserve* to be punished in proportion to their bad deeds, even if this provides no benefits to the individual or society. Since it focuses almost exclusively on the individual and their responsibility, and not on the social determinants of criminal behavior, retributive justice tends to favor punitive approaches to crime rather than policies aimed at targeting the social structures and causes of criminal behavior. The retributive approach maintains that it is the individual who is responsible for criminal wrongdoing, and thus criminal justice is primarily about giving wrongdoers their *just deserts*. Perhaps nobody embodied this ethos of individual responsibility more than Ronald Reagan, who famously said: "We must reject the idea that every time a law's broken, society is guilty rather than the lawbreaker. It is time to restore the American precept that each individual is accountable for his actions."[28]

The problem, however, is that the more we learn about criminal behavior, the more it becomes obvious that crime has more to do with places and circumstances than people. In fact, look closely and you will find that there are lifetimes of trauma, poverty, and social disadvantage that fill the prison system (see Chapter 7). Failing to recognize this has profound consequences. James Dunlea and Larisa Heiphetz (2020), for instance, have studied how adults and children think of people's moral character:

> [They find] that both children and adults often assume that people go to jail or prison because of internal characteristics – that is, something about their personal character led them to the justice system. [Their] research suggests that people very rarely spontaneously think about the social forces, like poverty, housing, and racism, that are enormous contributors to criminal behavior. Instead, they attribute being in jail or prison with internal characteristic ("They're bad people") or behavioral characteristics ("They did a bad thing"). (LaBouff and Dustin 2020)

Importantly, Dunlea and Heiphetz find that these assumptions have consequences. When we think about someone's "badness" as an essential personal quality because we're ignoring the situational forces, we treat them worse and are less generous to them. We adopt punitive reactive responses to crime rather than targeting the situational causes of criminal behavior. We need to radically change our assumptions about criminal behavior and focus instead on those situational forces and changeable behaviors when making policy decisions (LaBouff and Dustin 2020).

Hence, if we seek to reject retributivism and adopt a more holistic and systematic approach to criminal behavior, the belief in free will potentially stands in the way since it encourages punitiveness and is driven by a desire to blame and hold others morally responsible. It sees criminal behavior as primarily a matter of individual responsibility and as a result ends the investigation at precisely the point it should begin. The criminal law, with its assumptions about free will, encourages us to adopt what I call a *time slice approach* to criminal behavior. It asks, at a particular moment in time (the time of the crime), was the agent competent? Were they reasons-

---

[28] From Reagan's speech at the Republican National Convention, Platform Committee Meeting, July 31, 1968.

responsive? Did they have a guilty mind or criminal intent? Did they understand that their actions were wrong or unlawful? Etc. Etc. If the answers are yes, yes, yes, and yes, then they are legally culpable and it is legitimate to punish them – all things considered and assuming there are no excusing conditions. Of course, the criminal law occasionally considers prior circumstances as relevant (e.g., in cases of domestic violence), but it is primarily focused on establishing *actus reus*, *mens rea*, and the state of mind of the offender at the time of the crime.[29] Unfortunately, adopting such a time slice approach abstracts individuals from their lived circumstances and the social systems they are embedded in. It blinds us to the social determinants of criminal behavior, the causes and systems that shape us, and *how* individuals come to acquire a particular state of mind.

Once we adopt the skeptical perspective, on the other hand, we realize that the myopic focus on individual responsibility, blame, and punishment is mistaken and counterproductive. The skeptical perspective tells us that the lottery of life is not always fair, we do not all have equal starting points, and individuals are embedded in social systems that shape who we are and what we do. In contrast with the time slice approach, it encourages a *historical whole person approach* that sees individuals as byproducts of their histories and circumstances. It helps us to recognize that criminal behavior is often the result of social determinants and that the best way to reduce crime and increase human well-being is to identify and take action on these determinants. So while it is possible to embrace the public health–quarantine model without sharing my skepticism about free will and basic desert moral responsibility, continuing to believe in the latter will work at odds with properly implementing the former. As the empirical findings mentioned earlier indicate, belief in free will, besides being unjustified, is wrapped up in punitive and retributive desires. It keeps alive the notions that wrongdoers justly deserve to suffer for the wrongs they've done and are morally blameworthy in the backward-looking sense. It is time that we leave these antiquated notions behind, lose our moral anger, stop blaming those who find themselves in unfortunate circumstances, and turn our attention to the difficult task of addressing the *causes* that lead to criminality.

---

[29] Traditionally, juries evaluate two aspects of a case for reasonable doubt: whether the accused actually committed the crime (legally known as *actus reus*) and whether at the moment of the crime the accused understood that he or she was doing wrong (legally known as *mens rea*).

2

Free Will Skepticism

Hard Incompatibilism and Hard Luck

Over the next three chapters, I will present six distinct arguments for rejecting retributivism.

The first, which is the focus of this chapter, argues that free will skepticism is the only reasonable position to adopt when it comes to the problem of free will. And since retributive punishment requires the kind of free will associated with basic desert moral responsibility in order to be justified, free will skepticism implies that retributive punishment lacks justification. Hence, in so far as we demand *justified* legal punishment practices, we should reject retributivism in light of the philosophical arguments against free will and basic desert moral responsibility. We can call this argument the *skeptical argument* against retributivism since it maintains that free will skepticism undermines the retributivist notion that wrongdoers *deserve* to be punished in the backward-looking sense required.

The chapter begins, in Section 2.1, with an overview of the problem of free will and an outline of the various positions. Sections 2.2 and 2.3 then make the case for *free will skepticism* and argue that who we are and what we do is ultimately the result of factors beyond our control – whether those be determinism, indeterminism, or luck – and because of this we are never moral responsible for our actions in the basic desert sense. Section 2.2 presents the arguments in support of *hard incompatibilism* (Pereboom 2001, 2014a), the thesis that free will is incompatible with *both* causal determination by factors beyond the agent's control *and* with the kind of indeterminacy in action required by the most plausible versions of libertarianism. Section 2.3 then defends a form of *hard luck* (Levy 2011), which maintains that regardless of the causal structure of the universe, we lack free will and moral responsibility because free will is incompatible with the pervasiveness of *luck*. I conclude in Section 2.4 by discussing the implications of free will skepticism for retributive punishment.

2.1 THE PROBLEM OF FREE WILL: POSITIONS AND BACKGROUND

Contemporary theories of free will tend to fall into one of two general categories, namely, those that insist on and those that are skeptical about the reality of free will and moral responsibility. The former category includes *libertarian* and *compatibilist* accounts of free will, two general views that defend the claim that we have free will but disagree on its nature or its conditions. The second category comprises a family of skeptical views that doubt or deny human free will. The main dividing line between the two pro–free will positions, libertarianism and compatibilism, is best understood in terms of the traditional problem of free will and determinism. *Determinism*, as it is commonly understood, is the thesis that at any given time only one future is physically possible (van Inwagen 1983: 3). Or put differently, it is the thesis that facts about the remote past in conjunction with the laws of nature entail that there is only one unique future (McKenna and Pereboom 2016: 19). The traditional problem of free will and determinism therefore comes in trying to reconcile our intuitive sense of free will with the idea that our choices and actions may be causally determined by factors over which we have no ultimate control, that is, the past before we were born and the laws of nature.

Libertarians and compatibilists react to this problem in different ways. *Libertarians* acknowledge that if determinism is true, and all of our actions are causally determined by antecedent circumstances, we lack free will and moral responsibility. Yet they further maintain that at least some of our choices and actions must be free in the sense that they are not causally determined. Libertarians therefore reject causal determinism and defend an indeterminist conception of free will in order to save what they maintain are necessary conditions for free will – that is, the *ability to do otherwise* in exactly the same set of conditions and/ or the idea that we remain, in some important sense, the *ultimate source/originator* of action. *Compatibilists*, on the other hand, set out to defend a conception of free will that can be reconciled with determinism. They hold that what is of utmost importance is not the absence of causal determination, but that our actions are voluntary, free from constraint and compulsion, and caused in the appropriate way. Different compatibilist accounts spell out requirements for free will differently but widely endorsed views single out responsiveness to reasons or connection of action to what one would reflectively endorse.

Free will skepticism stands in contrast to these pro–free will positions since it takes seriously the possibility that human beings are never morally responsible in the basic desert sense. In the past, the leading form of skepticism was *hard determinism*: the view that determinism is true and incompatible with free will – either because it precludes the ability to do otherwise (*leeway incompatibilism*) or because it is inconsistent with one's being the ultimate source of action (*source incompatibilism*) – hence, no free will. For hard determinists, libertarian free will is an impossibility because human actions are part of a fully deterministic world and compatibilism is operating in bad faith. Hard determinism had its classic statement in the time when Newtonian physics reigned supreme and was thought to be deterministic. The development of quantum mechanics, however, diminished confidence in determinism, for the reason that it has indeterministic interpretations. This is not to say that determinism has been refuted or falsified by modern physics, because a number of leading interpretations of quantum mechanics are consistent with determinism (see, e.g., Bohm 1952, 1980; Vaidman 2014; Lewis 2016). It is also important to keep in mind that even if we allow some indeterminacy to exist at the microlevel of the universe, the level studied by quantum mechanics, there may still remain *determinism-where-it-matters* – that is, at the ordinary level of choices and actions, and even the electrochemical activity in our brains (Honderich 2002: 5). Nonetheless, most contemporary skeptics tend to defend positions that are best seen as distinct from, but as successors to, traditional hard determinism.

Most contemporary free will skeptics maintain that while determinism is incompatible with free will and moral responsibility, so too is *indeterminism*, especially if it is limited to the sort posited by certain interpretations of quantum mechanics (Pereboom 2001, 2014; Caruso 2012; Pereboom and Caruso 2018; Caruso and Pereboom 2021). Others argue that regardless of the causal structure of the universe, we lack free will and moral responsibility because free will is incompatible with the pervasiveness of *luck* (Levy 2011; Caruso 2019a). Others still argue that free will and ultimate moral responsibility are incoherent concepts, since to be free in the sense required for ultimate moral responsibly, we would have to be *causa sui* (or "cause of oneself") and this is impossible (Strawson 1994, 2010). Here, for example, is Nietzsche on the *causa sui*:

> The *causa sui* is the best self-contradiction that has been conceived so far; it is a sort of rape and perversion of logic. But the extravagant pride of man has managed to entangle itself profoundly and frightfully with just this nonsense. The desire for "freedom of the will" in the superlative metaphysical sense, which still holds sway, unfortunately, in the minds of the half-educated; the desire to bear the entire and ultimate responsibility for one's actions oneself, and to absolve God, the world, ancestors, chance, and society involves nothing less than to be precisely this *causa sui* and, with more than Baron Munchhausen's audacity, to pull oneself up into existence by the hair, out of the swamps of nothingness. (1886/1992: 218–219)

What all these skeptical arguments have in common, and what they share with classical hard determinism, is the belief that our choices, actions, and constitutive characters are ultimately the result of factors beyond our control – whether that be determinism, chance, or luck – and because of this we lack the kind of free will needed for basic desert moral responsibility.

Importantly, free will skepticism, while doubting or denying basic desert moral responsibility, is consistent with agents being responsible in other senses. For instance, *attributability* responsibility is about actions or attitudes being properly attributable to, or reflective of, an agent's self. That is, we are responsible for our actions in the attributability sense only when those actions reflect our identity as moral agents, that is, when they are attributable to us (see Watson 1996; Shoemaker 2011, 2015; Eshleman 2019). Since attributability makes no appeal to basic desert or backward-looking praise and blame, it remains independent of desert-based accountability and is consistent with free will skepticism. Consider, for instance, Albert Einstein. He was a free will skeptic who believed that his scientific accomplishments were not of his own making. In a 1929 interview in *The Saturday Evening Post*, he said: "I do not believe in free will ... I believe with Schopenhauer: we can do what we wish, but we can only wish what we must." He then went on to add: "My own career was undoubtedly determined, not by my own will but by various factors over which I have no control." He concludes the interview by rejecting the idea that he deserved praise or credit for his scientific achievements: "I claim credit for nothing. Everything is determined, the beginning as well as the end, by forces over which we have no control." While free will skeptics can agree with Einstein that he does not *deserve* praise (in the basic desert sense) for his various attributes and accomplishments, they can nevertheless *attribute* those attributes and accomplishments to him without inconsistency.

The *answerability* sense of responsibility defended by Thomas Scanlon (1998) and Hilary Bok (1998) is also claimed by some skeptics to be consistent with the rejection of basic desert (see Pereboom 2014a; Caruso and Pereboom 2021; cf. Jeppsson 2016). According to this conception of responsibility, someone is responsible for an action or attitude just in case it is connected to her capacity for evaluative judgment in a way that opens her up, in principle, to demands for justification from others. When we encounter apparently immoral behavior, for example, it is perfectly legitimate to ask the agent, "Why did you decide to do that?" or "Do you think it was the right thing to do?" If the reasons given in response to such questions are morally unsatisfactory, we regard it as justified to invite the agent to evaluate critically what her actions indicate about her intentions and character, to demand an apology, or request reform. According to Derk Pereboom (2014a), engaging in such interactions is reasonable in light of the right of those harmed or threatened to protect themselves from immoral behavior and its consequences. In addition, we might have a stake in reconciliation with the wrong doer, and calling her to account in this way can function as a step toward realizing this objective. We also have an interest in her moral formation, and the address described functions as a stage in the process. On this forward-looking reading, answerability responsibility is grounded, not in basic desert, but in three nondesert-invoking desiderata: *future protection, future reconciliation*, and *future moral formation* (see Pereboom 2014a).

Basic desert moral responsibility should also be distinguished from *take charge responsibility* (see Waller 1989, 1990, 2004, 2011, 2014). Bruce Waller, for instance, has argued: "Just deserts and moral responsibility require a godlike power – the existential power of choosing ourselves, the godlike power of making ourselves from scratch, the divine capacity to be an uncaused cause – that we do not have" (2011: 40). Yet, he maintains, "[Y]ou [nevertheless] have take-charge responsibility for your own life, which is a responsibility you deeply value and enjoy exercising" (2011: 108). *Taking responsibility* is distinguished from *being morally responsible* in that, if one takes responsibility for a particular outcome it does not follow that one is morally responsible for that outcome. One can take responsibility for many things, from the mundane to the vitally important. For example, one can take responsibility for teaching a course, organizing a conference, or throwing a birthday party. The responsibility taken, however, is profoundly different from the moral responsibility that would justify blame and punishment, praise and reward (see Pereboom 2001: xxi; Waller 2011: 105).

In this chapter, I will present two distinct arguments in support of free will skepticism. I will begin, in Section 2.2, by arguing that the sort of free will required for basic desert moral responsibility is incompatible with *both* causal determination by factors beyond the agent's control *and* with the kind of indeterminacy in action required by the most plausible versions of libertarianism. Since this view maintains that free will is incompatible with both determinism and indeterminism, I follow Derk Pereboom in labeling it *hard incompatibilism* so as to distinguish it from traditional hard determinism (Pereboom 2001, 2014a; Pereboom and Caruso 2018). In Section 2.3, I then present a second, independent argument for skepticism that maintains that regardless of the causal structure of the universe, free will and basic desert moral responsibility are incompatible with the pervasiveness of *luck* – a view Neil Levy (2011) calls *hard luck*. As we will see, the arguments for hard luck are intended not only as an objection to libertarianism but extend to compatibilism as well. In the end, I conclude that the arguments for hard incompatibilism and hard luck provide more than sufficient reason for concluding that who we are and what we do is ultimately the result of factors beyond our control, and because of this nobody is ever morally responsible for their actions in the basic desert sense – the sense needed to ground retributive punishment.

I should acknowledge upfront that I do not claim originality over the arguments presented in this chapter, since most have already been developed elsewhere by others – especially by Pereboom (2001, 2014a), Levy (2011), and Waller (2011, 2015). It is also true that I have already presented these and other arguments for rejecting free will in my first book, *Free Will and Consciousness: A Determinist Account of the Illusion of Free Will* (Caruso 2012). What I offer here, then, is a summary of what I consider the best and most up-to-date reasons for doubting or denying the existence of free will.

2.2 HARD INCOMPATIBILISM

My first path to free will skepticism features distinct arguments that target three rival views, *event-causal libertarianism*, *agent-causal libertarianism*, and *compatibilism*, and then claims that the skeptical position is the only defensible position that remains standing. Section 2.2.1 focuses on libertarian accounts of free will. Section 2.2.2 focuses on compatibilist accounts. I argue that both fail to preserve the control in action required for basic desert moral responsibility, but for different reasons. The result is a defense of the hard-incompatibilist thesis that free will is incompatible with both determinism and indeterminism.[1]

2.2.1 Libertarianism

Libertarian accounts of free will can be divided into two general categories. According to *event-causal libertarianism*, actions are caused solely by way of events, and some type of indeterminacy in the production of actions by appropriate events is held to be a decisive requirement for moral responsibility (Kane 1996; Ekstrom 2000; Balaguer 2009; Lemos 2018). According to *agent-causal libertarianism*, on the other hand, free will of the sort required for moral responsibility is accounted for by the existence of agents who possess a causal power to make choices without being causally determined to do so (Taylor 1974; Chisholm 1976; Kant 1781/1787/1987; Reid 1788/1983; O'Connor 2000a; Clarke 2003; Griffith 2010). On this view, it is essential that the causation involved in an agent's making a free choice is not reducible to causation among events involving the agent – that is, it must irreducibly be an instance of the agent-as-substance causing a choice not by way of events. Hence, according to agent-causal libertarianism, it as an *agent*, understood fundamentally as a substance, that has the causal power to cause choices without being determined to do so.

Given that libertarians are *incompatibilists*, they maintain that neither free will nor moral responsibility is compatible with the truth of determinism. But since they also believe that agents are sometimes free and morally responsible, they defend an *indeterminist* conception of free will according to which agents retain the *ability to do otherwise* in exactly the same circumstances, keeping the past and the laws of nature fixed. That is, libertarians maintain that given the same antecedent conditions at a particular time *t* (including upbringing, education, genes, social conditions, and the like), and the same laws of nature at *t*, an agent remains undetermined and has the power to choose from branching paths that are metaphysically open – that is, it is somehow *up to the agent* what the world will look like after *t*. For libertarian free will to exist, however, agents must satisfy both a positive and negative constraint. The negative constraint stipulates that the agent must not be wholly

---

[1] I do not consider here *noncausal libertarian accounts*, such as Carl Ginet's (see 1990, 1997, 2007, 2008). But for criticisms of such accounts, see Pereboom (2014a: 39–43) and Clarke (2002). I also do not discuss Christian List's (2019) emergentist account of free will, which attempts to reconcile indeterminism at the agential level with determinism at the physical level. Elsewhere, however, I have argued that List's account succumbs to the same kind of concerns raised in this section (see Caruso 2020). At the agential level, for instance, List defends an indeterminist account of free will. Even if we were to grant List's highly contentious claim that deterministic laws at the physical level are consistent with genuine indeterminacy at the agential level (something many would challenge), List fails to provide us with an account of *how* such indeterminism preserves the control in action required for basic desert moral responsibility and how it overcomes the luck and disappearing agent objections discussed in this section (see Caruso 2020 for details).

determined by conditions that they themselves do not control. The libertarian Thomas Reid puts the negative point as follows:

> If, in any action, he had power to will what he did, or not to will it, in that action he is free. But if, in every voluntary action, the determination of his will be the necessary consequence of something involuntary in the state of his mind, or of something in his external circumstances, he is not free; he has not what I call the liberty of a moral agent, but is subject to necessity. (1895: 2:599)

Contemporary philosophers sometimes express this negative constraint more technically in terms of cross-world analysis. Al Mele, for instance, maintains that an agent can only freely A at time *t*, in the libertarian sense, if there is another possible world with the same past up to *t* and the same laws of nature in which the agent does not do A at *t* (2006, 2017). Most libertarians, however, are also quick to point out that it is not enough to simply introduce some indeterminism into the system. In addition, agents must also have some degree of *positive control* over what they do, such that their "free actions" are intelligible, purposive, and non-random. But as we will soon see, libertarian accounts have had an extremely difficult time explaining how we can satisfy this positive constraint in a way that fits ourselves as free agents into the natural world characterized by science.

2.2.1.1 Event-Causal Libertarianism

I would like to begin by focusing on Robert Kane's well-known event-causal account since it promises a naturalized account of libertarian free will (Kane 1996, 1999, 2002, 2007, 2011, 2016). As Kane describes it, his theory is an attempt "to see how far one can go in making sense of libertarian freedom without appealing either to sui generis kinds of agency or causation" (2002: 416). Explaining why he rejects earlier agent-causal attempts to account for libertarian free will, Kane writes:

> Libertarian responses invariably followed a certain pattern. Since agents had to be able to act or act otherwise, given exactly the same prior psychological and physical history (as indeterminism seems to require), some "extra (or special) factors" had to be introduced over and above the normal flow of events in order to explain how and why agents acted as they did ... But, whatever form they have taken, extra factor strategies have tended to reinforce the widespread view that notions of free will requiring indeterminism are mysterious and have no place in the modern scientific picture of the world. More importantly, as I see it, extra factor strategies give only the appearance of solving the problems of indeterminism, while creating further problems of their own. (2002: 415)

While I agree with Kane about "extra (or special) factor" strategies (see Section 2.2.1.2), I also acknowledge that if Kane were successful in providing an intelligible account of libertarian freedom, one that avoided such extra (or special) factors, such an account would need to be taken seriously by naturalists like myself. Unfortunately for libertarians, Kane's account fails to deliver on its promise – or so I will now argue. This is because (a) it fails to preserve the control in action required for basic desert moral responsibility since agents are left unable to *settle* which decision occurs, (b) it requires an unintelligible notion of dual efforts, and (c) it posits several highly speculative and empirically unsupported assumptions that are unlikely to all be true. And while my focus will primarily be on Kane's account in this section, I will also consider alternative accounts by John Lemos (2018, 2019) and Al Mele (2006, 2017) and argue that they too fail to salvage event-causal libertarianism.[2] I begin, however, with a brief review of Kane's account.

According to Kane, while the kind of free will required for basic desert moral responsibility does not require that we could have done otherwise for *every* act performed, it *does* require that we could have done otherwise (in the unconditional indeterminist sense) with respect to *some* acts in our past life histories by which we formed our present character. That is, while many of the free acts for which we are morally responsible may be causally determined, on Kane's account such causally determined free acts get their freedom from the fact that they proceed from a character or a motivational state that was shaped by earlier causally undetermined free acts. Kane calls these causally undetermined free acts which shape our character or motivational states *self-forming actions* (SFA). On Kane's account, then, basic desert moral responsibility requires indeterminism, but indeterminism does not have to be involved in all acts done "of our own free will." Only those choices or acts in our lifetimes by which we make ourselves into the kinds of persons we are have to be undetermined.

Self-forming actions, according to Kane, occur in situations of deep moral conflict where there is tension and uncertainty in our minds about what to do. Kane often provides the following example to help illustrate such moments:

> Consider a businesswoman who faces a conflict of this kind. She is on the way to a meeting important to her career when she observes an assault taking place in an alley. An inner struggle ensues between her moral conscience, to stop and call for help, and her career ambitions that tell her she cannot miss this meeting. She has to make an effort of will to overcome the temptation to go on to her meeting. If she overcomes the temptation, it will be the result of her effort, but if she fails, it will be because she did not *allow* her effort to succeed. And this is due to the fact that, while she wanted to overcome temptation, she also wanted to fail, for quite different and incommensurable reasons. When agents, like the woman, decide in such circumstances, and the indeterminate efforts they are making become determinate choices, they *make* one set of competing reasons or motives prevail over the others then and there *by deciding*. (2002: 471)

According to Kane, in this kind of situation the agent actually exerts efforts to choose to do each act she is contemplating – that is, she tries to make the choice to stop and

---

[2] For similar objections against Mark Balaguer's (2009) event-causal account, see Pereboom (2014a).

prevent the assault and she tries to make the choice to go on to her business meeting. Furthermore, Kane has us suppose that, whichever choice she ends up making, her ultimate decision is causally undermined, which is required for it to count as a self-forming action.

Kane goes on to speculate how these causally undetermined self-forming actions can be explained in a way that fits with a modern scientific understanding of the world. He suggests that when we are confronted with difficult moral decisions, like the one of the businesswomen:

> [T]here is tension and uncertainty in our minds about what to do . . . that is reflected in appropriate regions of our brains by movement away from thermodynamic equilibrium – in short, a kind of stirring up of chaos in the brain that makes it sensitive to micro-indeterminacies at the neuronal level. The uncertainty and inner tension we feel at such soul-searching moments of self-formation would thereby be reflected in the indeterminacy of our neuronal processes themselves. What is experienced personally as uncertainty corresponds physically to the opening of a window of opportunity that temporarily screens off complete determination by influences of the past. (2002: 417)

Kane's account therefore proposes that the uncertainty we experience from conflicting motivations "corresponds physically" with genuine indeterminacy at the neuronal level. Being torn due to such conflicts creates chaotic conditions that amplify quantum indeterminacy so that its effects percolate up – that is, they are first manifested at the level of individual neurons and then at the level of neural networks (Kane 1996: 128–130). Kane also maintains that the indeterministic noise experienced during "soul-searching moments of self-formation" creates the conditions in which quantum indeterminacies can be amplified and manifested in our deliberative processes. He writes:

> Let us imagine, in cases of SFAs like the businesswoman's, where the agents' wills are conflicted, that the indeterministic noise which is obstructing her will to overcome temptation (and do the moral thing) is not coming from an external source, but from her own will, since she also deeply desires to do the opposite (go on to her meeting). Imagine that in such conflicting circumstances, two competing (recurrent) neural networks are involved. (These are complex networks of interconnected neurons in the brain circulating impulses in feedback loops of a kind generally involved in high-level cognitive processing.) The input of one of these networks is coming from the woman's desires and motives for stopping to help the victim. If the network reaches a certain activation threshold (the simultaneous firing of a complex set of "output" neurons), that would represent her choice to help. For the competing network, the inputs are her ambitious motives for going on to her meeting, and its reaching an activation threshold represents the choice to go on . . . Now imagine further that these two competing networks are connected so that the indeterministic noise that is an obstacle to her making one of the choices is coming from her desire to make the other. Thus, as

suggested for SFAs generally, the indeterminism arises from a tension-creating conflict in the will. (2002: 419)

On Kane's account, then, what makes a person become sensitive to microlevel indeterminacy in the brain, leading to the indeterministic causation of action in a self-forming action, is the presence of competing efforts of will that cannot both be satisfied. And as John Lemos describes:

> It is important to understand that on Kane's view when we engage in an SFA we don't merely want to do one act, A, and another act, B, and then choose one or the other. Rather, on his view in deliberating about whether to A or to B, we actually are trying/exerting effort to A and simultaneously trying/exerting effort to B. The physical correlates of these competing efforts are competing neural networks in the brain. In these situations the choice or action is caused by processes in the brain, but the choice is not deterministically caused. So, in the case of the businesswoman, whichever course of action she takes, her action will be caused but undetermined by one of her efforts of will – her efforts to prevent the assault or her effort to go on to her meeting. (2019: 4)

Kane also maintains that "when either of the [neural] pathways 'wins' (that is, reaches an activation threshold)," this amounts to a genuine example of *choice* (2002: 419). For Kane, in cases of self-forming actions, the neural correlates of our efforts of will represent our competing motivations. And although it will be causally undermined which choice we ultimate make, since it is causally undetermined which neural network or "volitional stream" (Kane 2016) will "win" out, Kane nonetheless maintains that we will be morally responsible for that choice since it will be the result of one of our efforts of will succeeding at reaching its goal.

Kane therefore maintains that under these conditions, the choice (either way) will *not* be "inadvertent," "accidental," "capricious," or "merely random" *because* it will be *willed* by the agent either way, done for *reasons* either way, which the agent then and there endorses. In these self-forming actions, whichever way the agents choose, they will have succeeded in doing what they were trying to do *because they were simultaneously trying to make both choices*. According to Kane, "when we do decide under such conditions of uncertainty, the outcome is not determined because of the preceding [neuronal] indeterminacy – and yet it can be willed (and hence rational and voluntary) either way because, in such self-formation, the agents' prior wills are divided by conflicting motives" (2002: 471). For instance, Kane maintains that the neuronal indeterminacy that accompanies the businesswoman's uncertainty satisfies the incompatibilist demand for undetermined action, nonetheless the action is still intelligible *because* it will be *willed* by the woman either way, done for *reasons* either way – moral conviction if she turns back, ambitious motives if she goes on. Even though the outcome of the businesswoman's deliberation is indeterminate, it is *backed by reasons* since each of the competing courses of action is.

2.2 Hard Incompatibilism

While Kane's account succeeds in avoiding sui generis kinds of agency and causation, I maintain that it fails to preserve libertarian free will for three main reasons. First, for an agent to be morally responsible for a decision in the basic desert sense, she must exercise a certain type and degree of control in making that decision. In the event-causal libertarian picture, only events are causes, and free decisions are causally undetermined. The causally relevant events antecedent to a decision – most prominently agent-involving events – accordingly leave it open whether the decision occurs, and thus do not *settle* whether it occurs. Settling whether a decision occurs is a kind of control in action, and the event-causal libertarian is a causalist about control, specifying that control in action is a causal matter. But because on this view all causation is event-causation, the agent can have no role in settling whether a decision occurs beyond the role it plays in agent-involving events. Hence, given the indeterminism required for a free decision, the agent cannot settle whether the decision occurs. Therefore, in the event-causal libertarian picture an agent cannot have the control required for being morally responsible in the basic desert sense for a decision. Since the agent "disappears" at the crucial juncture in the production of the decision – when its occurrence is to be settled – Pereboom calls this the *disappearing agent objection* (Pereboom 2004, 2007, 2014a, 2017), and it is one kind of *luck objection* (Waller 1988; Allen 1995; Mele 1998, 2006; Haji 1999, 2005; Clarke 2002). I contend that this objection is a devastating one, not only for Kane's account but for all event-causal libertarian accounts (Caruso 2012; Pereboom 2014a, 2018).

The core concern is that because event-causal libertarian agents lack the power to settle which decision occurs, they lack the role in action necessary to secure the control that basic desert moral responsibility requires. As Pereboom spells out the objection:

> Suppose that a decision is made in a deliberative context in which the agent's moral motivations favor deciding to A, her prudential motivations favor her deciding to not-A, and the strength(s) of these motivations are in equipoise. A and non-A are the options she is considering. The potentially causally relevant events, typically belief- or desire-involving events, thus render the occurrence of each of these decisions equiprobable. But then the potentially causally relevant events do not settle which decision occurs, that is, whether the decision to A or the decision to not-A occurs. Since, given event-causal libertarianism, only events are causally relevant, *nothing* settles which decision occurs. Thus it can't be the agent or anything about the agent that settles which decision occurs, and she therefore lacks the control required for moral responsibility for it. (Pereboom 2018; see also 2014a, 2017)[3]

Imagine, for example, that Farah is torn between two courses of action: (a) attending an important meeting at work tomorrow morning or (b) calling in sick and spending

---

[3] Note that while Pereboom formulation of the problem cites the equipoise situation as a paradigm case, the objection about settling equally arises in non-equipoise situations as well.

the day with a friend who is in town for just one day. She has good reasons for doing (a) but she also has good reasons for doing (b). Whatever she ends up doing, we can say that it was intentionally endorsed and that she had "reasons for doing it." Consistent with Kane's account, we can also presuppose that Farah exerts "dual efforts of will" by trying to choose to do each act she is contemplating. But if indeterminacy is genuinely involved in the agential causal sequence, then it really is a matter of luck which action she ends up performing. To make vivid the lack of control agents have over genuinely undetermined events, consider what would happen if God rolled back the relevant stretch of history to some point prior to an undetermined event and then allowed it to unfold once more. Since events would *not* unfold in the same way on the replay as they did the first time around, since these are genuinely undetermined, and nothing the agent does (or is) can ensure which undetermined possibility is realized, the outcome of this sequence (in this case the agent's decision) is a matter of luck. Such luck, skeptics argue, is responsibility-undermining.

Since Kane's account rejects "extra (or special) factors" and "sui generis kinds of agency or causation," he is left unable to explain how agents can settle which option for action occurs. This is because, even if quantum indeterminacies were capable of percolating up to the level of neural networks during self-forming actions, as Kane proposes, his account leaves us unable to settle which neural network "wins" out. And on the account of *settling* I favor, the ability to settle which option for action occurs is an exercise of control in action with two main characteristics: *determination* and *difference making*. Following Pereboom (2017), I propose, first, that to settle whether to A or B, or equivalently, which of A or B occurs, is to *determine* which of these options occurs (Pereboom 2017, 2018). But there is also more to the notion of settling than determining whether an action or decision to act occurs. Helen Steward (2012), for instance, has argued that settling must also involve *difference making* – that is, making the difference as to which option for actions occurs. Putting the two suggestions together, Pereboom proposes the following characterization: An agent settles which option for action occurs just in case she determines which action occurs, and she makes the difference as to which action occurs (2017). Since event-causal libertarianism lacks this ability to settle which option for action occurs, it is unable to preserve the control in action required for basic desert moral responsibility.

Control, on Kane's account, essentially comes down to the agent being motivated by various wants, desires, and values – and the outcome, whatever it ends up being, being backed by reasons the agent there and then endorses. No indeterminist control is imparted to the agent as it is in agent-causal accounts. For this reason, Randolph Clarke has argued, "[A]n event-causal libertarian view adds no new types of causes to those that can be required by a compatibilist account, and hence the former appears to add nothing to the agent's positive power to determine what he does" (2002: 374). Clarke argues that causal indeterminist theories like Kane's provide "leeway" for

2.2 Hard Incompatibilism

choice, but no more control over actions than compatibilists offer – and more control, argues Clarke, is needed for libertarian freedom and responsibility. Timothy O'Connor (2000a) presents a similar argument against Kane. He argues that positing causal indeterminism in the triggering of an action is not enough – a successful account of libertarian freedom "must further explain how it could be up to the agent which option is realized" (2004: 24). Indeterminacy may open the door for libertarian free will, but it does not explain the control needed to carry out such freedom.

Defenders of event-causal libertarianism have attempted to respond to this objection in different ways (cf. Mele 2006, 2017; Lemos 2018, 2019). John Lemos (2019), for instance, argues that Kane's account of dual efforts can help answer the luck or disappearing agent objection. Kane's notion of dual efforts, recall, is an essential component of his account of self-forming actions. In the businesswoman example, Kane's account requires that she actually exerts efforts to choose to do each act she is contemplating – that is, she tries to make the choice to stop and prevent the assault and she tries to make the choice to go on to her business meeting. Because of these dual efforts, Kane maintains that whichever choice she makes it will be the product of one of these efforts. Appealing to this notion of dual efforts, Lemos argues: "[E]fforts are things we *do*, we *engage* in them; as such, they are not like merely having reasons or being in a certain motivational state" (2019: 8). For this reason, Lemos maintains that

> the agent doesn't disappear in the performance of an SFA [self-forming action]. The agent is on the scene engaged in these efforts and whichever choice is made it will be a product of one of her efforts, which is something she *does*. As such, her choice doesn't just happen to her; rather, her effort is an activity which is under her control and it provides a causal link between her motivation states and her choice. (2019: 8)

These considerations lead Lemos to conclude, "[D]ual efforts reveal that the idea that agents 'disappear' in causally undetermined choices is misguided" (2019: 8).

Setting aside for the moment the intelligibility of Kane's notion of dual efforts, something I will question in a moment, I contend that Lemos is mistaken in thinking such dual efforts of will help resolve the luck or disappearing agent objection. For one thing, Pereboom's objection is that the agent "disappears" at the crucial juncture in the production of the decision – that is, when its occurrence is to be *settled*. Nothing Lemos argues above refutes that. For an agent to be able to settle which option for action occurs, they must determine and make the difference as to which action occurs. Exerting dual efforts of will does not satisfy this level of control. Hence, even if an individual is "engaged" in a self-forming action in the manner described earlier, their choice is still a matter of luck. The disappearing agent objection is not that individuals play *no role* in which option for action occurs; rather it maintains that, given event-causal libertarianism, only events can be causally relevant, which leaves agents unable to settle which choice is ultimately made.

At this point, Lemos shifts gears and instead argues that the fact that the agent's choice is undetermined does not mean it is a matter of luck. In defending this claim, he appeals to Kane's argument from analogy:

> Kane notes that when we make an effort to do something and it is causally undermined whether we will succeed in doing it, we are still responsible for our action when we succeed. For instance, he has us suppose that an angry husband tries to break a glass tabletop and it is causally undetermined whether he will succeed in doing so. Kane notes that if he intentionally and without manipulation or coercion tried to break the tabletop and despite the indeterminacy he succeeds, then he is responsible for doing so. By analogy, he believes it follows that our businesswoman will also be responsible for what she does either way, since either way she will succeed at doing something which she without manipulation or coercion intentionally tried to do. (Lemos 2019: 8)

Lemos goes on to argue:

> [E]ven if Kane's view leaves room for chance in settling which particular choice gets made, it's not the kind of chance that reduces the agent's responsibility in any way. Again, think about the angry husband who breaks the tabletop. It was causally undetermined that it would break, but it breaks because he tried to break it and he's no less responsible for it than he would be had his effort *determined* its breaking. So, too, whichever particular choice our businesswoman ... makes she will be no less responsible for her choice than if her effort to make that choice had determined her choice. (2019: 9)

There is something odd, however, about this analogy. For one thing, the kind of effort the angry husband exhibits when he forcefully slams his fist on the table is *different in kind* from the kind of effort the businesswoman exhibits. The former involves a set of intentional movements and behaviors that are (presumably) under the direct control of the agent, even if the outcome of those actions (i.e., the table breaking) is not. The latter, however, involves an altogether different notion of effort, an *effort of will* – one that is, itself, ill-defined and controversial. Furthermore, in the case of the angry husband, the indeterminacy is presumably located *outside* the agent and occurs *after* he has already deliberated, chosen, and acted – that is, what is indeterminate is whether the tabletop breaks or not. In the businesswoman case, on the other hand, the indeterminacy is located at the level of neuronal processes *within* the agent and just *prior* to one effort of will winning out over the other, presumably the result of one neural network indeterminately reaching an activation threshold. Given these differences, the analogy does not go through. From the fact that the angry husband may be responsible for breaking the table despite the indeterminacy, at least for those who believe in moral responsibility, it does not follow that the businesswoman in Kane's example is equally morally responsible. To assume that she is would be to beg the question.

This brings me to my second objection to Kane's account, which questions his notion of *dual efforts* itself (see, e.g., Caruso 2012, 2015a; Vincent 2015). The problem, I contend, is with the rationality and intelligibility of positing an agent who *actively* and *simultaneously* tries to bring about two inconsistent ends. When an agent is confronted with a difficult moral choice – like whether they should accept the sexual advances of a stranger or stay faithful to their partner – it is easy to imagine the agent experiencing a conflict of desires. But to say that in such a situation the agent is actively willing *both* the moral choice to stay faithful to their partner *and* the choice to give in to their temptation makes the agent appear irrational. Such simultaneous but inconsistent efforts of will amount to the agent willing P and not-P at the same time. Not only is this of dubious coherence, it is far from the model of rationally guided behavior we were promised. It is also worth noting how counterintuitive this is as an account of "overcoming temptation." Try explaining to your partner that you *actively willed* (hence *tried*) sleeping with another person but was unsuccessful because the competing neural network won out – the result of an indeterminate process! I doubt you will have much success persuading them that your behavior was praiseworthy or that you have the requisite control over your ability to resist temptation.

I also see no principled reason why Kane should limit his account to just *dual* efforts. His account is consistent with the possibility of self-forming actions in which an individual is torn between three or more competing options and simultaneously tries to will all of them. Imagine, for example, that a bright philosophy student is torn between three career options after graduation. They have been accepted into both top-tier law schools and graduate philosophy programs, but a family member has also offered them a high-paying job in finance. If they accept the finance job, they will make a lot of money without the need for any additional schooling. On the other hand, they had always wanted to be a philosophy professor but are concerned about finding a position after graduate school. Law school seems like a good compromise, especially since they also have an interest in criminal law, but they're not sure whether it is a better option than either taking the finance job or going to graduate school for philosophy. They need to make a decision this week and are torn between the three options. In this situation, we can imagine that the student has reasons backing all three options and they simultaneously try to will all of them. Kane's account therefore allows for the possibility of *dual, triple*, and *quadruple efforts of will*. Such efforts of will, however, highlight just how irrational it is for an agent to actively and simultaneously try to bring about such inconsistent ends.

Lastly, I am not at all clear what an "effort of will" actually is. Kane and Lemos suggest that it is more than just "merely having reasons or being in a certain motivational state" (Lemos 2019: 8). But what more is required? On Kane's account, the dual efforts involved in self-forming actions appear to be efforts to *make a choice*, which Kane defines as "the formation of an intention ... to do something" (2007: 33). But as Leigh Vicens has argued, "[I]t does not make sense to speak of *efforts* to form particular *intentions* at all" (2015: 93). I agree with Vicens when she questions, "[W]hat exactly does it mean to make an effort *to intend* to do something?" (2015: 96). This component of Kane's theory leads to conceptual confusion. For instance, when we speak of an agent "making an effort" what we typically have in mind is the agent making an effort to do something *intentional*. But if this is what "making an effort" means, then to say that someone is making an effort to form a particular intention would imply that she is *intending to form a particular intention*, "which would seem nonsensical" (Vicens 2015: 96).[4] Kane's account of dual efforts therefore suffers from a number of devastating difficulties. Not only is the rationality of positing an agent who actively and simultaneously tries to bring about two inconsistent ends questionable, there is the problem of triple and quadruple efforts, and there is the intelligibility of talking about *efforts* to form particular *intentions*. And on top of all this, even if dual efforts *were* intelligible, they would still not resolve the luck or disappearing agent objection for the reasons argued earlier.

Before moving on, let me briefly consider a second possible reply to the luck or disappearing agent objection. While officially agnostic about libertarianism, Al Mele has defended event-causal libertarianism as a viable option (2006, 2017). He calls his alternative account the *daring libertarian view* (DLV) (2006, 2017) and distinguishes it from Kane's. As he describes it:

> [The daring libertarian view] ... is similar to Kane's view. The main difference is that where Kane postulates concurrent competing indeterministic efforts to choose, I postulate an indeterministic effort to decide (or choose) what to do. That effort can result in different decisions, holding the past and the laws of nature fixed. For example, in Bob's story ... [e.g., Bob lives in a town in which people make many strange bets, including bets on whether the opening coin toss for football games occur on time. After Bob agreed to toss a coin at noon to start a high school football game, Carl, a notorious gambler, offered him $50 to wait until 12:02 to toss it. Bob is undecided about what to do as noon approaches (Mele 2006: 73–74; 2017: 112–113)], there are no concurrent competing efforts to choose. Instead, there is a possible world in which Bob's effort to decide what to do about the coin toss issues at *t* in a decision to cheat, and in another world with the same past up to *t* and the same laws of nature, that effort issues at *t* in a decision to toss the coin right then. Bob has competing reasons at the time, and the decision he makes – whether it is to cheat or to do the right thing – is made for the reasons that favor it. (2017: 206)

[4] Vicens (2015) offers an alternative libertarian account that she maintains avoids these objections about dual efforts. She proposes that we place the indeterminism earlier in the sequence – that is, instead of viewing conflicting desires as leading to competing *efforts of will*, which is then only settled by one neural network temporarily winning out over another, Vicens suggests that we instead conceive of the conflict between our desires as being resolved *before* they lead to competing volitional efforts. While this is an intriguing proposal, I have argued elsewhere that it does not succeed and instead leads to a number of additional challenges. For details, see Caruso (2015a).

The core difference between Kane's account and Mele's is that Kane would represent Bob (and other event-causal agents) as trying to make each of two different competing choices, while Mele represents Bob as simply trying to decide what to do (Mele 2017: 207–208). Mele therefore rejects Kane's notion of dual efforts. The reasons he gives for doing so are similar to the one's above, but he also adds the following phenomenological point:

> [A]lthough Kane is ordinarily pretty sensitive to the phenomenology of agency, trying to choose to A while also trying to choose to do something else instead seems remote from ordinary experience ... We may occasionally have an experience of trying to bring it about that we choose to A. (For example, someone who knows that it would be best to quit smoking but who has not yet chosen to quit may try to vividly represent to himself the most important reasons for quitting, including the dangers of not quitting, with a view to bringing it about that he chooses to quit.) But how many of us have experienced simultaneously trying to bring it about that we choose a particular course of action and trying to bring it about that we choose a competing course of action instead? If such dual efforts never occur, they never underwrite free choices. (2017: 200)

Mele goes on to write, "[P]eople like me have their doubts about whether normal human beings ever simultaneously try to make each of two (or more) competing choices or decision, and phenomenological considerations are among the considerations we cite in support of the doubts" (2017: 200). I concur. Phenomenological considerations provide an additional reason for doubting Kane's account of dual efforts, an essential component of his overall account of self-forming actions.

While I think Mele is right about dual efforts, the question at hand is whether his daring libertarian view provides a better solution to the disappearing agent objection than Kane's. I do not think it does. In response to the luck or disappearing agent objection, Mele challenges Pereboom's claim that, given event-causal libertarianism, "only events are causally relevant" and neither "the agent nor anything about the agent" can settle which decision occurs (Pereboom 2001, 2014a, 2018). According to Mele:

> Proponents of event-causal views of decision-making will complain about the characterization of their view here. According to such views, it is agents who decide. Agents who decide (at least when they decide) are able to decide and have the power to decide. Proponents of event-causal theories of decision-making do not view an "agent's states, or else agent-involving events" as exercising the power or ability to make decisions. This is as it should be. States and events are not able to make decisions and therefore not able to exercise the power or ability to make decisions. Only agents can decide what to do. (2017: 164)

He goes on to write:

> It is agents who make decisions ... When they do, we say that such things as intentions, beliefs, and desires (or their physical realizers, or facts about what agents intend, believe, and desire) are among the causes of the decision. But we do not say

that things such as these decide or make decisions. We ascribe the decision-making to the agent, just as we ascribe the free-throw sinking to Sam. (2017: 165)

Mele goes on to add that "in my view, an agent's deciding to A ... does not depend on his having agent-causal powers and is accommodated by an event-causal libertarian view" (2017: 165–166). He calls this thesis *T* and maintains that if it is true, then "if an agent's deciding to A in a case of the kind in question is sufficient for his settling whether he is in one decision state or another, such settling does not depend on agent-causal powers and the disappearing agent objection fails" (2017: 166).

While Mele is, of course, free to describe his event-causal account however he wishes, the language he adopts when he describes *agents* as making decisions comes very close to violating the event-causal prohibition on appealing to "sui generis kinds of agency and causation." Pereboom expresses this concern rather well in his review of Mele's (2017) book:

> Note that Mele's suggestion is formulated in terms of *an agent* deciding. A concern that might be raised is that given the commitments of the event-causal libertarian position, this formulation is apt to convey the impression that his suggestion has more credibility than it in fact does. Mele argues, plausibly, that on event-causal libertarian reviews it remains correct to say that agents, and not events, decide and make decisions. "[Sam] has and exercises the ability or power to sink free throws, and he sinks many of them. His intentions, beliefs, skills, and the like do not sink free throws – alone or in combination with one another. And that is no surprise, because they are not able to sink free throws" (Mele 2017: 164). To be sure, retaining ordinary agent talk is legitimate for the event-causal libertarian. The view is not committed to linguistic reform. But it is committed to the metaphysical thesis that all causation is event-causation. Regarding Mele's contention that Sam's "intentions, beliefs, skills, and the like do not sink free throws," it's not open to the event-causal libertarian to affirm that in the sinking of the free throw Sam is a causal influence distinct from Sam-involving events. What's at issue here isn't how we ordinarily speak, but rather the commitments of an event-causal theory of action. (2018)

The problem is that event-causal libertarians, while free to retain ordinary agent talk, are committed to refrain from ascribing causal powers to agents separate from the causal powers of agent-involving events. Hence, it is hard to understand what Mele means when he says that *agents* "have the power to decide." Does he mean that they as agents, and not by virtue of the events in which they have a role, have the *causal* power to decide? If so, then he is guilty of smuggling in sui generis kinds of agency and causation and his account is no longer a pure event-causal account. If not, then it is hard to see how his reply to the disappearing agent objection adds anything new. Given Mele's resolute causalism (2017), he needs to explain how agents are capable of exercising the control needed for basic desert moral responsibility, which in the context of the disappearing agent argument requires the ability to settle which option occurs, without smuggling in agent-causal powers. I do not see how Mele's account does this.

Mele, in fact, is rather forthright about the fact that luck, in one form or another, remains an essential and unavoidable component of any and all libertarian accounts of free will (2006, 2017). And while he thinks the problem of luck actually counts more strongly against agent-causal libertarian accounts, he acknowledges that a degree of luck is still present in his own event-causal account. This is because, on both his account and Kane's, "what an agent does at *t* in one possible world and what he does at *t* in another possible world with the same past up to *t* and the same laws of nature is just a matter of luck" (Mele 2017: 204). When comparing the relative costs of his account against Kane's, Mele makes the following refreshingly honest points (this is a direct quote):

1. *On cross-world luck.* When an agent's choice-making occurs in a way that fits my [daring libertarian view (*DLV*)], the cross-world difference in what he chooses is, in Kane's words, "a matter of luck or chance" (2014: 207). When the agent's choice making occurs in a way that fits Kane's concurrent-efforts view, the cross-world difference in which of his efforts to choose wins out is no less a matter of luck or chance.
2. *On empirical burdens.* Kane's concurrent-efforts view requires more for basically free decisions [e.g., self-forming actions] than *DLV* does. It requires that the agent simultaneously makes competing efforts to choose. Ordinary experience supports the claim that normal human agents sometimes make an effort to decide what to do. The same cannot plausibly be said for the claim that agents sometimes make concurrent efforts to choose of the kind featured in Kane's view. And, to the best of my knowledge, there is no direct evidence of any kind that normal agents ever make Kane-style concurrent efforts to choose. (Mele 2017: 209–210)

Mele contends that the conjunction of 1 and 2 is motivation for his thesis that "event – causal libertarians should prefer *DLV* to Kane's concurrent-efforts view" (2017: 2010). Kane's view, he contends, has "a significantly heavy burden – and therefore carries a significantly higher cost – on the empirical front, and, as far as I can see, it has no advantage over *DLV* on the cross-world luck at the time of choice or decision" (2017: 210).

While I will leave it to event-causal libertarians to decide which account is preferable, *neither* account, I contend, resolves the luck or disappearing agent objection. Kane's account suffers from the problems outlined earlier. Mele's account, on the other hand, just bites the bullet and claims that libertarians simply need to come to terms with the fact that a degree of luck will remain present in any libertarian account that maintains that self-forming actions (or what Mele calls "basically free actions"[5]) are indeterministically caused by their proximal causes. Mele, for example, writes:

---

[5] Mele defines a *basically free action* as follows: "An agent performs a basically free action *A* at time *t* only if there is another possible world with the same past up to *t* and the same laws of nature in which he does not do *A* at *t*" (2017: 198).

"The typical libertarian wants both indeterminism and significant control at the moment of decision. That is the desire that prompts a serious version of the worry about luck ... I argue that neither agent causationists nor event-causal libertarians have laid the worry to rest" (2006: 14). While Mele does not think this worry provides *enough* reason to abandon libertarianism, I think it does. Such luck, I've argued, undermines the control in action, that is, the free will, required for basic desert moral responsibility, since it leaves agents unable to settle which option for action occurs. The task of event-causal libertarians is not just to make indeterminate actions intelligible, explaining how they can be done *for reasons*, they must also preserve the *control in action* needed for free will. They fail to do this.

My last and final objection to event-causal libertarian accounts is that they posit highly speculative and empirically unsupported assumptions that are unlikely to all be true. Kane's account, for instance, not only posits the possibility of microlevel neuronal indeterminacy, but also the chaotic amplification of such indeterminacy up to the level of neural networks. It is worth considering just how demanding the theory's empirical commitments are. As Manuel Vargas points out:

> [N]ot only do agent mental processes have to turn out to be indeterministic, but they must also be indeterministic in a very particular way. If multiple mutually exclusive aims did not cause the brain to go into a chaotic state the theory would be disproved. If it turned out that neurological systems weren't sensitive to quantum indeterminacies the theory would be disproved. If it turned out that neurological systems were sensitive to quantum indeterminacies, but not sufficiently sensitive to amplify quantum indeterminacies in a way that affects the outcome of choice, this too would disprove the theory. These are not marginal or insubstantial bets about what brain science will reveal to us. (2007: 143)

Similar empirical constraints apply to the event-causal accounts of Lemos (2018, 2019), Mele (2006, 2017), Ekstrom (2000), and Balaguer (2009), since they all posit indeterminacies at the level of brain processes. As a result, if quantum indeterminacy were shown not to exist at the appropriate neuronal level, then all these accounts would be empirically falsified. They would also be falsified if indeterminacy were not to exist at the right *temporal* moment in the proximate causal chain leading up to an agent deciding or making a choice, since each theory places the posited indeterminacy at some precise moment in the causal sequence. Mele, in fact, remains agnostic about libertarianism partly for this reason:

> Two things have kept me from being a libertarian. First, I have not been persuaded by any argument for incompatibilism. Second, for reasons I have set out elsewhere (Mele 2006), I take (a naturalistic) event-causal libertarianism to be the most promising brand of libertarianism, and I do not know of strong evidence that human brains work as they would need to work if a theoretically attractive event-causal libertarian view is true. Both of these things stand in the way of my endorsing the darling libertarian view that I floated. (Mele 2017: 205)

Lemos also admits: "It is my view that at this point in time we simply don't have sufficient experimental/empirical evidence nor sufficient metaphysical nor logical nor intuitive evidence to establish that libertarian free will exists" (2018: 6). These acknowledgments are extremely important, since they reveal that belief in libertarian free will does not meet the high epistemic standard needed to justify retributive legal punishment (see the Epistemic Argument in Chapter 3 for more on this point).

2.2.1.2 Agent-Causal Libertarianism

Let me now turn to agent-causal libertarian accounts. In the previous section we saw that because of the disappearing agent objection, if we are to be free in the sense required for basic desert moral responsibility, agents must have an enhanced kind of control in action relative to the control we would have if our actions are event-causally undermined. Agent-causal libertarians respond to this difficulty by specifying a new way in which the agent might possess the required power to *settle* which outcome occurs in indeterministic contexts. The solution they offer is to reintroduce the *agent as a cause*, this time not merely as involved in events, but rather fundamentally as a substance. Agent-causal theorists propose that we possess a distinctive causal power – a power for an agent, fundamentally as a substance, to cause a decision without being causally determined to do so, and thereby to settle whether it occurs (Chisholm 1966, 1971, 1976; Griffith 2010; Kant 1781/1787/1987; O'Connor 2000a, 2002, 2011; Clarke 1993, 2000, 2002, 2003).

Timothy O'Connor, for instance, regards the apparent failure of event-causal libertarian views as motivation for libertarians to embrace agent-causation. Since on event-causal accounts, "which choice occurs on a given occasion seems, as far as the agent's direct control goes, a matter of chance" (2000a), O'Connor argues that what is missing, and what libertarian accounts of free will require, is an "active power" – that is, "the power to freely choose one's course of action *for reasons*" (2000a: 95). As he describes it, "[E]xerting active power is intrinsically a direct exercise of control over one's own behavior" (2000a: 61). It is this active power that is supposed to provide agent-causal accounts with the control in action missing from event-causal accounts. Randolph Clarke similarly argues that "what is wanted from an account of free will is an account of an agent's *control* over which decisions he makes and which actions he performs" (2000: 22). He adds, "An agent's exercise of control in acting is an exercise of a positive power to determine what he does" (2002: 374). In this section, I will examine libertarian agent-causal accounts to see if they fare any better in preserving the kind of free will required for basic desert moral responsible. I will argue that they do not. I begin with a brief overview.

The most prominent agent-causal theorists have included the eighteenth-century Scottish philosopher Thomas Reid (1788/1983), who taught at the University of Aberdeen where I am currently writing this book, and such contemporary philosophers as C. A. Campbell (1957, 1967), Roderick Chisholm (1966, 1971, 1976),

Richard Taylor (1966, 1974), Randolph Clarke (1993, 1996, 2002, 2003), and Timothy O'Connor (1995, 1996, 2000a, 2000b, 2002). Common to all agent-causal accounts is the belief that an intelligible notion of an agent's causing an event can be given according to which the kind of causation involved is fundamentally distinct from the kind that obtains between events. The traditional notion of event causation assumes that all caused events are caused, either deterministically or indeterministically, by prior events. But instead of appealing to event causation, agent-causal theorists introduce a new type of causation, *agent-causation*, to account for human agency and freedom. According to this notion of agent-causation, it is the agent him- or herself that causes, or initiates, free actions. And the agent, which is the cause of their own free actions, is a *self-determining being*, causally undetermined by antecedent events and conditions.

While agent-causal theorists differ over whether they view all intentional actions as agent-causal in nature or just some intentional actions, they all agree that agent-causation is a necessary condition for an action's being free. The following passage by Richard Taylor does a good job summing up the basic position:

> The only conception of action that accords with our data is one according to which people ... are sometimes, but of course not always, self-determining beings; that is, beings which are sometimes the causes of their own behavior. In the case of an action that is free, it must be such that it is caused by the agent who performs it, but such that no antecedent conditions were sufficient for his performing just that action. In the case of an action that is both free and rational, it must be such that the agent who performed it did so for some reason, but this reason cannot have been the cause of it. (1974: 51)

Roderick Chisholm, another leading defender of agent-causal libertarianism, further elaborates this notion of self-determination when he writes:

> If we are responsible, and if what I have been trying to say [about agent causation] is true, then we have a prerogative which some would attribute only to God: each of us, when we act, is a prime unmoved mover. In doing what we do, we cause certain events to happen and nothing – or no one – causes us to cause those events to happen. (1964: 32)

O'Connor prefers the expression "not wholly moved movers" (2000a: 67), but the point is similar: According to agent-causal accounts, the agent must be the cause of their decision or action but themselves not causally necessitated to perform just that action – that is, the agent must be a kind of uncaused cause. This is what separates agent-causal accounts from all other accounts of free will. The reason agent-causal theorists view the agent, or self, as a prime unmoved mover is that they believe it is the only way to avoid the following dilemma. Free will skeptics and agent-causal libertarians largely agree that if determinism is true, human choice and action are not free since they are determined by antecedent conditions beyond the control of the agent, but if event-causal indeterminism is true, human actions are also not free since they would then be just a matter of luck. Agent-causal theorists present their view as a way to split the horns of this dilemma. As Taylor puts it: "The theory of agency avoids the absurdities of simple indeterminism by conceding that human behavior is caused [by the agent], while at the same time avoiding the difficulties of determinism by denying that every chain of causes and effects is infinite" (1974: 52).

While it is unclear whether agent-causal libertarianism actually avoids the problem of luck, for reasons that have been explored by Mele (2006), Haji (2004, 2016), Levy (2011), and others, I will focus most of my attention here on the metaphysical commitments of the view (although I will briefly return to the issue of luck and agent-causal libertarianism in Section 2.3). In this section, I will argue that (a) our best philosophical and scientific theories about the world count strongly against the metaphysical commitments of agent-causation; (b) by conceived of agents as non-reducible *substances* capable of causing physical events, agent-causal accounts run into difficulties accounting for mental causation, a necessary condition for free will; (c) the theory appears not to be reconcilable with a deterministic law-governed physical world (Pereboom 2001, 2014); and (d) on such an account, reasons are not causes for action, which is potentially problematic. Since I've previously spelled out these objections at great length in my first book, *Free Will and Consciousness* (2012), I will keep my presentation of them here brief. But there are overwhelming reasons for why we should reject agent-causal libertarianism, even if I cannot discuss all of them in detail here (see, e.g., Pereboom 2001, 2014a; Dennett 1984, 2003; Waller 2011; Buckareff 2001, 2011, 2012, 2017; Haji 2005; Widerker 2005; Caruso 2012).

First, let us examine more closely the metaphysical commitments of the view. According to agent-causal libertarians, an agent, understood as a substance and not just a collection of events, has the ontologically primitive causal power to cause or initiate an action. On some accounts, like that of O'Connor's (2000a), this is done by causing an action-triggering intention. This intention then immediately causes the action. Through this action-triggering intention, agent-causal theorists maintain that the agent is in control of the action and hence free and morally responsible (O'Connor 2000a: 108–125). As O'Connor describes it:

[A]gent causation (whether actual or merely possible) is an ontologically primitive type of causation, one that is uniquely manifested by (some possible) persons and is inherently goal-directed and nondeterministic. It is not directed to any particular effects, but instead confers upon an agent a power to cause a certain type of event within the agent: the coming to be of a state of intention to carry out some act, thereby resolving a state of uncertainty about which action to undertake. (2011: 313)

In addition to this ontologically primitive causal power, agent-causal theories require a metaphysically robust notion of the *self* or *agent*. Some agent-causal accounts view the self as a nonphysical, non-material substance (e.g., Foster 1991; Eccles 1994; Swinburne 1986), others view the self as a radically emergent entity (e.g., O'Connor 2000a; Hasker 1999), and others still view the self simply as an unexplained mystery (Taylor 1966, 1974). But whether viewed as a Cartesian soul, emergent systems feature, or unexplained mystery, agent-causal libertarian accounts view the agent/self as primitive and basic.

William Hasker (1999), for example, defends a radically emergentist account of agent-causal libertarianism, which he calls *emergent dualism*. He argues that the radical emergence required for agent-causation is an emergence not of properties but of a new *substance*. According to Hasker, "it is not enough to say that there are emergent properties here; what is needed is an *emergent individual*, a new individual which comes into existence as a result of certain functional configurations of the material constituents of the brain and nervous system" (1999: 190). He goes on to write:

> The most plausible example we have seen of [a radically emergent] property is libertarian free will, and it seems clear that this cannot be a property that consists of properties of, and relations between, the parts that make up a system of objects. If we are to include libertarian free will as an attribute of persons, it seems we shall need to recognize persons, or minds, or souls, as unitary subjects, not analyzable as complexes of parts ... this means we shall have to acknowledge the existence of minds as *emergent individuals*. (1999: 178)

O'Connor likewise argues that agent-causal libertarians should embrace an emergentist account of "active power" (2000a: 121–123). And in explaining how the emergence of active power differs from the "emergence of phenomenal consciousness," he writes:

> The agency theorist is committed ... to the emergence of a very different sort of property altogether. Instead of producing certain effects in the appropriate circumstances itself, of necessity, this property enables the individual that has it in a certain range of circumstances to freely and directly bring about (or not bring about) any of a range of effects. (2000a: 121)

O'Connor recognizes that many will find this emergent active power difficult to accept. He writes:

> This further commitment leaves the theory's proponent open to special objection, not applicable to emergentist claims generally: given the unique nature of the type of property the theory postulates, it is doubtful whether it could emerge from other natural properties. It will be claimed that this property would require a very different kind of *substance* than material substances, as is posited by Cartesian dualism. (2000a: 121)

While O'Connor thinks this objection "does not bear well under scrutiny" (2000a: 121), he does acknowledge that "taking the agency theory seriously within an emergentist framework raises a whole host of more detailed theoretical problems and issues" (2000a: 121). The most fundamental, he says, "is determining the precise underlying properties on which an agent-causal capacity depends" (2000a: 121).

2.2 Hard Incompatibilism

It is important to acknowledge the truly radical nature of these metaphysical commitments. In fact, some agent-causal libertarians find it hard to put forth their theory with "complete comfort . . . and not wholly without embarrassment" (Taylor 1974: 53). Richard Taylor, for instance, when laying out his agent-causal account, admits that it involves "two rather strange metaphysical notions that are never applied elsewhere in nature." As Taylor, himself, puts it:

> Now, this conception of activity, and of an agent who is the cause of it, involves two rather strange metaphysical notions that are never applied elsewhere in nature. The first is that of a *self* or *person* – for example, a man – who is not merely a collection of things or events, but a self-moving being. For on this view it is a person, and not merely some part of him or something within him, that is the cause of his own activity. Now, we certainly do not know that a human being is anything more than an assemblage of physical things and processes that act in accordance with those laws that describe the behavior of all other physical things and processes. Even though he is a living being, of enormous complexity, *there is nothing, apart from the requirements of this theory*, to suggest that his behavior is so radically different in its origin from that of other physical objections, or that an understanding of it must be sought in some metaphysical realm wholly different from that appropriate to the understanding of nonliving things. (1974: 52; italics added)

The second "strange metaphysical notion" referred to by Taylor is the rejection of our ordinary understanding of event causation:

> Second, this conception of activity involves an extraordinary conception of causation according to which an agent, which is a substance and not an event, can nevertheless be the cause of an event. Indeed, if he is free agent then he can, on this conception, cause an event to occur – namely, some act of his own – without anything causing him to do so. This means that an agent is sometimes a cause, without being an antecedent sufficient condition. (1974: 52)

Taylor openly admits that this conception of the causation of events by things that are not events is, in fact, so different from the usual philosophical conception of a cause that "it should not even bear the same name, for 'being a cause' ordinarily just means 'being an antecedent sufficient condition or set of conditions.'" Instead, then, of speaking of agents as *causing* their own acts, Taylor suggests, "[I]t would perhaps be better to use another word entirely, and say, for instance, that they *originate* them, *initiate* them, or simply that they *perform* them" (1974: 52).

Now that we have a better understanding of the "strange metaphysical" commitments of agent-causation, we can ask (a) whether we are warranted in positing such commitments and (b) whether doing so would help preserve and account for libertarian free will? My first objection to agent-causation focuses on the former question and maintains that we should reject the metaphysical commitments of the view since they are fundamentally at odds with our best physical theories about the world and our understanding of the natural world characterized by science. As Kane correctly notes, "[E]xtra factor strategies have tended to reinforce the widespread view that notions of free will requiring indeterminism are mysterious and have no place in the modern scientific picture of the world" (2002: 415). The debate over free will is often about intuitions, presuppositions, and starting points. If you begin with the assumption that agents are, at least sometimes, free and morally responsible in the basic desert sense, and you are willing to do whatever is necessary to preserve that assumption, then you might be willing to accept God-like abilities and "strange metaphysical notions that are never applied elsewhere in nature." If, on the other hand, you begin with the assumption of *physicalism* – the thesis that the world is ultimately physical and there is nothing over and above physical properties and events in the universe (e.g., Dowel 2006: 25) – then you will likely reject agent-causal libertarianism.

I take the latter approach and view the metaphysical commitments of agent-causation as sufficient reason for rejecting the theory. The agent-causal theorist reasons that since our belief in libertarian free will is primitive and non-negotiable, and since physical causal closure and naturalism are at odds with agent-causation, we should reject these theses. I, on the other hand, go the other way and argue that since physical causal closure and naturalism are essential components of our best physical theories about the world, we should reject the notion of agent-causation.[6] Now, one may think that this is just another case of one person's *modus ponens* being another's *modus tollens* – and of course that is somewhat true. But importantly these moves are not equally justified. Not only do we have strong prima facie reason to preserve physical causal closure and naturalism when it comes to theorizing about the world – since they are, after all, among the most inductively justified assumptions we have in science – but by giving up these commitments agent-causal accounts run into difficulties accounting for mental causation, a necessary condition for free will. This brings me to my second objection. Normal intuitions tell us that certain mental events cause, and are caused by, certain physical events. I desire a beer and believe there is one in the refrigerator so off the couch and into the kitchen I go. I decide to bring an umbrella with me to campus today because I believe it is going to rain later today and I wish not to get wet. I intentionally decide to use examples referencing beer and umbrellas and hence type these sentences. The combination of my beliefs, desires, and intentions, which are mental events, seems to cause my ensuing movements, which are physical events. The notion of mental causation typified in these examples is basic to our understanding of human behavior.

Libertarians *must* preserve our intuitive sense of mental causation for two reasons. First, mental causation is a necessary condition for free will, for without mental

---

[6] Physical causal closure is a metaphysical theory about the nature of causation. It says that "all physical states have *pure* physical cause" (Kim 1993: 280) or that "physical effects have *only* physical causes" (Vicente 2006: 150).

causation there would be no way to account for *agency* and all events would become mere happenings. If libertarians want to preserve free will, they need to preserve the ability of agents to mentally cause their choices and actions. Second, the idea that mental states, including intentions, cause actions is a basic premise of criminal law (Morse 2008, 2016; Sifferd 2006, 2014; Humbach 2019). Legal blame, punishment, and responsibility presuppose that criminal acts are products of the defendant's mind. As Stephen Morse explains:

> [T]he law implicitly adopts the folk-psychological model of the person, which explains behavior in terms of desires, beliefs, and intentions. If practical reason plays no role in explaining our behavior ... current responsibility doctrines and practices would have to be radically altered or jettisoned altogether. (2008: 2–3)

He goes on to add:

> The capacity for intentional activity or stillness – the capacity for agency – is a central aspect of personhood and is integral to what it means to be a responsible person. We act because we intend. Responsibility judgments depend on the mental states that produce and accompany bodily movement and stillness. This is how we think about ourselves, and this is the concept of the person that morality and law both reflect. (2008: 4)

As US Supreme Court Justice Oliver Wendell Holmes famously observed, "[E]ven a dog distinguishes between being stumbled over and being kicked" (1963). And, as Justice Jackson wrote in *Morissette v. U.S.*:

> The contention that an injury can amount to a crime only when inflicted by intention is no provincial or transient notion. It is as universal and persistent in mature systems of law as belief in freedom of the human will and a consequent ability and duty of the normal individual to choose between good and evil. A relation between some mental element and punishment for a harmful act is almost as instinctive as a child's familiar exculpatory "But I didn't mean to." (1952, U.S. 246, 250–252)

Since the "law properly treats persons generally as intentional creatures and not as mechanical forces of nature" (Morse 2008: 5), libertarians who want to preserve moral and legal responsibility must preserve mental causation.

Unfortunately, agent-causation, which requires either substance dualism, radical emergentism, or some form of mysterianism, becomes unacceptable once we realize that not only does it require us to give up important metaphysical and scientific assumptions, but it also fails to account for *how* the agent, conceived of as a substance and not just a collection of physical events, is able to cause various physical events within the agent. In *Free Will and Consciousness* (2012) I argued at great length that agent-causal theorists are ultimately confronted with the following dilemma: To make sense of libertarian free will, they need to preserve the agent's ability to causally interact with various physical states of their body through their beliefs, desires, intentions, choices, or willings (mental causation), yet, to preserve mental causation, they must relinquish the ontology of agent-causation and accept *some form* of mind-body physicalism according to which mental states are *identical* to, *supervenient* on, or *emergent* from physical states (see 2012: chapter 2). And as I conceive it, the kind of mind-body physicalism that is required to preserve mental causation is consistent with a host of reductionist and nonreductionist options, including weak and moderate forms of property emergentism – but not the *substance dualism* or *radical emergentism* of agent-causal libertarians.

The difficulty confronting agent-causation is that both substance dualism and radical emergentism violate the widely embraced *principle of causal closure*, which maintains that if x is a physical event and y is a cause or effect of x, then y, too, must be a physical event. It follows then from physical causal closure that we would never need to go outside the physical domain to explain the occurrence of a physical event. This principle is commonly assumed in scientific theorizing – in fact, one could argue that it is indispensable to scientific reasoning. The problem facing both substance dualism and radical emergentism, however, is the following. If the mental is fundamentally distinct from the physical, either because it is a unique substance (e.g., a Cartesian soul or mind) or because it has radically emergent causal powers not determined by physical properties or relations, then the mental could not affect the course of the physical events without violating the causal closure of the physical (Kim 1990, 1999; Papineau 2002; Caruso 2012). With regard to substance dualism, this problem is well known. Ever since the time of Descartes, it has been objected that substance dualism ultimately founders over its inability to explain how, even in theory, the two distinct substances can causally interact. As Michael Levin states the objection:

> [T]he anti-dualist presses what appears to be the empirical fact that for every physical event *e* involving a human body, there is some preceding physical event which is *the* cause of *e*. As far as anyone knows there are no gap in the sequence of bodily events to be bridged by a mental event, or into which a mental event might slip. There is no physical event whose cause is mental, in the dualist's intended sense. (1979: 82)

Of course, no amount of empirical evidence will ever *prove* that the physical domain is causally closed. However, since the assumption of physical causal closure provides invaluable pragmatic advantage, inference to the best explanation would suggest that *even* in cases where a physical cause currently eludes detection, it is still wise to posit such a cause. Given the practical significance of the principle, along with its empirical support, the burden of proof falls on the dualist to show, persuasively, that the assumption is false.

Furthermore, even if one were to reject physical causal closure, any hypothesis proposing that nonphysical minds exist, and that such minds play an active role in influencing physical events, requires the violation of fundamental physical laws (Wilson 1976, 1995, 1999; Papineau 2002; Dennett 1991). This objection goes all the way back to Leibniz (1898) who objected that Descartes's interactive substance dualism was predicated on an overly lax conception of the fundamental conservation principles of physics. Energy conservation states that energy can neither be created nor destroyed. The fundamental problem then facing the dualist is the following: "If immaterial mind could move matter, then it would create energy; and if matter were to act on immaterial mind, then energy would disappear. In either case energy would fail to be conserved. And so physics, chemistry, biology, and economics would collapse" (Bunge 1980: 17). Daniel Dennett spells out the difficulty in more detail:

> Let us concentrate on the return signals, the directives from mind to brain. These, *ex hypothesi*, are not physical; they are not light waves or sound waves or cosmic rays or streams of subatomic particles. No physical energy or mass is associated with them. How, then, do they get to make a difference to what happens in the brain cells they must affect, in mind is to have any influence on the body? A fundamental principle of physics is that any change in the trajectory of any physical entity is an acceleration requiring the expenditure of energy, and where is this energy to come from? It is this principle of conservation of energy that accounts for the physical impossibility of "perpetual motion machines", and the same principle is apparently violated by dualism. This confrontation between quite standard physics and dualism has been endlessly discussed since Descartes' own day, and is widely regarded as the inescapable and fatal flaw of dualism. (1991: 35)

Since it would be foolish to give up the law of conservation of energy, an empirically justified principle, to accommodate the hypothesis of interactive substance dualism, a hypothesis that is itself controversial, one could view this as a refutation of the position.

What, then, of the notion of radical emergentism? Does it fare any better? The notion of emergence has been employed with a variety of different meanings, and it is therefore necessary to clarify exactly which *type* of emergence is required for agent-causation. Robert Van Gulick (2001) has discerned ten varieties of the conception of emergence. Some of these varieties are benign and need not cause ontological concern to most physicalists, while others are highly controversial and run counter to certain centrally held physicalist principles. For the sake of brevity, I will only differentiate three types of emergence – hopefully this will be sufficient to bring out the needed contrast. First, there is the ever-popular *epistemic conception of emergence*. According to the epistemic conception: P emerges from properties or constituent components $a, b, c, \ldots$, if you cannot predict the presence of P from the presence of $a, b, c, \ldots$. Note, however, that this is much too weak for agent-causation, since P could be determined by, or even identical to, $a, b, c, \ldots$, even though nobody did or could recognize this. A second type of emergence, which we can call *modest kind (or system features) emergence*, maintains that a system's feature P is emergent in the sense that the system exhibits different features than its constituent components *a, b, c*, ... The basic idea is that the whole has properties or features that are *different in kind* from those of its parts. For example, a piece of cloth might be purple in hue even though none of the molecules that make up its surface could be said to be purple. Or water might have the properties of transparency and liquidity even though none of the constitutive molecules do. The problem with this kind of emergence is that it is again too weak to support agent-causation. Although the whole exhibits features that are different in kind from those of its parts, modest emergent systems features may nonetheless be determined by the features of their parts, their mode of combination, and the law-like regularities governing the features of their parts. Hence, if P is inevitably present when *a, b, c*, ... are, perhaps by metaphysical necessity, we still do not get the indeterminacy agent-causation requires.

Those agent-causal libertarians that embrace emergence therefore embrace a kind of *radical emergence*. Although there are different ways to state even this thesis, we can say, in general terms, that something is radically emergent if and only if the whole has features that are both (a) different in kind from those of its parts and (2) of a kind whose nature and existence are not necessitated by the features of its parts (Van Gulick 2001). Or put more precisely, we can say that radically emergent properties are those that are not necessitated by the lower-level base, where that base includes the lower-level laws but not the emergence laws (see Pereboom 2011, 2021). Whether or not there are any cases of radical emergence is, however, controversial and highly questionable. Furthermore, accepting radical emergence would be, as Van Gulick points out, "conceding that there are real features of the world that exist at the system or composite level that are not determined by the law-like regularities that govern the interactions of the parts of such systems and their features" (2001: 18). Hence:

> The notion that causal powers might exhibit radical-kind emergence merits special attention since it poses perhaps the greatest threat to physicalism. If wholes or systems could have causal powers that were radically emergent from the powers of their parts in the sense that those system-level powers were not determined by the laws governing the powers of their parts, then that would seem to imply the existence of powers that could override or violate the laws governing the powers of the parts; i.e., genuine cases of what is called "downward causation" (Sperry 1983, 1991; Kim 1992, 1999; Hasker 1999) in which the macro powers of the whole "reach down" and alter the course of events at the micro level from what they would be if determined entirely by the properties and [non-emergent] laws at that lower level. (Van Gulick 2001: 19)

The notion of radical emergence is troubling precisely because it challenges the idea that nothing outside the physical realm of events and laws causally affects the course of physical events (Kim 1990, 1999). It is in this respect that radical emergent causal powers would "pose such a direct challenge to physicalism, since they would threaten the view of the physical world as a closed causal system" (Van Gulick 2001: 19). Not surprisingly, though, the features that make radical emergence so threatening to physicalism are the very ones that make it attractive to agent-causal emergentists.

The problem is that radical emergentism suffers from many of the same problems as substance dualism, even if it appears to embrace a more modest ontology (see Caruso 2012). In particular, it too requires a violation of the principle of physical causal closure and again leaves unexampled how a radically emergent substance, whose nature and existence are not necessitated by the features of its parts, is able to causally interact with physical events within the agent. For radically emergent agent-causal theorists, agents are radically emergent objects or substances that cause their own intentions when they make free decisions. On this view, agents *qua* substances are not just bundles of properties, since agents *qua* substances *possess* properties (see Buckareff 2011).[7] Instead, it is the agent him- or herself, *qua* substance, that causes the agent's intention to act (O'Connor 2009a: 197). Yet, for physics to be causally closed, all physical events and states must be caused by other physical events and states. This claim is a crucial premise in the *causal exclusion* or *no overdetermination* argument for physicalism (see Kim 1990, 1999; Papineau 2002; Caruso 2012). Given this plausible premise, anything else that has physical effects – such as mental causation – must be identical with, supervene on, or be emergent from (in the modest or epistemic sense) something physical unless we are prepared to accept systematic overdetermination. Radical emergentists, however, like interactive substance dualists, deny the completeness of physics since they allow for genuine cases of downward causation where physical events are at least partly due to nonphysical causes. I therefore maintain that agent-causal libertarians are left in an untenable position. If they want to make sense of the basic conception of agent-causation, they must posit "a *sui generis* form of causation by an agent that is irreducible (ontologically as well as conceptually) to event-causal processes within the agent" (O'Connor 1995: 7). On the other hand, to make sense of mental causation, a necessary condition for free will, libertarians must relinquish their anti-naturalist metaphysics that make agent-causation possible. Either way, agent-causation fails to preserve libertarian free will. Not only are the metaphysical commitments of agent-causation inconsistent with our scientific worldview, the theory itself makes mental causation, and by extension free will, impossible.

A third objection to agent-causal libertarianism has been presented by Derk Pereboom (2001, 2014a), who has argued that such accounts are not reconcilable with a deterministic law-governed physical world. Immanuel Kant (1781/1787/1987), for instance, expresses a significant concern for his libertarian view, that it might not be reconcilable with what we would expect given our best empirical theories. He

[7] I am here defining *substances* as the basic entities that are the *bearers* of properties (Heil 2003: 171).

held that the physical world, as part of the world of appearance, is governed by deterministic laws, whereas the "transcendentally free" agent-cause would exist not as an appearance, but as a thing in itself. In his agent-causal picture, when an agent makes a free decision, she causes the decision without being causally determined to do so. On the route from this undetermined decision to its effects, changes in the physical world, for example, in the agent's brain or some other part of her body, are produced. However, Pereboom argues that it would seem that we would at these points encounter divergences from the deterministic laws, since the changes in the physical world that result from the undetermined decision would themselves not be causally determined. One might respond that it is possible that the physical alterations that result from free decisions just happen to dovetail with what could in principle be predicted on the basis of the deterministic laws, so nothing actually occurs that diverges from them. But this reconciliationist proposal would appear to involve coincidences too wild to be credible (see Pereboom 1995, 2001, 2014a).

Pereboom also argues that similar sorts of wild coincidences would plague a view according to which agent-caused free choices would reconcile with indeterministic and probabilistic laws (2014a). He writes:

> More recent expositors of the agent-causal view, such as Clarke (1993, 2003) and O'Connor (2000a, 2009), suggest that quantum indeterminacy can help with the reconciliation project. On one interpretation of quantum mechanics, the physical world is not in fact deterministic, but is rather governed by laws that are fundamentally merely probabilistic or statistical. Suppose, as is controversial, that significant quantum indeterminacy percolates up to neural indeterminacy at the level of decision or intention-formation. Then it might seem that agent-causal libertarianism could be reconciled with the claim that the laws of physics govern the physical components of human action. Still, it appears that wild coincidences would also arise on this suggestion. (2014a: 66)

He goes on to explain:

> Consider the class of possible human actions each of which has a physical component whose antecedent probability of occurring is approximately 0.32. It would not violate the statistical laws in the sense of being logically incompatible with them if, for a large number of instances, the physical components in this class were not actually realized close to 32 percent of the time. Rather, the force of the statistical law is that for a large number of instances it is correct to *expect* physical components in this class to be realized close to 32 percent of the time. Are free choices on the agent-causal libertarian model compatible with what the statistical law leads us to expect about them? If agent-causal free action were compatible with what according to the statistical law is overwhelmingly likely, then for a large enough number of instances the possible action in our class would have to be freely chosen close to 32 percent of the time. Then, for a large enough number of instances, the possible actions whose physical components have an antecedent probability of 0.32 would almost certainly be freely chosen close to 32 percent of the time. But if the

occurrence of these physical components were settled by the choices of agent-causes, then, their actually being chosen close to 32 percent of the time would amount to a coincidence no less wild then the coincidence of possible actions whose physical components have an antecedent probability of about 0.99 being chosen, over a large enough number of instances, close to 99 percent of the time. The proposal that agent-causal free choices do no diverge from what the statistical laws predict for the physical components of our actions would run so sharply counter to what we would expect as to make it incredible. (Pereboom 2014a: 67; see also Pereboom 1995, 2001)

This is a serious problem since it reveals that agent-causal libertarianism is unable to reconcile agent-causes acting at the macrolevel (decisions and actions) with the microlevel being causally closed under the statistical laws.

Hence, while it is *possible* that agent-causes act in accord with probabilistic microlevel laws, we should not *expect* such conformity. Recall that to answer the disappearing agent objection, the causal powers exercised by agents as substances must be of a different sort from those of the physical events that are causally relevant to the action, and on the occasion of free decision, the exercise of the agent-causal power must be token-distinct from the exercise of the causal powers of these events (Pereboom 2014a: 67). Given this requirement, Pereboom writes:

[W]e would expect the decisions of the agent-cause to diverge in the long run from the frequency of choices that would be extremely likely on the basis of these events alone. If we nevertheless found conformity, we have good reason to believe that the agent-causal power was not of a different sort from the causal powers of the events after all, and that on the occasion of particular decisions, the exercise of these causal powers was not token-distinct. Or else, this conformity would be a wild coincidence, which we would not expect and would have no explanation. (2014a: 67)

At this point, the libertarian might abandon the reconciliationist project and venture that there are indeed departures from the probabilities that we would expect on the basis of the physical laws, and they are likely to be found in the brain. Roderick Chisholm (1964) proposes a solution of this sort. But an objection to this proposal is that we would seem to lack any evidence that departures from the known physical laws occur in the brain when we make decisions. Hence, "without evidence for the departures from natural law that this view predicts, we have insufficient reason to accept it" (Pereboom 2014a: 69).

I turn now to my last objection to agent-causation. Some philosophers have argued that human action is caused by the reasons or desires of agents. The *causal theory of action*, for instance, is often referred to as the "standard story" of human action and agency in the philosophy of action (Aguilar and Buckareff 2010). In broad terms, it maintains that any behavior A (whether overt or mental) of an agent S is an action if and only if S's A-ing is caused in the right way and causally explained by some appropriate non-actional mental item (s) that mediates or constitutes S's reasons for

A-ing (Aguilar and Buckareff 2010). The touchstone essay for contemporary formulation of the causal theory of action is Davidson's "Actions, reasons and causes" (1963) but other defenders of the view include Bishop (1989), Mele (1992, 2001), Stout (1996), Enc (2003), and Aguilar and Buckareff (2010). Agent-causal libertarians, however, deny the causal theory of action. This is because, for them, human action is caused by the agent him- or herself, and not only by her reasons or desires.

O'Connor, for instance, contends that an agent (qua substance) has the power to cause an action-triggering intention, which in turn causes the action to occur. Reasons and desires do not play any direct causal role in the coming about of action, though they can influence the agent in her decision (O'Connor 2000a). As Andrei Buckareff explains:

> The agent-causalist will not want to allow for the occurrence of a reason for action to be even partially constitutive of an agent's exercise of agent-power, playing a role in the causal production or triggering of an agent's causing an intention. To do so would be to concede too much to proponents of reductive accounts of agent-causation. (2011)

So what role do reasons play in the etiology of action for agent-causal libertarians? According to O'Connor, reasons can be causally relevant as *structuring-features* of action, but they cannot be causes themselves (2005: 216; 2009a: 197; 2009b: 120). As Auke Alesander Montesano Montessori explains:

> We usually have reasons for our actions, such as desires, long term plans or moral principles. Many philosophers believe that these reasons should play a causal role during the creation of our actions. O'Connor disagrees. The agent is the origin of action, not the agent's reasons. The influence of reasons is explained through the way they structure how we can act. When we consider acting, we usually have a limited set of options. If I am hungry, then I might eat some bread or fruit. But I will not take a nap. Taking a nap does not come to mind as a serious option because I have no reason to take one. My reasons structure my action in such a way that I want to eat either bread or fruit, but leave me without an interest in a nap. In this way, reasons limit and structure my options for action. These reasons are often not equal in strength. Perhaps I dislike fruit and strongly prefer the taste of bread. In that case, I realise that I could eat some fruit and consider it as an option, but I have a stronger urge to opt for bread instead. I have multiple options because I have multiple conflicting reasons. I now get to decide, as an agent, what action to take. In most cases, I will eat some bread because I have stronger reasons to eat bread than to eat fruit. But I still consider fruit an option and in some cases I decide to go for it. Which scenario actually comes about depends fully on the agent. The reasons do not cause anything directly, they just form a non-causal propensity to act in a certain manner. (2017: 4; see also O'Connor 2000a: 91–101)

For O'Connor, then, "reasons for action are among the influences that causally structure, and hence, constrain the exercise of agent-causal power," but "they do not, along with the agent *qua* substance at the time, causally *produce* an intention" (Buckareff 2011).

One concern for this view is that reasons for action appear to be merely *causally relevant* to an agent's making a decision without being *causally efficacious* (Steward 1997: 186–190; see also Buckareff 2011). As a result, agent-causal theories must reject the causal theory of action, a widely embraced account in action theory, and offer an alternative explanation of how our beliefs and desires factor into our decisions and actions. O'Connor and other agent-causal theorists therefore need to find a different, indirect route to explain the relation between reasons and action. O'Connor attempts to do this by providing the following theory of *acting for a reason*. He states:

The agent acted in order to satisfy his antecedent desire that X if

1. prior to this action, the agent had a desire that X and believed that by so acting he would satisfy (or contribute to satisfying) that desire;
2. the agent's action was initiated (in part) by his own self-determining causal activity, the event component of which is the-coming-to-be-of-an-action-triggering-intention-to-so-act-here-and-now-to-satisfy-X;
3. concurrent with this action, he continued to desire that X and intended of this action that it satisfy (or contribute to satisfying) that desire; and
4. the concurrent intention was a direct causal consequence (intuitively, a continuation) of the action-triggering intention brought about by the agent, and it causally sustained the completion of the action. (2000a: 86)

While this is an intriguing proposal, several critics have noted that O'Connor's account of the relation between reasons and action is inadequate (see Clarke 2003: 138–144; Feldman and Buckareff 2003; Van Mitenburg 2015; and Montesano Montessori 2017).

Richard Feldman and Andrei A. Buckareff (2003), for instance, have argued that such an account appeals to something that is not necessary for the truth of the kind of reason-explanation we are seeking. On O'Connor's account, we can only say that we acted because of a desire or a reason if the desire or reason is part of the content of our intention. So only if our intention is "to do action A in order to satisfy reason X" can we say of A that X is the reason we did it. But Feldman and Buckareff convincingly argue that one can decide on the basis of a certain desire, and citing that desire can yield a true reason-explanation of one's desire, even if the intention that one forms in deciding is not a second-order attitude, that is, an attitude *about* (in part) another of one's attitudes (a certain desire) (Clarke and Capes 2017). As Montesano Montessori explains Feldman and Buckareff's (2003) objection:

Imagine an agent with two desires, D_1 and D_2. D_1 is "I want beer," D_2 is "I want something to drink." The agent decides, on the basis of D_1 and D_2, to go to a nearby pub. She causes intention 1 to occur. Intention 1 is "I will go to the bar in order to get a drink." The intention only refers to D_2 and not to D_1. So, O'Connor would be forced to accept that only D_2 explains the agent's behaviour. This despite the fact that D_1 was also a significant influence on the agent. It gets even worse when we imagine the agent causing the intention "I will go to the bar." C Intention 2, as we might call is, does not refer either to D_1 or D_2. It now seems that neither D_1 or D_2 can explain the agent's behaviour. The consequences of both intention 1 and 2 are destructive of O'Connor's theory. It seems undeniable that D_1 and D_2 are both important to the agent's actions. Deny one or both of these desires the status of explanation for the action can only be described as an error. (Montesano Montessori 2017: 19; Feldman and Buckareff 2003: 137–142)

Cases such as those described by Feldman and Buckareff cannot be dismissed in any obvious way.[8] And since O'Connor's theory (which is the most developed agent-causal account out there) is unable to pick the right reasons as explanations, we should conclude that O'Connor's theory fails (see also Van Mitenburg 2015; Montesano Montessori 2017).

I conclude, then, that we should reject agent-causal accounts of libertarian free will for the following four reasons: (a) our best philosophical and scientific theories about the world count strongly against the metaphysical commitments of the theory; (b) by conceived of agents as nonreducible *substances* capable of causing physical events, agent-causal accounts run into difficulties accounting for mental causation, a necessary condition for free will; (c) the theory appears not to be reconcilable with a deterministic law-governed physical world (Pereboom 2001, 2014); and (d) on such an account, reasons are not causes for action, and we have not been given a satisfying alternative account of the relationship between reasons and action.

2.2.2 Compatibilism

The remaining and most popular alternative to skepticism about free will is *compatibilism*. Compatibilists maintain that the kind of free will required for basic desert moral responsibility can be reconciled with determinism. They hold that what is of utmost importance is not the absence of causal determination, but that our actions are voluntary, free from constraint and compulsion, and caused in the appropriate way. Early on, classical compatibilists maintained that "[a] physical barrier or even an internal compulsion or addiction can be an impediment to action; but when one acts simply because one wants to, one is not being impeded from acting otherwise. Hence, one is expressing one's freedom by doing what one wants" (Berofsky 2002:

[8] O'Connor might reply by arguing that intentions 1 and 2 are not possible in these cases since the content of our intentions always refers to the desires that were important for bringing those intentions about. But as Montesano Montessori has argued: "I cannot see any reason why this would be so, apart from the fact this would be very convenient for O'Connor. Supposedly, we cause these intentions ourselves through our agent-causal powers. It would be strange if some automatic process filled in the content of our intentions. O'Connor might of course attempt to describe and justify such a view of our psyche, or find some other way to ensure that the content of our intentions always mention the relevant desires or reasons. But . . . O'Connor has not done this" (2017: 19).

182).[9] Contemporary compatibilists, however, often demand that additional requirements be met, with widely endorsed views singling out responsiveness to reasons or connection of action to what one would reflectively endorse (e.g., Fischer and Ravizza 1998; Fischer 1995, 2007; Frankfurt 1971; Dworkin 1970a, 1970b; Neely 1974; Wallace 1994; Mele 2006; McKenna 2005, 2013).

Harry Frankfurt (1971), for instance, has argued that free will requires that we assess our first-order desires and form "second-order volitions" about which of our first-order desires should move us to action. The first-order desires that move us to action are free, according to Frankfurt, when they conform with our second-order volitions – that is, when we have the will (first-order desires) we want to have (second-order desires). When this occurs, we *identify* with or *endorse* our wills. John Martin Fischer and Mark Ravizza (1998), on the other hand, have argued that *guidance control* is the freedom-level condition that is sufficient for moral responsibility. On their account, guidance control does not require the existence of genuine alternative possibilities. Instead, Fischer and Ravizza argue that moral responsibility should be understood in terms of the notion of *reasons-responsiveness*. Their idea is that we are morally responsible for an action when the mechanism that issues in that action is *moderately reasons-responsive* – that is, our choices and actions can be modified by, and some of them arise from, the rational consideration of our reasons.[10]

The arguments against compatibilism, on the other hand, typically take the form of one of two different types: *leeway incompatibilism* or *source incompatibilism*. The first maintains that determinism is incompatible with an agent's ability to do (or choose) otherwise, where the *ability to do otherwise* is considered a necessary condition for the kind of free will required for basic desert moral responsibility. The standard argument for leeway incompatibilism typically runs as follows:

(1) The existence of alternative possibilities (or the agent's power or ability to do or choose otherwise) is a necessary condition for acting freely.
(2) Determinism is not compatible with alternative possibilities (since it precludes the power or ability to do or choose otherwise).
(3) Therefore, determinism is not compatible with acting freely.

---

[9] A number of well-known philosophers have held versions of this position, including Thomas Hobbes (1654), David Hume (1743/1960), John Stuart Mill (1860/1947), W.T. Stace (1952), A.J. Ayer (1954), Moritz Schlick (1939, 1966), and Donald Davison (1973).

[10] More specifically, the mechanism M that issues in an agent's S's f-ing must be S's own, and M must be (at least) moderately reasons-responsive – where a mechanism M is moderately reasons-responsive *iff* M is *regularly reasons-receptive* and *weakly reasons-reactive*. A mechanism M that issues in S's f-ing is (at least) regularly reasons-receptive *iff* there is some set x of nomologically identical worlds (i.e., words with the same laws of nature as the world in which M issues in S's f-ing) in which there is sufficient reason for S to refrain from f-ing, and S recognizes (through M) that there is sufficient reason to refrain from f-ing. Lastly, a mechanism M that issues in S's f-ing is (at least) weakly reasons-reactive *iff* there are some worlds that are members of x in which S refrains from f-ing (through M) (Fischer and Ravizza 1998: 44; see also Fischer 1995, 2007; McKenna 2013).

In response to this argument, compatibilists have offered two different types of replies. *Traditional* or *classical* compatibilists typically grant that the agent's power or ability to do otherwise is necessary condition for acting freely but deny that determinism precludes this power – that is, they accept premise (1) but deny premise (2). In arguing against premise (2), classical compatibilists usually maintain that terms like *can*, *power*, and *ability* should be given a *conditional* or *hypothetical* analysis. They maintain that when we say that an agent *can* (i.e., has the *power* or *ability* to) do something, we mean the agent *would* do it *if* the agent wanted (desires or chose) to do it. According to classical compatibilism, this type of conditional analysis fits common usage and allows us to see how the power and freedom *to do otherwise* can be reconciled with determinism. To say "you could have done otherwise" would amount to the counterfactual claim that you would have done otherwise, if (contrary to fact) the past (or the laws of nature) had been different in some way. Conditional analyses of this type have been defended by the likes of G. E. Moore (1912), A. J. Ayer (1954), Kai Nielsen (1971), and David Lewis (1981). There is growing agreement, however, among compatibilists and incompatibilists alike that this approach fails.[11] Compatibilist Bernard Berofsky, for example, writes: "The rebuttal of [the incompatibilist] position based on a hypothetical analysis of power is a failure" (2002: 198). In fact, most contemporary compatibilists have abandoned conditional analyses, insisting that if compatibilism is to succeed it must find an alternative strategy (e.g., Lehrer 1976; Audi 1974; Berofsky 1987, 2002; Frankfurt 1969, 1971; Fischer and Ravizza 1998; Fischer 1995, 2007; Dworkin 1970a, 1970b; Neely 1974; Wallace 1994; Dennett 1984; Mele 2006; McKenna 2005, 2013).

The problem with analyzing *I could have done otherwise* as *I would have done otherwise if I wanted (or chose) to* is that it only invites the obvious question: Do I have the freedom or ability to want (or choose) differently? For the compatibilist argument to work, it would have to show that the *ability to want otherwise* is itself compatible with determinism, and here the conditional approach will not help without causing a regress (see, e.g., Broad 1952; Chisholm 1964, 1966; Lehrer 1964). Furthermore, this analysis fails to preserve the *unconditional ability to do otherwise*, which is what many philosophers claim is required for premise (2). That is, agents would still *lack the ability to do otherwise in exactly the same set of circumstances* – that is, keeping the laws of nature and antecedent conditions fixed. In the end, then, attempts to preserve the ability to do otherwise by means of conditional analysis amounts to nothing more than "the little *could* that *would* but *can't* so *won't*."

Because of the various problems with conditional analyses, many (perhaps most) contemporary compatibilists have opted for an alternative approach. Instead of arguing against premise (2), contemporary compatibilists have decided to question premise (1). These compatibilists attack the basic assumption upon which the

---

[11] See Campbell (1951, 1957), Broad (1952), Ginet (1995), Austin (1961, 1966), Chisholm (1964, 1966), van Inwagen (1983), and Lehrer (1964, 1968), and Caruso (2012).

leeway incompatibilist argument rests – that is, that the existence of alternative possibilities (or the agent's ability to do otherwise) is a necessary condition for acting freely. There are generally two types of arguments in the compatibilist literature for denying premise (1). The first kind of argument appeals to what has been called "character examples."[12] The second kind appeals to what have come to be known as "Frankfurt-style examples" – named after Harry Frankfurt, who introduced the first example of this kind in his influential article "Alternative Possibilities and Moral Responsibility" (1969). Although there are numerous versions of Frankfurt-style examples in the literature, such examples typically involve a neuroscientist (or controller) who can make an agent do whatever the neuroscientist wants (perhaps by direct control over the agent's brain), yet the neuroscientist will not intervene if the agent is going to do on their own what the controller wants. In examples of this sort, an agent considers performing some action (say, voting for candidate A while standing in the voting booth), but the neuroscientist is concerned that they will not come through (they want the agent to vote for candidate A and will intervene, if necessary, to make sure they do). So, if the agent were to manifest an indication that they will not or might not perform the desired action (i.e., voting for A), the neuroscientist would intervene. But as things actually go, the neuroscientist remains idle, since the agent performs the desired action on their own. The idea is that even though the agent could not have avoided the action they performed, they are intuitively morally responsible for their action. Contemporary compatibilists generally take such examples to show that the *ability to do otherwise* is *not* a necessary condition for moral responsibility.

This conclusion, however, is hotly debated and, personally, I am not convinced that Frankfurt-style cases succeed in refuting premise (1).[13] That said, I would prefer to avoid going down that rabbit hole here since the Frankfurt literature is vast and complex, and it would save us a lot of time and effort if we could side-step it altogether. I will therefore set aside the argument for leeway incompatibilism outlined earlier and opt instead for a form of *source incompatibilism*, which is independent of concerns about alternative possibilities. Source incompatibilists maintain that determinism makes it impossible for us to *cause and control our actions in the right kind of way*. On this view, an action is free in the sense required for basic desert moral responsibility only if it is not produced by a deterministic process that traces back to causal factors beyond the agent's control. As McKenna and Pereboom explain:

---

[12] One of the best-known arguments that appeal to *character examples* comes from Daniel Dennett's discussion of Martin Luther (see 1984: 133). For objections to this approach, see Caruso (2012).

[13] A number of critics have argued that Frankfurt-style arguments fail to refute the principle of alternative possibilities. Objections include the "flicker of freedom" reply (see Fischer 1994: 134–47), the dilemma defense (Kane 1996, 2000; Widerker 1995, 2006; cf. Pereboom 2014a), and the timing defense (Ginet 1996, 2002).

While leeway incompatibilists would also argue that the actual causal history of a morally responsible action must be indeterministic, they maintain this is so only because an indeterministic history is required to secure alternative possibilities. Source incompatibilists, by contrast, contend that the role the indeterministic causal history plays in explaining why an agent is morally responsible is independent of facts about alternative possibilities. On their view, it's that an indeterministic history allows the agent to be the source of her action in such a way that they are not causally determined by factors beyond her control. (2016: 105)

In the remainder of Section 2.2, I offer what I believe to be the best argument for source incompatibilism: the *manipulation argument* (see, e.g., Taylor 1974; Kane 1985, 1996; Ginet 1990; Pereboom 1995, 2001, 2014a; Mele 1995, 2006, 2019; Todd 2011, 2012, 2013, 2017). Later, in Section 2.3, I offer a second independent argument against compatibilism based on the pervasiveness of *luck* and Neil Levy's *luck pincer* argument (Levy 2011; Caruso 2019a). My two preferred arguments against compatibilism, then, are the *manipulation argument* and the *luck pincer*.

2.2.2.1 The Manipulation Argument

One way to argue against compatibilism begins with the intuition that if an agent is causally determined to act by, for example, scientists who unbeknownst to them manipulate their brain, then they are not morally responsible for that action, even if they satisfy the prominent compatibilist conditions on moral responsibility (Taylor 1974; van Inwagen 1983; Kane 1985, 1996; Ginet 1990; Pereboom 1995, 2001, 2014a; Mele 1995, 2006, 2019; Todd 2011, 2012, 2013, 2017). The argument then continues and maintains that there are no relevant differences between such manipulated agents and their ordinary deterministic counterparts that can justify the claim that the manipulated agents are not morally responsible while the determined agents are. Hence, if agents are not free and morally responsible under conditions of manipulation, then they are also not free and morally responsible in the case of ordinary determinism where their actions are causally determined by natural factors beyond our control. For sake of brevity, I will focus on Pereboom's *four-case* version of the manipulation argument since I think it is the most convincing. After providing a brief summary of the argument, I will consider a number of possible replies and argue that they all fail.

Pereboom's four-case argument sets out three examples of actions that involve manipulation. The first features the most radical sort of manipulation consistent with the proposed compatibilist conditions and with intuitive conditions on agency, each progressively more like the fourth, which is a case of ordinary determinism where the agent's action is causally determined in a natural way. The challenge is for the compatibilist to point out a relevant and principled difference between any two adjacent cases that would show why the agent might be morally responsible in the latter example but not in the earlier one. Pereboom maintains that "this can't be done, and that the agent's nonresponsibility therefore generalizes from the first of the manipulation examples to the ordinary case" (2014a: 75). Furthermore, since the first three cases set out examples of actions that involve manipulation, and in which the prominent compatibilist causal conditions on moral responsibility are satisfied, they also indicate that these conditions are inadequate.

Here is the setup. In each of the four cases Professor Plum decides to murder White for the sake of some personal advantage and succeeds in doing so. The action under consideration is his decision to kill White – "a basic mental action" (Pereboom 2014a: 75). Pereboom specifies that in each of the four cases, Plum's decision to kill White satisfies the relevant compatibilist conditions. For instance, Plum's decision to kill White satisfies David Hume's (1739/1978) condition that the decision not be out of character, since for Plum it is generally true that selfish reasons weigh heavily – too heavily when considered from the moral point of view. In addition, the desire that motivates Plum to act is nevertheless not irresistible for him, and hence he is not constrained to act. The action also meets the compatibilist condition proposed by Harry Frankfurt (1971) – that is, Plum's effective desire (i.e., his will) to murder White conforms appropriately to his second-order desire for which effective desire he will have. That is, Plum wills to murder White and wants to will to do so. In addition, the action satisfied the reasons-responsiveness condition advocated by John Martin Fisher and Mark Ravizza (1998) – that is, Plum's desire can be modified by, and some of them arise from, the rational consideration of his reasons, and if he believed that the bad consequences for himself that would result from killing would be more severe than he actually expects them to be, he would not have decided to kill her. Finally, the action also satisfies the related condition advanced by Jay Wallace (1994) – that is, Plum has the general ability to grasp, apply, and regulate his actions by moral reasons. For instance, when egoistic reasons that count against acting morally are weak, he will typically act for moral reasons instead.

The question, then, is that supposing Plum is causally determined by factors beyond his control to decide as he does, is it plausible that he is morally responsible for his decision in the basic desert sense? The following four cases exhibit varying ways in which Plum's decision to kill White may be causally determined by factors beyond his control. Case 1 involves manipulation by a team of neuroscientists:

> **Case 1:** A team of neuroscientists has the ability to manipulate Plum's neural states at any time by radio-like technology. In this particular case, they do so by pressing a button just before he begins to reason about his situation, which they know will produce in him a neural state that realizes a strongly egoistic reason process, which the neuroscientists know will deterministically result in his decision to kill White. Plum would not have killed White had the neuroscientists not intervened, since his reasoning would then not have been sufficiently egoistic to produce this decision. But at the same time, Plum's satisfies all the compatibilist conditions specified in the previous paragraph (e.g., Plum is not constrained to act in the sense that he does

not act because of an irresistible desire, he does not act contrary to character, he is moderately reasons-responsible, he approves of his decision to kill White, etc.). (Pereboom 2014a: 76–77)

In this case, it is intuitive to conclude that Plum is not morally responsible despite the fact that his actions satisfy each of the compatibilist conditions. And Plum's lack of moral responsibility is explained by the fact that his decision is causally determined by the neuroscientists' intervention, which is beyond his control, together with the fact that he would not have decided to kill White had the intervention not occurred (Pereboom 2014a: 77).

The next case is more like the ordinary situation than Case 1 but still involves manipulation.

> **Case 2:** Plum is just like an ordinary human being, except that a team of neuroscientists programmed him at the beginning of his life so that his reasoning is often but not always egoistic (as in Case 1), and at times strongly so, with the intended consequence that in his current circumstances he is causally determined to engage in the egoistic reasons-response process of deliberation and to have the set of first- and second-order desires that result in his decision to kill White. Plum has the general ability to regulate his actions by moral reasons, but in his circumstances, due to the strongly egoistic nature of his deliberative reasoning, he is causally determined to make his decision to kill. Yet he does not decide as he does because of irresistible desire. The neural realization of his reasoning process and of his decision is exactly the same as it is in Case 1 (although their causal histories are different). (Pereboom 2014a: 77)

Here again it is intuitive to conclude that Plum is not morally responsible for his decision since "it would seem unprincipled to claim that here, by contrast with Case 1, Plum is morally responsible because the length of time between the programming and his decision is now great enough" (2014: 77–78). It is irrelevant whether the programming occurs a few seconds before or forty years prior to the action. What *is* of relevance is that in both cases Plum's decision to kill White is causally determined by factors beyond his control. As Pereboom correctly explains: "Causal determination by what the neuroscientists do, which is beyond his control, plausibly explains Plum's not being morally responsible in the first case, and it's intuitive that he is not morally responsible in the second case for the same reason" (2014a: 78). Furthermore, if Plum lacks moral responsibility in Case 2, this once again indicates that the compatibilist conditions specified, either individually or in conjunction, are not sufficient for moral responsibility.

Case 3 is more similar yet to our ordinary situation. It supposes that Plum was brought up in an environment in which self-interest and violence are more strongly encouraged than they are in ours, even though morality also has a part.

> **Case 3:** Plum is an ordinary human being, except that the training practices of his community causally determined the nature of his deliberative reasoning process so

that they are frequently but not exclusively rationally egoistic (the resulting nature of his deliberative reasoning process are exactly as they are in Cases 1 and 2). This training was completed before he developed the ability to prevent or alter these practices. Due to the aspect of his character produced by this training, in his present circumstances he is causally determined to engage in the strongly egoistic reasons-responsive process of deliberation and to have the first- and second-order desires that issue in his decision to kill White. While Plume does have the general ability to regulate his behavior by moral reasons, in virtue of this aspect of his character and his circumstances he is causally determined to make his immoral decision, although he does not decide as he does due to an irresistible desire. The neural realization of his deliberation is just as it is in Cases 1 and 2. (Pereboom 2014a: 78)

The challenge for the compatibilist is to explain how Plum could be morally responsible in Case 3 but fail to be morally responsible in Case 2. To successfully do this he must identify a feature of these scenarios that would explain the difference. But this is impossible, argues Pereboom, since "there is no such feature" (2014a: 78). Hence, Plum's exemption from responsibility in Cases 1 and 2 generalizes to the near-to-normal Case 3.

Case 4 deals with ordinary determinism. It differs from the previous cases in that other agents do not bring about Plum's decision, but in all the other relevant respects it is similar.

> **Case 4**: Everything that happens in our universe is causally determined by virtue of its past states together with the laws of nature. Plum is an ordinary human being, raised in normal circumstances, and again his reasoning processes are frequently but not exclusively egoistic, and sometimes strongly so (as in Cases 1–3). His decision to kill White issues from his strongly egoistic but reasons-responsive process of deliberation, and he has the specific first- and second-order desires. The neural realizers of Plum's reasoning process and decision is exactly as it is in Cases 1–3; he has the general ability to grasp, apply, and regulate his actions by moral reasons, and it is not because of an irresistible desire that he decides to kill. (2014a: 79)

For proponents of this argument, Plum's exemption from moral responsibility generalizes to this ordinary case because there are no differences between Case 3 and Case 4 that would justify the claim that Plum is not responsible in Case 3 but is in Case 4. The fact that in Case 4 other agents do not bring about the causal determination of Plum's decision is not a relevant difference (see Section 2.2.2.4). Since Plum would lack moral responsibility here as well, we should conclude that "causal determination by other agents was not essential to what was driving the intuition of nonresponsibility in the earlier cases" (2014a: 79). Instead, what is responsibility-undermining in all four cases is the fact that Plum's action is causally determined by factors beyond his control. And since Plum is not morally responsible in Case 1, and there are no differences between Cases 1 and 2, 2 and 3, and 3 and 4 that can explain in a principled way why he would not be responsible in the former of each pair but would be in the latter, "we are thus driven to the conclusion that he is not responsible in Case 4" (2014a: 29). This result, I contend, undermines the compatibilist thesis.

2.2.2.2 Objections and Replies to the Manipulation Argument

In response to this argument, compatibilists tend to adopt either *hard-line* or *soft-line* replies (see McKenna 2008). Hard-line replies insist that Plum is morally responsible in all four cases, or at the very least that it is not clear that Plum is not responsible in these cases, while a soft-line reply claims that he is responsible in some of the cases although not in others. Hard-liners grant that there is no relevant difference between agents in the various manipulated scenarios and ordinary (non-manipulated) agents in deterministic settings; instead they attack the intuition that agents are not morally responsible in the manipulated cases. They maintain that as long as the various compatibilist conditions for moral responsibility are satisfied, manipulated agents are just as free and morally responsible as determined agents – despite what might be our initial intuition. Soft-line replies, on the other hand, try to differentiate between the various cases. They search for relevant differences between the cases, differences that would account for why manipulated agents are not free and morally responsible, but non-manipulated and causally determined agents are. There are, however, problems with both types of replies.

2.2.2.3 Hard-Line Replies

The first problem with the hard-line approach is that it conflicts too deeply with our intuitions about *sourcehood* and the relevant class of manipulation cases (Capes 2021). Many people find it highly implausible that Plum, say in Case 1, could be morally responsible in the basic desert sense for his behavior given how the behavior came about (cf. Fischer 2011, 2014; McKenna 2008, 2014; Sartorio 2016; Tierney 2013, 2014; Capes 2013). And it is not just a matter of intuition that leads us to conclude this. The incompatibilist can argue that "[w]hatever sourcehood is at the end of the day, Plum (in Case 1) clearly doesn't have it. And since sourcehood is required for basic desert moral responsibility, we must conclude that Plum is not morally responsible" (see Tognazzini 2014). Now some, like Matt King (2013), have argued that appealing to sourcehood in this way is question-begging, but that need not be the case (see Tognazzini 2014; Matheson 2016). As Neal Tognazzini has argued, "[F]ar from *presupposing* an incompatibilist conception of sourcehood, the manipulation argument is meant to *give us reason to adopt* that conception" (2014). According to Tognazzini (2014), the dialectic of such an argument runs as follows:

(1) The incompatibilist presents an allegedly disturbing manipulation scenario [or a series of scenarios], and then says: "Whatever sourcehood is at the end of the day, this guy clearly doesn't have it, and since sourcehood is required for moral responsibility, this guy ain't morally responsible either." It's this thought which gets regimented as [the first premise in manipulation arguments], the claim that the manipulated agent is not morally responsible for acting on his implanted psychological states.
(2) Then the incompatibilist points out that there seems to be no difference between the manipulated scenario and a plain old deterministic world, at least as far as responsibility is concerned.
(3) The incompatibilist then concludes that since the agent in the manipulated scenario isn't responsible for his action, and since a plain old deterministic world isn't relevantly different, the merely determined agent isn't responsible for his action either. And since the problem with the manipulated agent was a lack of sourcehood, that must also be the problem with the merely determined agent. Thus, the proper understanding of sourcehood must be one that is incompatible with determinism.

Tognazzini argues, persuasively in my opinion, that the judgment of nonresponsibility in the first premise is not inferred from the question-begging premise that sourcehood is incompatible with determinism; rather it is inferred from the intuition that, *whatever sourcehood requires*, it cannot be had by the agent in the manipulated scenario (together with the claim that sourcehood, whatever it requires, is itself required for moral responsibility). In other words, "the proponent of the manipulation argument wants to stay neutral, at first, on the correct conception of sourcehood, and the manipulation scenario is supposed to serve up a desideratum of any adequate conception of sourcehood: 'I think we'd all agree,' the incompatibilist says, 'that this guy isn't the source of his action'" (Tognazzini 2014).

Of course, not everyone *does* agree. But as Tognazzini correctly points out, that does not mean that the proponent of the manipulation argument has begged any question: "After all, I can't give a valid argument for a conclusion with which you disagree without presenting a premise with which you'll degree, but it can't be the *every* valid argument with a controversial conclusion begs the question" (2014). Furthermore:

> The fact that the first premise of the manipulation argument will be contested by compatibilists perhaps means, not that the argument begs the question against them, but rather simply that they won't find the argument compelling. That's no doubt true, but again, it would be an unreasonably high standard to require an argument to convince its opponents in order to be worth discussing. In fact, I think a more useful way to conceive of philosophical argumentation is to invoke an *idealized agnostic*, a person who is neutral about the debate in question. (2014)

This brings me to my second objection.

The second problem with the hard-line approach has to do with the *initial attitude* it adopts toward Case 4, the case of natural determinism, and how it proceeds to argue in the opposite direction that manipulation cases are no threat to free will and moral responsibility. Consider, for instance, the *resolute compatibilist* who adopts an unapologetic hard-line approach that maintains that Plum is morally responsible in all four cases. The problem with this approach is that any argument for Plum's responsibility in Case 1 will have to overcome the initial intuition that extreme, covert manipulation threatens moral responsibility. Furthermore, this approach "would not only require casting doubt on Plum's nonresponsibility, but making a case strong enough that inclines us toward Plum's being responsible" (Paskell 2016). But how can the hard-liner establish or show that Plum is responsible in Case 1? What kind of argument can they provide? It would not help to reason in the opposite direct, as hard-liners do, and argue that *since Plum is morally responsible in Case 4* (the case of natural determinism), Plum's responsibility must transfer to Case 1 since there is no relevant difference between agents in Cases 4 and 3, 3 and 2, and 2 and 1. This, of course, would be question-begging. Since the responsibility or nonresponsibility of an ordinary determined agent is exactly what is at issue, it cannot be claimed or assumed that Plum in Case 4 is morally responsible.

There is, however, a less ambitious hard-line approach that maintains that to successfully counter the four-case manipulation argument all that the compatibilist needs to do is show that Plum's nonresponsibility in Case 1 *cannot be taken for granted*. This is the kind of hard-line reply that Michael McKenna's (2008, 2014) develops. McKenna's central idea is that whatever attitude it is rational initially to have about Plum's responsibility in the ordinary deterministic example transfers to the manipulation cases. He begins with Pereboom's Case 4, Plum as an ordinary determined agent, and argues that it would be question-begging to claim outright that Plum is not morally responsible in such a situation. Instead, he maintains that the appropriate initial attitude to adopt in Case 4 is some form of *agnosticism*. He then proceeds to argue that since all relevant features of Plum are meant to carry over in all cases, the appropriate initial attitude that is informed by those features should also be preserved. Hence, according to McKenna, if we run the generalization backward, from Case 4 through to Case 1, then the attitude toward Plum in Case 1 should also be some form of agnosticism. As Pereboom describes the objection:

> In his view, since it is at the outset rational for us to have an agnostic attitude about the claim that Plum is morally responsible in the ordinary deterministic example ..., the absence of relevant differences [between the cases] allows this rational agnosticism to transfer unimpeded to the manipulation cases, thereby depriving them of counting in favor of incompatibilism. (2014a: 91)

The difference, then, between McKenna's account and the resolute or intransigent compatibilist response discussed earlier is that, for McKenna, the initial attitude we should have in the ordinary deterministic example is *not* that Plum is morally responsible but that it is *not clear* that Plum is *not* morally responsible.

While I think McKenna's characterization of the hard-line reply is clearly better, I also agree with Pereboom (2008, 2014a) that "if we are precise about the attitude it is rational to have about Plum in these examples, we will see that the force of this hard-line compatibilist response is compromised" (2014a: 91). According to Pereboom, McKenna is mistaken about the rationality of his initial attitude. As he describes it:

> I have a different take on the dialectic ... In everyday life, we assume that people can be, and often are, morally responsible in the basic desert sense for their actions. However, we ordinarily do not bring to bear on this assumption any theory about the general causal nature of the universe that might threaten its rationality. For example, we do not seriously question the rationality of this assumption given the theory they every event, including choices and actions, result from deterministic causal processes that trace back to a time before agents existed. (2014a: 92)

Pereboom maintains that if we did engage in such questioning, the epistemically rational attitude to adopt would be the *neutral inquiring attitude* rather than McKenna's *confirmed agnostic attitude*.

There are a number of different initial attitudes one can bring to the ordinary deterministic example. As Pereboom identified them, the *resolute compatibilist* response is to "deny that under these circumstances causal determination poses even a prima facie threat to our everyday assumption, and that it is rational to refuse to take seriously any further consideration for there being such a threat" (2014a: 93). A distinct approach affirms that causal determination provides a reason for giving up the responsibility assumption but claims that so far the issue has not been settled. This is the *neutral inquiring* response. "By this response it is initially epistemically rational not to believe that the agent in an ordinary deterministic example is morally responsible in the basic desert sense, and not to believe that he isn't, but to be open to clarifying considerations that would make one or other of these beliefs rational" (2014a: 93). It is crucial to note that the neutral inquiring attitude differs significantly from that of the *confirmed agnostic*. The confirmed agnostic claims that it is not clear that the ordinary causally determined agent is morally responsible in the sense at issue, and that it is not clear that he is not, but, like the resolute compatibilist, maintains that it is rational to consider enquiry into the issue closed, "and for this reason it is not open to further clarifying considerations" (Pereboom 2014a: 93).

I agree with Pereboom that the confirmed agnostic response, the response that generates McKenna's hard-line conclusion, is not the appropriate response to take. Instead, "the most attractive way of conceiving manipulation arguments involves supposing that the neutral inquiring attitude about ordinary determined agents is initially epistemically rational" (Pereboom 2014a: 94). The reason the neutral inquiring attitude is the appropriate attitude to adopt is that it allows for clarifying considerations to alter our thinking and "it's the best one for the opposing parties in the debate to make if there is to be a productive engagement" (Pereboom 2014a: 94). As Pereboom explains:

> Fruitful discussion requires participants to find common ground by setting aside at least some points of disagreement. It's also plausible that this supposition is substantively the reasonable one to make. My sense of this dialectic is that the resolute compatibilist and confirmed agnostic initial attitudes toward the agent in the ordinary deterministic cases are unreasonable. I think this is also true for a resolute incompatibilist stance. These attitudes are unreasonable because they are not open to the further clarifying considerations. As a result, the similarities of the cases will not yield a sound argument for the epistemic rationality of the attitudes specified by these positions toward agents in the remote and local manipulation cases. (2014a: 94)

Once we adopt the neutral inquiring attitude, however, we can see how an analogous manipulation case functions as a clarifying consideration that makes rational the belief that the ordinary causally determined agent is not morally responsible. While the confirmed agnostic rules out this possibility, the neutral inquirer leaves it open.

McKenna's argument therefore fails since he cannot *guarantee* that the initial agnosticism he adopts in Case 4 can be preserved through to Case 1. Such a guarantee is precluded by the possibility of clarifying considerations altering the agnostic position upon encountering the manipulation cases (Pereboom 2014a: 100). The neutral inquiring response – the most epistemically rational attitude to adopt – is open to the potential rational influence of manipulation examples, and so we cannot assume that it transfers to the manipulation cases unaltered. As a result, "an argument that begins with the neutral inquiring response for the ordinary deterministic case will not secure agnosticism about manipulation cases" (2014a: 94). Contra McKenna, then, "the neutral inquiring agnostic's position thus cannot be run backward through the cases with assurance that the agnosticism would survive through to the first case, since encountering the manipulation cases have the potential to sway the agnostic toward incompatibilism" (2014a: 100).

Furthermore, if we adopt the neutral inquiring attitude and reason in the order that Pereboom and I suggest (from Case 1 to 4), manipulation cases, like Cases 1–3, can then be used to clarify our intuitions in a situation where it is clear that an agent's inner psychological states are causally determined by factors beyond their control (i.e., a team of external manipulators), and we can then use those clarifying considerations to inform our thinking in the ordinary deterministic case. While McKenna contends that manipulation cases are artificial, and we should be more confident in our judgments about ordinary, non-artificial cases, I maintain that the artificiality is required to make the deterministic causation salient. As Pereboom explains:

[W]e do not ordinarily bring to bear on our judgments of responsibility any theory about the general causal nature of the universe that might threaten their rationality. The Spinozian concern is that in ordinary cases such judgments will have been shaped by a supposition of indeterministic free will. (2014a: 95)

I therefore think the artificiality of the local and remote manipulation cases are needed to make the deterministic causation salient. As Dana Nelkin writes:

[O]ne might argue that their unrealistic quality helps ensure that we are focused on the stipulated features, and that we aren't implicitly but unconsciously relying on background assumptions that we bring to ordinary life. In this way, the intuitions are arguably *more* reliable than the real life ones. (2012)

I therefore contend that we should reject the hard-line approach since the resolute compatibilist simply begs the question and the confirmed agnostic refuses to allow for clarifying considerations to alter their thinking. Yet once we adopt the neutral inquiring attitude, manipulation cases can function as a clarifying consideration that makes rational the belief that the naturally determined agent is not morally responsible.[14]

2.2.2.4 Soft-Line Replies

Let me know turn to soft-line replies. Unlike the previous approach, the challenge here is to point to a difference between two adjacent cases that can explain in a principled way why Plum is not morally responsible in the former case but is in the latter. The main problem with the soft-line approach, however, is that any difference identified as the relevant one between manipulated agents and ordinary determined agents may be a difference that applies only to current manipulation

---

[14] In response to these objections, Daniel Haas (2013) has attempted to defend the hard-line reply by arguing for an alternative reasonable initial attitude that is friendlier to compatibilist intuitions about moral responsibility. For a reply to Haas, see Pereboom (2014a: 99–100). Another approach hard-liners have taken is to argue that moral responsibility comes in degree and that, provided that agents like Plum (in Cases 1–3) satisfy the relevant compatibilist conditions for free agency and moral responsibility, compatibilist should insist that the agent acted freely and that he bears at least *some* responsibility for action, but that his responsibility is (or may be) diminished in that he deserves less praise and blame, less punishment and reward, for what he did than he would have if his action hadn't been causally determined in the way it was (see Tierney 2013, 2014; Capes 2013). The main challenge with this reply, however, is that it faces Patrick Todd's question: "[I]f the compatibilist admits that determinism itself is mitigating, a fair question is, in virtue of what?" (2011: 131). Todd argues that proponents of manipulation arguments have assumed too heavy a burden: they do not need to make it plausible that manipulated agents are not morally responsibility, only that their responsibility is mitigated (2011, 2013). This is because compatibilists will have as difficult a time accounting for mitigated responsibility in a manipulation case as they would have explaining nonresponsibility. If, for instance, the compatibilist were to agree that Plum's blameworthiness in Case 1 or in Case 2 is mitigated, what would, on the compatibilist view, account for this? If it is deterministic manipulation, then because there is no relevant difference between determinist manipulation and natural determination, the compatibilist's position would be compromised (Pereboom 2014a: 81; Todd 2011).

cases but not future cases. A number of leading soft-line replies point, for instance, to responsibility-conferring conditions not specified in a particular manipulation case (Lycan 1987; Baker 2006; Feltz 2012; Murray and Lombrozo 2017). But even if one could point to a relevant difference between an agent in an extant manipulation case and an agent in the naturally determined case, this may only serve as an invitation for proponents of the manipulation argument to revise the vignette on which their argument is based so that the agent now satisfies the relevant condition on which the soft-liner insists (Capes 2021). The challenge, then, for defenders of the soft-line approach is to show that there is some kind of requirement for free action and moral responsibility that can be satisfied by agents in deterministic settings, but which cannot, *even in principle*, be satisfied by agents in manipulation cases.

Unfortunately, as McKenna points out, there is "no way to foreclose the metaphysical possibility that the causes figuring in the creation of a determined morally responsible agent could not be artificially fabricated" (2008: 144). The problem for all soft-line replies, then, is that

> [e]ven if the compatibilist argued that a manipulation case has yet to be constructed properly, it would be quite a leap to suggest that a manipulated agent who satisfies any and all compatibilist conditions for responsibility is *inconceivable*. After all, what factor could we point to in a case of a manipulated agent that could not also arise in a determined world? The primary difference between a relevantly described manipulated agent and an ordinary determined agent seems to lie in the source of determination rather than in the type of determination, and the source of determination could hardly be relevant to responsibility. (Paskell 2014: 6)

Soft-line replies are therefore unconvincing because, at best, they can only show that *a particular* manipulation example has failed to capture *all* the relevant compatibilist conditions for moral responsibility, *not* that manipulation arguments fail *tout court*.

Consider, for instance, William Lycan's (1997) soft-line reply that the distinguishing feature of Case 4 is that the causal determination of Plum's decision is not brought about by other agents. Since most extant manipulation cases involve external agents who act as intentional manipulators, whereas this is missing in the normal case of natural determinism, proponents of soft-line replies might be tempted to point to this as the relevant difference. There are, however, two key problems with this reply. First, it is question-begging to assume that this is the relevant difference since incompatibilists would insist that it is completely irrelevant whether the inner states of the agent which (according to compatibilism) allegedly prompt my "free" activity are determined by another agent or by perfectly impersonal forces. If free will and moral responsibility are to be compatible with the determination of our actions by factors beyond our control, as compatibilists maintain, it should not matter whether those factors are personal or impersonal.

Second, new manipulation cases can easily be devised that avoid external agents altogether. Imagine, for instance, the following case:

Brain-Implant Malfunction Case: Imagine that Plum has a devise implanted in his brain for medical purposes (e.g., to control seizures or trembling due to Parkinson's disease), not for the purpose of manipulation. When operating normally, the device does not affect Plum's reasoning. One day the device malfunctions and ends up triggering in Plum a strongly egoistic reasoning process that deterministically results in his decision to kill White. And it does so in a way that satisfies all the prominent compatibilist conditions (e.g., Plum is moderately reasons-responsible, approves of his decision to kill White, is able to grasp, apply, and regulate his actions by moral reasons, etc.). Here we have a case of accidental manipulation due to a malfunctioning device implanted in Plum's brain. (We could easily imagine variations on this case, where the triggering of the device was the result of a cat walking across a keyboard that remotely controlled the implanted device.)

The case mentioned here provides an example of a manipulated agent who is determined to commit a criminal action *without external agents acting as intentional manipulators*. And it would not aid the soft-liner to reply that since the device was intentionally implanted the case fails, since the fact that the device was intentionally implanted (for medical purposes) in no way undermines the main philosophical point: the malfunctioning of the device, and the subsequent manipulation, was *not the result of external agents acting as intentional manipulators*. Hence, the presence of intentional manipulation by external agents cannot be the relevant difference soft-line theorists are after.[15]

What other approach, then, can soft-liners take to show that there is a relevant and significant difference between manipulated agents and ordinarily determined agents, a difference that cannot be accounted for, even in principle, by modified, carefully constructed, manipulation cases? Oisin Deery and Eddy Nahmias (2017) have recently developed a compatibilist account of *causal sourcehood* that they claim undermines all manipulation arguments. According to Deery and Nahmias:

> Even if causal determinism is true ..., an agent can be the causal source of her actions, since often no variable beyond the agent's control will have a stronger causal-explanatory relationship with her actions than relevant variables within her control. On the other hand, the causal source of a manipulated agent's actions lies beyond the agent's control in the intentions of the manipulator. As a result, determined agents can be free and responsible, contrary to what Manipulated Arguments conclude, whereas manipulated agents have, at best, reduced freedom and responsibility. (2017: 1256)

In defending this view, Deery and Nahmias appeal to *interventionist* theories of causation which maintain that X causes Y just in case, for at least some state of the model, there is an intervention on X that would reliably change the value of Y. On this framework, an intervention is an exogenous experimental manipulation of X to

---

[15] Pereboom (2001: 115) and Mele (2006) also offer examples of manipulation cases that do not require intentional manipulation by external agents.

find out whether X causes Y. Building on this account of causation, Deery and Nahmias develop an account of *causal sourcehood* which maintains that, for a variable to be the causal source of an event, that variable must bear the *strongest causal invariance relation* to it among all the variables that are causally connected to the event. And as they define it:

> A causal invariable relation, R_1, that obtains between two causal variable, X and Y, is stronger than another such relation, R_2, obtaining between Y and another of its prior causal variables – for instance, W – if:
>
> (1) holding fixed the relevant background conditions, C, R_1 predicts the value of Y under a wider range of interventions on X than R_2 does under interventions on W; and
> (2) R_1 predicts the value of Y across a wider range of relevant changes to the values of C than R_2 does. (Deery and Nahmias 2017: 1262–1263)

Deery and Nahmias then argue that a naturally determined agent, like Plum in Case 4, can be the causal source of their action since nothing beyond the agent's control will have a stronger causal-explanatory relationship with their action than relevant variables within their control; while in the case of manipulated agents, things are importantly different.

The central idea is that causal variables that can result in an outcome by more than one means – that is, in response to a wider range of changes to the background conditions – bear stronger causal invariable relations to their outcome variables than variables that cannot, or than variables that only result in the outcome across a narrower range of changes to the background conditions (2017: 1263). In the case of natural determinism, Deery and Nahmias argue that the output of deliberative activity within the agent's compatibilist agential structure bears a stronger causal invariance relation to their actions than any other variable – that is, the output of the compatibilist agential structure will cause the action across a wider range of circumstances. In manipulation cases, on the other hand, Deery and Nahmias argue that this is not the case. Instead, they contend, the strongest causal invariable relation exists between the manipulator(s) decision to manipulate the agent. In Pereboom's Case 1, for instance, Deery and Nahmias would argue that the relation between the neuroscientists' decision and Plum's action is such that, across a maximally wide range of changes to background conditions, the variable representing Plum's decision to kill White does not change in value without a change in the value of the variable representing the neuroscientists' decision, and changes in the value of the variable representing the neuroscientists' decision correspondingly change the value of the variable representing Plum's decision to kill. In this way, Deery and Nahmias claim to have isolated a relevant difference between naturally determined agents and manipulated agents.

While this is an interesting and novel way of defending the soft-line approach, Deery and Nahmias's account faces significant problems. First and foremost, they do not take into account that both the nature of manipulation and the nature of the manipulated agent can be made to vary, with the result that the two can be made to match in degrees and kinds of invariance (Pereboom, in correspondence). For Deery and Nahmias, it is important that the team of neuroscientists *intend* for Plum to decide to kill White, and that they are able to *ensure* that he does so. In fact, it is the combination of these two factors that allows Deery and Nahmias to claim that the strongest causal invariance relation exists between the manipulators' intention/decision and the agent's action. Deery and Nahmias make this clear in their use and discussion of Al Mele's famous *Zygote* example. In this scenario, a powerful Goddess, Diana, has the power to know what will happen in the future and to act in ways that ensure that specific events occur in the distant future. Diana has these abilities in part because she exists in a deterministic universe and is able to get enough information about events occurring in it to deduce exactly what she needs to do at that time to ensure that a particular event occurs thirty years later. As the example is described:

> Diana assembles atoms in a specific way at t_1 so as to create a zygote that develops into a child, grows up, finds a wallet 30 years later, and at t_{30} decided to keep the money it contains. For some reason, Diana wants to ensure that this occurs at t_{30} and she possess the power to alter events at t_1 precisely so that she ensures that it does occur. (Deery and Nahmias 2017: 1257)

The life of this intentionally created person, who is called *Manny* (since he is *Ma*nipulated), is contrasted with *Danny*, an ordinarily (non-manipulated) determined agent. We are told that the lives of Manny and Danny follow the exact same course, both are determined by factors beyond their control, both decide to steal the money from the wallet at t_{30}, and there is no difference between them when it comes to their abilities to consider options, weigh reasons, and make decisions.

Now, according to Deery and Nahmias, the reason why Danny can be held morally responsible for stealing the money, while Manny cannot, is that the output of the deliberative activity within Danny's compatibilist agential structure bears a stronger causal invariance relation to his actions than any other variable – that is, the output of the compatibilist agential structure will cause the action across a wider range of circumstances. Whereas for Manny, Deery and Nahmias argue:

> [S]ince we are assuming that Diana is able to *ensure* (30 years prior to the event in question) what Manny will do, there are no relevant changes to conditions C that could possibly interfere with Manny's stealing, since Diana (we are assuming, along with advocates of the Manipulation Argument) has foreseen all such possibilities. As a result, [Diana's decision] bears a stronger causal invariance relation to *Steal* than any other prior causal variable does. (2017: 1265)

The problem with this soft-line reply, however, is manipulation cases need not assume such invariance, nor must they require manipulators to be able to "ensure" specific outcomes. Manipulation cases can be devised where the manipulation is neither intended nor ensured. In such cases, the responsibility-undermining manipulation would *not* provide the strongest causal invariance relation to the agent's action, since small changes in the background conditions would not result in the same output. In fact, my Brain-Implant Malfunction Case is just such an example, since in that scenario it is simply *false* that there are very few changes in background circumstances that could break the causal connections between the malfunctioning of the brain-implant and Plum's decision to kill White. That is, unlike Deery and Nahmias's preferred example of Manny – who is *intentionally* manipulated by Diana, a goddess, who can *ensure* that Manny does exactly as she wants[16] – my Brain-Implant Malfunction Case provides a case where small differences in background conditions result in different outcomes and there is no intentional manipulator who ensures and bears the strongest causal invariance relation to the agent's action.

Other manipulation cases can also be devised that undercut Deery and Nahmias's soft-line reply. Here, for instance, is a case by Pereboom and McKenna (2021). It is based on a modified version of the Manny example:

> Suppose Diana is quite powerful, but not omniscient or omnipotent, but due to her impending death, she has only one shot at manipulating Manny. She does what's specified in Deery and Nahmias description, but due to lack of information, she believes she has only a small chance of succeeding. But what she does succeeds in causally determining Manny to steal. Let's imagine the other possibilities for manipulation she was considering would have failed. In this case she can't ensure that Manny steals, but our intuition that Manny isn't responsible is still in place. However, in this example, it's false that there are very few changes in background circumstances that could break the causal connection between Diana's intention and Manny stealing the money. Moreover, Manny's abilities can be specified so that the degrees of invariance relative his stealing the money match hers precisely. In this scenario, it's false, on the interventionist approach, that Manny is not the causal source of his stealing. (Pereboom and McKenna 2021)

Here we have a case that involves a covert, intentional, manipulator (Diana) who causally determines an agent (Manny) to act in a certain way (i.e., to steal money from a wallet he finds on the ground). From the soft-liner's perspective, Manny is not morally responsible for his action due to the manipulation (this is what differentiates the soft-line approach from the hard-line approach). The problem, however, for Deery and Nahmias's account is that the manipulator's intentions (just like the malfunctioning of the brain-implant in my example) do *not* provide the strongest

---

[16] According to Deery and Nahmias: "Diana creates Manny's zygote (event MZ) in such a way (z) that Manny's own deliberations ($Manny = m$) bring about exactly what she wants ($Steal = s$). The reason that Diana's decision (DD) bears the strongest causal invariance relation to *Steal* is that Diana can (we are assuming) ensure that Manny steals as she intends across the widest possible range of changes to C" (2017: 1266).

invariance relation to Manny's action, nor can it "ensure" that Manny steal the money.

One of the central problems, then, with Deery and Nahmias's account is that they overlook the fact that both the nature of manipulation and the nature of the manipulated agent can be made to vary, with the result that the two can be made to match in degrees and kinds of invariance. And this failure is made even greater when it is combined with the following rule (proposed by Pereboom 2014): The best strategy for manipulation arguments requires as close a causal match as possible between the manipulation cases and the natural determinism case while preserving the intuition of nonresponsibility in the manipulation case. When we apply this rule to the case mentioned earlier, we can see that the resulting manipulation matches natural determinism better than Mele's original Zygote case – that is, just as nature does not exercise intentional invariant control, neither does Diana. Given, then, that Pereboom and McKenna's modified Manny case, as well as my Brain-Implant Malfunction Case, better match natural determinism in this way, and given that Deery and Nahmias's account fails to establish a relevant difference in causal sourcehood in those cases, we should reject their soft-line reply.

Additional difficulties exist as well. Hannah Tierney and David Glick (2020), for instance, have criticized Deery and Nahmias's analysis of sourcehood by drawing on a distinction between two forms of causal invariance that can come into conflict on their account. They argue that any attempt to resolve this conflict will either result in counterintuitive attributions of moral responsibility or will undermine their response to manipulation arguments. Following Woodward (2007: 76–77), Tierney and Glick call invariance under changes of background conditions *stability*. And they call invariance under changes of the value of the causal variables *reliability*. Tierney and Glick then wonder how these two forms of invariance should be weighed against one another in cases where they indicate different causal sources. For instance, "suppose variables A and B are both actual causes of C, but A → C is more reliable then B → C while B → C is more stable than A → C. Is A or B the causal source of C?" (2020: 959). Tierney and Glick provide the following example to help illustrate the problem:

> Imagine that a mafia boss decided to hire an assassin to kill an enemy. The assassin takes the job and decided to kill the enemy by poisoning the enemy's dinner on a Thursday evening and then goes on to do just this ... What is the causal source of the murder: the boss's decision or the assassin's decision? (2020: 959)

On the one hand:

> [T]he relationship between the assassin's decision and the murder (R_1) appears to be more reliable than the relationship between the boss's decision and the murder (R_2). This is because there is a narrower range of values that the boss's decision can take that will predict the murder of the enemy as compared to the range of values that the assassin's decision can take. While the boss can plausibly

decide only whether to hire an assassin and which assassin to hire, we can assign a much broader range of values to the assassin's decision. For example, we can imagine a number of different ways the assassin could decide to kill the enemy: by different means, at different times, on a different day, etc. Thus, holding fixed the relevant background conditions, C, R_1 predicts the value of M [murder] under a wider range of interventions on A [assassin's decision] than R_2 does under interventions on B [boss's decision]. (2020: 959–960)

On the other hand:

R_2 is more stable than R_1. By hiring the assassin to kill the enemy, the boss provides the assassin with an incentive to perform the murder. The assassin would most likely successfully commit the murder under a wide range of changes in the background circumstances because she was hired to do so. For example, we can easily imagine the assassin successfully following through on the mafia boss's orders if it suddenly began raining outside, or is she came down with a cold, or if it was announced that her favorite movie was playing on TV. But when evaluating the relationship between only A and M, we must ignore the contribution of B. Without the contribution of the boss's orders, there are far more circumstances in which the assassin's decision could be thwarted. If the assassin decided to murder the individual for fun or for practice, then a sudden change in the weather, her health, or access to less violent entertainment could all cause the assassin to not act on her decision. But these are precisely the kinds of changes in circumstances in which the boss's orders would still carry weight. Furthermore, if the assassin attempted to murder the enemy, but failed due to a change in the background conditions, the boss could go on to hire as many assassins as is necessary to complete the murder. Thus, there are plausibly fewer circumstances in which the assassin's decision would lead to the murder of the enemy than circumstances in which the boss's decision would. So, R_2 predicts the value of M across a wider range of relevant changes in the background conditions than R_1. (Tierney and Glick 2020: 260)

The example mentioned here reveals how the two forms of causal invariance can come into conflict with one another. Hence, we can ask if R_1 is more reliable than R_2 and R_2 is more stable than R_1, which relation is more invariant on Deery and Nahmias's view?

According to Tierney and Glick, "[Deery and Nahmias] give us no way to weigh reliability and stability against one another when determining the invariance of causal relationships, and without such a mechanism it is impossible to determine which agent's decision, the boss's or the assassin's, is the causal source of the murder" (2020: 961). And after exploring several potential ways of resolving the conflict between reliability and stability in Deery and Nahmias's account of causal sourcehood, Tierney and Glick conclude that "each attempt at resolution either produces counterintuitive judgments about free will and moral responsibility or undermines [Deery and Nahmias's] soft-line response to manipulation arguments" (2020: 961). If this is correct, and I believe it is, we have additional reasons for rejecting Deery and Nahmias's soft-line reply (see Tierney and Glick (2020) for further details).

Given the failure, then, of both hard-line and soft-line replies, manipulation arguments, like Pereboom's four-case argument, should lead us to conclude that determinism is incompatible with an agent being the *appropriate source* of their actions or controlling them in the right kind of way. This conclusion, a form of *source incompatibilism*, is the only reasonable position to adopt given the arguments discussed earlier. We should therefore conclude that "[a]n action is free in the sense required for moral responsibility only if it is not produced by a deterministic process that traces back to causal factors beyond the agent's control" (Pereboom 2001: 34). But once we combine this conclusion with the conclusions of the previous sections – that is, that event-causal and agent-causal libertarian accounts of free will *also fail* to preserve the control in action required for basic desert moral responsibility – we see that *hard incompatibilism* is the only reasonable position to adopt. Hence, the conclusion of Section 2.2 is that we have sufficient reason for adopting the skeptical thesis that who we are and what we do is ultimately the result of factors beyond our control, and because of this we are never morally responsible for our actions in the basic desert sense.

2.3 HARD LUCK

In this section, I would like to present a second, independent argument for free will skepticism based on the pervasiveness of luck. It is my contention that, while the arguments for hard incompatibilism are sufficient on their own for rejecting free will, *so too* are the arguments for hard luck. If that is correct, then defenders of free will, as well as retributivists who ground their justification for punishment in the notion of *just deserts*, must overcome both sets of arguments. It is not enough to argue that one of these routes to free will skepticism fails. Since either is sufficient on its own, free willists must successfully refute both sets of arguments.

Consider the significant roll luck plays in our lives. First, there is the initial "lottery of life" or "luck of the draw," over which we have no say. Whether we are born into poverty or affluence, war or peace, abusive or loving homes, is simply a matter of luck. It is also a matter of luck what natural gifts, talents, predispositions, and physical traits we are born with. Beyond this initial lottery of life, there is also the luck of what breaks one encounters during one's period of self-formation and what environmental influences are most salient on us. Combined, these matters of luck determine what Nagel famously calls *constitutive luck* – luck in who one is and what character traits and dispositions one has. Since our genes, parents, peers, and other environmental influences all contribute to making us who we are, and since we have no control over these, it seems that who we are is at least largely a matter of luck. And since how we act is partly a function of who we are, the existence of constitutive luck entails that what actions we perform depends on luck (Nelkin 2013).

Some philosophers, myself included, believe that constitutive luck raises serious problems for moral responsibility, but not all philosophers agree. Daniel Dennett, for example, writes:

> Suppose – what certainly seems to be true – that people are born with noticeably different cognitive endowments and propensities to develop character traits; some people have long lines of brilliant (or hot-blooded, or well-muscled) ancestors, for instance, and seem to have initial endowments quite distinct from those of their contemporaries. Is this "hideously unfair" – to use a phrase of Williams (1981, p. 228) – or is this bound to lead to something hideously unfair? Not necessarily. (1984: 95)

Dennett proceeds to give the example of a footrace where some are given a head start based on when they were born (an arbitrary fact). He argues that this would be unfair if the race were a hundred yard dash but *not* if it's a marathon: "In a marathon such a relatively small initial advantage would count for nothing, since one can reliably expect other fortuitous breaks to have even greater effects" (1984: 95). According to Dennett, "[a] good runner who starts at the back of the pack, if he is really good enough to deserve winning, will probably have plenty of opportunity to overcome the initial disadvantage" (1984: 95). Since life is more like a marathon than a sprint, Dennett maintains that "luck averages out in the long run" (1984: 95).

While this folksy example may have intuitive appeal for some, it is demonstrably false. Luck does *not* average out in the long run. Those who start from a disadvantaged position of genetic abilities or early environment do not always have offsetting luck later in life. The data clearly show that early inequalities in life often compound over time rather than average out, affecting everything from differences in health and incarceration rates to success in school and all other aspects of life. Malcolm Gladwell (2008), for example, documents the rather strange fact that there are more players in the National Hockey League born in January, February, and March than any other months. His explanation is that in Canada, where children start playing hockey at a very young age, the eligibility cutoff for age-class hockey programs in January 1. At the ages of six and seven, being ten or eleven months older gives one a distinct advantage over one's competitors. Since the older players tend to do better, they end up getting more playing time, and as they progress through the ranks they are selected for better teams and more elite programs, receive better coaching, and play more games against better competition. What begins as a small advantage, a mere matter of luck, snowballs and leads to an ever-widening gap of achievement and success.

This kind of phenomenon can be found throughout society. Studies show, for instance, that low socioeconomic status (or SES) in childhood can affect everything from brain development to life expectancy, education, and income (Farah 2012; Avants et al. 2012; Mariani 2017; Nobel et al. 2005; Farah et al. 2006; Nobel et al. 2007). Educational inequity also has a snowball effect. As Bruce Waller writes, "[T]he child of a wealthy family who receives the benefits of excellent (and expensive) preschools also has the benefits of superb prep schools ..., more advanced placement courses, tutors for the SAT, and probably a legacy advantage in applying to the most selective universities" (2015: 68). Dennett is simply mistaken then in thinking that luck averages out in the long run – it does not. His marathon example also suffers from the fact that it focuses only on constitutive luck, but there are additional kinds of luck that need to be considered – for example, resultant, circumstantial, and causal luck (Nagel 1979).

Resultant luck is luck in the way things turn out. Examples of resultant luck include the drunk driver who hits a pedestrian when his car swerves on to the sidewalk versus the drunk driver who does not. While both engaged in the same reckless behavior, it is a matter of luck that only the former can be held morally and legally accountable for manslaughter. *Circumstantial luck*, on the other hand, is luck in the circumstances in which one finds oneself. As Nagel states, "The things we are called upon to do, the moral tests we face, are importantly determined by factors beyond our control" (1979: 33). Nagel provides the example of Nazi collaborators in 1930's Germany:

> Ordinary citizens of Nazi Germany had an opportunity to behave heroically by opposing the regime. They also had the opportunity to behave badly, and most of them are culpable for having failed this test. But it is a test to which the citizens of other countries were not subjected, with the result that even if they, or some of them, would have behaved as badly as the Germans in like circumstances, they simply did not and therefore are not similarly culpable. (1979: 34)

Circumstantial luck highlights the fact that "one is morally at the mercy of fate" (Nagel 1979: 34), and not only with regard to factors that form our characters and the consequences of our actions but also with the circumstances with which we are confronted. While it is easy to want to morally judge and blame those who are tested morally by circumstantial factors and fail, there is also truth to the old proverb, "There but for the grace of God (or circumstantial luck), go I."

The last of Nagel's four kinds of luck is *causal luck*, or luck in how one is determined by antecedent circumstances. This kind of luck is essentially the traditional problem of free will. As Nagel puts it:

> If one cannot be responsible for consequences of one's acts due to factors beyond one's control, or for antecedents of one's acts that are properties of temperament not subject to one's will, or for the circumstances that pose one's moral choices, then how can one be responsible even for the stripped-down acts of the will itself, if *they* are the product of antecedent circumstances outside of the will's control?" (1979: 35)

Nagel fears that the more we examine the problem the more the "area of genuine agency, and therefore of legitimate moral judgment, seems to shrink under this scrutiny to an extensionless point" (1979: 35). While some philosophers may think this problem arises only if determinism is true, this is not the case. As Dana Nelkin notes, "Even if it turns out that determinism is false, but events are still caused by prior events according to probabilistic laws, the way that one is caused to act by antecedent circumstances would seem to be equally outside of one's control" (2013; see also Pereboom 2001, 2014; Caruso 2012).

In what follows, I will cease talking about resultant, circumstantial, and causal luck and talk instead of only two kinds of luck: *present luck* and *constitutive luck*. I will set aside any further consideration of resultant luck since it goes beyond the question I am interested in here. And causal luck, on this classification, becomes redundant since what it covers is completely captured by the combination of constitutive and present luck. While constitutive luck remains the same, present luck (Mele 2006; Levy 2011) is the luck at or around the moment of a putatively free and morally responsible action or decision. While present luck may include features of circumstantial luck, it is a much broader concept. It also includes any genuine indeterminism that may exist in the proximal causal chain leading to action, as libertarians posit, as well as any circumstantial or situational influences that may affect an agent's choice or action in a way that is outside her control. It can also include features of what Heather Gert (2017) calls *awareness luck* – luck in how aware we are of the morally significant features of our surroundings. As she points out: "[I]ndividuals placed in the same situation will often notice different aspects of it. Some will notice more of what matters morally, while others notice less" (2017).[17]

2.3.1 *The Luck Pincer*

I will now argue that regardless of the causal structure of the universe, free will and basic desert moral responsibility are incompatible with the pervasiveness of *luck* (Levy 2009a, 2011; cf. Haji 2016). This argument is intended not only as an objection to event-causal libertarianism, as the *luck objection* is, but extends to compatibilism as well. At the heart of the argument is the following dilemma: either actions are subject to *present luck* (luck around the time of the action), or they are subject to *constitutive luck* (luck that causes relevant properties of agents, such as their desires, beliefs, and circumstances), or both. Either way, luck undermines moral responsibility since it undermines responsibility-level control. This is what Neil Levy calls the *Luck Pincer* and it can be summarized as follows (2011: 84–97; as summarized by Hartman 2017: 43):

[17] It is important to note that awareness luck has both occurant and dispositional forms. As Gert describes: "A person might merely be more aware than others of the morally relevant aspects of a particular situation. But he might also have the disposition to be unusually aware of what matters morally. Although it is possible to be especially aware in a particular situation without having this general disposition, for ease of exposition I will assume that individual who exhibit exceptional awareness in specific cases do so because they are so disposed" (2017). It is only the occurant form of awareness luck that can be considered a form of present luck. Dispositional awareness luck, on the hand, would fall more properly under constitutive luck.

Universal Luck Premise: Every morally significant act is either constitutively lucky, presently lucky, or both.

Responsibility Negation Premise: Constitutive and present luck each negate moral responsibility.

Conclusion: An agent is not morally responsible for any morally significant acts.

Let us examine the argument in more detail, focusing first on what exactly is meant by "luck."

While there are several competing accounts of luck in the literature,[18] I favor the modal account developed by Levy (2011). The modal account defines luck by way of possible worlds without reference to indeterminism or determinism, and it classifies luck as either *chancy* or *not chancy*. An agent's being *chancy lucky* is defined as follows:

> An event or state of affairs occurring in the actual world is chancy lucky for an agent if (i) that event or state of affairs is significant for that agent; (ii) the agent lacks direct control over the event or state of affairs; and (iii) that event or state of affairs fails to occur in many nearby possible worlds; the proportion of nearby worlds that is large enough for the event to be chancy lucky is inverse to the significance of the event for the agent. (Levy 2011: 36)

On the other hand:

> An event or state of affairs occurring in the actual world that affects an agent's psychological traits or dispositions is non-chancy lucky for an agent if (i) that event or state of affairs is significant for that agent; (ii) the agent lacks direct control over that event or state of affairs; (iii) events or states of affairs of that kind vary across the relevant reference group, and ... in a large enough proportion of cases that event or state of affairs fails to occur or be instantiated in the reference group in the way in which it occurred or was instantiated in the actual case. (Levy 2011: 36)

Note that the first two conditions are the same for an agent's being chancy and non-chancy lucky – that is, (i) *significance*, and (ii) *lack of direct control*. And we can say that an event is *significant* for an agent if she cares about the event and it can have either good or bad significance for her (Levy 2011: 13). It may, for instance, be chancy whether I have an odd or even number of hairs on my head at twelve noon, but it would be strange to say that this is a matter of luck since we generally reserve the appellation "luck" for events that *matter* (Levy 201: 13) – that is, we do not generally speak of entirely trivial events as lucky (i.e., as good or bad for an agent).

With regard to the second condition, we can say that an agent has *direct control* over an event if the agent is able (with high probability) to bring it about by intentionally performing a basic action and if the agent realizes that this is the case (Levy 2011: 19; cf. Coffman 2007). As Levy puts it, an agent has direct control

---

[18] cf. Pritchard, 2005, 2014; Driver, 2012; Levy 2011; Hales, 2016; Latus, 2000, 2003; Hartman, 2017; Zimmerman, 1987, 2002; Coffman, 2007.

over E's occurrence when he can bring about E's occurrence, or act to ensure E's non-occurrence, by virtue of performing some basic action which (as he knows) will bring about or prevent E's occurrence (2011: 19, 150). This is only a first pass account of direct control and may not be entirely adequate, according to Levy, but it will do for almost all purposes.

To help understand how the third condition differs in the two definitions – that is, the *modal condition* (chancy luck) and the *uncommon instantiation condition* (non-chancy luck) – let us consider some examples. A paradigmatic example of a chancy lucky event is Louis's winning the lottery. This is because (i) he lacks direct control over winning the lottery since there is no basic action that he can perform to bring it about, (ii) the event of his winning the lottery is also at least minimally significant, and (iii) – the modal condition – in most close possible worlds with a small divergence from the actual world, Louis does not win. On the other hand, Elaini may be non-chancy lucky for being a genius with a high IQ in comparison with her peers.[19] This is because (i) Elaini lacks direct control over being a genius, (ii) it is significant for her, and (iii) – the uncommon instantiation condition – being a genius is not commonly instantiated in that reference group (assuming, of course, that most of her actual peers are not geniuses).

With these three conditions in place, we can now better understand the distinction between *present luck* and *constitutive luck*. We can say that an agent's decision is the result of present luck if a circumstantial factor outside of the agent's control at or near the time of action significantly influences the decision. Such circumstantial factors could include the agent's mood, what reasons happen to come to her, situational features of the environment, and the like. For instance: "Our mood may influence what occurs to us, and what weight we give to the considerations that do cross our mind ... Our attention may wander at just the wrong moment or just the right one, or our deliberation may be primed by chance features of our environment" (Levy 2009a: 245; see also 2011: 90). In contrast, we can say that an agent's decision is the result of constitutive luck if that decision is partially settled by her dispositional endowment, which is outside of her control. Finally, while present luck is limited to cases of chancy luck, constitutive luck can be a subspecies of both chancy and non-chancy luck since it can refer to a disposition that an agent possesses in either a chancy or a non-chancy way (Levy 2011: 87).

Let us now return to the *Luck Pincer* and see how libertarian and compatibilist accounts fare against it. Libertarian accounts famously face the problem of explaining how a decision or action can be free, given the libertarian demand for indeterminacy immediately prior to directly free action. Moral responsibility skeptics and compatibilists alike have long argued that such indeterminacy makes the action unacceptably chancy, in a way that is responsibility-undermining (see, e.g., Waller 1988; Mele 1999, 2006; Haji 2002, 2004, 2013;

---

[19] This is an altered example from Hartman (2017: 44–46).

2016; Pereboom 2001, 2014a; Levy 2009a, 2011; Caruso 2012). In the previous section, we saw how this objection applies to event-causal libertarian accounts. But it is important to note that it also applies to agent-causal versions of libertarianism (see Mele 2005, 2006; Haji 2004, 2016; Levy 2011). Al Mele, for instance, in criticizing Timothy O'Connor's agent-causal account, asks us to imagine an agent, Tim, who has agent-causal powers and "feely chooses" at time t between taking a break or continuing to work. He then argues:

> [O]n O'Connor's view, Tim "had the power to choose to continue working or to choose to stop, where this is a power to cause either of these mental occurrences. That capacity was exercised at t in a particular way (in choosing to continue working), allowing us to say truthfully that Time at time t causally determined his own choice to continue working" ([O'Connor] 2000, p.74). Suppose that the position reported in the preceding two sentences is true. Why should we suppose that the following cross-world difference is not a matter of chance or luck: that Tim exercises the capacity at issue at t in choosing to continue working rather than in choosing to do something else, as he does in some possible worlds with the same past and laws of nature? Grant that Tim "causally determined his own choice to continue working." Why aren't the differences in his causal determinings at t across worlds with the same past and laws of nature a matter of chance or luck? Tim was able to causally determine each of several choices, whereas a counterpart who fits the event-causal libertarian's picture was able to make – but not to causally determine – each of several choices. If it is a matter of chance that the latter agent chooses to keep working rather than choosing to do something else, why is it not a matter of chance that the former agent causally determines the choice he causally determines rather than causally determining a choice to do something else? (Mele 2006: 54–55)

The kind of luck that is problematic here is *present chancy luck*, since the agent's putatively "free" decision is chancy (i.e., the same decision would fail to occur in many nearby possible worlds), significant, and the circumstantial factor outside of the agent's control occurs just prior to the decision (i.e., the indeterminate event(s)).

Peter van Inwagen (2000) makes vivid the lack of control a libertarian agent has over genuinely undetermined events by considering what would happen if God rolled back the relevant stretch of history to some point prior to an undetermined event and then allowed it to unfold once more (Levy 2009a: 238). Since events would not unfold in the same way on the replay as they did the first time round, since these are genuinely undetermined, and nothing the agent does (or is) can ensure which undetermined possibility is realized, the outcome of this sequence (in this case the agent's decision) is a matter of luck. Such luck, skeptics argue, is responsibility-undermining. Sometimes this is expressed in terms of contrastive explanation – an explanation that explains not only why some event A occurred, but why A occurred *as opposed to* some alternative event B. If an agent's choice cannot be contrastively explained, it is, in some crucial sense, inexplicable, and an agent cannot be responsible for an inexplicable happening since such happenings would be a matter of luck and outside the control of the agent. Since contrastive explanations cannot be offered for causally undetermined events, libertarian accounts introduce luck of the sort that undermines, rather than enhances, freedom and moral responsibility (see Mele 1999, 2005, 2006; Almeida and Bernstein 2003; Haji 2000, 2001; cf. Elzein 2018).

Compatibilist accounts of moral responsibility, on the other hand, are vulnerable to their own powerful luck objection. We can divide compatibilist accounts into two main categories: *historical* and *nonhistorical*. Historical accounts are sensitive to the manner in which an agent comes to be the kind of person they are, in the circumstances in which they find themselves (see Mele 1995, 2006; Fischer and Ravizza 1998). If an agent, for instance, decides to donate a large sum of money to Oxfam, historical accounts of moral responsibility hold that it is important how the agent came to have such a generous nature and make the decision they did – for example, did the agent have a normal history and acquire the disposition to generosity naturally, or did a team of neuroscientists (say) engineer them to have a generous nature? Nonhistorical accounts, on the other hand, maintain that moral responsibility depends instead on nonhistorical factors – like whether an agent identifies with his/her own desires (Frankfurt 1988) or the quality of an agent's will (Scanlon 1998).

The main problem with historical accounts is that they cannot satisfactorily explain how agents can take responsibility for their constitutive luck. The problem here is analogous to the problem raised by manipulation arguments. Manipulated agents are the victims of (very bad) luck – that is, the manipulation is significant for them, they lack control over its (non-)occurrence, and it is chancy, in as much as there are nearby possible worlds in which the manipulation does not occur (Levy 2009a: 242). The problem of constitutive luck is similar in that an agent's *endowments – that is*, traits and dispositions – likewise result from factors beyond the agent's control, are significant, and are either chancy or non-chancy lucky. A historical compatibilist could respond, as they often do to manipulations cases, that as long as an agent *takes responsibility* for her endowments, dispositions, and values, over time she will *become* morally responsible for them. The problem with this reply, however, is that the series of actions through which agents shape and modify their endowments, dispositions, and values are themselves significantly subject to present luck – and, as Levy puts it, "[W]e cannot undo the effects of luck with more luck" (2009a: 244). Hence, the very actions to which history-sensitive compatibilists point, the actions whereby agents take responsibility for their endowments, either *express* that endowment (when they are explained by constitutive luck) or reflect the agent's present luck, or both (see Levy 2009a: 247; 2011).

Hence, present luck is not only a problem for libertarianism it is also a problem for historical compatibilism. And while present luck may be a *bigger* problem for libertarians, since they require the occurrence of undetermined events in the causal chain leading to free action, the problem it creates for historical compatibilists is nonetheless significant. With compatibilism, we need to assess the implications of present luck *in conjunction* with the implications of constitutive luck. When we do, we see that though it might often be the case that the role played by present luck in the decisions and actions of compatibilist agents is relatively small, it is the agent's endowment – directly, or as modified by the effects of present luck, or both – that explains why this is so. An agent's preexisting background of reasons, desires, attitudes, belief, and values – against which an agent deliberates – is the endowment from constitutive luck, inflected and modified, to be sure, but inflected and modified by decisions which either *express* constitutive luck, or which were not settled by the endowment, *and therefore were subject to present luck* (Levy 2009a: 248). Hence, the Luck Pincer: actions are either the product of constitutive luck, present luck, or both.

Nonhistorical accounts, on the other hand, run into serious difficulties of their own with the epistemic condition on control over action. The epistemic condition maintains that moral responsibility for an action requires that the agent understands that, and how, the action is sensitive to her behavior, as well as appreciation of the significance of that action or culpable ignorance of these facts (Levy 2011: chapter 5; cf. Rosen 2002, 2004, 2008; Zimmerman 1997, 2009). Because the epistemic condition on control is so demanding and itself subject to the Luck Pincer, nonhistorical accounts of compatibilism (as well as other accounts that may survive the arguments mentioned earlier) face a serious challenge (see Levy 2011, 2009b). Consider cases of non-culpable ignorance. Imagine, for instance, that a sixteenth-century surgeon operates on a patient without washing his hands or sterilizing his equipment, and as a result his patient gets an infection and dies. The surgeon would not be blameworthy in this situation because he was non-culpably ignorant of the risks of non-sterilization, since germ theory was not established until much later. In this and other cases of non-culpable ignorance, the fact that agents are ignorant of the relevant details is frequently a matter of luck – either present luck or constitutive luck or both.

We can say that non-culpable ignorance is chancy lucky when an agent fails to know that p (where p is significant for her) lacks direct control over whether she knows that p, and in a large proportion of nearby possible worlds does know that p. Let's say I drop my daughter Maya off at a friend's house for a play date. She has a peanut allergy and I forget to inform the other parent at the time of drop-off. When I get to the coffee shop, I realize this and immediately text the parent about the allergy, but because I am in a "dead zone" the message does not go through. Not having received my text, the parent proceeds to give the kids a snack with peanut butter in it, resulting in Maya having a near-fatal reaction. The parent's non-culpable ignorance in this case is chancy lucky since in a large portion of nearby possible worlds she would have received the text. The sixteenth-century surgeon example, on the other hand, is better seen as an example of non-chancy luck, since his ignorance is the result of bad luck inasmuch as beliefs about germs vary across agents in different historical periods (the relevant reference group here), rather than nearby possible worlds.

Since non-culpable ignorance is responsibility-undermining and much more common than philosophers typically think (see Zimmerman 1997, 2009), it gives additional force to the Luck Pincer. Thanks to luck, distant or present, agents who perform wrongful actions *typically* lack freedom-level control over their actions because they fail to satisfy the epistemic condition on such control (Levy 2011: 115–116). In cases of unwitting wrongdoing, there often is no plausible candidate for a culpable *benighting* action that could ground blameworthiness (Levy 2011: 131). Furthermore, it is often the case that we cannot reasonably demand of agents that they do not act in ways that express their epistemic vices (Levy 2011: 126). When an agent does not see that she is managing her moral views badly, it would be unfair to blame her for doing wrong if she had no internal reasons for omitting her bad behavior. This is because, when an agent is managing her moral views badly from the point of view of *objective* morality, it is often the case that her *subjective* moral values and beliefs – which ex hypothesi she does not know are wrong – are governing herself in a perfectly rational and consistent way. Agents cannot govern themselves by the standards of objective morality when they do not accept those standards by way of a reasoning procedure. Since these internal moral values and beliefs are themselves a matter of luck – either present, constitutive, or both – we once again arrive at the Luck Pincer. It would seem, then, that present luck, constitutive luck, or both swallow all, and both libertarian and compatibilist accounts fail to preserve moral responsibility.

2.3.2 *Defending the Luck Pincer*

Let me now consider some objections to the argument mentioned earlier, focusing on Robert Hartman's (2017) recent defense of moral luck and his criticisms of the skeptical view. Hartman argues that premise (2) of the luck pincer, the responsibility negation premise, is false because "the compatibilist has distinctive resources to show that circumstantial and constitutive luck do not necessarily undermine moral responsibility" (2017: 7).[20] The luck pincer maintains that luck undermines basic desert moral responsibility since it violates the following *principle of fairness*: Agents do not deserve to be praised or blamed, punished or rewarded, in the basic desert sense unless there is a desert-entailing difference

---

[20] I should note that Hartman begins by arguing that the Universal Luck Premise is subject to three classes of counterexamples. I will not discuss these counterexamples here, however, since Hartman himself offers a more modest version of premise (1) that is able to circumvent the supposed counterexamples (see 2017, pp. 46–51). See also Levy (forthcoming) for a detailed reply to these counterexamples. Since it is Hartman's objections to premise (2) that are intended to establish that the luck pincer is "unsound," I will focus my attention on these.

between them.[21] It goes on to argue that since a lucky difference between two individuals is not a desert-entailing difference, luck undermines basic desert moral responsibility. Hartman challenges this claim and instead argues that a lucky difference *can* constitute a desert-entailing difference (2017: 51).

He begins by examining the conditions of constitutive and present luck that are supposed to negate praiseworthiness and blameworthiness – that is, their control undermining properties. Following Franklin (2015: 755–756), Garrett (2013: 212), and Tognazzini (2012: 819), Hartman asserts that the significance, modal, and uncommon instantiation conditions appear to be superfluous for the negation of moral responsibility. Furthermore, the direct control condition represents no new challenge to compatibilism since (a) indirect control is often sufficient for basic desert moral responsibility, and (b) if compatibilism is true and "an act's being causally determined does not even diminish responsibility-level control" (2017: 53), then neither does the lack of control intrinsic to the present and constitutive source conditions.

Let me quickly deal with the significance condition since I am willing to grant that an event's being significant for an agent – the agent's caring about the event – "in no way diminishes her responsibility-level control over it" (Hartman 2017: 51). Condition (i) of present and constitutive luck does not mitigate responsibility-level control; rather it is a necessary condition for an event being a matter of *luck* at all. We can therefore set it aside and focus on Hartman's arguments against the direct control, modal, and uncommon instantiation conditions.

With regard to the lack of direct control condition, Hartman maintains that it is compatible with responsibility-level control. He writes, "Agents have mere indirect control over actions that involve a process, and agents are plausibly morally responsible for at least some of those actions" (2017: 52). He provides the following example as evidence:

> I do not directly control the event of giving charitably online when I am away from my phone or computer. But there are basic actions that I can perform that culminate in my giving online such as walking to my computational device and punching keys in the relevant order. Since I enjoy direct control over each of these events in the process, it is plausible that I also possess responsibility-level control over giving online. It follows, then, that we may have responsibility-level control with regard to some events over which we lack direct control. Thus, condition (ii) of present and constitutive luck does not itself negate responsibility-level control. (2017: 52)

In response I would argue that, contra Hartman, either the lack of direct control in the example does undermine moral responsibility, or it is not located in the right

---

[21] Levy provides the following similar principle: "[A]gents do not deserve to be treated differently unless there is a desert-entailing difference between them" (2011, p. 9). Our principles are essentially the same, since basic desert for me is what would justify any deserved difference in treatment, but I prefer my formulation since it retains the language of basic desert.

place for the counterexample to succeed. Consider the following dilemma: If an agent, let us call him *Bob*, lacks direct control over giving charitably online because he is away from his phone or computer, *and this prevents him from acting on his charitable desire*, then it is reasonable to conclude that Bob is not morally responsible. On the other hand, if there are basic actions that Bob could perform that would culminate in his giving online, and these basic actions were all under his direct control, then Hartman's objection fails for a different reasons – that is, the lack of direct control is not located in the right place for the counterexample to succeed since under such a description the agent *would* have direct control over giving charitably online.

Furthermore, Hartman's contention that he enjoys direct control over each of the basic actions involved in the process raises questions of its own. If this is meant as a stipulation of the example, then we are back into the dilemma just outlined – since Bob would in fact retain direct control over his ability to give and hence there would be no counterexample. If, on the other hand, it is meant as an empirical claim, I contend that it is highly questionable. This is because it is reasonable to think that at least some of these more basic actions would themselves be subject to either constitutive luck, present luck, or both – in which case, the lack of direct control condition would remain relevant. We can imagine Bob is sitting on his couch, not near his phone or computer, when he is struck with the desire to get up, locate his phone, and give to his favorite charity. A defender of the luck pincer could argue that the decision to act on this desire would either be the result of a long-standing charitable predisposition that was beyond the direct control of the agent (and hence a matter of constitutive luck), the result of present luck (e.g., a commercial that came on the television or some other situational or circumstantial factor), or both. Hartman's example either begs the question by assuming that direct control is retained throughout the process, or it fails to address why luck would not be a problem at these other moments in the process.

Lastly, it is unclear what Hartman's argument is actually an argument against. The luck pincer maintains that luck undermines every instance of direct control. Hartman replies by arguing that we can be morally responsible in virtue of exercising indirect control. But everyone accepts that you cannot just exercise indirect control – rather, indirect control is exercised in virtue of some instance of direct control. So saying that we can have indirect control over giving charitably online is just not a response to the argument at all.

Moving on the Hartman's objection to the modal condition, he argues that "it is implausible that the *mere fact* that and event fails to occur in a broad range of nearby possible worlds itself mitigates the agent's control over the actual event" (2017: 52). He maintains that there is no necessary connection between the satisfaction of the modal condition and an agent having less control over an event. What is of importance, according to Hartman, is not the chanciness of an event, but that it can be *reasonably foreseen*. He writes, "[I]n moral philosophy, there is widespread agreement that an agent is not morally responsible for a consequence of an action that she could not even reasonably have been expected to foresee" (2017: 53). So in the case where some indeterminism is introduced into an otherwise deterministic chain of causes, Hartman agrees with Levy that the agent would not be responsible in the basic desert sense. But, Hartman contends, this is because the unforeseeability of the result undermines his praiseworthiness and blameworthiness, not its chanciness. He concludes, "[C]ondition (iii) of present luck and chancy constitutive luck do not necessarily even partially mitigate responsibility-level control" (2017: 53).

My first reply would be that Hartman's focus on foreseeability rather than chanciness or the modal condition may amount to a difference without much of a difference – in which case, moral responsibility may still be threatened by chancy luck but for different reasons. In most cases, an event that is chancy lucky will also be reasonably unforeseeable. While I can hope and even foresee winning the lottery, I cannot reasonably foresee winning. And this is because in most nearby possible worlds I will not win. If it turns out that the satisfaction of the modal condition tracks the lack of reasonable foreseeability, Hartman's shift in responsibility-undermining properties may still fail to save moral responsibility when it comes to chancy luck. For me, however, it is precisely because winning the lottery is chancy lucky that I cannot expect or reasonably foresee winning – that is, the lack of reasonable foreseeability is not what undermines moral responsibility; rather it is parasitic on the chanciness involved. And while I acknowledge that lack of foreseeability can be due to factors other than its chanciness, in such cases I would argue that luck may still be a factor since awareness luck or constitutive features of the agent may be responsible for the lack of foreseeability.

Second, and more importantly, I disagree with Hartman that there is no necessary connection between the satisfaction of the modal condition and an agent having less control over an event. An agent has direct control over E's occurrence if he can bring about E's occurrence by virtue of performing some basic action which (he knows) will bring about E's occurrence. The probability of his basic action having the intended effect need not be 100 percent, but it should be high (Levy 2011: 19). I would argue that the fact that an event or state of affairs fails to occur in many nearby possible worlds *does* indicate that the agent lacks the direct control needed to bring about that event or state of affairs with high probability. Saying this is still consistent, of course, with the agent being able to *influence* the relative probabilities of some event's occurrence. As Levy writes: "We *can* influence the probability of lucky events. I am lucky if I win the lottery, but I can certainly influence the probability of my winning the lottery: I can buy two tickets, or three, or one hundred" (2011: 19). The problem, however, is that it is precisely "because agents can influence the probability of chance events but cannot ensure their occurrence that they lack *direct* control over them" (2011: 19). Hartman provides no argument against this other than to say that "it is implausible."

Turning now to the uncommon instantiation condition, Hartman once again maintains that it does not diminish responsibility-level control. He writes:

> The way in which a disposition mitigates control over an action is exhausted by the disposition's intrinsic nature, by its being unsheddable, or by its having been acquired non-voluntarily. But the satisfied uncommon instantiation condition refers merely to the fact that a disposition is relatively rare within a reference group. But being rarely instantiated is not an intrinsic property of a disposition. And a disposition's being unsheddable or non-voluntarily acquired has no necessary connection with its being rarely instantiated. So, then, because the only ways in which a disposition could mitigate an agent's control over the action are not necessarily related to the uncommon instantiation condition, the satisfaction of that condition does not mitigate an agent's responsibility-level control. (2017: 53)

Here I agree with Hartman that there is no necessary connection between a disposition being rarely instantiated and its being unsheddable or nonvoluntarily acquired. But there are two possible replies a skeptic could make here. The first is to argue that Hartman is simply mistaken when he says that "the only ways in which a disposition could mitigate an agent's control over the action" is when the disposition is unsheddable or nonvoluntarily acquired. Hartman provides no argument for the claim that these two features exhaust the control-mitigating options. And it seems questioning-begging to simply rule out non-chancy luck as possibly relevant here.

Second, a defender of the luck pincer could argue that the uncommon instantiation condition, while a necessary condition for non-chancy luck, does not diminish responsibility on its own. Rather, when a psychological trait or disposition is rarely instantiated it means that non-chancy luck is involved (assuming the other conditions are satisfied), but it is the fact that *constitutive or present factors beyond the direct control of the agent are the source of the trait or disposition* that is responsibility-mitigating. This second reply would concede Hartman's main point but it would not undermine the skeptical view or the force of the luck pincer. Consider, again, the example of Elaini being non-chancy lucky for being a genius with a high IQ in comparison to her peers. We can say that (i) being a genius is significant for her, (ii) she lacks direct control over it, and (iii) being a genius is uncommonly instantiated in her reference group. But we can add that it is the fact that the *source* of this uncommonly instantiated psychological trait is constitutive factors beyond the direct control of the agent that undermines responsibility and praiseworthiness for it. In some cases, such as this one, the constitutive source of the uncommonly instantiated trait or disposition will be indicative of the fact that it was involuntarily acquired. In other cases, the trait or disposition may be acquired voluntarily but only as a result of other features of the agent that are the result of constitutive luck, present luck, or both. Either way, uncommonly instantiated traits or dispositions would remain subject to the luck pincer.

This second reply brings me to Hartman's final objection. Hartman acknowledges that the present and constitutive source conditions "mitigate the agent's control in certain ways," but he also maintains that "the compatibilist should resist thinking that they even partially diminish responsibility-level control" (2017: 53). This is because

> [t]he compatibilist affirms that past states of affairs and the laws of nature outside of an agent's control can decisively influence which action she performs without even partially attenuating responsibility-level control. And if causal determinism does not even partially diminish responsibility-level control, then circumstantial factors and constitutive properties outside of the agent's control do not even mitigate responsibility-level control. (2017: 53)

Hartman offers two interrelated arguments for this conclusion. The first, the *a fortiori argument*, runs as follows:

> Assume that compatibilism is true. As a result, an act's being causally determined does not even diminish responsibility-level control. But the lack of control intrinsic to a causally determined act is great (even though it is not great enough even to partially mitigate responsibility-level control), because the agent has no control over the laws of nature or the events prior to her birth that jointly causally determine her actions. In comparison, the lack of control intrinsic to the present and constitutive source conditions is weaker, because each kind of factor outside of agent's control is merely one among many that contribute to her performing an action. Since the greater lack of control does not even partially diminish responsibility-level control, neither does the lesser. Therefore, neither circumstantial factors nor constitutive properties beyond an agent's control that decisively influence her decisions even partially mitigate her responsibility-level control. (2017: 54)

The second argument, the *proper part argument*, maintains:

> The causal deterministic process that produces an agent's causally determined action also generates whatever circumstantial factors or constitutive properties influence her action – that is, the causal deterministic process that is sufficient to bring about an agent's performing an action is also sufficient to bring about her being in a particular circumstance with particular dispositions. We might roughly think of the influence that circumstantial factors and constitutive properties have on one's action as proper parts of the influence that causal determinism has on one's action. But if a proper part of the causally deterministic process even partially rules out responsibility-level control, then an agent cannot be fully morally responsible for a causally determined act. In other words, if the relevant circumstantial or constitutive factors even partially undermine responsibility-level control, then so does causal determinism. (2017: 54)

He goes on to argue that since "the dialectic of Levy's argument assumes that compatibilism is true" – and "causal determinism's decisive influence on an agent's decision does *not* even partially mitigate responsibility-level control" – the circumstantial factors and constitutive properties that decisively influence an agent's decision "do not even partially diminish responsibility-level control either" (2017: 54).

While the *a fortiori* argument and the proper parts argument may have some force against Levy's own particular set of views, they beg the question against incompatibilists like myself. Levy may be willing to assume the truth of compatibilism as part of his dialectic but I am not. I argued earlier that both determinism and indeterminism are incompatible with free will and basic desert moral responsibility, and as a result we should adopt the skeptical perspective. While my argument here is independent of those arguments, neither of Hartman's arguments is effective against my view since I do not concede their main assumption – the truth of compatibilism. Hartman begins with the truth of compatibilism and then proceeds to argue that if the lack of control in the case of determinism does not undermine responsibility, neither does it undermine responsibility in the case of present and constitutive luck. I go in the opposite direct. I contend that the control in action required for basic desert moral responsibility is undermined by *both* determinism and the luck pincer.

To be clear, my point is not that one needs to be an incompatibilist to find the luck pincer convincing. Rather, it is that the lack of control involved in present and constitutive luck resembles the lack of control involved in the manipulation argument. Hence, both the *a fortiori* argument and the proper parts argument are question-begging since they assume the truth of compatibilism. What Hartman needs is an independent argument for why the lack of control intrinsic to present and constitutive luck are not a threat to moral responsibility, one that does not assume the very thing under debate. He has not provided that.

Conclusion: I have here argued that the skeptical view remains the most justified position to adopt since the pervasiveness of luck undermines free will and basic desert moral responsibility. I began by examining the different varieties of luck. I then introduced the luck pincer and argued that all morally significant actions are either subject to constitutive luck, present luck, or both, and since constitutive and present luck each negate basic desert moral responsibility, we should conclude that agents are never morally responsible in the relevant sense. I then concluded by addressing Robert Hartman's many objections to the luck pincer, arguing that each can be satisfactorily dealt with.

2.4 IMPLICATIONS OF FREE WILL SKEPTICISM FOR RETRIBUTIVE PUNISHMENT

If what I've argued in this chapter is correct, we have one very powerful reason for rejecting retributivism already in hand. The arguments in favor of hard incompatibilism and hard luck reveal that what we do and the way we are is ultimately the result of factors beyond our control and because of this we are never morally responsible for our actions in the basic desert sense. But if agents are never morally

2.4 Implications of Free Will Skepticism for Retributive Punishment

responsible for their actions in the basic desert sense, then they never deserve to suffer for the wrongs they have done in the purely backward-looking sense required for retributivism. This is not to say, of course, that other conceptions of responsibility cannot be reconciled with determinism, chance, or luck. Nor is it to deny that there remain good reasons for incapacitating dangerous criminals and engaging in forms of moral protest in the face of bad behavior. Rather, it is to insist that to hold people *truly* or *ultimately* morally responsible for their actions – that is, to hold them responsible in a non-consequentialist desert-based sense – would be to hold them responsible for the results of the morally arbitrary, for what is ultimately beyond their control, which is fundamentally unfair and unjust. Free will skepticism therefore presents a powerful challenge to retributivism since it does away with the idea of basic desert.

Since retributive punishment requires basic desert in order to be justified, free will skepticism implies that retributive punishment lacks justification. And in so far as we demand *justified* legal punishment practices, we need to revise the legal system and replace it with a justification that does not rely on desert (Stråge 2019: 38). Alva Stråge (2019) calls this the *Revision Argument*, which maintains that in light of the philosophical arguments against basic desert, we should revise the legal system so that any retributive justification of punishment is removed. Neil Levy echoes this demand for revision of the legal system when he correctly notes:

> Central elements of the criminal justice system are ... justified only if agents are morally responsible for their actions. The sanctions this system imposes – especially the deprivation of liberty – are morally serious and require an equally weighty rationale for their imposition. Traditionally, incarceration is seen as justified, in part, by the *desert* of offenders: because they are *guilty* – morally, and not merely legally, guilty – we can impose significant sanctions on them; the more weighty the sanction, the more such a justification is required ... But if [free will and] moral responsibility skeptics are right, agents are never deserving of the imposition of such sanctions. This moral responsibility skepticism has practical implications: it apparently entails that major elements of the criminal justice system are unjustified (2012: 480–481).

The *skeptical argument* against retributivism therefore maintains that since free will skepticism is the only reasonable position to adopt, we must conclude that agents are never morally responsible in the basic desert sense, but since this conclusion undermines the retributivist notion that wrongdoers *deserve* to be punished in the backward-looking sense required, we should reject retributivism and revise those elements of the criminal justice systems that depend upon it.

The skeptical argument therefore provides the most direct and comprehensive argument against retributivism. It goes directly at the philosophical foundations of retributivism by arguing that no one is ever morally responsible for their actions in the sense required for retributive punishment to be justified. But what if one is not convinced by the arguments against free will and basic desert moral responsibility? What if they claim that the arguments for hard incompatibilism and hard luck fail? This, of course, is one way to resist the conclusion of the skeptical argument. But, in reply, I would first want to know *where* they think those arguments fail. Since *each* set of arguments is sufficient on its own for rejecting free will and basic desert, defenders of retributivism would need to overcome *both* the arguments for hard incompatibilism (or some aspect of them) *and* the arguments for hard luck. It would not be enough on its own to refute only one of those arguments – since if the right hand does not get you, the left hand will. Furthermore, *even if* the retributivist thought they could overcome the overwhelming case for free will skepticism, they would still need to face the five additional arguments against retributivism developed in this book – that is, the Epistemic Argument, the Limited Effectiveness Argument, the Misalignment Argument, the Poor Epistemic Position Argument (or PEPA), and the Indeterminacy in Judgment Argument. Each of these arguments, I contend, presents powerful reasons on their own for rejecting retributivism.

3

The Epistemic Argument against Retributivism

In this chapter, I would like to develop a second independent argument against retributivism, which I call the *Epistemic Argument*. The argument maintains that even if one is not convinced by the arguments against free will and basic desert moral responsibility, it remains unclear whether retributive punishment is justified. This is because the burden of proof lies on those who want to inflict intentional harm on others to provide good justification for such harm (see Pereboom 2001, 2014; Vilhauer 2009, 2012, 2015; Shaw 2014; Corrado 2017; Caruso 2020). This means that retributivists who want to justify legal punishment on the assumption that agents are free and morally responsible (and hence *justly deserve* to suffer for the wrongs they have done) must justify that assumption. And they must justify that assumption in a way that meets a high epistemic standard of proof since the harms caused in the case of legal punishment are often quite severe. It is not enough to simply point to the mere possibility that agents possess libertarian or compatibilist free will. Nor is it enough to say that the skeptical arguments against free will and basic desert moral responsibility fail to be conclusive. Rather, a positive and convincing case must be made that agents are in fact morally responsible in the basic desert sense, since it is the backward-looking desert of agents that retributivists take to justify the harm caused by legal punishment. The problem, however, is that all extant accounts of basic desert moral responsibility fail to satisfy the high burden of proof required to justify intentionally inflicting harm on others. Hence, even if one is not completely convinced by the arguments against free will and basic desert moral responsibility, there remains a strong argument against causing harm on retributivist grounds that undermines both libertarian and compatibilist attempts to justify it. This is because the Epistemic Argument requires only a weaker notion of skepticism than the one defended in the previous chapter, namely one that holds that the justification for believing that agents are morally responsible in the basic desert sense, and hence justly deserve to suffer for the wrongs they have done, is too weak to justify the intentional suffering caused by retributive legal punishment.

3.1 THE EPISTEMIC ARGUMENT AGAINST RETRIBUTIVE LEGAL PUNISHMENT

Recall that the retributivist justification for punishment maintains that those who commit certain kinds of wrongful acts, paradigmatically serious crimes, morally deserve to suffer (Walen 2014). Unlike theories of punishment that aim at deterrence, rehabilitation, or moral education, retributivism grounds punishment in the blameworthiness and desert of offenders and holds that punishing deserved wrongdoers is justified regardless of whether it benefits society or the individual. For the retributivist, wrongdoers deserve a punitive response proportional to their wrongdoing, even if their punishment serves no further purpose. Legal punishment, on the other hand, involves one person's deliberately harming another on behalf of the state in a way that is intended to constitute a fitting response to some offense and to give expression to the state's disapproval of that offense (see Zimmerman 2011: 1–19; Boonin 2008: 3–26). The question, then, is whether *retributive legal punishment* is ever justified.

I will now argue that the retributive justification of legal punishment fails to meet the burden of proof required to justify the intentional harms it causes. My argument for this conclusion runs as follows:

(1) Legal punishment intentionally inflicts harms on individuals and the justification for such harms must meet a high epistemic standard. If it is significantly probable that one's justification for harming another is unsound, then, prima facie, that behavior is seriously wrong.
(2) The retributive justification for legal punishment assumes that agents are morally responsible in the basic desert sense and hence justly deserve to suffer for the wrongs they have done in a backward-looking, non-consequentialist sense (appropriately qualified and under the constraint of proportionality).
(3) If the justification for the assumption that agents are morally responsible in the basic desert sense and hence justly deserve to suffer for the wrongs they have done does not meet the high epistemic standard specified in (1), then retributive legal punishment is prima facie seriously wrong.
(4) The justification for the claim that agents are morally responsible in the basic desert sense provided by both libertarians and compatibilists faces powerful and unresolved objections and as a result falls far short of the high epistemic bar needed to justify such harms.
(5) Hence, retributive legal punishment is unjustified and the harms it causes are prima facie seriously wrong.

3.1 The Epistemic Argument against Retributive Legal Punishment

I call this the *Epistemic Argument* and it maintains that no extant account of basic desert moral responsibility has the evidentiary support needed to justify retributive legal punishment.[1]

Premise (1) places the burden of proof on those who want to justify legal punishment, since the harms caused in this case are often quite severe – including the loss of liberty, deprivation, and in some cases even death. As Victor Tadros spells out these harms:

> Punishment is probably the most awful thing modern democratic states systematically do to their own citizens. Every modern democratic state imprisons thousands of offenders every year, depriving them of their liberty, causing them a great deal of psychological and sometimes physical harm. Relationships are destroyed, jobs are lost, the risk of the offender being harmed by other offenders is increased, and all at great expense to the state. (2011: 1)

Given the gravity of these harms, the justification for legal punishment must meet a high epistemic standard. If it is significantly probable that one's justification for harming another is unsound, then, prima facie, that behavior is seriously wrong (Pereboom 2001: 199; see also Vilhauer 2009).

Support for premise (1) can be found both in the law and everyday practice. As Michael Corrado writes:

> The notion of a burden of proof comes to us from the adversarial courtroom, where it guides the presentation of evidence. In both criminal and civil cases the defendant is presumed not guilty or not liable, and it is up to the accuser to persuade the finder of fact. The only difference between the two cases lies in the measure of the burden that must be carried, which depends upon the seriousness of the outcome. When all that is at issue is the allocation of a loss that can be measured in financial terms, the accuser needs only to prove the defendant's fault by a preponderance of the evidence, but where the defendant's very life or freedom is at stake the burden is considerably higher: the prosecutor must prove beyond a reasonable doubt. (2017: 1)

Our ordinary everyday practices also place the burden of proof on those who knowingly and intentionally cause harm to others. In fact, even in cases where harm is *foreseeable* but not intended, we often demand a high level of justification. Let us say a newspaper receives a tip on a story that will likely cause great harm to a public figure, potentially sinking their career. In such circumstances, good journalistic standards demand that the story be independently verified and properly vetted before it is run. If the newspaper were to run the story without properly vetting it, and later discover that the tip came from an organization who seeks to undermine

---

[1] The basic idea behind the Epistemic Argument was first introduced by Pereboom in *Living without Free Will* (2001: 161). Benjamin Vilhauer then developed the argument at length in a series of papers (2009, 2012, 2015). I presented my own version of it in Caruso (2018). Others who have also defended versions of the Epistemic Argument include Double (2002), Shaw (2014), Corrado (2017), and Jeppson (2020).

the public's trust in the media, we would rightly condemn the newspaper for not applying a higher epistemic standard. Things are even clearer when the harm caused is intentional, like in the case of a just war or when a nation decides to use deadly force. The use of deadly force, we feel, is only justified under conditions of extreme necessity, when all lesser means have failed or cannot reasonably be employed. And while we may acknowledge that the level of justification required may vary depending on the severity of harm involved, we typically demand that one must have good justification for intentionally harming another.

In the case of legal punishment where the severity of harm is beyond question, I maintain that we should place the highest burden possible upon the state. If the state is going to punish someone for first-degree murder, say, then the epistemic bar that needs to be reached is guilt beyond a reasonable doubt. But does this burden of proof carry over to theoretical debates – for example, the debate over free will and moral responsibility? Here I follow Pigliucci and Maarten (2014) as well as Corrado (2017: 3) in distinguishing between *evidential* burden of proof, which comes into play only when there is no costs associated with a wrong answer, and *prudential* burden of proof, which comes into play precisely when there are significant costs associated with a wrong answer. As Corrado applies the distinction to theoretical matters:

> [I]n a purely philosophical contest where nothing of a practical nature hangs on the outcome it is the evidential burden of proof that is required, and the standard of proof must be "by a preponderance of the evidence": whoever simply has the better evidence must win. On the other hand, if something practical does depend on the outcome of the philosophical debate, then what would matter is the prudential burden. The costs on either side would determine the allocation of the burden and the standard by which satisfaction of the burden is to be measured. (2017: 3)

I contend that given the practical importance of moral responsibility to legal punishment, and given the gravity of harm caused by legal punishment (to the individuals punished as well as those family and friends who depend upon the imprisoned for income, love, support, and/or parenting), the proper epistemic standard to adopt is the prudential burden of proof beyond a reasonable doubt.

Benjamin Vilhauer, for instance, has persuasively argued that "[i]f it can be reasonably doubted that someone had free will with respect to some action, then it is a requirement of justice to refrain from doing serious retributive harm to him in response to that action" (2009: 131). Derk Pereboom has also proposed applying the reasonable doubt standard – in fact, he was probably the first to do so, when in *Living without Free Will* he wrote:

> Punishment – in particular, punishment designed to satisfy the retributive goals – harms people. If one aims to harm another, the justification must meet a high epistemic standard. If it not beyond reasonable doubt that retributivist justifications are disguised vengeful justification, and vengeful justification are illegitimate, then there is reason to believe that it is immoral to justify punishment policy

retributivistically. More generally, where there is a substantial likelihood that one's justification for harming someone is illegitimate, then harming that person on the basis of that justification could well be morally wrong. (2001: 161)

The proof-beyond-a-reasonable-doubt standard is the appropriate epistemic standard to apply when we are talking about intentional harm and institutional punishment. When the stakes are high, as they are with legal punishment, both the law and everyday practice demand that we set the epistemic bar accordingly. As Vilhauer notes, the prudential burden of proof beyond a reasonable doubt has a close kinship to another "reasonable doubt" principle, which is widely recognized to be a requirement of justice: "[T]hat is the requirement in Anglo-American criminal legal proceedings that the accused can only be convicted of a crime if it is proven beyond reasonable doubt that he acted criminally" (2009: 133). The grounds for accepting this high epistemic standard for criminal conviction are the same as the grounds for accepting it with regard to premise (1).

When premise (1) is combined with (2), which is simply a statement of the retributivist justification for legal punishment, we get the requirement that retributivists must justify their core assumption – that is, that agents are free and morally responsible in the basic desert sense and hence justly deserve to suffer for the wrongs they have done. As Vilhauer puts it:

> When the claim that someone has free will plays a role in a retributive justification of serious harm, that claim must be held to the same standard [as criminal conviction], for the same reason. That is, in this context, the claim that someone has free will plays a role in an argument for seriously harming someone, just as the claim that someone has committed a crime typically does. For this reason, it must be held to the "reasonable doubt" standard, just as the claim that someone has committed a crime must be. (2009: 134)

While this demand for justification is reasonable given the strength of (1), many retributivists simply deny or ignore it. For instance, Larry Alexander, Kimberly Kessler Ferzan, and Stephen Morse – in their book *Crime and Culpability: A Theory of Criminal Law* – maintain that "[w]e need take no stand on the freewill-determinism issue" (2009: 15).[2] They go on to explain:

> Two of us – Ferzan and Morse – are persuaded by the arguments for compatibilism. One of us – Alexander – is not. His view is that compatibilism provides only a hollow form of moral responsibility, not the full-blooded form that our reactive attitudes

---

[2] In the book, Alexander, Ferzan, and Morse set out to explain what the criminal law would look like if structured by moderate retributivism: "What we intend to do in this book is to explore what the doctrines of the criminal law would look like if they were structured (primarily) by the concern that criminal defendants receive the punishment they deserve, and particularly that they receive no more punishment than they deserve ... In our view, it is the defendant's decision to violate society's norms regarding the proper concern due to the interests of others that establishes the negative desert that in turn can both justify and limit the imposition of punishment" (2009: 6–7).

assume. In particular, it seems unresponsive to the worry that what appears to an actor to be a reason, or a reason with a particular positive or negative weight, seems to be beyond the actor's proximate control. On the other hand, he also believes that libertarianism cannot deliver a form of moral responsibility worth wanting because, just like determinism, its foil, libertarianism takes control out of the agent's hands and relinquishes it to chance – or else just makes it utterly mysterious. (2009: 15)

How, then, does Alexander justify doing harm on retributive grounds when "neither determinism nor indeterminism can provide a satisfactory account of moral responsibility, and together they appear to exhaust the possibilities" (2009: 15)? We are provided with the following, rather unsatisfying, answer:

> Alexander believes, as a metaphilosophical position, that the freewill-determinism puzzle is one of those antinomies of thought that we are incapable of resolving, along with the mind-body and infinity puzzles. For him, the freewill-determinism puzzle will always dog practices of holding people morally responsible, practices that we nevertheless cannot imagine dispensing with. *Because we cannot dispense with such practices, a retributivist regarding criminal punishment need not resolve or even take sides on the freewill issue.* (2009: 15 [italics added])

Alexander's position seems to be that while we will never be able to comprehend the basis of moral responsibility (see 2009: 15n22), we should nevertheless continue causing harm on retributivist grounds since "we cannot dispense with such practices."

There are, however, at least two major problems with this reply. First, why think that we can never dispense with our retributive practices when it comes to the criminal law? If Alexander were limiting his comments to our interpersonal reactive attitudes, arguing (à la Strawson) that they were indispensable or centrally important, that would be one thing. But in the comment quoted and the book from which it is drawn, Alexander is discussing legal punishment. I see no reason to think that retributivism is indispensable to the criminal law. The fact that several countries have moved away from retributive models of legal punishment (to greater or lesser extent) is evidence enough that this is false. It is also important to distinguish between *narrow-profile* and *wide-profile* reactive attitudes (Nichols 2007: 25). Narrow-profile attitudes are local or immediate emotional reactions to situations, whereas wide-profile responses are not immediate and involve rational reflection. While we may be unable to appreciably reduce narrow-profile retributive reactions in some cases, it is open for us to diminish or even eliminate retributive reactions in wide-profile cases. If I am hurt in an intimate personal relationship, for example, it may be beyond my ability to resist feeling resentment or anger. But when it comes to the law, which involves wide-profile rational reflection, we can indeed disavow retributivism in the sense of rejecting any force it may be assumed to have in *justifying* a harmful response to wrongdoing.

Second, to continue doing harm on retributivist grounds even though one acknowledges that the philosophical foundations of the view can never be comprehended or justified violates the basic precept, both widespread and intuitive, that one should restrain from intentionally doing harm unless otherwise justified. Note that Alexander is *not* saying that despite our inability to justify, in some foundational way, basic desert moral responsibility, we should consider libertarianism or compatibilism as providing *justification enough*. Instead, he explicitly states, "[C]ompatibilism provides only a hollow form of moral responsibility" and "libertarianism cannot deliver a form of moral responsibility worth wanting." Since this is a conclusion shared by many free will skeptics, it is unclear why he thinks we should continue holding agents morally responsible in the basic desert sense, let alone subject them to severe and often painful forms of legal punishment. It in no way helps to claim that the problem of free will is an antinomy. One does not get off the justificatory hook with regard to legal punishment by simply throwing their hands up in the air and saying, "Since there is no satisfying solution to the problem of free will we should continue assuming agents are morally responsible and hence justly deserve to suffer for the wrongs they have done." Rather, one needs to provide a positive and compelling reason *for* believing that agents are free and morally responsible in the sense required.

Morse and Ferzan at least claim they are "persuaded by the arguments for compatibilism." But how persuaded? In answering this, I will focus on Morse's take on compatibilism since he spells it out at great length elsewhere (2013, 2015a, 2015b, 2018). He begins by noting that

> [t]he criminal law is a thoroughly folk-psychological enterprise. Doctrine and practice implicitly assume that human beings are agents, creatures who act intentionally for reasons, who can be guided by reasons, and who in adulthood are capable of sufficient rationality to ground full responsibility unless an excusing condition obtains. We all take this "standard picture" for granted because it is the foundation not just of law but of interpersonal relations generally, including how we explain ourselves to others and to ourselves. (2015a: 40)

He goes on to argue that the standard picture is thoroughly compatibilist in nature. He acknowledges that "metaphysical assumptions matter" (2015a: 44), especially when it comes to the criteria for moral responsibility, but adds: "The question is whether one must resolve or even defend one's metaphysical and other philosophical foundations in these fraught areas. I think not" (2015a). According to Morse, "when philosophy is foundational and practically important, one's position must be acknowledged but need not be defended or, *a fortiori*, resolved" (2015a: 45).

When it comes to the free will debate, Morse maintains that "[t]here will always be good arguments for and against the various positions" (2015a: 45). With no ability to declare a winner, he asks himself: "What is a poor, country lawyer-scholar to do in such circumstances when trying to make normative arguments about doctrine, practice, and policy?" (2015a: 45). His answer is to start with a normative position that is attractive at the non-metaphysical level of applied ethical, moral, political, and legal theory. If this position is consistent with a reasonable metaphysics that does not conflict with relatively uncontroversial, or at least plausible, empirical accounts about the world and with other reasonable philosophical theories, then one can proceed without defending the metaphysics, the empirics, and other philosophical positions. (2015a: 46)

According to Morse, compatibilism provides just such a reasonable metaphysics. And while incompatibilists are likely to point to all the arguments against compatibilism that suggest that the normative position adopted is unjustified, Morse maintains that "a sophisticated metaphysician who adheres to the chosen metaphysics would have answers, and there would be no decisive arguments to refute the sophisticate" (2015a: 46). It is this lack of decisiveness that Morse points to as key. He also maintains that any position that wants to deny the "standard picture" should carry the burden of proof, since "[a]ny position that violates common sense should meet the most demanding burden of persuasion" (2015a: 46). For these reasons, he concludes: "I am a compatibilist, a perfectly plausible metaphysics, and will continue to believe that robust responsibility is possible until an incontrovertible argument that all would accept requires me to jettison this view" (2015a: 49).

While Morse's reasoning is quite sophisticated, I contend that it gets things exactly backward. First, free will skepticism also offers a reasonable metaphysics, one that is consistent with our best philosophical and scientific accounts of the world. While Morse might find it is unattractive at the level of applied moral, political, and legal theory (2018), *optimistic skeptics* argue that adopting the skeptical perspective actually has distinct advantages in these areas (Caruso 2013, 2016, 2017a, 2017b; Pereboom and Caruso 2018; see also Pereboom 2001, 2014; Waller 2011, 2015). Second, I disagree with Morse on who carries the burden of proof. He claims the burden falls on those who want to reject basic desert moral responsibility (what he calls "robust responsibility"). I, on the other hand, maintain that if one is going to cause harm on the assumption that compatibilism is true and agents are morally responsible in the sense required for retributive justice, then the burden is on them to establish beyond a reasonable doubt that this is the case. While Morse is correct that in *certain circumstances* the burden falls on those who advance philosophical views contrary to common sense, things change dramatically when significant harm is involved. Perhaps it is acceptable to adopt a reasonable metaphysics with regard to, say, realism about the external world, but this is significantly different than adopting compatibilism about moral responsibility since it is not used to justify retributive harm.

My proposal is that we adopt the following *precautionary principle* when it comes to unresolved metaphysical/philosophical positions that are likely to cause severe harm:

Precautionary Principle: In the context of philosophical uncertainty about an issue that has significant costs associated with a wrong answer, precautionary measures should be taken to protect individuals from unjustified harm.

The principle is analogous to the ones adopted by the United Nations General Assembly, various legally binding international treaties (e.g., the Montreal Protocol, Rio Declaration, and Kyoto Protocol) and the law of the European Union. The precautionary principle has been used by policy makers to justify discretionary decisions in situations where there is the possibility of harm from a decision, course of action, or policy, and extensive scientific knowledge on the matter is lacking. The principle implies that there is a social responsibility to protect the public from exposure to harm, when scientific investigation has found a plausible risk.[3] The principle has been adopted in numerous contexts, including in response to climate change skeptics who argue that we should do nothing to cap CO_2 and other greenhouse gas emissions in the face of (what they consider to be) scientific uncertainty about man-made climate change. The 1992 United Nations Framework Convention on Climate Change, for instance, states: "When an activity raises threats of harm to human health or the environment, precautionary measures should be taken even if some cause and effect relationships are not fully established scientifically."

In the current context, I propose that we employ a precautionary principle that constrains which "reasonable metaphysics" one adopts in the face of philosophical uncertainty – or, at least, constrains the practical implementation of that metaphysics in the arena of criminal law. If, as Morse thinks, the free will debate is currently unresolvable (something I disagree with but will grant for the moment), then on precautionary grounds we should prohibit causing retributive harm in the case of legal punishment until and unless the high epistemic standard of proof outlined earlier is met. Just like tobacco executives who challenged the link between smoking and cancer by appealing to scientific uncertainty, desertists who justify retributive harm on the grounds that no "incontrovertible argument that all would accept" has yet been presented against the notions of desert and moral responsibility are violating a pretty reasonable precautionary principle. The principle demands that in the context of uncertainty, when there are significant costs associated with a wrong answer, precautionary measures should be taken to protect individuals from unjustified harm.

But what about those philosophers who are more confident about the existence of free will and basic desert moral responsibility? Both Morse and Alexander appear willing to accept premise (4) of the Epistemic Argument, which states that the philosophical arguments for libertarianism and compatibilism are subject to powerful and unresolved objections. They instead reject the demand for a high level of justification for the claim that agents are morally responsible and hence justly deserve to suffer for the wrongs they have done. Yet philosophers who defend libertarian and compatibilist accounts of free will are more likely to challenge

---

[3] See *Wikipedia* entry for "precautionary principle": https://en.wikipedia.org/wiki/Precautionary_principle.

premise (4). In defending premise (4) against these accounts, I will take as my starting point Bruce Waller's powerful insight – spelled out and defended at great length in his recent book *The Stubborn System of Moral Responsibility* (2015) – that *belief* in basic desert moral responsibility is stronger than the philosophical arguments presented in their favor. More specifically, I will argue that the philosophical arguments presented in favor of basic desert moral responsibility, which are needed to justify retributive harm, are either scientifically implausible (as in the case of agent causation), empirically unwarranted (as in the case of event causal libertarianism), beg the question (as in the case of Strawson and other forms of compatibilism), or end up "changing the subject" (as in the case of Dennett and others).

Let me begin with a rather obvious case of a philosopher who believes more strongly in moral responsibility than the philosophical arguments he presents in its favor, that of Peter van Inwagen. After championing the *consequence argument* in favor of incompatibilism,[4] van Inwagen proceeds to argue that we *must* reject determinism even though it means free will "remains a mystery" (1983, 2000). He acknowledges that libertarian free will is difficult to make sense of, yet he also claims that to "deny the free-will thesis is to deny the existence of moral responsibility, which would be absurd" (1983: 223). According to van Inwagen, "free will undeniably exists and there is a strong and unanswered prima facie case for its impossibility" (2000: 1–2). It is the *absurdity* of denying moral responsibility that leads van Inwagen to favor libertarianism (and embrace a mystery) over its incompatibilist alternative of free will skepticism.[5] But he does not stop there. He continues to say that *if* science were one day able to present us with compelling reasons for believing in determinism, "[t]hen, and only then, I think, should we become compatibilists" (1983: 223). Essentially, after several decades of heroically defending the consequence argument, van Inwagen would be willing to chuck it out the window (if need be) to preserve moral responsibility. Such a defense of moral responsibility (if one can call it that) is a far cry from the level of justification needed to license the kind of harm caused by retributive legal punishment – which is all I am concerned with here.

Additional evidence of the kind of stubbornness Waller has in mind can be found among agent-causal libertarians – such as C. A. Campbell (1957), Richard Taylor (1974), and Roderick Chisholm (1982) – who are willing to embrace mysterious and "god-like" powers and abilities to preserve moral responsibility. Chisholm, for example,

---

[4] Although there are many different formulations of the consequence argument, van Inwagen summarizes the basic idea as follows: "If determinism is true, then our acts are the consequences of the laws of nature and events in the remote past. But it is not up to us what went on before we were born; and neither is it up to us what the laws of nature are. Therefore, the consequences of these things (including our present acts) are not up to us" (1983: 16).

[5] Part of the problem with van Inwagen's view is that he does not distinguish backward-looking from forward-looking responsibility. It might indeed be at least practically absurd to deny that we can ever engage in moral remonstration with wrongdoers. But once we recognize that denying basic desert leaves the forward-looking part in place, it is no longer practically absurd to deny "moral responsibility" (i.e., in the backward-looking sense).

3.1 The Epistemic Argument against Retributive Legal Punishment

famously argued: "If we are responsible, and if what I have been trying to say is true, then we have a prerogative which some would attribute only to God: each of us, when we really act, is a prime mover unmoved" (1982: 32). While Chisholm appears to gleefully embrace such miraculous powers, Taylor is at least more willing to acknowledge the embarrassment of such a move. He says, for instance, of his own theory:

> One could hardly affirm such a theory of agency with complete comfort, however, and not wholly without embarrassment, for the conception of agents and their powers which is involved in it is strange indeed, if not positively mysterious. In fact, one can hardly be blamed here for simply denying our data outright, rather than embrace this theory to which they do most certainly point. (1974: 53)

This is a far cry from the epistemic standard needed to justify punishing someone on the grounds that they possess libertarian free will and therefore deserve it. And as Waller so eloquently points out: "When contemporary philosophers are willing to posit miracles in order to save moral responsibility, the philosophical belief in moral responsibility obviously runs deep and strong" (2015: 3).

Naturalistically minded event-causal libertarians have the advantage of avoiding miraculous sui generis kinds of causal powers, but when it comes to providing the epistemic justification needed to ground retributive punishment, they too fall far short. Consider, for instance, the prominent event-causal libertarian accounts of Robert Kane (1996), Mark Balaguer (2009), and Al Mele (2006, 2017). None of these philosophers claim to have provided reason to believe that their accounts are true rather than false or that the necessary empirical requirements posited on their respective accounts actually obtain. Rather, they all settle for the much weaker claim that their theories are *consistent* with our best scientific theories and have *not yet* been ruled out. The *mere possibility* that one of these accounts may be true, however, is simply not enough to provide the epistemic justification needed to ground retributive harm. This becomes especially clear when one considers what *actually* needs to be the case for these accounts to be true. For example, in the previous chapter we say that Kane's account requires not only that agent mental processes be indeterminist, but that they be indeterminist in a very particular way. Hence:

> If multiple mutually exclusive aims did not cause the brain to go into a chaotic state the theory would be disproved. If it turned out that neurological systems weren't sensitive to quantum indeterminacies the theory would be disproved. If it turned out that neurological systems were sensitive to quantum indeterminacies, but not sufficiently sensitive to amplify quantum indeterminacies in a way that affects the outcomes of choice, this too would disprove the theory. These are not marginal or insubstantial bets about what brain science will reveal to us. (Vargas 2007: 143)

To justify retributive practices, including in some instances excessively punitive practices, on the off chance that all these empirical conditions will be met is akin to moral malpractice.

The fact that libertarian accounts of free will fail to provide the epistemic justification needed to ground retributivism, yet continue to hold agents morally responsible in the basic desert sense, is why Richard Double famously charges them with "hard-heartedness" (2002, 2017). Double's argument can be summarized as follows. Any thinker who holds the following three theses is hard-hearted (i.e., morally unsympathetic, not morally conscientious): (1) We may hold persons morally responsible only if they make libertarian choices, (2) we should hold persons morally responsible, and (3) there is scant epistemic justification that persons make libertarian choices. Statement (1) is true of all libertarians by definition and (2) reflects the motivation that drives most libertarians to the theory. Thesis three, on the other hand, is acknowledged by many prominent libertarians, including Immanuel Kant, William James (1884/1956), Robert Kane (1996), Peter van Inwagen (2000), and John Lemos (2018). In fact, some are rather forthright about it, as Lemos is when he writes: "It is my view that at this point in time we simply don't have sufficient experimental/empirical evidence nor sufficient metaphysical nor logical nor intuitive evidence to establish that libertarian free will exists" (2018: 6). Instead of arguing for libertarianism on evidentiary grounds, then, Lemos offers a pragmatic argument in favor of the view – arguing, as Kant does, that it is necessary for certain "deontological considerations centered around an unabashed moral realism, the Principle of Ends, [and] the dictum that 'ought' implies 'can'" (Double 2020: 1).[6] While other libertarians may not be so upfront about the lack of epistemic justification for their view, most are willing to acknowledge it if pushed. To the extent, then, that (3) is true, which it is, it would be hard-hearted for libertarians to hold persons morally responsible. The reasoning here is analogical. Just as it would be hard-hearted to punish subjects for actions if we lacked strong evidence that those subjects did those actions, it would likewise be hard-hearted to blame subjects (in the backward-looking sense) for actions if we lacked strong evidence that those subjects did those actions from free will.

While Double restricts his charge of hard-heartedness to libertarians, I think a similar argument can be made against compatibilists who want to continue harming individuals on retributivist grounds. In the case of compatibilism, however, the lack of epistemic justification comes at a different point than that of libertarianism. The epistemic challenge facing libertarianism is to justify the claim that we

---

[6] I should note that Lemos's (2018) pragmatic argument for libertarian free will rests upon a number of questionable assumptions (see Double 2020). For instance, Lemos maintains that we have a moral duty to treat all persons as ends and not as mere means (the Principle of Ends), yet he also claims we are morally obligated to abide by the Principle of Ends *only if* persons have libertarian free will. This is incorrect. In subsequent chapters, I will argue that free will skeptics can indeed preserve respect for persons and the prohibition on manipulative use in a way that is consistent with the Principle of Ends. Lemos also assumes that libertarians are morally justified in holding persons morally responsible for libertarian choices, even if they have no epistemic justification for the existence of libertarian choices (see Double 2020). This chapter is a prolonged argument against that claim that at least when holding agents morally responsible it is taken to license retributive legal punishment. For additional objections, see Double (2020).

3.1 The Epistemic Argument against Retributive Legal Punishment

actually possess the powers and abilities posited by such accounts. There is no equivalent debate with regard to compatibilism. All parties agree, including skeptics, that we have the abilities discussed by most leading compatibilist accounts – for example, reasons-responsiveness, voluntariness, the capacity to act in accordance with moral reasons or one's Deep Self, etc. The question instead is whether such abilities are *enough* to justify basic desert moral responsibility and along with it retributive harm in the case of legal punishment. It is here that scant epistemic justification is generally provided.

While compatibilists reject miracles and propose accounts of moral responsibility consistent with both naturalism and determinism, they seldom provide justification for the moral responsibility system itself. In lieu of justifying the moral responsibility *system*, compatibilists typically take the system as given and instead focus on what attitudes, judgments, and treatments are justified from *within* the system. P. F. Strawson (1962) is a good example of this. His defense of the reactive attitudes takes our normal moral responsibility practices as given and proceeds from there to articulate special circumstances when it is acceptable *not* to hold someone morally responsible or to excuse them – for example, when they are profoundly impaired by delusion or lack any moral capacity, either temporarily or permanently. In these special circumstances, Strawson claims it is acceptable to adopt the *objective attitude* toward them. But according to Strawson and his followers, the denial of *all* moral responsibility is unacceptable, self-defeating, and/or impossible, since to permanently excuse everyone would entail that "nobody knows what he's doing or that everybody's behavior is unintelligible in terms of conscious purposes or that everybody lives in a world of delusion or that nobody has a moral sense" (1962: 74).

The problem with this defense of moral responsibility, however, is that it takes for granted the very thing in need of justification. To quote Waller once again:

> [I]f we start from the assumption of the moral responsibility system (assumptions that are so common and deep that they are difficult to escape), then the denial of moral responsibility is absurd and self-defeating. But the universal denial of moral responsibility does *not* start from the assumption that under normal circumstances we are morally responsible, and it does *not* proceed from that starting point to enlarge and extend the range of excuses to cover everyone (so that *everyone* is profoundly flawed). That is indeed a path to absurdity. Rather, those who reject moral responsibility reject the basic system which starts from the assumption that all minimally competent persons (all who reach the plateau level) are morally responsible. For those who deny moral responsibility, it is never fair to treat anyone as morally responsible, no matter how reasonable, competent, self-efficacious, strong-willed, and clear-sighted that person may be. (2015: 103)

Since skeptics who globally challenge basic desert moral responsibility – for example, Waller (2011, 2015), Pereboom (2001, 2014), Levy (2011), G. Strawson (1986, 1994), and myself (2012; Dennett and Caruso 2021) – do not accept the rules of that desert-based system, it is question-begging to assume our ordinary moral responsibility practices are justified without refuting the arguments for global skepticism.

Furthermore, even if Strawson were correct about the necessity of holding each other responsible in our interpersonal exchanges, it is another thing altogether to think retributive legal punishment is justified. Perhaps one could justify adopting an evidential burden of proof by limiting one's compatibilism to our interpersonal reactive attitudes where the level of harm involved is significantly lower than legal punishment (though still not inconsequential). But in the case of legal punishment, retributivists who adopt compatibilism need to meet a higher burden of proof. It also does not help if one decides to shift the focus away from Strawson's reactive attitudes and toward an account of what those attitudes might rightfully be reacting to – namely some capacity or feature of the agent. While contemporary compatibilists have conceived of this capacity in a number of different ways – including the capacity to act in accordance with one's Deep Self, the capacity for rational review of actions, the capacity to act in accordance with moral reasons, and the capacity for reasons-responsiveness – the central question remains: Are these capacities (alone or combined) *enough* to ground basic desert moral responsibility? Given that extant compatibilist accounts still face powerful and unresolved objections – such as the manipulation argument (Mele 2006), Pereboom's four-case argument (2001, 2014), van Inwagen's consequence argument (1983), Galen Strawson's basic argument (1986, 1994), Fischer's no-forking-paths argument (1994), Levy's luck pincer (2011), etc. – they fail to meet the prudential burden of proof. For a retributivist to assume that compatibilism is true and proven beyond a reasonable doubt is to beg the question against incompatibilists and permit unjustified harm.

While some (or most) forms of compatibilism beg the question, others simply change the subject. Daniel Dennett is a good example of the latter since the kind of free will he argues for does not attempt to justify retributivism or what I have called basic desert moral responsibility. In fact, Dennett makes this clear in our recent exchange/debate – see *Just Deserts: Debating Free Will* (Dennett and Caruso 2021). After pushing him on whether his account of compatibilism is capable of preserving retributive punishment, he writes: "I too reject retributivism. It's a hopeless muddle, and so is any doctrine of free will that aspires to justify it" (Dennett and Caruso 2021). He makes the same point in a revealing exchange with Tom Clark and Bruce Waller – on Waller's book *Against Moral Responsibility* (2011). After explaining how Waller rejects retributive punishment and basic desert moral responsibility, Dennett writes:

> [L]et me say right away that I agree with Waller's main conclusion in one important sense: *that* kind of absolutistic moral responsibility – insisting as it does on what I have called guilt-in-the-eyes-of-God – is incompatible with naturalism and has got to go. (2012)

3.1 The Epistemic Argument against Retributive Legal Punishment

Rejecting what he considers to be an untenable retributivist system of legal punishment and the strong type of basic desert moral responsibility that it relies upon, Dennett proposes "a consequentialist defense of just deserts" (2012) and punishment. He reiterates this point in *Just Deserts*, writing: "I have all along stressed the 'forward-looking' justification [of punishment]. There are non-retributive, non-deontological, consequentialist justifications of punishment" (Dennett and Caruso 2021).

While many compatibilists want to secure a justification for retributive blame and punishment, Dennett does not seem to be among them. Instead, he espouses a nonretributivist, consequentialist concept of moral responsibility and punishment. What is of paramount importance for Dennett is that we find a naturalistic way to justify punishment so as to maintain a "secure and civil society" (see Dennett and Caruso 2021). The justification Dennett provides for punishment, however, is decidedly different than what many compatibilists would endorse since he acknowledges that we must abandon retributivism and basic desert moral responsibility and replace it with an "ultimately consequentialist" (2012) conception of punishment and reward. Given that most free will skeptics would agree, Dennett's account fails to preserve what is of central philosophical and practical importance – the claim that people deserve to be praised and blamed, rewarded and punished, on strictly retributivist and non-consequentialist grounds. In fact, Dennett admittedly does not attempt to preserve this sort of moral responsibility and cheerfully wishes it "good riddance" (Dennett and Caruso 2021).

One important difference, however, between Dennett's consequentialist justification of punishment and that of free will skeptics is that Dennett prefers to retain the notion of *just deserts*. I contend that this is inconsistent with Dennett's reformed consequentialist account of moral responsibility. As Tom Clark notes:

> Whether as consequentialists we should still talk of just deserts is debatable, given the strong deontological, retributive connotations ... What you're advocating is the *practical necessity* of punishment, not its intrinsic goodness, but "just deserts" strongly implies that the offender's suffering is intrinsically good, which you don't think is the case. So I think we should drop talk of just deserts so we don't mislead people about what we believe are defensible justifications for punishment. (2012)

Given the canonical understanding of *just deserts* and how it is used to justify various retributive attitudes, judgments, and treatments, Dennett's use of the term lends itself to easy confusion and gives the mistaken impression that he is setting out to preserve something that he is not. Rather than defending or justifying just deserts, Dennett ends up changing the subject. His brand of compatibilism does not justify retributive harm – it does not even attempt to. His justification for punishment, being consequentialist in nature, is completely consistent with the skeptic's rejection of free will and just deserts.

So while libertarian accounts of free will fail to satisfy the high epistemic bar needed to justify retributive legal punish, so too do compatibilist accounts. The former tend to be either scientifically implausible or empirically unwarranted, while the latter either beg the question or change the subject.

3.2 DOES THE EPISTEMIC ARGUMENT ALSO APPLY TO THE PUBLIC HEALTH–QUARANTINE MODEL?

Before concluding, I would like to address a potential objection against the non-retributive model I develop later in the book. Michael Corrado (2019a) has argued that the considerations just discussed can be turned against my own public health–quarantine model. Corrado argues that in the face of epistemic uncertainty about the existence of free will, we should prefer punishment to my own nonretributive, nonpunitive alternative. [I should note that for Corrado, "punishment just is retribution, retribution just is punishment, so that punishment is justified if and only if retribution is justified" (2019a: fn.5).] His argument is predicated on the following two claims: (1) that "the methods associated with [retributive] punishment are preferable to the methods associated with criminal quarantine" (2019a); and (2) "a system of quarantine, in spite of all good intentions to the contrary, imposes tremendous hardship and would deprive those considered dangerous of many of the protections associated with [retributive] punishment" (2019a). According to Corrado, retributive punishment provides certain important protections, including the principle of proportionality and respect for human dignity. He argues that it would be "callous to deprive offenders of the protections of punishment unless we can prove, with evidence that would support a strong conviction," that they lack the kind of control in action required for basic desert moral responsibility. These assumptions lead Corrado to conclude:

> If I am right in thinking that there is not enough evidence to support either the conclusion that human beings are never free or the conclusion that human beings are at least sometimes free, then neither the institution of state punishment nor the proposed institution of universal criminal quarantine can be fully justified. But if I am also right in thinking that the methods associated with [retributive] punishment are preferable to the methods associated with criminal quarantine, then a state that must act to reduce harm to the community should (with regret) prefer punishment to quarantine. (2019a)

While Corrado's objection is an interesting one, I think it fails for three main reasons.

First, both of Corrado's key assumptions can be challenged. I maintain that Corrado is mistaken about *both* the putative protective power of retributive punishment *and* the risks of giving up such punishment and adopting the public health–quarantine model. While I must put off a fuller discussion of these claims until later in the book, it is important that I say a few words about them now. Defenders of retributive punishment typically maintain that it would be bad to punish a wrongdoer more than they deserve, where what they deserve must be in some way proportional to the gravity of their crime. For retributivists, the principle of proportionality is needed to guarantee respect for persons since it treats them as autonomous, morally responsible agents and not just objects to be "fixed" or used as a means to an end. Retributivists fear that without this principle in place, there will be no limit to the harshness of punishment meted out and no way to block treating individuals as a mere means to an end. Yet, in Chapter 4, I will argue that the putative protections provided by the principle of proportionality are more apparent than real. In particular, I will argue that retributivism does not provide the protections it promises with regard to proportionality. This is because, how the state goes about judging the gravity of wrong done, on the one hand, and what counts as proportional punishment for that wrong, on the other, are highly sensitive to subjective and cultural biases and prejudices, and as a result, the principle of proportionality in *actual practice* does not provide the kind of protections against abuse it promises.

Furthermore, in Chapter 8, I will argue that we should resist narrowly conceiving of respect for persons in terms of giving wrongdoers their just deserts. Instead, respecting human dignity demands, at a minimum, that the capabilities and well-being of wrongdoers be taken into consideration, that we avoid punishments that dehumanize and disenfranchise individuals, and that we do everything we can to rehabilitate and reintegrate offenders back into the community. The public health–quarantine model does a better job at respecting human dignity in this sense than does retributivism. I also respond to several of Corrado's other objections and argue that they too can be reasonably dealt with. For example, while my public health–quarantine model does reject the retributive principle of proportionality, I argue that it has a proportionality principle of its own. I also argue that Corrado is simply mistaken that my model flattens out the distinction between agents who are reasons-responsive and those who are not. It does not. If it turns out, then, that the putative protections provided by retributive punishment are more apparent than real, and/or that adopting the public health–quarantine model would *not* lead to "tremendous hardship," then Corrado's pragmatic argument in favor of punishment fails.[7]

Second, I think there is a more fundamental problem with Corrado's argument, since it fails to recognize that there is an important difference between the state *intentionally harming* individuals (which is an essential component of punishment)

---

[7] I should note that Corrado, himself, is not a retributivist. Instead, he defends a nonretributive model he calls "correction" (2013a, 2019b). According to Corrado, correction involves "intentional harsh treatment" aimed at changing behavior. It is justified, not on the grounds of desert, but by the "benefit it offers the one corrected" (2013a). While correction is consistent with free will skepticism, Corrado also believes it retains the protective features of punishment mentioned earlier. But if I am correct that these protections are more apparent than real, then my criticism of retributive punishment discussed in the following chapter would equally apply to Corrado's model of correction.

and the state causing *unintentional harm* (which would apply to any harms caused by a nonpunitive system of incapacitation). Arguably, the former must meet a higher epistemic bar, especially when it is unclear that the alternative would have the negative effects Corrado contends. If we are unsure agents are morally responsible in the basic desert sense, which Corrado concedes, then the justification for *intentionally harming* wrongdoers should carry a higher burden of proof than adopting a nonpunitive approach that *may or may not* have unintended negative consequences. As we will see later, the public health–quarantine model is not only a nonretributive model, it is also a nonpunitive one since it does not satisfy the standard definition of punishment. Seeing as though it does not seek to intentionally harm perceived wrongdoers and communicate disapproval, I contend that it is easier to justify than retributive punishment. Hence, if we are uncertain about the existence of free will, the default position should be to adopt an approach that does not seek to intentionally harm perceived wrongdoers on the assumption that they deserve it.

Third, I disagree with Corrado when he says that under conditions of epistemic uncertainty about the existence of free will, "neither the institution of state punishment nor the proposed institution of universal criminal quarantine can be fully justified" (2019a). The justification of quarantine (in the case of disease) and incapacitation (in the case of dangerous criminals) is, on my model, grounded in the right of self-defense and defense of others. It in no way depends upon the questionable notions of free will and basic desert moral responsibility, nor is it justified on purely utilitarian or consequentialist grounds. As a result, any harm it causes those individuals who are quarantined or incapacitated *would* be justified on the grounds of self-defense and prevention of harm to others (even if such harms remain regrettable). The right of self-defense and defense of others justifies temporarily limiting one's liberty under certain constraints and restrictions, even it does not justify punishment in the traditional sense. This is because, just as we do not seek to intentionally harm or punish those contagious individuals we are forced to quarantine, we do not seek to intentionally harm or punish those dangerous individuals we are forced to incapacitate. The aim of incapacitation is not to intentionally harm or punish wrongdoers, it serves a different purpose altogether. As a result, epistemic uncertainty about the existence of free will does not undermine the justification for incapacitating seriously dangerous criminals.

For these reasons, I contend that the burden of proof remains on the retributivist. This conclusion also seems to follow from the precautionary principle defended earlier, which demands that in the context of uncertainty, precautionary measures should be taken to protect individuals from unjustified harm. Since Corrado acknowledges that retributive punishment *cannot* be fully justified under conditions of epistemic uncertainty about the existence of free will, and since such practices involve intentionally inflicting harm on individuals, the precautionary principle would count strongly against it. The public health–quarantine model, on the other hand, does not involve the intentional infliction of harm as a means of punishment or communicating disapproval – it is a completely nonpunitive approach. I also contend that the harms it causes would be justified even if we lack free will and basic desert moral responsibility, since the right of self-defense and defense of others allows us to take the least restrictive steps necessary to protect public health and safety (see Chapter 7). Furthermore, I contend that Corrado is mistaken about *both* the putative protective power of retributive punishment *and* the risks of giving up such punishment and adopting the public health–quarantine model (see Chapters 5, 8, and 9). Hence, I conclude that the justification for *intentionally harming* wrongdoers should carry a higher burden of proof than adopting a nonpunitive approach that *may or may not* have unintended negative consequences.

3.3 CONCLUSION

In this chapter, I have argued that the burden of proof is on the retributivist to justify legal punishment – and given the severity of harm involved, the highest epistemic standard should be adopted. Drawing from the criminal law, I argued that the proper place to set the epistemic bar is at the prudential standard of beyond a reasonable doubt. I further argued that all extant accounts of libertarianism and compatibilism fail to satisfy this burden of proof since they either tend to be scientifically implausible (as in the case of agent causation), empirically unwarranted (as in the case of event causal libertarianism), question-begging (as in the case of Strawson and other forms of compatibilism), or end up changing the subject (as in the case of Dennett and others). If what I have argued is correct, the Epistemic Argument provides sufficient reason, on its own, for rejecting retributive legal punishment.

4

Additional Reasons for Rejecting Retributivism

We have now seen two distinct arguments against retributive legal punishment: (1) the Skeptical Argument and (2) the Epistemic Argument. In this chapter, I would like to consider additional reasons for rejecting retributivism that are independent of worries over free will and basic desert moral responsibility. I will argue that even if one does not share my skepticism about free will, there still remain good reasons for wanting to reject retributivism. This is because, even if we assume, for the sake of argument, that the requisite capacity for control is in place and agents are morally responsible in the basic desert sense, retributivism still faces a number of powerful philosophical and practical objections. In particular, I will argue that (3) it is philosophically problematic to impart to the state the function of intentionally harming wrongdoers in accordance with desert since it is not at all clear that the state is capable of properly tracking the desert and blameworthiness of individuals in any reliable way. This is because criminal law is not properly designed to account for all the various factors that affect blameworthiness, and as a result the *moral criteria of blameworthiness* is often misaligned with the *legal criteria of guilt* (Kelly 2018). Furthermore, (4) for the state to be able to justly distribute legal punishment in accordance with desert, it needs to be in the proper epistemic position to know what an agent basically deserves, but since the state is (almost) never in the proper epistemic position to know what an agent basically deserves, it follows that the state is not able to justly distribute legal punishment in accordance with desert. Assuming retributivists can overcome these hurdles, there still remains the additional worry that (5) how the state goes about judging the gravity of wrong done, on the one hand, and what counts as proportional punishment for that wrong, on the other, are wide open to subjective and cultural biases and prejudices, and as a result, the principle of proportionality in *actual practice* does not provide the kind of protections against abuse it promises. Lastly, (6) there are simply good pragmatic reasons for rejecting retributivism since it has "limited effectiveness in promoting important social goals such as rehabilitation and reforming offenders" (Shaw 2019).

This chapter will conclude my case against retributivism and in total we will have seen that there are at least six powerful reasons for rejecting retributivism: (1) the Skeptical Argument, (2) the Epistemic Argument, (3) the Misalignment Argument, (4) the Poor Epistemic Position Argument (PEPA), (5) the Indeterminacy in Judgment Argument, and (6) the Limited Effectiveness Argument.[1] Subsequent chapters will then take up the search for an alternative to retributive legal punishment. In Chapter 5, I examine forward-looking justifications of punishment and argue that, although they are consistent with free will skepticism, they face significant moral concerns of their own. I also examine *mixed theories* of punishment, which combine forward- and backward-looking justifications, and argue that they too fail. I then spend the remainder of the book developing and defending my novel alternative: the public health–quarantine model.

4.1 THE MISALIGNMENT ARGUMENT

I would like to begin with an objection that warrants more attention than it has received. It has to do with the fact that it is not at all clear that the criminal law is capable of properly tracking the blameworthiness of individuals in any reliable way. This is because criminal law is not properly designed to account for all the various factors that affect blameworthiness, and as a result the moral criteria of blameworthiness is often misaligned with the legal criteria of guilt. Erin Kelly (2018) makes a strong case for this claim in her excellent book, *The Limits of Blame: Rethinking Punishment and Responsibility*. In it she takes issue with a criminal justice system that aligns legal criteria of guilt with moral criteria of blameworthiness – where *blameworthiness* is understood in the backward-looking basic desert sense. She argues that many incarcerated people do not meet the criteria of blameworthiness, even when they are guilty of crimes:

> People who think carefully about criminal justice must address the problem that the *legal* criteria of guilt do not match familiar *moral* criteria for blame. Conditions that excuse moral failings – such as ignorance, provocation, and mental illness – have limited application in law. This demonstrates a lack of alignment between law and morality. Considerations that mitigate moral blame are often irrelevant to legal findings of criminal guilt. For example, poverty and other unjust deprivations of opportunity have no mitigating relevance in the courtroom; nor do serious mental illnesses such as sociopathy and schizophrenia. Some criminal defendants have diminished moral culpability and others should not be seen as morally blameworthy at all, yet such factors have no bearing on determinations of legal guilt. (2018: 3–4)

---

[1] I say "at least" because there are additional reasons for rejective retributivism not discussed here (see, e.g., Boonin 2008; Tadros 2011; Zimmerman 2011; Brooks 2012; Zaibert 2018).

Kelly's argument underscores the problem of exaggerating what criminal guilt indicates, particularly when it is tied to the illusion that we know how long and what ways criminals should suffer.

According to Kelly, the notion of individual moral responsibility central to retributive punishment "masks the systematic nature of social inequality that is solidified by the criminal justice system, especially that found in the United States" (2018: 11). She writes:

> A conception of responsibility that connects wrongdoers and moral desert is used to rationalize indefensible criminal-justice practices. We are encouraged to think that criminal conviction metes out verdicts of individual blameworthiness, and this judgment, in turn, functions, by way of its alleged ground in criminal guilt per se, as a basis for thorough-going social typecasting. The very point of criminal justice, so understood, is to assign moral responsibility to individual wrongdoers through findings of criminal guilt and the impositions of a stigmatizing punishment they are thought morally to deserve. (2018: 11)

But she goes on to argue:

> We should resist this form of moral identity-making because it normalizes social injustice, narrows our moral perspective, and precludes a morally sensitive appreciation of the psychological and social adversity confronting many people who commit crimes. A blaming perspective focused predominately on manifestations of *ill will* too readily overlooks the social and psychological context in which person's beliefs and attitudes are formed, and this focus distorts its moral findings. For example, when poverty and racial injustice are ignored, and the significance of mental illness, immaturity, or mental deficiency is disregarded, conclusions about the blameworthiness of many criminally guilty persons are exaggerated. When the relationships between criminal justice and social justice and between individual responsibility and collective responsibility are not thoughtfully calibrated, they become dangerously unbalanced. As a result, criminal justice institutions are permitted – and exploited – to punish without measure or shame. This is what happens in the United States. (2018: 11)

At the core of Kelly's criticism is the claim that since the criminal law fails to properly track desert and blameworthiness, since it fails to take seriously the way blameworthiness is affected by poverty and social injustice, mental illness, addiction, and various other mitigating factors, we must reject retributivism and with it any criminal justice system that attempts to align legal criteria of guilt with moral criteria of blameworthiness.

For instance, Kelly correctly notes that "courts have thrown out racial discrimination as a basis of challenging criminal conviction and sentencing – for the perverse reason that such discrimination is too common" (2018: 8). It is also problematic that many of those actually caught up in our criminal legal system are among the most economically disadvantaged and the least psychologically healthy. The American Psychological

Association, for instance, notes that "over the past four decades, the nation's get-tough-on-crime policies have packed prisons and jails to the bursting point, largely with poor, uneducated people of color, about half of whom suffer from mental health problems" (2014). Regarding the economically disadvantaged, Kelly writes:

> People should not be burdened with serious, harmful consequences for breaking the law when they have been deprived of a reasonable opportunity to lead a satisfactory, law-abiding life. Social injustice undermines legitimate law enforcement and dooms prospects for achieving justice through criminal law. (2018: 15)

And regarding psychological health, she urges:

> The criminal law is indifferent to individual capacities partly because it does not want to invite defendants to argue, as some surely would, that they are morally dense or unmoved by moral reasons, thereby leaving jurors to sort out whether such claims are true, on a case by case basis. In other words, it is sometimes by design, rather than by accident – or viciousness or racism on the part of judges and legislatures – that criminal law's specification of the conditions under which one is subject to legal punishment departs from morality's specification of when a person can be blamed. (2018: 38)

Proponents of retributivism will, no doubt, point out that criminal law allows for various excusing condition, like the insanity defense, but it is important to recognize that these defenses are limited in scope, seldom successful, and are by no means fine-grained enough to properly track the basic desert and blameworthiness of individuals in any reliable way.

Mental illness, for instance, functions as an excuse only when it fits the legal definition of insanity, a highly specialized notion that typically does not include bipolar disorder, autism, Alzheimer's, brain damage due to injury, or many other forms of mental illness or diminished capacity (Kelly 2018: 8). The problem is that the insanity defense is a legal concept, not a clinical (or medical) one (see Bada Math et al. 2015; Fingarette 1966). This means that, first, "just suffering from a mental disorder is not sufficient to prove insanity" (Bada Math et al. 2015: 381). Second, the defendant has the burden of proving the defense of insanity by "clear and convincing evidence" (18 U.S. Code §17(B)).[2] And third, "[i]t is hard to determine legal insanity, and even harder to successfully defend it in court" (Bada Math et al. 2015: 381).[3] Consider, for example, the case of Eddie Ray Routh, who was convicted in Texas for killing two men at a shooting range, one of whom was

---

[2] The new US Federal code for the insanity defense states that "(a) Affirmative Defense: It is an affirmative defense to a prosecution under any Federal statute that, at the time of the commission of the acts constituting the offense, the defendant, as a result of a severe mental disease or defect, was unable to appreciate the nature and quality or the wrongfulness of his act. Mental disease or defect does not otherwise constitute a defense. (b) Burden of Proof: The defendant has the burden of proving the defense of insanity by clear and convincing evidence" (18 U.S. Code §17 [2020]).

[3] To make matters even worse, four US states (Montana, Idaho, Kansas, and Utah) have banned the insanity defense. And, as one NPR headline put it, "With No Insanity Defense, Seriously Ill People

celebrated sniper Chris Kyle (the former Navy Seal, who has the most recoded kills of any US sniper). A former marine, Routh had been diagnosed with post-traumatic stress disorder (PTSD) and schizophrenia. On the day of the killing, Kyle and his friend, Chad Littlefield, took Routh with them to the shooting range after Routh's mother asked Kyle for help in dealing with her troubled son. According to defense attorneys, Routh was under extreme mental distress and was convinced the two men (Kyle and Littlefield) would turn on him on the day of the killing. Routh's counsel sought the insanity defense but failed to convince the jury that Routh did not know his actions were wrong (King and May 2018: 11). The district attorney, Alan Nash, won the jury over, stating, "I am tired of the proposition that if you have a mental illness, you can't be held [legally] responsible for what you do" (Dart 2015).

This cavalier attitude toward mental illness, combined with the extremely limited scope of the insanity defense, results in a severe and troubling misalignment between the legal criteria of guilt and the moral criteria of blameworthiness. In fact, most (non-skeptical) moral responsibility theorists acknowledge that different forms of mental illness can, and often do, mitigate or fully exculpate moral blameworthiness and desert (see, e.g., Wallace 1994; Elliot 1996; Fine and Kennett 2004; Callender 2010; Shoemaker 2009, 2010, 2015; Ciurria 2014; Scholten 2016; Baird, Kennett, and Schier 2020). David Shoemaker (2015), for example, has argued that people with high-function autism have "significantly mitigated accountability" in virtue of their empathetic impairments (2015: 173). Matthé Scholten (2016) has argued that it would be inappropriate to morally blame people suffering from mental disorders that fall within the schizophrenia spectrum. And Amee Baird, Jeanette Kennett, and Elizabeth Schier (2020) have argued that individuals with dementia are unfit for retributive punishment. If these theorists are correct, or correct about at least some of these conditions, then retributivism faces an alignment problem.

Consider dementia. After studying an increasing number of criminal cases in Australia where the accused had, or may have had, dementia, Baird, Kennett, and Schier found that "current sentencing guidelines do not accommodate progressive cognitive impairment" (2020: 1). This is problematic since "offenders with dementia will be progressively unable to meet the minimum moral or rational agency requirement presumed by our legal system and are thus unable to comprehend or respond to the key retributive and communicative purposes for which punishment is imposed, and by which it is justified" (2020: 1). According to Baird, Kennett, and Schier, these individuals "are, or will become, *unfit* for punishment" (2020: 1). Yet "they are regularly sentenced to forms of detention that are in fact and intent, punitive" (2020: 1). Moral responsibility theorists who are sensitive to the various ways an agent's diminished capacities can affect moral

End up in Prison" (www.npr.org/sections/health-shots/2016/08/05/487909967/with-no-insanity-defense-seriously-ill-people-end-up-in-prison).

blameworthiness and desert[4] should therefore acknowledge that the legal criteria of guilt is often poorly aligned with the moral criteria of blameworthiness.

This misalignment is especially troubling when one considers how pervasive mental illness is among inmates in the United States. One recent study found that 64 percent of jail inmates, 54 percent of state prisoners, and 45 percent of federal prisoners report mental health issues (National Research Council 2014). And the mental health crisis is especially pronounced among women prisoners, with one study by the US Bureau of Justice Statistics finding that 75 percent of women incarcerated in jails and prisons having mental illness. Another study found that there are currently three times more seriously mentally ill persons in jails and prisons than hospitals in the United States, with the ratio being nearly ten to one in states like Arizona and Nevada (Torrey et al. 2010). The study further found that 16 percent of the jail and prison population in the United States has a "serious mental illness," defined as someone diagnosed with schizophrenia, bipolar disorder, or major depression. This is extremely problematic for retributivists, since many, if not most, of these individuals likely fail to satisfy the various moral criteria of blameworthiness (or, put more carefully, their conditions likely significantly reduce their blameworthiness), yet when it comes to the criminal legal system, they are found to satisfy the legal criteria of guilt. It is exactly this disconnect that makes retributivism practically problematic, since in the real world it is virtually impossible to accurately distribute punishment in accordance with moral desert.

Misalignments can also occur in cases of psychopathy. Many philosophers and psychologists have argued that psychopaths' impaired capacity for empathy, diminished responses to fear-inducing stimuli, and failure to conform to social norms indicate that they are not fully responsible for their actions,[5] yet the law continues to hold them legally responsible. As Glenn, Raine, and Laufer argue:

> Psychopaths know the difference between right and wrong, yet emotionally lack the *feeling* of what is right and wrong. Unlike individuals with mental disorders such as schizophrenia or dementia who may have impaired cognitive capacity, psychopathic individuals understand that specific actions are against the law or violate social norms; however, although they may be able to make accurate judgments about legal or moral violations, they appear to lack an important factor that motivates individuals to behave morally – emotional capacity. Psychological and neuroscientific studies are providing increased empirical evidence demonstrating the importance of emotion in moral judgment and behavior, and charactering the deficits observed in psychopathy. Such evidence provides empirical support for

---

[4] See, e.g., Kennett (2001, 2007, 2010), Kennett and Matthews (2002, 2009), Kennett and Fine (2004), Shoemaker (2010, 2015), Nelkin (2017, 2019), Hirstein, Sifferd, and Fagan (2018), King and May (2018), Ciurria (2014, 2020).

[5] See, e.g., N. Levy (2007, 2014), Morse (2008), Kennett and Fine (2004), Kennett (2010), Haji (2010), Glen, Raine, and Laufer (2011), Shoemaker (2009, 2011), Nelkin (2015), Vierra (2016). Cf. Sifferd and Hirstein (2013), Hirstein, Sifferd, and Fagan (2018), Jefferson and Sifferd (2018), Greenspan (2016), Pilsbury (2013), Godman and Jefferson (2017), K. Levy (2011).

the recent argument ... that "severe" psychopaths are neither morally responsible nor deserving of blame and punishment because they do not understand the point of morality, lack a conscience and the capacity for moral understanding and rationality ... [W]e suggest that the criminal law should accommodate increasing psychological and neuroscientific evidence that emotional capacity is an important factor for translating factual knowledge about right and wrong into moral behavior, and that psychopathic individuals have deficits primarily in this domain. (2011: 302)

To the extent that these philosophers are correct that psychopaths are neither fully morally responsible nor deserving of blame and punishment, yet the law fails to recognize this, we have another case where the moral criteria of blameworthiness and the legal criteria of guilt fail to track each other.

Another example of this disconnect can be found in the rather common practice of prosecuting children as adults. Thirteen states in the United States have no minimum age for prosecuting a child as an adult, leaving eight-, nine-, and ten-year-old children vulnerable to extreme punishment, trauma, and abuse within adult jails and prisons. Australian law also currently allows children as young as ten to be charged with a criminal offense, falling below the average minimum age of criminal responsibility worldwide of 12.1 years.[6] Around 600 children under 14 are locked up in Australia prison cells every year. While it may be possible for children to satisfy the legal criteria of guilt, since they tend to be rather permissive, it is not at all clear children satisfy the moral criteria of blameworthiness – assuming again that agents are sometimes morally responsible in the basic desert sense. Since children under 14 are especially immature and impulsive and have not yet developed mature judgment or the ability to accurately assess risks and consequences, it is unclear they have the executive functioning needed for basic desert moral responsibility. William Hirstein, Katrina Sifferd, and Tyler Fagan argue, for example, that "[e]xecutive functions – such as attentional control, planning, inhibition, and task switching – are ... uniquely well suited to ground a reasons-responsiveness account of the capacities necessary for moral responsibility, including both sensitivity to morally or legally relevant reasons and the volitional control to act in accordance with those reasons" (2018: 13). But they also argue that children who commit criminal offenses are typically "too young at the time of the offense to have had a minimally mature set of executive capacities" (2018: 14). If this is correct, then children are not morally responsible in the sense required for retributive punishment, yet in many states and countries they can still satisfy the legal criteria of guilt.[7] This is problematic.

In addition, there are other potential sources of misalignment as well. For instance, a growing number of theorists have argued that deeply disadvantaged backgrounds, poverty, and pervasive and systemic social injustice can affect blameworthiness and basic desert moral responsibility but are seldom considered

---

[6] See YouthPolicy.org.
[7] For a different type of argument for why children should not be held criminally responsible, see Gideon Yaffe (2018).

mitigating in the criminal law (see, e.g., Murphy 1973; Bazelon 1976; Delgado 1985; Tonry 2004, 2020; Kelly 2018; Heffernan and Kleining 2000). In fact, some legal scholars have even proposed that we adopt a "social adversity" or "rotten background" defense, analogous to the insanity defense, allowing that testimony be permitted in appropriate cases concerning the influence of deep disadvantage and requiring that the jury be directed "that a defendant is not responsible if at the time of his unlawful conduct his mental or emotional processes or behavior controls were impaired to such an extent that he cannot justly be held responsible for his action"[8] (see also Tonry 2020). Unfortunately, the criminal law does not currently permit social adversity as an affirmative defense, nor does it (generally) view deep disadvantage and adversity as mitigating of desert and punishment.[9]

Of course, philosophers have long been sympathetic to social adversity, though they have tended to pay more attention to the state's moral authority (or standing) to punish than to whether disadvantage sometimes lessens or in extreme cases negates blameworthiness (Tonry 2020: 17). For instance, philosopher Jeffrie Murphy rejected his own retributive "benefits and burdens" theory of punishment because of the social adversity problem. A large proportion of defendants in criminal courts, he noted, are deeply disadvantaged and cannot reasonably be said to enjoy the benefits of living in a secure, ordered society. That being so, their retributive punishment cannot be justified until "we have restructured society in such a way that criminals genuinely do correspond to the only model that will render punishment permissible – i.e., make sure that they are autonomous and that they do benefit in the requisite sense" (1973: 243; as quoted by Tonry 2020: 6). Retributivist Andreas von Hirsh further observed in *Doing Justice* that "as long as a substantial segment of the population is denied adequate opportunities for a livelihood, any scheme for punishment must be morally flawed" (1976: 149; as quoted by Tonry 2020). And perhaps the most influential punishment theorist in our time, British philosopher Antony Duff, offered an ideal retributive punishment theory in *Trials and Punishments* but concluded that "punishment is not justifiable within our present legal system; it will not be justified unless and until we have brought about deep and far-reaching social, political, legal, and moral changes in ourselves and our society" (1986: 294).

Another potential source of misalignment has to do with the epistemic condition for moral responsibility. Most moral responsibility theorists maintain that for an agent to be morally responsible in the basic desert sense they must satisfy two

---

[8] Chief Judge Bazelon, *United States v. Brawner* (1972) 471 F.2d 969 (D.C. Cir.): 1032
[9] There are, however, a few notable exceptions, such as US Supreme Court Justice Elena Kegan's description of the life of Evan Miller in *Miller v. Alabama* (567 U.S. 460, 2012), the decision that declared mandatory life imprisonment without parole for offenders under age 18 unconstitutional: "[I]f ever a pathological background might have contributed to a 14-year-old's commission of a crime, it is here. Miller's stepfather physically abused him; his alcoholic and drug-addicted mother neglected him; he had been in and out of foster care as a result; and he had tried to kill himself four times, the first when he should have been in kindergarten" (567 U.S. 460 [2012]).

necessary and jointly sufficient conditions: a *control condition* (also called the freedom condition) and an *epistemic condition* (also called the knowledge, cognitive, or mental condition) (see Rudy-Hiller 2018). The first condition has to do with the kind of free will, that is, control in action, required for basic desert moral responsibility that I challenged in the previous two chapters. It prompts us to ask: "Was the agent acting *freely* when they did A?" The epistemic condition, on the other hand, is concerned with a different question: "Was the agent *aware* of what they were doing (of its consequences, moral significance, etc.) when they did A?" The epistemic condition, then, is concerned with whether the agent's epistemic or cognitive state was such that they can properly be held accountable for the action and its consequences (see Rudy-Hiller 2018). Another way, then, for the legal criteria of guilt to be misaligned with the moral criteria of basic desert and blameworthiness is for the former to not properly track and account for failures of the epistemic condition for moral responsibility.

Douglas Husak (2016), for instance, has recently argued that ignorance of the law – or more exactly, ignorance of the morality underpinning the law – ought to serve as an excuse to criminal guilt in most cases (cf. Sifferd 2018). He argues that ignorance of the law ought to excuse in the same way that ignorance of an important fact regarding one's crime excuses. A person, for instance, who honestly believes they are in immediate danger from an armed aggressor, though in reality the aggressor is carrying a toy gun rather than a real one, is less than fully blameworthy for killing that aggressor even if they were mistaken about the threat. Similarly, says Husak, ignorance that some act is morally wrong clearly matters to moral blameworthiness: other things being equal, a person who is ignorant of the moral wrongness of their act is less blameworthy than someone who is aware that what they are doing is wrong (2016: 31). According to Husak, when ignorance that an action violates a criminal law is related to ignorance regarding the morality of the act a person is less than fully culpable (2016: 97). For reasons such as these, the epistemic condition for moral responsibility raises another potential problem for retributivists who wish to punish in accordance with basic desert.

Given, then, the various ways moral and legal culpability can be misaligned, retributivism suffers from the fact that a person can easily be found criminally guilty and eligible for retributive punishment without being (fully) morally blameworthy for their criminal wrongdoing. Excuses, whether morally or legally established, indicate diminished responsibility, even for those theorists who believe in basic desert moral responsibility. Yet the legal criteria of guilt is not sufficiently sensitive to all the various excusing conditions that can diminish or remove moral blameworthiness. Yes, the law allows for certain excusing conditions (e.g., insanity, self-defense, automatism, etc.), but these are by no means sensitive enough to track moral blameworthiness in any kind of reliable way. Criminal law often dismisses ignorance, age, systemic injustice, and diminished capacities short of insanity, as legitimate excuses. For this reason, "the notion of moral blameworthiness will not function well as the basis of legal guilt" (Kelly 2018: 46). I therefore agree with Kelly that "[w]e should abandon efforts to justify state-imposed punishment as morally deserved. We should reform the criminal justice system without aiming for moral desert and retribution" (2018: 46).

4.2 THE POOR EPISTEMIC POSITION ARGUMENT

Perhaps, at this point, a retributivist could argue that these problems are more indicative of our broken criminal justice system, not retributivism per se, and that a properly reformed criminal justice system could better align the legal criteria of guilt with the moral criteria of basic desert and blameworthiness, thereby avoiding the previous objection. But I think there are in principle reasons to doubt this. This brings me to my next objection, which I will label the *Poor Epistemic Position Argument* (or PEPA) so as to distinguish it from the Epistemic Argument developed in the previous chapter. PEPA can be summarized as follows: (a) for the state to be able to justly distribute legal punishment in accordance with desert, it needs to be in the proper epistemic position to know what an agent basically deserves, but since (b) the state is (almost) never in the proper epistemic position to know what an agent basically deserves, it follows that (c) the state is not able to justly distribute legal punishment in accordance with desert.[10]

Retributivists, I assume, will try to resist this argument by challenge (b), the key premise. They could do this by arguing either that retributivism is no more epistemically worse off than its alternatives, or that the state *can* properly assess what wrongdoers justly deserve in all, or almost all, relevant cases. But there are serious problems with each of these responses. The problem with the first reply is that it in no way aids retributivism to point to the epistemic limitations of other theories. While it may be true that forward-looking justifications of punishment, like, say, consequentialist deterrence theories, may have their own epistemic worries – for instance, knowing, ahead of time, what types of punishments will successfully deter crime – this in no way gets retributivism off the hook. Intentionally inflicting harm on wrongdoers in accordance with desert requires a way of properly assessing desert, and this remains true regardless of whether the alternatives generate their own epistemic worries. Furthermore, given the centrally important role desert plays in retributivism, and given its commitment to proportionality, it is natural to think that retributivism carries a heavier epistemic burden than other views since it would be wrong, on its own terms, to punish any individual more severely than they deserve. But this means that it would be morally unacceptable for the retributivist to acknowledge that the state is not in a good epistemic position to know what agents truly deserve – especially given the amount of harm caused by legal punishment. Rather than saving retributivism, the first strategy essentially acknowledges

---

[10] When I say "basically deserves," I mean "deserves" in the basic desert sense.

that it would be practically impossible for the state to punish in accordance with desert, *without this leading to injustice*, since, due to the state's epistemic limitations, some people will inevitably end up getting more punishment than they deserve (and some less).

What, then, of the second reply, that the state can, in fact, properly track the desert of offenders? The problem here is that the state (or representatives of the state) is almost never in a good epistemic position to know what an individual basically deserves. There are several reasons for this. First and foremost, for the state to be able to justly punish in accordance with basic desert, it would need to be capable of obtaining, processing, and weighing far more information than is typically available in a normal criminal trial. But as Kelly and others have argued, the moral criteria of blameworthiness and accountability is more sensitive to the capacities and epistemic states of agents, as well as the way poverty, racism, and prior abuse can affect blameworthiness, than is the criteria of legal guilt. Since the state is epistemically limited in what it can know and what it can consider, it is virtually impossible for it to epistemically determine what an individual basically deserves. To further complicate matters, the lives of individuals are complex and the line between victim and criminal is not always clear. Research shows that violent offenders, more often than not, are victims long before they commit their first crime.[11] The complex reality of the lives of these offenders, as both violent perpetrator and violence victim, is one the criminal justice system is ill-prepared to acknowledge or treat. The depressing truth is that most people who go to prison have had to deal with violence all their lives. A recent Boston Re-entry Study (2015) found that half of the people interviewed had been beaten by their parents; 40 percent had witnessed someone being killed; 30 percent grew up with other family violence; and 16 percent reported being sexually abused. Nine out of ten of the people interviewed got in fights throughout adolescence. An additional 50 percent said they were seriously injured in assaults or accidents as children.

While it is easy to portray violence as a characteristic of certain people – thugs who are beyond redemption, people with no conscience – the violent offender of political debates is mostly a fiction. Violence is as much a characteristic of places and circumstances as of people. Analysis of the life histories of the men and women who end up in prison indicates that violence typically arises in the context of poverty where conditions are "chaotic" and "lack informal sources of social control" (Western 2015: 14). Look closely and you will find that there are lifetimes of trauma that fill the prison system. And as Western writes, "This situational perspective on violence diverges from the criminal justice perspective in which offenders and victims represent distinct classes of people and punishment involves the assessment of individual culpability" (2015: 14). This divergence has led some, like Michael

---

[11] See, e.g., Boston Re-entry Study (2015), Western (2015), Western et al. (2015), Wachs and Evans (2010), Tonry (1995, 2014), and Callender (2010, 2019).

4.2 The Poor Epistemic Position Argument

Tonry (2014), to argue that deep social disadvantages should be recognized as an excusing or mitigating defense in the criminal law, as well as be recognized as an appropriate basis for mitigating the severity of punishment. Views that deny this, he argues, "fail to acknowledge the existence of social science evidence on human development that makes clear that many offenders offend for reasons for which no plausible case can be made that they are morally responsible" (2014).

If retributivists want to reform the criminal justice system so as to be more sensitive to these mitigating factors, then they need to squarely face the problem of PEPA, since the state is often not in a position to discern the relevant mitigating factors, let alone properly weigh them so as to determine how much they should mitigate moral and legal culpability. And not only is the state epistemically limited in what it can know and properly track, it is also limited in terms of the time, effort, and resources it can dedicate to each individual case. Due to these practical limitations, the state often resorts to plea-bargaining and settling cases prior to a trail, which deprives poor and disadvantaged defendants from a proper hearing of the facts or a close examination of their moral and legal guilt. In fact, in the United States 97 percent of federal cases and 94 percent of state cases end in plea bargains, with defendants pleading guilty in exchange for a lesser sentence.[12] The image of a criminal justice system where defendants get their fair day in court and a fair and just sentence once a trial is concluded is very different from the real, workaday world inhabited by prosecutors and defense lawyers in the United States.

In recent decades, American legislators have criminalized so many behaviors that police are arresting millions of people annually – almost 11 million in 2015, the most recent year for which figures are available. Taking to trial even a significant proportion of those who are charged would grind proceedings to a halt. As Emily Yoffe writes:

> Because of plea bargains, the system can quickly handle the criminal cases of millions of Americans each year, involving everything from petty violations to violent crimes. But plea bargains make it easy for prosecutors to convict defendants who may not be guilty, who don't present a danger to society, or whose "crime" may primarily be a matter of suffering from poverty, mental illness, or addiction. And plea bargains are intrinsically tied up with race, of course, especially in our era of mass incarceration. (2017)

Since low-income people are less likely to afford bail, the bulk of America's jailed population is made up of people whose incarceration stems from being poor. And studies show that people in jail are more likely to plead guilty because it is typically the fastest track to getting home.[13] As a result, many poor and disadvantaged people plead guilty to crimes they may not have committed because they fear that without

---

[12] See *New York Times* (March 22, 2012), "Strong Hand for Judges in the 'Bazaar' of Plea Deals": www.nytimes.com/2012/03/23/us/stronger-hand-for-judges-after-rulings-on-plea-deals.html.

[13] See, e.g., Dobbie, Goldin, and Yang (2018), Gupta, Hansman, Frenchman (2016).

proper representation they will end up with longer sentences if they risk going to trial. Retributivists need to explain how, in the imperfect world we occupy, the state – with its limited resources and poor epistemic position – is to justly distribute legal punishment in accordance with desert. Retributivists seldom address such concerns, but they are of serious practical importance.

And as if these hurdles were not enough, there is also the fact that humans are both fallible and prone to asymmetric biases where they overestimate their own merit and underestimate the merit of others, as well as judge the bad behavior of others as more blameworthy than their own bad behavior. Such biases put representatives of the state in an even poorer epistemic position, since data clearly show that we often exaggerate a person's actual or potential control over an event to justify our blame judgments and we will even change the threshold of how much control is required for a blame judgment.[14] Other biases, such as implicit racial biases, can also affect judgments of desert. There is no denying that race matters in the criminal justice system. Black defendants appear to fare worse than similarly situated white defendants:

> In a study of bail-setting in Connecticut, for example, Ian Ayres and Joel Waldfogel (1994) found that judges set bail at amounts that were twenty-five percent higher for black defendants than for similarly situated white defendants. In an analysis of judicial decision making under the Sentencing Reform Act of 1984, David Mustard found that federal judges imposed sentences on black Americans that were twelve percent longer than those imposed on comparable white defendants (Mustard 2001). Finally, research on capital punishment shows that "killers of White victims are more likely to be sentenced to death than are killers of Black victims" and that "Black defendants are more likely than White defendants" to receive the death penalty (Banks et al. 2006). (Rachlinski et al. 2009: 1196)

Implicit racial biases may account for these racially disparate outcomes in the criminal justice system. A recent study involving a large sample of trial judges drawn from around the United States found, for example, that "judges harbor the same kinds of implicit biases as others" and that "these biases can influence their judgments" (Rachlinski et al. 2009: 1195).[15]

---

[14] See, e.g., Alicke et al. (2008), Alicke (1994, 2000, 2008), Clark et al. (2014), Everett et al. (2018), Berg and Vidmar (1975), Eften (1974), Lagnado and Channon (2008).

[15] Another problem, not discussed here, has to do with racial discrimination in jury selection and how this affects both judgments of guilt and sentencing. When prosecutors (and defense attorneys) select jurors for a trial, they slowly eliminate prospective jurors from the jury pool. So-called peremptory challenges by the prosecutor can be used to eliminate prospective jurors and they do not require any justification and need not be approved by a judge. A recent study by the Michigan State University College of Law detailed a persistent and consistent pattern of discrimination in North Caroline, to mention just one example. For more than twenty years, state prosecutors had removed more than twice the number of black jurors as nonblack jurors in capital cases; and in cases involving a black defendant, prosecutors had eliminated nearly three times the number of black jurors as nonblack jurors.

It would seem, then, that the state is epistemically and practically compromised in a number of important ways. These include being unable to properly track and weigh the extent to which prior abuse and disadvantage should mitigate responsibility, being unable to dedicate the time, resources, and effort needed to accurately assess desert and blameworthiness in most cases, cognitive biases that cloud our judgments, and the general difficulty of knowing how addiction, diminished capacities, social injustice, and other relevant factors should affect judgments of desert.

These considerations lead me to conclude that the state is almost never in the proper epistemic position to determine what an agent basically deserves. The Poor Epistemic Position Argument (PEPA) therefore provides a powerful reason for rejecting retributivism. Of course, defenders of retributivism could try to avoid PEPA by limiting the scope of considerations to something like the current criteria of legal guilt, arguing that the kinds of mitigating factors discussed earlier are irrelevant to desert. But this would only bring us back to the previous objection that the legal criteria of guilt is not properly aligned with the moral criteria of blameworthiness. It appears that whichever path the retributivist chooses they face serious difficulties. These difficulties are best captured in the following dilemma:

> **Retributivist Tracking Dilemma:** If retributivists resist broadening the range of considerations by which legal guilt can be mitigated, they end up with an unacceptable misalignment between the legal criteria of guilt and the moral criteria of blameworthiness. On the other hand, if they attempt to properly align the legal criteria of guilt with the moral criteria of blameworthiness so that that former accurately tracks the various factors that mitigate basic desert moral responsibility, they will end up confronting epistemic and practical limitations that make it virtually impossible for the state to properly distribute punishment in accordance with desert. This is because the state is in a poor epistemic position to properly track and weigh the appropriately expanded set of considerations.

I contend that however the retributivist attempts to resolve this dilemma, they will end up with an unacceptable outcome. And this conclusion is reached on the retributivist's own terms, since either option will inevitably lead to some people getting more punishment than they deserve on the retributivist's own standards.

4.3 INDETERMINACY IN JUDGMENT ARGUMENT

Another practical problem confronting retributivism has to do with how the state goes about judging and ranking such things as *gravity of wrong*, on the one hand, and what counts as *proportional punishment*, on the other. I contend that such judgments are wide open to subjective and cultural biases and prejudices, and as a result, the principle of proportionality in *actual practice* does not provide the kind of protections against abuse it promises. There simply is no magic ledger to look to that objectively and impartially spells out a rank order of wrongs in one column and the punishment deserved for each in another. This is obvious from the fact that retributivists often disagree with one another about how to measure each. If the history of punitive practices and institutions has taught us anything, it is that judgments of what counts as a grievous wrong are hypersensitive to cultural biases, prejudices, and power relations. And even when there is wide agreement on the gravity of a wrong, there is still often disagreement about what kind of punishment is deserved. For instance, all retributivists can agree that murdering an innocent person is a grievous wrong, but they can, and often do, disagree on what count as "proportional" punishment. Kant proposed death. Other retributivists propose life in prison. Still others think life in prison is too harsh. How do we decide questions like these on the principle of proportionality?

To see just how wide-open deontological judgments of gravity and proportionality are to cultural influence, examine the criminal codes and punitive practices of other cultures, times, and places. For instance, the law code set out in the Book of Deuteronomy in the Hebrew Bible provided instructions covering "a variety of topics including religious ceremonies and ritual purity, civil and criminal law, and the conduct of war" (Coogan 2009: 149). Not only does it prohibit things like plowing with "an ox and an ass together" (Duet 22:10) and wearing "wool and linen together" (Duet 22:11), it also covers criminal law and provides rules for witnesses (Duet 19:15–21), procedures for slander (Duet 22:13–21), and various laws concerning adultery and rape (Duet 22:22–29). For instance:

> If a man be found lying with a woman married to a husband, then they shall both of them die, the man that lay with the woman, and woman; so shalt thou put away the evil from Israel. If there be a damsel that is a virgin betrothed unto a man, and a man find her in the city and lie with her; then ye shall bring them both out unto the gate of that city, and ye shall stone them with stones that they die; the damsel, because she cried not, being in the city; and the man, because he hath humbled his neighbor's wife; so though shalt put away the evil from the midst of thee. But if the man find the damsel that is betrothed in the field, and the man take hold of her, and lie with her; then the man only that lay with her shall die. But unto the damsel thou shalt do nothing; there is in the damsel no sin worthy of death ... For he found her in the field; the betrothed damsel cried, and there was none to save her. (Duet 22:22–27).

These punishments were thought to be retributively just at the time, proportional to the "sin" and wrong done, and justified on largely backward-looking and deontological grounds. Of course, we no longer think adulterers deserve to be stoned to death, but that is exactly my point. Judgments about gravity and proportionality are shaped by, and often change in accordance with, cultural attitudes.

Consider the shifting attitudes about homosexuality. In the past, many countries viewed homosexuality as a grave wrong, punishable by the state. For instance, in the United Kingdom, under the Buggery Act of 1533, same-sex sexual activity was characterized as "sinful" and was outlawed and punishable by death. The Offences Against the Person Act of 1861 removed the death penalty for homosexuality, but male homosexual acts remained illegal and were punishable by imprisonment. And while many liberal democracies have now abandon such laws, there are unfortunately still many countries around the world where homosexuality is illegal and deemed a punishable offense – including, Afghanistan, Algeria, Bangladesh (male only), Bhutan (male only), Brunei (male only), Burundi, Cameroon, Chad, Egypt, Ethiopia, Gambia, Chana, Guinea, Indonesia (in some areas), Iran, Iraq (de facto), Kenya (male only), Kuwait (male only), Lebanon (male only), Liberia, Livia, Malaysia, Morocco, Myanmar (male only), Nigeria, Oman, Pakistan (male only), Qatar, Saudi Arabia, Senegal, Sierra Leone (male only), Singapore (male only), Somalia, South Sudan, Singapore (male only), Sri Lanka, Sudan, Syria, Tanzania, Togo (male only), Tunisia, Uganda, United Arab Emirates, Uzbekistan (male only), Zambia, Zimbabwe (male only), and Yemen.

Michael Zimmerman provides another nice example from the history of ancient Indian and Brahmanic jurisprudence:

> As in medieval Europe, so too in ancient India there existed a rich and imaginative set of customs concerning the measures to be applied when it came to punishing criminals and violators of traditional codes of behavior. The old textbooks on jurisprudence, the *dharmasūtras* and *dharmaśāstras*, the composition of which began in the last centuries before the Common Era and clearly bear the imprints of a brahmanically dominated society, prescribe a wide variety of such punishments. Among them we find, just to mention a number of them: money fines, forced labor, confiscation of (all) property, banishment, imprisonment; branding, beating, whipping, mutilation of bodily parts (finger, hand, foot, nose, ear, lips, tongue, male organ), pouring boiling oil in mouth and ears; death penalty through a sharp weapon, poisoning, hanging, trampling to death by an elephant, burning or drowning, impalement, beheading, being devoured by gods, being gored by horns of a bull, being torn apart by oxen, being roasted in fire, being shot to death with arrows. (2006: 214)

Examples like these reveal that what was once thought a grave wrong may no longer be. And what was once thought just and proportional punishment may later appear cruel, inhumane, and disproportionate. Acknowledging this, however, raises a serious problem for the purported protective power of retributivism: How can the principle of proportionality prevent, in any reliable way, disproportionate punishment when there is no objective and impartial way to rank-order wrongs and determine what is to count as proportional punishment for each?

A more contemporary example of how cultural biases and prejudices can influence judgments of gravity and proportionality can be found in the sentencing disparity in the United States between crack cocaine and powder cocaine. The Anti-Drug Abuse Act of 1986 established for the first time mandatory minimum sentences triggered by specific quantities of cocaine, along with much tougher sentences for crack cocaine offenses than for powder cocaine cases. For example, distribution of just 5 grams of crack carried a minimum five-year federal prison sentence, while for powder cocaine, distribution of 500 grams – 100 times the amount of crack cocaine – carried the same sentence. We know, of course, that this 100-to-1 ratio has no scientific or penological justification (see ACLU 2006). The United States Sentencing Commission (USSC), created by Congress in 1984 to develop fair federal sentencing guidelines, long ago concluded that crack is not appreciably different from powder cocaine in either its chemical composition or the physical reactions of its users (see USSC Report 1995). And on three separate occasions, the USSC urged Congress to reconsider the statutory penalties for crack cocaine. In fact, back in 1995, more than twenty years ago, the USSC recommended equalizing the ratio between crack and powder cocaine, but Congress rejected the recommendation, waiting another fifteen years to address the issue at all.

The 100-to-1 ratio and the sentencing disparity it caused are a good example of how subjective and cultural biases, prejudices, and power relations can influence judgments of gravity and proportionality. If legislators were to conclude that crack cocaine is significantly worse than powder cocaine, then it is only natural for them to seek a proportional difference in punishment. But what makes the sale of crack cocaine worse, let alone a hundred times worse? Since there is no scientific evidence for thinking crack cocaine is more addictive or harmful than powder cocaine – a fact already known back in 1995 (USSC Report 1995) – it cannot be that this judgment is based on the increased harm done by crack. Numerous scientific and medical experts have determined that in terms of pharmacological effects, crack cocaine is no more harmful than powder cocaine, with the effects on users being the same regardless of form (USSC Report 2002: Appendix E). In addition, research indicates that the negative effects of prenatal crack cocaine exposure are identical to the negative effects of prenatal powder cocaine exposure (USSC Report 2002: 94). Other assumptions, such as the epidemic of crack use by youth, never materialize to the extent feared (USSC Report 2002: 96). And while this scientific information has been available for many years, unjust cocaine laws have remained largely in place for decades – though in 2010 Congress passed the Fair Sentencing Act, which reduced the 100:1 ratio to an 18:1 ratio and eliminated the five-year mandatory minimum sentence for simple possession of crack cocaine. As with many things in America, especially with regard to the criminal justice system, the explanation, I think, comes down to race. In saying this, I am not suggesting that legislators were motivated by overt racism – although that is impossible to rule out in particular instances. Rather, what I am suggesting is that in judging gravity and proportionality, legislators were likely influenced by implicit biases and prejudices.

For the twenty-year anniversary of the Federal law, the ACLU (2006) put out a comprehensive report discussing the "extremely arbitrary" justification of the sentencing disparity and how it has had a disproportionate impact on the African American community. The report concluded:

> [T]his sentencing disparity is extremely arbitrary for several reasons. First, the current 100:1 drug quantity ratio promotes unwarranted disparities based on race. Because of its relative low cost, crack cocaine is more accessible for poor Americans, many of whom are African Americans. Conversely, powder cocaine is much more expensive and tends to be used by more affluent white Americans. Nationwide statistics compiled by the Sentencing Commission reveal that African Americans are more likely to be convicted of crack cocaine offenses, while whites are more likely to be convicted of powder cocaine offenses. Thus, the sentencing disparities punishing crack cocaine offenses more harshly than powder cocaine offenses unjustly and disproportionately penalize African American defendants for drug trafficking comparable to that of white defendants. (2006: i)

The report adds:

> Compounding the problem is the fact that whites are disproportionately less likely to be prosecuted for drug offenses in the first place; when prosecuted, are more likely to be acquitted; and even if convicted, are much less likely to be sent to prison. Recent data indicates that African Americans make up 15% of the country's drug users, yet they comprise 37% of those arrested for drug violations, 59% of those convicted, and 74% of those sentenced to prison for a drug offense. Specially with regard to crack, more than 80% of the defendants sentenced for crack offenses are African American, despite the fact that more than 66% of crack users are white or Hispanic. (2006: i)

These racial disparities are even more troubling considering the devastating collateral consequences that the nation's drug policy and mandatory minimums have on African American men, women, and families (ACLU 2006).

For instance, in 1986 before the enactment of federal mandatory minimum sentencing for crack cocaine offenses, the average federal drug sentence for African Americans was 11 percent higher than for whites. Four years later, the average federal drug sentence for African Americans was 49 percent higher (ACLU 2006; Drug Policy Alliance 1992). In 2000, there were more African American men in prison and jails than there were in higher education, leading scholars to conclude that our crime policies are a major contributor to the disruption of the African American family (ACLU 2006; Justice Policy Institute 2009). As the ACLU report highlights, the effects of mandatory minimums not only contribute to these disproportionately high incarceration rates, but also separate fathers from families, separate mothers with sentences for minor possession crimes from their children, create massive disfranchisement of those with felony convictions, and prohibit previously incarcerated people from receiving some social services for the betterment of their families (2006: ii; USSC Report 2002: 96). By criminalizing one set of actions more than another, on what most agree are arbitrary grounds, such unjust sentencing disparities result in prejudicial forms of punishment that disproportionately impact one group of people, primarily African Americans.

These historical and contemporary examples highlight just how easy it is for judgments about gravity and proportionality to be influenced by cultural biases, prejudices, and power relations. Retributivists may wish to dismiss these examples as historical curiosities, or the problem of judging gravity as merely a practical one, but the putative protections provided by the proportionality principle require a mechanism for resolving such disagreements. As philosopher Julian Lamont has put it, desert is a highly indeterminate concept that "requires external values and goals to make it determine" (1994: 45). He goes on to elaborate:

> When people make desert-claims they are not simply telling us what desert itself requires. They unwittingly introduce external values, and make their desert-judgments in light of these values. The reason why so many writers have been able to affirm so confidently such a diverse and conflicting set of desert-claims in debates over distributive [and criminal] justice is not because the true conceptual and moral core of desert is so complex and difficult to discern. It is because the true conceptual and moral core of desert allows the introduction of external values and goals. It is the diversity and conflicting nature of these values which explains the diversity and conflicting nature of desert-claims. This is why differences of opinion over what should constitute the desert-base are not going to be solved by examination of desert itself. The differences do not lie at that level, but rather at the level of values. (1994: 49)

And radical changes in values and desert judgments need not take hundreds of years to occur. As Ristroph observes, "[P]erceptions of deserved penalty (not simply the optimal deterrent or necessary incapacitation, but the *deserved* penalty) for smuggling dangerous items onto airplanes or violating airport security regulations probably changed dramatically after September 11, 2001" (2006: 1309).

Beyond these kinds of concerns, there are additional problems as well. For instance, the problem of measuring gravity is an important one for retributivists since what punishment is deserved is going to be determined by this. Yet the proportionality principle leaves unanswered several important questions beyond the ones just raised. For one, "does it matter if harm is caused, or is the gravity of the wrong set fully by the wrong risked or intended?" (Walen 2014).[16] Second, what significance, if any, should be given to the difference between being punished for the first time, and having been punished before and then having committed the same or a similar wrong again? As Walen writes:

> Many retributivists resist the idea that past convictions should matter, on the grounds that having been punished already, more severe punishment for the next wrong would effectively constitute double punishment for the first (Fletcher 2000: 462; Singer 1979: chapter 5). Others think there is a way around this problem. One approach is to hold the repeat offender guilty of a culpable omission: the failure "to

---

[16] For the position that harm does not matter, see Feinberg (1995) and Alexander, Ferzan, and Morse (2009). For a criticism of that view, see K. Levy (2005) and Walen (2010).

organize his life in a way that reduces the risk of his reoffending" (Lee 2009: 578). Another is to defend a first-offender discount, reflecting human susceptibility to temptation (frailty). This discount would progressively diminish for subsequent comparable offenses, effectively raising the offender's culpability (von Hirsch and Ashworth 2005: 148–155), and it would apply only to lesser wrongs, as it is hard to sympathize with frailty when it comes to serious crimes such as rape or murder (Duff 2001: 169). (2014)

Until retributivists can agree on how to resolve these problems it remains unclear how gravity should be measured, which needs to be settled if we are to know how to apply the proportionality principle in practice.

Assuming for the moment, however, that a rank order of gravity is possible, there still remains the problem of determining what counts as proportional punishment. There are two basic senses of proportionality that can be found in the literature: *cardinal* and *ordinal*. Cardinal proportionality sets absolute measures for punishment that is proportional to a given crime. Ordinal proportionality, on the other hand, requires only that more serious crimes should be punished more severely. There are, however, problems with both approaches. Cardinal proportionality, for instance, tends to lead to unacceptable extremes. For example:

Lex Talionis (section 3.4) offers a theory of cardinal proportionality. In its traditional form – an eye for an eye, a tooth for a tooth – it seems implausible, both for being too lenient in some cases (take $10 from a thief who stole $10), and too extreme in others (repeatedly torture and rape someone who had committed many such acts himself). Kant proposed what might be thought a better version, saying that the thief should lose not just the value of what he stole, but instead all rights to property (1797: 142), and prohibiting those forms of "mistreatment that could make the humanity in the person suffering it into something abominable" (ibid.). Nonetheless, his measure for theft swings to the overly punitive side, leaving the convicted thief a dependent on the state, and thereby "reduced to the status of a slave for a certain time, or permanently if the state sees fit" (ibid.). Others have tried to rehabilitate *lex talionis*, arguing, for example, that it can be rendered plausible if interpreted to call for punishment that "possess[es] some or all of the characteristics that made the offense wrong" (Waldron 1992: 35). But however one spells out the wrong-making characteristics, it seems likely that *lex talionis* will provide a measure either too vague to be of much help (see Shafer-Landau 1996: 299–302; 2000: 197–198), or too specific to be plausible (at least in some cases). (Walen 2014)

Ordinal proportionality, on the other hand, faces a different problem:

If all that were required to do justice is to rank order wrongs by their gravity and then provide a mapping onto a range of punishments that likewise went from lighter to more serious – respecting the norms of rank-ordering and parity – then neither the range of punishments from a fine of $1 up to a fine of $100, nor from 40 years to 60 years in prison, would provide disproportionate punishment, no matter what the crimes. This seems wrong. Murder should not be punished with a $100 fine, and littering should not be punished with 40 years in prison. Some vague degree of cardinality therefore seems to be called for, punishing grave wrongs with heavy penalties and minor wrongs with light penalties. (Walen 2014)

Such problems reveal that the principle of proportionality is too ambiguous to guarantee respect for persons since it is unable to draw a clear line in the sand between deserved punishments on the one hand and cruel and inhumane punishment on the other. As a result, cultural and societal pressure can easily affect how gravity and proportional punishment are measured, and this can easily lead to excessively punitive forms of punishment.

At this point, a retributivist may acknowledge that the concept of desert is indeterminate and that judgments of proportionality are elastic, but nonetheless argue that limiting retributivism at least tells us that some punishments are *too much*. The problem, however, is that "experience shows that desert does not function as an effective limiting principle. Instead, the concept of desert is sufficiently elastic that almost any existing sanction can plausibly be defended as deserved" (Ristroph 2009: 741). For instance, the American criminal justice system has long been committed to the principle of proportionality and limited retributivism, a commitment reaffirmed by the recent revision of the Model Penal Code. Yet, despite this commitment, the principle of proportionality has not prevented the rise of mass incarceration or the large number of people serving life sentences. In fact, judgments of desert and proportionality often lead to judges and juries favoring excessively harsh sentences. For instance, in sentencing the notorious 71-year-old charlatan financier Bernie Madoff to 150 years in prison, Judge Denny Chin said, "[A]n offender should be punished in proportion to his blameworthiness." Since Madoff's acts were "extraordinarily evil," Judge Chin chose the extraordinarily harsh sentence to send a message that Madoff would "get what he deserves."[17] The Supreme Court has also maintained that retributivism is the "primary justification for the death penalty"[18] This reveals that retributivism fails to provide the kind of protections against inhumane and disproportionate punishment it claims. In fact, the rise of the American carceral state appears to coincide directly with the rise of retributive philosophical rhetoric (Enns 2006; Ristroph 2009; Gruber 2010).

Retributivism "tells us to punish those who deserve it but fails to give any indication of who deserves it and how much they deserve" (Gruber 2010). As Alice Ristroph (2006, 2009) and Aya Gruber (2010) have noted, while there have been attempts to resolve this problem, such as the currently popular "empirical retributivism," which defines retributive justice with reference to shared social intuitions of what is deserved and how bad certain crimes and criminals are, serious problems still remain. For instance, "the social intuitionism school is particularly disturbing in

---

[17] See Benjamin Weiser, "Judge Explains 150-Year Sentence for Madoff," NY *Times* (June 28, 2011): www.nytimes.com/2011/06/29/nyregion/judge-denny-chin-recounts-his-thoughts-in-bernard-madoff-sentencing.html.

[18] *Spaziano v. Florida*, 468 U.S. at 461.

light of studies that reveal social intuitions of justice to be largely racialized" (Gruber 2010). In this sense, "judgments of 'desert' may serve as an opportunity for racial bias to enter the criminal justice system" (Ristroph 2009: 749). Furthermore, in the eyes of ordinary citizens, many criminals fail to get as much punishment as they deserve (Ristroph 2006). Factoring these intuitions into our judgments of what wrongdoers deserve will only lead to more punitive responses.

Appeals to desert can also serve to shelter the most severe punishment regimes from claims of disutility and being opposed to other important social goods (Ristroph 2009; Gruber 2010). As Ristroph notes, we can "hope that the facts will speak for themselves ... that once people see how much sentences cost, and how little they apparently deter, the only rational response will be to reduce the length of prison sentences and look for alternatives" (2009: 748). Unfortunately, this hope is often undermined by the retributivist belief that wrongdoers deserve to be punished in proportion to their wrongdoing, no matter how much it costs, how little it deters, or how much this "deserved" punishment happens to disproportionately impact certain populations (Gruber 2010). Hence, "[t]he danger of desert is that it preserves the possibility that some will say the costs are worth it, the inequities deserved" (Ristroph 2009: 748).

In light of these considerations, retributivists may simply retreat to the notion of *negative desert* and argue that at least the negative component of retributivism provides one very important kind of protection. As Walen examples, "Retributivism ... involves both positive and negative desert claims. The positive desert claim holds that wrongdoers morally deserve punishment for their wrongful acts." On the other hand, "[t]his positive desert claim is complemented by a negative one: Those who have done no wrong may not be punished" (2014, s. 3.1). Retributivists could, I imagine, acknowledge that the principle of proportionality provides no real-life protections when it comes to positive desert, but nonetheless argues that negative desert at least prohibits punishing those not guilty of wrongdoing (who deserve no punishment). There are, however, two essential problems with this move. First, it would be a major concession for retributivists to acknowledge that the principle of proportionality provides no real-life protections when it comes to positive desert. Since almost all accounts of retributivism accept both the positive and negative components of the view, to retreat only to the protections of negative desert would be to abandon a core component of the view.[19]

---

[19] Mario DeCaro (2019), for instance, has recently defended a limited form of retributivism that preserves only the notion of negative desert. On DeCaro's account, we should abandon the notion of positive desert for the reasons outlined in the previous two chapters. That is, DeCaro accepts the basic conclusion of the Epistemic Argument and thinks doubts about the existence of free will are sufficient to reject positive retributivism. Nevertheless, he proposes that we maintain the protections of negative desert. While I am sympathetic to his position and think it is a marked improvement over traditional retributivism, it is important to recognize that it has much more in common with my free will skepticism than it does with most traditional forms of retributivism. Such a view would likely be

Second, negative desert is not the only, or even best, way to provide the protections we seek. As Ristroph correctly argues:

> Desert is not the only or best source of proportionality restrictions on criminal sentences. Indeed, proportionality principles are often invoked as limitations on government power outside the contest of punishment, and it is this non-punitive proportionality that is most likely to limit the power to punish. (2009: 741)

In following chapters, I will argue that the public health–quarantine model has a non-desert-based principle of proportionality of its own, one that is capable of securing respect for persons and protecting innocent people from being used simply as a means to an end (see Chapters 6 and 8). Consider the prohibition on punishing innocent people. Retributivists will argue that this prohibition follows from the protections provided by negative desert since only individuals who deserve to be punished should be punished – hence, innocent people should not be punished since they do not deserve it. The public health–quarantine model, however, could achieve the same prohibition on punishing innocent people who pose no threat to society by arguing that the right of self-defense only permits the limiting of liberty in cases when an individual poses a serious threat, and only then in accordance with the principle of least infringement, but since innocent people pose no such threat, it would be wrong to incapacitate them. If this is correct, as I will argue it is, then appeals to negative desert are not needed to secure such protections.

In conclusion, I maintain that the principle of proportionality cannot protect against inhumane and disproportionate punishment. The fundamental problem is that the principle is utterly vague and indeterminate, and judgments of gravity and proportionality are easily influenced by subjective and cultural biases and prejudices. And whatever protections negative desert are thought to provide, adopting a nonpunitive proportionality principle grounded in the right of self-defense and the principle of least infringement can provide the same protections.[20]

4.4 LIMITED EFFECTIVENESS

Lastly, there are good pragmatic reasons for rejecting retributivism since it has limited effectiveness in promoting important social goals such as rehabilitation and reform of offenders. The retributive justification of legal punishment maintains that, absent any excusing conditions, wrongdoers are morally responsible for their actions and deserve to be punished in proportion to their wrongdoing, even if this provides no forward-looking benefits to the individual or society. As Michael Moore

---

unacceptable to most retributivists. Furthermore, I think the preservation of negative desert is unnecessary for the reasons explained in what follows.

[20] See Chapters 5, 6, and 8; especially my defense of the *conflict resolution principle*, the *principle of least infringement*, and the *prohibition on manipulative use*.

puts it, "Punishment is justified, for a retributivist, solely by the fact that those receiving it deserve it" (1997: 153). He goes on to add:

> Punishment may deter future crime, incapacitate dangerous persons, educate citizens in the behaviour required for a civilized society, reinforce social cohesion, prevent vigilante behaviour, make victims of crime feel better, or satisfy the vengeful desires of citizens who are not themselves crime victims. Yet for the retributivist these are a happy surplus that punishment produces and form no part of what makes punishment just: for a retributivist, deserving offenders should be punished even if the punishment produces none of these other, surplus goof effects. (1997: 153)

Given its purely backward-looking focus, retributivism is simply not designed, nor does it even attempt, to promote important social goals such as safety and rehabilitation. For this reason, it tends to be ineffective at making us safer, reforming offenders, and reducing recidivism. To the extent that these social goods *are* important and *should* be something we care about, retributive justice is suboptimal when compared to alternatives. On purely pragmatic grounds, then, we should seek a more effective alternative.

Consider, for instance, the negative affects punitive imprisonment can have on offenders, families, and communities. While not all criminals deserve imprisonment, according to retributivism, some do. And since prisoners are meant to serve a punitive purpose for retributivists, not a rehabilitative one, they tend not to focus on the well-being, rehabilitation, and reintegration of offenders. If prisons provide opportunities for rehabilitation, that would be a "happy surplus that punishment produces" but it would "form no part of what makes punishment just." On the other hand, for those who care about human well-being and safety, the affects of imprisonment are not of secondary concern. Instead, they comprise important social goods that society should aim to achieve. And there is good reason to believe that imprisonment, in the kind of conditions normally found in United States, United Kingdom, and Australian prisons, actually increases crime and makes society less safe (Raphael and Stoll 2009; Harding 2019). This is because the harsh prison environment can exacerbate mental health problems, make people more prone to aggression, isolate prisoners from their friends and family, deprive them of educational and employment opportunities, and make them cynical and distrustful of the legal system (Raphael and Stoll 2009; Harding 2019).

In fact, "decades of research have shown that prison is the least effective place to rehabilitate offenders" (Bartle 2019), especially when prisons are designed for punitive purposes. As Jarryd Bartle explains:

> Studies have indicated that a stint in prison increases the likelihood that inmates will reoffend ... There are many reasons for this: whether because they have been rendered incapable of functioning on the outside by the trauma of incarceration or because being housed with the country's worst-of-the-worse has rubbed off. Ultimately, prisons institutionalise inmates into a highly regulated way of life

completely foreign to the real world ... Young people are particularly ill-suited to prison – detention renders them more likely to graduate from low-level juvenile offenders to lifetime criminals via a stint in corrections. (2019)

Rather than employ punitive imprisonment, I contend that we need to reimagine both the physical design and purpose of our institutions of incapacitation (see Chapters 7 and 8). The current punitive approach to incarceration instills a kind of learned helplessness that is counterproductive from the perspective of rehabilitation and reintegration – which, I contend, should be the primary aim of incapacitation. The retributive approach to imprisonment simply doesn't work.[21] And this remains true even if retributivists acknowledge that we currently imprison too many people and for a disproportionate length of time for some offenses. Retributivists must admit that punitive imprisonment is at least sometimes justified, and by its very nature punitive imprisonment does not seek to rehabilitate offenders or reintegrate them back into society as quickly as possible.

Punitive imprisonment also tends to do more harm than good. For instance, studies have shown that imprisonment can exacerbate preexisting mental health problems or cause new ones that may increase the risk of engaging in violence or being victimized by violence.[22] There is also ample evidence showing that imprisonment can erode social networks that support health and well-being and introduce obstacles in finding housing, employment, and healthcare after release, as well as encourage the formation of pro-criminal social networks.[23] Studies also show that those who have served a prison sentence are far more likely to commit suicide.[24] Even short prison sentences can have these negative effects since it only takes a brief interruption in employment for an offender, and their family, to become homeless and to lose their healthcare coverage. In fact, the impact on the families of those incarcerated is often immense. This is especially true for large and growing proportion of children growing up with an incarcerated parent.

A growing body of research has examined the effects of parental incarceration on children and has found that parental incarceration exposure leads children to develop greater behavioral problem trajectories (Johnson 2009; Murphey and Cooper 2015). For instance, a study conducted by Child Trends found that after controlling for effects associated with demographic variables such as race and income, parental incarceration was associated with a higher number of other

---

[21] Of course, most retributivists will not be moved by this objection since they view rehabilitation, reintegration, and safety as "surplus" goods that "form no part of what makes punishment just" (Moore 2010: 153). But part of what I am arguing is that any plausible normative ethics *should* be concerned with rehabilitation, reintegration, and safety, and the actual costs of retributively justified punishment, as it is played out in the United States, United Kingdom, and Australia, are too high for it to be justified all things considered.

[22] See, e.g., Dumont et al. (2012), Schnittker et al. (2012), Schnittker and John (2007), Swanson et al. (2015), and Caputo-Levine (2013).

[23] See, e.g., Pager (2007), Kling (2006), Loeffler (2013), Granovetter (1973), Tyler and Kling (2007).

[24] See Haglund et al. (2014), Zlodre and Fazel (2012), Pratt el al. (2006), Binswanger et al. (2007).

major, potentially traumatic life events – stressors that are most damaging when they are cumulative; more emotional difficulties, low school engagement, and more problems in school, among children ages 6 to 11; and a greater likelihood of problems in school among older youth (12 to 17), as well as less parental monitoring (Murphy and Cooper 2015: 2). With regard to the correlation with increased traumatic life events, the study found among children who ever had an incarcerated parent, more than half had lived with someone who had a substance abuse problem, compared with less than 10 percent among children with no parental incarceration; and nearly three in five had experienced parental divorce or separation, compared with one in five among children without parental incarceration (Murphy and Cooper 2015). This is particularly troubling when one considers the fact that *more than five million* children in the United States, representing seven percent of all US children, have had at least one parent in prison at one time or another (Murphy and Cooper 2015). Furthermore, "the phenomenon has a clear racial implication as well, as black children are far more likely than white children to have a parent involved in the criminal justice system" (Raphael and Stoll 2009: 17). And this contributes to "the growing gulf between the early-life experiences of white and black children, and the profound effects on their later-life socioeconomic attainments" (Raphael and Stoll 2009: 17; see also Johnson 2009). Incarceration therefore negatively impacts more than just the person incarcerated. Since retributivism does not consider these external costs when making judgments about desert, it is poorly positioned to address the problem.

Given that punitive imprisonment has these negative effects on offenders and their families, perhaps we should seek, on purely pragmatic grounds, a more effective approach to addressing criminal behavior, keeping our communities safe, and rehabilitating and reintegrating individuals back into the community. Drug courts, for example, have been found to reduce recidivism more effectively than conventional custodial sentences. "The key to effective drug courts is the ability to make drug treatment orders, calling for the intensive treatment and monitoring of offenders with substance issue" (Bartle 2019). Special jurisdictions have also been created to deal with offenders with mental health issues. For example, the Assessment and Referral Court List in Victoria (Australia) deals with accused persons who have mental illness or cognitive impairment, lining them up with treatment agencies to deal with the underlying causes of offending. These too have been shown to reduce recidivism. Of course, not all forms of offending can be traced to addiction or underlying mental health issues, "but for those offenders who do require treatment, it is the single most effective way to reduce reoffending" (Bartle 2019). And even for those offenders not suffering from addiction or mental health issues, I propose that we adopt a nonretributive approach that seeks alternatives to incarceration and applies a holistic public health approach to identifying and treating the underlying causes and circumstances of offending. Such an approach, I contend, is fundamentally at odds with retributivism since it does not seek to punish in accordance with desert but rather adopts a *historical whole person approach* that sees individuals as byproducts of their histories and circumstances.

4.5 CONCLUSION

In previous chapters, I argued that retributive legal punishment should be rejected because it is unclear that agents have the kind of free will and basic desert moral responsibility needed to justify it. I presented stronger and weaker arguments for this skeptical conclusion. In Chapter 2, I argued that who we are and what we do is ultimately the result of factors beyond our control and because of this we are never morally responsible for our actions in the basic desert sense – the sense that would make us truly deserving of praise and blame, punishment and reward. The truth of free will skepticism, I argued, undermines the retributive justification of punishment since it undermines the notion that wrongdoers are morally responsible for their actions in the relevant sense. In Chapter 3, I then introduced the Epistemic Argument, which required only a weaker notion of free will skepticism – one that claimed that the justification for believing that agents are morally responsible in the basic desert sense, and hence justly deserve to suffer for the wrongs they have done, is too weak to justify the intentional suffering caused by retributive legal punishment.

In this chapter, I introduce four additional reasons for rejecting retributivism. First, I argued that it is philosophically problematic to impart to the state the function of intentionally harming wrongdoers in accordance with desert since it is not at all clear that the state is capable of properly tracking the desert and blameworthiness of individuals in any reliable way. This is because criminal law is not properly designed to account for all the various factors that affect blameworthiness, and as a result the moral criteria of blameworthiness is often misaligned with the legal criteria of guilt (Kelly 2018). Second, I argued that (a) for the state to be able to justly distribute legal punishment in accordance with desert it needs to be in the proper epistemic position to know what an agent basically deserves, but (b) since the state is (almost) never in the proper epistemic position to know what an agent basically deserves, it follows that (c) the state is not able to justly distribute legal punishment in accordance with desert. Practically speaking, then, retributivism will almost certainly lead to injustice, judged on its own terms, since due to the state's epistemic limitations some people will inevitably end up getting more punishment than they deserve (and some less). Third, I argued that retributivism faces difficulties fairly and impartially judging the gravity of wrong done, on the one hand, and what counts as proportional punishment for that wrong, on the other. As a result, the principle of proportionality in *actual practice* does not provide the kind of protections against abuse it promises. This is because judgments of gravity and proportionality are wide open to subjective and cultural biases and prejudices – as witnessed by the sentencing disparity between crack cocaine and powder cocaine and numerous historical and cultural examples. Lastly, I argue that retributive justice has limited

4.5 Conclusion

effectiveness in promoting important social goals such as rehabilitation and reforming offenders, and as a result it does not make us safer or reduce recidivism. On purely pragmatic grounds, then, we should seek a more effective alternative.

In the end, I conclude that we have at least six powerful reasons for rejecting retributivism: (1) the truth of free will skepticism; (2) the Epistemic Argument; (3) the Misalignment Argument; (4) the Poor Epistemic Position Argument (PEPA); (5) the fact that the principle of proportionality is too ambiguous and easily influenced by biases and prejudices to guarantee respect for persons and prevent cruel and inhumane punishment (the Indeterminacy in Judgment Argument); and (6) the Limited Effectiveness Argument.

5

Consequentialist, Educational, and Mixed Theories of Punishment

With the case against retributivism complete, we can now ask: If we come to doubt or deny the existence of free will, or reject retributivism for other reasons, where does that leave us with regard to criminal justice? Traditionally, in addition to pure retributivism there have been a number of other common justifications of legal punishment, including consequentialist deterrence theories, moral education theories, and a variety of expressive, communicative, and mixed theories of punishment. In this chapter, I will examine these other approaches in an attempt to show that they face significant moral concerns of their own – or, in the case of mixed theories, retain certain retributive components that are unjustified. My aim will not be to refute these theories or establish that punishment is never justified. Instead, I simply want to argue that there are sufficient reasons for seeking an alternative to these nonretributive justifications of punishment. In the remainder of the book, I will then argue that the public health–quarantine model offers the best alternative.

Before beginning, though, it is important to note that the *problem of punishment* is a difficult one – perhaps more difficult than some realize. As David Boonin describes it:

> [P]unishment involves not merely acts that predictably harm offenders, but acts that are carried out precisely in order to harm them. Since it is considerably more difficult to justify intentionally harming someone than it is to justify merely foreseeably harming her, the problem of punishment is even greater than it might at first seem: we must explain not only why the line between offenders and nonoffenders is morally relevant at all but, in particular, how it can be important enough to justify not merely harming those on one side of the line but intentionally harming them. Punishment, in short, involves the state's treating some of its citizens in ways that it would clearly be wrong to treat others. The problem is to explain how this can be morally permissible. (2008: 28–29)

In light of this problem, a number of theorists have argued that legal punishment can never be justified (see, e.g., Honderich 2006; Boonin 2008; Zimmerman 2011). If these theorists are correct, the public health–quarantine model would again have an advantage over rival approaches since it offers an alternative to legal punishment generally, rather than a justification of it. That is, the public health–quarantine model is consistent with (though does not require) the complete rejection of all justifications of punishment. That said, I must reiterate that my goal in this chapter is not to argue that legal punishment is never justified, since that is a stronger claim than I need to defend here. Instead, my goal is simply to argue that we have sufficient reason to seek an alternative to these forward-looking and mixed justifications of punishment since they face a number of serious and powerful objections.

5.1 CONSEQUENTIALIST DETERRENCE THEORIES

Consequentialist deterrence theories have probably been the most discussed alternative to retributivism. According to these theories, the prevention of criminal wrongdoing serves as the good on the basis of which punishment is justified. The classic deterrence theory is Jeremy Bentham's, one of the founders of *utilitarianism* – a consequentialist moral theory that judges actions in terms of the aggregate good (i.e., the amount of pleasure and happiness over pain and suffering) it produces overall. Bentham's justification for legal punishment maintains that the immediate end of punishment is to deter future crime. For Bentham, punishment is an evil since it causes pain, but it is a justified evil since the pain it causes is outweighed by the good consequences it produces overall.[1]

Bentham claims that utilitarianism underlies not only human actions in general but legal punishment in particular: "The business of government is to promote the happiness of society, by punishing and rewarding ... In proportion as an act tends to disturb that happiness, in proportion as the tendency of it is pernicious, will be the demand it creates for punishment" (1823/1948, s. I, chapter 7). Since punishment involves pain or unhappiness, it can only be justified in terms of the forward-looking benefits it produces in terms of pleasure or happiness, for either the individual punished or society as a whole. As Pereboom summarizes the view:

> In [Bentham's] conception, the state's policy on criminal behavior should aim at maximizing utility, and punishment is legitimately administered if and only if it does so. The pain or unhappiness produced by punishment results from the restriction on freedom that ensues from the threat of punishment, the anticipation

---

[1] In the following quote, Bentham makes clear that he conceives of punishment as an evil: "The general object which all laws have, or ought to have in common, is to augment the total happiness of the community: and therefore, in the first place, to exclude, as far as may be, everything that tends to subtract from the happiness: in other words, to exclude mischief. But all punishment is mischief: all punishment in itself is evil. Upon the principle of utility, if it ought at all to be admitted, it ought only to be admitted in as far as it promises to exclude some greater evil" (1823/1948, chapter 13). Bentham appears to be following Hobbes here, who argued in the *Leviathan*: "A punishment, is an evil inflicted by public authority, on him that hath done, or omitted that which is judged by the same authority to be a transgression of the law; to the end that the will of men may thereby the better be disposed to obedience" (Part II, chapter 28).

of punishment by the person who has been sentenced, the pain of actual punishment, and the sympathetic pain felt by others such as the friends and family of the criminal (Bentham 1823). The most significant pleasure or happiness that results from punishment derives from the security of those who benefit from its capacity to deter. (2014: 163–164)

This capacity to deter can be divided into two different types: *general deterrence* and *specific (or special) deterrence*. General deterrence can be defined as the deterrence achieved from the threat of legal punishment on the public at large. Specific, or special, deterrence is deterrence aimed at previous offenders in order to reduce the likelihood of their re-offending. Thus, general deterrence results from the perception of the general public that criminal laws are enforced and that there is a risk of detection and punishment when they are violated. Specific deterrence results from an individual's actual experiences with detection, prosecution, and punishment.

Consequentialist (or utilitarian) deterrence theories maintain that we should only punish wrongdoers when it is rational to expect that it would maximize utility, or consequentialist value, relative to all the other options. These future benefits primarily include deterrence and increased safety. Bentham, for example, makes clear that compensation, or a "pleasure or satisfaction to the party injured," is not the primary purpose of punishing, because "no such pleasure is ever produced by punishment as can be equivalent to the pain" (1823/1948, s. II, chapter 13; quote from Tunick 1992: 71). Instead, Bentham points to the deterrence function of punishment as primary: "Example [by which Bentham means deterrence] is the most important end of all, in proportion as the number of persons under temptation to offend is to one" (1823/1948, s. II, chapter 13). Bentham therefore provides a classic statement of the consequentialist deterrence-based justification of punishment – we punish to deter future crime.

While consequentialist deterrence theories are completely compatible with free will skepticism, they face several well-known moral objections.[2] Pereboom, for instance, identifies the following three and argues that they provide sufficient reason for seeking an alternative. The first is that deterrence theories have the potential to justify punishments that are intuitively too severe. This is because in certain cases harsh punishment would be more effective deterrents than milder forms, "while the harsh punishments are intuitively too severe to be fair" (2014: 164). The second concern is that such accounts would seem to justify punishing the innocent. Pereboom provides the following example: "If after a series of horrible crimes the actual perpetrator is not caught, potential criminals might come to believe that they can get away with serious wrongdoing. Under such circumstances it might maximize utility to frame and punish an innocent person" (2014: 164). Lastly, there is the "use" objection, which is a problem for utilitarianism more generally. Utilitarianism

---

[2] See, e.g., Ten (1987), Montague (1995), Pereboom (2001, 2014), Boonin (2008), Zimmerman (2011), Tadros (2011), Honderich (2006), Zaibert (2018).

"sometimes requires people to be harmed severely, without their consent, in order to benefit others, and this is often intuitively wrong" (2014: 165). In addition to these objections, there is also the more general concern that in many cases, especially cases of violent crime, punitive punishment may not successfully deter, since "the notion that offenders are 'rational agents' weighing up the cost and benefits of offending has been largely debunked" (Bartle 2019). In such cases, the right of self-defense can provide a justification for incapacitating seriously dangerous criminals even when it is not an effective deterrent and, for that reason, has a distinct advantage over consequentialist deterrence theories.

Let us examine each of these objections in turn. The first has to do with the potential of consequentialist theories to justify punishments that are intuitively too severe to be fair. Take, for instance, the following example from C. L. Ten:

> Suppose ... that petty thefts are rife in a society and literally hundreds of cases occur weekly, and the thiefs [sic] are so efficient that it is rare for one to be caught. Although the harm caused by each theft is small, the total harm caused by all the thefts is, from the utilitarian point of view, great, and may well outweigh the harm caused by the severe punishment of one petty thief. Suppose that in such a situation the application of a newly enacted law imposing a punishment of 10 years' imprisonment on a convicted petty thief, and the threat of repeating the penalty on future offenders will be sufficient to deter all other thiefs [sic], and no lesser penalty will have any deterrence effect. It is arguable that the utilitarian would have to condone the imposition of 10 years' imprisonment on the one unfortunate petty thief who was unlucky enough to be caught. (1987: 143–144; as quoted by Murtagh 2019: 141)

This example provides a conceivable set of circumstances in which consequentialist deterrence theories can justify very harsh punishments for relatively minor crimes. If the harsh punishment successfully deterred and produced the best overall outcome, compared with available alternatives, then it would appear to be justified on consequentialist grounds. This is because even though the ten-year prison sentence will cause a great deal of pain and unhappiness for the one petty thief (and their family and friends), an even greater amount of pain and unhappiness will be avoided by preventing the larger number of thefts that would have otherwise occurred (Murtagh 2019: 141). This, however, seems intuitively wrong and unfair. And since consequentialist deterrence theories allow for this possibility, they are morally problematic.

A consequentialist could, of course, reply that while it *appears* as though such punishment is intuitively unfair, our intuition is simply wrong. The consequentialist could simply bite the bullet and let their theoretical commitments drive their intuitions – arguing that if the harsh punishment does, in fact, successfully deter and produce better outcomes on balance, then it *would be the morally right thing to do*. While this is a legitimate move for a consequentialist to make, many would view it as a *reductio* of the consequentialist perspective. Ten years in prison for petty theft not only violates our intuitions about fairness, it also seems emblematic of a failed moral theory – one that would allow such harsh punishment in this hypothetical case. Imagine, for instance, that instead of fining speeders we decided to confiscate their vehicles every time they were caught speeding. This would surely deter speeding and save thousands of lives a year that would otherwise be lost to car accidents. It would also create a great deal of revenue for the state through the sale of the confiscated vehicles, which (we can imagine) was then used to fund important social programs. The problem for the consequentialist is that even if a policy of confiscation were to deter speeding in this, as well as produce these other beneficial outcomes, it would be a draconian measure where (at least for many) the ends would not justify the means – which in this case involves the violation of property rights as well as being excessive.[3] A theory that would allow such outcomes is morally problematic.

The second objection is that such accounts would also seem to justify punishing the innocent under certain circumstances.[4] Consider, for instance, the following scenario. Imagine that a cybercriminal hacks into the US banking system and successfully steals more than a billion dollars – the largest attack of its kind in history. Instead of keeping the money for him/herself, the money is distributed around the world to hundreds of millions of individual bank accounts, with most people receiving an average of one to two dollars. The routing codes used to steal the money are untraceable and the authorities are unable to catch the hacker. Authorities fear that if no one is prosecuted for the crime, foreign governments and other would-be hackers might come to believe that they too can get away with similar cyberattacks. It would also expose the weaknesses of our current security systems and remove any confidence investors have in the banking system. This could have devastating effects on the economy and by extension hundreds of thousands of lives, since many retirement plans are dependent on the markets. Under such circumstances, it would seem that the only way to maintain the appearance of security and deter similar attacks is to frame and punish an innocent person – say another hacker who is known to be innocent or someone with experience working in cybersecurity. We could even imagine that the initial deterrence provided by framing the innocent person would provide cyber security experts with enough time to diagnose the vulnerabilities in the current system and safeguard it against future attacks.

---

[3] Note that eminent domain – the right of a government to expropriate private property for public use – is often thought to be justified on consequentialist ground, which indicates that property rights are not absolute for consequentialists. Hence, consequentialists cannot object to this example on the grounds that it violates property rights. Non-consequentialists, however, could make just such an argument.

[4] See, e.g., McCloskey (1972) and Pereboom (2001, 2014). For the history of this objection, see Sverdlik (2012).

In this example, it would seem that consequentialists would need to recommend framing and punishing an innocent person, since doing so would be the only way to safeguard the economy, protect the retirement savings of hundreds of thousands of people, and deter other would-be attackers. To the extent this conclusion is unacceptable – that is, to the extent that any morally acceptable justification of punishment must safeguard against framing and punishing innocent people – we must reject purely consequentialist deterrence-based justifications of punishment. Of course, defenders of such theories would likely respond by arguing that there are good consequentialist reasons for not punishing the innocent. For instance, if such a scheme were uncovered, this would erode the public's trust in the criminal justice system and likely result in greater disutility in the long run. Furthermore, there are good consequentialist reasons for punishment policy to be general, stable, and public. If such policies allowed for the framing and punishment of innocent people, such stability would be undermined, and this would likely result in massive disutility. These replies, however, suffer from two general problems.

First, according to utilitarian and consequentialist theories, no actions are intrinsically right or wrong – you always need to consider the specifics of the case, the likely consequences, and what course of action would produce the greatest aggregate good compared to available alternatives. In this example, it is easy to imagine the FBI framing and punishing the innocent person in a covert manner and trying the case in secret, claiming the evidence is a matter of national security. If only a small number of trustworthy agents are involved, and the evidence is classified as top secret, it would seem that the chances of the public ever finding out are vanishing low. In this particular case, then, the general stability of the system would be retained (assuming we limit the use of deceptive punishment to only this case). And with regard to other utilitarian concerns, like the possible erosion of important protections, it would seem that, at least in this case, the benefits of deceptively punishing an innocent person would outweigh them since the secrecy of the trail and the nature of the evidence (being classified as top secret) would make it unlikely to affect other normal criminal proceedings. The problem is that when considerations of utility are applied to individual actions, considered on a case-by-case basis, it is easy to imagine special circumstance (i.e., like this one) where framing an innocent person would produce the greatest aggregate good and hence be justified. And even if one adopted a *rule utilitarianism*, which applies utilitarian calculations to rules directly rather than actions, there is still the problem of what to do when two rules conflict as well as special circumstances when it would be permissible to override a given rule. Without appealing to certain deontological constraints, which consequentialism and utilitarianism rule out, it is difficult, perhaps impossible, to establish an *absolute* prohibition on punishing the innocent.

Second, even if consequentialists/utilitarians could successfully argue against the practicality of punishing the innocent, claiming that it would erode important protections and produce poorer outcomes in the long run, such a reply would remain insensitive to the fundamental unfairness of doing so, pointing only to practicality as a reason to avoid it. This is intuitively unsatisfying since it provides no insights into the fundamental unfairness of punishing the innocent and it allows for the possibility of framing and punishing an innocent person when where there is little to no chance of getting caught.[5]

Pereboom's final objection is known as the "use" objection. It stems from the fact that utilitarianism "sometimes requires people to be harmed severely, without their consent, in order to benefit others, and this is often intuitively wrong. Punishing criminals for the security of society would appear to be just such a practice" (2014: 165). I think it best to understand this objection in terms of Victor Tadros's (2011) distinction between *manipulative use*, where someone is used in order to promote some further independent goal, and harming someone to *eliminate* a threat they pose. In cases of manipulative use, we use individuals as a means to an end. And Tadros (2011) cites a wide range of examples where it is intuitively objectionable to use someone manipulatively in this way. On the other hand, "harming someone to *eliminate* a threat they pose is much easier to justify, based on the right of self-defense" (Shaw 2019: 101; see also Tadros 2011; Pereboom 2020). As Tadros puts it:

> If the *means principle* is a principle that prohibits using other people as a means, it necessarily involves intentions. For we can be regarded as using a person to achieve some goal only if we intend to harm that person in order to achieve the goal. But not all intentional harming involves using. Sometimes we intentionally harm a person simply to eliminate the harm that they pose to us. This is often true in cases of self-defense. When I defend myself against an attacker I do not use the attacker as a means to avert a threat. That person is the threat. The *mean principle* is best understood as a principle that prohibits a subset of the set of intentional harming: that where the person is harmed for some further goal. In other words, the *means principle* prohibits manipulative rather than eliminative harming. (2011: 14)

I maintain that the "use" objection is best characterized as an objection against manipulative use, not eliminative harming. The right of self-defense and defense of others permits certain harms that do not count as "manipulative use" (see Tadros 2011; Shaw 2019; Pereboom 2020). I will have more to say about the distinction between eliminating harm and manipulative use in the following chapter, but for the moment I will assume it is a valid distinction and I will focus on why consequentialist deterrence theories run afoul of the prohibition on manipulative use.

Concerns over manipulation use are particularly acute with regard to general deterrence, since punishing a person in order to deter others from crime would be to use that individual as an instrument (or a means-to-an-end) to affect the behavior of others. To see why, it might be instructive to first consider a slightly different

---

[5] In the following chapter, I will argue that the public health–quarantine model has an advantage here since it can provide an account of why framing an innocent person would be wrong; that is, it would be a violation of the *conflict resolution principle*.

example: the problem of evil. Many find it hard or impossible to understand why an all-knowing, all-powerful, all-loving God would allow the suffering of, say, innocent children. For instance, a child born with Tay-Sachs disease, a genetic disorder that results in the destruction of nerve cells in the brain and spinal cord, will live a life of nothing but pain and suffering and die sometime in early childhood. Around three to six months of age, the baby will lose the ability to turn over, sit, or crawl, followed by seizures, hearing loss, the inability to move, and finally death. Some theodicies attempt to explain such suffering by pointing to the potential benefits it may have on others. For instance, the child with Tay-Sachs may be used to test the parents' faith, help us understand the contrast between good and evil, or challenge society to be more loving, compassionate, and cooperative. Such replies, however, are thoroughly unconvincing and morally problematic. They run afoul of what I like to call the *Jack and Jill problem*, since they're analogous to a parent beating the hell out of Jack to teach Jill a lesson, which does not explain Jack (pun intended)! That is, the use of Jack for the benefit of Jill does not explain the necessity of Jack's suffering (or the child with Tay-Sachs) and is intuitively wrong.

Consequentialist deterrence theories have a similar problem. Recall the example of Leandro Andrade, who as a result of California's three strikes law was given twenty-five years to life for stealing some VHS tapes from Kmart. Three strikes laws were implemented across the United States in the 1990s in an attempt to deter crime. It is important to note that their justification was largely consequentialist and *not* retributivist. Advocates of such laws maintained that, although individuals like Leandro Andrade may not be much of a threat to public safety, having fixed and harsh penalties for those who commit three felonies will help deter would-be criminals. Unfortunately, these laws ended up resulting in extremely harsh penalties for minor crimes. The case of Leandro Andrade is just one example, but there are many others. The core problem with three strikes laws is that when individuals who are not a serious threat to public safety are sent away for life in an attempt to deter others, they are treated as a means-to-an-end to be used for the benefit of others. In this way, Leandro Andrade resembles Jack in that both are harmed severely, without their consent, for the sake of others and in a manner most would consider unacceptable.

Deterrence theorists could, perhaps, argue that while many of the architects of three strikes laws *thought* such laws would deter and reduce crime, in actual fact more recent empirical research does not support these claims (see, e.g., Vitiello 2002, 2004). But even if this is true, these laws were put in place largely on the *assumption* that they would deter future crime. Concerns over manipulative use did not prevent their implementation. This is an important point, since it reveals that consequentialists are at least theoretically willing to use individuals in certain ways so as to deter others – for instance, sentencing them to life in prison, if this were to deter others from committing felonies. The public health–quarantine model has an advantage here, since it would be opposed to both the sentence of life in prison and three strikes laws. This is because such policies prevent individual cases from being judged on their own terms, which would be needed if we are to accurately assess the threat posed by an individual to society moving forward. The fact that one person has committed three strikes does not mean they represent the same threat to society as another. Second, such policies exclude from the outset the chance of rehabilitation. Lastly, three strikes laws often run afoul of the principle of least infringement, an essential component of the public health–quarantine model. The public health–quarantine model also has the advantage of being consistent with the *prohibition on manipulative use principle*, which maintains that it is generally wrong to use someone merely as a means in order to promote some further independent end – in contrast to harming someone to eliminate a threat they pose based on the right of self-defense, which can be justified. Consequentialist deterrence theories run afoul of this principle, while the public health–quarantine model does not.

I would like to end with one last objection. Note that all the objections mentioned earlier assume that punishment can successfully deter criminal behavior. Imagine that this was wrong. What if it turned out, even if only hypothetically, that punishing murders, rapists, and serial killers had no deterrence effect at all, not on them or others? Would deterrence theorists then conclude that we should let them run free? If not, how would they go about justifying punitive imprisonment? Appeals to deterrence would not provide the justification needed. Perhaps they could appeal to incapacitation? But that would turn their account into a variant of my own, which maintains that incapacitation is justified, since it is necessary to protect public safety, but not punitive imprisonment. Punitive imprisonment, which involves intentional harm in response to wrongdoing, requires a different type of justification than incapacitation. And in a world where deterrence was ineffective, consequentialist deterrence theories would be unable to justify it.

A deterrence theorist could reply that, although this objection has traction in a hypothetical world where punishment has no deterrence effect, in the *actual world* punishment (including punitive imprisonment) does, in fact, deter and is therefore justified on consequentialist grounds. But is that true? Clearly, it is an empirical question what forms of punishment deter, if any, and how much they deter. A recent study by Harding et al. (2019) found, for instance, that prison has no preventive effect on violence in the long term among violent offenders who might have been sentenced to probation. Using a data set covering more than 100,000 convicted criminals in the United States, the study compared the rates of violent crime committed by individuals sentenced to prison with those of individuals sentenced to probation using a natural experiment based on the random assignment of judges to criminal cases. The study found that being sentenced to prison had no significant effects on arrests or convictions for violent crimes after release from prison, although the "effects of incapacitation during imprisonment" did reduce the probability of violence. The authors of the study conclude: "These results suggest that for individuals on the current policy margin between prison and probation, imprisonment is an ineffective long-term intervention for violence prevention, as it has, on balance, no rehabilitative or deterrent effects after release" (2019: 671).

Additional studies have also shown that prison is not a very effective way to deter crime (see, e.g., Levin 1971; Song and Lieb 1993; Gendreau et al. 1996; Nagin and Pogarsky 2001; Doob and Webster 2003; Sentencing Project 2010; National Research Council 2012; Nagin 2013). For instance, a 1999 study tested the deterrence effect of imprisonment in a meta-analysis reviewing fifty studies dating back to 1958 involving a total of 336,052 offenders with various offenses and criminal histories (Gendreau et al. 1999). Controlling for risk factors such as criminal history and substance abuse, the authors assessed the relationship between length of time in prison and recidivism and found that longer prison sentences were actually associated with a 3 percent *increase* in recidivism. Offenders who spent an average of thirty months in prison had a recidivism rate of 29 percent, compared to a 26-percent rate among prisoners serving an average sentence of 12.9 months. The authors also assessed the impact of serving a prison sentence versus receiving a community-based sanction. Here too they found that being incarceration versus remaining in the community was associated with a 7 percent increase in recidivism. The assumption, then, that putting people in prison for years and even decades will prevent offenders from re-offending by deterring them from committing future crimes is simply wrong. Contrary to deterrence ideology, the bulk of research on the deterrent effects of harsh sentences fails to support this assumption (Doob and Webster 2003; Sentencing Project 2010). And this is especially true for violent crimes.

There is no proof, for instance, that the death penalty has any deterrent effect on homicide rates (National Research Council 2012; Nagin 2013). In fact, scientists agree, by an overwhelming majority of 88.2 percent, that the death penalty has no deterrent effect (Radelet and Lacock 2009). And this scientific consensus is supported by empirical evidence that shows that the murder rate in non-death penalty states has remained consistently lower than the rate in states with the death penalty.[6] As Amnesty International explains:

> The threat of execution at some future date is unlikely to enter the minds of those acting under the influence of drugs and/or alcohol, those who are in the grip of fear or rage, those who are panicking while committing another crime (such as robbery), or those who suffer from mental illness or mental retardation and do not fully understand the gravity of their crime.[7]

For the same reason, the threat of imprisonment does not deter most violent crime. None of this should be surprising since violent crime is "largely impulsive or driven by complex external factors on decision-making – the notion that offenders are 'rational agents' weighing up the cost and benefits of offending has been largely

---

[6] See the Death Penalty Information Center: https://deathpenaltyinfo.org.
[7] Amnesty International, "The death penalty and deterrence." Available at: www.amnestyusa.org/issues/death-penalty/death-penalty-facts/the-death-penalty-and-deterrence/.

debunked" (Bartle 2019). As the Sentencing Project explains: "One problem with deterrence theory is that it assumes that human beings are rational actors who consider the consequences of their behavior before deciding to commit a crime; however, this is often not the case" (2010: 2). For example, half of all state prisoners were under the influence of drugs or alcohol at the time of their offense (Mumola 1999). It is unlikely, then, "that such persons are deterred by either the certainty or severity of punishment because of their temporarily impaired capacity to consider the pros and cons of their actions" (Sentencing Project 2010: 2).

I am not suggesting that punishment never deters – surely it has some effect in some cases, especially when the level of certainty of getting caught is high. What I am suggesting is that the date clearly shows that imprisonment and long sentences do little to deter people from committing future crimes,[8] and this is particular problematic in cases of violent crime since consequentialist deterrence theories rely on the effectiveness of deterrence to justify imprisonment in such cases. I contend that the public health–quarantine model has another distinct advantage here, since in the case of seriously violent crime the right of self-defense can provide a justification for incapacitation even when it is not an effective deterrent. That is, the public health–quarantine model has no problem justifying the incapacitation of seriously dangerous criminals, even if the threat of loss of liberty does not effectively deter, since the right of self-defense and defense of others would provide the grounding needed. Deterrence theories would have a difficult time justifying imprisonment in such cases. Of course, this objection is an empirical one, since *if* deterrence theorists *could* show that punitive imprisonment successfully deters violent crime, they could regain some justification for it (assuming they could also overcome the objections raised earlier). I therefore leave it to the consequentialist to make the empirical case.

5.2 MORAL EDUCATION THEORIES

Let me now turn to moral education theories, which maintain that "punishment should not be justified as a deserved evil, but rather as an attempt, by someone who cares, to improve a wayward person" (Hampton 1984: 237). Perhaps the best known of these theories is the one proposed by Jean Hampton in "The Moral Education Theory of Punishment" (1984), although she later abandoned the view in favor of an expressive theory of retribution.[9] According to the theory, punishment is justified if and only if it gets wrongdoers, "to reflect on the moral reasons for that barrier's existence [i.e., the law's prohibition] so that he will make the decision to reject the

---

[8] See, e.g., Nagin (2013), National Research Council (2012), Sentencing Project (2010), Nagin and Pogarsky (2001), Doob and Webster (2003), Gendreau et al. (1996), Gendreau et al. (1999), Levin (1971), Song and Lieb (1993).
[9] See Section 5.3 for details. See also Hampton (1991, 1992a).

prohibited action for *moral* reasons, rather than for the self-interested reason of avoiding pain" (1984: 212). Furthermore, it maintains that

> on the moral education view it is incorrect to regard simple deterrence as the aim of punishment; rather, to state it succinctly, the view maintains that punishment is justified as a way to prevent wrongdoing insofar as it can teach both wrongdoers and the public at large the moral reasons for *choosing* not to perform an offense. (1984: 213)

According to Hampton, the moral education theory provides a "full and complete justification" of punishment (1984: 209). The theory seeks to reveal that certain actions are unacceptable not only because they are forbidden by law, but because they are morally wrong. The goal is not merely to set boundaries of behavior or action, but to show that such behavior or actions are not acceptable because they are immoral. As Hampton puts it: "Wrong occasions punishment not because pain deserves pain, but because evil deserves correction" (1984).

Moral education theories typically draw on an analogy with the justification of the punishment of children. As Pereboom points out, "Children are typically not punished to exact retribution, but rather to educate them morally" (2014: 161). Since moral education is a generally acceptable goal, a justification for criminal punishment based on this analogy is one the free will skeptic can potentially accept. But despite its consistency with free will skepticism, a serious concern for this type of theory is that it is far from evident that punishing adult criminals is similarly likely to result in moral improvement (Pereboom 2014: 161). Children and adult criminals differ in significant respects. For example, "[a]dult criminals, unlike children, typically understand the moral code accepted in their society" (Pereboom 2014: 161). Furthermore, "[c]hildren are generally more psychologically malleable than adult criminals are" (Pereboom 2014: 162). Because of these disanalogies, serious doubt is cast on the practical viability of moral education theories.

Furthermore, Hampton herself later came to acknowledge several defects in the moral-education approach to punishment. One of these defects is that there are "too many criminals on whom such a [morally educative] message would be completely lost; for example, amoral risk-takers, revolutionary zealots, sociopathic personalities" (1992a: 21). As Richard Dagger explains, "If moral education provides the 'full and complete justification' for punishment that [Hampton] once sought, then it would seem that there is no good reason to punish such people, no matter how heinous the crimes they committed" (2011: 7). The core problem is that by justifying punishment on the grounds of moral education and claiming it is the "full and complete justification," we are left unable to successfully address violent criminals who, for various reasons, may be unable to benefit from such "moral education." Here again the public health–quarantine model would have an advantage since the justification for incapacitation is not grounded in the ability of wrongdoers to be morally improved.

Additionally, it is unclear that punishment is even the best way to educate individuals morally. To return to the analogy of children, it was once thought acceptable to spank and/or slap children as a way to teach them about right and wrong. We no longer think such corporal punishment of children is ever acceptable. This is because we have come to realize that spanking children often does more harm than good and can permanently damage children.[10] The same may be true of criminal punishment generally, at least as it is commonly practiced. If so, then punishment would not have the desired morally educative benefits the theory presupposes. I acknowledge, of course, the empirical nature of this conditional. But it does place the burden of proof on defenders of the moral-education approach to establish the putative value of punishment.

Hampton also later felt that the moral-education approach elided the significance of victims (Hampton and Murphy 1988: 132). By focusing on the "wayward person" who is to be improved through punishment, she felt the moral education theory deflects attention from those who suffer at the hands of the offender (Dagger 2011: 7). This concern led Hampton to latter adopt a theory of expressive retribution (1991, 1992b). I will have more to say about Hampton's expressive theory of retribution in the following section. I will also argue in later chapters that the public health–quarantine model can accommodate concerns about victims' rights without the intentional infliction of suffering or harsh treatment on wrongdoers imposed by retributive punishment. But given all I have argued thus far, a return to retribution, in any form, would be a significant step backward. At least the moral education theory attempts to provide a rational and compassionate justification of punishment that in no way depends upon the unjustified notions of free will and just deserts. Unfortunately, the theory faces a number of serious challenges – challenges its most famous proponent eventually came to acknowledge. I therefore recommend that we seek an altogether different nonretributive alternative, one that avoids such difficulties. I will introduce my preferred alternative in the following chapter, but only after considering one last class of positions.

5.3 EXPRESSIVE, MIXED, AND COMMUNICATIVE THEORIES

In addition to deterrence and moral education theories, there are also a diverse array of expressive, communicative, and mixed justification theories of punishment. Take, for a start, Joel Feinberg's work on the expressive function of punishment. Feinberg writes, "Punishment is a conventional device for the expression of attitudes of resentment and indignation, and judgments of disapproval and reprobation, on the part either of the punishing authority himself or of those 'in whose name' the

---

[10] See, e.g., Afifi et al. (2017), Benjeta and Kazdin (2003), Durrant and Ensom (2012). See also Marshall (2002), who argues that it is inconsistent to both morally educate children and punish them. This is because the aims of punishment, according to tradition theories, are, in the case of children, incompatible with the aims of moral education.

punishment is inflicted" (1970: 96). Feinberg argues that punishment must be characterized with reference to both some sort of "hard treatment" and this symbolic significance. Condemnation without the imposition of any additional cost is not punishment. And hard treatment without condemnation is merely, what Feinberg calls, *penalties*.[11] Furthermore, the hard treatment itself expresses condemnation: "To say that the very physical treatment itself expresses condemnation is simply to say that certain forms of hard treatment have become the conventional symbols of public reprobation" (1970:100).

According to Feinberg, the expressive function of punishment serves important social purposes. These include authoritative disavowal (e.g., by punishing the soldier who commits war crimes, the government expresses that it does not condone his actions), symbolic nonacquiescence (punishment may be a refusal to acquiesce in being involved in or condoning certain crimes), vindicating the law (if perjury is never punished, then the law against it is dead letter), and absolution of others (punishment of one person for a crime relieves others of suspicion and blame). As Heather Gert, Linda Radzik, and Michael Hand explain:

> It maintains the normative force of the law. Were infractions of the law not condemned, law would lose its authority. Public condemnation of the guilty through punishment also removes suspicion from other parties. Furthermore, symbolic condemnation of wrongdoing enables the state to disavow the wrongful act. Feinberg argues that these social functions of punishment are all performed through the expression of condemnation that is conventionally associated with punishment, rather than through anything intrinsic to the hard treatment itself. (2004: 79–80)

But this leads Feinberg to wonder whether the imposition of suffering (or "harsh treatment") on wrongdoers is really necessary: "One can imagine an elaborate public ritual, exploiting the most trustworthy devices of religion and mystery, music and drama, to express in the most solemn way the community's condemnation of a criminal for his dastardly deed" (1970: 116). He continues: "The only point I wish to make here is one about the nature of the question. The problem of justifying punishment, when it takes this form, may really be that of justifying our particular symbols of infamy" (1970: 116). We can call this *Feinberg's challenge* and it questions the necessity of "hard treatment" (or punishment) to communicate disapproval.

This is a real problem for all expressive accounts of punishment: hard treatment, such as imprisonment, seems neither necessary (at least in principle) nor sufficient (as mere penalties show) for such symbolic significance. Once we

---

[11] According to Feinberg, punishment should be distinguished from penalties. Penalties include "the infliction of hard treatment by an authority on a person for his prior failing in some respect (usually an infraction of a rule or command)." Punishment, on the other hand, must also include a symbolic or expressive significance that other penalties lack. Hence, harsh treatment without this expressive component does not constitute punishment.

distinguish symbolic condemnation from harsh treatment, each seems vulnerable to objection. Against symbolic condemnation without harsh treatment, Feinberg worries it would have no deterrence effect: "We need penalties for deterrence. But condemnation [alone] serves no useful social purpose" (1970: 116). Against hard treatment, on the other hand, Feinberg writes: "It is clear why we should condemn crimes. But why must this condemnation involve any further pain or hardship? Why should the condemnation come through the 'usual physical media – incarceration and corporal treatment'?" (1970: 116). For expressive accounts of punishment that do not also rely on retributive justifications, the challenge is to explain why our particular expressive symbols of disapproval *must* include the intentional "infliction of hard treatment by an authority on a person for his prior failing in some respect (usually an infraction of a rule or command)" (Feinberg 1970a). While retribution aims to *appropriate suffering to moral desert*, expression aims only to *communicate society's condemnation*. And as Feinberg acknowledges:

> Given our conventions, of course, condemnation is expressed by hard treatment, and the degree of harshness of the latter expresses the degree of reprobation of the former. Still, this should not blind us to the fact that it is social disapproval and its appropriate expression that should fit the crime, and not hard treatment (pain) as such. Pain should match guilt only insofar as its infliction is the symbolic vehicle of public condemnation. (1970)

If social disapproval could be expressed without harsh treatment, which at least in theory is possible, there would be no grounds, on this account, for punishing wrongdoers. Hence, the connection between a society's expression of disapproval, on the one hand, and punishment, on the other, is only a contingent one. The expressive function of punishment does not itself provide a necessary justification of punishment.

Hampton, after rejecting her moral education theory, takes up Feinberg's challenge by developing a theory of *expressive retribution*. She agrees that punishment serves an expressive function, and also that it is a means of condemning the wrongdoer (1994: 163–164). But, she adds, punishment also reaffirms the moral equality of the victim and the wrongdoer in a way that makes it a uniquely appropriate response to wrongdoing. As Gert, Radzik, and Hand explain:

> According to Hampton, punishment is justified because, qua expressive act, it is a required response to another expressive act: the wrong. When one person intentionally wrongs another (as opposed to merely harming another), he acts on the assumption that the victim's value does not preclude this action. To intentionally wrong another person is to treat that person as having lower value than oneself; it is to demean her. The wrongful act thus expresses this view of the victim's value. In fact, Hampton goes so far as to say that wrongful acts are wrong *because* they make a false and insulting claim about the value of the victim. They deny the moral truth that all people are of equal, immutable value. (2004: 80)

On Hampton's account, then, the moral obligation to punish wrongdoing stems from the obligation to defend this moral truth. As she states in her own words:

> A retributivist's commitment to punishment is ... a commitment to *asserting* moral truth in the face of its denial ... By victimizing me, the wrongdoer has *declared* himself elevated with respect to me ... A *false moral claim* has been made. Moral reality has been *denied*. The retributivist demands that the false claim be corrected ... If I cause the wrongdoer to suffer in proportion to my suffering at his hands, his elevation over me is denied, and moral reality is *reaffirmed*. (Hampton and Murphy 1988: 125; emphases added)

Thus, on Hampton's account, it is by means of just punishment that we reassert the moral equality of victim and wrongdoer.

> [R]etributive punishment is the defeat of the wrongdoer at the hands of the victim (either directly or indirectly through an agent of the victim's, e.g., the state) that symbolizes the correct relative value of wrongdoer and victim. It is a symbol that is conceptually required to reaffirm a victim's equal worth in the face of a challenge to it. (Hampton and Murphy 1988: 125–126)

For Hampton: "The retributive punisher uses the infliction of suffering to symbolize the subjugation of the subjugator, the domination of the one who dominated the victim. And the message carried in this subjugation is 'What you did to her, she can do to you. So you're equal'" (1992: 13). In contrast, then, to the moral education theory she once defended, "[R]etribution isn't about making a criminal better; it is about denying a false claim of relative value" (Hampton and Murphy 1988: 133).

There are, I contend, several serious problems with Hampton's theory of expressive retribution. First and foremost, it is retributive through and through. For Hampton, wrongdoers *deserve* to suffer for the wrongs they have done, where these wrongs include the expression of one's superior value over that of the victim. Retribution, for Hampton, is understood not only as a way of paying back the offender for the wrong they have done, but also as an expression of society's refusal to accept the wrongdoer's implicit claim to be more important or valuable than their victims. But independent of the expressive component of Hampton's account, it is still at bottom retributive, and as such it presupposes that wrongdoers deserve (in the basic desert sense) to suffer proportionally for the wrongs they have done. If what I have argued is correct, such claims are unjustified. Hence, we must reject Hampton's account.

But beyond the already-discussed problems with retributivism, there are additional concerns as well. For instance, Hampton's account is highly moralistic and places on the state the obligation to correct the "false moral claim" expressed by criminal acts. But is it really the job of the state to correct all false moral claims or to use "the infliction of suffering to symbolize the subjugation of the subjugator" as a way of reestablishing the value of those who have been demeaned or degraded? I find such a suggestion deeply disturbing. As David Dolinko has pointed out:

> If someone publishes a book asserting that men are superior to women, or Jews to gentiles, or blacks to Latinos, or a book asserting that its author is an *Übermensch* greater in moral value than any other human being on the face of the earth, we do not regard it as obligatory of the government to see that a reply is published forthwith. Still less would we think government ought to clap the author in jail. (1991: 551; as quoted by Gert et al. 2004)

In fact, as Gert, Radzik, and Hand note:

> [M]ost of us believe that states that punish people simply for making false moral claims are *unjust*. This is part of what it means to be committed to a right to free speech. But if we cannot punish someone for publishing a book that literally asserts that one person is inferior to another, then how can we punish assault or rape on the grounds that it expresses the same idea? The need to answer false moral claims with true ones does not permit the restriction of speech. Why should we believe that it justifies the even harsher responses of criminal punishment? (2004)

This is a serious problem for Hampton's theory, since her account imparts to the state a moral obligation to punish wrongdoing for expressions of superiority. Requiring the state to carry out such a function seems both inappropriate and way too broad. If it were applied universally, it would lead to all kinds of injustices.

Another concern is that not all criminal acts are best seen as attempts to demean or degrade others. Some criminal acts, such as illegally crossing a border or stealing food to feed a family, may perhaps be better understood as crimes of necessity. Others, such as shoplifting or tax evasion, may be forms of free riding. And others still, such as speeding or driving drunk, may be forms of reckless behavior but not necessarily expressions of one's superior value. It is not at all clear that criminals always seek to lower, demean, or degrade their victims, which throws into doubt Hampton's account of what criminal acts express and what the state expresses when it retributively punishes wrongdoers. If Hampton's account is meant as a universal justification of legal punishment, then she needs to explain how it applies to cases such as these. Is it that, despite appearances, offenders in such circumstances are *always* acting on the belief that they are of greater value or worth than others? If not, how does Hampton revise her account to include a plurality of different expressive functions of crime? Much more needs to be said.

Gert, Radzik, and Hand have also argued that Hampton's defense of retributive punishment is at odds with her commitment to egalitarian moral values. As they explain:

> Hampton recognizes that those who take greater power to be evidence of greater value are committed to a false theory of human value ... But Hampton frequently insists that we must reassert moral truth in the face of its denial. So if Hampton

believes that most people adhere to this false theory of human value, we should expect her to provide an argument against the theory. But ... this is not what she does. (2004)

Instead of sending the message that the offender's exercise of power says nothing about his value:

> Hampton insists that allowing the victim (by means of the state) to exert power over the wrongdoer is the best way to communicate their relative equality. Hampton not only tells us that by punishing the wrongdoer the victim says, "I master the purported master, showing that he is my peer," she endorses this claim: "What you did to her, she can do to you. So you're equal." Hampton allows that punishment can say something about value *because* it is an exercise of power. (2004)

The core problem here is that rather than correcting false moral views, "Hampton's theory of punishment reinforces at least one false claim: that power is correlated with human value" (Gert, Radzik, and Hand 2004). That is, if there is no connection between power and moral value, then the victim's later defeat of the wrongdoer (by means of the state) cannot give us any evidence of their equality either. For this reason, Gert, Radzik, and Hand conclude: "Rather than dispelling the impression that retributivism is morally repugnant, Hampton's version of retributivism makes it appear more troubling than ever" (2004: 80).

In fact, Hampton seems perfectly willing to use the powers of the state to demean and degrade wrongdoers in an attempt to express the state's disapproval and redress the wrong done. For instance, Hampton claims we are justified in denying voting rights to offenders during their prison terms as a form of *expressive punitive response*. As she explains:

> When we vote, we do something ... Our hands are on the levers of political power. Now we would not give that lever to an enemy of our state – someone who would want to destroy it, or who wants to undermine the values animating it. We would not do such a thing because it would be a betrayal both of our country and of the values we believe it stands for, especially the values of freedom and equality. (1998: 41)

According to Hampton, because offenders have acted in ways that "undermine the values animating" the democratic state, it is entirely proper that their punishment includes disenfranchisement while they are imprisoned. But comparing criminal offenders with enemies of the state seems profoundly unfair. Most criminal offenses do not, in intention or consequence, aim to destroy or undermine the values of society in the same way acts of sedition, treason, and terrorism (both domestic and foreign) do. By drawing the comparison, Hampton has also opened the door for all kinds of dehumanizing forms of treatment. In fact, Hampton's retributive account, perhaps more than any other, seems animated by a desire for payback. It recommends using the powers of the state to demean, degrade, and disenfranchise offenders so as to lift others up. Such a retaliatory philosophy, even on Hampton's own account, appears guilty of trying to cancel out one wrong with another.

Let me now turn to Antony Duff's well-known *communicative* theory of punishment (1996, 1999, 2001, 2003). To begin, I would like to note that Duff's account is a subtle and nuanced one. He also seems to share with me the belief that the current US criminal justice system is broken and in need of major reform. If either one of us was put in charge of reforming the system, I imagine we would agree on a lot, as long as we focused on institutional design and practice rather than the reasons behind them. That said, there are still important philosophical differences between us, and it is those that I will now focus on. On Duff's theory, legal punishment is pro tanto justified because it communicates the censure that offenders deserve for their crimes. According to Duff, legal punishment should be understood as a kind of secular penitential burden that is placed upon offenders to censure them for their crimes, with the aim that they will then come to repent, reform themselves, and reconcile with those whom they have wronged. It is a mixed theory since it retains the retributive belief that punishment is justified in accordance with desert, but it also holds that punishment should bring about at least some future good. It treats offenders as responsible moral argents who are asked to understand the wrong they have done and to repent it, but it also attempts to explain the rational for inflicting hard treat upon the offender by claiming that punishment is an integral part of the communicative process and not just a supplement to it. As such, the hard treatment of punishment, according to Duff, is essential to the communicative process: It serves as a penance that the offender is required to undergo in order to focus their mind on their wrongdoing and to repair the broken relationship with those they have wronged, which includes the wider community (see Cochrane 2017).

For Duff, when serious wrongs are committed, more is needed than just verbal censure and apology: "To think that [the offender] could just apologize, and then return to her normal life, would be to portray the wrong as a relatively trivial matter that did not seriously damage the victim or their relationship" (2001: 95). Instead, the wrong committed requires some kind of redress. This redress is delivered through "hard treatment" or punishment, which is intended as a two-way dialogue. As Duff explains:

> Criminal punishment, I argue, should communicate to offenders the censure they deserve for their crimes and should aim through the communicative process to persuade them to repent those crimes, to try to reform themselves, and thus to reconcile themselves with those whom they have wronged. (2001: xvii)

Legal punishment therefore demonstrates to offenders the extent to which they have done wrong and focuses their attention on their crime and its consequences. At the same time, the hard treatment constitutes a message from the offender. As Duff explains, it is "a material and forceful expression of the apology that the [offender] owes to those whom she wronged – to the direct victim of her crime, if there was one, and to the wider community whose values she flouted" (2003: 300).

Duff acknowledges that punishment will not always achieve its communicative aims and for some offenders, like psychopaths, effective moral communication may even prove impossible (see Duff 1996: 54). He also acknowledges that such communication will be ineffective for offenders who have already acknowledged the wrongfulness of their actions and the need for reform in advance of receiving punishment (1996: 54). But according to Duff, it is not the *actual success* of communication that justifies punishment, it is instead the attempt to communicate censure that is *deserved* for a moral wrongdoing. Hence, Duff's claim is not that punishment will always be effective in establishing communicative dialogue; instead, as Cochrane explains, "[H]e is making the much more modest claim that each of these forms of [punitive] sanctions, when appropriately employed, is rationally connected to the communicative enterprise of punishment" (2017). Punishment, for Duff, ensures that the retributive condition of imposing a penance for moral wrongdoing is satisfied, even if the wrongdoer does not actually repent. Furthermore, while the hard treatment entailed by punishment is retributive, Duff contends that it also serves a forward-looking communicative purpose: It helps offenders understand the nature and implications of their crimes.

According to Duff, while "the punishments imposed by our legal system are not *purely* symbolic," since they "are burdensome independently of any condemnatory meaning they might have," they "*can* communicate censure" (2001: 29). That is:

> Given an appropriate set of conventions and a shared understanding of those conventions, a term of imprisonment or compulsory community service, or a fine, can communicate to those on whom it is imposed (and to others) an authoritative censure or condemnation of the crime for which it is imposed. Such punishments are then no longer *merely* hard treatment, but also symbolic acts of censure. (Duff 2001: 29)

Duff, however, acknowledges that this "raises the crucial question that faces any communicative or expressive account of punishment" (2001: 29):

> That question concerns the gap between "can" and "should". Granted that we *can* express or communicate the censure that criminals deserve through hard treatment punishment, why *should* we do so? Since that censure could also be expressed by formal conventions or declaration, or by purely symbolic punishments, what can justify the choice of penal hard treatment as the mode of expression – given the pains and burdens that such hard treatment imposes on those subjected to it? If a communicative theory is to justify hard treatment punishments, it must show that penal hard treatment is not just a *possible*, but a *necessary*, method of communicating the censure that offenders deserve. (2001: 29).

It appears we have once again returned to Feinberg's challenge, which Duff acknowledges "faces any communicative or expressive account of punishment."

Duff attempts to bridge this gap by means of two important further claims: the claims that the state should, in fact, censure those who break the law, and the claim that "penal hard treatment is not just a *possible*, but a *necessary*, method of communicating the censure that offenders deserve" (2001: 29). As Duff explains:

> I offer an alternative account of why we should use penal hard treatment to communicate the censure that offenders deserve by portraying punishment as a species of secular *penance*. That accounts is retributivist: it justifies punishment as the communication of deserved censure. Unlike other forms of retributivism, however, it also gives punishment the *forward-looking* purpose of persuading offenders to repent their crimes (communicate actions in general typically have a forward-looking purpose). This is not to say, however, that my account is a partly consequentialist one – that it seeks to marry a retributivist concern for desert with a consequentialist concern for future benefits: for the relation between punishment and its aim is not, as it is for consequentialists, contingent and instrumental ... but internal. The very aim of persuading responsible agents to repent the wrongs they have done makes punishment the appropriate method of pursing it. (2001: 30)

Like Hampton, then, Duff answers Feinberg's challenge by appealing to retributivism and the intrinsic value of punishment. But if what I have argued thus far is correct, no individuals intrinsically deserve censure or harsh treatment in the basic desert sense. Hence, Duff's way of bridging the gap between "can" and "should" must be rejected. In fact, all mixed theories of punishment must be rejected to the extent they retain the core retributive claim that punishment is justified in accordance with desert.

Communicative and expressive theories therefore face the following dilemma: If they wish to remain free of retributivism and assumptions about the desert of offenders, they end up running afoul of Feinberg's challenge and are unable to explain the necessary connection between expressions of condemnation and punishment. On the other hand, if they respond to Feinberg's challenge by going retributivist (as Duff and Hampton do), their account falls victim to the challenge of free will skepticism, the Epistemic Argument, and the various other problems confronting retributivism.

Since Duff's account remains commitment to retributivism it must be rejected. And to see just *how* committed it is to retributivism, consider again what Duff says about individuals who are impervious to the communicative effects of punishment. According to Duff:

> [T]he law should aim to bring him to recognize and repent that wrongdoing: not just because that is a method of persuading him not to repeat it, but because that is owed to him and to his victim. To take wrongs seriously as wrongs involves responding to them with criticism and censure; and the aim internal to censure is that of persuading the wrongdoer to recognize and repent his wrongdoing. This is not to say that we should censure a wrongdoer only when we believe that there is

some chance of thus persuading him. We may think that we owe it to his victim, to the values he has flouted, and even to him, to censure his wrongdoing even if we are sure that he will be unmoved and unpersuaded by the censure. But our censure still takes the form of an attempt (albeit what we believe is a futile attempt) to persuade him. (2001: 81–82)

It seems, then, that despite Duff's forward-looking focus on communication and secular penance, it is a "mistake to suppose that on this theory punishments are justified only when they are likely to result in repentance, reform, and reconciliation of an offender with respect to his wrongdoing" (Honderich 2006: 186). Instead, as Ted Honderich explains:

A punishment on this view does not have to have even a chance of reforming in order to be justified. It is not that we are to go ahead with it because we cannot be sure it won't work. What the view comes to, we can take it, is that punishment is right when it tells an offender something, and in some way he [can] understand it, even if it and his understanding have no reformative effect on him. The thought may incline us to suppose this is more a retribution theory than so far supposed, purer retribution than supposed. (2006: 186)

Duff's account therefore remains committed to the retributivist claim that wrongdoers deserve punishment and censure regardless of whether it results in repentance, reform, or reconciliation.

I could end my discussion of Duff here by simply reiterating my objections against retributivism, but, as with Hampton, there are some additional objections worth mentioning (see, e.g., Von Hirsch 2003; Matravers 2006, 2011; Boonin 2008; Tadros 2011). First, it is unclear that punishment, especially harsh punishment like incarceration, matches Duff's normative theory of criminal punishment as moral communication. Although Duff acknowledges that punishment will not always have its desired communicative effect, his theory nevertheless depends on punishment being capable of bringing about repentance and behavioral change. Punishment, on Duff's account, is, after all, enforced secular penance, which ideally leads to the offender accepting responsibility and changing their ways (Duff 1999). Marguerite Schinkel (2014), however, conducted twenty-seven narrative interviews with men at different stages of a long-term prison sentence and found that Duff's normative vision of punishment as moral communication may be difficult to realize in *actual practice* because of the inevitable pressures on defendants in the courtroom and on prisoners during their incarceration. The study found that in the court process the attention of offenders was "focused on the length of the sentence imposed" and as a result they were "often overwhelmed by emotion and did not interact with the court as a moral arena" (2014: 578). And within prison, the study found that offenders tended to "accept their sentence in order to make bearing their incarceration easier" (2014: 578). The study therefore suggests that Duff's normative theory fails to comport with the lived experience of punishment, at least for the men interviewed, which raises important questions for the theory's potential implementation. Perhaps punishment, especially incarceration, is simply not well suited for producing repentance and reconciliation.[12]

David Boonin has also argued that Duff's first claim (that the state should, in fact, censure those who break the law) can only be sustained in a sense too weak to do the work needed of it, and that his second claim (that "penal hard treatment is not just a *possible*, but a *necessary*, method of communicating the censure that offenders deserve") cannot be sustained at all (2008:172–176). Boonin begins his criticism by noting that the claim that the state has a particular right can be understood in one of two ways. On a relatively weak reading, the claim means merely that the state has the right as a prima facie right: "[T]he right permits the state to do something provided that, in doing so, it does not employ any means that are themselves independently objectionable" (2008: 173). He provides the example of the state's right to print its own currency. He notes: "[T]his does not mean that it can do any act at all so long as it does the act as a means of printing currency. It means merely that so long as nothing involved in its printing of currency is independently morally objectionable, it may print its own currency" (2008: 173). On a much stronger reading, the claim that a certain right exists means that "behavior that would otherwise be impermissible is rendered permissible by the existence of the right" (2008: 173). Here, the right of self-defense is standardly viewed as an example: "Normally, it would be impermissible for me to kill you, but if your attacking me activates my right to self-defense, then this right makes it permissible for me to do what would otherwise be impermissible" (2008: 173–174). With this distinction in place, Boonin argues:

> This distinction between two senses in which it might be claimed that a certain right exists undermines the reprobative solution to the problem of punishment for the combination of two reasons. The first is that the solution can succeed only if it can justify the claim that the state has a right to censure people who break the law in the stronger sense of having such a right. Since legal punishment involves the state's treating people in ways that would ordinarily be impermissible, that is, the claim that the state has the right to censure people who break the law can only show that it has the right to punish them for breaking the law if the right to censure is strong enough to render permissible what would otherwise be impermissible. But – and this is the second reason – the claim that the state has a right to censure those who break the law is plausible only when it is constructed in the weak sense. The reprobative solution, therefore, is undermined by an equivocation over what it is for the state to have a right to censure those who break the law. (2008: 174)

If this is correct, then Duff's claim that the state has a right to censure wrongdoers is guilty of an equivocation of sorts – it confuses a prima facie right to censure with one

---

[12] I should note that the forward-looking aims of reconciliation and moral change may be easier to achieve in the context of restorative justice and victim-offender mediation programs. But even here, I contend, these aims would be better achieved without backward-looking blame and other retributive components (see Chapter 8 for more on this).

5.3 Expressive, Mixed, and Communicative Theories

that permits the state to impose "harsh treatment" and/or intentional harm that would otherwise be impermissible.

But what if this objection is mistaken and the state's right to censure is as strong as a person's right to self-defense? Well, there still may be good reason to think the reprobative solution must be rejected. As Boonin explains:

> In the case of self-defense, after all, the right makes it permissible to kill someone whom it would otherwise be impermissible to kill, but only if there are no other means of self-defense. If you can safely escape an attacker without harming him, for example, then the right to self-defense does not give you the right to kill him. And this suggests that even if the state has the right to censure an offender in the strong sense, in which the right can render it permissible to treat the offender in ways that would otherwise be impermissible, this will justify the permissibility of punishment only if there are no nonpunitive forms of censure. And it seems clear that the state could censure an offender without punishing him. It could, for example, issue an official statement of denunciation, in much the same way that legislative bodies sometimes issue a statement censuring one of their members. (2008: 176–177)

Since nonpunitive forms of censure exist, it seems that even if we agree that the state has the right to express disapproval of offenders in the strong sense of having such a right, "this concession cannot be used to justify the conclusion that the state has the right to punish him, so the reprobative solution will again fail the entailment test" (Boonin 2008: 177).[13] The central problem is that if nonpunitive alternatives of censure exist, and they do, the state's right to express disapproval (even if interpreted in the strong sense) would require it to always opt for the nonpunitive alternative before using punishment to express censure.

The objections just mentioned present a formidable challenge to Duff's account, even if we set aside the more general objections to retributivism. And there are other difficulties as well. For instance, as Ambrose Lee argues:

> One prominent objection to Duff's communicative theory is that it just seems improper for the state to induce and elicit repentance from offenders. This objection is based on the idea that in doing so, the state seems to be doing something that an abbot would be doing in a monastery, when he imposes penance on sinners so that they come to repent and expiate their sins, and thereby achieve absolution and salvation. Thus despite Duff's claim that it is a *secular* form of penance, it is unclear that this is something a *secular* liberal democratic state like ours should be doing when responding to crimes. (Lee 2017)

And note that there are actually two issues raised in this objection:

> The first one concerns whether the *aim* of inducing and eliciting repentance from offenders is itself a proper one for a liberal democratic state; and the second one is

---

[13] Boonin considers three possible replies to this objection but argues they all fail. See Boonin (2008: 177–179) for details.

about the proposed *means* that are to be used in the pursuit of that aim: whether it is proper for a liberal democratic state to burden offenders with hard treatment (just as the penance imposed by the abbot burdens the sinner) to induce offenders to repent for their crimes. (Lee 2017)

These concerns are important for a number of reasons, not the least of which is that they get to core questions about the aims and methods of punishment. Let me briefly say something about each.

With regard to the first, it is an open question whether the proper role of the state should include aiming to induce and elicit repentance from offenders. The legitimate functions of the state are generally held to include protecting its citizens from significant harm and providing a framework for human interaction to proceed without significant impairment. These roles arguably underwrite justification that in the first instance appeals to prevention of crime (Pereboom 2014). But these roles have no immediate connection to the aim of apportioning punishment in accord with desert or seeking to stimulate repentance in offenders. It is conceivable that the state can serve its legitimate function of protecting its citizens by means of incapacitation, rehabilitation, and adopting crime prevention measures aimed at altering social conditions and addressing the social determinates of crime – and it is conceivable that this can be done without secular penance. It is at least an open question whether repentance is needed to achieve these goals. Duff could respond that rehabilitation is important for promoting safety and protecting citizens, and rehabilitation requires repentance, but it is unclear that it does. I will argue later that means of rehabilitation are available that do not presuppose basic desert moral responsibility or aim at offenders repenting in the sense retributivists have in mind. If this is correct, then additional argument is needed to establish that repentance is *necessary* for the proper function of the state.

With regard to the second concern, the worry here is that on Duff's account it is not clear what exactly is the hard treatment that is justifiable to burden offenders with. As Lee correctly notes, it certainly cannot be whatever best induces offenders to repent their crimes: "If this was the case, then it could end up justifying widely disproportionate punishment; for the severity of punishment would then be tied to how 'thick-skinned' an offender is, and not to the severity of the crimes in question" (2017). Again, there are really two aspects to this concern (Lee 2017). The first concerns the *duration* of hard treatment – that is, "just how long is it justifiable to burden an offender with a particular kind of hard treatment in order to induce his repentance?" (Lee 2017). The second concerns the *kind* of hard treatment in question – that is, "just what exactly is the appropriate kind of hard treatment that is justifiable to burden an offender with for his particular crime?" (Lee 2017). Let us examine how Duff would respond to each of these concerns, beginning with the latter.

According to Duff, the hard treatment of punishment is absolutely essential to the communicative process: It serves as a penance that the offender is required to

5.3 Expressive, Mixed, and Communicative Theories

undergo in order to focus their mind on their wrongdoing and to repair the broken relationship with those they have wronged, which includes the wider community. As Duff writes: "On the account I have developed and defended ... the communicative purpose of criminal punishment runs all the way down, even to the justification ... of particular kinds of hard treatment punishment" (2001: 51). So what kinds of punishment does Duff see as appropriate methods within a wider system of communicative criminal justice? Duff discusses a number of options including victim-offender mediation programs, probation, education programs, and community service as effective examples of communicative punishments (see 2001, 1992, 1996). But Duff also sees punitive imprisonment as having a role within his account of punishment. While Duff is absolutely clear that the use of imprisonment should be reduced dramatically in a society with a properly communicative criminal justice system, he is also explicit that imprisonment ought to hold a prominent place within it (2001: 149–251; 1986: 282–283; 1999: 60).

Three separate rationales for the use of imprisonment can be found within Duff's writing (see Cochrane 2017). First, he argues that imprisonment is required as the ultimate sanction for those that willfully fail to comply with all other forms of punishment (2001: 152). Second, he claims that prison can form an appropriate shock or stimulus to an offender's repentance (1986: 283). Lastly, and most prominently, Duff argues that imprisonment serves as a "symbolically appropriate" form of punishment for those who have committed crimes which seriously undermine the "social and moral bonds," which hold a community together (2001: 148). For instance, Duff argues that "[t]he message of imprisonment is that the offender has not just damaged or threatened, but has *broken*, the normative bonds of the community" (2001: 145). This last response, however, is problematic. As Lee explains:

> One worry about this response is that this would then make "the appropriate kind of hard treatment" depend on the kind of account that we hold for the nature of crimes. If all crimes are, according to some social contract theories, wrongs that violate the terms of the social contract of the political community in question, then arguably all crimes involve breaking "the normative bonds" of the community in question. That would then lead to the rather implausible conclusion that imprisonment is appropriate for all crimes, regardless of their severity as wrongs. (2017)

And similar concerns remain if you replaced social contract theory with a different account of the nature of crimes, since it is likely that whatever account one provides, crime will still be understood, at some level, as "breaking the normative bonds" of the community in question.

Furthermore, it is also unclear that Duff's response to the first question about the duration of hard treatment is adequate (Lee 2017). Here Duff argues that we should only do so much when it comes to inducing offenders to repent for their crimes. This is because to properly respect individuals as responsible autonomous agents, we should leave them room in the end to not accept, and therefore not come to judge and recognize, that they have done wrongs, despite our best efforts to persuade them otherwise (Duff 2001: 36–39). The problem, however, is that "it is unclear, according to this argument, just when we are doing more than we should" (Lee 2017). Should the state give serious offenders ten years' punitive imprisonment to repent and then decide, after they have not repented, enough is enough, we should *now* respect their autonomy not to repent and release them? Should it be twenty years? Thirty years? Furthermore, it is hard to know just how much weight the state should give these considerations about respect for an individual's right not to repent when it comes to limiting the duration of hard treatment. How does the state go about weighing these competing interests? And how do we reconcile this respect for individuals not to repent with Duff's earlier claim that punishment and hard treatment remain justified even when it is unlikely to lead to repentance? A lot more needs to be said to address these concerns about duration.[14]

Duff's communicative account therefore not only remains retributivist in ways that I have argued are unjustified and problematic, it also faces a number of additional challenges. And while the objections to retributivism presented earlier are sufficient for rejecting mixed theories like Duff's, these additional objections remain important since they reveal that attempts to reform or soften the appeal of retributivism by bringing in forward-looking considerations are going to have their own set of problems. These problems include satisfactorily resolving Feinberg's challenge, explaining how "secular penance" and other forward-looking goods are to be realized in actual practice when punitive punishment often undermines these goals, dealing with the kinds of objections raised by Boonin and Lee and explaining how (if at all) these forward-looking features are to constrain the duration and methods of punishment.

5.4 CONCLUSION

In this chapter, I have examined several leading alternatives to pure retributivism and argued that they each face significant moral concerns of their own – and in the case of mixed theories, they retain certain retributive components that are unjustified. Against consequentialist deterrence theories, I raised a number of objections, including concerns over excessively harsh punishments that successfully deter, punishing the innocent, the "use" objection, and empirical data that indicate that punitive imprisonment and even the death penalty do not successfully deter violent crime. Against moral education theories, I argued, first, that adult prisoners differ in significant ways from children, where a moral educative approach seems most natural and appropriate; second, there are, as Hampton

---

[14] See Lee (2017) for an attempt to respond to these concerns and defend a modified communicative account. For additional criticisms of communicative theories, see Tadros (2011), Bulow (2018), Engen (2014), Hanna (2008), and Sverdlik (2014).

herself later came to acknowledge, many cases where the morally educative message would be completely lost – for example, "amoral risk-takers, revolutionary zealots, sociopathic personalities" (1992: 21) – and in such cases, the public health–quarantine model has the distinct advantage since it can still justify incapacitation; and third, it is unclear that punishment is the best way to educate individuals morally.

Finally, I examined expressive and communicative theories of punishment. Here I argued that all such accounts face Finberg's challenge of explaining why punishment or "harsh treatment" is *necessary*. If social disapproval could be expressed without harsh treatment, which at least in theory is possible, there would be no grounds, on Finberg's account, for punishing wrongdoers. Hence, the connection between a society's expression of disapproval, on the one hand, and punishment, on the other, is only a contingent one. The expressive function of punishment does not itself provide a necessary justification of punishment. On the other hand, communicative and expressive theories that attempt to resolve this difficulty by appealing to retributivism end up confronting the arguments developed in the first half of the book – that is, the truth of free will skepticism, the Epistemic Argument, and the four objections discussed in the previous chapter. They also face a number of other powerful objection and concerns. For these reasons, I contend that we should seek an alternative that does not suffer from these difficulties. That alternative, I will now argue, is the public health–quarantine model.

6

The Public Health–Quarantine Model I

A Nonretributive Approach to Criminal Behavior

One of the most frequently voiced criticisms of free will skepticism is that it is unable to adequately deal with criminal behavior and that the responses it would permit as justified are insufficient for acceptable social policy. This concern is fueled by two factors – both of which we have now seen. The first is that one of the most prominent justifications for punishing criminals, retributivism, is incompatible with free will skepticism. The second concern is that alternative justifications that are not ruled out by the skeptical view per se face significant independent moral objections. Yet despite these concerns, I will now argue that free will skepticism leaves intact other ways to respond to criminal behavior – in particular incapacitation, rehabilitation, and alteration of relevant social conditions – and that these methods are both morally justifiable and sufficient for good social policy. The position I defend is similar to Derk Pereboom's (2001, 2013, 2014), taking as its starting point his quarantine analogy, but it sets out to develop the quarantine model within a broader justificatory framework drawn from public health ethics. The resulting model – which I call the *public health–quarantine model* – provides a framework for justifying quarantine and incapacitation that is more humane than retributivism and preferable to other nonretributive alternatives. It also provides a broader approach to criminal behavior than the quarantine analogy does on its own.

I begin by introducing Pereboom's formulation of the quarantine model, explain how it justifies the incapacitation of dangerous criminals, and then argue that the quarantine analogy should be understood within the larger justificatory framework of public health ethics. I explain the public health framework and offer a *conflict resolution principle* designed to deal with conflicts between public health and safety (on the one hand) and individual liberty and autonomy (on the other). I conclude by defending a *capabilities approach* to social justice and explain how it is consistent with free will skepticism. In subsequent chapters, I then expand on the public health–quarantine model, respond to objections, and discuss its practical implications for public policy and the criminal law.

6.1 THE PUBLIC HEALTH–QUARANTINE MODEL

Despite the various problems facing the other nonretributive alternatives, there is, I contend, an acceptable approach for addressing dangerous criminal behavior that is neither undercut by free will skepticism nor by other moral considerations. The theory begins with Pereboom's quarantine analogy, which draws on a comparison between treatment of dangerous criminals and treatment of carriers of dangerous diseases. In its simplest form, it can be stated as follows: (1) Free will skepticism maintains that criminals are not morally responsible for their actions in the basic desert sense. (2) Plainly, many carriers of dangerous diseases are not responsible in this or in any sense for having contracted these diseases. For instance, the vast majority of those who contracted Ebola during the West African epidemic in 2014 were not morally responsible for having contracted the disease. And yet (3) we generally agree that it is sometimes permissible to quarantine them, and the justification for doing so is the right to self-protection and the prevention of harm to others. (4) For similar reasons, even if a dangerous criminal is not morally responsible for their crimes in the basic desert sense (perhaps because no one is ever in this way morally responsible) it could be as legitimate to preventatively detain them as to quarantine the non-responsible carrier of a serious communicable disease (Pereboom 2014, 2001, 2013; Pereboom and Caruso 2018; Caruso and Pereboom 2020).

The first thing to note about the theory is that although one might justify quarantine (in the case of disease) and incapacitation (in the case of dangerous criminals) on purely utilitarian or consequentialist grounds, Pereboom and I resist this strategy (see Pereboom and Caruso 2018; Caruso and Pereboom 2020). Instead, we maintain that incapacitation of the seriously dangerous is justified on the ground of the right to harm in self-defense and defense of others. That we have this right has broad appeal, much broader than utilitarianism or consequentialism has. In addition, this makes the view more resilient to a number of objections and provides a more resilient proposal for justifying criminal sanctions than other nonretributive options. One advantage it has, say, over consequentialist deterrence theories is that it has more restrictions placed on it with regard to using people merely as a means. For instance, as it is illegitimate to treat carriers of a disease more harmfully than is necessary to neutralize the danger they pose, treating those with violent criminal tendencies more harshly than is required to protect society will be illegitimate as well. In fact, the model requires that we adopt the *principle of least infringement*, which holds that the least restrictive measures should be taken to protect public health and safety. This ensures that criminal sanctions will be proportionate to the danger posed by an individual, and any sanctions that exceed this upper bound will be unjustified.

Second, the quarantine model places several constraints on the treatment of criminals (Pereboom 2001, 2014). First, as less dangerous diseases justify only preventative measures less restrictive than quarantine, so less dangerous criminal tendencies justify only more moderate restraints (Pereboom 2014: 156). We do not, for instance, quarantine people for the common cold even though it has the potential to cause others some harm. Rather, we restrict the use of quarantine to a narrowly prescribed set of cases. Analogously, the use of incapacitation should be limited to only those cases where offenders are a serious threat to public safety and no less restrictive measures were available. In fact, for certain minor crimes perhaps only some degree of monitoring could be defended. Secondly, the incapacitation account that results from this analogy demands a degree of concern for the rehabilitation and well-being of the criminal that would alter much of current practice. Just as fairness recommends that we seek to cure the diseased we quarantine, so fairness would counsel that we attempt to rehabilitate the criminals we detain (Pereboom 2014: 156). Rehabilitation and reintegration would therefore replace punishment as the focus of the criminal justice system. Lastly, if a criminal cannot be rehabilitated and our safety requires his indefinite confinement, this account provides no justification for making his life more miserable than would be required to guard against the danger he poses (Pereboom 2014: 156).

Summarizing Pereboom's proposal, then, the core idea is that the right to harm in self-defense and defense of others justifies incapacitating the criminally dangerous with the minimum harm required for adequate protection. The resulting account would not justify the sort of criminal punishment whose legitimacy is most dubious, such as death or confinement in the most common kinds of prisons in our society (2014: 174). The account also demands a certain level of care and attention to the well-being of criminals, which would change much of current policy. In the following section I will defend and expand on Pereboom's quarantine analogy by considering it within the broader justificatory framework of public health ethics. The resulting account, the *public health–quarantine model*, will not only provide a justification for the incapacitation of dangerous criminals but it will also provide a broader and more comprehensive approach to criminal behavior generally. Its advantages include the prioritization of prevention, a focus on social justice, and a more detailed set of principles for resolving the conflict between individual liberty and public safety. This combined approach, I maintain, is sufficient for dealing with dangerous criminals, leads to a more humane and effective social policy, and is actually preferable to the harsh and often excessive forms of punishment that typically come with retributivism.

6.1.1 *The Public Health Framework*

The public health–quarantine model places the quarantine analogy within a broader justificatory framework drawn from public health ethics. It makes use of the public health framework but also places some constraints on it and draws some insights from the four core principles of traditional health care ethics (aka medical ethics). The traditional health care ethics approach emphasizes four key dimensions – *autonomy*, *beneficence*, *nonmaleficence*, and *justice* (see Beauchamp and Childdress 1989) – and focuses primarily on the individual (e.g., the patient-doctor relationship). The broader public health framework, on the other hand, focuses on groups and larger populations. For example, Ruth Faden and Sirine Shebaya (2015) have detailed a public health ethic that weighs such factors as overall benefit to society, fairness in the distribution of burden, and the harm principle. While it is not always easy to reconcile these two approaches since conflicts and dilemmas arise (see Phua 2013), a successful justification of quarantine, not to mention many other ethical and public policy issues, requires that a resolution be sought. In what follows, I will provide a public health justification for quarantine, one that incorporates (as best as possible) the individualistic concerns of the traditional health care ethics approach but provides a method for conflict resolution when it cannot.

Let me begin with a brief summary of Faden and Shebaya's (2015) framework for a broad public health ethic. At its core, public health is concerned with promoting and protecting the health of populations, broadly understood. Public health ethics deals primarily with the moral foundations and justifications for public health, the various ethical challenges raised by limited resources for promoting health, and real or perceived tensions between collective benefits and individual liberty. There are two different ways of viewing the moral foundation of public health ethics:

> One view of public health ethics regards the moral foundation of public health as an injunction to maximize welfare, and therefore health as a component of welfare (Powers and Faden 2006). This view frames the core moral challenge of public health as balancing individual liberties with the advancement of good health outcomes. Consider for example, how liberties are treated in government policies that fluoridate municipal drinking water or compel people with active, infectious tuberculosis to be treated ... An alternative view of public health ethics characterizes the moral foundation of public health as social justice. While balancing individuals' liberties with promoting social goods is one area of concern, it is embedded within a broader commitment to secure a sufficient level of health for all and to narrow unjust inequalities (Powers and Faden 2006) ... Understood this way, public health ethics has deep moral connections to broad questions of social justice, poverty, and systematic disadvantage. (2015)

Whichever foundation one favors, obvious analogies exist here with nonretributive approaches to criminal justice. From the skeptical perspective, we have to reconcile the fact that dangerous criminals do not *justly deserve* to be blamed or retributively punished for their actions with a more general concern for the well-being and safety of society. We need, therefore, to confront the moral challenge of balancing individual liberties with the advancement of the public good. But beyond balancing individual liberties against public health and safety, I also maintain that a comprehensive approach to criminal justice will need to be embedded within a broader commitment to social justice and addressing unjust inequalities. I therefore favor an account of public health ethics that takes as its moral foundation social justice. (I will argue in Section 6.2 for a *capabilities approach* to social justice and explain how it is consistent with free will skepticism – but more on that in a moment.)

On the social justice approach to public health ethics, questions of justice in health policy cannot, at their foundation, be tackled without an understanding of the relation of health to other dimensions of well-being and of the historical and social factors in which actual opportunity for well-being is situated (Powers and Faden 2006). In particular, we need to focus on "those contexts where multiple dimensions of well-being are affected by multiple social determinants in ways that systematically disadvantage some socially situation groups" (Powers and Faden 2006). The public health–quarantine model I defend therefore has deep moral connections to broad questions of social justice, poverty, and systematic disadvantage.

Public health has four unique characteristics: (1) it is a public or collective good; (2) its promotion involves a particular focus on prevention; (3) its promotion often entails government action; and (4) it involves a forward-looking outcome orientation (Faden and Shebaya 2015, s. 1). These four characteristics can equally be applied to the concept of public safety. First, in public health the object of concern is populations, not individuals: "Public health is, by its very nature, a public, communal good, where the benefits to one person cannot readily be individuated from those to another" (2015, s. 1). We can say the same for public safety – it too is a communal good. The societal goods we seek in the criminal justice system (e.g., safety, security, justice, etc.) are aimed at the collective good and the policies we employ to achieve them are designed and implemented with the public good in mind.

The second characteristic of public health deals with prevention. In particular, promoting public health involves a high degree of commitment to the prevention of disease and injury (Faden and Shebaya 2015, s. 1). In the United States, public health agencies like the Centers for Disease Control and Prevention, the Food and Drug Administration, the Environmental Protection Agency, and the Consumer Protection Agency focus heavily on this preventive task. The primary function of these agencies is to *prevent* disease, food-borne illnesses, environmental destruction, injuries, and the like. A nonretributive approach to criminal justice modeled on public health ethics would similarly focus on prevention. Preventing criminal behavior from occurring in the first place is not only preferable in terms of public safety, it is more consistent with the commitments and beliefs of free will skeptics. Skeptics acknowledge how patently unfair the lottery of life can be – we are not all born with the same set of mental capacities, psychological propensities, economic and educational opportunities, and the like. Instead of focusing on punishing criminals and building more prisons, the public health model would advocate addressing the systemic causes of crime, such as social injustice, poverty, systematic disadvantage, mental health issues, and addiction.

This focus on prevention is one of the key contributions of the public health–quarantine model. Rather than focusing narrowly on justifying the incapacitation of dangerous criminals, the public health model makes prevention a *primary function* of the criminal justice system. Public health ethics not only justifies quarantining carriers of infectious diseases on the grounds that it is necessary to protect public health, it also requires that we take active steps to prevent such outbreaks from occurring. Quarantine, in a sense, is only needed when the public health system fails in its primary function. Since no system is perfect, quarantine will likely be needed for the foreseeable future, but it should *not* be the primary means of dealing with public health. The same would hold true for the use of incapacitation in criminal justice. The public health–quarantine model justifies the incapacitation of dangerous criminals, but the primary focus should always be on preventing crime from occurring in the first place by addressing the systemic causes of crime. Prevention is always preferable to incapacitation.

The third defining feature of public health ethics highlights the fact that achieving good public health results frequently requires government action: "[M]any public health measures are coercive or are otherwise backed by the force of law" (Faden and Shebaya 2015, s. 1). The same holds true for criminal justice. Criminal justice, like public health, is focused on regulation and public policy and relies less often on individual actions and services. Any comprehensive approach to criminal justice therefore needs to address potential conflicts concerning justice, security, and the scope of legal restrictions and regulations. While this problem is not unique to the public health–quarantine model (it is a problem for all theories of punishment), there is good reason to think that the quarantine model is better suited than retributivism for dealing with it. The quarantine model places several important constraints on the treatment of criminals. First, as less dangerous diseases justify only preventative measures less restrictive than quarantine, so less dangerous tendencies justify only more moderate restraints. Secondly, the incapacitation account that results from the quarantine model demands a degree of concern for the rehabilitation and well-being of the criminal that would alter much of current practice. Lastly, if a criminal cannot be rehabilitated, and our safety requires his indefinite confinement, the quarantine model provides no justification for making his life more miserable than would be required to guard against the danger he poses (Pereboom 2014: 156). Retributivism does not include such constraints and in actual practice often leads to excessively punitive systems of punishment and inhumane treatment of prisoners.

Finally, the last defining feature of public health ethics is that it has a forward-looking outcome orientation. As Faden and Shebaya write:

> Promoting public health means seeking to avoid bad health outcomes and advance good ones. As noted at the outset, in some discussions of public health ethics, this outcome-orientation is viewed as the moral justification and foundation of public

health and, as with all consequentialist schemes, is presented as needing to be constrained by attention to deontological concerns such as rights, and by attention to justice-related concerns such as the fair distribution of burdens (Kass 2001; Childress et al. 2002). While public health ethics has to engage with the traditional problems raised by its consequentialist commitments, for those who view social justice as the moral foundation of public health, considerations of justice provide the frame within which the moral implications of public health's consequentialist orientation are addressed. (2015, s. 1)

Since my own public health–quarantine model takes social justice as its foundation, it seeks to restrict the consequentialist orientation of public health ethics by considering the justification of quarantine within a broader social justice framework. Considerations of social justice and fairness regarding groups and individuals are important foundational principles in my public health–quarantine model and need to be kept in mind at all times. I will say more about the importance of social justice to public health and safety in a moment.

Now that we have a better understanding of the scope of public health ethics, it is time that I turn to the principles of traditional health care ethics: autonomy, beneficence, nonmaleficence, and justice. In the remainder of this section, I will provide a justification of quarantine that relies on public health ethics but incorporates (as best as possible) the principles of autonomy, beneficence, nonmaleficence, and justice. Where conflicts arise, as they do with the principle of autonomy, I will provide a method for conflict resolution consistent with public health ethics. The resulting justificatory framework will serve as the foundation for my public health–quarantine model of criminal behavior.

6.1.2 *Autonomy*

The individualist approach to autonomy places primary emphasis on the liberty, privacy, and informed consent of individual persons in the face of a health intervention carried out by other parties. It acknowledges a person's right to make choices, to hold views, and to take actions based on personal values and beliefs. It is the principle of autonomy that precludes running experiments on humans without their informed consent. It is also the principle of autonomy that grants patients the right to refuse or deny medical treatment – for example, the right of cancer patients to refuse chemotherapy or the right of Jehovah's Witnesses to refuse blood transfusions. When it comes to quarantine, however, the principle of autonomy needs to be weighed against the broader public health framework that requires us to consider the well-being and safety of society. The public health framework maintains that the control of infectious diseases necessitates public health interventions that often infringe on the autonomy of individuals. While such infringement is unfortunate it is also sometimes morally justified because such diseases can spread from the infected individual to other people, with the young, the elderly, and the immune-compromised often at highest risk. The broad public health framework therefore justifies quarantine on the grounds that it is needed to prevent harm from occurring to others.

While I accept this public health justification of quarantine, I see the sacrifice of autonomy as regrettable, but sometimes morally justified. Given that free will skepticism rejects the notion that individuals justly deserve to be punished, I believe the justificatory burden is always on those who want to limit one's liberty and autonomy by means of incarceration or incapacitation. In the case of dangerous criminals who pose a continued threat to society, the public health–quarantine model can meet this justificatory burden without appealing to notions of basic desert and retribution. In those cases where the threat of harm to others is very low, however, I maintain that significant weight should be given to the principle of autonomy. This raises an interesting question: How should we go about deciding when autonomy should be preserved and when it should be overridden? It is here that the public health approach appeals to the right of self-defense and the prevention of harm to others.

As Faden and Shebaya note, "[N]o classic philosophical work is cited more often in the public health ethics literature than John Stuart Mill's *On Liberty* (Mill 1869)" (2015, s. 2.4). Mill's famous *harm principle* maintains that the only justification for interfering with the liberty of an individual, against her will, is to prevent harm to others. As Mill states the principle:

> [T]he sole end for which mankind are warranted, individually or collectively, in interfering with the liberty of action of any of their number, is self-protection. That the only purpose for which power can be rightfully exercised over any member of a civilized community, against his will, is to prevent harm to others. He cannot rightfully be compelled to do or forbear because it will be better for him to do so, because it will make him happier, because, in the opinion of others, to do so would be wise, or even right. (1869)

The principle includes two main components: one asserting that self-protection or the prevention of harm to others is sometimes a sufficient warrant for limiting liberty, and the other claiming that the individual's own good is never a sufficient warrant for the exercise of compulsion either by society as a whole or by its individual members.

While the harm principle has been hotly debated, it may nevertheless serve as a useful guide in the domains of public health ethics and criminal justice even if it is not endorsed as a solution to all questions of political liberty. First, the principle helps justify various infectious disease control interventions including quarantine. In fact, "the harm principle is often viewed as the most compelling justification for public health policies that interfere with individual liberty" (Faden and Shebaya 2015, s. 2.4). Infectious diseases put at risk not only the carrier but also the health and well-being of others, hence self-protection and the prevention of harm to others justify quarantine. The same is true for the incapacitation of seriously dangerous criminals who pose a continued risk to society. Second, the harm principle can also be used to carve out a protected space for autonomy. If a cancer patient wishes to refuse life-saving treatment, say chemotherapy, the harm principle dictates that we must respect their wishes. Even if the treatment could save the individual's life, their autonomy should be respected since the decision to forgo treatment is self-regarding and poses no significant harm to others. The same can be said for the Jehovah's Witness who refuses a blood transfusion. According to the harm principle, then, autonomy should be preserved when self-protection and the prevention of harm to others are not at issue.

The harm principle is therefore useful in justifying the use of quarantine/incapacitation in terms of self-protection and prevention of harm to others, while at the same time protecting liberty and autonomy as much as possible. I therefore accept it as a generally good guide. I would, however, like to supplement the harm principle with my own more exact principle, one that I believe captures all the right restrictions on overriding autonomy and individual liberty in the context of public health and criminal justice. I propose the following *conflict resolution principle*, designed to deal with conflicts between public health and safety (on the one hand) and individual liberty and autonomy (on the other). It states:

> **The Conflict Resolution Principle**: When there is a significant threat to public health and safety, individual liberty can be limited but only when it is (a) in accordance with the right of self-defense and the prevention of harm to others, where (b) this right of self-defense is applied to an individual threat and is calibrated to the danger posed by that threat (not some unrelated threat), and (c) it is guided by the principle of least infringement, which holds that the least restrictive measures should be taken to protect public health and safety.

Let me discuss each of these components in turn. The first condition (a) maintains that liberty can be limited in cases of quarantine and incapacitation but only in accordance with the general right of self-defense and defense of others. This is significant because it distinguishes the public health–quarantine model from more general utilitarian and consequentialist approaches to punishment. Rather than appealing to an increase in some aggregate good (e.g., pleasure) or the benefits of general deterrence as a liberty-limiting justification, the conflict resolution principle states that liberty can only be limited in accordance with the right of self-defense and the defense of others. This, I contend, avoids the objections raised in the previous chapter to consequentialist theories – for example, the "use objection" and cases where framing innocent individuals or using harsh and severe punishment would be the most effective way to deter crime.

Take the example of framing an innocent person to prevent a riot. Imagine you are the sheriff in a racially volatile community (McCloskey 1957). For years you have worked to calm racial tensions and have achieved some small level of success. But one day a crime occurs, and it is perceived by the community to be racially motivated. You know that if you do not find someone guilty of the crime quickly, a riot will occur. In your expert opinion, the riot will cause immense pain and suffering for the community, much like the LA riots in 1992. Individuals will be injured, businesses will be destroyed, violent attacks will occur, and the community will suffer long-term economic and psychological damage. You know, however, that you can easily frame an innocent homeless person for the crime. The person was near the scene of the crime and by using footage from local surveillance cameras and, perhaps, some planted evidence, you can easily make your case. We can even add that the individual has no close family or friends, so no one but they will suffer. Despite the fact that the individual is innocent, a consequentialist may have to conclude that the pain and suffering caused by the riot would far outweigh the pain and suffering experienced by the innocent homeless person.

While consequentialists may argue against the practicality of engaging in such practices, claiming that it would erode important protections and produce poorer outcomes in the long run, they must nonetheless allow for the possibility of exceptions. Furthermore, as noted in the previous chapter, this reply remains insensitive to the fundamental unfairness of punishing an innocent person, pointing only to practicality as a reason to avoid it. While some critics worry that the public health–quarantine model would likewise allow for the framing of an innocent person, the conflict resolution principle reveals why this is not the case. Consider the following objection by Hazem Zohny:

> [I]t is unclear that appealing to a right to harm defensively would offer any guarantee against framing individuals … .[S]uppose the failure to frame someone for a crime would lead to massive riots that entail many more innocent deaths. In such extreme cases, the utilitarian sheriff may concede that framing someone is required. But would a sheriff appealing to a right to harm defensively necessarily reach a different conclusion? It is not obvious they would, given a duty to protect others, and given intelligence denoting that a great many will be in serious danger of their lives if no one is framed for the crime, a right to harm someone in order to defend against the eventuality may well be justified on such grounds. That is to say, if the stipulated choice really is between the town being torn by riots with much loss of life, and framing someone, an appeal to defensive harm to avoid such an eventuality may well justify the framing, despite the wronging of the framed individual. (Zohny, personal correspondence)

This objection, however, overlooks several important points. The first and most obvious is that innocent people do not pose a threat to society, and as a result the right of self-defense would not justify incapacitating them. Second, condition (b) of the conflict resolution principle states that the right of self-defense and prevention of harm to others only apply to the danger posed by individualized threats, not general threats. That is, the right of self-defense only applies to the source of an individual threat and must be calibrated to the danger posed by *that* threat, not some unrelated threat. Accordingly, it would be wrong to incapacitate an innocent person because *that* person, being innocent, is not a danger to society nor are they the source of the threat posed by the impending riot. To limit the liberty of an individual because of concerns about the safety of society that emanate from a *different source* would be a violation of the conflict resolution principle and any intuitive understanding of the right of self-defense.

Conditions (a) and (b) are also consistent with the *prohibition on manipulative use principle* discussed in the previous chapter, which maintains that it is generally wrong to use someone merely as a means in order to promote some further independent end – in contrast to harming someone to eliminate a threat they pose based on the right of self-defense. According to Victor Tadros, *eliminative harming* is much easier to justify than *manipulative harming* since the former is based on the right of self-defense, whereas there are a wide range of cases where it is intuitively objectionable to use someone manipulatively (Tadros 2011).[1] The prohibition of manipulative use principle therefore provides an additional explanation of why framing an innocent person is wrong and unjust – it involves using that individual as a means in order to promote some further independent end (see also Shaw 2019). On the other hand, harming someone to eliminate the harm they pose does not involve manipulative use. This is because in cases of self-defense, a person is typically harmed to avert a threat emanating from themselves and not as a means to some independent end. Common examples include using physical force to defend oneself against attack. Such harming is widely perceived to be justified (see Thomson 1986, 1991; Wasserman 1987; Uniaske 1994; Ferzan 2005; Wallerstein 2005, 2009; Leverick 2006; Ferzan and Grabczynska 2009; Frowe 2009).

I contend that this right of self-defense, in accordance with the conflict resolution principle, extends to cases of state action where it is justifiable for the state to restrict the liberty of individuals who pose a serious threat to public health and safety. And the state's right to restrict liberty on the grounds of self-defense and defense of others in no way requires that agents are free and morally responsibility in the basic desert sense. As Ferdinand Schoeman (1979) and Pereboom (2001, 2014) have argued, "[I]f in order to protect society, we have the right to quarantine people who are carriers of severe communicable diseases, then we also have the right to isolate the criminally dangerous to protect society" (Pereboom 2001: 174). This is because in the case of contagious disease

> [i]f the danger to society is great enough, it is acceptable to deprive carriers of their liberty to the degree that the safety of society requires it. This is true irrespective of the carriers' moral responsibility for the disease. If a child is a carrier of the Ebola

---

[1] I should note that while I endorse this distinction, I do not endorse Tadros's use of it in arguing for his instrumentalist, duty-based justification of punishment. For criticisms of Tadros's account, see Nelkin (2019), Uniacke (2015), Lippert-Rasmussen (2015), Ferzan (2013), Bergelson (2013), and Duff (2013).

virus by its being passed on to her at birth from her parent, quarantine is nevertheless intuitively legitimate. (Pereboom 2001: 174)

The same is true for incapacitating the criminally dangerous: They need not be morally responsible in the basic desert sense to justify restricting their liberty. Importantly, though, the state's right to incapacitate on the grounds of self-defense and defense of others does not extend to manipulative harming. As Pereboom notes:

> If our guide is the right of self-defense, what we can legitimately do to a criminal in custody to protect ourselves against him will be determined by the minimum required to protect ourselves against him in his actual situation. If one would want to harm him more severely – say in the interests of providing plausibility for a system of threats – the right of self-defense could not provide the required justification, and one would again be in danger of endorsing a view that is subject to the "use" objection. (Pereboom 2001: 173–174).

Hence, conditions (a) and (b) of the conflict resolution principle do not violate the intuitive prohibition on manipulative use. Yes, they allow for the limiting of individual liberty, which causes harm, but only in cases of eliminative harming.

Condition (c) of the conflict resolution principle simply reiterates that while the right of self-defense and defense of others may justify limiting liberty, such infringements of liberty should be guided by the principle of least infringement, which holds that the least restrictive measures should be taken to protect public health and safety. To successfully implement the public health–quarantine model in the criminal justice system, then, we would need to reevaluate the harms posed by various crimes so as to determine the appropriate reaction. Justice and fairness demand that we undertake this reevaluation so that liberty is limited no more than is absolutely necessary. Condition (c) provides the public health–quarantine model with a kind of proportionality principle of its own. It ensures that the sacrifice of autonomy and liberty will be proportionate to the danger posed by an individual, and any sanctions that exceed this upper bound will be considered unjustified. In the case of "victimless crimes" where no one is harmed save the person engaged in the act, assuming such cases exist, the harm principle would recommend decriminalization. The private use of marijuana may be such a case. But even if it is not, one thing is clear: Many of the low-level crimes we currently incarcerate people for (sometimes for many years) would be judged from the perspective of the public health model as excessively punitive and unjustified.

The upshot of this discussion, then, is that while significant weight should be given to autonomy and protecting individual liberty, such considerations can be outweighed when there is a significant danger to public health and safety but only in accordance with the conflict resolution principle. Of course, determining what counts as a significant threat to public health and safety is not always easy. But with regard to criminal justice, the kinds of threats we are most often concerned with involve physical and bodily harm and threats to life, liberty, and property. I therefore contend that the right of self-defense can justify limiting one's liberty when that individual's actions seriously threaten another's life, liberty, property, or physical well-being. Note that on this conception of harm, finding a particular action offensive does not constitute the kind of liberty-limiting harm at issue. If, for instance, someone was offended by a particular work of art at the Museum of Modern Art, that does not provide grounds for limiting the liberty of the artist to create it or the museum to exhibit it. Likewise, if one were left out of their grandmother's last will and testament, this may cause them some financial harm. But this is not enough to limit the liberty of the grandmother since the individual is not entitled to the money, nor are they harmed with respect to their rights of personal property, autonomy, or physical well-being. Purely self-regarding acts and consensual acts between two adults, such as private sexual acts, would also be outside the scope of the right of self-defense since they do not harm any third parties, hence liberty should be preserved. Lastly, the right of self-defense would provide no grounds for limiting the liberty of individuals based purely on considerations of sexual orientation, religious belief, or freedom of conscience and expression since that would violate the harm principle and the conflict resolution principle.

6.1.3 Beneficence and Nonmaleficence

The principles of beneficence and nonmaleficence are closely related. The principle of beneficence refers to an action done for the benefit of others. The word "beneficence" comes from the Latin for "doing good." Beneficent actions can be taken to help prevent or remove harms or to simply improve the situation of others. The principle of nonmaleficence, on the other hand, means to "do no harm." This means that physicians must refrain from providing ineffective treatments or acting with malice toward patients. Since many treatments involve some degree of harm (e.g., side effects from drugs, chemotherapy, etc.) the principle of nonmaleficence is typically interpreted as implying that the harm should not be disproportionate to the reasonably expected benefits of treatment. The justification for these principles is drawn from the goals and purpose of health care itself. The goal of health care is to help people get and stay healthy. It exists to do people good and not harm. Health care is an essentially beneficent phenomenon. Public health ethics is also a beneficent phenomenon since it aims at promoting public health.

When it comes to the justification of quarantine, the principles of beneficence and nonmaleficence are applied to society as a whole. Quarantine is consistent with the principles of beneficence and nonmaleficence since it seeks to benefit society and prevent harm from occurring. Of course, when beneficence and nonmaleficence are applied to society rather than individuals, conflicts can arise. This is why the restrictions outlined in the previous section are designed to protect individual autonomy to the fullest extent possible consistent with a concern for public health and safety. Additionally, the principles of beneficence and nonmaleficence further add that quarantine is only justified when (a) the benefits to society (protection from infectious disease) are greater than the burdens placed upon those in quarantine; (b) the burdens placed on those in quarantine cause the least harm possible; and (c) those placed in quarantine are provided with adequate care (including treatment).

Furthermore, the treatment of those *in* quarantine and the rehabilitation of those incapacitated should *itself* be guided by the principles of beneficence and nonmaleficence. This is an extremely important point, since it constitutes another significant departure from punitive approaches to criminal behavior. On my model, once one is quarantined or incapacitated, treatment and rehabilitation programs should be guided by the principles of beneficence and nonmaleficence. I will say more about this is Chapter 8 when I discuss various approaches to rehabilitation. For present purposes, it is simply important to note that once we move to the individual level of treatment and rehabilitation – that is, once we have determined that we are justified in quarantining or incapacitating someone for the safety of society – there is no inconsistency in adopting the principles of beneficence and nonmaleficence on my account. In fact, I believe the treatment of those we are attempting to rehabilitate *should* be guided by these principles.

Applying these principles to the criminal justice system would require major reform. Consider, for instance, the use of extended solitary confinement in many supermax prisons. Prisoners are isolated in windowless, soundproof cubicles for 23 to 24 hours each day, sometimes for decades. The cell itself is usually smaller than a typical horse stable, approximately 80 square feet, and furnished with a bed, a sink and toilet, but rarely much else. Food is delivered through a slot in the door, and each day inmates are allowed just one hour of exercise, in a cage. Under such conditions, prisoners experience severe suffering, often resulting in serious psychological problems. Supreme Court Justice Anthony Kennedy recently stated that "solitary confinement literally drives men mad"[2] and the United Nations agrees. In 2011 the United Nations issued a report claiming that long-term solitary isolation is a form of torture – a cruel, inhuman, and degrading treatment prohibited by international law.

The practice of solitary confinement is clearly inconsistent with the principles of beneficence and nonmaleficence and the public health approach more generally. If we were to adopt the public health approach to criminal behavior, the practice would need to be ended immediately. While the public health–quarantine model justifies the incapacitation of dangerous criminals, it does not justify treating them cruelly. The principles of beneficence and nonmaleficence require us to do what we can to rehabilitate criminals and perhaps even provide them with continued support upon release. Of course, strong retributivist intuitions often get in the way of such progress. While most reasonable retributivists, and I know many, acknowledge that

---

[2] He made this statement before the House Appropriations Subcommittee on Financial Services and Federal Government, as reported on in the Huffington Post on March 24, 2015: www.huffingtonpost.com/2015/03/24/anthony-kennedy-solitary-confinement_n_6934550.html.

the United States imprisons far too many people in far too harsh conditions, retributivism nonetheless remains committed to the core belief that criminals *deserve* to be punished and suffer for the harms they have caused. This retributive impulse in actual practice, rather than in pure theory, often leads to practices and policies that try to make life in prison as unpleasant as possible. It was this retributive impulse, for instance, that was recently behind the effort in England and Wales to create a blanket ban on sending books to prisoners, and previous efforts in the United States to cut educational programs and college Pell Grants for offenders.[3] The public health–quarantine model, with its focus on prevention, rehabilitation, and reintegration, would strongly oppose these moves, especially since a 2016 RAND Corporation study found that prison education programs, including both academic and vocational programming, were associated with a 43 percent reduction in recidivism – saving $4 to $5 for each dollar spent.

6.1.4 *Justice*

The last principle of traditional health care ethics deals with justice. In this context, the principle of justice demands that we treat others equitably and distribute benefits and burdens fairly. It is the principle of justice that requires scarce medical resources be distributed fairly and consistently. Organ transplantation is a good example since there is more demand for organs than there is supply. In deciding who should receive a heart or live transplant first, the principle of justice demands that we treat all parties fairly, consistently, and non-prejudicially. Whatever procedural method we agree on, it must be applied consistently across all cases and not discriminate between potential recipients in an unjust manner.

When applied to quarantine, the principle of justice means that decisions for the application of quarantine be made using a fair process and include a publicly available rationale for those decisions, a mechanism for dispute resolution, and a regulatory body to enforce decisions (Baum, Gollust, and Jacobson 2007). In addition, officials need to exhibit transparency regarding the goals to be accomplished and whether the benefits and burdens of their decisions are expected to be distributed equally throughout the community. Where inequality exists, there must be a rationale and justification for that disparity (Baum, Gollust, and Jacobson 2007). The principle of justice is therefore extremely important to the proper justification and application of quarantine. Its importance to public health ethics, however, goes far beyond this.

---

[3] Although there has been some improvement in prison education programs in recent years, in 2016 the Vera Institute of Justice reported that only 35 percent of state prisons provided college-level courses, and these programs only serve 6 percent of incarcerated individuals nationwide. Report available at: https://storage.googleapis.com/vera-web-assets/downloads/Publications/making-the-grade-postsecondary-education-programs-in-prison/legacy_downloads/making-the-grade-postsecondary-education-programs-in-prison.pdf.

In the version of public health ethics I defend, social justice is a foundational cornerstone. And even for those who do not share this foundational commitment, there is wide agreement that social justice is important:

> Whether social justice is viewed as a side constraint on the beneficence-based foundation of public health, or as foundational in its own right, there is broad agreement that a commitment to improving the health of those who are systematically disadvantaged is as constitutive of public health as is the commitment to promote health generally (Kass 2001; Thomas, Sage, Dillenberg & Guillory 2002; Institute of Medicine (USA) 2003; Powers & Faden 2006; Nuffield Council on Bioethics 2007; Venkatapuram 2011; Gostin 2012). (Faden and Shebaya 2015, s. 3)

In public health ethics, a failure on the part of public health institutions to ensure the social conditions necessary to achieve a sufficient level of health is considered a grave injustice. For many in the public health sector, "the extraordinary disparities in life expectancy, child survival and health that distinguish those living in rich and poor countries constitute a profound injustice that is the duty of the global community to redress" (Faden and Shebaya 2015, s. 3). An important task of public health ethics, then, is to identify which inequalities in health are the most egregious and thus which should be given the highest priority in public health policy and practice.

The public health approach to criminal behavior likewise maintains that a core moral function of the criminal justice system is to identify and remedy social and economic inequalities responsible for crime. Just as public health is negatively affected by poverty, racism, and systematic inequality, so too is public safety. Faden and Shebaya eloquently describe how health can be affected in this way:

> When inequalities in health exist between socially dominant and socially disadvantaged groups, they are all the more important because they occur in conjunction with other disparities in well-being and compound them (Powers & Faden 2006; Wolff & de-Shalit 2007). Reducing such inequalities are specific priorities in the public health goals of national and international institutions ... Whether through processes of oppression, domination, or subordination, patterns of systemic disadvantage associated with group membership are invidious and profoundly unjust. They affect every dimension of well-being, including health. In many contexts, poverty co-travels with the systematic disadvantage associated with racism, sexism, and other forms of denigrated group membership. However, even when it does not, the dramatic differential in material resources, social influence and social status that is the hallmark of severe poverty brings with it systematic patterns of disadvantage that can be as difficult to escape as those experienced by the most oppressed minority groups. Even when these patterns are lessened, the life prospects of persons living in severe poverty or in dominated groups often continue to be far below that of others. A critical moral function of public health is to vigilantly monitor the health of systematically disadvantaged groups and intervene to reduce the inequalities so identified as aggressively as possible. (2015, s. 3)

The broad approach to criminal justice provided by the public health–quarantine model therefore places issues of social justice at the forefront. It sees racism, sexism, poverty, and systematic disadvantage as serious threats to public safety and it prioritizes the reduction of such inequalities.

By placing social justice at the foundation of my public health approach, the realms of criminal justice and social justice are brought closer together. I see this as a virtue of the theory since it is a mistake to hold that the criteria of individual accountability can be settled apart from considerations of social justice. As Erin Kelly correctly notes: "It is not clear ... that we should think of criminal justice in retributive terms. I believe our understanding of criminal justice is ethically distorted when we understand criminal justice apart from the framework of premises and principles that comprise a conception of distributive [or social] justice and its associated notion of collective responsibility" (2012: 66). Making social justice foundational, as my account does, places on us a collective responsibility, which is forward-looking and perfectly consistent with free will skepticism, to redress unjust inequalities and to advance collective aims and priorities such as public health and safety. This means that "criminal justice cannot be individualist in the way proponents of the retributive view suppose" (Kelly 2012: 66).

While some critics have argued that free will skeptics are not entitled to such appeals to social justice, since talk of justice presupposes deontological and/or desert-based claims that we are not entitled to (e.g., Smilansky 2019), I have never quite understood this charge. Unless one were to think that *all* theories of justice had to be *desertist* (i.e., grounded in desert), there is no reason to think this claim has any merit. Yes, there are desertist theories of justice that hold that justice is fundamentally a matter of receipt in accord with desert. The idea seems to be present, for example, in certain passages in Aristotle, Leibniz, Mill, Sidgwick, and Ross (see Feldman and Skow 2015). There are, however, several prominent theories of justice that are not desertist, including the well-known theory of John Rawls (1971). In A *Theory of Justice*, Rawls stresses the fact that inequalities of birth are types of underserved discrimination and claims that desert does not apply to one's place in the distribution of native endowments, one's initial starting point in society, the familial or social circumstances into which one is born, or to the superior character that enables one to put forth the effort to develop one's abilities. Rawls' theory therefore suggests a *metaphysical argument* against desert, according to which "since most of who we are and what we do is greatly influenced by underserved native endowments and by the undeserved circumstances into which we are born, one cannot deserve anything, or, at best, one can deserve very little" (Celello 2014). For Rawls, desert should not have any role in distributive justice, since these underserved factors have a major influence on all would-be desert bases (Sher 1987: 22ff; cf. Moriarty 2002: 136–137).

Another philosopher who proposes a non-desertist theory of justice is David Hume (1983). And as Peter Celello explains, Hume's insights can be used to develop *epistemological* and *pragmatic arguments* against desert:

> Hume argued that since humans are both fallible in their knowledge of the factors that would establish others' merit and prone to overestimating their own merit, distributive schemes based on merit could not result in determinate rules of conduct and would be utterly destructive to society (Hume [1983], 27). This thinking is captured in the epistemological and pragmatic argument against desert. According to the epistemological argument, since we cannot know the specific details of the lives of every member in a community or society, we cannot accurately treat people according to their desert ... The pragmatic argument against desert is that, regardless of whether we could gain the knowledge needed to treat people according to their desert accurately, attempting to do so would have overriding negative consequences. Such negative consequences could include expending large amounts of time and resources in an effort to make accurate desert judgments and, perhaps, losses of personal privacy as one delves into the details of others' lives. Both the epistemological and pragmatic arguments must be accounted for when attempting to explain how a true meritocracy could and should be arranged. (2014)

These metaphysical, epistemic, and pragmatic considerations count strongly against desertist theories of justice. And Rawls's theory of justice, which he calls *justice as fairness*, provides one potential non-desertist approach to social and distributive justice.

On the other end of the political spectrum, political libertarian accounts of justice also tend to be non-desertist. For the political libertarian, the primary goal of justice is the protection of negative liberty – that is, the absence of constraints on an individual's actions. In *Anarchy, State, and Utopia* (1974), Robert Nozick advances one of the best-known libertarian accounts of justice – his entitlement theory of justice. On this view, a just distribution is one where each person is entitled to the holdings that he/she possesses according to the principles of justice in acquisition, transfer, and rectification. Nozick describes his entitlement theory as "historical," because it determines the justice of holdings on the basis of how those holdings came to be held, and "unpatterned," because the justice of holdings is not determined on the basis of some additional normative criteria, such as merit, need, or effort (1974: 155ff). But as Celello explains:

> Because meritocracies are patterned, Nozick would reject them. Right-libertarians [like Nozick] would be concerned with liberty-restricting attempts at distributing or redistributing resources according to prevailing conceptions of merit or desert. Therefore, the concept of desert does not have a major role in their theories of justice. (2014)

Of course, political libertarians need not reject the concept of desert entirely. Nozick, for example, offers various arguments against Rawls's rejection of desert

(1974: 215ff). Nevertheless, for the right-leaning political libertarian, "desert could be a concept for the individual to consider in his personal decision-making processes, but not one that the state should use to try to guide allocations or distributions of resources" (Celello 2014).

As long as we understand social justice in terms of a non-desertist theory, there is no reason free will skeptics cannot appeal to the notion of justice and all that it entails. But rather than simply point out that these non-desertist options exist, I will now endorse a particular theory of social justice and explain how it is consistent with free will skepticism. Of course, the public health–quarantine model is not dependent on the particular theory I favor, since other non-desertist options may be compatible as well, but I believe the two theories work nicely together and the theory of social justice sketched in the following section provides a solid foundation for public health ethics generally.

6.2 A CAPABILITIES APPROACH TO SOCIAL JUSTICE

While there are different ways of understanding social justice and different philosophical accounts of what a non-desertist theory of justice aims to achieve, I favor a *capabilities approach* according to which the development of capabilities – what each individual is able to do or be – is essential to human well-being.[4] For capability theorists, human well-being is the proper end of a theory of justice. And on the particular capability approach I favor, social justice is grounded in six key features of human well-being: *health, reasoning, self-determination* (or *autonomy*), *attachment, personal security*, and *respect*. This list is drawn from the work of Powers and Faden (2006) who specifically developed their capabilities account of social justice to serve as the moral foundations of public health and health policy. While I am not dogmatically attached to this list and would consider revisions and additions – Martha Nussbaum, for instance, offers an alternative list(s) (cf. 1988, 2000, 2011) – I do think each of these six dimensions is an essential feature of well-being such that "a life substantially lacking in any one is a life seriously deficient in what it is reasonable for anyone to want, whatever else they want" (Powers and Faden 2006: 8). On this account, then, the job of justice is to achieve a sufficiency of these six essential dimensions of human well-being, since each is a separate indicator of a decent life.

The key idea of capability approaches is that social arrangements should aim to expand people's capabilities – their freedom to promote or achieve *functionings* that are important to them. *Functionings* are defined as the valuable activities and states that make up human well-being, such as having a healthy body, being safe, or having a job. While they are related to goods and income, they are instead described in

---

[4] See, for instance, Sen (1980, 1984, 1985, 1999), Nussbaum (1988, 2003, 2011), Anderson (1999), Power and Faden (2006), Robeyns (2017).

terms of what a person is able to do or be as a result. For example, when a person's need for food (a commodity) is met, they enjoy the functioning of being well nourished. Examples of functionings include being mobile, being healthy, being adequately nourished, and being educated. The genuine opportunity to achieve a particular functioning is called a *capability*. Capabilities are "the alternative combination of functionings that are feasible for [a person] to achieve" – they are "the substantive freedom" a person has "to lead the kind of life he or she has reason to value" (Sen 1999: 87).

As Tabandeh, Gardoni, and Murphy describe:

> Genuine opportunities and actual achievements are influenced by what individuals have and what they can do with what they have. What they can do with what they have is a function of the structure of social, legal, economic, and political institutions and of the characteristics of the built-environment (i.e., infrastructure). For example, consider the functioning of being mobile. The number of times an individual travels per week can be an indicator of mobility achievement. When explaining a given individual's achievement or lack of achievement, a capability approach takes into consideration the conditions that must be in place for an individual to be mobile. For instance, the possession of certain resources, like a bike, may influence mobility. However, possessing a bike may not be sufficient to guarantee mobility. If the individual has physical disabilities, then the bike will be of no help to travel. Similarly, if there are no paved roads or if societal culture imposes a norm that women are not allowed to ride a bike, then it will become difficult or even impossible to travel by means of a bike. As this example makes clear, different factors will influence the number of times the individual travels. (Tabandeh, Gardoni, and Murphy 2017)

Thinking in terms of capabilities raises a wider range of issues than simply looking at the amount of resources or commodities people have, because people have different needs. In the example just given, just providing bicycles to people will not be enough to increase the functioning of being mobile if you are disabled or prohibited from riding because of sexist social norms. A capabilities approach to social justice therefore requires that we consider and address a larger set of social issues.

Martha Nussbaum does a nice job summarizing the core features of the capabilities approach in her book *Creating Capabilities*:

> The Capabilities Approach can be provisionally defined as an approach to comparative quality-of-life assessments and to theorizing about basic social justice. It holds that the key question to ask, when comparing societies and assessing them for their basic decency or justice, is, "What is each person able to do and to be?" In other words, the approach takes *each person as an end*, asking not just about the total or average well-being but about the opportunities available to each person. It is *focused on choice or freedom*, holding that the crucial good societies should be promoting for their people is a set of opportunities, or substantial freedoms, which people then may, or may not exercise in action: [T]he choice is theirs. It thus

commits itself to respect for people's powers of self-definition. The approach is resolutely *pluralist about values*: [I]t holds that the capability achievements that are central for people are different in quality, not just in quantity; that they cannot without distortion be reduced to a single numerical scale; and that a fundamental part of understanding and producing them is understanding the specific nature of each. Finally, the approach is *concerned with entrenched social injustice and inequality*, especially capability failures that are the result of discrimination or marginalization. It ascribes an urgent *task to government and public policy* – namely, to improve the quality of life for all people, as defined by their capabilities. (2011: 18–19)

Although Nussbaum refers to "substantial freedoms" (2011: 18) and Sen to "substantive freedom" (1999: 87) in defining capabilities, the set of (usually interrelated) opportunities to choose and to act, these notions are perfectly consistent with free will skepticism and the rejection of basic desert moral responsibility. As Nussbaum explains, capabilities "are not just abilities residing inside a person but also the freedoms or opportunities created by a combination of personal abilities and the political, social, and economic environment" (Nussbaum 2011: 20). Nussbaum refers to these "substantial freedoms" as *combined capabilities* (2011: 21). And since combined capabilities do not assume agents are morally responsible in the basic desert sense for either their personal abilities or the political, social, and economic environment, there is no reason to think free will is required for the exercise of combined capabilities.

Combined capabilities are defined as internal capabilities plus the social, political, and economic conditions in which functioning can actually be chosen (Nussbaum 2011: 22). According to Nussbaum:

> Of course the characteristics of a person (personal traits, intellectual and emotional capacities, states of bodily fitness and health, internalized learning, skills of perception and movement) are highly relevant to his or her "combined capabilities," but it is useful to distinguish them from combined capabilities, of which they are but a part. I call these states of the person (not fixed, but fluid and dynamic) *internal capabilities*. They are to be distinguished from innate equipment: they are trained or developed traits and abilities, developed, in most cases, in interaction with the social, economic, familial, and political environment. (2011: 21)

The innate powers we are born with, on the other hand, Nussbaum labels *basic capabilities* (2011: 23). These can be nurtured or neglected and are "the innate faculties of the person that makes later development and training possible" (2011: 24). Of course, individuals are not morally responsible in the basic desert sense for basic capabilities. But neither must they be morally responsible in this way for internal capabilities. Internal capabilities are simply attributability characteristics of a person that work in combination with external social, political, and economic conditions. While they may be developed, to greater or lesser extent, they are subject to the same kind of luck and hard-incompatibilist arguments presented in Chapter 2. Since free will skepticism can and should acknowledge the importance of internal capabilities to what each individual is able to do or be, even if people are not morally responsible for them in the basic desert sense, it is consistent with the capabilities approach and the relevant notion of freedom.

When Sen and Nussbaum, the two chief architects of the capabilities approach, talk about capabilities as freedoms, what they have in mind is *opportunity freedoms* (see Robeyns 2017: 102–105). In his *Dewey Lectures*, Sen defends a conceptualization of well-being freedom in terms of capabilities and defines well-being freedom as "whether one person did have the opportunity of achieving the functioning vector that another actually achieved. This involves comparisons of actual opportunities that different persons have" (1985: 201). Similarly, in *Inequality Reexamined*, Sen writes:

> A person's position in a social arrangement can be judged in two different perspectives, viz. (1) the actual achievement, and (2) the freedom to achieve. Achievement is concerned with what we *manage* to accomplish, and freedom with the *real opportunity* that we have to accomplish what we value. (1992: 31)

Nussbaum also defines freedoms in terms of opportunities: "[T]he crucial good societies should be promoting for their people is a set of opportunities, or substantial freedoms, which people then may, or may not exercise in action" (2011: 18–19). Given Sen's and Nussbaum's descriptions of the freedoms that the capability approach is concerned with in terms of opportunities, we can say that the nature of capabilities is best captured by the concept of *opportunity freedom* or *option freedom* – that is, "[w]hat counts in the capability approach is indeed the access that a person has to a wide range of valuable alternative options" (Robeyns 2017: 105).

Opportunity freedoms are the alternatives that an agent is in a position to realize. They include *negative* freedom (Berlin 1969), or freedom from external constraints and obstacles, but they go beyond this. Appealing to the work of Philip Pettit (2003: 394–395), Robeyns describes this wider notion of opportunity or option freedom as follows:

> Pettit argues that option freedom is a function of two aspects: the character of access to options, and the character of options themselves. First, option freedom is a function of the character of the agent's *access* to the options. Some philosophers would hold that the physical possibility of carrying out an option is sufficient for access, and this would conclude that the agent has option freedom. Alternatively, one could defend the position that access to an option does not only depend on the physical possibility of carrying out the option, but that non-physical barriers are relevant too. Pettit distinguishes two possibilities: either an agent is objectively more burdened than another agent when trying to access an option, whether by difficulty or by penalty, or an agent is subjectively burdened in the sense that he believes that access to an option is not possible. The second aspect of option freedom is the

character of the options. Here a wide range of views exist, such as the number of options that are accessible, their diversity, and whether they are objectively significant or subjectively significant (Pettit 2003: 389–392). (Robeyns 2017: 105)

We can say that capabilities are precisely this kind of opportunity freedom. Robeyns provides an excellent example of this wider understanding of opportunity freedom, which highlights how it goes beyond mere negative freedom and the absence of external or physical barriers:

> If, in a patriarchal community, men have all the power, and in a verbally aggressive manner they teach girls and remind women that their place is inside the house, then surely these women do not have the same opportunity freedom to find employment in the nearest city where women from more liberal communities are holding jobs. In formal terms, the women from both communities may be able to work outside the home since there are jobs available to women in the city, they are able-bodied and are able to commute to the city. Yet women from the patriarchal community would face much bigger costs and would need to gather much more courage, and resist the subtle working of social norms, before they could effectively access this formal opportunity. Put in capability terms, we would say that the first group of women has a much smaller capability to work outside the home than the women living in less patriarchal communities. If the costs and burdens borne by the women from strongly patriarchal communities are excessive, we could even conclude that the capability to work in the city is virtually nonexistent. (2017: 104)

To avoid confusion, we can call this understanding of opportunity freedom *social freedom*, so as to distinguish it from the metaphysical conception of freedom that is associated with free will and basic desert moral responsibility. Free will skepticism only rejects the latter. It can easily accommodate the former since social freedoms are about the set of opportunities an individual can realize given their combined capabilities, which has nothing to do with basic desert moral responsibility.

According to the capabilities approach, then, when asking normative questions, we should ask what people are able to do and what lives they are able to lead. The approach is concerned with aspects of people's lives such as their health, the education they enjoy, the support they receive from their social networks, and much more. In the example given earlier, the capabilities approach requires that we not only support the development of internal capabilities for the women in the patriarchal community – through "education, resources to enhance physical and emotional health, support for family care and love," etc. (Nussbaum 2011: 21) – but that we also redress the wider social, political, and economic conditions that negatively affect their opportunities. As Nussbaum notes, "A society might do quite well at producing internal capabilities but might cut off the avenues through which people actually have the opportunity to function in accordance with those capabilities" (2011: 21). For instance, "[m]any societies educate people so that they are capable of free speech on political matters – internally – but then deny them free expression in practice through repression of speech" (2011: 21). Since combined capabilities are defined as internal capabilities plus the social/political/economic conditions in which functioning can actually be chosen (Nussbaum 2011: 22), the capabilities approach requires societies to address a wide set of issues to help expand people's opportunities to promote or achieve functionings that are essential for well-being.

Over time, at least two general applications of the capabilities approach have emerged: one more practical and empirical, the other theoretical. These two different applications can partially be traced in the divergent directions Sen and Nussbaum have developed the approach. Sen's primary concern has been to identify capabilities as the most pertinent space of empirical comparison for the purposes of quality-of-life assessment, thus changing the direction of the development debate. Largely due to the work of Sen, the capabilities approach is now applied and developed in a wide range of empirical fields, including global public health, human development, environmental protection, ecological sustainability, education, technological design, welfare state policies, and many, many more (see Robeyns 2017). As Nussbaum describes:

> [Sen's] version of the approach does not propose a definite account of basic justice, although it is a normative theory and does have a clear concern with issues of justice (focusing, for example, on instances of capability failure that result from gender or racial discrimination). In consequence, Sen does not employ a threshold or a specific list of capabilities, although it is clear that he thinks some capabilities (for example, health and education) have a particular centrality. Nor does he make central theoretical use of the concept of *human dignity*, though he certainly acknowledges its importance. (2011: 19–20)

On the more theoretical application, Nussbaum and others have put the capabilities approach to work in constructing a theory of basic social justice.[5] As a theory of fundamental political entitlements, Nussbaum's version of the approach employs a specific list of the *central capabilities* (see 2011:chapter 2). It also gives a central theoretical role to the concept of human dignity.

While I think both of these applications are important and the capabilities approach provides a relatively unified approach to a set of normative questions about both quality of life assessments and basic justice, I follow Nussbaum in using the capabilities approach to construct a basic theory of social justice. My own account, however, resembles Nussbaum's in some respects and differs in others. For instance, while Nussbaum offers a list of ten central capabilities (2011: chapter 2), my list consists of just six: *health, reasoning, self-determination* (or *autonomy*), *attachment, personal security,* and *respect.* I will discuss each of these in a moment, but on my theory the central job of justice is to achieve a sufficiency of

---

[5] See Nussbaum (1992, 1997, 2000, 2003, 2006, 2011), Anderson (1999), Powers and Faden (2006), Claasen (2016), Robeyns (2017).

(at least) these six essential dimensions of human well-being, since each is a separate indicator of a decent life – that is, "a life substantially lacking in any one is a life seriously deficient in what it is reasonable for anyone to want, whatever else they want" (Powers and Faden 2006: 8). Another difference is that I view the capabilities approach to social justice as providing the moral foundation for public health ethics generally. That is, rather than view public health ethics as grounded in the purely utilitarian injunction to maximize welfare and balance individual liberties against the advancement of good health outcomes, I conceive of it as grounded in a notion of social justice understood in terms of the capabilities approach. Understanding the moral foundation of public health ethics in this way further constrains its outcome orientation by giving pride of place to the notion of human dignity and the six central capacities listed earlier and discussed later in this chapter.

Despite these differences, though, Nussbaum and I both agree that it is the job of justice to promote the most important human capabilities and address the social, political, and economic conditions that prohibit their exercise, "especially capability failures that are the result of discrimination or marginalization" (2011: 19). I further agree with Nussbaum that well-being is best understood as involving plural, irreducible dimensions, each of which represents something of independent moral significance (Power and Faden 2006: 6). Finally, I agree that the capabilities approach, as well as the public health–quarantine model, "ascribes an urgent *task to government and public policy* – namely, to improve the quality of life for all people, as defined by their capabilities" (2011: 18–19).

Grounding public health in such a capabilities conception of social justice makes a number of things clear. As Powers and Faden explain:

> The positive point of justice for public health is to secure a sufficiency of the dimension of health for everyone. The negative point of justice, which in our view requires a commitment to policing patterns of systematic disadvantage that profoundly and pervasively undermine prospects for well-being, shines the spotlight of moral urgency on the health needs of oppressed and subordinate groups, on people whose prospects for well-being, including for health, are so limited that their life choices are not even remotely like those of others, and on children, whose prospects for well-being, not only in childhood but throughout life, are at risk because of the locking in of systemic constraints at an early age. (Power and Faden 2006: 9)

This view of both the negative and positive aims of justice nicely captures, I believe, the twin moral impulses that animate public health: "to improve human well-being by improving health and related dimensions of well-being and to do so in particular by focusing on the needs of those who are the most disadvantaged" (Power and Faden 2006: 10). My public health–quarantine model simply expands the application of the public health framework, and with it considerations of social justice, to the promotion of public safety and the prevention of criminal behavior. The public health–quarantine model recognizes that just as there are multiple causes of ill and good health, there are multiple causes of criminal behavior. Furthermore, it recognizes that health and safety are themselves sometimes a causal factor with regard to other important human goods. Lastly, it maintains that a holistic approach to criminal behavior, just like poor health outcomes, requires society to address various issues of social justice, especially capability failures that are the result of discrimination or marginalization.

We can say, then, that my public health–quarantine model adopts an approach to public health grounded in social justice, understood in terms of capabilities and those dimensions of well-being that "are of special moral urgency because they matter centrally to everyone, whatever the particular life plans and aims of each has" (Powers and Faben 2006: 15). While it is not my goal to defend an exhaustive, mutually exclusive list of these discrete elements of well-being, my account (following Powers and Faden 2006) is built around six distinct dimensions of well-being, each of which merits separate attention within a theory of justice. I will now discuss each in turn.

6.2.1 Health

On the theory I endorse, one central task of justice is to secure a sufficient level of health for each individual, insofar as possible, where health reflects a moral concern with the rich and diverse set of considerations characteristic of public health and clinical medicine, including premature mortality and preventable morbidity, malnutrition, pain, loss of mobility, mental health, the biological basis of behavior, reproduction, and sexual functioning (Powers and Faben 2006: 17). It is important to note that this definition of health is rather broad and consumes multiple dimensions of Nussbaum's list of central capabilities. That is, while it includes what Nussbaum calls *bodily health* – that is, "[b]eing able to have good health, including reproductive health; to be adequately nourished; to have adequate shelter" (2011: 33) – it goes beyond this. It also includes what Nussbaum calls *life* – "Being able to live to the end of a human life of normal length; not dying prematurely, or before one's life is so reduced as to be not worth living" (2011: 33) – as well as aspects of what she calls *play*. Following Powers and Faben, we can say that

> [w]hile health is a state or condition that in many respects can be described in organic or functional terms, it is important ... to note that the absence of health refers to more than biological malfunctioning or impairments to some functional ability such as mobility, sight, or hearing. Being in pain, even if that pain does not impede proper biological function, is also incompatible with health. So, too, are sexual dysfunction and infertility. (Powers and Faben 2006: 17)

All of these matter crucially in sustaining a human existence across the whole life span. Moreover, health is of independent (although not exclusive) moral concern when threatened by war, violence, environmental hazards, consumer products, and natural disasters, "all of which have been claimed, to one degree or another, as public health problems as well" (Powers and Faben 2006: 17).

Given that health, thus understood, matters centrally to everyone, whatever a person's particular life plans and personal commitments, it is an essential dimension of my capabilities theory of social justice and an important moral foundation for public health and health policy generally. Importantly, though:

> Although health as a dimension of well-being is offered as the primary moral foundation for public health and health policy, there is no reason to suppose that every policy decision that bears on public health and medical care rests on the single moral foundation of health any more than any other intellectual discipline, profession, or social institution necessarily rests on a single moral foundation. For example, policies against female genital mutilation rest on concerns for health, the physical and psychological inviolability encompassed by the dimension we label as personal security, and self-determination. In this case, the moral foundation in justice for the policies draws upon three dimensions of well-being, none of which is reducible to the others. Each signals a separate kind of injustice produced through the mutilation. (Powers and Faben 2006: 17)

So, while health comprises an important moral foundation for public health ethics, it is not the only component that matters since other dimensions of social justice may also be relevant to public health and health policy. Free will skeptics, I contend, can appeal to these various aspects of social justice since they in no way depend upon the control in action required for basic desert moral responsibility. This should be clear with health, but some of the other dimensions of well-being discussed in the following sections may require a bit more explanation.

6.2.2 *Reasoning*

Like health, the capability of reasoning is centrally important to a diverse array of functionings essential for well-being. Reasoning, we can say, refers to a broad set of diverse skills and abilities, including those classified within philosophical discussions since Aristotle under the headings of practical and theoretical reason. It also includes what the psychological literature has subsumed under the label cognitive reasoning – that is, a "combination of skills, including attention, learning, memory, praxis (skill motor behaviors), and so-called executive function, such as decision making, goal setting, and judgment" (Whitehouse et al. 1997). While the nature and degree of reasoning skills and abilities needed for well-being varies in historical and situational contexts, humans need some level of ability to reason deductively and inductively (Powers and Faden 2006: 20). They also need the ability to "make logical connections and detect logical errors; to communicate effectively with others in a culture; and to make causal inferences" (Powers and Faden 2006: 20). Without these capabilities, whatever other dimensions of well-being we may have, we lack something crucial to our ability to function.

The abilities we associate with practical reason, for instance, include the ability to form and revise a conception of how we each wish to live, to conform behavior to ideals and ends that are part of that conception, and to deliberate among alternative means to achievement of those ends (Powers and Faden 2006: 20). Given its importance, Nussbaum places practical reasoning on her list of ten central capabilities and defines it as "[b]eing able to form a conception of the good and to engage in critical reflection about the planning of one's life" (2011: 54). Practical reasoning, however, is valuable for more than just the development of individual life plans or settling one's own personal goals or ends: "It is necessary for the very possibility of other-regarding morality" (Powers and Faden 2006: 20). That is, in order to function as a member of a moral community, "we need to be able to deliberate with others about the reasonableness of our actions and choices and to reflect on those actions and choices from the perspectives of others affected by them" (Powers and Faden 2006: 20).

While reasoning clearly captures a morally salient aspect of human flourishing, one may wonder whether it is consistent with free will skepticism. I contend that it is. To see why, I will focus on the issue of *rational deliberation* for a moment, since it is here that the debate is often engaged. *Deliberation* is a process or activity in which one figures out what to do. As Richard Taylor (1966: 168) notes, deliberation has "as its aim or goal a decision to act," as opposed to the goal of merely forming a *belief* about which action one will perform. And as Yishai Cohen writes, "Unlike the epistemic activity of inferring or predicting what will occur, deliberation is an activity or process that is intended to play an explanatory role with respect to what one ends up doing" (Cohen 2018: 86). For the sake of clarity, we can adopt the following definition of deliberation offered by Derk Pereboom:

> (D) S deliberates just in case S is engaged in an active mental process whose aim is to figure out what to do from among a number of distinct, i.e., mutually incompatible, alternatives, a process understood as one that can (but need not) include the weighing and evaluating of reasons for the options for what to do. (2014: 110)

Rational deliberation, as distinct from deliberation simpliciter, requires that in addition to (D) the beliefs salient to an agent's deliberation be consistent. That is, in order to rationally deliberate about whether to do A1 or A2, where A1 and A2 are distinct actions, an agent must not have any inconsistent beliefs that are salient to her deliberation about whether to do A1 or A2 (Cohen 2018: 86). This means that I cannot rationally deliberate about whether I should walk home from campus today or use my powers of flight and fly, while also believing that I am human and humans are incapable of flight.

We can now ask: Is free will skepticism compatible with rational deliberation? First, note that the belief that we lack moral responsibility in the basic desert sense does not by itself conflict with the conception of ourselves as rational, deliberative agents: "[S]uch a belief about basic desert is unrelated to the general presuppositions of rational deliberation" (Pereboom 2014: 104). That said, rational deliberation may conflict with conditions free will skeptics are open to accepting – that is, the causal determination of all of our actions by factors beyond our control. Recall that my hard incompatibilism is neutral regarding the truth of determinism but it is open to its being true. It maintains that causal determinism, if true, is one way the control in action, that is, the free will, required for basic desert moral responsibility is ruled out. Some philosophers contend that in addition to the usual threats causal determinism poses to free will and basic desert moral responsibility, *belief* in the truth of causal determinism also poses a threat to rational deliberation (see, e.g., Taylor 1966; Ginet 1966; Kant 1795/1981; Haji 2012). Those who find this threat illusory are deliberation-compatibilists:

Deliberation-Compatibilism: S's deliberating and being rational is compatible with S's believing that their actions are causally determined by antecedent conditions beyond their control.

Their opponents are deliberation-incompatibilists:

Deliberation-Incompatibilism: S's deliberating and being rational is incompatible with S's believing that their actions are causally determined by antecedent conditions beyond their control.

I will now briefly defend deliberation-compatibilism and argue that a coherent account of rational deliberation can be made consistent with belief in causal determinism.[6]

One of the main concerns deliberation-incompatibilists have with determinism is that it appears to rule out the kind of *openness* of options required for rational deliberation. When we deliberate, we typically believe that we have more than one distinct option available to us for which action to perform, each of which is available to us in the sense that we "can" or "could" perform each of these actions. It is often argued that belief in such openness is required for deliberation or at least for rational deliberation. For example, Peter van Inwagen writes, "[I]f someone deliberates about whether to do A or to do B, it follows that his behavior manifests a belief that it is *possible* for him to do A – that he *can* do A, that he has it within his power to do A – and a belief that it is possible for him to do B" (van Inwagen 1983: 155; cf. Kant 1795/1981, AK IV 448; Taylor 1966: chapter 12; Ginet 1966; Stapleton 2010). Some philosophers maintain that belief in this kind of openness conflicts with the truth of determinism in the sense that, in any deliberative situation, the truth of determinism would rule out the availability to us of all but one distinct option for what to do, and thus would rule out the

---

[6] For more detailed arguments, see, e.g., Pereboom (2014), Kapitan (1986), Pettit (1989), Nelkin (2004, 2011), Jeppsson (2016).

openness about what to do. Accordingly, this line of reasoning supports a kind of deliberation-incompatibilism (see, e.g., Ginet 1966; Taylor 1966), which maintains that S's deliberating and being rational is incompatible with S's believing that their actions are causally determined.

But does determinism conflict with the kind of openness required for rational deliberation? Most deliberation-compatibilists acknowledge that deliberation requires a kind of openness, but rather than interpret it metaphysically they provide an epistemic interpretation of "can" or "could." As Pereboom explains:

> It does seem plausible that when we deliberate about what to do, we typically presuppose that we have more than one distinct option for which action to perform, each of which is available to us in the sense that we can or could perform each of these actions. But the sense of "can" or "could" featured in such beliefs might not always or even typically be metaphysical. It might well be that in some such cases, it is epistemic, and in many others it is indeterminate between a metaphysical and epistemic sense. On certain epistemic interpretations, such beliefs would not conflict with a belief in determinism. When I am deliberating whether to do A, supposing I correctly believe determinism is true, I would not know whether I will in fact do A since I lack the knowledge of the antecedent conditions and laws that would be required to make the prediction based on these factors, not to mention the time and wherewithal. So even if I believe that it is causally determined that I will not do A, I might without inconsistency believe that it is in a sense epistemically possible that I do A, and that I could do A in this epistemic sense. (2014: 107)

Epistemic accounts of this kind have been developed by a number of deliberation-compatibilists – including Dennett (1984), Kapitan (1986), Pettit (1989), Nelkin (2004, 2011), and Pereboom (2014). The account I prefer maintains that the beliefs about the possibility of acting salient for deliberation are in some key respects epistemic but that there are *two* key compatibilist epistemic states. One of these specifies an epistemic notion of openness for what to do, and the other is an epistemic condition on the efficacy of deliberation (see, e.g., Kapitan 1986; Pereboom 2014). In what follows, I will focus on Pereboom's formulations of these conditions since they plausibly deliver a coherent way of making sense of the relevant epistemic notions of openness and deliberative efficacy, while at the same time avoiding some of the more well-known counterexamples that have plagued other extant accounts (see, e.g., Pereboom 2014: chapter 5).

The *epistemic openness* condition I endorse can be articulated as follows:

> (EO) In order to deliberate rationally among distinct actions A1 ... An, for each Ai, S cannot be certain of the proposition that she will do Ai, nor of the proposition that she will not do Ai; and either (a) the proposition that she will do Ai is consistent with every proposition that, in the present context, is settled for her, or (b) if it is inconsistent with some such proposition, she cannot believe that it is. (Pereboom 2014: 113)

This condition maintains that in order for an agent to deliberate rationally among distinct actions, say what shirt to wear from an array of options, the agent cannot be certain of the proposition that they will pick shirt*, nor of the proposition that they will not pick shirt*. Furthermore, the proposition that they will pick shirt* must be consistent with every proposition that, in the present context, is settled for them – where "[a] proposition is settled for an agent just in case she believes it and disregards any uncertainty she has that it is true, e.g., for the purpose of deliberation" (2014: 133). Clause (b) is required because although there may be certain cases in which I can rationally deliberate about whether to do Ai even if in fact my doing Ai is inconsistent with a proposition I regard as settled in that context, "it is crucial that I then not believe that it is inconsistent" – since, "if I did believe this, it's intuitive that I couldn't rationally deliberate about whether to do A" (2014: 114). I contend that (EO) provides a plausible understanding of the kind of epistemic openness required for rational deliberation, and in no way conflicts with the belief that one's actions are causally determined by antecedent conditions beyond their control.

On its own, however, the epistemic openness condition does not provide a successful compatibilist account of rational deliberation. Belief in the efficacy of deliberation is required in addition. To see why, consider the following example provided by van Inwagen:

> [I]magine that [an agent] is in a room with two doors and that he believes one of the doors to be unlocked and other door to be locked and impassable, though he has no idea which is which: let him then attempt to imagine himself deliberating about which door to leave by. (1983: 154)

About this example, Dana Nelkin remarks: "While it seems that I can deliberate about which door to decide *to try* to open and even which door handle to decide to jiggle, if I know one of them to be locked and impassable, it also seems that I cannot deliberate about which *door to open* – or even which door to *decide* to open" (Nelkin 2011: 130). Van Inwagen's example poses a problem for deliberation-compatibilists since it satisfies (EO) but is also plausibly a case where rational deliberation about which door to open is ruled out. What is more:

> [I]f an agent believed determinism and its consequences, then in any deliberative situation she would believe that all but one option for what to do was closed off; "locked and impassable," so to speak (although she would ordinarily not have a belief about which one was not closed off). If in the example one cannot deliberate about which door to open, and one believed determinism and its consequences, then it seems that one would never be able to deliberate about what to do. A compatibilist account would need to explain why rational deliberation is not possible in the two-door case, but nonetheless possible for the determinist. (Pereboom 2014: 116)

To solve this problem, several deliberation-compatibilists have suggested that rational deliberation also requires a belief in the efficacy of deliberation (see

Kapitan 1986: 247; Nelkin 2004; Pereboom 2014). That is, rational deliberators must believe that for each of the options for action under consideration, deliberation about it would, under normal conditions, be efficacious in producing the choice for that action and the action itself (Pereboom 2014: 117). In van Inwagen's example, then, we can say that it is not the absence of a belief in openness that precludes deliberation about which door to open. Rather, what precludes such deliberation is that given the agent's belief that one of the two doors is locked, if he is rational he will believe that his deliberation would not ultimately be efficacious for him opening one of the doors (Pereboom 2014: 117). This is not the case, however, in the normal case of determinism. That is, unlike the two-door case, when a determinist is deliberating under ordinary doxastic circumstances, he can, upon proper reflection, form the true belief that his deliberation makes a difference with respect to which action he performs. So there is an explanation for why the agent cannot rationally deliberate in the two-door case that does not apply to ordinary doxastic scenarios in which a determinist deliberates (Cohen 2018: 91).

We therefore need to add to (EO) a second *deliberative-efficacy condition*. Nelkin (2011: 142) and Kapitan (1996: 436) each offer formulations of their own, but I will once again focus on Pereboom's formulation:

> **(DE)** In order to rationally deliberate about whether to do A_1 or A_2, where A_1 and A_2 are distinct actions, an agent must believe that if as a result of her deliberating about whether to do A_1 or A_2 she were to judge that it would be best to do A_1, then, under normal conditions, she would also, on the basis of this deliberation, do A_1; and similarly for A_2. (2014: 118–119)

The important thing to note is that while (DE) is not met by the agent in the two-door situation, it is satisfied by someone in an ordinary deliberative situation in which they believe that determinism is true and that they therefore have only one possibility for decision and action – but they do not know which. Hence, (DE) avoids van Inwagen's counterexample while making sense of the belief in deliberative efficacy under ordinary doxastic circumstances in which a determinist deliberates. If an agent believes that because determinism is true they cannot either do A_1 or A_2 on the basis of deliberation, but they do not know which, they can still meet condition (DE): For they might still rationally believe that if they were to judge doing A_1 best, they would do A on the basis of deliberation, and similarly for A_2.

I maintain that (EO) and (DE), together with other uncontroversial conditions necessary for rational deliberation, provide a plausible and coherent account of how I can deliberate about, say, what to wear today *and* believe, without inconsistency, that my actions are causally determined by antecedent conditions beyond my control. Rational deliberation only requires epistemic openness and an epistemic condition on the efficacy of deliberation, neither of which conflict with believing in causal determinism. So, when I engaged in an active mental process aimed at figuring out what to wear this morning, my deliberation in no way conflicted with my belief in causal determinism, since I satisfied the epistemic openness condition (EO) and the deliberative-efficacy condition (DE). To the extent this epistemic strategy succeeds, free will skeptics can resist the arguments of rational-deliberation-incompatibilists. They can also conceive of reasoning as I do – that is, as an essential dimension of well-being.

Reasoning, I contend, captures a morally salient aspect of human flourishing that, while related to other dimensions of well-being on my list, is not reducible to them. And from the perspective of justice, "deficits in reasoning abilities matter morally, apart from how they are caused and independent of what else they enable us to do" (Powers and Faden 2006: 21). To achieve a sufficient level of reasoning ability, considerations of justice must go beyond health and nutrition:

> Above and beyond the biological and physiological substrate of reasoning abilities, we can see that much more is required for their exercise than health brain structures and the nutrition, physical environment, and medical care needed to sustain them. Certain kinds of health states are necessary for reasoning, but they are not sufficient. What further distinguished reasoning abilities from healthy functioning of the brain is that the former also requires an understanding of the world that must be *learned*. (Powers and Faden 2006: 21)

What is learned in the first few years of life, for instance, has a profound effect on our abilities to reason across the life span. As Powers and Faden explain:

> [T]he impact of learning in early childhood is mediated through the brain, whose continued development throughout childhood is influenced by environmental learning. Thus, reasoning abilities are affected not only by physical well-being during childhood but also by characteristics of the social world in which childhood is experienced. (Powers and Faden 2006: 21)

In contemporary society, we often think of reasoning capabilities as promoted most directly by access to education:

> Schooling provides the skills of literacy and mathematics, skills that in many contexts are important, if not essential, for the exercise of reason in everyday life. Schooling also provides knowledge about the physical and social world which forms the basic data for cognition and which prepares us to assume responsibility of democratic participation and to protect our interests in the marketplace. Without the knowledge gained through education, it is in many contexts difficult if not impossible to exercise the capabilities of reason. (Powers and Faden 2006: 21)

Schooling, however, is but a part of the story since cognitive capacities are shaped by far more than formal education (see Buchanan 2002). So-called epistemic authorities, or persons whose judgment is routinely respected and often deferred to within a culture, also play a role in "transmitting moral beliefs, inculcating virtue, shaping patterns of sympathy, and providing the factual beliefs underlying the formation of social bonds" (Powers and Faden 2006: 22). Such authorities, of course, may or may not be worthy of their trusted status, and their beliefs can be false, distorting, or self-serving. Because of this, in order to exercise abilities of practical reason so that our beliefs are adopted on due reflection and not just inherited, individuals need to develop sufficient critical thinking skills and faculties (Powers and Faden 2006: 22). It is the job of justice to provide access to, and help foster the development of, these various reasoning capabilities, since they are essential for human flourishing.

6.2.3 Self-Determination

Third on my list of essential dimensions of well-being, which it is the job of justice to secure a sufficient level of, is self-determination. Here self-determination has nothing to do with metaphysical free will or the control in action required for basic desert moral responsibility. Rather, it is the linchpin of liberal political theory and a foundation for other conclusions about what a just social structure requires. It is a broad and encompassing category of human good. On the political front, it includes, as Nussbaum puts it, "[b]eing able to participate effectively in political choices that govern one's life; having the right of political participation, protections of free speech and association" (2011: 34). Materially, it also includes "[b]eing able to hold property (both land and movable goods), and having property rights on an equal basis with others; having the freedom from unwarranted search and seizure" (Nussbaum 2011: 34). In work, it includes "being able to work as a human being, exercising practical reason and entering into meaningful relationships of mutual recognition with other workers" (ibid.). Perhaps the most straightforward moral justification of this liberal conception of self-determination is that "being self-directed, or living one's life from the inside, according to one's own inclinations and values, is itself a constituent of human well-being" (Powers and Faden 2006: 26).

Self-determination, thus understood, does not conflict with the kind of free will skepticism I have advanced. Yes, in addition to the reasoning abilities that are necessary to set and revise our own ends, and in addition to the political liberties that are necessary means to their pursuit, self-determination consists in being in a condition in which our ends contribute effectively to the shaping of the course of our lives. But free will skeptics need not deny, and I do not deny, the causal efficacy of our choices and intentions (see Pereboom and Caruso 2018). Unlike some neuroscientific arguments for skepticism, ones that deny the causal efficacy of conscious will, the philosophical arguments I've advanced allow for agents to make choices, for mental states to be causally efficacious, and for there to exist various degrees of autonomy. Skeptics are able to acknowledge the distinctions compatibilists have made regarding the different degrees of control agents possess, while simultaneously denying that these differences provide the control in action necessary for basic desert moral responsibility. Acting in accordance with our own ends does not mean those ends, or the ability to act on them, are not themselves ultimately the result of factors beyond our control. Furthermore, skeptics are perhaps better able to acknowledge the degree to which our ability to act in accordance with our own ends is dependent upon various political, economic, and environmental factors. And it is these factors that belong to the domain of liberal political theory.

A just social structure therefore requires political liberties along with the other conditions necessary for individuals to achieve the kind of self-determination required for well-being. As Powers and Faden describe:

> [D]oors will not open without political liberties. Some large area of noninterference is necessary as a means for leading self-determining lives, but political liberties too are not sufficient for leading a self-determined life ... Unless legal system and cultural norms are structured in ways that provide social room for meaningful choices and their implementation, then leading a self-determined life is unlikely. More to the point, without the proper economic, legal, and social structures, one's chances for being self-determining are thwarted. Perhaps most fundamentally, certain material conditions are essential to our being self-determined. People who live meal to meal; who do not know if tomorrow there will be food for themselves or their children; who are dying of exposure, starvation, or exhaustion are not positioned to be self-determining in any meaningful respect. (2006: 27–28)

Self-determination as an essential dimension of well-being therefore rests on simple and widely shared views about having some control over who we are and who we will become. It does not depend on some controversial metaphysical claims about free will or basic desert moral responsibility. Aristotle's example of the helmsman provides an excellent illustration of the kind of self-determination I have in mind (*Politics* 129a: 1–5).

> The helmsman sets a course on an open sea, but does not command the winds nor decide the boundaries between land and sea. Her choices are therefore bounded. She cannot decide to sail upon the land, and she cannot will the wind to blow in the desired direction or at the desired velocity. She does not choose her course wholly without regard to necessity or need, and she does not proceed on any course without the help or hindrance of luck. And yet the helmsman charts her own course within the parameters of these external influences. Charting her course is not possible, however, when the seas are so rough and her vessel so damaged that the helmsman must work feverishly just to keep from drowning. (Powers and Faden 2006: 28–29)

Self-determination thus requires some material basis for its exercise – a sturdy boat, so to speak. Furthermore, the successful exercise of self-determination, like the successful navigation of the helmsman, "will depend also on the favorable circumstances in which other dimensions of well-being, health, personal security, attachment, respect and the exercise of reason, are present in sufficient quantity" (Powers and Faden 2006: 29). Self-determination is not something that depends on reasoning capacities alone, or that can be achieved outside of a web of interdependences, or that needs only an absence of human interference. Rather, "self-determination is a valuable state or condition for which enough is required for our well-being, and without which the prospects for a decent life are undermined in ways not reducible to deficits in other valuable dimensions of well-being" (ibid.).

6.2.4 Attachment

A fourth central dimension of human well-being is attachment. It includes both friendship and love in their most intimate expressions, as well as a sense of solidarity or fellow-feeling with others within one's community (Powers and Faden 2006: 24). As Nussbaum correctly observes (with reference to what she labels "affiliation"), such bonds matter for reasons of both friendship and justice. Attachment requires: "Being able to live with and toward others, to recognize and show concern for other human beings, to engage in various forms of social interaction; to be able to imagine the situation of another" (2011: 34). Protecting this capability, Nussbaum argues, "means protecting institutions that constitute and nourish such forms of affiliation, and also protecting the freedom of assembly and political speech" (2011: 34). Furthermore, attachment means having the "social bases of self-respect and non-humiliation; being able to be treated as a dignified being whose worth is equal to that of others" (Nussbaum 2011: 34). This, according to Nussbaum, "entails provisions of nondiscrimination on the basis of race, sex, sexual orientation, ethnicity, caste, religion, national origin" (2011: 34). Such attachment is an essential dimension of well-being, since a life significantly lacking in it is a life seriously deficient in what it is reasonable for anyone to want, whatever else they want.

On the personal level, attachment engages the capacities for love, friendship, emotional engagement, compassion, and sympathetic identification with others (Powers and Faden 2006: 24). The bonds created by attachment – to care for and to be cared for by others, to feel longing in their absence, and to grieve for their loss – are matters that are essential to well-being, whatever else is valuable (Nussbaum 2000: 79). Beyond the personal, attachment is also a prerequisite for the formation and perpetuation of a just society:

> Attachment is essential ... to justice in the same way that respect and reasoning ability are. The level of emotional engagement and sympathetic identification with others is what ... distinguishes attachment as an essential, irreducible element of what is necessary for the processes of forging bonds of mutual forbearance and mutual aid and for participation in the responsibilities of caring for one another. (Powers and Faden 2006: 25)

Given that attachment is essential to both justice and well-being generally, the capabilities theory of justice requires that its basic social institutions conform to and reproduce capacities for human attachment. That is, unlike traditional theories of justice that primarily condemn infringements of liberties or seek to curb material inequality, the capabilities approach seeks to address the importance of developing and cultivating capabilities for attachment and for living lives characterized by dependence and interdependence, vulnerability, and the potential for exploitation. Following Powers and Faden, I maintain that "internal to a theory of social justice is the requirement that the totality of social institutions and social conventions should be such that it *does fit* people for lives in which the bonds of attachment and capacities for sympathetic identification with others are cultivated" (Powers and Faden 2006: 25). This means that in some instances, "the injustice of a particular social arrangement consists not simply in the fact that a valuable social opportunity or good is unavailable to some members of society, but that those arrangements do not cultivate the kinds of relations among persons that justice demands" (Powers and Faden 2006: 25).

Since viewing the bonds of attachment as an essential dimension of well-being in no way presupposes the existence of free will, this dimension of well-being, like the others, is open for free will skeptics to embrace. Even if agents lack the kind of free will required for basic desert moral responsibility, they are still capable of experiencing the bonds of attachment as well as finding their well-being diminished when such bonds are limited or absent. The importance of attachment to well-being is particularly acute when considering the incarceration of offenders. Separating individuals from their loved ones, their family and friends, and their communities, almost always has a negative effect on well-being. This is why the use of incarceration to punish offenders must carry a high burden. Of course, the public health–quarantine model, while not providing a justification of punishment, does allow for the incapacitation of seriously dangerous offenders. But the model also requires a number of important reforms, not the least of which is that we must consider the well-being of offenders.

With regard to attachment, the well-being of offenders requires retaining and fostering, as much as possible, their attachment relations even when incapacitation is required. For instance, following the lead of the Norwegian Correctional Service, I propose that we adopt the *principle of normality*. This principle states three things:

(1) Incapacitation is the restriction of liberty, "but no other rights have been removed by the sentencing court." Therefore, the sentenced offender has all the same rights as all other citizens.
(2) "No-one shall serve their sentence under stricter circumstances than necessary for the security in the community." Therefore, offenders shall be placed in the lowest possible security regime.
(3) "During the serving of a sentence, life inside will resemble life outside as much as possible."[7]

Consistent with this principle, I propose that our institutions of incapacitation should encourage attachment relations between offenders, offenders and guards,

---

[7] For an official statement of the principle, see www.kriminalomsorgen.no/information-in-english.265199.no.html.

and offenders and family/community. There are a number of different ways this can be done, and drawing on some innovative prison designs from Norway, I will offer up some concrete proposals in the following chapter (see Chapter 7). These proposals, however, are drastically different than most US, UK, and Australian prisons, which are designed for punitive purposes and tend to isolate prisoners, minimize their interaction, and control every aspect of their daily lives. This is not only counterproductive from the perspective of rehabilitation and reintegration, since it can instill a kind of learned helplessness that makes the transition back into society extremely difficult, it is also an injustice since it intentionally cuts off many of the meaningful attachment relations necessary for human well-being.

This is particularly harmful when mothers are separated from their children (80 percent of women jailed each year are mothers)[8] and primary wage earners are removed from their households. But this is not the only injustice done by our current criminal justice system. Offenders are also detached from their communities, often transported hundreds of miles away to serve their sentence, as well as striped of their voting rights. The public health–quarantine model, grounded as it is in concerns about social justice, therefore demands that (a) in addition to redesigning prisons so that "life inside will resemble life outside as much as possible," (b) the attachment relations of offenders be retained and fostered as much as possible, which minimally requires that (c) those we incapacitate be kept as close as possible to the communities from which they come, allowing them to retain their attachment to family and friends through visitation, (d) the voting rights of offenders be retained while incapacitated and thereafter, since other than liberty "no other rights have been removed by the sentencing court," and lastly, (e) all attempts be made to allow mothers, especially single mothers, to continue to care for their children. These recommendations minimally follow from the capabilities approach to justice and the importance of attachment as a central dimension of well-being.

6.2.5 Personal Security

Like health, reasoning, self-determination, and attachment, it is a central task of justice to secure a sufficient level of personal security for each individual, insofar as possible, since it is an essential dimension of well-being. Personal security includes maintaining physical and bodily integrity and psychological inviolability. It means being "secure against violent assault, including sexual assault and domestic violence" (Nussbaum 2011: 33) as well as psychological abuse, threat, or fear of attack. As Powers and Faden explain:

> Criminal acts such as rape or battery do more than harm the body. Assault (placing another in fear of imminent bodily harm) and intimidation are invasions of personal security, even when they do not eventuate in bodily injury or pain. It is

---

[8] Prison Policy Initiative: www.prisonpolicy.org/blog/2018/05/13/mothers-day-2018/.

arguably extremely difficult if not impossible to live a decent life if one is in constant fear of physical or psychological abuse. Experiencing such abuse is surely a setback to well-being, regardless of who we are or what values we might otherwise have. Violations such as rape, assault, and torture are of concern to the public health community because of their impact on health, but even more so they are the objects of concern for those persons and institutions having a special focus on human rights abuses, domestic violence, crime, war, and terrorism. (2006: 19)

Personal security as a dimension of well-being provides one of the primary moral foundations for adopting a public health approach to preventing criminal behavior. But just as with health, there is no reason to suppose that every policy decision that bears on public safety rests on the single moral foundation of personal security. In fact, as we will see in the following chapter, criminal behavior *itself* it often a result of offenders themselves experiencing injustices involving assault, degradation, rape, domestic violence, and other violations of personal security, along with other capability failures that are the result of systematic disadvantage, discrimination, and marginalization. Public health policies aimed at addressing these social injustices will often appeal to moral foundations beyond personal security, since they also involve violations of respect, self-determination, and even health.

Personal security, though, is an independent dimension of well-being, and as such it is the job of justice to secure a sufficient level of it for each individual. The best way to do this, I maintain, is to adopt the public health–quarantine model sketched in this chapter. Instead of focusing on punitive approaches to crime, the public health approach prioritizes prevention and adopts a holistic approach to social justice that meaningfully addresses the capability failures often responsible for criminal behavior. It acknowledges that violent crime is a public health issue and securing a sufficient level of personal security for all provides one of the moral foundations for addressing it.

6.2.6 Respect

Lastly, there appears to be some convergence on the final dimension of well-being on my list, since philosophers of widely divergent perspectives have all argued that respect is an essential element of human flourishing and that it is a proper concern of justice (Rawls 1971; J. Cohen 1989; Sen 1992; Anderson 1999; Nussbaum 2000; Powers and Faden 2006). Respect for others requires an ability to see others as independent sources of moral worth and dignity and to view others as appropriate objects of sympathetic identification (Powers and Faden 2006: 22). Respect for others is also closely linked to self-respect: "A capacity for self-respect involves an individual's capacity to see oneself as the moral equal of others and as an independent source of moral claims based on one's own dignity and worth" (Powers and Faden

2006: 22). Respect then matters to human well-being in two related ways: (1) a life lacking in the respect of others is seriously deficient in something crucial to well-being; and (2) so too is a life lacking in self-respect. On the flip side, we can say:

> Lack of respect is a dimension of well-being characteristically under assault when an individual is the object of discrimination based on judgments of intrinsic inferior social status, often linked to properties of group membership, such as ethnicity, gender, or social class, or to ability or appearance. While it is possible for individual members of a socially disfavored group to retain their self-respect under discriminatory and oppressive social conditions, they are able to do so only with heroic efforts or good fortune. Being respected and retaining one's self-respect, however, are of much too great moral importance for human development and flourishing to be left to the vicissitudes of individual luck or heroism. That individuals can, with hard work and good luck, be self-respected does nothing to vitiate the injustice of being disrespected by others. A lack of respect from others and an awareness of one's own exclusion from the reciprocal system of mutual respect that others in one's society enjoy are profound injustices in their own right. (Powers and Faden 2006: 23)

Hence, respect and well-being are set back whenever we are perceived of as being lesser value because of membership in a particular race, gender, economic class, or some other group about whom invidious judgments are made. In this way, the well-being of individuals is often tied to the well-being of groups (Powers and Faden 2006: 23).

Can this understanding of respect be reconciled with free will skepticism? I believe it can. First, we need to recognize that there is no inconsistency in accepting a Kantian regard for respect, dignity, and treating individuals as ends-in-themselves, without accepting Kant's particular attitudes on free will (see Pereboom 2001: 150–152; Vilhauer 2009, 2013a, 2013b). Pereboom has argued, for instance, that there is nothing in Kant's second formulation of the categorical imperative – which maintains that you should "[a]ct so that you treat humanity, whether in your own person or in the person of any other, always at the same time as an end, never merely as a means" – that requires agents be free in the sense required for basic desert moral responsibility. He considers the following concern:

> Perhaps a more threatening conflict is suggested by Fischer's claim that on the hard determinist position, we cannot retain a conception of ourselves as persons. The Kantian conception of morality provides one interpretation of this thesis: If hard determinism is true, then the basis for respecting human beings will be undermined, and thus any claim to moral dignity will have to be relinquished. For Kant, moral dignity is ascribed to human beings because they possess certain kinds of capacities. First, humans have dignity insofar as they are capable of rationality – in particular, rationality of a practical sort ... [P]ractical rationality allows us to set ends or goals for ourselves, to reason about means for achieving those goals, to set goals and choose means in accord with principles that specify respect for all

humanity, to formulate such principle and to make a commitment to them. (2001: 151)

But Pereboom correctly notes that "none of these capacities is threatened by hard determinism, nor, for similar reasons, by hard incompatibilism" (2001: 151). Of course, if hard incompatibilism is true, then agents are not morally responsible in the basic desert sense for setting ends and choosing means, or for formulating principles and making commitments to them. Nevertheless, the capacities for these activities can remain intact (Pereboom 2001: 151).

A second sort of capacity that in Kant's view confers dignity and respect is autonomy. Perhaps one might think that hard incompatibilism undermines autonomy, and that hence hard incompatibilists are barred from adopting the most central component of Kantian ethics. But as I have already argued, the skeptical perspective (including hard incompatibilism) is capable of acknowledging that agents have varying degrees of autonomy, self-determination, and the like. According to Kant, to have autonomy is to have the capacity to commit oneself to certain principles of conduct as rationally binding (see Pereboom 2001: 151–152). No feature of hard incompatibilism or skepticism is incompatible with autonomy thus understood, for having this capacity is clearly consistent with lacking free will. To the extent, then, that the capacities of practical reasoning and/or autonomy are what confer respect on persons, free will skeptics (and hard incompatibilists) are able to retain them.

Furthermore, the capabilities account of social justice I defend holds that respect is something of independent moral significance regardless of whether individuals poses free will, since it matters centrally to everyone, whatever the particular life plans and aims each has. To the extent that a human life is seriously deficient in respect, it is likely a life lacking a sufficient level of well-being. To help make my account more concrete, it might be useful to draw upon a distinction Stephen Darwall makes between what he calls "appraisal respect" and "recognition respect." As Powers and Faden explain the distinction:

> Appraisal respect involves the judgment by others that our conduct or projects are estimable or worthy of praise. Such judgments are matters of degree, and not all people are equally worthy of appraisal respect (Darwall 1992, 77, n.18). Some deserve Nobel Prizes for what they have accomplished or praise and admiration for the obstacles they have overcome, but many are not so worthy. By contrast, recognition respect is what is owed to each of us as agents entitled to treatment worthy of members of the moral community on a par with all others. Recognition respect, then, is what our theory is concerned with. Respect in this sense is what is characteristically lacking in invidious judgments of persons on the basis of their group membership, as in the phenomenon of racism or sexism. It is also what is lacking centrally in self-respect where individuals internalize the belief that they are worthless and not deserving of the treatment others are entitled to expect. (Powers and Faden 2006: 23)

Arguably, appraisal respect requires free will since it involves judgments about praiseworthiness. And for those who believe praiseworthiness is justified in the basic desert sense, it comes in degrees since we are not equally worthy of it. Recognition respect, on the other hand, applies to all equally and does not require an appeal to free will or basic desert. It instead maintains that all agents are entitled to respect on a par with all others.

Critics may object that recognition respect, like appraisal respect, appeals to a notion of desert since it holds that all individuals are *deserving* of respect and equal regard. But Benjamin Vilhauer (2009, 2013a, 2013b) has argued, convincingly in my opinion, that there is an important, often overlooked, distinction between "action-based" desert claims and "personhood-based" desert claims. The former is the kind of desert claim at issue in the free will debate, while the latter is not. Consider again the backward-looking justification of blame and praise, punishment and reward:

> [T]he only sort of reference event that mainstream ethicists typically accept in backward-looking justifications is action – more specifically, actions that they take agents to be morally responsible for performing (if they suppose that there are such things). According to backward-looking justifications of this form, we deserve to be treated in particular ways because of how we have acted. I ... refer to such justifications as *action-based desert claims*. Since we can only deserve to be treated in particular ways based on our actions if we are morally responsible, action-based desert claims imply that the agent at issue acted with free will. (Vilhauer 2013a: 149)

Hence, action-based desert claims presuppose the existence of free will.

Personhood-desert claims, on the other hand, arguably do not. Like Pereboom, Vilhauer maintains that we can ground respect for persons in the Kantian principle that *persons must always be treated as ends, and never as mere means*, without adopting Kant's own particular metaphysical commitments. Yes, Kant claimed that personhood itself implies free will so that human beings cannot have the moral status of persons unless they are free (see Kant 1996, 6: 223). But as Vilhauer points out:

> Kant does not need to define persons in this way. He can define persons as beings who autonomously set their own ends, and who must therefore be treated only as they would rationally consent to be treated. Free will skeptics can follow Kant in making respect for our right to independently set our own ends a central moral principle. So long as we understand the influence that we are independent from, in autonomously setting our own ends, as the undue influence of others, rather than the influence of the causal nexus constituting the world, this view is entirely compatible with free will skepticism. (Vilhauer 2003a: 150)

Skeptics can therefore adopt a robust Kantian respect of persons without looking backward to action-based desert. That is, they "can make such dignity and respect for persons a central moral principle if they respect people as *rational* agents rather than as *free* agents, and if they regard agents as autonomous not with respect of the laws of nature, but instead with respect to the undue influence of other agents" (2013a: 148). This is what Vilhauer means by personhood-desert claims:

> We need only look to the people with whom we are interacting to find a basis for desert-claims that constrain consequentialist justifications. Personhood can provide a basis for desert-claims which is irreducibly different from action, and which does not depend upon free will in the way action-based desert does. Persons deserve to be treated only as they would rationally consent to be treated, just because they are persons. (Vilhauer 2013a: 151)

Since personhood-based desert does not depend on how we act, we do not need to appeal to moral responsibility to make sense of it. Free will skeptics can therefore endorse personhood-based desert claims even though they must reject action-based desert claims. And it is personhood-based desert that is appealed to in recognition respect – hence, it is consistent with free will skepticism.

Where my view differs from Vilhauer's is that he proceeds to understanding personhood-based desert, rational consent, human rights, and distributive justice, by means of a Rawlsian social contract theory that appeals to original position deliberation and Rawls's "veil of ignorance" (see 2013a, 2013b for details). While I have sympathies with Vilhauer's approach, my own preferred way of conceiving of justice – and along with it recognition respect, human rights, and the other essential dimensions of well-being – is by means of the capabilities approach discussed earlier. Respect for persons, that is, what Darwall calls recognition respect, simply follows from the fact that it is an essential dimension of well-being. As Nussbaum states, "Governments must treat all people respectfully and should refuse to humiliate them" (2011: 26). This is because of the "centrality of notions of dignity and respect in generating the entire capabilities list" (ibid.). The capabilities approach is normative in nature:

> The Capabilities Approach is not a theory of what human nature is, and it does not read norms off from innate human nature. Instead, it is evaluative and ethical from the start: it asks, among the many things that human beings might develop the capacity to do, which ones are the really valuable ones, which are the ones that a minimally just society will endeavor to nurture and support? An account of human nature tells us what resources and possibilities we have and what our difficulties may be. It does not tell us what to value. (2011: 28)

For both Nussbaum and me, respect and dignity are centrally important for establishing political principles that can provide the grounding for constitutional law and public policy in a nation aspiring to social justice. This is because "human dignity, from the start, is equal to all who are agents in the first place ... All, that is, deserve equal respect from the laws and institutions" (Nussbaum 2011: 31). Respect, thus understood, means "some living conditions deliver to people a life that is worthy of the human dignity that they possess, and others do not" (Nussbaum 2011: 30). In the later circumstances, "they retain dignity, but it is like a promissory note whose claims have not been met. As Martin Luther King, Jr., said of the promises inherent in national ideals: dignity can be like a check that has come back marked 'insufficient funds'" (ibid.).

In general, then, my version of the capabilities approach focuses on the protection of the dimensions of well-being so central that their removal makes life not worthy of human dignity. It maintains that respect for human dignity requires that individuals be provided a sufficient level of well-being in all six of the dimensions just discussed. The list I offer is, of course, a proposal. It may be contested by arguing that one or more of the items is not so central and thus should be left to the ordinary political process rather than being given special protection. But I think a strong case can be made that all six of these dimensions contribute in such a manner that is not merely instrumental but partly constitutive of a worthwhile human life. It is the essential nature of these dimensions of well-being that make them a constitutive component of a worthwhile human life and a proper concern of justice.

6.3 CONCLUSION

Bringing everything together, my public health–quarantine model characterizes the moral foundation of public health as social justice, not just the advancement of good health outcomes. That is, while promoting health is one area of concern, public health ethics as I conceive it is embedded within a broader commitment to secure a sufficient level of human well-being for all and to narrow unjust inequalities. More specifically, I see the capabilities approach to social justice as the proper moral foundation of public health ethics. This means that the broader commitment of public health should be the achievement of those capabilities needed to secure a sufficient level of human well-being – including, but not limited to, health, reasoning, self-determination, attachment, personal security, and respect. This account "rejects the separate-spheres view of justice in which it is possible to speak about justice in public health and health policy without reference to how other public policies and social environments are structured or to how people are faring with regard to the rest of their lives" (Powers and Faden 2006: 9–10).

By placing social justice at the foundation of the public health approach, the realms of criminal justice and social justice are brought closer together. I see this as a virtue of the theory since it is hard to see how we can adequately deal with criminal justice without simultaneously addressing issues of social justice. Retributivists tend to disagree since they approach criminal justice as an issue of individual responsibility and desert, not as an issue of prevention and public safety. I believe it is a mistake to hold that the criteria of individual accountability can be settled apart from considerations of social justice and the social determinants of criminal behavior. Making social justice foundational, as my public health–quarantine model does, places on us an obligation to redress unjust inequalities and to advance collective aims and priorities such as public health and safety. The capability approach and the public health approach therefore fit nicely together. Both maintain that poor health and safety are often the byproducts of social inequities, and both attempt to identify and address these social inequities in order to achieve a sufficient level of health and safety.

Summarizing the public health–quarantine model, then, the core idea is that the right to harm in self-defense and defense of others justifies incapacitating the criminally dangerous with the minimum harm required for adequate protection. The resulting account would not justify the sort of criminal punishment whose legitimacy is most dubious, such as death or confinement in the most common kinds of prisons in our society. The model also specifies attention to the well-being of criminals, which would change much of current policy. Furthermore, the public health component of the theory prioritizes prevention and social justice and aims at identifying and taking action on the social determinants of health and criminal behavior. This combined approach to dealing with criminal behavior, I maintain, is sufficient for dealing with dangerous criminals, leads to a more humane and effective social policy, and is actually preferable to the harsh and often excessive forms of punishment that typically come with retributivism.

7

The Public Health–Quarantine Model II

The Social Determinants of Health and Criminal Behavior

In this chapter, I will further develop the public health–quarantine model by exploring the relationship between public health and safety. I will focus on how social inequalities and systemic injustices affect health outcomes and crime rates, how poverty affects incarceration rates, how offenders often have preexisting medical conditions including mental health issues, how involvement in the criminal justice system itself can lead to or worsen health and cognitive problems, how treatment and rehabilitation methods can best be employed to reduce recidivism and reintegrate offenders back into society, and how a public health approach could be successfully applied within the criminal justice system. My approach will draw on research from the health sciences, social sciences, public policy, law, psychiatry, medical ethics, epidemiology, neuroscience, and philosophy. I will argue that there are number of important links and similarities between the social determinants of health (SDH) and the social determinants of criminal behavior (SDCB), and that the public health–quarantine model provides the most justified, humane, and effective approach for addressing criminal behavior.

I begin, in Section 7.1, by discussing recent empirical findings in psychology, neuroscience, and the social sciences that provide us with an increased understanding of the social determinants of health and criminal behavior. While this section is filled with a wealth of information, the purpose of so much detail is to make vivid the fact that poor health outcomes and criminal behavior are more a characteristic of places and circumstances than of people. In fact, analysis of the life histories of the men and women who end up in prison indicates that they have been exposed to a number of powerful social determinants. Look closely and you will find that there are lifetimes of trauma, poverty, and social disadvantage that fill the prison system. In Section 7.2, I then explain how the public health–quarantine model, with its focus on prevention and its grounding in the capabilities approach to social justice, can be implemented to identify, prioritize, and target the social determinants of criminal behavior. I argue that we cannot successfully address concerns over public health and safety without simultaneously addressing issues of social justice – including the social determinants of health and the social determinants of criminal behavior.

I conclude, in Section 7.3, by offering eleven distinct policy proposals that are consistent with my model and motivated by the analysis (in Section 7.1) of the various factors that cause criminal behavior.

7.1 THE SOCIAL DETERMINANTS OF HEALTH AND CRIMINAL BEHAVIOR

The *social determinants of health* are the conditions in which people are born, grow, work, live, and age, and the wider set of forces and systems shaping the conditions of daily life. These forces and systems include economic policies and systems, development agendas, social norms, social policies, and political systems. A core function of the public health framework is to identify and take action on the social determinants of health to address health inequities. One of the things I want to argue in this chapter is that, just as it is important to identify and take action on the *social determinants of health* (SDH) if we want to improve health outcomes, it is equally important to identify and address the *social determinants of criminal behavior* (SDCB) if we want to reduce crime and improve public safety. Since the social determinants of health and criminal behavior are broadly similar, or so I will argue, I contend that we should adopt a broad public health approach focused on prevention and social justice for identifying and taking action on these shared social determinants.

7.1.1 *Poverty and Socioeconomic Status*

One of the most important determinants of health and criminal behavior is poverty and socioeconomic status. While poverty rates have declined over the years, there are still a large number of people living in poverty in the United States, United Kingdom, and around the world. In 2018, 38.1 million Americans (about one in eight) lived below the official poverty line, which is defined as $25,465 for a family with two adults and two children (United States Census Bureau 2019). In the United Kingdom, there are more than 14 million people living in poverty (about one in five), including 4.6 million children, with an extra 2.5 million people living just above the poverty line (Social Metrics Commission 2019). The rate of poverty worldwide is measured a bit differently, with 10 percent of the world's population living on less than $1.90 a day (The World Bank 2015). These numbers are significant because we know that poverty or low *socioeconomic status* (SES) can have profound negative effects on health. Numerous studies have shown that individuals with lower socioeconomic status have higher rates of mortality and morbidity, including obesity, cardiovascular disease, and mental illness (see, e.g., Adler et al. 1994; Anderson and Armstead 1995; Chen et al. 2002; Chen 2004; Berkman and Epstein 2008; Akil and Ahmad 2011; Franks et al. 2011).[1] One study found that low SES had almost the same impact on health than

---

[1] *Socioeconomic status* (SES) is a multidimensional construct. It typically combines a number of objective factors such as an individual or parent's education, occupation, and income, as well as subjective perceptions of social status and social class (McLoyd 1998; Brito and Noble 2014: 1).

smoking or a sedentary lifestyle and was associated with a reduced life expectancy of 2.1 years (Stringhini et al. 2016). Interestingly, the relationship between SES and health holds true whether it is measured as the prevalence rate of illness, the severity of illness, or the likelihood of mortality, and it is true for most types of diseases, as well as for many risk factors for disease (Chen 2004: 112; Berkman and Epstein 2008). It also holds true across the life span, from childhood to older adulthood. And perhaps most intriguing, the relationship between SES and health exists as a gradient – that is, it is not just that poor people have poorer health than rich people. Rather, "each step increase in SES is accompanied by incremental benefits in health" (Chen 2004: 112).

In addition to low SES, higher levels of income inequality have also been shown to have a negative effect on health, including higher rates of mortality and morbidity (see Kennedy et al. 1996; Kawachi et al. 1997; Diez-Roux 2000; Pickett et al. 2005; Pickett and Wilkinson 2010; Johnson et al. 2015). In a survey of data from twelve developed countries, Pickett and Wilkinson (2010) discovered that countries with higher income-inequality had three times as many individuals with mental illness than those with lower income-inequality. And Kahn et al. (2000) found that those living in states with higher income inequality had higher rates of depressive symptoms and poorer self-rated health in mothers at the bottom 20 percent of household income.

Unfortunately, these negative effects of socioeconomic status are not limited to poor health. A number of studies have also found that poverty and low SES during childhood are a distal risk factor for subsequent criminal and substance misuse behaviors (Carlen 1988; William and McShane 1998; Wright et al. 1999; Fergusson, Swain-Campbell, and Horwood 2004; Galloway and Shardhamar 2010; Sareen et al. 2011; Webster and Kingston 2014). A Norwegian total population study found that children of parents in the lowest income decile were twice as likely to be convicted of a violent or drug crime compared with their peers in the fifth decile (Galloway and Shardhamar 2010; Sariaslan et al. 2014: 286). Similarly, a number of longitudinal US studies have linked low-income levels with substance use disorders (McMillan et al. 2010; Sareen et al. 2011). Additional studies have found that childhood socioeconomic disadvantage is associated with increases in rates of both self-reported crime and officially recorded convictions (Fergusson, Swain-Campbell, and Horwood 2004) and that poverty increases the likelihood that a person will commit crime, be apprehended, and be the victim of crime (Lewontin 2000; Sampson and Laub 2003). The relationship between poverty and violence also appears to hold across different sorts of violent crimes, including murder, assault, and domestic violence (Parker 1989; Martinez 1996; Kelly 2000; Pridemore 2011).

This does not mean, of course, that poverty *alone* is responsible for these antisocial behaviors since, as we will see in the following sections, there are other important social determinants of drug misuse and violent behavior. We also know that poverty and low SES can cause depression in adolescents, and studies have found that an increase in depressive symptoms is associated with a significant elevated risk of subsequent violence

(Yu et al. 2017). Behavioral genetic investigations also indicate that the likelihood for both violent offending and substance misuse is influenced by shared genetic and family environmental factors (Frisell et al. 2011; Kendler et al. 2012). The few studies, however, that have controlled for these genetic factors have found that there still remains an inverse association between parental income during childhood and development of behavioral problems (Blau 1999; Hao and Matsueda 2006; D'Onofrio et al. 2009; Jaffee et al. 2012; cf. Sariaslan et al. 2014). It would seem, then, that poverty or low SES remains a risk factor for substance misuse and criminal behavior.[2]

Determining exactly why this is the case is no doubt difficult to do, but we are beginning to understand some of the causal mechanisms at play. We know, for instance that "[h]uman development does not occur within a vacuum. The environmental contexts and social connections a person experiences throughout his or her lifetime significantly impact the development of both cognitive and social skills" (Brito and Noble 2014: 1). Numerous studies have shown that socioeconomic disparities profoundly affect physical health, mental well-being, and cognitive development (Anderson and Armstead 1995; Brooks-Gunn and Duncan 1997; Duncan et al. 1998; McLoyd 1998; Evans 2006; Brito and Noble 2014; Nobel et al. 2015a). Studies indicate, for instance, that SES accounts for approximately 20 percent of the variance in childhood IQ (Gottfried et al. 2003) and it has been estimated that by age five, chronic poverty is associated with 6- to 13-point IQ reduction (Brooks-Gunn and Duncan 1997; Smith et al. 1997; as cited by Brito and Noble 2014). Evidence suggests multiple possible, and non-mutually exclusive, explanations for these findings (Brito and Nobel 2014: 2). Socioeconomically disadvantaged children, for instance, tend to experience less linguistic, social, and cognitive stimulation from their caregivers and home environments than children from higher SES homes (Hart and Risley 1995; Bradley et al. 2001; Bradley and Corwyn 2002; Rowe and Goldin-Meadow 2009; Brito and Nobel 2014: 2). Additionally, individuals from lower SES homes report more stressful events during their lifetime, and the biological response to stressors has been hypothesized as one of the underlying mechanisms for health and cognitive disparities in relation to SES (Adler et al. 1994; Anderson and Armstead 1995; Cohen et al. 1999; Wilkson 1999; Hackman and Farah 2009; Nobel et al. 2012a; Brito and Nobel 2014: 2).

These experiential differences are also "likely to have specific downstream effects on particular brain structures" (Brito and Noble 2014: 2). Disparities in the quantity and quality of linguistic stimulation in the home, for instance, have been associated with developmental differences in language-supporting cortical regions in the left hemisphere (Kuhl et al. 2003; Conboy and Kuhl 2007; Kuhl 2007; as cited by Brito and Noble 2014: 2). We also know that the experience of stress has important negative effects on the hippocampus (Buss et al. 2007; McEwen and Gianaros 2010;

---

[2] Studies also reveal that societies with greater inequality have higher rates of violent crime (see, e.g., Ouimet 2010; Enamorado and Rodrigiez-Castelan 2015; Vives-cases et al. 2015).

Tottenham and Sheridan 2010), the amygdala (McEwen and Gianaros 2010; Tottenham and Sheridan 2010), and areas of the prefrontal cortex (Liston et al. 2009; McEwen and Gianaros 2010) – structures that are linked together anatomically and functionally (Brito and Noble 2014: 2). Several recent studies, in fact, have directly studied the connection between socioeconomic parameters (e.g., family income and parental education) and cognitive and neurological development (see, e.g., Hackman and Farah 2009; Hackman et al. 2010; Lawson et al. 2013; Mackey et al. 2015; Noble et al. 2015b; Piccolo et al. 2016; Crooks et al. 2018). They found that lower SES is related to smaller overall cortical surface and thinner prefrontal cortex (Lawson et al. 2013; Nobel et al. 2015b; Crooks et al. 2018), that both family income and parental education moderate nonlinear age-related variations in cortical thickness (Piccolo et al. 2016), and that female adolescents in neighborhoods with high-inequality and low household income displayed a significant age-related decrease in cortical thickness compared to their peers (Parker et al. 2017).

We can conclude that while we may not yet fully understand all the causal mechanisms by which socioeconomic factors affect health and safety, poverty and socioeconomic status are important social determinants of both. Poverty and low SES can increase levels of stress, expose agents to more negative life events, limit educational opportunities, and profoundly affect the social, cognitive, and neurological development of agents. To reduce crime and increase health we need to adopt policies that directly address these socioeconomic factors. And the justification for doing so can be found in the public health framework and the capabilities approach defended in the previous chapter – that is, poverty and low SES seriously diminish the capabilities needed to achieve a sufficient level of human well-being and they negatively effect health and safety.

7.1.2 Abuse and Domestic Violence

In addition to poverty and socioeconomic status, there are also a number of other social determinants of health and criminal behavior that a public health approach would need to address. These include education, housing, healthcare, childhood abuse, and domestic violence to name just a few. Take, for example, exposure to violence. While it transcends age and SES and affects all levels of income, education, and occupation, it overlaps with these other social determinants of health and crime since youth from lower SES backgrounds tend to have increased exposure and likelihood of suffering from detrimental future outcomes. We know that safe, stable, nurturing relationships and environments are essential to prevent child maltreatment and to assure that children reach their full potential (Centers for Disease Control and Prevention 2014; American Psychological Association Fact Sheet 2017). And child maltreatment takes a large economic toll on our society through child welfare costs, physical and mental health costs, special education costs, and legal system costs (Fang et al. 2012; APA 2017). Research shows that adverse childhood experiences are associated with risky health behaviors, crime, chronic health conditions, low life potential, and early death (Centers for Disease Control and Prevention 2016) – all of which have a profound negative impact on the health and opportunity of individuals.

Exposure to violence during adolescence, for instance, has been shown to correlate with reduced educational attainment, decreased odds of getting married, reduced income and net worth in adulthood, and increased instances of delinquency and violent behavior (Stouthamer-Loeber et al. 2002; Weaver, Borkowski, and Whitman 2008; Covey, Menhard, and Franzese 2013). A study conducted by Weaver, Borkowski, and Whitman (2008) found that witnessing violence and victimization prior to age ten predicted delinquency and violent behaviors even after controlling for prenatal maternal and early childhood externalizing problems. Violence victimization, in fact, has been found to be the single best predictor of juvenile violent behaviors for both boys and girls in a nationally representative sample of adolescents (Blum, Ireland, and Blum 2003). Among urban black adolescents, retrospective reports of witnessing violence and victimization were the strongest predictor of current use of violence, such as involvement in fights and carrying weapons (Durant et al. 1994; Weaver, Borkowski, and Whitman 2008: 96).[3] And Flannery et al. (1998) found that violent behavior among adolescents who were exposed to high levels of home violence were three times higher for girls and two times higher for boys when compared with adolescents from low-violence homes (see also Stouthamer-Loeber et al. 2002). Additional studies have found that exposure to violence at school is associated with concurrent violent behavior as well as psychological trauma (Flannery, Wester, and Singer 2004), that observing violence and family conflict is correlated with increased depressive symptoms during high school (Lambert et al. 2010; Eisman et al. 2015), that adolescents exposed to community violence have lower high school grade point averages and decreased enjoyment and interest in school (Borofsky et al. 2013; Strom et al. 2013), and that neighborhood violence has a negative impact on children's math and reading scores on standardized tests (Milam, Furr-Holden, and Leaf 2010) (see also American Psychological Association Fact Sheet 2017).

Domestic violence is another social determinant of health and safety and has been shown to have long-term negative effects on employment, mental health, and incarceration rates, especially for women. Studies have found that women in abusive relationships frequently lose their jobs, experience high job turnover, and are fired or forced to quit more frequently (Crowne et al. 2011; Adams et al. 2013). And the negative effects of abuse on the ability to remain employed are not just short term; they also inhibit women's ability to maintain a job for some time after the abuse ends (Adams et al. 2013). Domestic violence has also been identified as the primary cause

---

[3] It should be noted that the carrying of weapons is often done out of fear of victimization rather than violent or malicious intent (Jenkins and Bell 1994).

of family homelessness in 17 percent of cities across the United States (United States Conference of Mayors 2015). Other studies have found that 85–90 percent of women in prison have a history of being victims of violence prior to their incarceration, including domestic violence, sexual violence, and child abuse (ACLU 2011). One reasons for this is that women are often coerced into criminal activity by their abusers or forced to fight back to defend their lives or their children's lives (Gilfus 2002).

A study of women incarcerated in New York's Rikers Island found that most of the domestic violence survivors interviewed reported engaging in illegal activity in response to experience of abuse, the threat of violence, or coercion by a male partner (Richie and Johnsen 1996). Another study found that, of 525 abused women at a mental health center who had committed at least one crime, nearly half had been coerced into committing crimes by their batterers as "part of a structural sequence of actions in a climate of terror and diminished, violated sense of self" (Loring and Beaudoin 2000). Women, however, are more likely to be incarcerated for drug and property crimes compared to men and less likely to be incarcerated for violent crime (Carson 2016). Furthermore, women of color and low-income women are disproportionately affected by mandatory arrest policies for domestic violence. A New York City study found, for example, that of women who had been arrested with their abusers (dual arrest cases) or arrested as a result of a complaint lodged by their abusers (retaliatory arrest cases), 66 percent were African American or Latina, 43 percent were living below the poverty line, and 19 percent were receiving public assistance at the time (Haviland et al. 2001).

Sadly the incarceration of women has additional negative consequences. Studies indicate that 70 percent of women in prison are mothers (Bloom 2004) and many of them are the primary caretakers of their children at home (Richie 2000). In fact, 1.3 million children are affected by female imprisonment, including the children left at home when the mother is imprisoned and the babies born and raised in prison (Poehlman 2003). The impact of this on children and families is profound and hard to fully calculate. The statistics are even more disturbing when one looks at the number of children who have *either* parent in prison or jail. Between 1991 and 2007, the number of children with a parent in state or federal prison grew 80 percent. Today, an estimated 2.7 million children in the United States have a parent in prison or jail – that is, one in every twenty-eight children (3.6 percent of all children) (Pew Charitable Trust 2010).

7.1.3 Housing, Mental Illness, and Healthcare

Housing, mental illness, and access to healthcare are also social determinants of health and criminal behavior and quite often overlap for vulnerable populations. For example, about a fifth of the 1.7 million homeless people in the United States suffer from untreated schizophrenia or manic-depressive illness. And not surprisingly, mental illness often prolongs homelessness. Approximately 26 percent of homeless adults staying in shelters live with serious mental illness and an estimated 66 percent live with severe mental illness and/or substance use disorders. Mental illness and homelessness also puts people at an increased risk of being the victim of a crime as well as being arrested for a crime, particularly disorderly conduct and property theft. In 2005, more than half of all people incarcerated in prisons and jails had a mental illness: 56 percent of state prisoners, 45 percent of federal prisoners, and 64 percent of jail inmates (James and Glaze 2006). Of those who had a mental illness, about three quarters also had a co-occurring substance use disorder (James and Glaze 2006). Researchers have also found that of more than 20,000 adults entering five local jails, 14.5 percent of the men and 31 percent of the women had serious mental illnesses, which, taken together, comprises 16.9 percent of those studied – rates in excess of three to six times those found in the general population (Steadman et al. 2009). And the numbers are even worse for juvenile offenders. Approximately 60–70 percent of youth in juvenile justice detention, correctional, or community-based facilities have a diagnosable mental illness and more than 27 percent have a serious mental illness that impairs his or her ability to function (Skowyra and Cocozza 2006).

Studies have also found that homelessness significantly increases the risk of incarceration (Greenberg and Rosenheck 2008). One national survey of jail inmates found that prison inmates who had been homeless (i.e., those who reported an episode of homelessness anytime in the year before incarceration) made up 15.3 percent of the US jail population or 7.5 to 11.3 times the standardized estimate of 1.36 percent to 2.03 percent in the general US adult population (Greenberg and Rosenheck 2008). For those with mental illnesses, the rates of homelessness are even higher – about 20 percent (Greenberg and Rosenheck 2008). And in comparison with other inmates, those who were homeless were more likely to be currently incarcerated for a property crime, but they were also more likely to have past criminal justice system involvement for both nonviolent and violent offenses, to have mental health and substance abuse problems, to be less educated, and to be unemployed (Greenberg and Rosenheck 2008). Other studies have estimated that 25–50 percent of people experiencing homelessness also have a history of incarceration (Doherty 2015). Additional studies have found that the relationship between homelessness and prison runs in the other directions as well – that is, upon release from prison those who were previously homeless often return to homelessness while many others experience homelessness for the first time. There are a number of reasons for this including decreased employability, stigmatization, and exclusion from public housing in some states due to a felony conviction. These findings suggest that homelessness and incarceration increase the risk of each other, and these factors seem to be mediated by mental illness, substance abuse, education, and low SES. Adopting a public health approach to health and safety would require tackling the problem of homelessness and working to more effectively transition offenders back into society. And the justification for this would again be provided by the capabilities approach to social justice, since homelessness is an injustice that leads to numerous capability failures.

Access to healthcare is another social determinant of health and criminal behavior. For many vulnerable populations, including the homeless, poor, and mentally ill, not having access to affordable and consistent healthcare means forgoing treatment for mental illness, substance use, chronic health conditions, acute care, and injuries. Those without health insurance have less access to recommended care, receive poorer quality of care, and experience worse health outcomes than insured adults do (Institute of Medicine 2002; McWilliams 2009; National Immigration Law Center 2014). Uninsured adults are more than 25 percent more likely to die prematurely than adults with health insurance (Bailey 2012). The Institute of Medicine (2009) estimates that lack of health insurance led to the death of 18,000 adults in the year 2000, making it the sixth most frequent cause that year of death among people aged 18 to 64. Those without access to healthcare typically avoid seeking medical care unless they are faced with an emergency, or they delay care until their symptoms become intolerable (K. Davis 2003; National Immigration Law Center 2014). As a result, "the uninsured are less likely to receive a diagnosis in the early stages of a disease and are more likely to suffer complications from aggravated medical conditions" (National Immigration Law Center 2014). They are more likely to receive, say, an initial diagnosis of cancer at a later stage of the disease and die within less time after diagnosis (K. Davis 2003). And with acute or sudden conditions, such as injuries, the uninsured tend to experience poorer medical outcomes, are less likely to fully recover, and are more likely to die as a result of the injury (McWilliams 2009). The uninsured (and underinsured) are also more likely to be crushed by the healthcare costs associated with these treatments, forcing many to go bankrupt. According to Health Affairs, nearly two million Americans filed for medical bankruptcy in 2001 due to unexpected health problems (Hummelstein et al. 2005).

Studies have also found that people in the criminal justice system experience chronic health conditions, infectious diseases, substance use disorders, and mental illnesses at much higher rates than the general population (see, e.g., National Commission on Correctional Health Care 2002; Cloud 2014; Rich et al. 2014). And since more than 95 percent of prisoners eventually return to the general population, bringing their health conditions with them, and 80 percent are without health insurance upon reentry into the community (Rich et al. 2014), treatment initiated during incarceration frequently stops when an individual returns to society – including even HIV care, which often receives priority treatment in the incarcerated setting (Rich et al. 2011; Montague et al. 2012). This has, as one would predict, profound negative health consequences. Numerous studies have found that risk of emergency care, hospitalization, and death is exceptionally high after release from jail or prison (Binswanger et al. 2007; Binswanger et al. 2013; Frank et al. 2013; Wang, Wang, and Krumholz 2013; Rich et al. 2014). If we want to improve public health and safety, we should heed the advice of Rich et al. (2014) and view incarceration as a public health issue and draw those who are incarcerated into the healthcare system. This is "critical for the nation" and "is especially relevant for poor communities, communities of color, and other socially marginalized groups that are both disproportionately imprisoned and often disenfranchised from medical care" (2014: 463).

7.1.4 Education, Environment, and Nutrition

We also know that education, environmental health, and poor nutrition are important social determinants and have a profound negative affect on public health and safety. Beginning with education, studies indicate that only about half of incarcerated adults have a high school degree or its equivalent (Harlow 2003) and youth in the juvenile system are significantly more likely than other youth to have academic skills well below their grade level, possess a learning or developmental disability, and drop out of school (Katsiyannis et al. 2008). According to the Urban Institute, employment rates and earning histories of people in prison and jail are often low before incarceration as a result of limited education, low job skill levels, and the prevalence of physical and mental health problems – and incarceration only exacerbates these challenges (Holzer, Raphael, and Stoll 2003). A three-state recidivism study conducted from 2001 to 2006 found that less than half of people released from prison had secured a job upon their return to the community (Visher, Debus, and Yahner 2008). Almost all experts agree that education is important for preventing the occurrence of crime before it occurs and can help lower recidivism rates, especially if educational opportunities (including job training) are extended into prison. In fact, numerous studies show that enrollment in school and academic achievement are associated with lower levels of criminal behavior, re-offending, and better outcomes into adulthood (see, e.g., Katsiyannis et al. 2008). And a 2013 RAND Corporation study showed that participation in prison education, including academic and vocational programming, was associated with more than 40 percent reduction in recidivism – while also saving $4 to $5 for each dollar spent (Davis et al. 2013).

Environmental health and nutrition are also important determinants of public health and safety. As Georges Benjamin, the Executive Director of the American Public Health Association (APHA), writes: "Many communities lack access to nutritious, affordable food; are denied safe places to walk and exercise; or live near polluting factories." And as a result, the "health risks for these families are greater" (APHA 2017). The World Health Organization (WHO) defines *environment*, as it relates to health, as "all the physical, chemical, and biological factors external to a person, and all the related behaviors" (WHO 2006b). And *environmental health* consists of preventing or controlling disease, injury, and disability related to the interaction between people and their environment. As APHA puts it:

Environmental health is the branch of public health that focuses on the relationships between people and their environment; promotes human health and well-being; and fosters healthy and safe communities. Environmental health is a key part of any comprehensive public health system. The field works to advance policies and programs to reduce chemical and other environmental exposures in air, water, soil and food to protect people and provide communities with healthier environments. (2017)

A comprehensive public health approach should therefore incorporate a focus on, and concern for, air quality, surface and groundwater quality, toxic substances and hazardous wastes, climate change, exposure to lead in homes and schools, epidemiology, and other environmental factors, since we know that these can (and do) have profound effects on public health and safety.

Given limited space, I can only briefly mention a few of these determinants of health here – for a more comprehensive understanding of these issues see World Health Organization (2002, 2006a). Let me begin with air quality. We know that poor air quality is linked to premature death, cancer, and long-term damage to respiratory and cardiovascular systems (WHO 2005, 2006a, 2013, 2016a). And while we have made some progress reducing harmful air emissions, the EPA estimates that in 2008 approximately 127 million people lived in US counties that exceeded national air quality standards (US Environmental Protection Agency 2010). The World Health Organization (WHO) further estimates that in 2014, 92 percent of the world population was living in places where WHO air quality guidelines levels were not met (WHO 2016a). These are troubling statistics since outdoor air pollution was estimated to cause 3 million premature deaths worldwide in 2012 (WHO 2016a).

Surface and groundwater quality is another major determinant of environmental health. Worldwide, water-related disease remains one of the major health concerns. Diarrheal diseases, which are largely derived from poor water and sanitation, accounted for 1.8 million deaths in 2002 and contributed around 62 million Disability Adjusted Life Years per annum (WHO 2004a). According to the World Health Organization, "this places diarrhoeal diseases as the sixth highest cause of mortality and third in the list of morbidity and it is estimated that 3.7 per cent of the global disease burden is derived from poor water, sanitation and hygiene (Pruss-Ustun et al. 2004)" (WHO 2006b: 3). It was estimated that in 2002, roughly one-sixth of humanity (1.1 billion people) lacked access to any form of improved water supply within 1 kilometer of their home, and approximately 40 percent of humanity (2.6 billion people) lack access to some form of improved excreta disposal (WHO and UNICEF 2000). This is clearly a public health crisis and needs to be given urgent attention. To properly address it, though, a number of other social inequities will need to be addressed as well, since these negative health consequences are primarily borne by populations in developing counties and by children.

Exposure to lead is another major determinant of health. It can be caused (as we know from the tragic events in Flint, Michigan) by contamination from lead pipes or by inhalation of lead particles, ingestion of lead-contaminated dust or paint chips, or eating food from lead-glazed containers. Lead is a cumulative toxicant that affects multiple body systems and is particularly harmful to young children. When it enters the body it is distributed to the brain, liver, kidney, and bones – and no known level of lead exposure is considered safe. According to the World Health Organization, young children are particularly vulnerable to the toxic effects of lead and can suffer profound and permanent adverse health effects, particularly affecting the development of the brain and nervous system (WHO 2010, 2016b). Lead also causes long-term harm in adults, including increased risk of high blood pleasure and kidney damage. And exposure to pregnant women to high levels can cause miscarriage, stillbirth, premature birth, and low birth weight, as well as malformations (WHO 2010, 2016b). Children who survive lead poisoning may be left with mental retardation and behavioral disorders. As the WHO describes, "[L]ead affects children's brain development resulting in reduced intelligence quotient (IQ), behavioral changes such as reduced attention span and increased antisocial behavior, and reduced educational attainment" (WHO 2016b; see also 2010). In fact, numerous studies have found that the brain damage caused by exposure to lead and the neurobehavioral changes associated with it are irreversible and untreatable (Needleman et al. 1990; Bellinger, Stiles, and Needleman 1992; Burns et al. 1999; Rogan et al. 2001; Wright et al. 2008).

Given the focus of this book, a few additional facts are worth mentioning. First, exposure to lead is often a byproduct of other social injustices and is completely preventable. As the WHO describes:

> Although lead can affect children from every socioeconomic stratum, socially and economically deprived children in low-income countries carry the greatest burden of disease due to lead. Poor people are more likely to be exposed to lead and to be at risk of exposure to multiple sources. They are more likely to dwell on marginal land (near landfills and polluted sites), to live in substandard housing with ageing and deteriorating lead-based paint, and to live near industry sites where waste is burned. (2010: 35)

The WHO report goes on to say:

> Communities that lack political influence, communities that are disenfranchised, and ethnic minority groups have repeatedly been shown to be at greater risk of exposure to lead than other populations. Such communities typically lack the power to force companies, such as lead recyclers or smelters, to stop polluting their environment. (WHO 2010: 35; see also American Pediatrics Committee on Environmental Health 2003)

A comprehensive public health approach, like the one I advocate, will require our institutions to address these social injustices since they not only negatively affect public health and safety but also lead to a number of other capability failures.

The second thing I want to note is that since lead exposure at young ages leaves children with problems like learning disabilities, ADHD, and impulse control, it has also been proposed that it can lead to increases in criminal behavior (Billings and Schnepel 2015; Feigenbaum and Muller 2016; Aizer and Currie 2017). Three different research teams have recently studied the effects of lead exposure on juvenile delinquency and crime rates, and each found some support for the claim. Feigenbaum and Muller (2016) used homicide rates between 1921 and 1936 and compared them to cities with municipal water systems that used either lead or iron service pipes. They found support for the hypothesis that lead service pipes considerably increased city-level homicide rates. Aizer and Currie (2017), on the other hand, used data linking preschool blood lead levels with data on school detention and suspension for 120,000 children born between 1990 and 2004 in Rhode Island. They found that a one-unit increase in lead increased the probability of suspension from school by 6.4–9.3 percent and the potential of detention by 27–74 percent, though the latter applied only to boys. Billings and Schnepel (2015) took a different approach and studied the effect of CDC-recommended interventions for kids with elevated blood lead levels. Since kids are required to test positive for lead twice to get services, they hypothesized that the random noise in the test could be used to study the effects of treatment – that is, they presumed that a lot of kids who test over the threshold once but not a second time do so for reasons other than their actual lead exposure. Using data on kids born between 1990 and 1997 in Charlotte, NC, and comparing blood lead level tests with school records and adult arrests, they found that kids who received the intervention exhibited substantially less antisocial behavior, including suspensions, absences, school crimes, and violent crime arrests. While much more work in this area needs to be done, these findings suggest that lead exposure is potentially a public health *and* safety issue (see also Drum 2016).

Climate change is another determinant and is likely to have profound negative effects on public health and safety. The Intergovernmental Panel on Climate Change (IPCC) projects, for example, that climate change will impact sea level, patterns of infectious diseases, air quality, and the severity of natural disasters such as floods, droughts, and storms (IPCC 2014a, 2014b, 2014c; see also Patz et al. 2005; Kinney 2008). And while many are beginning to understand that we need to combat climate change for the sake of society and its environmental health (although, perhaps, not enough), very few realize that climate change is also a "threat multiplier" and will likely increase the incidents of war, conflict, and violence (Department of Defense 2015; NATO Science and Technology Committee 2017; Weaver et al. 2017). A new NATO special report concludes that climate change is the ultimate "threat multiplier" – meaning that it can exacerbate political instability in the world's most unstable regions. By intensifying extreme weather events like droughts, climate change stresses food and water supplies. In poor, arid countries already facing food and water shortages, this increased stress can lead to disputes and violent conflict over scarce resources. Rising sea levels can also cause refugee crises as large numbers of people are forced to relocate, and this too can cause conflict as resources get stretched and cultures clash.

The US Department of Defense (DoD) has also concluded that climate change is a threat multiplier and that "climate change is an urgent and growing threat to national security, contributing to increased natural disasters, refugee flows, and conflicts over basic resources such as food and water" (DoD Report 2015: 3). Former Defense Secretary Chuck Hagel said, for example: "Rising global temperatures, changing precipitation patterns, climbing sea levels and more extreme weather events will intensify the challenges of global instability, hunger, poverty, and conflict." He went on to say that "[t]hey will likely lead to food and water shortages, pandemic disease, disputes over refugees and resources, and destruction by natural disasters in regions across the globe" (DoD News 2014). The U.N. Secretary-General Antonio Guterres has also made similar statements (U.N. Press Release 2017). And in 2016, a coalition of twenty-five military and national security experts, including former advisers to Ronald Reagan and George W. Bush, warned that climate change poses a "significant risk to U.S. national security and international security" and requires immediate attention from the US federal government (Center for Climate and Security 2016). It would seem, then, that climate change is not only an environmental issue, it is a major public safety concern.

One last social determinant worth mentioning here is diet and nutrition. We know that access to food, diet, and good nutrition are a critical pathway in influencing chronic conditions such as hypertension, diabetes, cardiovascular disease, obesity, cancer, osteoporosis, and dental disease (WHO 2002a, 2002b, 2004; Viswanath and Bond 2007). A joint report put out by the World Health Organization (WHO) and the Food and Agriculture Organization (FAO) (2003) found, for example, that many of the deaths and disabilities caused by the major nutrition-related chronic diseases are due to risk factors that could easily be prevented. The report goes on to make a number of recommendations to help prevent death and disability from major nutrient-related chronic diseases. Unfortunately, many poor, disadvantaged, and marginalized people find it difficult (or even impossible) to follow these guidelines due to larger systemic social inequities. This is why concern for public health and safety cannot be separated from issues of social justice – that is, we will need to address these larger social issues if we want to promote public health and safety. With regard to diet and nutrition, these include addressing household food security (e.g., access to affordable and appropriate food), national and regional food security (e.g., the ability to provide adequate nutrition within a country without relying heavily on imported products), and cold-chain reliability (the safety of transporting products that deteriorate microbiologically in the heat).

It should also be noted that like many of the other social determinants discussed thus far, there is good reason to think that poor nutrition and diet can also negatively impact public safety, not just health. For instance, several studies now suggest that nutrient-poor diets can contribute to violent criminal acts and psychopathology (see, e.g., Hibbeln 2001; Gesch et al. 2002; Zaalberg et al. 2010; Deans 2011). In one study conducted by Bernard Gesch and colleagues (2002), 231 adult male prisoners received a daily vitamin, mineral, and essential fatty acid supplementation or a placebo. After 142 days, Gesch et al. found that the disciplinary incidents per 1,000 person-days dropped from 16 to 10.4 in the active group, which is a 35 percent reduction, whereas the placebo group only dropped 6.7 percent – and for especially violent incidents, the active group dropped by 37 percent. Zaalberg and colleagues (2010) were able to replicate these findings – the only difference was that in their study the supplements used included increased doses of omega-3 fatty acids compared to Gesch. These results, especially with regard to omega-3s, are interesting since there is growing evidence that low levels of omega-3 alongside other micronutrient deficits may be linked to antisocial and aggressive behavior (Schoenthaler 1983a, 1983b; Corrigan et al. 1994; Schoenthaler and Bier 2000; Gesch et al. 2002).

Two randomized clinical trials have found that anger scores were reduced among substance abusers and participants with borderline personality disorder when administered omega-3s (Zanarini and Frankenburg 2003; Buydens-Branchey, Branchey, and Hibbeln 2008). And a study by Gow and colleagues (2013) conducted in children and adolescents with ADHD and symptoms of conduct disorder found that low blood levels of omega-3 were negatively associated with high scores on callous and unemotional (CU) traits. This is particularly interesting since callous and unemotional traits are a sizeable risk factor for the later development of psychopathy and antisocial behaviors. These and other findings lead Adrian Raine to suggest that omega-3s might be a place to intervene given everything we know about the neuroanatomy of violent criminals (Raine et al. 2016) – since it has been shown that omega-3 supplementation increases the function of the dorsolateral prefrontal cortex, a region Raine found to have higher rates of damage or dysfunction in criminal offender (Raine et al. 2000; Raine 2014).

In one study, Raine and colleagues (2014) conducted a longitudinal study of children in the small island of Mauritius and found that omega-3 may have long-term neurodevelopmental effects that ultimately reduce antisocial and aggressive behavior in children. The study tracked the development of children who had participated in an enrichment program at three years old, as well as the development of children who did not participate. The enrichment program had additional cognitive stimulation, physical exercise, and nutritional enrichment – including an extra two and a half portions of fish a week. They found that at eleven years old, participants in the enrichment program showed a marked improvement in brain function as measured by EEG, as compared to those who did not participate. And at age twenty-three, they showed a 34 percent reduction in criminal behavior. In a more recent study, Raine et al. (2016) found that nutritional supplementation of omega-3, multivitamins, and minerals for more than three months, combined with cognitive behavior therapy, reduced childhood aggression in eleven- to twelve-year-olds.

These findings not only highlight the importance of diet and nutrition with regard to public health and safety, they also suggest that supplements, including omega-3s, can potentially be used (along with more traditional therapies) to help reduce aggression, violence, and crime.

7.1.5 The Neuroscience of Psychopathy

Let me conclude this section with a brief discussion of psychopathy since it is, perhaps, the best-known personality disorder associated with violent antisocial behavior. Psychopathy is a "personality construct characterized by deficits in interpersonal relations and affect processes (e.g., fearlessness, callousness, failure to form close emotional bonds, dishonesty, deficits in passive avoidance learning, and deficient empathic responses) as well as antisocial and impulsive behavior" (Hare and Neumann 2008; Leutgeb et al. 2015: 195). Psychopathy is strongly associated with violence and criminal recidivism (Hare 1991, 2003; Kiehl and Hoffman 2011) – and the conning, manipulative, interpersonal style of psychopaths typically has a broad, destructive impact on the individuals' life, work, and relationships (Anderson and Kiehl 2014: 103). The Psychopathy Checklist-Revised is widely used as the measure to identify psychopathic traits and it comprises two factors reflecting emotional and interpersonal detachment (Factor 1) as well as antisocial behavior and parasitic lifestyle (Factor 2) (Hare 2003). Given its connection with violence and criminal behavior, psychopathy is clearly relevant to our discussion of public health and safety.

Measures of psychopathy have proven to be valuable for risk assessment in violent criminals. As Anderson and Kiehl summarize the findings:

> While only about 1% of the adult general population would be classified as such by Hare's Psychopathy Checklist-Revised, psychopaths make up around 20% of the prison population in North America (Hare 2003). Above and beyond criminal activity, psychopaths are particularly prone to violence, demonstrating increased aggressive behavior and committing a greater number of violent attacks than non-psychopaths (Salekin et al. 1996) ... Psychopathy is also a strong predictor of how likely one is to re-offend after release from prison (Hart et al. 1988; Porter et al. 2001), and it is a particularly strong predictor of violent recidivism (Cornell et al. 1996; Harris et al. 1991; Porter et al. 2009). Within one year of release psychopaths are about three times more likely to recidivate than non-psychopaths, and four times more likely to violently recidivate (Hemphill et al. 1998). Indeed, after 10 years, 77% of psychopaths had committed a violent offense compared to 40% of the sample in a large follow-up assessment (Harris et al. 1991). Non-psychopathic offenders' violent recidivism rates appear to plateau at about 40%; however after 20 years, it was reported that 90% of psychopaths had committed another violent crime (Rise and Harris 1997). Furthermore, these trends remain consistent outside North America, generalizing across a variety of cultures (Hare et al. 2000). (Anderson and Kiehl 2014: 107–108)

Since the core features of psychopathy appear to be developmental in nature, with relatively persistent traits becoming apparent before the age of ten, the better we understand how "neurocognitive peculiarities can hijack the development of our moral sensibility" (Anderson and Kiehl 2014: 103) the more successful we will be in developing new strategies for managing the specific deficits responsible for this altered developmental trajectory.

Over the last few decades, neuroscientists have begun to study the neuronal basis of psychopathy (see e.g., Raine et al. 2000; Glenn et al. 2010; Glenn, Yang, and Raine 2012; Viding, McCory, and Seara-Cardoso 2014; Leutgeb et al. 2015). Leutgeb et al. (2015), for example, compared structural imaging data from forty male high-risk violent offenders and thirty-seven non-delinquent healthy controls via voxel-based morphometry. They then correlated psychopathic traits and risk for violence recidivism with gray matter volume of regions of interest previously shown relevant for criminal behavior. They found that (a) relative to controls, criminals showed less gray matter volume in the prefrontal cortex and more gray matter volume in cerebellar regions and basal ganglia structures; (b) within criminals, there was a negative correlation between prefrontal gray matter volume and psychopathy; (c) there was a positive correlation between cerebellar gray matter volume and psychopathy as well as risk of recidivism for violence; (d) gray matter volumes of the basal ganglia and supplementary motor area were positively correlated with antisociality, and (e) that gray matter volume of the amygdala was negatively correlated with dynamic risk for violence recidivism (Leutgeb et al. 2015). They concluded that in violent offenders, deviations in gray matter volume of the prefrontal cortex as well as areas involved in the motor component of impulse control (cerebellum, basal ganglia, supplementary motor area) are differentially related to psychopathic traits and the risk of violence recidivism. Other neuroimaging investigations have found reductions in orbitofrontal gray matter in psychopaths (e.g., de Oliveira-Souza 2008; Tiihonen et al. 2008; Boccardi et al. 2011) as well as volume reduction in the most anterior frontopolar regions of the prefrontal cortex (de Oliveira-Souza 2008; Tiihonen et al. 2008).

The amygdala also features prominently in theories of psychopathy due to its role in forming stimulus-reinforcement association, conditioned fear responses, and the initiation of affective states (Davis 1997; Davis and Whalen 2001; Anderson and Kiehl 2014: 111). And recent neuroimaging data have strongly implicated the involvement of the amygdala in psychopathy-related deficits (Anderson and Kiehl 2014: 111). In one large-scale investigation involving nearly 300 incarcerated subjects, Ermer and colleagues (2011) found that psychopathy was associated with decreased regional gray matter in several paralimbic and limbic areas, including the amygdala. Yang et al. (2010) also found that volume reductions in both the prefrontal cortex and the amygdala were more pronounced in psychopaths with criminal convictions compared to both controls and "successful" psychopaths. And in their overview of the neuroscientific literature on psychopathy, Anderson and Kiehl describe a number of other findings related to the amygdala and prefrontal cortex:

> Kiehl and colleagues (2001) were the first to report amygdala dysfunction in criminal psychopaths using fMRI, demonstrating reduced activity there when comparing emotional and non-emotional words. Amygdala deficits in psychopathy have also been demonstrated during aversive conditioning (Birbaumer et al. 2005; Rilling et al. 2007; Veit et al. 2002), when viewing pictures depicting moral violations (Harenski et al. 2009), viewing pictures of facial affect (Gordon et al. 2004), when viewing pictures depicting moral violations (Harenski et al. 2010), and when viewing fearful faces (Dolan and Fullam 2009). Many of these reports are the same as those indicating lower prefrontal activity in psychopaths, and this likely speaks to the extensive connections between the amygdala and prefrontal cortex. Building on the pattern noted above, youth with callous/unemotional traits and conduct disorder also show lower amygdala activity when engaged in passive avoidance learning (Finger et al. 2011) and viewing fearful faces (Jones et al. 2009). This result suggests that disruption in affective processing evident in adults is a deficit which begins early in life, having persistent effects into adulthood. (2014: 112)

Additional studies have found reduced gray matter volumes in psychopaths' cingulate cortex and other paralimbic structures (Boccardi et al. 2011), tissue reduction in the temporal pole (Muller et al. 2008) and insula (de Oliveira-Souza et al. 2008), and tissue reduction in the posterior cingulate (Ermer et al. 2011).

Given these new insights into the neurological correlates of psychopathy, neuroscientific methods may have the potential to improve existing tools for prediction of violence recidivism (Leutgeb et al. 2015: 194; see also Meixner 2014). But unlike the social determinants of health and criminal behavior discussed earlier, I want to flag a few potential ethical concerns about the use of neuroscience in predicting future violent behavior. The use of neuroscience in criminal law has recently become a topic of much debate and has even given birth to a new area of study called *neurolaw* (see, e.g., Shen 2010; Jones 2013; Jones et al. 2013a, 2013b; Meixner 2014). John Meixner identifies three major areas of interest regarding the application and use of neuroscience within the law: (1) neuroscience-based credibility assessments, which seeks to detect lies or knowledge associated with a crime; (2) application of neuroscience to aid in assessment of brain capacity for culpability, especially among adolescents; and (3) neuroscience-based prediction of future recidivism (Meixner 2014). I am only concerned here with the last of these – the potential use of neuroscience to predict violent and criminal behavior before it occurs. While a public health approach to criminal behavior should welcome any and all improvements in our current risk assessment instruments, including those provided by neuroscience, I fear that these measures can potentially be used to justify preemptive incapacitation for those who are deemed a risk to society. There is also the very real potential for stigmatization – identifying children who exhibit early psychopathic traits, for example, may be helpful in providing early interventions, but it can also stigmatize them by labeling them as potential future criminals.

Since these issues are important, I would like to make a few broad suggestions now before returning to the issue again in the following chapter. First, on my model, preemptive incapacitation should be prohibited in all but the most extreme circumstances (see Chapter 8 for more details). Given that we are unable to assess with certainty the likelihood of future violent behavior, and given the potential for false positives, I maintain that significant weight should be given to protecting individual liberty. Just as we adopt the *presumption of innocence* in the context of criminal law, I propose that we likewise adopt the *presumption of harmlessness* in the context of prediction (Floud and Young 1981). The burden of proof should always be on the one who wants to limit liberty. Imagine, for example, that the social and neurological determinants of crime outlined earlier are like individual dials on a vast combination lock. Even if nineteen out of, say, twenty dials are in place, the lock will not open until the last dial (e.g., the last environmental or neurological trigger) is put in place. Of course, in real life the number of variables responsible for violent behavior is much greater. I therefore contend that since we are in a poor epistemic position to judge when (if ever) certain factors will trigger a violent episode, and since this will likely remain true for the foreseeable future, we should put a bright line in the sand in favor of protecting individual liberty and against preemptive incapacitation – especially with regard to risk assessed by brain scans or other demographic risk factors.

Second, since the potential for stigmatization in youth who exhibit callous-unemotional traits (an early indicator of psychopathy) is a serious one, I recommend that we favor interventions that (a) maximize the autonomy of agents, (b) acknowledge the potential for change, and (c) focus on current antisocial behavior rather than future risk of offending. In fact, studies have found that not all children that exhibit callous-unemotional traits grow up to be adult psychopaths, which is important. This challenges us to find the right interventions – and there are some promising treatment approaches out there for young people. As Anderson and Kiehl point out:

> [The] patterns of delinquency [in psychopaths] are persistent from a young age, and are a conspicuous cause for concern that the developmental nature of psychopaths may place even the very young on a trajectory for incorrigible antisocial deviance. Evidence suggests, however, that such a bleak outlook may only apply when traditional intervention strategies are implemented ... In fact, alternative strategies which incorporate knowledge of psychopaths' impaired forms of social reasoning have proven to be more effective, particularly, when applied to younger offenders. (2014: 113)

Anderson and Kiehl go on to outline a number of these alternative strategies, including targeted treatments tailored for specific groups of offenders (see also

Andrews et al. 1990). They acknowledge that therapeutic interventions and rehabilitation strategies with adult psychopaths have traditionally proven ineffective and even occasionally counterproductive, but they also note that "successful interventions might be more likely at an earlier stage when the focused reinforcement of socially adaptive behaviors is likely to have a more robust impact on the developing personality and behavioral habits of the fledgling psychopath" (2014: 115). The Mendota Juvenile Treatment Center (MJTC) in Madison, Wisconsin, for example, has designed and implemented an ambitious treatment program that employs intensive one-on-one therapeutic attention, several hours a day, for a minimum of six months (Caldewll and Van Rybroek 2001). Studies indicate that this intensive treatment protocol may cut violent recidivism rates in half, compared to juveniles receiving standard group therapy sessions (Caldewll and Van Rybroek 2001, 2005).

It is also worth noting that recent research has found that psychopaths – especially those with antisocial personality disorder and psychopathy – *do not learn well with punishment* (Gregor et al. 2015). A recent study by Gregor et al. (2015) found that people with antisocial personality disorder and psychopathy appear to have reinforcement-learning systems that do not operate in the "normal" way. In particular, the behavior of men with antisocial personality disorder "seems to be driven more by potential rewards than potential punishments (reward dominance)" (2015: 153). This suggests that punitive approaches to criminal behavior, like those currently favored in the United States, are not likely to be effective in altering the antisocial behavior of psychopaths. When it comes to adult criminal psychopaths, "the best strategy might be to focus on minimizing the harm they cause others by reinforcing specific behavioral patters and self-control" and the most effective means of doing this "might be to promote such behavior with measured rewards" (Anderson and Kiehl 2014: 114).

7.2 ADOPTING A PUBLIC HEALTH APPROACH

Everything we know about the social determinants of health and criminal behavior indicates that the best way to protect public health and safety, and to promote the capabilities needed for human well-being, is to adopt a public health approach aimed at addressing poverty, educational inequity, abuse, domestic violence, unemployment, housing, healthcare, mental health, and other structural factors. This conclusion is in line with the recommendations of the World Health Organization Commission on Social Determinants of Health (2008), the Vera Institute of Justice (Cloud 2014), the American Public Health Association (2018), Public Health England (2019), the Acheson Report in Britain (Acheson et al. 1998), and the National Criminal Justice and Public Health Alliance (Heller 2016) (see also Lee 2005; Irwin et al. 2006). I contend that if we really want to improve public health and safety it is imperative that we use the power of the public health framework to reenvision and change our criminal justice system and all its component parts (see also Heller 2016). I concur with Jonathan Heller that we need to start thinking about criminal justice as a public health issue by "changing behaviors related to violence; addressing the traumas that victims face and how those perpetuate crime; reducing adverse childhood experiences; ensuring those leaving prison [have access to healthcare]; and working to reinvest savings from criminal justice reform back into our hardest hit communities" (2006).

In public health ethics, a failure on the part of public health institutions to ensure the social conditions necessary to achieve a sufficient level of health is considered a grave injustice. For instance, the extraordinary disparities in life expectancy, child survival, and health that distinguish those living in rich and poor countries constitute a profound injustice that is the duty of the global community to redress. An important task of the public health approach, then, is to identify which inequalities in health are the most egregious and thus which should be given the highest priority in public health policy and practice. The public health approach to criminal behavior likewise maintains that a core moral function of the criminal justice system is to identify and remedy social and economic inequalities responsible for crime. Just as public health is negatively affected by poverty, educational inequity, abuse, unemployment, homelessness, and other social determinants, so too is public safety. The broad approach to criminal justice provided by the public health–quarantine model therefore places issues of social justice at the forefront. It sees social injustice and systematic disadvantage as serious threats to public safety and it prioritizes the reduction of such inequalities.

Furthermore, as we saw in the previous chapter, I view the capabilities approach to social justice as the proper moral foundation of public health ethics. According to the capabilities approach, when asking normative questions, we should ask what people are able to do and what lives they are able to lead. The approach is concerned with aspects of people's lives such as their health, the education they enjoy, the support they receive from their social networks, and much more. This means that the broader commitment of public health should be the achievement of those capabilities needed to secure a sufficient level of human well-being – including, but not limited to, health, reasoning, self-determination, attachment, personal security, and respect. By placing social justice at the foundation of the public health approach, the realms of criminal justice and social justice are brought closer together – and I view this as a virtue of the theory since it is impossible to adequately deal with criminal justice without simultaneously addressing issues of social justice.

But what exactly does a "public health" approach to criminal behavior look like? To get more concrete, we can say, first, that a public health approach to criminal behavior is one that (a) focuses on the health, safety, and well-being of entire populations; (b) is focused on prevention – that is, by tackling "upstream" risk factors, it aims to lessen "downstream" consequences; (c) takes a system-wide multi-agency approach, recognizing that preventing criminal behavior requires the cooperation of multiple agencies, institutions, and stakeholders; (d) requires long-term commitment; and (e) seeks to build an evidence base that recognizes the complexity of the issues involved (Jones and Zoete 2018). Second, the public health approach understands that, like illness, criminal behavior can be encouraged or discouraged by structural factors. Taking a public health approach means "looking behind an issue or problem or illness to understand what is driving it" (Public Health England & College of Policing 2019: 4). Third, it typically involves taking epidemiology (the study of the distribution of risk and disease in space and time) and turning it into a study of variables, vectors, and factors that affect distribution of crime and risk (McManus 2018). These variables include upstream ones like the physical environment, opportunity for offending, and circumstances that lead people to offending rather than non-offending; as well as downstream ones like rehabilitation to reduce recidivism (McManus 2018). Epidemiology is a quantitative public health discipline that looks at the frequency and patterns of events in a group of people and what the risk and protective factors are. "This is often the starting point for public health approaches to violence prevention, some of which use epidemiology to understand the patterns of violent events" (Public Health England & College of Policing 2019: 5).

Lastly, all public health approaches share a basic methodology, which generally involves four key stages (CDC 2019):

(1) **Step 1: Define and Monitor the Problem:** The first step in preventing criminal behavior is understanding the scale and nature of the problem. We need to understand the "who," "what," "where," and "how" of the problem. As the CDC describes: "Grasping the magnitude of the problem involves analyzing data such as the number of violence-related behaviors, injuries, and deaths. Data can demonstrate how frequently violence [and criminal behavior generally] occurs, where it occurs, trends, and who the victims and perpetrators are" (CDC 2019).

(2) **Step 2: Identify Risk and Protective Factors:** In addition to understanding the scale and nature of the problem, it is also important to understand what factors protect people or put them at risk for experiencing or perpetrating criminal behavior. The CDC defines a *risk factor* as a "[c]haracteristic that increases the likelihood of a person becoming a victim or perpetrator of violence [or criminal behavior]" (2019). On the other hand, a *protective factor* is a "[c]haracteristic that decreases the likelihood of a person becoming a victim or perpetrator of violence because it provides a buffer against risk." Understanding the social determinants of health and criminal behavior is, therefore, essential to Step 2. They provide us with an understanding of the risk factors associated with criminal behavior and inversely direct us to important protective factors. For instance, we know that witnessing domestic violence as a child is a well-established risk factor for either perpetrating or experiencing violence later in life, while a close relationship with parents or friends can protect against violent behaviors (Public Health England and

College of Policing 2019). The same is true with many other social determinants of criminal behavior.

(3) **Step 3: Develop and Test Prevention Strategies:** This step involves designing interventions and policies to tackle the problem using multiple services, as well as monitoring and evaluating the impact of those interventions. This step requires an evidence-based approach to program planning. Once a program or policy has been implemented, it should be evaluated rigorously to determine its effectiveness.

(4) **Step 4: Assure Widespread Adoption:** Once prevention programs have been proven effective, they must be implemented and adopted more broadly. Step 4 therefore involves scaling up successful strategies. This may require dissemination techniques to promote widespread adopting including training, networking, technical assistance, and evaluation.

The public health approach to criminal behavior is therefore a multidisciplinary, evidence-based approach. It relies on knowledge from a broad range of disciplines including medicine, epidemiology, sociology, psychology, criminology, education, and economics (Dahlberg and Krug 2002). It also emphasizes input from diverse sectors including health, education, social serves, business, community groups, and criminal justice (Dahlberg and Krug 2002). In practice, this means addressing criminal behavior requires collective action on the part of numerous agencies, institutions, and stakeholders.

The American Public Health Association (APHA) describes the public health approach to violence and criminal behavior as follows:

> The recognition of violence as a health issue is founded on an understanding of violent behavior as arising from contextual, biological, environmental, systemic, and social stressors [Dahlberg and Mercy 2009]. Violence is defined as "the intentional use of physical force or power, threatened or actual, against oneself, another person, or against a group or community, which either results in or has a high likelihood of resulting in injury, death, psychological harm, maldevelopment, or deprivation" [WHO 2019]. A "trauma-informed" approach suggests that violence is not symptomatic of "bad people" but, rather, is a negative health outcome resulting from exposure to numerous risk factors [Center for Nonviolence and Social Justice 2019]. The public health approach to violence focuses on prevention through addressing the known factors that increase or decrease the likelihood of violence. Within the health system, every interaction is an opportunity to prevent violence directly. Thus, the public health system must play a primary role in preventing the spread of violence, with the public health workforce involved in the critical functions of training, educating, and analyzing, and there must be an explicit focus on addressing inequalities and reducing racial bias in the system's institutions. This approach not only prevents harm and injustice but also saves a significant amount in funding. (APHA 2018)

This statement builds on a growing body of research, including the 2001 report of the US Surgeon General on youth violence, showing that the public health approach to violence can be extremely effective. In this foundational document, Dr. David Satcher stated that "the key to preventing a great deal of violence is understanding where and when it occurs, determining what causes it, and scientifically documenting which of many strategies for prevention and intervention are truly effective" (Office of the Surgeon General, 2001). In fact, more than thirty years ago, the then Surgeon General C. Everett Koop issued a public health call to action that included the following components: "education of the public on the causes and effects of violence, education of health professionals as to better care for victims and better approaches to violence prevention, improved reporting and data-gathering, some additional research, and increased cooperation and coordination ... among health and health-related professions and institutions" (Koop 1985). The American Public Health Association described Dr. Koop's statement as "a prescient vision for a health-centered response to violence in which the health system assumes a central role in both treatment and prevention" (2018).

To see how effective the public health approach to criminal behavior could be, consider the case of Scotland. In 2005, the United Nations published a report declaring Scotland the most violent country in the developed world. That same year, a study by the World Health Organization (WHO) examined data from twenty-one European countries and found that Glasgow was the "murder capital" of Europe. At its peak, more than 1,000 people a year required treatment for facial trauma alone:

> Sometimes, the injuries were caused by a baseball bat, with shattered bones and bruising as bad as that from a car accident. More often than not, it was a knife. A slash across the forehead or cheek, leaving a scar etched across the face; a machete wound to the jaw, slicing through the skin and breaking the bone underneath. (Shackle 2018)

In response, Scotland adopted a public health approach to tackling violent crime. In 2005, a team of analysts for the Strathclyde Police Department wrote a report pointing out that traditional policing was not actually reducing violence. They started pulling together evidence on the social determinants of violent crime and found that "[p]articularly in Scotland, it was poverty, inequality, things like toxic masculinity, [and] alcohol use" (Shackle 2018). Next, they looked around the world to find and learn from pioneering programs working to prevent violent crime. This was the foundation of the Violence Reduction Unite (VRU), which took elements of those programs and focused on garnering support from a range of Scottish agencies – the health services, addiction support, job centers, and a host of others. Since the VRU was launched in 2005, the murder rate in Glasgow has dropped by 60 percent and facial traumas by more than half (American Public Health Association 2018; Shackle 2018). And countrywide, Scotland has seen homicide rates fall to their lowest level since 1976. By aligning the work of police officers, social workers, teachers, and doctors to support at-risk residents with new services – including housing support and employment advice – Scotland's public health approach has been able to reduce violent crime dramatically.

The Scottish government website now states that "Scotland has adopted a public health approach to tackling violence, as advocated by the World Health Organization. This includes prevention activity such as education and early intervention coupled with appropriate law enforcement when necessary."[4] While Scotland has the world's only police force to have formally adopted a public health model, with support from the Scottish government, the police work alongside a whole range of public agencies and stockholders, including doctors and social workers (Shackle 2018). Medics Against Violence, for example, is a program that goes into schools to educate children about knife crime. It also employs "navigators" who intervene in hospitals directly after violent incidents to defuse tension and help people find support: "After an initial conversation, the navigator follows up by helping the person get drug or alcohol treatment, job opportunities or therapy" (Shackle 2018). One of the key assumptions of the public health approach is that violent crime can be prevented and its impact reduced. As the World Health Organization writes:

> Despite the fact that violence has always been present, the world does not have to accept it as an inevitable part of the human condition ... Violence can be prevented and its impact reduced, in the same way that public health efforts have prevented and reduced pregnancy-related complications, workplace injuries, infectious diseases, and illness resulting from contaminated food and water in many parts of the world. The factors that contribute to violent responses – whether they are factors of attitude and behavior or related to larger social, economic, political and cultural conditions – can be changed. (WHO 2002: 3)

Given the success of Scotland's public health approach, the Mayor of London, Sadiq Khan, recently announced plans to adopt a similar program and "establish a new Violence Reduction Unit of specialists in health, police and local government to lead and deliver a long-term public health approach to tackling the causes of violent crime."[5]

Scotland, however, is only one example. In Medellín, Colombia, mapping the locations and drivers of violence allowed the city to target infrastructure spending to offer poor residents a path out of poverty and violent crime (Cerdá et al. 2012). As part of their public health approach, Medellín pioneered "urban acupuncture," a tactic using urban design to solve social problems. For instance, in one of the city's most

---

[4] For more information, please see the Scottish Government's policy on "Crime Prevention": www.gov.scot/policies/crime-prevention-and-reduction/violence-knife-crime/.
[5] Mayor of London, Press Release, September 19, 2018: www.london.gov.uk/press-releases/mayoral/new-public-health-approach-to-tackling-violence.

violent neighborhoods, they built a cable car to help residents reach other parts of the city. The public transit system connected isolated low-income neighborhoods to the city's urban center, which "helped them find jobs, and made them feel more included" (Siddons 2018). Elsewhere in the city, money was invested into the provisions of basic services – particularly libraries and schools (Siddons 2018). Better education and improved mobility helped cut the city's homicide rate from a world-record-breaking 380 per 100,000 to around 20 in 2015 (see Cerdá et al. 2012; Siddons 2018). A study by Cerdá et al. (2012) analyzed the effects of these neighborhood-level interventions in Medellín and compared them to control neighborhoods with no interventions. They found that the decline in homicide rate was 66 percent greater in intervention neighborhoods than in control neighborhoods, and resident reports of violence decreased 75 percent more in intervention neighborhoods. The study concluded that "[t]hese results show that interventions in neighborhood physical infrastructure can reduce violence" (2012: 1045).

In Chicago, a "Cure Violence" program using public health methods to interrupt violence, reduce risk, and change neighborhood norms reduced homicides and shootings by up to 70 percent and retaliations by 100 percent (Skogan 2008; Hemenway and Miller 2013; American Public Health Association 2018). One of the innovative techniques used in Chicago was to employ "violence interrupters" to intervene in the aftermath of a shooting to prevent retaliations, and to calm people down before a dispute escalates to violence (Shackle 2018). As Samira Shackle explains:

> Interrupters' ability to be effective depends on their credibility. Many ... have served long prison sentences and can speak from experience. Most also have a close relationship with the local community. They respond when a shooting takes place, for instance by convincing loved ones not to retaliate. But they are also aware if conflict is brewing between two individuals or rival groups, and can move in to defuse the tension or suggest peaceful alternatives. (2018)

Although it must always be adapted for each location, the Cure Violence program follows roughly the same steps when establishing itself in a new community. First, it maps the violence to see where it clusters. Then it hires credible workers with a local connection. Such methods have proven quite successful, not only in Chicago but elsewhere as well.

In Baltimore, for instance, one historically violent neighborhood went more than twenty-two months without a homicide after implementation of the same model (Webster et al. 2013; American Public Health Association 2018). In New York City, the John Jay College of Criminal Justice Research and Evaluation Center released an extensive independent evaluation of the local Cure Violence program that showed a 37 percent to 50 percent reduction in gun injuries in the two communities examined, a 14 percent reduction in attitudes supporting violence (with no change in the control group), and increased confidence in and willingness to contact police

(Butts and Delgado 2017; American Public Health Association 2018). Cure Violence is a community-based public health approach that uses three key components to stop the transmission of violence: (1) working with friends and families of victims to prevent retaliation and mediate ongoing disputes, (2) changing the thinking of those at high risk of perpetrating violence, and (3) changing group norms about violence in the broader community (Butts et al. 2015). Cure Violence has been implemented in major urban areas across the United States with a great deal of success (see, e.g., Picard-Fritsche and Cerniglia 2013; Butts et al. 2015; Butts and Delgado 2017; Delgado et al. 2017; Cerda, Tracy, and Keyes 2018).

These are just some examples of how adopting a public health approach can successfully prevent criminal behavior, reduce violence, and even reduce costs overall. For instance, the Safe and Successful Youth Initiative in Massachusetts, which requires cities to focus on using a street outreach model to provide comprehensive services and mentoring to at-risk young men 17 to 24 years of age, resulted in a 25 percent reduction in violence and a cost saving of $7 per dollar invested (Cooper et al. 2006). In fact, the American Public Health Association notes that "numerous studies show that our nation is paying extremely high costs [for violent crime], many of which are avoidable by investing in prevention and intervention" (2018). For instance, hospital-based violence intervention programs (HVIP) have been proven to be cost-effective. In San Francisco, researchers found that, for approximately every 100 young adult patients served annually, the city's program generated 24 quality-of-life years and produced hospital savings of $4,100 (APHA 2018; San Francisco Violence Prevention Services 2019). In addition, it has been estimated that providing HVIPs to all violently injured hospitalized patients would result in a national Medicaid savings of $69 million (Daily Caller 2014). Hence, the objection that public health initiatives are too costly is completely misguided – it cost us way more to do nothing.

The real challenge for the public health approach is not its costs, it is that it challenges our prevailing ways of thinking about criminal behavior. It recommends that we replace the current *reactive approach* to criminal justice with a *preventive approach*. Rather than reacting to crime after it occurs with punishment and indignation, the public health approach views criminal behavior as "a negative health outcome resulting from exposure to numerous risk factors" (APHA 2018). As a result, it views criminal behavior as preventable and therefore takes proactive steps to identify, prioritize, and address the social determinants of criminal behavior and intervene, where possible, to interrupt the transfer of violence. Some, however, resist this shift in focus since it downplays or eliminates the role of individual responsibility. For instance, Mark Moore, a critic of the public health approach, writes:

> Obviously, the ideas of individual guilt, blame, and accountability are central to the criminal justice approach to "intentional violence." The moral ... justification of punishment depends on assuming that individuals are accountable for their own

actions and that their degree of culpability depends on whether or not they intended to inflict injury on their fellow citizens. That is generally what is at issue in a criminal trial – not the question of what would be effective in controlling future offending by the particular offender being tried or by the general population. (1993: 43)

He goes on to say:

> In contrast, the public health approaches want to deemphasize and make unnecessary these difficult judgments of moral accountability. They would prefer to get at the problem by attacking the antecedent causes or the risk factors that shape the context of offending rather than the motivations and values of individual offenders. They would prefer to find the causes of violence in society than in the evil intentions of individual offenders. (1993: 43–44)

Moore wants to retain the reactive approach since he finds it simply "true" that "intentionally injuring a fellow citizen is morally offensive and should be responded to with moral indignation" (1993: 44). I, on the other hand, welcome the shift away from the reactive approach and toward a preventive approach for three main reasons.

First, while I acknowledge that one could adopt a public health approach to criminal behavior without sharing my free will skepticism, I nonetheless maintain that free will skepticism remains the most justified position to adopt. This is because all the other positions fail to preserve the control in action needed for basic desert moral responsibility. Furthermore, my epistemic argument maintains that if there is sufficient doubt that agents possess the kind of free will needed to justify the reactive approach, especially with regard to legal punishment, it would be seriously wrong to continue such practices. In addition, I also believe that free will skepticism and the public health approach work better in conjunction. I contend that there are a number of distinct advantages of rejecting the notions of free will and basic desert moral responsibility, and with them backward-looking blame and retributive punishment. First and foremost, once we abandon these antiquated notions, we can "look more clearly at the causes and more deeply into the systems that shape individuals and their behavior" (Waller 2011: 287) – and doing so will allow us to adopt more humane and effective approaches to criminal justice and social policy. Furthermore, belief in free will can stifle personal development, encourage punitive excess in criminal justice, and perpetuate social and economic inequalities (Pereboom 2001; Waller 2011).

Lastly, I contend that the skeptical perspective best captures the fact that the lottery of life is not always fair. The simple truth is that we do not all have equal starting points in life, and luck profoundly affects our life outcomes. The data on the social determinants of health and criminal behavior should make this point clear. I therefore agree with Gary Slutkin, the Founder and Executive Director of Cure Violence, when he says:

The idea that's wrong is that these people are "bad" and we know what to do with them, which is punish them. That's fundamentally a misunderstanding of the human. Behavior is formed by modeling and copying. When you're in a health leans, you don't blame. You try to understand, and you aim for solutions. (As quoted in, Shackle 2018)

Of course, the public health–quarantine model is able to justify incapacitating seriously dangerous criminals and, in that sense, is capable of reacting to criminal behavior when it occurs, but it does so without punishment or backward-looking blame. Furthermore, its focus remains squarely on prevention, employing public health methods to prevent criminal behavior from occurring in the first place. The public health approach therefore requires a shift in the way our society address violence, from a focus on reacting to violence after it occurs to a focus on changing the social, behavioral, and environmental factors that cause violence (Mercy et al. 1993).

7.3 PUBLIC POLICY PROPOSALS

Before concluding, I would like to offer up eleven distinct policy proposals for implementing a preventive approach to criminal behavior. Each is consistent with the public health framework and everything we know about the social determinants of health and criminal behavior. I do not intend for these proposals to be exhaustive, nor do I wish for them to be too specific. This is because the public health approach always needs to be sensitive to the specific factors and drivers of crime in the communities it is employed. What works in Chicago may not work in Scotland, and what works in Scotland may not work in Colombia. That said, certain social determinants impact individuals in such predictable ways that we should adopt policies aimed at addressing them. The proposals I favor are wide-reaching and ambitious, but my intent is for each to serve as a general principle by which more specific policy proposals can be generated. In all cases, we must take a system-wide, multi-agency approach, recognizing that preventing criminal behavior requires the cooperation of multiple agencies, institutions, and stakeholders. Furthermore, for these policies to be effective they need to be backed up with investment and accompanied by grassroots efforts.

Here are my proposals:

(1) Invest in programs and policies aimed at reducing poverty, homelessness, abuse, and domestic violence. As we have seen, poverty, low socioeconomic status, homelessness, abuse, and domestic violence are important social determinants of health (SDH) and criminal behavior (SDCB). They also severely diminish human well-being by limiting an individual's ability to secure a sufficient level of health, personal security, meaningful attachment, and self-determination. Under the capabilities approach, poverty is a capability deprivation rather than a mere lack of money. It severally limits what each individual is able to do or be and, in some cases, makes certain essential functionings impossible. For example, decent and stable housing is essential for human survival and dignity, a principle affirmed both by US policy and international human rights law. Without access to housing or the ability to secure housing, this essential function for human well-being cannot be met. The capabilities approach and the public health approach work well together here since both maintain that we need to take into consideration the conditions that must be in place for an individual to be capable of achieving a sufficient level of health and safety. Adequate housing and freedom from abuse are often essential for this. Hence, our health, safety, and justice institutions should work together to reduce the instances of abuse and domestic violence and address the social inequities responsible for poverty and homelessness.

(2) **Increase funding for mental health services with a focus on the early and active treatment of mental illness.** Mental illness can severally impact an individual's life-potential and negatively affect his/her health and well-being. It can also impact public safety. As we saw earlier, more than half of all people incarcerated in prisons and jails in 2005 had a mental illness: 56 percent of state prisoners, 45 percent of federal prisoners, and 64 percent of jail inmates (James and Glaze 2006) – and of those who had a mental illness, about three quarters also had a co-occurring substance use disorder (James and Glaze 2006). Consider depression as just one example. A recent longitudinal study by Yu et al. (2017) examined the association between depression and subsequent violence from three representational samples in the Netherlands, United Kingdom, and Finland. They found a consistent pattern of increased relative risk for violence in adolescents with depressive symptoms. In the Finnish sample, for example, the odds of violence in individuals with a diagnosis of depression were increased two-fold, compared to those without depression. We also know that higher rates of depression have been reported among adolescents in juvenile detention and correctional facilities (e.g., 11 percent in boys and 29 percent in girls). These findings highlight the need for active and early treatment of mental illness, especially in adolescents and young people.

(3) **Develop, implement, and fund hospital, community, and government agency health programs aimed at preventing and interrupting criminal behavior.** I wish to include here a number of action steps proposed by the American Public Health Association (APHA 2018). For instance, the APHA calls on "health departments to assess and analyze data on violence to provide improved health information related to violence and implementation of violence prevention models (e.g., Cure Violence)" (2018). They also call on "hospitals, societies of health professionals, and academic institutions to train health professionals, including doctors and nurses, in identifying risks, detecting signs of violence and trauma, responding in a trauma-informed manner, and ensuring appropriate referrals to services and treatment" (2018). With regard to community programs, they write:

APHA calls on entities implementing or funding community health programs, including nonprofit foundations and associations, to initiate programs to prevent violence that include detection and interruption of violence on the part of professionally trained workers and that identify and change behaviors and social norms among at-risk individuals and the community. Community health workers, nurses, patient navigators, and promotors are often aware of potentially violent circumstances within homes and communities long before they manifest in a hospitalization or in a police or child protective services report. Linkage to mediation, child protective, or crisis management services allow providers to address the critical need for safety among their clients. Providers must be equipped to deliver trauma-informed and culturally relevant services that recognize that patients may bring with them a history of traumatic experience and a need for emotional support, and they must identify those at risk for violence in order to intervene effectively. Specific attention must be paid to those disproportionately impacted by violence, including communities of color, women, children youths, and LGBTQIA and religious groups. All community health programs should be able to implement violence prevention and trauma initiatives that include training of frontline staff as a core component. (APHA 2018)

Lastly, the APHA calls on local, state, and federal government agencies to adopt, invest in, expand, and support evidence-based and promising public health approaches to violence and criminal behavior, including screening practices related to intimate partner violence, elder abuse, and abuse of vulnerable adults as detailed in the US Preventive Services Task Force recommendations.[6]

(4) Secure universal access to affordable and consistent healthcare for all. Access to affordable and consistent healthcare is essential for human well-being. It is also key from the perspective of public health and safety. As we saw earlier, for many vulnerable populations, including the homeless, poor, and mentally ill, not having access to affordable and consistent healthcare means forgoing treatment for mental illness, substance use, chronic health conditions, acute care, and injuries. This in turn has profound negative effects on public health and safety. To prevent these deleterious effects, we should adopt policies that strive to make healthcare accessible and affordable for all. We should also extend health services to those in the criminal justice system and do everything we can to improve the health of offenders and link them up with programs and services that will provide continued access to healthcare. Doing so would not only help improve public health and safety, it would also help address a number of other social inequities. As Rich et al. argue, "Given the racial disparities of incarceration, if criminal justice involvement were to lead to increased access to health care upon release, this could cause a decrease in the racial disparities regarding health and health care in the community" (2014: 464). Public health and safety affects all of us and it should be the goal of everyone to provide affordable and consistent healthcare to all members of society. The capabilities

---

[6] See: www.uspreventiveservicestaskforce.org/Page/Name/recommendations.

approach to social justice also demands it, since lack of access to affordable and consistent healthcare negatively affects not only health but several other dimensions of human well-being as well (Powers and Faden 2006: 17–18).

(5) **Redesign prisons and institutions of incapacitation specifically for the purpose of *rehabilitation* and *reintegration*, not punishment**. With few exceptions, US, UK, and Australian prisons are harsh, restrictive institutions, designed to enable maximum control over the behavior of inmates at all times. As Lutham and Klippan write: "Their scale and appearance instill mistrust and anonymity ... The ability to personalise space, have ownership and have personal control over one's situation is intentionally absent. Mostly, these are overtly punitive environments, unlike any other" (2016). These "cold" prison environments have an effect on the people inside them and they are typically not good. Just consider the rates of suicide and self-harm in US and UK prisons. According to the US federal Bureau of Justice Statistics, suicides account for more deaths in state and federal prisons than drug and alcohol intoxication deaths, homicide, and accidents combined. And things are even worse in county jails where the suicide rate was 46 per 100,000 in 2013. Incidents of self-harm in England and Wales are also at an all-time high (Ministry of Justice 2016). Furthermore, US and UK prisons are also breeding grounds for violence (Bowker 1980; Irwin 1980; Ministry of Justice 2016), which is not surprising given that they typically confine large numbers of people in overcrowded quarters and in conditions characterized by material and social deprivation (Bowker 1980; Wortley 2005).

In his book *Situational Prison Control* (2005), former prison psychologist Richard Wortley articulates strategies to reduce negative behavior in prison contexts, including through physical design. He suggests (a) setting positive expectations through domestic furnishings that confer trust; (b) reducing anonymity through small prison size; (c) personalizing victims through humane conditions; (d) enabling a positive sense of community through ownership and personalization of the space; and (e) reducing provocation and stress by designing in the capacity for inmates to enact control over environmental conditions and personal space. The current model of US correctional facilities is the antithesis of each of these strategies. Lutham and Klippan correctly note, "When we create environments that fuel the negative behaviors we naturally associate with criminals, we are caught in a vicious cycle: harsh community and political attitudes toward prisons and prisoners are perpetuated, and overtly punitive prisons continue to be built" (2016).

Some good examples of innovating prison design exist in Scandinavian countries, including Bastoy Island and Halden Prison in Norway, and Mark Prison in Denmark. There are also some good examples in Austria (e.g., the Justice Center at Leoben) and Germany. These prisons are purposely designed to reduce crime. Lutham and Klippan explain:

> They do this by providing positive opportunities for inmates and building a greater sense of optimism for their future ... These spaces are designed to more closely

reflect environments in the outside community. The design treats these people not solely as "prisoners" but also as community members – with all the social, vocational and emotional responsibility that this entails. (Lutham and Klippan 2016)

Halden Prison in Norway, for example, has trees intentionally scattered across its 75-acre site, whereas US prisons are usually devoid of vegetation to maximize visibility. In addition, to help inmates develop routines and to reduce the monotony of confinement, designers spread Halden's living quarters, work areas, and activity centers across the prison grounds. This provides offenders with some degree of autonomy and encourages interpersonal interactions – mirroring the kinds of conditions they will return to upon release. I propose that we follow the lead of the Norwegian Correctional Services and officially adopt the *principle of normality*.[7] The principle maintains that (1) during the serving of a sentence life inside prison should resemble life outside as much as possible. It further states that (2) no one shall serve their sentence under stricter circumstances than necessary for the security of the community. Therefore, offenders shall be placed in the lowest possible security regime. Lastly, it states that (3) prison should be a restriction of liberty but nothing more, that is, "no other rights have been removed by the sentencing court." According to the normality principle, then, an offender should have all the same rights as other people living in Norway and life inside should resemble life outside as much as possible. All Norwegian prisoners, for example, have the right to study and they are all allowed to vote. Sentences are also kept short. On average, they are no more than eight months long, and nearly 90 percent of sentences are for less than a year. Additionally, the longest sentence permitted by law is twenty-one years, but that can be extended in five-year increments if a prisoner is not rehabilitated and is considered a continued risk to society. Since most prisoners will eventually return to society, Norwegian prisons prepare inmates for reintegration by mimicking the outside world as much as possible.

These innovative designs also treat inmates with respect and dignity. In Austria, the Justice Center at Leoben was designed by architect Joseph Hohensinn. There are two inscriptions on the prison's perimeter. The first reads: "All human beings are born free and equal in dignity and rights," which is taken from the Intentional Covenant of Civil and Political Rights. The second reads: "All persons deprived of their liberty shall be treated with humanity and with respect for the inherent dignity of the human person." These sentiments are in stark contract with the way individuals are treated in US, UK, and Australian prisons. At Leoben, inmates are able to move freely through their cells and shared spaces, and each prisoner has his own bathroom, kitchen area, and floor-to-ceiling window that opens onto a balcony. There are also three courtyards and multiple outdoor communal spaces. Treating individuals with respect, maximizing the autonomy of inmates, and explicitly

---

[7] For more details, see the Norwegian Correctional Service's full document: www.kriminalomsorgen.no/information-in-english.265199.no.html.

designing spaces with the purpose of rehabilitation in mind have been extremely successful in driving down recidivism and reintegrating individuals back into society (see the following chapter for more details).

If we are to adopt a public health approach to criminal behavior, we must reexamine the design of those physical spaces and environments in which we house individuals. We should aim for the rehabilitation and reintegration of offenders back into society and we should adopt practices and policies that best achieve this goal. The *normality principle* is just one example of a policy specifically designed with this goal in mind, but other policies will be needed as well. Unfortunately, retributivism and purely punitive approaches to criminal behavior remain a stumbling block in the way of progress. It is imperative that we reject these and consider anew the aims and ends of criminal justice.

(6) Shift to a "holistic defense" approach to legal representation. "Holistic defense" is a form of legal representation pioneered in the Bronx two decades ago. Using this method, public defender's offices not only help clients with their court cases but also try to address the life circumstances that led them to commit crimes in the first place (Hager 2018).

> Holistic defense first emerged in the 1990s as a new paradigm for legal representation of indigent clients. In contrast to the traditional public defense model, with its emphasis on criminal representation and courtroom advocacy by a single lawyer, the holistic defense model is base on the idea that to be truly effective advocates for their clients, defenders must adopt a broader understanding of the scope of their work. To this end, defenders must address not only the immediate case at hand but also the enmeshed, or collateral, legal consequences of criminal justice involvement (such as loss of employment, public housing, custody of one's children, and immigrant status) and the underlying life circumstances and nonlegal issues that so often play a role in driving clients into the criminal justice system in the first place (such as drug addiction, mental illness, or family or housing instability). Holistic representation requires an interdisciplinary team that includes not just criminal defense lawyers and related support staff ... but also civil, family, and immigrant lawyers, as well as social workers and nonlawyer advocates – all working collectively and on an equal footing with each other. (Anderson, Buenaventura, and Heaton 2019: 1)

According to one of the first ever large-scale, empirical studies by the RAND Corporation, holistic representation can "reduce incarceration and save taxpayer dollars – without harm to public safety" (Anderson, Buenaventura, and Heaton 2019). The study compared outcomes in the Bronx between a holistic defender's office and a more traditional one using court data from more than 587,000 cases spanning 2000 through 2007 and 2012 through 2014. The report found that defendants offered holistic services were about 16 percent less likely to get locked up. They also served 24 percent shorter jail and prison sentences, without leading to any increase in crime (Hager 2018; Anderson, Buenaventura, and Heaton 2019). In drug cases, those represented holistically saw their likelihood of serving time decreased by 25 percent and their expected sentence length reduced by 63 percent. More than ten years, those defendants under the holistic model spent 1.1 million fewer days behind bars. And with regard to cost, the RAND study found that holistic defense saved New York taxpayers $165 million in incarceration costs more than a decade, offsetting the high price tag of hiring social workers and staffing for a range of client needs.

(7) **End policies that disenfranchise ex-offenders, making it more difficult for them to reintegrate back into society.** In 2016, an estimated 6.1 million people were prohibited from voting due to laws restricting voting rights for those convicted of felony-level crimes (Uggen, Larson, and Shannon 2016). The African American community has been disproportionately impacted by these felony disenfranchisement policies, with a recent report from the Sentencing Project estimating that one in every thirteen black Americans has lost their voting rights (Chung 2016). Voter disenfranchisement, however, is not the only barrier ex-prisoners face. Under the Personal Responsibility and Work Opportunity Reconciliation Act (PRWORA), thirteen states fully prohibit anyone with a drug-related conviction from receiving public assistance under the Temporary Assistance to Needy Families (TANF) program – and twenty-three other states maintain a partial ban. Additionally, people with a felony criminal record are restricted from jury service in forty-seven states (Love 2016), and the American Bar Association has documented 27,254 state occupational licensing restrictions nationwide for people with a criminal record (Love, Roberts, and Klingele 2013). Public housing is also restricted for many ex-offenders. In fact, under current housing policies, everyone convicted of a felony is automatically ineligible for a minimum of five years – condemning people with criminal records to homelessness or transient living at precisely the moment when reintegration is most important. Policies like these make it more difficult for ex-offenders to reintegrate back into society and end up increasing the chances of recidivism. They are counterproductive from the perspective of public health and safety. Rather than making us safer, these policies are a hangover from an antiquated and largely discredited approach to criminal justice – one grounded in the retributive impulse for payback and the desire to give offenders their *just deserts*. If we wish to adopt effective, data-driven policies aimed at promoting public health and safety, as I believe we should, these disenfranchisement policies need to be abandoned.

(8) **Prioritize and properly fund education, especially in low-income areas, and support educational programs in prison.** Research has shown that education is an important SDH and SDCB. Not only can it have a profound impact on an individual's life-potential, receiving an adequate education is an important (and perhaps essential) functioning for human well-being. Yet despite its obvious importance, there still remains enormous educational inequity within the United States and around the world. We need to adopt programs and policies aimed at leveling the

playing field. In particular, we need to make it a public health priority to provide low-income communities with adequate educational opportunities. We also need to support and fund educational programs in prison. We know that correctional education improves inmates' chances of not returning to prison. A major 2013 study by the RAND Corporation found, for example, that inmates who participate in correctional education programs have 43 percent lower odds of recidivating than those who do not (Davis et al. 2013). This translates to a reduction in the risk of recidivating of 13 percentage points. These programs also improve the chances of offenders obtaining employment after release. The odds of obtaining employment post-release among inmates who participated in correctional education were 13 percent higher than the odds for those who did not (Davis et al. 2013). Furthermore, providing correctional education is cost-effective when it comes to reducing recidivism – saving $4 to $5 for each dollar spent.

(9) **Adopt policies that protect the environmental health of our communities by combating climate change, protecting air and water, and reducing/eliminating harmful toxins**. As we saw in Section 7.1.4, public health and safety can be negatively affected by environmental factors such as poor air and water quality, exposure to lead and toxins, and climate change. Exposure to lead, for instance, can cause long-term harm in adults, including increased risk of high blood pressure, kidney failure, and, in pregnant women, miscarriage, stillbirth, premature birth, and minor malformations (WHO 2016b). Young children are particularly vulnerable to the toxic effects of lead and "can suffer profound and permanent adverse health effects, particularly affecting the development of the brain and nervous system" (WHO 2016b). Furthermore, lead exposure is also a potential threat to public safety since studies have found that it can lead to increases in criminal behavior (Billings and Schnepel 2015; Feigenbaum and Muller 2016; Aizer and Currie 2017). This is just one example since there are many other toxins and environmental factors that affect health and safety.

For instance, a recent study conducted in China by researchers from the Yale School of Public Health showed that high air pollution levels were correlated with lower test scores in language and math. The study estimates that this reduction in intelligence had a similar impact of losing a year of education (Zhang, Chen, and Zhang 2018). Climate change is also a threat to public health and safety since it is likely to cause more variable weather, heat waves, heavy precipitation events, flooding, droughts, more intense storms, sea-level rise, and air pollution (IPCC 2014a, b, c) – each of which has the potential to negatively affect public health as well as be a threat multiplier, increasing conflict and military involvement around the world.

If we wish to adopt a broad, holistic approach to public health and safety – one grounding in social justice and aimed at promoting health and preventing criminal behavior – we need to adopt practices and policies that address these environmental threats. Robert Bullard (2010), for example, proposes a number of helpful solutions in his discussion of overcoming racism in environmental decision-making. He begins by noting that

> [d]espite the recent attempts by federal agencies to reduce environmental and health threats in the United, States, inequities persist. If a community is poor or inhabited largely by people of color, there is a good chance that it receives less protection than a community that is affluent or white. This situation is a result of the country's environmental policies, most of which distribute the costs in a regressive pattern while providing disproportionate benefits for the educated and wealthy. (2010: 644)

Bullard provides numerous examples of environmental discrimination and argues that unequal environmental protection undermines three basic types of equity: procedural, geographic, and social (2010; see also Bullard 1983, 1987, 1990). Some examples of environmental discrimination include how the US government cleans up toxic waste sites and punishes polluters, for example, white communities see faster action, better results, and stiffer penalties than communities where black, Hispanic, and other minorities live (see, e.g., Lavelle and Coyle 1992); the geographical placement of landfills, incinerators, sewage treatment plants, lead smelters, refineries, and other noxious facilities, which are more often put in poor and minority communities (see, e.g., Costner and Thornton 1990); and the role of sociological factors, such as race, ethnicity, class, culture, lifestyle, and political power, in environmental decision-making (Bullard 1983, 1987, 1990, 2010).

To correct for these inequities and to end unequal environmental protection, Bullard proposes the following five principles of environmental justice (abstracted from 2010: 647–655):

(a) **The Right to Protection:** Every individual has a right to be protected from environmental degradation. Protecting this right will require enacting a federal "fair environmental act." The act could be modeled after the various federal civil rights acts that have promoted nondiscrimination – with the ultimate goal of achieving "zero tolerance" – in such areas as housing, education, and employment. The act ought to address both the intended and unintended effects of public policies and industrial practices on ethnic minorities and other vulnerable groups.

(b) **Prevention of Harm:** Preventing, the elimination of the threat before harm occurs, should be the preferred strategy of government. For example, to solve the lead problem, the primary focus should be shifted from treating children who have been poisoned to eliminating the threat by removing lead from houses, replacing lead pipes, etc.

(c) **Shift the Burden of Proof:** Under the current system, individuals who challenge polluters must prove that they have been harmed, discriminated against, or disproportionately affected. Few poor or minority communities have the resources to hire the lawyers, expert witnesses, and doctors needed to sustain such a challenge. Thus, the burden of proof must be shifted to the polluters who do harm, discriminate, or do not give equal protection to minorities and other overburdened classes. Environmental justice would require the entities that are applying for operating permits for landfills, incinerators, smelters, refineries, and chemical plants, for example, to prove that their operations are not harmful to human health, will not disproportionately affect minorities or the poor, and are nondiscriminatory.

(d) **Obviate Proof of Intent:** Laws must allow disparate impact and statistical weight – as opposed to "intent" – to infer discrimination because proving intentional and purposeful discrimination in a court of law is next to impossible.

(e) **Redress Inequity:** Disproportionate impact must be redressed by targeting action and resources. Resources should be spent where environmental and health problems are greatest, as determined by some ranking scheme – but one not limited to risk assessment. Such targeting should channel resources to the hot spots, communities that are burdened with more than their fair share of environmental problems.

Each of these proposals would, I believe, be an improvement over existing practices since they go a long way in correcting for the procedural, geographic, and social inequities that currently exist. I present them here, however, only as an example of what a more specific set of proposals might look like. Of course, one or more of Bullard's principles might be debated and additional proposals will still need to be added – for example, ones that directly address climate change, global environmental justice, and the allocation of scarce resources. But whatever more specific set of proposals we adopt, if they are to be consistent with the general public health framework I have outlined, they will need to identify and address social inequities in environmental health and aim to promote human well-being by seeking to achieve a sufficient level of health and personal security for all members of society.

(10) Research more effective interventions and rehabilitation strategies for psychopathy. The success of the Mendota Juvenile Treatment Center (MJTC) program indicates that certain interventions and treatment protocols can in fact work in cutting violent recidivism rates in juveniles who exhibit callous-unemotional traits (Caldewell and Van Rybroek 2001, 2005). While genetic factors and neurobiological deficits are widely believed to be involved in the development of psychopathy, early identification of the personality traits associated with psychopathy, as well improvement in the social conditions identified earlier, can help mitigate the development of psychopathy. Furthermore, as we come to better understand psychopathy and its neurological correlates, we can potentially develop better "intervention strategies that are informed by an understanding of the neuropsychological obstacles to healthy development" (Anderson and Kiehl 2014: 116). The MJTC program is one intervention strategy that needs to be studied further – and, as Anderson and Kiehl point out, "[I]t will be necessary to carry out rigorous investigations of changes in functional circuitry over the course of reasonably successful intervention efforts" (2014: 116).

The use of neurofeedback in correctional settings has also been suggested as "an innovative approach that may ultimately lessen criminal behavior, prevent violence, and lower recidivism" (Gkotsi and Benaroyo 2012: 3; see also Quirk 1995; Smith and Sams 2005; Evans 2006). As Gkotsi and Benaroyo describe:

> Neurofeedback or neurotherapy is a relatively new, noninvasive method which is based on the possibility of training and adjusting the speed of brainwaves, which normally occur at various frequencies (Hammond, 2011). An overabundance, or deficiency in one of these frequencies, often correlates with conditions such as depression, and emotional disturbances and learning disabilities, such as Attention Deficit Hyperactivity Disorder (ADHD) (Gretemann, 2009) ... Therapists attach electrodes to the patients' head and a device records electrical impulses in the brain. These impulses are sorted into different types of brain waves. Using a program similar to a computer game, patients learn to control the video display by achieving the mental state that produces increases in the desired brain wave activity. Neurofeedback has gained recognition for its potential benefits for children with ADHD, alcoholics and drug addicts. It can also enhance athlete and musician performance as well as improve elderly people's cognitive function. (Gretemann 2009) (2012: 3)

Douglas Quirk, a Canadian researcher, tested the effects of a neurofeedback treatment program on seventy-seven dangerous offenders in an Ontario correctional institute who suffered from deep-brain epileptic activity. The results demonstrated reduction in the subjects' criminal recidivism and suggested that "a subgroup of dangerous offenders can be identified, understood and successfully treated using this kind of biofeedback conditioning program" (Quirk 1995; as quoted by Gkotsi and Benaroyo 2012: 3). Additional studies by Smith and Sams (2005) on juvenile offenders with significant psychopathology and electroencephalographic abnormalities, and by Martin and Johnson (2005) on male adolescents diagnosed with ADHD, also demonstrated reduced recidivism, improved cognitive performance, improved emotional and behavioral reactions, and inhibition of inappropriate responses. Findings like these are promising and moving forward we will need to further investigate whether neurofeedback can produce similar results with psychopathy.

(11) **Make use of big data, neuroscience, and other predictive technologies to aid in identifying, tracking, and predicting violent behavior for the purposes of designing general and local interventions,** *but prohibit such technology from being used for the purpose of preemptive incapacitation*. This is extremely important. As the use of big data and other predictive technologies grows, it is inevitable that they will be employed by police departments and government agencies to help combat violent crime. It is occurring already. We know, for instance, that crime rates

go up on hot weather days in large cities. Algorithms can also be used to identify "hot spots" where crimes are more likely to occur based on previous activity. Such knowledge can be used to design certain preventive interventions, such as opening public air-conditioning centers, funding public pools, and introducing more violence interrupters into the community on hot days. These tools can be extremely helpful when used in conjunction with a public health approach to criminal behavior, but they can also be abused. For that reason, more work needs to be done to determine the appropriate uses and limits of such technology.

One important limit, however, is that such technologies should not be used for the purposes of preemptive incapacitation. There are several reasons for this. First, even with such technologies we remain in a poor epistemic position to determine, with any level of certainty, that an individual will commit a violent crime before they do so. The possibility of false positives is too great. My combination lock analogy discussed earlier helps illustrate that point. Second, the liberty of individuals must always be weighed heavily in decisions about incapacitation. The burden of proof should always be on the one who wants to limit liberty. Predictive technologies do not meet the burden of proof needed and it is unlikely that they will anytime soon, if ever, since the causes of human behavior are extremely complex and difficult to predict. Third, respect for individuals, which I argued in the previous chapter, is consistent with free will skepticism and the public health–quarantine model, demands that we adopt the presumption of harmlessness (analogous to the presumption of innocence) as a guiding principle and prohibit preemptive incapacitation in all but the most extreme cases. In the following chapter, I will discus what "extreme cases" may allow for exceptions, but importantly they will not involve cases of big data. It would be wise policy, then, to limit the use of predictive technologies to those interventions that focus on interrupting criminal behavior (on the community and local level) and designing policies (on the general level) to address the structural and environmental causes of criminal behavior.

7.4 CONCLUSION

In this chapter, I argue that the social determinants of health (SDH) are broadly similar to the social determinants of criminal behavior (SDCB). I identify poverty, socioeconomic status, abuse, violence, housing, mental health, access to healthcare, education, environmental health, and nutrition as key social determinants. I also argue that we should adopt a broad public health approach, focused on prevention and social justice, for identifying and taking action on these shared social determinants. I concluded by recommending eleven broad public policy proposals for moving forward. Examining the social determinants of health and criminal behavior revealed that we cannot successfully address concerns over public health and safety without simultaneously addressing issues of social justice. Criminal justice and social justice are intimately connected and as a result retributive and purely punitive approaches to criminal behavior end up missing the mark, since they see the problem as generally a matter of individual responsibility and desert. We need to abandon the reactive approach, with its myopic focus on punishment and individual responsibility, and instead adopt a preventive approach. And the best way to do this is to adopt the public health–quarantine model and the eleven proposals outlined in the previous section.

8

The Public Health–Quarantine Model III

Human Dignity, Victims' Rights, Rehabilitation, and Preemptive Incapacitation

In the final two chapters, I consider and address a number of objections to the public health–quarantine model. In this chapter, I will address concerns about proportionality, human dignity, victims' rights, rehabilitation, and preemptive incapacitation. In the following chapter, I will address concerns about deterrence, cost, evidentiary standards, and indefinite detention. I will argue that the public health–quarantine model can successfully deal with each of these concerns and as a result it offers a superior alternative to retributive punishment and other nonretributive accounts. My hope is that by addressing these concerns now, the case for the public health–quarantine model will be made even stronger. It will also provide me with the opportunity to flesh out some additional components of my account.

8.1 PROPORTIONALITY AND HUMAN DIGNITY

One concern critics have with the public health–quarantine model, and perhaps free will skepticism generally, is that they fear it will not protect human dignity and respect for persons in the same way that retributivism does. As Alec Walen describes: "Retributive justice holds that it would be bad to punish a wrongdoer *more* than she deserves, where what she deserves must be in some way proportional to the gravity of her crime. Inflicting disproportionate punishment wrongs her just as, even if not quite as much as, punishing an innocent person wrongs her (Gross 1979: 436)" (Walen 2014).[1] For retributivists, the principle of proportionality is needed to guarantee respect for persons since it treats them as autonomous, morally responsible agents and not just objects to be "fixed" or used as a means to an end. Hence, punishment administered because one is a morally responsible autonomous person who *justly deserves* punishment preserves one's status as a person and a member of the human community of responsible agents as long as it is not disproportionate (see

---

[1] Pereboom argues against this point that even if retribution is a state interest, protection is as well, and this is affirmed in virtually every jurisdiction that endorses retributivism. If a criminal has "paid for" their crime and yet remains a serious danger, they are kept in prison. So, in effect, retributivists will not let retributivism limit sentences when protection is at issue (see Pereboom 2019).

Lewis 1953; Oldenquist 1988; and H. Morris 1968). Critics contend that without this principle in place, there will be no limit to the harshness of punishment meted out and no way to block treating individuals as a mere means to an end.

Immanuel Kant, for example, famously argued that human beings possess a special dignity and worth that demands that they be treated as ends in themselves and never as mere means. According to Kant, imprisonment could only be justified on the grounds that the criminal conduct was a product of the free-willed choices of the criminal making them *deserving* of a punitive response. Kant, however, also believed that the death penalty was deserved, in fact obligatory, in cases of murder:

> But whoever has committed murder, must die. There is, in this case, no juridical substitute or surrogate that can be given or taken for the satisfaction of justice. There is no likeness or proportion between life, however painful, and death; and therefore there is no equality between the crime of murder and the retaliation of it but what is judicially accomplished by the execution of the criminal (Kant 1785/1981, Part II: 6).

While many retributivists disagree with Kant regarding the death penalty, they share his belief that punishment should not exceed what is *deserved*. They also agree with Kant that free will and (basic desert) moral responsibility are needed to maintain respect for persons. John Lemos, for example, has argued, "[T]he human capacity for moral responsibility gives human beings a special dignity and worth that is fundamental to a proper system of morality grounded on the concept of respect for persons" (2013: 78), and theories of punishment that reject basic desert moral responsibility are incapable of protecting this special dignity and worth (see Lemos 2013, 2016, 2018).

While I take these concerns seriously, it is wrong to think that free will skeptics cannot preserve respect for human dignity or protect against harsh and inhumane treatment without the notion of basic desert. In response to this objection, I offer three main replies. First, I contend that the principle of proportionality, *in actual practice*, does not guarantee respect for persons any better than the alternatives. This is because measurements of gravity and proportionality are hypersensitive to cultural biases, prejudices, and power relations, and there remain serious problems for both cardinal and ordinal ways of measuring proportionality (see Chapter 4). Second, the public health–quarantine model, has a non-desert-based principle of proportionality of its own, one which is capable of securing respect for persons and protecting innocent people from being used as a means to an end. Lastly, respecting human dignity, I argue, is not about giving wrongdoers their just deserts. Rather, it demands that the capabilities and well-being of wrongdoers be taken into consideration, that we avoid punishments that dehumanize and disenfranchise individuals, and that we do everything we can to rehabilitate and reintegrate offenders back into the community. The public health–quarantine model does a better job at respecting human dignity in this sense than does retributivism.

While I have already argued in Chapter 4 that the principle of proportionality does not provide the protections against abuse retributivists' claim, I would like to return to the issue one last time to focus on the question of human dignity. I will begin by empirically investigating whether belief in free will, just deserts, and retributive justice *ensure* punishment is proportionally any better than the alternatives. Since it is the *real-life effects* of free will skepticism that is being questioned, I think the empirical question is an important one. If the critics are wrong about the protective power of basic desert moral responsibility and the constraints it places on proportional punishment, then this concern loses much of its force. Empirically speaking, then, does belief in just deserts and retributive justice ensure punishment is proportional? I contend that it does not. Of course, there are many reasonable retributivists who acknowledge that we imprison far too many people, in far too harsh conditions, but the problem is that retributivism remains committed to the core belief that criminals *deserve* to be punished and suffer for the harms they have caused. Recall Kant's claim that we should execute the last prisoner on the island before we abandon it in order that everyone "realize the desert of his deeds." This retributive impulse in *actual practice*, despite theoretical appeals to proportionality by its proponents, often leads to practices and policies that try to make life in prison as unpleasant as possible.

Bruce Waller has done an excellent job examining this question empirically and he sets up the cultural expectations as follows:

> Belief in individual moral responsibility is deep and broad in both the United States and England; in fact, the belief seems to be more deeply entrenched in those cultures than anywhere else – certainly deeper there than in Europe. That powerful belief in moral responsibility is not an isolated belief, existing independently of other cultural factors; rather, it is held in place – and in turn, helps anchor – a neo-liberal cultural *system* of beliefs and values. At the opposite end of the scale are social democratic corporatist cultures like Sweden that have taken significant steps beyond the narrow focus on individual moral responsibility. With that picture in view, consider the basic protections which philosophers have claimed that the moral responsibility system affords: first, protection against extreme punitive measures; second, protection of the dignity and rights of those who are held morally responsible and subject to punishment; and third, a special protection of the innocent against unjust punishment. According to the claim that strong belief in individual moral responsibility protects against abuses, we would expect the United States and Great Britain (the neo-liberal cultures with the strongest commitment to individual moral responsibility) to score best in providing such protections; and we would predict that Norway, Sweden, and Denmark (the social democratic corporatist cultures, with much more qualified belief in individual moral responsibility) would be the worst abusers. (2014, 6; see also 2015)

What happens when we actually make the comparison, however, is that we find the exact opposite. That is, we find that the stronger the belief in moral responsibility (as in the United States), the harsher the punishment, the greater the skepticism of moral responsibility (as in Norway), the weaker the inclination toward punishment. A few cross-cultural statistics should help make this point salient.

In 2014, the Pew Research Center asked people whether they agreed or disagreed with the notion that personal success is determined by factors outside of oneself. While not exactly measuring belief in free will and moral responsibility, the survey was able to confirm that Americans are much more likely to see success or failure in personal terms. This is in line with the systems of thinking Waller describes and is unsurprising given the US emphasis on rugged individualism and individual responsibility – which, of course, is closely aligned with attitudes about just deserts, praise and blame, punishment and reward. For example, 57 percent of Americans disagreed with the statement "Success in life is determined by forces outside our control," which was the highest percentage among advanced countries. The United Kingdom was immediately behind the United States with 55 percent disagreeing. Unfortunately, Scandinavian countries were not included in the survey but European nations like Germany and Italy came in at 31 percent and 32 percent, respectively. Additional work by Clark et al. (2014) has also found that belief in free will is higher in countries like the United States than in Scandinavian countries where crime rates are much lower.

Now, retributivists would have us believe that given its strong commitment to individual moral responsibility, the United States can be expected to provide better protections against harsh and excessively punitive forms of punishment than countries with a weaker commitment to individual moral responsibility. The reality, however, is quite the opposite. Consider the problem of mass incarceration in the United States. While the United States makes up only 4.5 percent of the world's population, it houses 25 percent of the world's prisoners – that is, one of the highest rates of incarceration known to mankind. Despite a steady decline in the crime rate over the past two decades, the Unites States imprisons around 700 prisoners for every 100,000 of population.[2] That is a remarkable number. Compare that to the social democratic countries with a much weaker commitment to individual moral responsibility, such as Norway, Sweden, and Finland, where the imprisonment rate hovers around 60 per 100,000.[3] As a proportion of the population, then, the United States has more than ten times as many prisoners as these other countries.

Furthermore, the United States not only imprisons at a much higher rate, it also imprisons in notoriously harsh conditions and for longer periods of time. Even controlling for crime rates and population size, the United States hands down longer sentences, spends more money on prisons, and executes more of its citizens than every

---

[2] According to the Prison Policy Initiative, in 2018 the number was 698 per 100,000 (see www.prisonpolicy.org/global/2018.html). According to the International Centre for Prison Studies, it was 731 in 2010 and 672 in 2015 (see www.prisonstudies.org/sites/default/files/resources/downloads/wppl_12.pdf).

[3] According to the latest numbers, Norway imprisons 63 per 100,000, Sweden 59, Finland 51, and Denmark 63. See International Centre for Prison Studies, "World Prison Brief": www.prisonstudies.org/sites/default/files/resources/downloads/wppl_12.pdf.

other advanced industrial democracy (Farrell and Clark 2004; Blumstein, Tonry, and Van Ness 2005; Enns 2006: 3; Cowen 2010; Amnesty International 2012). For instance, a recent report by the Sentencing Project (2017) found that as of 2016, there were 161,957 people serving life sentences, or one of every nine people in prison. An additional 44,311 individuals are serving "virtual life" sentence, yielding a total population of life and virtual life sentences at 206,268 – or one of every seven people in prison. The pool of people serving life sentences has more than quadrupled since 1984. Furthermore, nearly half (48.3 percent) of life and virtual life-sentenced individuals are African American, equal to one in five black prisoners overall. More than 17,000 individuals with life without parole or virtual life sentences have been convicted of nonviolent crimes. The United States incarcerates people for life at a rate of 50 per 100,000, roughly equivalent to the entire incarceration rates of the Scandinavian nations of Denmark, Finland, and Sweden (The Sentencing Project 2017).

American prisons are also often cruel places, using a number of harsh forms of punishment including extended solitary confinement. The watchdog organization *Solitary Watch* estimates that up to 80,000 people in the United States are currently in some form of solitary confinement. These prisoners are isolated in windowless, soundproof cubicles for twenty-three to twenty-four hours each day, sometimes for decades. Such excessively punitive punishment not only causes severe suffering and serious psychological problems, it does nothing to rehabilitate prisoners nor does it reduce the rate of recidivism. In fact, the United States has one of the highest rates of recidivism in the world, with 76.6 percent of state prisoners being rearrested within five years of release (Bureau of Justice Statistics 2016). Norway, by contrast, averages around 20 percent (Kristoffersen 2010). Looked at empirically, then, it is nigh impossible to defend the claim that commitment to individual moral responsibility, just deserts, and retributivism *ensures* proportional and humane punishment. In fact, the opposite seems to be the case – the problem of disproportionate punishment seems to grow more out of a desire for retribution and the belief that people justly deserve what they get than from free will skepticism.

This claim is further supported by the fact that individual states *within* the United States with stronger belief in individual moral responsibility tend to have harsher forms of punishment (see Waller 2014, 2015; Everett et al. 2019). Consider, once again, incarceration rates. The relative distribution of the prison population in the United States is concentrated mostly in the southern states and states where the methodology of the rugged individual, the self-made man, the causa sui, are strongest. The ten states with the highest number of inmates per 100,000 residents are Oklahoma (1,079), Louisiana (1,052), Mississippi (1,039), Georgia (970), Alabama (946), Arkansas (900), Texas (891), Arizona (877), Kentucky (869), and Missouri (859).[4] Furthermore, many of these states favor "frontier justice," which

---

[4] See www.prisonpolicy.org/global/2018.html. Compare these numbers to Norway (63), Sweden (59), Finland (51), and Denmark (63). Compare them also to the Netherlands, where it is 59 per 100,000 – and they have a lot less crime, and also a non-homogenous society, with 1 million in the Islamic

leads to more punitive forms of punishment. Texas, for instance, has consistently led the states in number of executions per year, with 13 prisoners put to death in 2018, 16 in 2013, and a total of 566 since 1976.[5] Given these cross-cultural and interstate comparisons, I cannot help but conclude along with Waller that "commitment to moral responsibility exacerbates rather than prevents excessively harsh punitive policies" (2014: 7).

Recent work in experimental philosophy further reveals that where belief in free will is strongest we tend to find increased punitiveness (see Carey and Paulhus 2013; Shariff et al. 2014). Perhaps the strongest evidence for this linking comes from a set of recent studies by Shariff et al. (2014). Shariff and his colleagues hypothesized that if free will beliefs support attributions of moral responsibility, then reducing these beliefs should make people less punitive in their attitudes about punishment. In a series of four studies they tested this prediction. In Study 1 they found that people with weaker free will beliefs endorsed less retributive attitudes regarding punishment of criminals, yet their consequentialist attitudes were unaffected. In the study, 244 American participants completed the seven-item Free Will subscale of the Free Will and Determinism Plus scale (FAD+) (Paulhus and Carey 2011), which measures belief in free will. In order to further measure attitudes toward retributivist and consequentialist motivations for punishment, Shariff and his colleagues had participants read descriptions of retributivism and consequentialism as motivations for punishment and then indicate on two separate Likert scales (1 = *strongly disagree*, 7 = *strongly agree*) how important retributivism and consequentialism should be in determining motivation for criminal punishments. As predicted, Shariff et al. found that stronger belief in free will predicted greater support for retributive punishment but was not predictive of support for consequentialist punishment. The effects remained significant when statistically controlled for age, gender, education, religiosity, and economic and social political ideology. Study 1 therefore supports the hypothesis that free will beliefs positively predict retributive attitudes, yet it also suggests that "the motivation to punish in order to benefit society (consequentialist punishment) may remain intact, even while the need for blame and desire for retribution are forgone" (Shariff et al. 2014: 7).

Study 2 further highlights how stronger belief in free will and moral responsibility can lead to increased punitiveness. In the study, participants were randomly assigned to one of two groups. In the anti-free-will condition, participants were given a passage from Francis Crick's (1994) *The Astonishing Hypothesis*, which rejected free will and advocated for a mechanistic view of human behavior. In the neutral condition, the passage was unrelated to free will. Next, participants read a fictional vignette involving an offender who beat a man to death. Acting as hypothetic jurors,

---

predominantly North African community with a total population of 17 million (see www.usnews.com/news/best-countries/articles/2019-05-13/the-netherlands-is-closing-its-prisons).
[5] For statistics on executions by state and region since 1976, see: https://deathpenaltyinfo.org/executions/executions-overview/number-of-executions-by-state-and-region-since-1976.

participants recommended the length of the prison sentence (if any) that this offender should serve following a two-year, nearly 100 percent-effective, rehabilitation treatment. As Shariff et al. describe:

> The notion that the offender had been rehabilitated was used in order to isolate participants' desire for punishment as retribution. The passage further focused participants on retributive, rather than consequentialist, punishment by noting that the prosecution and defense had agreed that the rehabilitation would prevent recidivism and that any further detention after rehabilitation would offer no additional deterrence of other potential criminals. (Shariff et al. 2014: 4)

As predicted, participants who read the anti–free will passage recommended significantly lighter prison sentences than participants who read the neutral passage. In particular, participants who read the anti–free will passage recommended roughly half the length of imprisonment (~five years) compared with participants who read the neutral passage (~ten years). This study helps further confirm that it is actually commitment to retributivism that increases punitiveness, contrary to what its proponents claim.

Studies by Carey and Paulhus (2013) have also found a relationship between beliefs about free will and punishment. In particular, they found that believing more strongly in free will was correlated with increased punitiveness – that is, free will believers were more likely to call for harsher criminal punishment in a number of hypothetical scenarios. In the third of their studies, for instance, Carey and Paulhus presented two scenarios portraying serious crimes (child molestation and the rape of an adult woman) and tested the degree to which subjects' attitudes toward punishment of the criminals would be impacted by factors including the criminal having been abused as a child and assurance that a medical procedure would prevent the criminal from ever perpetrating similar crimes again. The fact that subjects who expressed the strongest belief in free will were essentially the only group of subjects whose attitudes toward punishment were not mitigated by environmental or consequentialist considerations led the researchers to conclude that "free will belief is related to retributivist punishment" (2013: 138). View collectively, these empirical considerations count strongly against the claim that commitment to retributivism, free will, and basic desert moral responsibility guarantee respect for human dignity and protection against disproportionate and inhumane forms of punishment.

Nevertheless, one may still wonder how the public health–quarantine model fares when it comes to protecting human dignity. This brings me to my second reply. To begin, let me note that while the model rejects the retributivist principle of proportionality, it has a proportionality principle of its own. This is because the public health–quarantine model maintains that legal sanctions should be proportionate to the danger posed by an individual, and any sanctions that exceed this upper bound will be unjustified. This is coupled with the principle of least infringement and the conflict resolution principle, which states:

When there is a significant threat to public health and safety, individual liberty can be limited but only when it is (a) in accordance with the right of self-defense and the prevention of harm to others, where (b) this right of self-defense is applied to an individual threat and is calibrated to the danger posed by that threat (not some unrelated threat), and (c) it is guided by the principle of least infringement, which holds that the least restrictive measures should be taken to protect public health and safety.

The conflict resolution principle and the principle of least infringement set strict limits on how individuals can and should be treated. They prohibit, for instance, the incapacitation of innocent people who pose no threat to society.[6] On the public health–quarantine model, the justification for incapacitation should not be understood in a strict consequentialist theoretical context. Rather, the model justifies incapacitation on the ground of the right to self-defense and defense of others. That right does not extend to people who are non-threats. It would therefore be wrong to incapacitate someone who is innocent since they are not a serious threat to society.

The right of self-defense can only justify limiting one's liberty when that individual's actions seriously threaten another's life, liberty, property, or physical well-being. Since *innocent people* do not pose such a threat, it would be a violation of the conflict resolution principle to incapacitate them. Hence, the public health–quarantine model, just like retributivism, is able to prohibit the punishment (or incapacitation) of innocent people. The principle of least infringement would also prohibit legal sanctions that exceed what is needed to protect public health and safety. As a result, it would oppose using individuals simply as a means to deter others by ratcheting up various punitive responses to crime, as three strikes laws did. For this reason, the public health–quarantine model also has certain advantages over consequentialist theories of punishment. I therefore contend that the public health–quarantine model is able to provide the kinds of protections needed to protect innocent people from legal sanctions and prohibit excessively punitive forms of punishment.

I also maintain that the public health–quarantine model does a better job respecting human dignity than does retributivism. Consider again the hypothetical scenario used in the Shariff et al. study. The fictional case involved an offender who beat a man to death but after serving two years in prison was nearly 100 percent effectively rehabilitated. The case further stipulated that "the prosecution and defense had agreed that the rehabilitation would prevent recidivism and that any further detention after rehabilitation would offer no additional deterrence of other potential criminals" (Shariff et al. 2014: 4). While this is clearly a contrived scenario, we can use it here as a test case. On my model, it would be unjust to continue to incapacitate this individual. Retributivists, on the other hand, will generally feel that this person *deserves* more than two years in prison (though they will likely disagree on

[6] By "innocent people" I here mean individuals who have not committed any criminal acts or otherwise pose a serious threat to society. In Section 8.4, I will take up the separate issue of incapacitating those who pose serious threats but have not yet committed a crime.

how much more). I wonder which of these views better respects human dignity. I contend that punishing someone who is no longer a threat to society, and in a way that exceeds effectiveness, is not the proper way to respect human dignity. Instead, I maintain that the public health–quarantine model actually respects human dignity more since it specifies that (a) individuals who are not a serious threat to society should not be incapacitated, (b) no one should be incapacitated longer than is absolutely necessary (where this is determined by the continued threat the individual poses to society), and (c) when it is necessary to incapacitate an individual, we must do so in a way that treats them humanely, with respect and dignity, and with rehabilitation as our goal.

Furthermore, the capabilities approach to social justice, which I use to ground my public health framework, demands that we take into consideration the well-being of wrongdoers, that we avoid punishments that dehumanize and disenfranchise individuals, and that we do everything we can to rehabilitate and reintegrate offenders back into the community. In Chapter 6, I argued that *respect* is one of the six dimensions of human well-being that it is the job of justice to secure a sufficient level of, and that it is completely compatible with free will skepticism. Unlike retributivists, I do not think respect for persons or concern for their well-being ends at the point of wrongdoing. Retributivists, however, appear to have a limited technical understanding of respect for human dignity in mind, one which focuses on giving wrongdoers their just deserts. They see this as the proper way to respect individuals as morally responsible agents. My account, on the other hand, is informed by the capabilities approach to justice and the public health approach to criminal behavior, both of which view respect more holistically.

Respect, as I conceive it, is an essential element of human flourishing. Well-being is therefore set back whenever individuals are perceived of as being lesser value because of membership in a particular group or because they are judged by their worst act and not their humanity. This is easy to see when invidious judgments are made about people based on race, gender, or economic class. But I also contend that the retributivist tendency to view offenders as simply "criminals" or "felons," and therefore deserving of punishment, stigmatization, and disenfranchisement, is also a form of disrespect and harmful to human flourishing. I agree with Elizabeth Shaw when she writes:

> When trying to understand concepts such as "dignity" and "respect" it is important to examine actual historical examples where people have been treated with disrespect and their dignity has been violated, rather than relying entirely on purely abstract accounts of such concepts. One of the main reasons why the concepts of "respect" and "dignity" remain a key part of moral discourse is because these ideas are necessary in order to capture the nature of wrongs against these victims. (2018: 10)

While retributivists like to see themselves as the champions of human dignity, in actual fact the practices they permit, and the violations of human dignity they encourage, provide exactly the kind of historical examples of disrespect Shaw speaks of. Individuals are wronged and their well-being diminished when they are subject to punitive practices that dehumanize, stigmatize, and disenfranchise them. On any neutral understanding of dignity and respect, such punitive practices would be considered textbook examples of violations of human dignity.

On my model, *all* individuals are worthy of respect, including those we incapacitate. My model provides no justification for dehumanizing, disenfranchising, or treating cruelly the individuals we must incapacitate. In fact, my model requires that we consider the well-being of those individuals and do everything we can to rehabilitate and reintegrate them back into society. The public health–quarantine model also endorses the principle of normality, which maintains that (a) life inside prison should resemble life outside as much as possible, (b) "[n]o one shall serve their sentence under stricter circumstances than necessary for the security of the community," and (c) criminal wrongdoing justifies "a restriction of liberty but nothing more" – that is, "no other rights have been removed by the sentencing court."[7] I view the principle of normality as a form of respect for human dignity, one that the retributivist fails to acknowledge or extend to criminal wrongdoers. Instead, the retributivist conception of human dignity is like a parent who, while spanking their child, says: "I'm not doing this for my own sake, I'm doing it to respect you as a morally responsible agent by giving you your just desert." Hogwash! This is a perverse notion of human dignity and should have never gained traction in the first place.

Lastly, I contend that free will skeptics can additionally justify the safeguards needed to protect the rights of offenders and accused people in virtue of the fact that they are *persons* (see Shaw 2019a). In Chapter 6, I argued that there is no inconsistency in accepting a Kantian regard for respect, dignity, and treating individuals as ends-in-themselves, without accepting Kant's particular attitudes on free will (see Pereboom 2001: 150–152; Vilhauer 2009, 2013a, 2013b; Shaw 2019a). This is because the capabilities account of social justice maintains that respect is something of independent moral significance regardless of whether individuals poses free will, since it matters centrally to everyone, whatever the particular life plans and aims each has. Appealing to Darwall's (1992) distinction between "appraisal respect" and "recognition respect," and Vilhauer's (2003a) distinction between "action-based" desert claims and "personhood-based" desert claims, I argued that free will skeptics are able to preserve the latter of each pair even if they must reject the former. This is because action-based desert claims may presuppose the existence of free will, while personhood-based desert claims arguably do not. As Vilhauer explains, free will skeptics "can make such dignity and respect for persons a central moral principle if

---

[7] For more details, see the Norwegian Correctional Service's full document: www.kriminalomsorgen.no/information-in-english.265199.no.html.

they respect people as *rational* agents rather than as *free* agents, and if they regard agents as autonomous not with respect of the laws of nature, but instead with respect to the undue influence of other agents" (2013a: 148). I also argued that respect for persons simply follows from the fact that it is an essential dimension of well-being. As Nussbaum states, "Governments must treat all people respectfully and should refuse to humiliate them" (2011: 26). This is because of the "centrality of notions of dignity and respect in generating the entire capabilities list" (2011: 26). On the capabilities approach, respect and dignity are centrally important for establishing political principles that can provide the grounding for constitutional law and public policy in a nation aspiring to social justice. Hence, the public health–quarantine model maintains that "human dignity, from the start, is equal to all who are agents in the first place" (Nussbaum 2011: 31).

The public health–quarantine model need not limit itself, then, to the safeguards provided by the principle of least infringement, the conflict resolution principle, and the nonretributive principle of proportionality discussed earlier. It can also appeal to a robust notion of respect for persons in arguing for various safeguards since this is perfectly consistent with the rejection of basic desert moral responsibility. In this way, Shaw, for instance, has argued that nonretributivists and free will skeptics can prohibit framing innocent people, "since it is plausible that all persons, regardless of their moral responsibility status, have the right not be lied about and not be treated merely as a means (in the sense of manipulative use)" (Shaw 2019a). She also argues that free will skeptics can "appeal to broader range of rights" than generally acknowledged, including reputational damage and the manipulative use prohibition. In this way, they can "identify one type of injustice that is involved in the framing of non-offender that does not depend on the ideas of moral responsibility and retribution" (2019a). She then proceeds to argue for additional safeguards on similar grounds, including due process safeguards. Principles of due process, for instance, typically do not depend on basic desert moral responsibility. Instead, they are grounded in respect for persons and the prohibition of manipulative use (see Shaw 2019a for details). The public health–quarantine model can therefore appeal to these additional grounds for safeguards, which only strengthens its position.

There is no reason to think, then, that giving up on basic desert moral responsibility will lead to abuses of human dignity, disproportionate punishment, or the absence of due process safeguards. The public health–quarantine model has the resources needed to protect against these concerns.

8.2 VICTIMS' RIGHTS

A second objection to my account is that victims of violent crime will never receive proper justice or satisfaction. This is because the public health–quarantine model rejects harsh punishment in favor of rehabilitating dangerous criminals and implementing the least restrictive forms of sanctions needed to secure public safety. Consider, for instance, the kind of "tough on crime" rhetoric often heard from politicians. Democratic Senator Dianne Feinstein and Republican Senator Jon Kyl have argued that "for too long, our court system has tilted in favor of accused criminals and has proven appallingly indifferent to the suffering of crime victims."[8] While I think this is a gross misrepresentation of the US criminal justice system over the last few decades – evidenced by the mass incarceration crisis in the United States, the heavy-handedness of mandatory minimums, and the three-strikes-you-are-out laws that have swept the nation – I mention it because it captures a common concern critics have with reformist proposals like my own. The concern is that such models put the rights of criminals above the concerns of victims and advocate for reforms that run contrary to the concerns of victims. While I take this objection seriously, I do not think the public health–quarantine model is "indifferent to the suffering of crime victims." Rather, I maintain that it better reflects the attitudes and preferences of most victims and does a better job preventing future victims.

First, I contend that this objection is predicated on a mistaken assumption. The underlying assumption seems to be that most victims of violent crime want retribution above all else and that to deny them the satisfaction of seeing the perpetrators suffer is an injustice. Proponents of the death penalty and other forms of excessively punitive forms of punishment typically argue, for instance, that whatever deterrence factor such punishment may or may not have, such punishment provides justice for the victims and their families since it satisfies their desire for retribution. Kant, for example, famously argued that if a people do not insist on the execution of murders, "blood guilt" would "cling" to them "as collaborators in this public violation of justice" (1785/1981: 142). Setting aside the issue of what counts as proportional punishment raised in Chapter 4, it is an empirical question what victims *actually* want, what their preferences and attitudes are, and what kind of justice they would like to see from the criminal justice system.

Fortunately, the Alliance for Safety and Justice has recently investigated exactly these questions. In its first-of-its-kind national survey, they found that victims of violent crime say they want to see *shorter* prison sentences, *less* spending on prisons, and a *greater* focus on the rehabilitation of criminals (2016). The survey polled the attitudes and beliefs of more than 800 crime victims pooled from a nationally representative sample of more than 3,000 respondents. According to the report:

> Perhaps to the surprise of some, victims overwhelmingly prefer criminal justice approaches that prioritize rehabilitation over punishment and strongly prefer investments in crime prevention and treatment to more spending on prisons and

---

[8] As reported on in the *Washington Post* (2016): www.washingtonpost.com/news/wonk/wp/2016/08/05/even-violent-crime-victims-say-our-prisons-are-making-crime-worse.

jails. These views are not always accurately reflected in the media or in state capitols and should be considered in policy debates. (2016: 4)

An examination of the data reveals that victims prefer an approach much closer to the public health–quarantine model, with its focus on prevention, social justice, and rehabilitation, than retributivism. For instance, the survey found the following:

- By a 2 to 1 margin, victims prefer that the criminal justice system focus more on rehabilitating people who commit crimes than punishing them.
- By a margin of 15 to 1, victims prefer increased investments in schools and education over more investments in prisons and jails.
- By a margin of 10 to 1, victims prefer increased investments in job creation over more investments in prisons and jails.
- By a margin of 7 to 1, victims prefer increased investments in mental health treatment over investments in prisons and jails.
- By a margin of nearly 3 to 1, victims believe prison makes people more likely to commit crimes than to rehabilitate them.
- By a margin of 7 to 1, victims prefer increased investments in crime prevention and programs for at-risk youth over more investments in prisons and jails.
- 6 in 10 victims prefer shorter prison sentences and more spending on prevention and rehabilitation to prison sentences that keep people incarcerated for as long as possible.
- By a margin of 4 to 1, victims prefer increased investments in drug treatment over more investment in prisons and jails.
- By a margin of 2 to 1, victims prefer increased investments in community supervision, such as probation and parole, over more investments in prisons and jails.
- 7 in 10 victims prefer that prosecutors focus on solving neighborhood problems and stopping repeat crime through rehabilitation, even if it means few convictions and prison sentences.
- 6 in 10 victims prefer that prosecutors consider victims' opinions on what would help them recover from the crime, even when victims do not want long prison sentences.

The report also found that victims' views remained consistent across demographics – that is, for each of the questions mentioned earlier, they found majority or plurality support across demographic groups, including age, gender, race, ethnicity, and political party affiliation. This skepticism about imprisonment is in line with most social science research, which has generally shown that mass incarceration causes more crime than it prevents, that institutionalizing young offenders makes them more likely to commit crime as adults, and that spending time in prison teaches people how to be better criminals (see, e.g., Weatherburn 2010).

It would seem, then, that those tough-on-crime proponents who invoke the names of victims of violent crime and claim to speak for them, such as Feinstein and Kyl, often misrepresent their actual preferences, attitudes, and desires. To say that approaches like the public health–quarantine model are "appallingly indifferent to the suffering of crime victims" is to discount what victims say they actually want. It also overlooks the fact that the best way to reduce crime and the suffering caused by it is to (a) prevent the crime from occurring in the first place by addressing the causal determinates of crime and (b) to rehabilitate criminals so as to reduce the likelihood of recidivism. The public health–quarantine model attempts to do both, retributivism by its very nature does neither. Since retributivism myopically focuses on justifying backward-looking blame and punishment, it does not have the resources needed to address rehabilitation or preventative measures. I question, then, the claim that retributivism reflects a deeper concern for victims and their families. If one really cares about victims and their suffering, the best way to honor this concern is to reject retributivism and adopt a more holistic approach to criminal behavior that focuses on preventing crime, rehabilitating criminals, and reducing the number of people who become victims of violent crime.

Second, *even if* victims of violent crime wanted to see criminals suffer and were on the whole indifferent to concerns about safety and rehabilitation – contrary to what appears to be the case – it does not provide strong reason that we should inflict such harm and suffering nor does it follow that denying victims the satisfaction of seeing their perpetrators suffer would be a violation of their rights. As Walen accurately points out, "[T]he view that it wrongs victims not to punish wrongdoers confuses vengeance, which is victim-centered, with retributivism, which is agent-centered: concerned with giving the wrongdoer the punishment *he* deserves" (2014). Paul Robinson (2008), for instance, has argued that retributivists must distinguish between vengeful and deontological conceptions of deserved punishment. The former urges punishing an offender in a way that mirrors the harm or suffering he/she has caused:

> Because of this focus on the harm done, the vengeful conception of desert is commonly associated with the victim's perspective. Retributive justice "consists in seeking equality between offender and victim by subjecting the offender to punishment and communicating to the victim a concern for his or her antecedent suffering" [(Fletcher 1999: 58).] ... And the association with the victim's suffering, in turn, associates vengeful desert with the feelings of revenge and hatred that we commonly see in victims. Thus, punishment under this conception of desert is sometimes seen as essentially an institutionalization of victim revenge; it is "injury inflicted on a wrongdoer that satisfies the retributive hatred felt by the wrongdoer's victim and that is justified because of that satisfaction" [(Feinberg and Coleman 2000: 793)]. (Robinson 2008: 147–148)

The problem, however, is that justifying punishment on the grounds of vengefulness or the satisfaction of retributive hatred fails to take into account the blameworthiness of the offender. The deontological conception of desert, on the other hand, focuses at least not on the harm of the offense but on the blameworthiness of the offender, as drawn from the arguments and analysis of moral philosophy (Robinson 2008: 148).

> Thus, the criterion for assessing punishment is broader and richer than that for vengeful desert: Anything that affects an offender's moral blameworthiness is taken into account in judging the punishment he deserves. The extent of the harm caused or the seriousness of the evil done will be part of that calculation but so too will be a wide variety of other factors, such as the offender's culpable state of mind or lack thereof and the existing conditions at the time of offence, including those that might give rise to claims of justification, excuse, or mitigation. (Robinson 2008: 148)

To the extent, then, that retributivists want to appeal to moral blameworthiness rather than vengeful desires in justifying punishment, denying victims the vengeful satisfaction they seek would not be a violation of their rights.

This brings me to my next reply. Punishment inflicts harm on individuals and the justification for such harm must meet a high epistemic standard. If it is significantly probable that one's justification for harming another is unsound, then, prima facie, that behavior is seriously wrong. But if free will skeptics are right, neither libertarians nor compatibilists satisfy this epistemic standard and hence individuals do not justly deserve to be punished. And if individuals do not justly deserve to be punished, there is no violation of the rights of victims to deny them the revenge they seek. Even retributivists would acknowledge that the desire for revenge and retribution has its limits. The principle of proportionality, despite its weaknesses, dictates that punishments that are disproportionate to the wrong done (whatever that ultimately amounts to) would be unjustified. Hence, if the victim of an armed robbery wanted to see their perpetrator executed, and this was deemed disproportionate punishment by the standards of retributivism, it would not be a violation of the victim's rights on that theory to prohibit said execution. By extension, if free will skeptics are right, and retributive punishment itself is unjustified, then to deny victims their desire for revenge (conceived here in a purely backward-looking, non-consequentialist sense) would likewise not be a violation of their rights. For victims to have the right to see suffering and harm imposed on their perpetrators, it would have to be the case that such harm was justified. According to free will skeptics, however, neither victims of violent crime nor the state acting on their behalf is justified in causing more harm than is minimally required for adequate protection.

Lastly, the public health–quarantine model is able, I contend, to deal with the concerns of victims, acknowledge the wrongs done to them, and help aid in recovery. First, recall that the Alliance for Safety and Justice Survey (2016) found that six in ten victims preferred that prosecutors consider victims' opinion on what would help them recover from the crime, even when victims do not want long prison sentences. Too often tough-on-crime-advocates and overzealous prosecutors speak for victims without listening to what they really want or considering what would help them recover. As the survey indicates, many victims prefer that the criminal justice system focus more on preventing crime by investing in job creation, education, and mental health services, as well as rehabilitating criminals rather than punishing them. Since the public health approach to criminal behavior similarly advocates for these reforms, it has the virtue of being sensitive to the concerns of victims. Many victims of violent crime want above all else to know that meaningful efforts are being made to guarantee that others do not suffer in the same way they have. Retributive punishment is unable to provide this and in many cases simply obfuscates the need to do so. The public health–quarantine model, on the other hand, is perfectly designed to address the forward-looking concerns of victims and it is able to do so in a manner that is acutely sensitive to the harms done to them.

Contrary to what some critics have argued, free will skepticism is consistent with acknowledging the moral wrongs done to victims. As Pereboom and I have argued:

> Accepting free will skepticism requires rejecting our ordinary view of ourselves as blameworthy or praiseworthy in the basic desert sense. A critic might first object that if we gave up this belief, we could no longer count actions as morally bad or good. In response, even if we came to hold that a serial killer was not blameworthy due to a degenerative brain disease, we could still justifiably agree that his actions are morally bad. Still, secondly, the critic might ask, if determinism precluded basic desert blameworthiness, would it not also undercut judgments of moral obligation? If "ought" implies "can," and if because determinism is true an agent could not have avoided acting badly, it would be false that she ought to have acted otherwise. Furthermore, if an action is wrong for an agent just in case she is morally obligated not to perform it, determinism would also undermine judgements of moral wrongness (Haji 1998). In response, we contend that even if the skeptic were to accept all of this (and she might resist at various points; cf. Pereboom 2014a:chapter 6; Waller 2011), axiological judgments of moral goodness and badness would not be affected (Haji 1998; Pereboom 2001). So, in general, free will skepticism can accommodate judgments of moral goodness and badness, which are arguably sufficient for moral practice. (Pereboom and Caruso 2018)

There is nothing preventing free will skeptics, then, from acknowledging the moral wrongness of criminal acts. There is also nothing preventing them from acknowledging the harm done to victims by these morally bad acts. Given that free will skeptics can retain axiological judgments of moral goodness and badness, the public health–quarantine model can recommend that one way to help aid victims in recovery is to have the wrong done to them acknowledged and a commitment made to rehabilitate the offender and protect others from similar crimes.

This brings me to my final point. On the forward-looking account of moral responsibility developed by Pereboom (2013, 2014), acknowledgement of wrongful behavior can be used for the purposes of future protection, future moral formation, and future reconciliation. In the following section, I will suggest how forward-looking moral responsibility can be used to help aid offenders in rehabilitation, but for the moment I will simply say that it can also be used to aid victims in their recovery and perhaps even achieve some form of reconciliation. *Restorative justice* models, for example, have been employed around the country over the last few decades with great success (see, e.g., Camp et al. 2013; Walgrave 2002). Restorative justice is an approach that emphasizes repairing the harm caused by criminal behavior by bringing together members of the community, victims, and offenders. As the Centre for Justice and Reconciliation describes it:

> Restorative justice views crime as more than breaking the law – it also causes harm to people, relationships, and the community. So a just response must address those harms as well as the wrongdoing. If the parties are willing, the best way to do this is to help them meet to discuss those harms and how to bring about resolution. Other approaches are available if they are unable or unwilling to meet. Sometimes those meetings lead to transformational changes in their lives.[9]

The restorative approach maintains that the best way to repair the harms caused by criminal behavior is to bring together all stakeholders for the purpose of making amends and reintegration. It focuses on repairing the harm caused by crime and reducing future harm through crime prevention.

Now it is true that most restorative justice methods require offenders to take responsibility for their actions and for the harm they have caused, but such responsibility *need not* be conceived in terms of basic desert. Most current restorative justice models probably do assume backward-looking blame and basic desert moral responsibility (e.g., Sommers 2016), but these are not essential components of the restorative approach. The same ends, I contend, can be achieved on a model that does not appeal to basic desert moral responsibility. For instance, a restorative justice model consistent with free will skepticism could appeal to *answerability* and *attributability* conceptions of moral responsibility rather than *accountability*. A conversational model of forward-looking moral responsibility like that proposed by Pereboom (2013, 2014) could, for example, serve as a basis for an exchange between victim and offender in a way that does not invoke backward-looking blame or basic desert (see Section 8.3). Such an exchange could aid both in the rehabilitation of offenders and in the recovery of victims.

8.3 REASONS-RESPONSIVENESS AND REHABILITATION

I would now like to turn to an objection concerning rehabilitation and the importance of reasons-responsiveness.[10] In his extensive criticisms of the public health–quarantine model, Michael Corrado has raised three main objections to my account (see 2016, 2017, 2018, 2019a, 2019b, 2019c), which leads him to reject the view in favor of an approach he calls *correction*. His position, while denying basic desert moral responsibility, endorses hard treatment of reasons-responsive criminals on the

---

[9] Please see: http://restorativejustice.org/restorative-justice/about-restorative-justice/tutorial-intro-to-restorative-justice/lesson-1-what-is-restorative-justice/.
[10] Most of the material in this section, as well as the next, is drawn from Pereboom and Caruso (2018).

ground of moral educational benefit to the criminal and deterrence of future crime. Corrado's first objection is that the view Pereboom and I endorse, unlike his, makes no distinction between people who are dangerous and yet have the sort of control captured by the reasons-responsiveness condition and those who are dangerous but lack this sort of control – instead we treat all criminals on the model of illness. The second is that, given our view, too many people will be drawn into the criminal justice system, since merely posing a danger is sufficient to make one a candidate for incapacitation. His third objection is that the public health–quarantine model allows for the possibility of indefinite detention if an offender remains a serious continued threat to society, whereas retributive punishment (and his own theory of correction) protects "the right to be held by the state only for a limited period of time" (2018: 10). I will address the first two objections in the remainder of this chapter and return to the last objection in the following chapter.

On the first concern, both Pereboom and I have distinguished the quarantine model from views according to which criminal tendencies are viewed exclusively as psychological illnesses modeled on physical illness (Pereboom 2001; Pereboom and Caruso 2018). It is true that on our view policies for making a detained criminal safe for release would address a condition in the offender that results in the criminal behavior. But such conditions are not restricted to psychological illnesses – they also include conditions that are not plausibly classified as illness, such as insufficient sympathy for others, or a strong tendency to assign blame to others and not to oneself when something goes wrong, etc. What unites policies for treatment of criminals on our view is not that they assume that they are psychologically ill and therefore in need of psychiatric treatment. Instead, they all aim to bring about moral change in an offender by nonpunitively addressing conditions that underlie criminal behavior.

What sets the illness model apart, and what makes it problematic, is that proposed treatment does not address the criminal's capacity to respond to reasons but circumvents such capacities. For example, consider the Ludovico method, made famous by Anthony Burgess's book and Stanley Kubrick's film *A Clockwork Orange*. Alex, a violent criminal, is injected with a drug that makes him nauseous while at the same time he is made to watch films depicting the kind of violence to which he is disposed. The goal of the method is that the violent behavior be eliminated by generating an association between violence and nausea. Herbert Morris's objection to therapy of this sort is that the criminal is not changed by being presented with reasons for altering his behavior that he would autonomously and rationally accept. But Pereboom and I have cited a number of programs for treating criminals that are not in accord with the illness model (see Pereboom 2001; Pereboom and Caruso 2018). The Oregon Learning Center, for instance, aims to train parents and families to formulate clear rules, to monitor behavior, and to set out fair and consistent procedures for establishing positive and negative incentives. The method involves presentation of reasons for acting and strategies for realizing aims in accord with these reasons. This program is successful: In one study, youth in ten families showed reductions of 60 percent in aggressive behavior compared to a 15-percent drop in untreated control families.[11]

Pereboom and I also cite therapeutic programs designed to address problems for the offender's cognitive functioning (see Pereboom and Caruso 2018). A number of cognitive therapy programs are inspired by S. Yochelson and S. Samenow's influential work *The Criminal Personality* (1976, 1977), which argues that certain kinds of cognitive distortions generate and sustain criminal behavior. Kris Henning and Christopher Frueh provide some examples of such cognitive distortions:

> Car thieves would be more likely to continue with their antisocial activities if they reasoned that *stealing cars isn't as bad as robbing people* (minimization of offense) or *I deserve to make a couple of bucks after all the cops put me through last time* (taking the role of the victim). Similarly, a rapist who convinces himself, *she shouldn't have been wearing that dress if she didn't want me to touch her* (denial of responsibility), would probably be at greater risk to reoffend than someone who accepts responsibility for his actions. (1996: 525)

In 1988, the State of Vermont put in place a therapeutic program inspired by the Yochelson and Samenow's cognitive distortion model. The *Cognitive Self-Change Program* was initially designed as group treatment for imprisoned male offenders with a history of interpersonal aggression, and it later included imprisoned nonviolent offenders. Henning and Frueh provide a description of the procedure:

> Treatment groups met 3–5 times per week. During each session, a single offender was identified to present a "thinking report" to the group. Typically, these reports documented prior incidents of anti-social behavior, although more current incidents were reported on when appropriate. At the beginning of each session, the offender would provide the group with an objective description of the incident. He would then list all of the thoughts and feelings he had before, during, and after the event. After the report was delivered, the group worked with the offender to identify the cognitive distortions that may have precipitated the antisocial response to the situation. Role plays sometimes were used during these sessions to develop a better understanding of the cognitions and emotions that led up to the offender's behavior. Once an offender learned to identify his primary criminogenic thought patterns, intervention strategies were discussed in the group to help him prevent such distortions from occurring in the future. These might include cognitive strategies (e.g. challenging one's cognitions, cognitive redirection) and/or behavioral interventions (e.g. avoidance of high-risk situations; discussion of cognitions and feelings with therapist, friend, or partner). (1996: 525)

Henning and Frueh found that in a group of 28 who had participated in this program, 50 percent (14) were charged with a new crime following their release.

---

[11] Patterson, Chamberlain, and Reid (1982), cited in Walters (1992: 143). Cf. Patterson (1982), Alexander and Parsons (1982). For a review of studies on family therapy, see Gendreau and Ross (1979).

In a control group of 96 who had not participated, 70.8 percent (68) were charged with a new offense. Twenty-five percent of offenders who had participated received a new criminal charge within one year, 38 percent within two years, and 46 percent within three. By contrast, in the comparison group 46 percent had been charged with a new crime within one year, 67 percent within two, and 75 percent within three. These results were found to be statistically significant.

Models of restorative justice proved another alternative for rehabilitating criminals in a way that respects the reasons-responsiveness of agents. It also has the additional benefit of addressing the rights of victims by having the criminal admit the wrong done, acknowledge the harm caused, and agree to work toward reconciliation with the victim or the victim's families. As I said earlier, models of restorative justice can be made consistent with free will skepticism as long as they are employed in a way that does not appeal to backward-looking blame in the restorative process. Consider, for instance, the recent success of schools in using restorative methods as an alternative to school suspension.[12] In traditional school-discipline programs, students face an escalating scale of punishment for infractions that can ultimately lead to expulsion. There is now strong research, however, that shows pulling students out of class as punishment can hurt their long-term academic prospects (Losen, Martinez, and Okelola 2014; Losen et al. 2015; Richmond 2015). Furthermore, data show that punishments are often distributed unequally. More black students, for example, are suspended nationally than white students (US Department of Education Office for Civil Rights 2014; Richmond 2015).

As an alternative, public schools from Maine to Oregon have begun to employ restorative justice programs designed to keep students in school while addressing infractions in a way that benefits both the offender and the offended. Here is one description of such a program:

> Lower-level offenses can be redirected to the justice committee, which is made up of student mediators, with school administrators and teachers serving as advisors. The goal is to provide a nonconfrontational forum for students to talk through their problems, addressing their underlying reasons for their own behaviors, and make amends both to individuals who have been affected as well as to the larger school community. (Richmond 2015)

Students are often given the option of participating in these alternative programs or accept traditional discipline, including suspension. As reported on in *The Atlantic*, "Early adopters of the practice report dramatic declines in school-discipline problems, as well as improved climates on campuses and even gains in student achievement" (Richmond 2015). Programs like this reveal that the more punitive option – for example, expulsion rather than restorative processes – is often less effective from

---

[12] See "Alternative to School Suspension Explored Through Restorative Justice" (Associated Press), December 17, 2014; and "When Restorative Justice in Schools Works" (*The Atlantic*), December 29, 2015.

the perspective of future protection, future reconciliation, and future moral formation. They also reveal how rehabilitating individuals can be done in a way that appeals directly to their reasons-responsive capacities.[13]

Contrary to Corrado's concerns, then, I maintain that methods of therapy that engage reasons-responsive abilities should be preferred. On the forward-looking account of moral responsibility Pereboom and I endorse (Pereboom 2013; 2014: chapter 6), when we call an agent to account for immoral behavior, at the stage of moral address we request an explanation with the intent of having the agent acknowledge a disposition to act badly, and then, if she has in fact so acted without excuse or justification, we aim for her to come to see that the disposition issuing in the action is best eliminated. In normal cases, this change is produced by way of the agent's recognition of moral reasons to eliminate the disposition. Accordingly, it is an agent's responsiveness to reasons – together with the fact that we have a moral interest in our protection, her moral formation, and our reconciliation with her – that explains why she is an appropriate recipient of moral protest in this forward-looking sense. While many compatibilists see some type of attunement to reasons as the key condition for basic desert moral responsibility, we instead view it as the most significant condition for a notion of responsibility that focuses on future protection, future reconciliation, and future moral formation.

Still, a concern for many forms of therapy proposed for altering criminal tendencies is that they circumvent, rather than address, the criminal's capacity to respond to reasons. I propose that forms of treatment that do address reasons-responsiveness are to be preferred. Typically, these will involve consoling and therapy combined with work training, educational programs, and social services aimed at addressing the situational features of crime. However, the fact that a mode of therapy circumvents rather than addresses the capacities that confer dignity on us should not all by itself make it illegitimate for agents who are in general responsive to reasons but not in particular respects. Imagine such an agent who is beset by bouts of violent anger that he cannot control in some pertinent sense. Certain studies suggest that this tendency is due to deficiencies in serotonin and that it can sometimes be alleviated by antidepressants.[14] It would seem mistaken to claim that such a mode of treatment is illegitimate because it circumvents capacities for rational and autonomous response. In fact, this sort of treatment often produces responsiveness to reasons

[13] Despite the benefits of restorative justice, it is important that I also acknowledge that the method is not without its problems, particularly in its advocacy of *shaming* as an essential element of the larger restorative process. John Braithwaite (1989, 2002), for instance, insists that shaming plays a vital role in restoring the offender to the community and restoring wholeness to the community. Braithwaite repeatedly insists that the essential *shame* is not the destructive shaming that *stigmatizes* the wrongdoer and marks that person as a permanent bad character; rather, the shaming is a *reintegrative* shaming that focuses on the wrongness of the *act* instead of the badness of the person performing the act. Critics, however, have noted that even reintegrative shaming can be extremely harmful, and once the Pandora's box of shaming is opened it is difficult to control what emerges (see White 1994; Retzinger and Sheff 1996; Whitman 1998; Morris 2001, 2002; Matthews 2006).

[14] Burlington Free Press (Associated Press), December 15, 1997, p. 1.

where it was previously absent (Pereboom 2001). A person beset by violent anger will typically not be responsive to certain kinds of reasons, to which he would be responsive if he were not suffering from this problem. Therapy of this sort can thus increase reasons-responsiveness. By analogy, medications are often used as an important part of the treatment of offenders with drug and alcohol addiction, especially when combined with behavioral therapies. By counteracting addiction in this way, these medications can result in enhanced reasons-responsiveness.

But what if even this approaches fail to rehabilitate? What if despite serious attempts at moral rehabilitation that do not circumvent the criminal's rational capacities, and despite procedures that mechanically increase the agent's capacities for reasons-responsiveness, the criminal still displays dangerously violent tendencies? Imagine that the choice is now between indefinite confinement without hope for release and the option (say) of chemical castration for violent sexual offenders. Chemical castration consists of a pharmacological therapy that reduces sex hormones (such as testosterone) and, in consequence, eliminates sexual desires. It is normally a reversible procedure, ending after the treatment is discontinued. Several countries offer sexual offenders this option on a *voluntary basis*, including Sweden, Finland, Denmark, Norway, and Germany. If it were shown that chemical castration significantly and effectively reduced recidivism, would it be wrong to give offenders the option on a voluntary basis? While I acknowledge that difficult ethical issues arise here, including concerns about consent and the potential for harmful side effects,[15] it is also not obvious that the option of chemical castration should be ruled out as morally illegitimate. One must assess the appropriateness of this option by comparing it with the other options. Suppose, for example, that the only legitimate alternative to confinement for life is for the offender to choose chemical castration. It is not clear that under such circumstances the moral problems with such a therapy are not outweighed – especially if it is carried out in a way that respects autonomy by leaving the decision up to the individual.

Pereboom and I propose, then, that rehabilitation methods that directly appeal to a criminal's rational capacities should always be preferred and attempted first (see Pereboom and Caruso 2018). When these fail, we contend that it is sometimes acceptable to employ therapies that mechanically increase an agent's capacities for reasons-responsiveness, but that these therapies should involve the participation of the subject to the greatest extent possible (e.g., talk therapies in conjunction with other forms of treatment), should involve the consent of the subject, and should be ordered such that noninvasive methods are prioritized. When all else fails and only more invasive methods are left, important ethical questions need to be considered and answers weighed but leaving the final choice up the subject is one possible option.

---

[15] See, e.g., Scott and Holmberg (2003), Douglas et al. (2013), Aagaard (2014), Douglas (2014, 2019), Shaw (2019b), Berryessa, Chandler, and Reiner (2016).

8.4 PREEMPTIVE INCAPACITATION

Corrado's second objection is that too many people will be drawn into the criminal justice system on the approach favored by the public health–quarantine model. First, Corrado intimates that many more people would be detained than is the case currently. Second, there is the issue of incapacitating those who pose threats but have not yet committed a crime. Corrado is reasonably concerned about the prospects of such a policy. Regarding the first issue, though, Pereboom and I have all along advocated for the *principle of least infringement*, which specifies that the least restrictive measures should be taken to protect public health and safety. While we do believe that we should indefinitely detain mass murderers and serial rapists who cannot be rehabilitated and remain threats, we do not believe that nonviolent shoplifters who remain threats and cannot be rehabilitated should be preventatively detained at all, by contrast with being monitored, for example. Our view does not prescribe that all dangerous people be detained until they are no longer dangerous. Certain kinds of persisting threats can be dealt with by monitoring by contrast with detention. Moreover, other behavior that is currently considered criminal might not require incapacitation at all. Our view is consistent, for example, with the decriminalization of nonviolent behavior such as recreational drug use and thus is consistent with many fewer people being detained than in the United States currently.

In response to the second concern, that is, the incapacitation of dangerous individuals who have not yet committed a crime, I argue that there are several moral reasons that count against such a policy. As Ferdinand Schoeman (1979) has argued and I have stressed, the right to liberty must carry weight in this context, as should the concern for using people as merely as means. In addition, the risk posed by a state policy that allows for preventative detention of non-offenders needs to be taken into serious consideration. In a broad range of societies, allowing the state this option stands to result in much more harm than good, because misuse would be likely. Schoeman also points out that while the kinds of testing required to determine whether someone is a carrier of a communicable disease may often not be unacceptably invasive, the type of screening necessary for determining whether someone has violent criminal tendencies might well be invasive in respects that raise serious moral issues. Moreover, available psychiatric methods for discerning whether an agent is likely to be a violent criminal are not especially reliable, and as Stephen Morse points out, detaining someone on the basis of a screening method that frequently yields false positives is seriously morally objectionable (Morse 1999; Nadelhoffer et al. 2012).

For these reasons, I propose we adopt an attitude of *epistemic skepticism* when it comes to judging the dangerousness of someone who has not yet committed a crime. Given the limitations of our current screening methods, their invasiveness, and the likelihood of false positives, our default position should be to respect individual liberty and prohibit the preventative detention of non-offenders.

8.4 Preemptive Incapacitation

Additionally, Jean Floud and Warren Young (1981) have argued that anyone who has not yet committed a crime should be entitled to a *presumption of harmlessness*, much as a person should be entitled to a presumption of innocence. Just as the presumption of innocence protects the unconvicted person against punishment, so the presumption of harmlessness protects the unconvicted person against preventive detention. And not only is the presumption of harmlessness consistent with the attitude of epistemic skepticism, it is also a presumption that should be afforded all rational individuals since respect for persons and considerations of justice demand it.

These considerations, I contend, will block preemptive incapacitation in all but the most extreme cases. But where and when should exceptions be made? What are the "extreme cases"? Here is one possible case:

> Imagine that someone has involuntarily been given a drug that makes it virtually certain that he will brutally murder at least one person during the one-week period he is under its influence. There is no known antidote, and because he is especially strong, mere monitoring would be ineffective. (Pereboom and Caruso 2018: 215)

In such a case, the public health–quarantine model may allow for preventative detention. But this should not count as a strong objection to the view since virtually everyone would agree that it would be at least prima facie permissible to preventatively detain this individual for the week. In fact, instead of being a weakness of the model, I think the possibility of exceptions in cases like this provides the model with an additional advantage over retributivism. In this situation, retributivists would have a hard time justifying preventive measures on the grounds that individual *deserves* punishment, since he has not yet done anything wrong. Yet the retributivists I have talked to about this example, as well as the many audiences I put the question to, have acknowledged that they too would detain the individual until the drug has worn off. This indicates to me that most retributivists are not pure retributivists but are willing to supplement their account with additional justifications when needed, such as the justification provided by the public health–quarantine model. But if one is going to be a *retributivist plus* – that is, if one is going to embrace retributivism but supplement it with additional justifications, like incapacitation, when needed – then they too must address concerns about preemptive detention.

Corrado, himself, acknowledges that he would also detain this individual for the week (Corrado 2018). In explaining why, he offers a few possible interpretations of the case. On one interpretation, he argues that we could view the drug as undermining the agent's reasons-responsiveness and that in such cases it is sometimes permissible to preemptively incapacitate non-reasons-responsive agents, as is currently permitted in cases of mental illness when an individual is involuntarily committed for being an imminent and serious threat of substantial harm to self or other. According to Corrado, there are two possible ways the drug could undermine the agent's reasons-responsiveness. First, he writes:

If because of the drug [the man in the example] will cause harm without ever intending to do anything wrongful (just as the highly contagious person might communicate her disease in spite of every effort to avoid doing so), then I would argue that preventing the harm is not within his practical control, and we may indeed restrict his behavior just as we restrict the behavior of the unavoidable contagious individual in the public health case. It would be foolish to expect the criminal laws to influence the harmful behavior of a man who could not be so influenced. (2018)

If, on the hand, the harm is to be brought about intentionally by the drugged man, which is consistent with the drug working through the agent's intentions, then Corrado suggests the question should be: "[C]ould he have responded to reasons not to have so intended?" (2018). If not, then Corrado once again concludes he fails to be reasons-responsive and "preventive detention – civil commitment – would be appropriate under existing law" (2018).

I agree with Corrado that existing law already allows for preventive involuntary commitment in certain rare and specifically defined cases. Consider the use of involuntary commitment for the mentally ill. While standards for involuntary commitment differ from state to state, they generally maintain something like the following (e.g., Alabama Code 22–52-10.4):

(a) A respondent may be committed to inpatient treatment if the probate court finds, based upon clear and convincing evidence that:
   i. the respondent is mentally ill;
   ii. as a result of the mental illness the respondent poses a real and present threat of substantial harm to self and/or others;
   iii. the respondent will, if not treated, continue to suffer mental distress and will continue to experience deterioration of the ability to function independently; and
   iv. the respondent is unable to make rational and informed decisions as to whether or not treatment for mental illness would be desirable.
(b) If the probate judge finds that no treatment is presently available for the respondent's mental illness, but that confinement is necessary to prevent the respondent from causing substantial harm to himself or to others, the order committing the respondent shall provide that, should treatment for the respondent's mental illness become available at any time during the period of the respondent's confinement, such treatment shall be made available to him immediately.

Under such conditions, the law allows for the involuntary commitment of the dangerously mentally ill. And I agree with Corrado that the justification for such commitment lies largely in the fact that such individuals "are not just dangerous but both dangerous and unable to confirm their behavior to the law (whether from a deficit of reason or of will)" (Corrado 2018: s.3).

I see no reason, however, why the public health–quarantine model cannot also make use of this distinction between agents who are suffering from mental illness and satisfy the conditions just stated, or are drugged and satisfy similar conditions, and agents who are competent and reasons-responsive. I propose that in cases when an individual is suffering from mental illness and satisfies the epistemic demand for "clear and convincing evidence" of conditions (i)–(iv), involuntary commitment may be justified, as long as it is also guided by the principles of least infringement, beneficence and nonmaleficence, and concern for the well-being of the individual. I contend the same is true for the drugged man since similarly he (i) is not in control of his actions; (ii) poses a real and present threat of substantial harm to others; (iii) is "virtually certain" to kill at least one person during the next week if not incapacitated; and (iv) is unable to make rational and informed decisions during the one-week period he is under the drugs influence. On the other hand, I contend that when agents are competent, moderately reasons-responsive, and able to make rational and informed decisions, the presumption of harmlessness and epistemic skepticism count strongly, perhaps even conclusively, in favor of allowing individuals the liberty to commit criminal acts before incapacitation can be justified. Moderately reasons-responsive agents are able to conform their behavior to the reasons they have for action (Fischer and Ravizza 1998). If we think that a reasons-responsive agent is going to harm another, we could reason with them or provide them with countervailing moral and/or legal considerations, but we should respect their liberty to conform with those reasons or not. And given that we have no way of determining ahead of time what reasons will ultimately move them, we should afford them the presumption of harmlessness.

I acknowledge that it is possible that this epistemic burden of proof can be overcome in certain hypothetical situations – like when we are "virtually certain" that an agent will cause severe and substantial harm to others. But in most real-world cases, since we lack a crystal ball, we are nowhere near certain that a reasons-responsive agent will cause severe and substantial harm to others until they do so. Furthermore, even when we have good indication that someone poses a serious threat of harm, there are countervailing moral considerations that must be taken into account. In many societies the danger of misuse posed by allowing the state to preventatively detain even highly dangerous non-offenders is a grave concern that stands to outweigh the value of the safety provided by such a policy. I therefore argue that the preemptive incapacitation of competent, reasons-responsive agents should be prohibited in practically all real-world cases. And in the cases where my model would allow exceptions, like the hypothetical example of the drugged man, virtually all theorists would agree that some preemptive measures should be taken.

Lastly, I would also suggest that in many real-world cases concerns about preemptive incapacitation are not pertinent. That is because, the actions and behaviors we often take to indicate that someone is a real, present, and substantial threat to others are *themselves* criminal acts, or least could be interpreted as such, in which case incapacitation, if it were deemed justified, would no longer be *preemptive*. Instead, it would be a reaction to criminal offenses already performed and hence justified on the right of self-defense. For instance, if a would-be school shooter makes a video expressing their intentions and plans and then posts it online before attempting the actual shooting, the video itself would likely be interpreted as a criminal act and itself grounds for restrictive measures. Similarly, a violent stalker who has not yet harmed their intended target may violate privacy and cyber laws before their action escalates to the point of violent behavior. If these are the signs by which we judge an individual is a significant threat to others, then any restrictive measures we take would no longer be *preemptive*; they would be responsive to an actual crime. Since most real-world grounds for thinking an individual poses a significant threat of harm will involve prior actions of this kind, the realm of cases where preemptive incapacitation is even a legitimate question may be vanishingly small. They will generally only arise when the grounds for thinking someone poses a significant and present threat come, not from their actions or behavior, but from sociological and/or neuroscientific data indicating an increased risk of violence. But as I already argued in Chapter 7, such data are generally insufficient to overcome the presumption of harmlessness and the epistemic burden of proof.

9

The Public Health–Quarantine Model IV

Funishment, Deterrence, Evidentiary Standards, and Indefinite Detention

In the previous chapter, I argued that the public health–quarantine model can successfully deal with concerns about proportionality, human dignity, victims' rights, rehabilitation, and preemptive incapacitation. In this chapter, I will argue that it can also successfully deal with concerns about funishment, cost, deterrence, evidentiary standards, and indefinite detention. In the process of defending my account, I will revisit the issue of prison design, explain one important difference between the views of Pereboom and myself, and argue that high evidentiary standards and the importance of *actus reus* and *mens rea* can all be preserved.

9.1 FUNISHMENT

I would like to begin with a rather interesting objection by Saul Smilansky (2011, 2016) against optimistic skeptics, like me, who maintain that we are better off without belief in free will and basic desert moral responsibility. According to Smilansky, free will skeptics are forced to seek to revise the practice of punishment in the direction of *funishment*, whereby the incarcerated are very generously compensated for the deprivation of incarceration, since those cannot be deserved. Yet Smilansky argues that such a policy would be extremely expensive – in fact, the cost of funishment, compared to punishment, would be so high that it would be intolerable. Smilansky summarizes his argument as follows (2016):[1]

1. Murderers, rapists, violent bullies, thieves, and other miscreants need to be kept apart from lawful society; we have no real choice, for otherwise they will kill, rape, steal, and make life miserable for the rest of us.
2. Since free will skepticism holds that no one deserves the hardship of being separated from regular society, this hardship needs to be compensated for. Hence a great effort and expense must be made, in order that a person undergoing

---

[1] This is drawn directly from Smilansky's own summary (2016) but with one change: I have replaced his reference to "hard determinism" with "free will skepticism" so as to remain consistent with my preferred terminology.

punishment will have a good life despite being separated from regular society, and deprived of the freedom and opportunity to move among the rest of us.

3. This effort at compensation morally must receive high social priority. We are at risk of ruining the lives of people who (again, assuming the skeptical perspective) in no way deserve this. Incarceration does not just occur. The criminals are proposed to become our victims: They will suffer grave deprivation and harm (in itself, and relatively to others on the outside), due to our own intentional actions and because this serves our interests. We, as a society, are proposing to target and injure them in a special way, which they do not deserve, for our own purposes. In order to be permitted to do so, we must provide adequate compensation.

4. So, instead of punishment, we should have *funishment*: Funishment would resemble punishment in that criminals would be incarcerated apart from lawful society, and institutions of funishment would also need to be as secure as current prisons to prevent criminals from escaping. But institutions of funishment would also need to be as delightful as possible. They would need to resemble five-star hotels, where the residents are given every opportunity to enjoy life.

5. This would go beyond material conditions: Each criminal will need to be permitted considerable leeway in running his or her own personal life, as well as a large measure of freedom of social interaction (including frequent visits from outsiders).

7. Criminals currently have to balance the temptations of crime with the risks of punishment: the risk that, if caught, they are likely to spend many of the best years of their lives in miserable, ugly, harsh, nasty, violent, and otherwise highly unpleasant institutions. Some people nevertheless take the risk, while many others are deterred. But, once funishment replaces punishment, matters change radically.

8. The potential offender knows that, if he is not caught, he can enjoy the spoils of his crime. But even if he is caught, he faces only some time in an institution of funishment, which – apart from being separated from lawful society – will be like a fabulous holiday. Funishment will greatly weaken the deterrence of institutions of punishment.

9. The claim that a system that could threaten potential offenders with, at worst, funishment would be challenged in its efforts to deter, while empirical, can hardly be controversial. Modern societies are finding it difficult to deter many people even with present, highly unpleasant prisons; a turn toward funishment must greatly weaken deterrence. Following free will skepticism would lead to a flood of crime. The number of people who would need to be kept apart from lawful society would increase enormously. Many people who would otherwise not have become involved in crime, nor ever suffer detention, would be caught up in that very life. In the meantime, the rest of us would be living in the worst possible world: suffering unprecedented crime

waves while paying unimaginable sums for the upkeep of offenders in opulent institutions of funishment.
10. Even in terms of free will skepticism, all this is a very bad state of affairs. Free will skeptics have sought to limit the number of people with which the justice system must deal, to reduce public hatred of offenders, and to beneficially reform the social conditions that generate crime. But free will skepticism itself defeats all those idealistic goals. If implemented, the view would generate more rather than less crime, more criminals would be caught up in the system and incarcerated apart from society (albeit under improved conditions), and public sentiment would hardly move toward an offender-sympathetic stance, once crime blossoms, and the taxation required to finance the regime of funishment mushrooms. This makes a backlash against funishment very likely.
11. In any case, a nonretributive order in line with free will skepticism would be nightmarish, even for free will skeptics, if correctly implemented. Free will skeptics themselves cannot desire the results of the reforms required by their own position (rising crime, much higher levels of incarceration, etc.). Free will skepticism is, in practice, self-defeating.

This argument represents a serious challenge to my view, but one that is significantly different than the kinds of objections already discussed. Previous objections feared that the public health–quarantine model would lead to cruel and inhumane treatment of prisoners. This objection maintains the exact opposite – that free will skepticism will lead to funishment where criminals are provided with accommodations resembling "five-star hotels." I find it a bit amusing that the public health–quarantine model has been charged with such diametrically opposed concerns. It appears critics cannot decide whether to accuse it of being too harsh or too lenient. Setting aside, though, the seemingly inconsistent nature of these criticisms, I will now address Smilansky's objection in detail and argue that it fails for three main reasons.

First, as Smilansky acknowledges, it is an empirical question whether strong punitive measures better deter crime than the alternatives. If Smilansky is correct, funishment will not have the deterrence factor needed to prevent society from falling into the abyss. For Smilansky, harsh and unpleasant punishment is required to deter crime. In fact, Smilansky states in premise (7) that even the potential cost of spending the "best years of their lives in miserable, ugly, harsh, nasty, violent, and otherwise highly unpleasant institutions" (2016) is often not enough to deter criminals in our current system. If we were to improve these conditions to the point of funishment, he argues, where accommodations would resemble "five-star hotels" (2016), all or most deterrence would be lost.[2] I would like to challenge this empirical

---

[2] It is an interesting question whether Smilansky's argument is consistent with prison reform at all, as he states it is (2016), since the argument seems to imply that each increment of improvement would result in a corresponding loss of deterrence. We could imagine that at one end of the punishment scale we had inquisition-like conditions, on the other end funishment. In between would be a sliding scale of humane treatment, comfort, levels of autonomy, living conditions, etc. While not committing

claim by examining some real-world examples and by once again drawing attention to the importance of prison design and environment on inmates' behavior.

As has already been discussed, typical US, UK, and Australian prisons are harsh, restrictive institutions, designed to enable maximum control over inmates' behavior at any time. "Their scale and appearance instill mistrust and anonymity ... The ability to personalise space, have ownership and have personal control over one's situation is intentionally absent. Mostly, these are overtly punitive environments, unlike any other" (Lutham and Klippan 2016). Such conditions are a breeding ground for violence and self-harm.[3] On the other hand, there are good examples of innovative, humanitarian, and rehabilitative prison design that exist in Scandinavian countries. These prisons resemble, in many ways, the conditions of funishment Smilansky finds problematic. Prisons such as Halden Prison in Norway, Leoben in Austria, and Enner Mark in Denmark are purposely designed to reduce crime. As Lutham and Klippan explain:

> They do this by providing positive opportunities for inmates and building a great sense of optimism for their future ... These spaces are designed to more closely reflect environments in the outside community. The design treats these people not solely as "prisoners" but also as community members – with all the social, vocational and emotional responsibilities that this entails. (Lutham and Klippan 2016)

A good example of this is the Norwegian prison island of Bastoy. By most accounts it is exactly what Smilansky has in mind when he speaks of funishment. Here, for example, is the BBC's description of life on Bastoy:

> Inmates ... are free to walk around in a village-style setting, tending to farm animals. They ski, cook, play tennis, play cards. They have their own beach, and even run the ferry taking people to and from the island. And in the afternoon when most prison staff go home, only a handful of guards are left to watch the 115 prisoners. (BBC News 2016)[4]

The *Guardian* further describes Bastoy as "cushy" and "luxurious." In an article titled "The Norwegian prison where inmates are treated like people," they write:

> I found that the loss of liberty was all the punishment [the prisoners] suffered. Cells had televisions, computers, integral showers and sanitation. Some prisoners were segregated for various reasons, but as the majority served their time ... they were offered education, training and skill-building programmes. Instead of wings and landings they lived in small "pod" communities within the prison, limiting the

---

Smilansky to the claim that the worst off conditions would deter the most, he would nonetheless have to acknowledge that there is some optimal or peak level that maximizes deterrence. Given this, it would seem that any deviation from this optimal or peak state would begin to bend the curve downward, resulting in a loss of deterrence.

[3] See, e.g., Bowker (1980), Irwin (1980), Ministry of Justice (2016), Wortley (2005).
[4] BBC News, "Andrew Breivik: Just how cushy are Norwegian prisons?" March 16, 2016. Available at: www.bbc.com/news/magazine-35813470.

spread of the corrosive criminal prison subculture that dominates traditionally designed prisons. (James 2013)

And the *Huff Post* adds:

Bastoy is an open prison, a concept born in Finland during the 1930s and now part of the norm throughout Scandinavia, where prisoners can sometimes keep their jobs on the outside while serving time, commuting daily. Thirty percent of Norway's prisons are open, and Bastoy ... is considered the crown jewel of them all. (2016)

Another Norwegian prison that resembles funishment more than punishment is Halden Prison, a high-security prison near the Swedish border that aims to rehabilitate criminals with comfortable and thoroughly modern facilities. At Halden, prisoners have access to steel cutlery in the kitchens, saws, pliers, and metal files in the workshop, and a music studio with guitars, keyboards, drums, and a mixing deck. *Time* magazine reports, to ease the psychological burden of imprisonment, the planners of Halden spent roughly $1 million on paintings, photographs and light installations.[5] Every ten to twelve cells share a kitchen and living room, where prisoners prepare their evening meals and relax after a day at work. None of the windows at Halden have bars. And in terms of recreational opportunities for prisoners:

Security guards organize activities from 8:00 in the morning until 8:00 in the evening. It's a chance for inmates to pick up a new hobby, but it's also part of the prison's dynamic security strategy: occupied prisoners are less likely to lash out at guards and one another. Inmates can shoot hoops on the basketball court, which absorbs falls on impact, and make use of a rock-climbing wall, jogging trials and a soccer field.[6]

Halden's designers also preserved trees across the 75-acre site, whereas US prisons are usually devoid of vegetation to maximize visibility. Lastly, to help inmates develop routines and to reduce the monotony of confinement, designers spread Halden's living quarters, work areas, and activity centers across the prison grounds.

These facilities are purposely designed with the philosophical goal of rehabilitation and reintegration squarely in mind. And as discussed previously, the Norwegian Correctional Service has officially adopted the *normality principle*, which maintains that during the serving of a sentence "life inside will resemble life outside as much as possible." Given that these Norwegian prisons resemble funishment in almost all salient respects – for example, the living conditions resemble the outside world as much as possible and individual autonomy is maximized so that inmates have considerable leeway in running their own lives and interacting socially – Smilansky's argument would predict that crime in Norway must be rampant and out of control. The reality, however, is the exact opposite. The crime rate in Norway

---

[5] See *Time* magazine's photo story, "Inside the world's most humane prison." Available at: http://content.time.com/time/photogallery/0,29307,1989083,00.html.
[6] Ibid.

is relatively low in comparison to the United States and Western European countries.[7] For instance, the United States has 87 percent more crime than Norway.[8] Norway also has one of the lowest murder rates in the world. In 2009, Norway had 0.6 intentional homicides per 100,000 people. In the same year, the United States had five murders per 100,000 people, meaning that the United States proportionally had eight times as many homicides. Norway's incarceration rate is also a fraction of that of the United States – which again runs contrary to Smilansky's prediction that "more criminals would be caught up in the system and incarcerated apart from society." The United States incarcerates around 700 prisoners for every 100,000 citizens, whereas Norway incarcerates around 60 per 100,000.

What about recidivism? Well, when criminals in Norway leave prison, they tend to stay out. Norway's recidivism rate of 20 percent is one of the lowest in the world. The recidivism rate of Bastoy Prison, for example, is about 16 percent. By contrast, in the United States more than 76 percent of state prisoners are rearrested within five years. The recidivism rate in the United Kingdom is lower, about 45 percent, but still more than double that of Norway. These statistics reinforce what researchers are finding, that prison has at best a negligible – and at worst a damaging – impact on the likelihood a person will re-offend (see Weatherburn 2010). Furthermore, as Lutham and Klippan note:

> Though these less conventional prison environments feature much "softer" forms of security, there has not been a correlating increase in security incidents within them. Most investigations of these places indicate fewer incidents and more positive interactions between staff and prisoners. This contradicts the idea that "hard" prison design is necessary for behaviour control. (2016)

Empirically speaking, then, it is hard to argue that shorter prison sentences and "luxury" conditions on their own will increase crime. If Norway is any indication, this is simply not the case.[9] And given that this empirical claim comprises the core of Smilansky's objection, the argument fails to be convincing. I see no reason for thinking that free will skeptics would be required to provide *more* than the kinds of conditions provided in Norwegian prisons – which are perhaps the most humane and comfortable in the world. And given that such conditions do not result in

---

[7] See the Norway 2015 Crime and Safety Report. www.osac.gov/pages/ContentReportDetails.aspx?cid=16970.
[8] Source: www.nationmaster.com/country-info/compare/Norway/United-States/Crime.
[9] Of course, Norway differs from the United States in a number of salient ways and this may in part account for the differences we see in crime, incarceration, and recidivism rates. Norway, for example, lacks the racial history of the United States. It is also a more egalitarian society with less concentration of wealth at the top, very little poverty, universal healthcare, and more comprehensive government services. These differences, however, simply reinforce the notion that a holistic approach to criminal behavior, like that offered by the public health–quarantine model, needs to deal not only with the treatment and rehabilitation of those we incapacitate but also with social justice – including racism, poverty, wealth inequality, access to healthcare, and the like.

"unprecedented crime waves" or the "worst possible world" Smilansky predicts, we should conclude that such fears are overblown.

Let me now consider a slightly different objection. Smilansky also claims that adopting the public health–quarantine model would require "paying unimaginable sums for the upkeep of offenders in opulent institutions of funishment" (2016). We can call this the *cost objection*, as opposed to the deterrence or rising-crime objection addressed earlier. We can state the objection as follows: (1) According to my model, just as we have a duty to do what we can, within reasonable bounds, to make a person with cholera in quarantine safe for release as quickly as possible and to house them in comfortable and reasonable conditions, we likewise have a duty to criminals to do what we can, within reasonable bounds, to rehabilitate them and house them in comfortable and reasonable conditions; (2) this will have a cost; (3) it would be seriously unfair for a society or state to be unwilling to pay this cost, especially since the deprivation experienced would not be deserved on my account; but (3) this would result in "unimaginable sums" and be prohibitively expensive.

My first reply to this objection would be that, *even if this were so* it would leave untouched the normative aspects of my argument. An analogy with public education is helpful here. Most people would agree with the following normative claim, which is meant to be analogous to premise (1) above: (1*) we have a duty to do what we can, within reasonable bounds, to provide access to public education for all – regardless of race, ethnicity, gender, class, sexual orientation, or ability to pay. Assuming (1*) for the moment, the analogous argument would run as follows: (2*) Paying for a system of public education will have a cost; and (3*) it would be unfair and unjust for a society or state to be unwilling to pay this cost. Now let us assume (as the argument just given does) that the costs of public education became prohibitively expensive – perhaps even that it became impossible for states to cover said costs without overburdening taxpayers. Even if this were so, it would not follow that premise (1*) is false or that we should disregard matters of justice and fairness. At most it would reveal a practical barrier in the way of achieving justice, but not that denying children a public education was *itself* just. I would say the same for criminal justice. Even if it was practically difficult or even impossible to implement my public health–quarantine model because it was too expensive, an assumption I will challenge in a moment and have challenged in the preceding chapter, it would neither follow that harsh or excessively punitive punishment would suddenly become justified, nor would it follow that retributivism was justified – the cost objection simply has no bearing on these matters.

That said, would the public health–quarantine model be prohibitively expensive? I contend that it would not. Let us drill down into the numbers. The American prison system is massive and extremely expensive – so massive that its estimated annual cost of $80 billion eclipses the GDP of 133 nations. Consider first the monetary costs to taxpayers. While the price of prisoners can vary greatly from state to state, a Vera Institute of Justice (VIJ) study of forty states found the cumulative cost of prisons in 2010 was $39 billion.[10] That is $5.4 billion more than the $33.5 billion provided by corrections budgets – an interesting accounting trick. The annual average public cost per prisoner in those same forty states was $31,286, with some states on the high end paying as much as $60,000 per prisoner annually. By comparison, the average cost per public school student nationwide was $11,184 in 2010. That means it is significantly cheaper to educate a child for a year than to house someone in prison. According to the Justice Department, the nationwide expense of incarceration in both state and federal budgets in 2010 was about $80 billion.[11] While it is true that Norway's per prisoner costs are higher than the United States – for instance, housing a prisoner in Halden prison runs $93,000 per inmate per year – this does not mean that the system as a whole is more expensive. *The New York Times* (2015) estimates that if the United States incarcerated its citizens at the same low rate as Norwegians do, it could spend that much per inmate and still save more than $45 billion a year.[12]

Furthermore, per prisoner annual costs are only part of the story, there are also hidden costs society pays for incarceration. And in the United States we pay a huge price for a largely ineffective system. As a report put out by the Pell Center for International Relations and Public Policy explains:

> The costs associated with incarceration and recidivism are not just financial. The toll on prisoners and their families is impossible to calculate. Loved ones can suffer from economic strain, psychological and emotional distress, and social stigma. Prisoners endure isolation from their families and the community. They are often housed in overcrowded and dangerous prisons. The stress of surviving in prison can lead to depression and anxiety. Inmates may leave prison worse off than when they arrived, which can be detrimental to communities and society as a whole. (2014, 2)[13]

In Norway and other Scandinavian countries, as well as in places like the Netherlands,[14] the emphasis is on rehabilitation and re-socialization rather than

---

[10] Christian Hendrickson and Ruth Delaney, "The Price of Prisons: What Incarceration Costs Taxpayers," Vera Institute of Justice, Center on Sentencing and Corrections, January 2012 (updated July 20, 2012). Accessed November 11, 2013, www.vera.org/publications/price-of-prisons-what-incarceration-costs-taxpayers.

[11] US Department of Justice, "Smart on Crime: Reforming the Criminal Justice System for the 21st Century," August 2013. Accessed November 13, 2013, www.justice.gov/ag/smart-on-crime.pdf.

[12] Jessican Benko, "The Radical Humaneness of Norway's Halden Prison," March 26, 2015. www.nytimes.com/2015/03/29/magazine/the-radical-humaneness-of-norways-halden-prison.html?_r=1.

[13] Carolyn W. Deady, "Incarceration and Recidivism: Lessons from Abroad," March 2014: www.salve.edu/sites/default/files/filesfield/documents/Incarceration_and_Recidivism.pdf.

[14] See, e.g., this US News story on "How the Dutch are closing their prisons": www.usnews.com/news/best-countries/articles/2019-05-13/the-netherlands-is-closing-its-prisons. The Dutch example is also a good one because, unlike the Scandinavian countries, it is a non-homogenous society, showing that this rehabilitative approach can also work in more diverse societies. By 2017, for instance, persons with an immigration background, both Western and non-Western, formed a majority in Amsterdam, Rotterdam, and the Hague, the three largest cities of the Netherlands (see: https://opendata.cbs.nl/statline/#/CBS/nl/dataset/70748NED/table?fromstatweb). Canada is also a good example – it has

just punishment. As a result, they provide work training and other educational opportunities for prisoners. This has proven to be extremely effective in reducing the rate of recidivism. Incarceration is also used less frequently and for shorter periods of time. By comparison, in the United States people are often imprisoned for crimes that would not lead to imprisonment in other countries, such as passing bad checks, minor drug offenses, and other nonviolent crimes. Also, prisoners in the United States are often incarcerated for a lot longer than in other countries. This emphasis on punishment rather than rehabilitation leads not only to increased costs associated with incarcerating more people for longer periods of time, but it also comes with a number of hidden and less-obvious costs. One is that prisoners are often released with no better skills to cope in society and are offered little support after release, increasing the chances of re-offending. This results in reduced public safety, higher rates of recidivism, increased unemployment, and numerous financial and emotional costs to the families of those imprisoned.

In 2015, the Ella Baker Center for Human Rights published a report investigating the criminal justice system's long-term effects on inmates, families, and society. The report found that the economic, social, and health-related burdens communities bear from incarceration result in "increased poverty, destabilized neighborhoods, and generations of trauma." The costs of even a minor offense can add up in thousands of dollars of debt, mental health issues, and the specter of a permanent record. The burden of judicial punishment, the report finds, is carried not only by offenders but also their families. For instance, families lose a source of income, must find a way to pay off legal fees, and must pay to stay in contact with their incarcerated loved one. And since no family or individual is an island, the economic setbacks can spread to the entire community. These costs pile up measurably at every stage of the system:

> While imprisoned, inmates' basic needs must be paid for by family, at absurd costs. Under these financial pressures, one in five families faces eviction during a loved one's incarceration because of housing unaffordability, and almost two in three struggle to afford other necessities. Economic strains continue after incarceration because of the stigma attached to a criminal record. 76 percent of former inmates found it "very difficult or nearly impossible" to get a job after prison, and less than half worked fulltime five years after release. Unpaid debts incurred during adult incarceration compound the effects of employment constraints, and 12 percent of former inmates are put back into prison for missing conviction-related debt payments.[15]

Ironically, government aid that could lift men and women back onto their feet during re-entry is denied even to minor offenders. In most states, past drug offenders

---

a diverse population on a number of dimensions but an incarceration rate of 114 per 100,000, which is low compared to the United States.

[15] Campaign for Youth Justice, "The Hidden Costs of Incarceration in the Adult System," September 29, 2015: www.campaignforyouthjustice.org/news/blog/item/the-hidden-costs-of-incarceration-in-the-adult-system.

are ineligible for federal welfare programs, and local housing authorities can deny public housing to individuals with a record. In the Ella Baker Center for Human Rights survey, they found that one in ten family members polled lost their public housing after a loved one with a record returned home. Unpaid criminal justice debts can also result in the denial of student loans, disability benefits, and Social Security.

Reports like this powerfully underscore the hidden costs of incarceration. When we lock somebody up, we destroy not just his or her economic and social opportunity, but in fact harm entire families and communities. Hence, we should not do so lightly. On the model I propose, we should only incapacitate individuals when they pose a serious threat to society and even then we should do so for the shortest period of time necessary and with a goal of rehabilitation and reintegration. While Smilansky objects that my model would be too costly for society, I contend that it is our *current* system of punishment that is actually too costly. When examined holistically, the public health–quarantine model is a far more cost-effective and humane alternative. Consider, for instance, how the public health approach could address homelessness and, as a result, reduce both the financial and human costs of incarceration and poor health.

Homelessness is a public health issue (see Donovan and Shinseki 2013). This is true in two directions: Poor health is a major cause of homelessness *and* homelessness creates new health problems and exacerbates existing one. As the National Health Care for the Homeless Council (NHCHC) explains:

> An injury or illness can start out as a health condition, but quickly lead to an employment problem due to missing too much time from work; exhausting sick leave; and/or not being able to maintain a regular schedule or perform work functions. This is especially true for physically demanding jobs such as construction, manufacturing, and other labor-intensive industries. Losing employment often means getting disconnected from employer-sponsored health insurance. The lack of both income and health insurance in the face of injury or illness then becomes a downward spiral; without funds to pay for health care (treatment, medications, surgery, etc.), one cannot heal to work again. Of the 1 million personal bankruptcies in 2007, 62% were caused by medical debt. In these situations, any savings accumulated are quickly exhausted, and relying on friends and family for assistance to help maintain rent/mortgage payments, food, medical care, and other basic needs can be short-lived. (2011)

In the other direction, living on the street or crowded homeless shelters is personally stressful and made worse by being exposed to communicable disease, violence, malnutrition, and harmful weather exposure (Singer 2003; O'Connell 2004; Wrezel 2009).

> Hence, common conditions such as high blood pressure, diabetes, and asthma become worse because there is no safe place to store medications or syringes

properly. Maintaining a healthy diet is difficult in soup kitchens and shelters as the meals are usually high in salt, sugars, and starch (making for cheap, filling meals but lacking nutritional content). Behavioral health issues such as depression or alcoholism often develop or are made worse in such difficult situations, especially if there is no solution in sight. Injuries that result from violence or accidents do not heal properly because bathing, keeping bandages clean, and getting proper rest and recuperation isn't possible on the street or in shelters. Minor issues such as cuts or common colds easily develop into large problems such as infections or pneumonia. (2011)

It is not surprising that those experiencing homelessness are three to four times more likely to die prematurely than their housed counterparts, and experience an average life expectancy as low as forty-one years (Song et al. 2007; Morrison 2009).

Homelessness and incarceration are also mutual risk factors for each other (Metraux and Culhane 2006; Greenberg and Rosenheck 2008). Researches estimate that 25–50 percent of the homeless population has a history of incarceration (Metraux and Culhane 2006; Tejani et al. 2013). Additionally, a greater percentage of inmates have been previously homeless when compared to adults in the general population, illustrating that homelessness often precipitates incarceration (see Greenberg and Rosenheck 2008; Tsai, Mares, and Rosenheck 2012; Tsai et al. 2013). Greenberg and Rosenheck (2008), for example, found that homelessness was 7.5 to 11.3 times more prevalent among jail inmates than the general population. As the National Health Care for the Homeless Council writes:

> Existing homelessness is daunting regardless of one's criminal record. However, individuals with past incarceration face even greater barriers to existing homelessness due to stigmatization, policies barring them from most federal housing assistance programs, and challenges finding employment due to their criminal records (Tejani et al. 2013). To meet basic necessities amidst these barriers, previously incarcerated individuals sometimes engage in criminal activities to get by, perpetuating the cycle of homelessness, re-arrest, and incarceration. (2013)

If we want to break this revolving door of risk between incarceration and homelessness, we need to shift to a *preventive* approach that is data driven, research informed, and prioritizes more immediate access to permanent housing. One such model is Housing First, an emerging, evidence-based best practice for assisting people experiencing chronic homelessness to obtain and maintain permanent housing – quickly, safely, and without prerequisites. As Donovan and Shinseki write:

> [T]he Housing First model also assists with access to health care, employment, and other supportive services that promote long-term housing stability, reduce recidivism, and improve quality of life. Investments in effective, evidence-based programs utilizing the Housing First model, such as rapid rehousing, Supportive Services for

Veteran Families (SSVF), and the Housing and Urban Development Veterans Affairs Supportive Housing (HUD-VASH) programs, along with unprecedented partnerships between federal and local partners, have yielded substantial reductions in veteran and chronic homelessness. (2013)

Since the Housing First model was first introduced, and despite an affordable housing crisis, an economic recession, and elevated poverty, the number of chronically homeless individuals has continued to decline (see Donovan and Shinseki 2013). These gains are evidence that the model is working.

Providing the homeless with housing not only improves health outcomes and reduces the chances of incarceration and recidivism, it is also more humane *and* saves money. One recent report estimates that giving housing to the homeless is three times cheaper than leaving them on the streets. The Central Florida Commission on Homelessness (CFCH) conducted a study in 2014 and found that the region spends $31,000 a year per homeless person on "the salaries of law-enforcement officers to arrest and transport homeless individual – largely for nonviolent offenses such as trespassing, public intoxication or sleeping in parks as well as the cost of jail stays, emergency-room visits and hospitalization for medical and psychiatric issues" (2014). By contrast, getting each homeless person a house and a caseworker to supervise their needs would cost only about $10,000 per person in Orange, Seminole, and Osceola counties, the counties included in the study. Additional studies around the country have also found a community cost savings associated with placement of chronically homeless individuals in housing compared to the cost of the same population while living on the streets and in the shelters. The CFCH report (2014) estimates that nationally the annual cost savings ranged from 79 percent in Los Angeles (Economic Roundtable 2009), 72 percent in Jacksonville (Nazworth 2014), 55 percent in Tulsa (Stromberg et al. 2007), 53 percent in Seattle (2009), and 49 percent in Louisville (Barber et al. 2008). These studies, comparing the cost of public services used by chronically homeless individuals to the costs of providing housing plus services for the same population, show that developing affordable Permanent Supportive Housing options reduces homelessness and saves millions of taxpayer dollars over time, improving the quality of life for everyone (see Gulcur et al. 2003; CFCH Report 2014; Tsemberis 2014). This is just one example of how a public health approach can save money while producing better outcomes.

Let me end with one final reply. If we consider Smilansky's punishment objection in conjunction with his other views, especially his *illusionism*, a troubling moral concern emerges. Smilansky seems to hold that while individuals are not truly morally responsible in the basic desert sense, we should nevertheless maintain a system of retributive punishment despite its lack of justification. Smilansky (2000) has famously argued that our commonplace beliefs in libertarian free will and desert-entailing ultimate moral responsibility are illusions, but he also maintains that if people were to accept this truth there would be wide-reaching negative intrapersonal and interpersonal consequences. According to Smilansky, "Most people not only believe in actual possibilities and the ability to transcend circumstances, but have distinct and strong beliefs that libertarian free will is a condition for moral responsibility, which is in turn a condition for just reward and punishment" (2000: 26–27). It would be devastating, he warns, if we were to destroy such beliefs: "[T]he difficulties caused by the absence of ultimate-level grounding are likely to be great, generating acute psychological discomfort for many people and threatening morality – if, that is, we do not have illusion at our disposal" (2000: 166). To avoid any deleterious social and personal consequences, and to prevent the unraveling of our moral fabric, Smilansky recommends *free will illusionism*. According to illusionism, people should be allowed their positive illusion of libertarian free will and with it ultimate moral responsibility; we should not take these away from people, and those of us who have already been disenchanted ought to simply keep the truth to ourselves (see Smilansky 2000).

While illusionism is something I reject, I think it is one thing to advocate for it when it comes to personal beliefs and an altogether different thing to hold that we should promote illusionism within our institutions of punishment and the criminal justice system. I contend that it is wholly unacceptable to punish someone on retributivists grounds if we lack epistemic justification for believing that they have the kind of control in action needed to ground basic desert moral responsibility. Richard Double (2002) famously criticized libertarians for their "hard-heartedness" on exactly these grounds. I would extend that criticism to illusionism as well, since I think it is hard-hearted to maintain a system of retributive punishment when you yourself believe it is founded on false beliefs.

My argument for the hard-heartedness of illusionism is that Smilansky is committed to the following five claims, which together are morally unsympathetic and hard-hearted: (1) Most people believe in libertarian free will and that it is necessary for moral responsibility; (2) libertarian free will is an illusion; (3) if people came to accept (2) it would be devastating; hence (4) we should promote the positive illusion of libertarian free will; yet (5) keeping the positive illusion of libertarian free will alive requires keeping the notion of just deserts alive and with it institutional retributive punishment. Since Smilansky accepts (2) and acknowledges that libertarian free will is an illusion and hence cannot provide the justification needed to ground backward-looking blame and retributive punishment, I conclude that it would be hard-hearted for him to continue endorsing institutional retributive punishment.

Now, Smilansky could appeal to his other main doctrine, *dualism*, and argue that while our commonplace beliefs in libertarian free will and desert-entailing ultimate moral responsibility are illusions, certain compatibilist insights are also true. As Smilansky describes his dualism:

I agree with hard determinists that the absence of libertarian free will is a grave matter, which ought radically to change our understanding of ourselves, of morality, and of justice. But I also agree with the compatibilists that it makes sense to speak about ideas such as moral responsibility and desert, even without libertarian free will (and without recourse to a reductionist transformation of these notions along consequentialist lines). In a nutshell, ... "forms of life" based on the compatibilist distinctions about control are possible and morally required, but are also superficial and deeply problematic in ethical and personal terms. (2000: 5)

Unfortunately, I do not think this helps. Smilansky's dualism is simply too weak to *justify* institutional retributive punishment. Smilansky admits in the quote that while his dualism allows him to adopt compatibilist ways of speaking about moral responsibility and desert, compatibilism nevertheless remains "superficial and deeply problematic in ethical and personal terms." Regardless, then, of which insights Smilansky wishes to retain from compatibilism, a view that admits hard-determinism (or hard-incompatibilism) contains important insights and truths, and that these insights "ought radically to change our understanding of ourselves, of morality, and of justice," is left in a seriously weakened position and without the justificatory power needed to defend our retributive practices. Smilansky's dualism falls far short of the high epistemic standard needed to justify harming another individual on the grounds of basic desert. My criticism, then, is that it is hard-hearted for Smilansky to continue to support institutional retributive punishment given his illusionism and dualism – since neither provides the epistemic justification needed.

9.2 DETERRENCE

I would now like to address some more general issues related to deterrence. Recently, Derk Pereboom, my inspiration and partner in developing the public health–quarantine model, has departed slightly from the core of the model in response to criticisms from general deterrence theorists (see Pereboom 2017, 2019, 2020). In this section, I will explain why I do not follow Pereboom in that departure and instead prefer to keep the model free of any justificatory appeals to general deterrence. Largely in response to considerations raised by Victor Tadros (2011, 2016, 2017), who has argued that concerns about manipulative use can sometimes be overridden,[16] Pereboom has conceded that perhaps a greater level of general deterrence might be desired than what is permitted by the right of self-defense. In particular, he has argued that with regard to "monetary fines and short prison

[16] Tadros (2011) has argued that while there are a wide range of cases where it is intuitively objectionable to use someone manipulatively, there are also exceptional cases where the prohibition on manipulative use can be overweighed. Tadros rejects basic desert but nevertheless aims to justify certain forms of punishment that are more severe than those that are justified on the grounds of self-defense. To justify these additional measures, he develops a theory that claims that the manipulative use objection can be answered by invoking duties that wrongdoers owe to victims (see Tadros 2011, 2016, 2017). For objections to Tadros's theory see Nelkin (2019) and Pereboom (2017, 2020).

9.2 Deterrence

terms" (2019: 104) it might sometimes be justified to "use unfree wrongdoers in ways that involve such penalties to subserve general deterrence" (2020: 7).

Before explaining why I do not share this aspect of Pereboom's view, we need to take a step back and recall the distinction between *special deterrence* and *general deterrence*. General deterrence is the deterrence achieved from the threat of legal punishment on the *public at large*. Special deterrence, on the other hand, is aimed at previous offenders in order to reduce the likelihood of *their* re-offending. Pereboom argues that it is significantly easier to ground a limited form of special deterrence in the right to harm in self-defense and defense of others than is general deterrence. This is because the use of preventive detention (or incapacitation) qualifies as a case of threat-elimination (or eliminative harming) and not as manipulative use (Pereboom 2020: 4). Pereboom argues that the use of preventive detention is justified "as special deterrence on the ground of the right to self-defense" (Pereboom 2019: 103), as long as it is in accordance with the principle of least infringement and the minimum harm required to protect ourselves and others. In this way, Pereboom justifies special deterrence, understood not as a form of punishment but as the right to use preventive detention and eliminative harming, by appealing to the right of self-defense and defense of others.

But what about general deterrence? Even if incapacitation and eliminative harming can be justified as special deterrence on the ground of the right to self-defense, does not general deterrence violate the prohibition on manipulative use? Here, Pereboom provides two separate answers – the first that I accept, and think is sufficient, and the second that I reject. Pereboom first correctly notes that a significant level of general deterrence will result as a natural side effect of a system based on incapacitation. He calls this "free general deterrence" (2019, 2020):

> [N]ote that preventive detention, justified as special deterrence on the ground of the right to self-defense, stands to have a significant general deterrent effect. For it's plausibly required that the state not conceal the fact that it detains violent criminals on such a ground, but to make this information publicly available. We have the right to know what the state does to its members, and why, when they are dangerous to others. But such a policy would serve to yield, as a side effect, general deterrence. Such preventive detention would not only have a deterrence effect on the actual unjust aggressors who are detained but also on others who are tempted to commit crimes. This general deterrent effect comes for free, so to speak, since it is a side effect of the state's satisfying a publicity requirement on special deterrence. I call general deterrent effects justified as special deterrence on the basis of the self-defense right *free general deterrence*. (2019: 103)

Free general deterrence follows from the state's requirement to be transparent about its practices regarding the incapacitation of the seriously dangerous. Importantly, though, it comes with "a significant limitation on how much harm can legitimately be inflicted – only the minimum harm required to protect against an aggressor can be justified" (Pereboom 2019: 103). Since it does not extend beyond the minimum harm required to eliminate a threat on the right of self-defense, it does not violate the prohibition on manipulative use.

While I agree with Pereboom that incapacitation justified on the right of self-defense will naturally produce free general deterrence, I contend that this is *all* we should seek to justify. I therefore disagree with Pereboom that we should seek to go beyond free general deterrence and justify "more exacting general-deterrence-subserving penalties" (2019: 103). But before explaining why I disagree, we should first get clear on Pereboom's position. In a series of recent papers, Pereboom (2017, 2019, 2020) has proposed a way to justify a "limited degree" of general deterrence that surpasses free general deterrence. As he describes it:

> First, I've argued that it's plausibly the right to life, liberty, and physical security of the person that have a key role in making the use objection to general deterrence intuitive. Those rights are grounded in the more general right to a life in which one's capacity for flourishing is not compromised in the long term. There is a heavily weighted presumption again punishment as use where that involves intentional killing, long-term confinement, and infliction of sever physical or psychological harm. But if the proposed penalties are significantly less extreme, such as monetary fines and short prison terms, it would be permissible to use unfree wrongdoers in ways that involve such penalties to subserve general deterrence. (2019: 104)

According to Pereboom, there "may well be many circumstances in which effective general deterrence would require modest penalties of these sorts" – that is, penalties that "involve the imposition of more harm than can be justified on special deterrence grounds; that is, as free general deterrence" (2019: 104–105). In such circumstances, Pereboom argues that it would be permissible to increase the severity of the penalty since "monetary fines ... don't hinder the prospects for a life lived at [a] reasonable level of flourishing" (2019: 105). On Pereboom's proposal, general deterrence not justified on special deterrence grounds is "plausibly justified if it substantially increases general deterrence value, and/or it substantially lowers the cost of deterrence, provided that the more exacting measure doesn't hinder the prospects for a life lived at a reasonable level of flourishing" (2019: 105).

While I acknowledge that Pereboom's proposal is an attractive option for those free will skeptics who wish to justify more exacting measures that go beyond what is permitted by the public health–quarantine model, I resist it for three main reasons. First, I think supplementing the public health–quarantine model with a limited form of general deterrence unnecessarily muddies the waters and sacrifices some of the distinct advantages the model has over rival accounts, including consequentialist deterrence theories. In my estimate, two of the most distinct features of the public health–quarantine model are that (a) it offers a nonpunitive approach to addressing criminal behavior, not just a nonretributive one, and (b) it does not run afoul of the prohibition on manipulative use. But in one fell swoop, Pereboom's proposal sacrifices both of these features. By allowing in limited general deterrence as a justification for monetary fines and short prison terms, Pereboom has introduced a punitive component. As a result, his newly expanded theory must squarely face the *problem of punishment* presented by David Boonin (2008), Michael Zimmerman (2011), and others, who argue that *all* forms of punishment are unjustified. My version of the public health–quarantine model remains pure and free of any punitive components and is therefore compatible with the complete rejection of all justifications of punishment. I see this as an advantage, since the problem of punishment is a serious one and Boonin and Zimmerman may well be right that punishment is never justified. Pereboom's proposal also requires defending exceptions to the prohibition on manipulative use, even if only in limited cases, since general deterrence involves manipulative use. The version of the public health–quarantine model I defend, on the other hand, is consistent with an absolute prohibition of manipulative use, which, again, I see as an advantage.

Second, I think Pereboom underestimates the extent to which monetary fines and short prison sentences can, and often do, "hinder the prospects for a life lived at a reasonable level of flourishing." Short prison sentences, for instance, can be extremely disruptive to the lives of those incarcerated as well as their family and friends. We know, for example, that prison sentences have a long-term and negative impact on a person's employment prospects (Ministry of Justice 2013) and even a short prison term will cause an interruption in employment and increase the possibility of homelessness, bankruptcy, suicide, loss of healthcare, stigmatization, and divorce (Prison Reform Trust 2018). Short prison terms also separate parents from children, which disrupts the development of positive relationships, and this can have long-term negative effects on children. Furthermore, short prison sentences are far less effective than community sentences at reducing re-offending (Ministry of Justice 2013, 2018; Prison Reform Trust 2018). In England and Wales, for instance: "[t]he reoffending rates for prison sentences of a year or less were at 65.5% in the last three months of 2016 – the last period for which statistics have been published – rising to 67% for sentences of six months or less" (Kay 2019). This is much higher than the 38 percent of people who re-offend after being served a court order, such as a community order or suspended sentence. As Christopher Kay correctly notes: "Reoffending rates from short sentences have been a cause for concern for years" (2019). Meanwhile, "research has shown the effectiveness of community-based sentences in reducing reoffending – at least compared to short prison sentences – and that community supervision is less likely to have a negative impact on employment and family time" (Kay 2019).

For these reasons, many experts now agree that we overuse short prison terms for nonviolent and persistent crime (Ministry of Justice 2018). David Gauke, the former Secretary of State for Justice in the United Kingdom, has, for instance, argued that short prison terms should only be used as a "last resort."[17] And Rory Stewart, the new Justice Minister, has called for a drastic reduction in the use of short prison sentences, writing:

> In March 2018 we launched our campaign that showed short sentences are short-sighted. We asked the government to review this issue and to consider introducing a new presumption against the use of short custodial sentences of less than six months. We also asked the government to strengthen community sentences so that they command public confidence and are better able to deal effectively with some of the underlying causes of persistent petty offending, including drug or alcohol addiction and mental ill-health. (Stewart 2019)

I endorse these recommendations and suggest that community sentences should be chosen over the use of short prison terms wherever possible. In fact, evidence from Scotland reveals that the presumption against prison terms of less than three months, introduced in 2010, has reduced use of short jail terms by 40 percent and in 2016/2017 crime in Scotland had fallen more than 18 percent with a 26-percent fall in property crime (Scottish Government 2019). Results like this have led the Revolving Door Agency to write:

> The evidence is clear. Short prison sentences are short-sighted because they disrupt family ties, housing, employment and treatment programmes, but they do not provide any meaningful rehabilitation. These sentences contribute to prison "churn" and volatility. They are ineffective at tackling petty crime. We can do better and should adopt a smarter approach.[18]

While Pereboom may now be willing to consider the use of short prison terms to subserve general deterrence, I do not think he realizes the extent to which such penalties are ineffective and how they can, and often do, hinder the prospects for a life lived at a reasonable level of flourishing.

But what about financial fines? Perhaps Pereboom could argue that fines, unlike short prison terms, can increase general deterrence value without significantly hindering human well-being and flourishing. It is not clear, however, that this is true. To see why, consider the following example. A few years back I received a series of speeding tickets in a short period of time. It is not something I am proud of but I was doing a lot of long-distance travel at the time and I occasionally had a heavy foot on those long stretches of empty highway. Each ticket cost me roughly $350 dollars. The last violation put me in jeopardy of losing my license. The officer who pulled me over told me that I could contact the District Attorney and pay him $200 dollars and he would petition the court to get the violation reduced or dismissed. So that is what I did. And as promised my speeding violation was reduced to a parking

---

[17] See, for instance: www.thetimes.co.uk/article/under-a-year-in-jail-must-be-last-resort-says-justice-chief-david-gauke-msdbmfmbb.
[18] See, for instance: www.revolving-doors.org.uk/file/2347/download?token=e9wtT41q.

violation, saving me around a $150, points on my license, an increase in my insurance premiums, and potentially the loss of my driver's license. Now, let us imagine the same scenario but with one small difference. In this case, let us assume the driver is someone who lives on the poverty line and who makes their living as a driver. Since they are unable to pay the District Attorney the $250, they obviously cannot pay the full $350-dollar fine. They plead not-guilty and are assigned a court date but they are unable to make it since they cannot afford to take the day off from work. After not paying the fine, the court notifies them that their driver's license has been suspended. Unfortunately, the individual's only source of income comes from being a driver. They could stop driving but that will significantly hinder their "prospects for a life lived at a reasonable level of flourishing." So they continue driving with a suspended license. They're careful not to speed again but one day they are pulled over for a front headlight that has gone out. As a result, they are assessed even heavier fines. But being unable to pay the fines, both old and new, the court eventually issues a warrant for their arrest. From here we can easily imagine a series of cascading events that leads to the arrest of the individual – which, turn, leads to additional lawyer fees, bail costs, and possibly even jail time.

Here we have a conceivable, and dare I say common, set of circumstances where an apparently "small" financial fine ends up hindering an individual's "prospects for a life lived at a reasonable level of flourishing" (2019: 105), since the cumulative costs incurred from the fine go well beyond the initial dollar amount and ultimately result in a significant diminishment in human well-being. As a result of the speeding tickets, this individual may lose their livelihood, their ability to pay their bills, and perhaps even their freedom. Small fines can have significant effects. As a recent article in *The Nation* explains: "Debtor's prisons have been illegal in America since 1833. But that doesn't matter. We know about some ways people can languish in jail for being poor – if they cannot pay bail, for example, or if they rack up fines related to imprisonment that must be paid upon release."[19] *Salon* magazine further explains:

> A symbol of Victorian England's inequitable nature made infamous by Charles Dickens, debtors' prisons were banned in the United States in 1833. The Supreme Court has affirmed the unconstitutionality of jailing those too poor to pay debts on three different occasions in the last century, finding that the 14th Amendment prohibits incarceration for non-payment of exorbitant court-imposed fines or fees without an assessment of a person's ability to pay and alternatives for those who cannot. "Punishing a person for his poverty" is illegal, the Court said. Yet in recent years the modern-day equivalent of debtors' prisons have returned, as cities have grown to rely on punishing regime of fines and fees imposed on their own residents as a major stream of revenue.[20]

[19] "Prosecutors and judges have brought back debtors' prisons," *The Nation*, February 22, 2018. Available at: www.thenation.com/article/archive/prosecutors-and-judges-have-brought-back-debtors-prisons/.
[20] "A return of debtors' prisons: Jeff Sessions' war on the poor," *Salon*, December 29, 2017. Available at: www.salon.com/2017/12/29/a-return-to-debtors-prisons-jeff-sessions-war-on-the-poor/.

The article goes on to write:

> Routine traffic tickets or even overdue student loan payments can set off a cycle of debt that also includes the suspension of a driver's license or professional license and, in some cases, jail time. A suspended driver's license makes it nearly impossible to get to work. When a person can't pay, courts add more fines on top of the original. If those fees aren't paid, a jail sentence is imposed. (Ibid.)

While I am certain Pereboom would oppose debtors' prison and the inequalities they reinforce, I do not think he fully appreciates the extent to which fines and short prison sentences can, and often do, interfere with an individual's ability to achieve a reasonable level of flourishing. Financial fines compound other existing social injustices and can have disproportionate effects on the poor. I therefore maintain that we should resist Pereboom's proposal to supplement the public health–quarantine model with "more exacting general-deterrence-subserving penalties" (2019: 103), since these can exacerbate existing social inequalities and negatively impact human well-being.

My last reason for rejecting Pereboom's proposal is that I think the public health–quarantine model already has the resources needed to deal with low-level, nonviolent crime, and as a result there is no reason to sacrifice the principle of least infringement in an effort to accommodate limited general deterrence. We should be content with free general deterrence and only what is permitted by the right of self-defense and defense of others. It is not at all clear that seeking "more exacting" penalties is either wise or justified. The right of self-defense and defense of others can, for instance, justify various liberty-limiting measures short of incapacitation and these can be used to address a host of nonviolent offenses like speeding, drunk driving, and shoplifting. And this can be done without appeal to free will or basic desert. Driving privileges, for example, can be limited, restricted, or removed for various reasons, including poor eyesight, age, and medical conditions that make driving unsafe. Such restrictions are widely seen as justified on the grounds that they are necessary for the protection of society and the prevention of harm to others. They are not forms of punishment nor are they implemented for the purposes of deterrence. By analogy, the public health–quarantine model can justify liberty-limiting policies for repeat speeders and drunk drivers since their actions manifest a blatant disregard for the safety of those around them. These restrictions can be implemented incrementally or all at once based on the nature of the violation and whether the individual is likely to re-offend.

With regard to speeding violations, my preference would be to avoid financial penalties for the reasons just indicated and because matters of justice need to be kept separate from the means of revenue creation. Unfortunately, our current system views fines and financial penalties as a major source of revenue, and when this occurs assessing fines becomes less about justice and more about generating more and more revenue for the state. Fines are assessed not so much to protect public safety but to create revenue. It is a bad idea, I contend, to conflate issues of justice with financial and budgetary considerations. This should never have occurred in the first place. One possible alternative is to have a point system where different traffic violations result in a specific number of points being added to your driver's license. When you reach a certain threshold, you trigger a liberty-limiting restriction. These could be staged so that one first loses their liberty to drive recreationally but maintains their right to drive to and from work. At the next stage they lose their liberty to drive altogether and are required to take certain steps to regain that privilege. Of course, this is only a suggestion. Others proposal may work just as well or better. My point is simply that the public health–quarantine model has the resources to justify liberty-limiting policies for nonviolent, low-level offenses based simply on the right of self-defense and defense of others. And, as Pereboom correctly notes, making these policies publicly known will produce, as a natural side effect, a free general deterrence effect. I see no reason why we should seek more than this and supplement the model with additional more exacting penalties that subserve general deterrence. Extending the model in that way only opens it up to the kinds of objections discussed in Chapter 5 and relinquishes its standing as a nonpunitive theory. I am not willing to do that.

9.3 EVIDENTIARY STANDARDS

Let me now turn to a recent objection by John Lemos (2016, 2018). Lemos has argued that my view too easily gives way to the use of legal practices that would increase the number of innocent people being detained for crimes they did not commit. He argues that my view exhibits insufficient respect for the rights and dignity of innocent human beings. In particular, he notes that the primary motivation for quarantine is to protect the rest of society from harm. As such, there is kinship between this approach and deterrence theories of punishment. He appeals to a recent criticism of deterrence theories that has been developed by Saul Smilansky (1990), who argues that if the sole motivation for punishment is deterrence, then we would be justified in lowering the evidentiary standards used for criminal conviction. In doing so, we could take more criminals off of the streets and this would increase the overall well-being of society while at the same time some more innocent people would end up being convicted and punished due to the use of a lower evidentiary standard. While Lemos acknowledges that the public health–quarantine model is not a deterrence theory of punishment, he argues it is still motivated to protect society from harm. Thus, it can be argued that to better protect society from dangerous criminals the evidentiary standards for criminal conviction should be lowered so as to capture more criminals offering more protection for society.

In response to this objection, I would first like to reiterate a point made several times now. The public health–quarantine model is not a strict consequentialist theory. Rather, it justifies incapacitation on the ground of the right to self-defense and defense of others. That right does not extend to people who are non-threats. The aim of protection is justified by a right with clear bounds and not by a consequentialist theory on which the bounds are unclear. It would therefore be wrong, according to the model, to incapacitate someone who is innocent since they are not a serious threat to society. Once this is fully appreciated, much of the force of Lemos's objection is lost. In fact, the public health–quarantine model provides a distinct advantage over consequentialist deterrence theories since it has more restrictions placed on it with regard to using people merely as a means. Concerns over the "use" objection, for example, count more heavily against punishment policy justified simply on consequentialist grounds than they do against incapacitation based on the quarantine analogy.

But to more fully address Lemos's concern, I would like to further explain what role I conceive evidentiary standards playing on my model. To begin, let me quote Stephen J. Morse on the criteria that the criminal law currently employs:

> Let us consider what the criteria are for allegedly deserved punishment. First, the agent must perform a prohibited intentional act (or omission) in a state of reasonably integrated consciousness (the so-called "act" requirement, usually confusingly termed the "voluntary act"). Second, virtually all serious crimes require that the person had a further mental state, the *mens rea*, regarding the prohibited harm. Lawyers term these definitional criteria for prima facie culpability the "elements" of the crime. They are the criteria that the prosecution must prove beyond a reasonable doubt. For example, one definition of murder is the intentional killing of another human being. To be prima facie guilty of murder, the person must have intentionally performed some act that kills, such as shooting or knifing, and it must have been his intent to kill when he shot or knifed. If the agent does not act at all because his bodily movement is not intentional – for example, a reflex or spasmodic movement – then there is no violation of the prohibition against intentional killing. There is also no violation in cases in which the further mental state required by the definition is lacking. For example, if the defendant's intentional killing action kills only because the defendant was careless, then the defendant may be guilty of some homicide crime, but not of intentional homicide. (2017: 337)

With regard to the "act" requirement, I maintain that on the public health–quarantine model high evidentiary standards remain centrally important since they are necessary to protect innocent people who are non-threats from being incapacitated. Consider a murder case where there is a dispute over who shot the victim. My model would require just as high an evidentiary standard as the current system in establishing the facts of the case since to justify incapacitating someone it would need to be established beyond a reasonable doubt that they performed the act in question. The finding of facts remains extremely important since we need to know that we have correctly identified the person who is *causally* responsible for the shooting. This is the only way we can then precede to judge whether the individual is a serious threat to society and if the right to self-defense and defense of others justifies incapacitation.

When it comes to judging *mens rea*, on the other hand, I have a rather radical proposal. I maintain that after the facts have established that we have identified the causally responsible agent, the defendant's state of mind at the time of the crime becomes more important in determining the continued threat of the agent and which sanctions, treatments, and forms of rehabilitation are most suitable, rather than establishing which punishment is deserved. Once we give up the notion of just deserts, the importance of establishing *mens rea* and distinguishing between, say, murder and negligent homicide becomes one of forward-looking relevance. Imagine, for instance, that a child is left in a hot car and dies as a result. After we have established who is causally responsible for the child's death (say, for example, the mother of the child), the agent's state of mind becomes relevant in determining their continued threat moving forward. If, say, the mother intentionally caused the death of her child and planned in advance to stage things so as to look like an accident, that is one thing. If, however, it was the result of a tragic oversight on the part of the mother resulting from lack of sleep due to a cold or flu that is another. The first would likely result in incapacitation and rehabilitation until we could be assured that the mother is no longer a serious threat to society, whereas the latter may not.[21] Furthermore, on my model we would adjust our methods of rehabilitation dependent on whether the mother is normally reasons-responsive or not (see s. IV). Hence, determining an agent's state of mind at the time of a crime as well as their overall ability to be reasons-responsive remains extremely important on my account.

There is no reason for thinking, then, that adopting the public health–quarantine model would result in the lowering of the evidentiary standards used for criminal conviction. Both the "act" requirement and the *mens rea* requirement would remain important in determining whether the right of self-defense and defense of others can, in any given situation, justify incapacitation. If, for instance, an individual was incapacitated for an action or omission that they were *not* causally responsible for, my account would consider this a grievous injustice. To prevent such grievous injustices from occurring, high evidentiary standards should be maintained. Second, my account would continue to require prosecutors to prove *mens rea* since agents who commit first-degree murder or other intentional crimes will often be judged more dangerous than those who inadvertently break the law by accident or out of negligence.[22]

Now, Lemos may be willing to acknowledge these points but nevertheless insists that I am overlooking a bigger problem – that is, that the way quarantine is actually

---

[21] Of course, much more would need to be known about these cases. In the latter case, for example, if it turned out that the mother's negligence was consistent with a persistent character flaw, we may conclude that mandatory counseling and/or monitoring would be justified.

[22] I should note that this will not always be the case. Someone who kills a family while driving under the influence, especially if this is after several previous drunk-driving infractions, may be a greater threat to society even though they lack *mens rea* than someone who intentionally steals a candy bar.

implemented in public health lends itself to an analogous justification for incapacitating innocent people. In developing his objection, he writes:

> It is not true that in matters of public health we detain only those known to carry infectious disease. Rather, we also detain those who are likely carriers of the disease, as sometimes people may have a disease and spread it before showing symptoms. The United States Center for Disease Control (CDC) actually distinguishes between isolation and quarantine. *Isolation* separates sick people with a contagious disease from people who are not sick. *Quarantine* separates and restricts the movement of people who were exposed to a contagious disease to see if they become sick. Those quarantined are not necessarily carriers of the disease; they are people who've been exposed and are likely carriers. Furthermore, federal and state laws allow for legally enforced quarantine of people who were merely exposed and who may not actually be carriers ... Thus, the quarantine model does not actually discourage quarantine of the innocent, rather it allows for it as long as those detained are likely to be criminals. Notice that this plays right into the hands of the kind of argument strategy employed by Smilansky. He argues that if no one is responsible in the basic desert sense and if the only point of punishment is to prevent crime then we might as well lower the evidentiary standards to get more criminals off the street. This is akin to saying that we should detain not only those who are known to be violent criminals but also those that are likely to be violent criminals. (2016; see also 2018)

Lemos is, of course, correct that the CDC and other public health organizations distinguish between isolation and quarantine. As it is applied in public health, quarantine does have a broader application. But in terms of the public health–quarantine model I have defended, there are several good reasons for restricting the use of incapacitation to only those who have, beyond a reasonable doubt, committed a serious crime.

To reiterate some of the points made earlier: (1) the right to liberty should carry significant weight and not be overridden lightly – I have attempted to highlight this point by arguing that the principle of autonomy needs to be weighed heavily against the public health justification for quarantine; (2) since the kinds of testing required to determine whether someone is a carrier of a communicable disease are often not unacceptably invasive, yet the types of screening necessary for determining whether someone has violent criminal tendencies might well be invasive in respects that raise serious moral issues, the former are much easier to justify than the latter; and (3) since the available psychiatric methods for discerning whether an agent is likely to be a violent criminal are not especially reliable and are capable of producing false positives, we should adopt an attitude of *epistemic skepticism* when it comes to judging the dangerousness of someone who has not yet committed a crime. In addition to these three points, I would add that the cost of being quarantined for a short period of time to assess one's health pales in comparison to being incapacitated for a crime one did not commit. This places a much higher evidentiary burden, I contend, on justifying criminal incapacitation.

9.3 Evidentiary Standards

If I am held for a few hours, or even a few days, after getting off a plane because it is suspected that I was exposed to a contagious disease, this is surely an inconvenience. This inconvenience, however, is relatively minor and a price most of us are willing to pay to help protect public health and prevent communicable diseases from spreading. On the other hand, incapacitating an innocent person because it is suspected that they might be dangerous, or because lowering our evidentiary standards marginally improves overall safety, results in far more than inconvenience. For one thing, those who are quarantined are quickly released once it is determined that they are healthy. This would not be the case when an innocent person is wrongly convicted for a crime they did not commit. Secondly, the violation of liberty is much greater in criminal incapacitation since it is usually of a longer duration and often accompanied by social stigmatization. For these reasons, I reject Lemos's false equivalency and maintain that the burden of proof must be significantly higher in cases of criminal incapacitation. From the fact that the right to self-protection and the prevention of harm to others may be able to justify quarantining people who are only potential threats when it comes to public health, it does not follow that it would likewise justify incapacitating innocent people when it comes to criminal justice. There are significant and important moral differences between the two cases that need to be taken into consideration and that ultimately demand a higher bar be applied in the latter case. Lastly, in the context of a criminal trial, the *immediate threat* posed by the accused is relatively low when compared to a likely carrier of a communicable disease – and this is because the crime has already occurred, the circumstances that gave rise to the crime have past, and the defendant is in custody. In such a situation, time, diligence, and high evidentiary standards can and should be employed.

Let me conclude with one last reply. Lemos suggests that it would be "unjustified discrimination against criminals" (2016) if moral responsibility skeptics like Pereboom and me were to argue that we should not lower the evidentiary standards to protect the freedom of those who have not committed crimes. This is because

> [o]n the responsibility denier's view, no one is responsible for what he does. On this view, the person who commits crimes is no more deserving of punishment than the person who never commits crimes. As I've argued, we could reduce crime more effectively by using lower evidentiary standards for criminal conviction and this would, of course, lead to punishment of more people who have not committed crimes. However, if the responsibility denier is correct in saying that no one is responsible, then, given the purpose of quarantine style criminal detention, it is unjust to expect only those who have actually committed crimes to be detained. Why should the criminals be the only ones to carry the burden of criminal detention for the sake of crime prevention if they are no more deserving of the detention than innocent people? (2016)

The answer to this question, however, should be obvious to anyone who acknowledges that incapacitation serves purposes other than the punishment of the guilty.

On the model defended here, the justification for why dangerous criminals should be the only ones to carry the burden of criminal detention is not because they deserve it, not because it will serve as a general deterrent, but because only those who pose a serious threat to society can be incapacitated on the grounds of self-defense and defense of others.

9.4 INDEFINITE DETENTION

I would like to conclude by considering one final objection. Michael Corrado (2018, 2019a, 2019b) has argued that one advantage retributive punishment (and his own theory of *correction*) has over the public health–quarantine model is that the former protects "the right to be held by the state only for a limited period of time" (2018: 10), whereas the latter allows for the possibility of indefinite detention if an individual is determined to be a continued serious threat to society. According to Corrado, the methods of quarantine allow for detention and other restrictions of freedom, "but impose no limits upon those restrictions except those that further the protection of the community" (2018: 11). He goes on to argue that "quarantine means a complete and unlimited surrender of autonomy to the state" since the person subject to quarantine or incapacitation "has no protection against the power of the state" – that is, "[i]f he should remain dangerous after treatment he may be detained indefinitely" (2018: 12).

In response, I would argue, first, that while I do acknowledge that on my model mass murderers and serial rapists who cannot be rehabilitated and remain serious threats would be indefinitely detained, this will not amount to a "complete and unlimited surrender of autonomy to the state," nor would it result in more people serving out their lives in prison. Second, I argue that the putative advantage Corrado claims retributive punishment (and correction) has is more apparent than real. This is because the principle of proportionality is inherently vague and indeterminate, and as a result it is consistent with the fact that one of every seven people currently in prison in the United States is serving life or virtual life sentences even though the American criminal justice system has long been committed to limiting retributivism and determinant sentencing. Third, I maintain that the rare cases where the public health–quarantine model would favor continuing to hold a violent criminal who cannot be rehabilitated are ones its critics, and the current law, would largely agree on. Furthermore, the conditions of detention for such individuals would be very different on my model from those vile conditions of the US prison system. Lastly, I argue that there are policy solutions available, such as setting the maximum prison term at twenty years but allowing for incremental extensions if absolutely necessary for public safety, as Norway does, as well as placing the burden of proof on the state to evaluate and establish, at regular intervals, that the threat posed by an offender warrants continued incapacitation. Let us take each of these points in turn.

First, there is no reason to think the public health–quarantine model amounts to a "complete and unlimited surrender of autonomy to the state." As we have now repeatedly seen, the model places a number of important constraints on the treatment of individuals, including the principle of least infringement, the prohibition on manipulative use, the principle of normality, the principles of beneficence and nonmaleficence, and concern for the well-being of offenders. Even in conditions of incapacitation, my model requires that the state respect human dignity by preserving the rights of offenders to vote, to not be dehumanized, and to be afforded as much autonomy and liberty as possible consistent with the minimum restrictions needed to protect public safety. According to the principle of normality, for instance, the only right an offender should lose when they are incapacitated is their liberty; they retain all their other rights. These include the right to vote (even while in prison), to health care, to attend school, to phone family and friends, etc. On almost every one of these points, our current methods of punishment sacrifice the autonomy of offenders more completely to the state. By limiting his concerns to indefinite detention, Corrado obfuscates this point and completely overlooks the fact that retributive punishment sacrifices more of an offender's rights to the state than the public health–quarantine model.

Second, with regard to the number of people who will never end up being released, which seems to be Corrado's driving concern with regard to indefinite detention, a strong case can be made that the public health–quarantine model far and away has the advantage here. Currently, one in seven people in prison in the United States is serving life or "virtual life" sentences, that is, sentences with a term of years that exceed an individual's natural life expectancy. These sentences are determinant in length and, at least conceivably, within the realm of what is permitted by the principle of proportionality. Of course, a retributivist could argue that the number of people serving life and virtual life sentences is excessive. But as I have already argued, the principle of proportionality is vague, elastic, and indeterminate when it comes to judging gravity and proportionality, hence it is virtually impossible to determine precisely what the upper limit of punishment should be for a violent crime. Findings complied by the Justice Policy Institute (2011), for instance, have found that sentencing times vary widely for the same crime across the globe. And the fact that a prison term is of determinant length, or specifies an acceptable range, by no means guarantees offenders will ever be released. In fact, of those serving a life sentence in the United States, about a third are without the chance of parole. Of the remainder, political considerations have made it increasingly difficult to secure parole in many states. In addition, a large number of offenders are serving "virtual life" sentence. For example, a forty-year prison term imposed on a thirty-five-year-old offender essentially equates to life imprisonment. And it is not uncommon for punitive systems to hand out impossible sentences, that is, multiple life sentences, to make a point or because they believe them to be proportional to the wrong done. For example, Terry Nichols, one of the accomplices in the 1995 Oklahoma City bombing, was given 161 life sentences with no possibility for parole.

In contrast, in Norway the maximum sentence one can get for any crime is twenty-one years. The public health–quarantine model would similarly require incapacitation be kept to an absolute minimum and life without parole be eliminated as an option. While Norway does allow for detention to be extended by five years at a time if an offender is still considered dangerous after serving their full sentence, the Norwegian approach at least has the benefit of requiring continued reevaluation and assessment and allowing for the possibility of rehabilitation and release. And unlike the United States, where one out of every seven people in prison is serving a life or virtual life sentence, very few offenders in Norway are held indefinitely. In fact, almost 90 percent of prisoners serve less than a year, and most offenders receive only community serve or another alternative to incarceration. If the Norwegian system is any indication, then, the fear that the public health–quarantine model will result in large numbers of offenders being held indefinitely, is overblown and unfounded. In fact, I maintain that there are good reasons to think that implementing the public health–quarantine model will actually result in a drastic reduction in the number of people incapacitated and the number of people held indefinitely. This claim is supported by a number of different considerations.

A recent study by the Brennan Center for Justice found, for instance, that 39 percent of the US prison population (roughly 576,000 people) are behind bars with little public safety rationale (Austin et al. 2016). According to the report, up to 25 percent of prisoners (364,000 people), almost all nonviolent, lower-level offenders, would be better served by alternatives to incarceration such as treatment, community service, and probation. They estimate that another 14 percent (212,000 people) have already served long sentences and can be safely set free with little or no risk to public safety. If these numbers are correct, adopting the public health–quarantine model would result in more than a half million people being released from prison with little to no increased risk to public safety. Furthermore, research indicates that the risk of recidivism drops dramatically as prisoners get older, and there will come a time when an additional year of prison no longer yields a meaningful reduction in the risk of recidivism among older prisoners (Kim and Peterson 2014; United States Sentencing Commission 2017). For instance, research by leading criminologists Alfred Blumstein and Kiminori Nakamura demonstrates that an eighteen-year-old arrested for robbery is no more likely to be arrested for this crime by the age of twenty-six than anyone in the general population. Additional research by the United States Sentencing Commission has found that older offenders are "substantially less likely than younger offenders to recidivate following release" (2017: 3). More specifically, they found that over an eight-year follow-up period, 13.4 percent of offenders aged sixty-five or older at the time of release were rearrested compared to 67.6 percent of offenders younger than age twenty-one at the time of release. Furthermore, for federal offenders under age thirty at the time of release, more than one-fourth (26.6 percent) who recidivated had assault as their most common new charge. By comparison, for offenders sixty years old or older at the time of release, almost one quarter (23.7 percent) who recidivated had a public order offense as their most serious new charge (2017: 3). So, while a retributivist could maintain that a 65- or 75-year-old should continue to be incarcerated because they *deserve* it, the public health–quarantine model would need to consider the chances of recidivism and the kind of harm they pose to society. Since the majority of elderly prisoners pose no serious public safety concerns, the public health–quarantine model would recommend release, with perhaps additional assistance and supervision. Of course, there will be occasional cases where an individual will need to be incapacitated indefinitely, but these will be the exception, not the norm. Given these considerations, I maintain that adopting the public health–quarantine model would drastically *reduce*, not increase, the number of people serving out their lives in prison.

Third, I maintain that there are additional policy solutions available for the public health–quarantine model to adopt, and these can provide additional protections against potential abuse. The public health–quarantine model already maintains the principle of least infringement, which requires that we always seek alternatives to incapacitation wherever and whenever possible. But beyond this, I also recommend establishing an upper limit of around twenty years in prison as a maximum penalty for the most dangerous of violent criminals, as Norway does, but to also allow for exceptional and incremental extensions when, say, a serial rapist or mass murderer has not been rehabilitated and continues to pose a serious threat to public safety (see Mauer 2016). This upper limit allows for rehabilitated offenders to be released at any point prior to the end of their term, but it prohibits handing down sentences longer than twenty years as a judicial option. As Marc Mauer explains: "The rationale for such a policy shift is grounded in both humanitarian and public-safety concerns. Life sentences ruin families and tear apart communities; they deprive the person of the chance to turn his or her life around. Moreover, it has long been known that individuals 'age out' of crime, and that this occurs at a surprisingly young age" (2016). I would also recommend placing the burden of proof on the state to establish, at regular intervals, that the threat posed by an offender warrants continued incapacitation. If the state cannot satisfy that burden of proof with documentation – for example, evidence of aggression and violence in prison, credible threats to continue to do harm upon release, etc. – then the offender should be released. As Mauer suggests: "A review board comprised of psychologists and other professionals could make recommendations either to a judge or a parole board regarding whether continued confinement is necessary for public safety. And in such cases, they should propose appropriate treatment interventions designed to produce behavioral change leading to eventual release" (2016). While some might think this unrealistic, it is important to recognize that "sentences of more than 20 years are quite rare in many democratic nations" (Mauer 2016). Additionally, most offenders age out of crime at a certain point, while others mature, educate, and rehabilitate themselves – especially when they are given support, counseling, and opportunity. I maintain that it is inhumane and contrary to the demands of public safety to continue to incapacitate such individuals. On the other hand, retributivists who favor life or virtual life sentences as deserved proportional punishment end up leaving offenders completely and utterly powerless and without the chance to alter a sentence that offers them no possibility of release or rehabilitation. This amounts to a "complete and unlimited surrender of autonomy to the state," but in the exact opposite direction then Corrado would have us believe. I therefore contend that the public health–quarantine model actually provides more protections and opportunities for offenders to be released than retributivism.

Finally, the kinds of cases where the public health–quarantine model would allow for indefinite incapacitation or quarantine are intuitively cases most would agree as justified. Consider the case of Mary Mallon, also known as "Typhoid Mary," who was the first person in the United States identified as an asymptomatic carrier of the pathogen associated with typhoid fever.[23] She was an Irish cook who from 1900 to 1907 worked in the New York City area for several families. She exhibited no outward signs of sickness but everywhere she worked people ended up getting sick and dying. She is believed to have infected more than fifty people. She was twice quarantined by public health authorities and eventually died after a total of nearly three decades in quarantine. The first time she was quarantined, Mary Mallon admitted she did not understand the purpose of hand washing because she did not believe that she posed a risk. She also refused to cease working as a cook since she did not believe she really carried the disease. Eventually, though, she was released when she finally agreed to stop working as a cook and take reasonable steps to prevent transmitting typhoid to others. However, upon her release she changed her name, disappeared, and returned to her former occupation as a cook despite having been explicitly instructed not to. As a result, she caused another major outbreak and was eventually located and quarantined for a second time. She was given the option of having her gallbladder removed, where the typhoid bacteria were believed to reside, but she refused. Given her continued threat to public safety, and her unwillingness to take reasonable precautions, she was held in quarantine for the rest of her life.

While this is a rare case, since very few people are ever indefinitely quarantined in this way, the right of self-defense and defense of others provides authorities with the grounds to indefinitely quarantine Mary Mallon in this way (assuming no other options are available). And I think most people, including Corrado, would agree such measures are justified. The same, I contend, is true with regard to seriously dangerous violent criminals who are unable to be rehabilitated. Furthermore, I maintain that existing punitive approaches, like retributivism, essentially allow for the same possibility in practice. Take, for example, the case of Andres Breivik

[23] Detail taken from the *Wikipedia* entry on Mary Mallon: https://en.wikipedia.org/wiki/Mary_Mallon.

who killed seventy-seven people in 2011, the worst case of mass murder in Norway's history. He was given the maximum sentence allowed in Norway, which is only twenty-one years. At the end of that period, the state can add five more years of civil incapacitation on the grounds of public safety if he has not been rehabilitated. It is conceivable that this can be done over and over again resulting in indefinite detention. Corrado might object that this violates "the right to be held by the state only for a limited period of time." But what, exactly, would a retributivist (or Corrado) do differently? In a case like Breivik's, there are generally two sentencing options available to retributivists (assuming he is judged competent): They could sentence him to life without the chance of parole right from the start, putting an end to his chances of ever being released, or they could give him a sentence that allows for the chance of parole after serving a minimum number of years in prison. The first option, I have argued, is inhumane since it precludes from the outset the possibility of rehabilitation, violates the principle of least infringement, discourages the state from working to rehabilitate offenders, and prevents the reassessment of individual cases as circumstances change. The second option, however, provides essentially the same possibility of indefinite detention since the parole board will have the power and discretion to determine whether Breivik should be released or not. If the board decides he should not be released, he will continue to be imprisoned. The key difference, however, between the retributivist approach and my own is that my approach (a) eliminates the option of life without parole, allowing for the possibility of rehabilitation and release, (b) establishes a maximum upper limit that will apply in all non-exceptional cases, (c) places the burden of proof on the state to justify any and all exceptions to that maximum, and (d) requires that no one is incapacitated longer than is absolutely necessary to protect public safety. My model also requires that offenders be housed in humane conditions and treated in accordance with the principle of normality, respect for persons, and concern for human well-being.

For the forgoing reasons, I maintain that the public health–quarantine model does not amount to a "complete and unlimited surrender of autonomy to the state," nor will it result in more people serving out their lives in prison. While it does allow for the possibility of indefinite detention in exceptional cases, which is not necessarily a bad thing as the Typhoid Mary example reveals, most criminal offenders will "age out" of crime or pose less of a threat over time, allowing for less restrictive measures to be taken to protect public safety. The public health–quarantine model also places several restrictions and humanitarian consideration on the treatment of offenders, which gives it a distinct advantage over current retributive policies.

9.5 CONCLUSION

The dual aims of this book have been to argue against retributivism and to develop and defend a viable nonretributive alternative for addressing criminal behavior that is both ethically defensible and practically workable. In the first half of the book,

I presented and defended six distinct arguments against retributivism – the Skeptical Argument, the Epistemic Argument, the Misalignment Argument, the Poor Epistemic Position Argument, the Indeterminacy in Judgment Argument, and the Limited Effectiveness Argument. In the second half of the book, I then developed and defended the public health–quarantine model, arguing that it is more humane than retributivism and preferable to other nonretributive alternatives. I argued that the model not only provides justification for the incapacitation of dangerous criminals, but it also provides a broader and more comprehensive approach to addressing criminal behavior since it prioritizes prevention and social justice. Criminal justice and social justice, I argued, are intimately connected, and the public health–quarantine model provides a number of preventative strategies for identifying and take action on the shared social determinates of health and criminal behavior. The model rejects the reactive approach of retributivism, with its myopic focus on punishment and individual responsibility, and instead adopts a preventive approach aimed at addressing the underlying causes of crime. Along the way, I also discussed the relationship between free will and criminal law, made the case for free will skepticism, argued against consequentialist, educational, and mixed theories of punishment, and defended a capabilities approach to social justice consistent with free will skepticism. I ended by addressing a series of objections to the public health–quarantine model and argued that the model can successfully deal with each.

References

1 FREE WILL, LEGAL PUNISHMENT, AND RETRIBUTIVISM

Alexander, L. 2013. You got what you deserved. *Criminal Law and Philosophy* 7: 309–319.
Alexander, L., K. Kessler Ferzan, and S. Morse. 2009. *Crime and Culpability: A Theory of Criminal Law*. New York: Cambridge University Press.
Alicke, M. D. 1994. Evidential and extra-evidential evaluations of social conduct. *Journal of Social Behavior and Personality* 9: 591–615.
Alicke, M. D. 2000. Culpable control and the psychology of blame. *Psychological Bulletin* 126: 556–574.
Alicke, M. D. 2008. Blaming badly. *Journal of Cognition and Culture* 8: 179–186.
Alicke, M. D., J. Buckingham, E. Zell, and T. Davis. 2008. Culpable control and counterfactual reasoning in the psychology of blame. *Personality and Social Psychology Bulletin* 34: 1371–1381.
Alicke, M. D., D. Rose, and D. Bloom. 2008. Causation, norm violation, and culpable control. *Journal of Philosophy* 108: 670–696.
Amnesty International. 2012. *Death Sentences and Executions 2011*. London: Amnesty International Publications.
Ashworth, A. 2015. *Sentencing and Criminal Justice*, 6th edition. Cambridge: Cambridge University Press.
Aspinwall, L. G., T. R. Brown, and J. Tabery. 2012. The double-edged sword: Does biomechanism increase or decrease judges' sentencing of psychopaths? *Science* 337: 846–849.
Austin, J., L-B. Eisen, J. Cullen, and J. Frank. 2016. *How Many Americans Are Unnecessarily Incarcerated?* Brennan Center for Justice at New York University School of Law. Available at: www.brennancenter.org/sites/default/files/publications/Unnecessarily_Incarcerated_0.pdf.
Berg, K. S. and N. Vidmar. 1975. Authoritarianism and recall of evidence about criminal behavior. *Journal of Research in Personality* 9: 147–157.
Berman, M. 2008. Punishment and justification. *Ethics* 18: 258–290.
Berman, M. 2011. Two kinds of retributivism. In *Philosophical Foundations of Criminal Law*, eds. R. A. Duff and S. Green, pp. 433–457. New York: Oxford University Press.
Berman, M. 2013. Rehabilitating retributivism. *Law and Philosophy* 32: 83–108.
Berman, M. 2016. Modest retributivism. In *Legal, Moral, and Metaphysical Truths: The Philosophy of Michael S. Moore*, eds. K. Kessler Ferzan and S. J. Morse, pp. 35–48. New York: Oxford University Press.
Blumstein, A., M. Tonry, and A. Van Ness. 2005. Cross-national measure of punitiveness. *Crime and Justice* 33(1): 347–376.

Boonin, D. 2008. *The Problem of Punishment*. New York: Cambridge University Press.
Carey, J. M. and D. L. Paulhus. 2013. Worldview implications of believing in free will and/or determinism: Politics, morality, and punitiveness. *Journal of Personality* 81(2): 130–141.
Carlsmith, K. M. and J. M. Darley. 2008. Psychological aspects of retributive justice. *Advances in Experimental Social Psychology* 40: 193–236.
Caruso, G. D. 2012. *Free Will and Consciousness: A Determinist Account of the Illusion of Free Will*. Lanham, MD: Lexington Books.
Caruso, G. D. (ed.). 2013. *Exploring the Illusion of Free Will and Moral Responsibility*. Lanham, MD: Lexington Books. Introduction, pp. 1–16.
Caruso, G. D. 2016. Free will skepticism and criminal behavior: A public health–quarantine model. *Southwest Philosophical Review* 32(1): 25–48.
Caruso, G. D. 2017. *Public Health and Safety: The Social Determinants of Health and Criminal Behavior*. London: ResearchLinks Books.
Caruso, G. D. 2018. Skepticism about moral responsibility. *Stanford Encyclopedia of Philosophy*. Available at: https://plato.stanford.edu/entries/skepticism-moral-responsibility/.
Caruso, G. D. 2019. Free will skepticism and its implications: An argument for optimism. In *Free Will Skepticism in Law and Society: Challenging Retributive Justice*, eds. Elizabeth Shaw, Derk Pereboom, and Gregg D. Caruso, pp. 43–72. New York: Cambridge University Press.
Caruso, G. D. 2020. Justice without retribution: An epistemic argument against retributive criminal punishment. *Neuroethics* 13(1): 13–28.
Caruso, G. D. and S. G. Morris. 2017. Compatibilism and retributive desert moral responsibility: On what is of central philosophical and practical importance. *Erkenntnis* 82: 837–855.
Caruso, G. D. and D. Pereboom. 2020. A non-punitive alternative to retributive punishment. In *Routledge Handbook of the Philosophy and Science of Punishment*, eds. F. Focquaert, B. Waller, and E. Shaw, pp. 355–365. New York: Routledge.
Chiesa, L. E. 2011. Punishment without free will. *Utah Law Review* 1403: 1–87.
Clark, C., R. Baumeister, and P. H. Ditto. 2017. Making punishment palatable: Belief in free will alleviates punitive distress. *Consciousness and Cognition* 51: 193–211.
Clark, C. J., J. B. Luguri, P. H. Ditto, J. Knobe, A. F. Shariff, and R. F. Baumeister. 2014. Free to punish: A motivated account of free will. *Journal of Personal and Social Psychology* 106: 501–513.
Clark, C. J., A. Shniderman, J. B. Luguri, R. F. Baumeister, and P. H. Ditto. (2018). Are morally good actions ever free? *Consciousness and Cognition* 63: 161–182.
Clark, C. J., B. M. Winegard, and R. F. Baumeister. 2019. Forget the folk: Moral responsibility preservation motives and other conditions for compatibilism. *Frontiers in Psychology*, February 7: https://doi.org/10.3389/fpsyg.2019.00215.
Clark, C. J., B. M. Winegard, and A. F. Shariff. 2019. Motivated free will beliefs: The theory, new (preregistered) studies, and three meta-analyses. www.researchgate.net/publication/333384764_Motivated_free_will_belief_The_theory_new_preregistered_studies_and_thre e_meta-analyses
Corrado, M. L. 2013. Why do we resist hard incompatibilism? Some thoughts on freedom and determinism. In *The Future of Punishment*, ed. T. Nadelhoffer, pp. 79–106. New York: Oxford University Press.
Corrado, M. L. 2017. Punishment and the Burden of Proof. UNC legal studies research paper. Available at SSRN: https://ssrn.com/abstract=2997654 or https://doi.org/10.2139/ssrn.2997654.

Cowen, N. 2010. *Comparison of Crime in OECD Countries*. London: CIVITAS Institute for the Study of Civil Society.

Cushman, F. A. 2008. Crime and punishment: Differential reliance on causal and intentional information for different classes of moral judgment. *Cognition* 108: 353–380.

Cotton, M. 2000. Back with a vengeance: The resilience of retribution as an articulated purpose of criminal punishment. *American Criminal Law Review* 37: 1313, 1326–1327, 1357.

Darwall, S. 1992. Internalism and agency. *Philosophical Perspectives* 6: 155–174.

Dennett, D. C. 1984. *Elbow Room*. Cambridge, MA: MIT Press.

Dennett, D. C. 2011. My brain made me do it. *Max Weber Lecture Series*. Available at: https://cadmus.eui.eu/bitstream/handle/1814/16895/MWP_LS_2011_01.pdf?sequence=1.

Dennett, D. C. and G. D. Caruso. 2021. *Just Deserts: Debating Free Will*. New York: Polity Books.

Dingwall, G. 2008. Deserting desert? Locating the present role of retributivism in the sentencing of adult offenders. *The Howard Journal of Crime and Justice* 47(4): 400–410.

Double, R. 2002. The moral harness of libertarianism. *Phil* 5: 226–234.

Duff, R. A. 2001. *Punishment, Communication, and Community*. New York: Cambridge University Press.

Dunlea, J. P. and L. Heiphetz. 2020. Children's and adult's understanding of punishment and the criminal justice system. *Journal of Experimental Social Psychology* 87: 103913. doi.org/10.1016/j.jesp.2019.103913.

Eftan, M. G. 1974. The effect of physical appearance on the judgment of guilt, interpersonal attraction, and severity of recommended punishment in a simulated jury task. *Journal of Research and Personality* 8: 45–54.

Encartele Inc. 2018. Scandinavian jails: Why is their recidivism rate so much better? Available at: www.encartele.net/2018/04/what-can-us-correctional-facilities-learn-from-scandinavian-jails/.

Enns, P. 2006. *Incarceration Nation: How the United States Became the Most Punitive Democracy in the World*. New York: Cambridge University Press.

Epley, N. and D. Dunning. 2000. Feeling "holier than thou": Are self-serving assessments produced by errors in self or social prediction? *Journal of Personality and Social Psychology* 79: 861–875.

Everett, J. A. C., C. J. Clark, J. B. Luguri, B. D. Earp, P. H. Ditto, and A. F. Shariff. 2018. *Political Differences in Free Will Beliefs are Driven by Differences in Moralization*. Available at: https://ssrn.com/abstract=3011597.

Farrell, G. and K. Clarke. 2004. What does the world spend on criminal justice? The European Institute for Crime Prevention and Control, affiliated with the United Nations. NEUNI Paper No. 20. www.heuni.fi/material/attachments/heuni/papers/6KtlkZMtL/HEUNI_papers_20.pdf

Feldman, G., K. F. E. Wong, and R. F. Baumeister. 2016. Bad is freer than good: Positive-negative asymmetry in attributions of free will. *Consciousness and Cognition* 42: 26–40.

Fischborn, M. 2018. How should free will skeptics pursue legal change? *Neuroethics* 11: 47–54.

Focquaert, F. 2019. Free will skepticism and punishment: A preliminary ethical analysis. In *Free Will Skepticism in Law and Society: Challenging Retributive Justice*, eds. E. Shaw, D. Pereboom, and G. D. Caruso, pp. 207–236. New York: Cambridge University Press.

Focquaert, F., G. D. Caruso, E. Shaw, and D. Pereboom. 2020. Justice without retribution: Interdisciplinary perspectives, stakeholder views and practical implications. *Neuroethics* 13 (1): 1–3.

Focquaert, F., A. Glenn, and A. Raine. 2013. Free will, responsibility and punishment of criminals. In *The Future of Punishment*, ed. T. Nadelhoffer, pp. 247–274. New York: Oxford University Press.

Focquaert, F., A. Glenn, and A. Raine. 2018. Free will skepticism, freedom, and criminal behavior. In *Neuroexistentialism: Meaning, Morals, and Purpose in the Age of Neuroscience*, eds. G. D. Caruso and O. Flanagan, pp. 235–250. New York: Oxford University Press.

Green, T. A. 2014. *Freedom and Criminal Responsibility in American Legal Thought*. New York: Cambridge University Press.

Hardcastle, V. 2018. The neuroscience of criminality and our sense of justice: An analysis of recent appellate decisions in criminal cases. In *Neuroexistentialism: Meaning, Morals, and Purpose in the Age of Neuroscience*, eds. G. D. Caruso and O. Flanagan, pp. 311–332. New York: Oxford University Press.

Hart, H. L. A. 2008. *Punishment and Responsibility: Essays in the Philosophy of Law*, 2nd edition. Oxford: Oxford University Press.

Husak, D. 2000. Holistic retributivism. *California Law Review* 88: 991–1000.

Jeppsson, S. M. I. 2020. Retributivism, justification and credence: The epistemic argument revisited. *Neuroethics*. doi.org/10.1007/s12152-020-09436-6.

Jones, M. 2003. Overcoming the myth of free will in criminal law: The true impact of the genetic revolution. *Duke Law Journal* 52: 1032–1053.

Kane, R. 1996. *The Significance of Free Will*. New York: Oxford University Press.

Kant, I. 1790. *The Metaphysics of Morals*. Hastie: Translation by Mary J. Gregor. New York: Cambridge University Press. 1991.

Kelly, E. 2018. *The Limits of Blame: Rethinking Punishment and Responsibility*. Cambridge, MA: Harvard University Press.

Kershnar, S. 2000. A defense of retributivism. *International Journal of Applied Philosophy* 14 (1): 97–117.

Kershnar, S. 2001. *Desert, Retribution, and Torture*. Lanham, MD: University Press of America.

Kristoffersen, R. 2010. Relapse study in the correctional services of the Nordic countries. *EuroVista* 2(3): 168–176.

LaBouff, J. and A. Dustin. 2020. Why we need to change our assumptions about incarceration. *Bangor Daily*. January 21. Available at: https://bangordailynews.com/2020/01/21/opinion/contributors/why-we-need-to-change-our-assumptions-about-incarceration/.

Langado, D. A. and S. Channon. 2008. Judgments of cause and blame: The effects of intentionality and foreseeability. *Cognition* 108: 754–770.

Lerner, M. J. and D. T. Miller. 1978. Just world research and attribution process: Looking back and ahead. *Psychological Bulletin* 85: 1030–1051.

Lerner, M. J., D. T. Miller, and J. G. Holmes. 1976. Deserving and the emergence of forms of justice. In *Advances in Experimental Social Psychology*, eds. L. Berkowitz and E. Walster, pp. 133–162.

Levy, N. 2011. *Hard Luck: How Luck Undermines Free Will and Moral Responsibility*. New York: Oxford University Press.

Levy, N. 2012. Skepticism and sanctions: The benefit of rejecting moral responsibility. *Law and Philosophy* 31(5): 477–493.

Levy, N. 2015. Less blame, less crime? The practical implications of moral responsibility skepticism. *Journal of Practical Ethics* 3(2): 1–17.

Levy, N. 2016. Does the desire to punish have any place in modern justice? *Aeon*. February 19, 2016. Accessed online: https://aeon.co/opinions/does-the-desire-to-punish-have-any-place-in-modern-justice.

Lewis, C. S. 1953. The humanitarian theory of punishment. *Twentieth Century: An Australian Quarterly Review* 3. Reprinted in C.S. Lewis, *God in the Dock*, edited by Walter Hooper, pp. 224–230. Grand Rapids: Willian B. Eerdmans.

Mabbott, J. D. 1939. Punishment. *Mind* 48: 150–167.
Marcus, M. H. 2007. Responding to the model penal code sentencing revisions: Tips for early adopters and power users. *Southern California Interdisciplinary Law Journal* 17: 67–138.
Monterosso, J., E. B. Royzman, and B. Schwartz. 2005. Explaining away responsibility: Effects of scientific explanation on perceived culpability. *Ethics and Behavior* 15: 139–158.
Moore, M. S. 1987. The moral worth of retribution. In *Punishment and Rehabilitation*, ed. J. G. Murphy, 3rd edition, pp. 94–130. New York: Wadsworth Publishing Company.
Moore, M. S. 1993. *Act and Crime: The Philosophy of Action and Its Implications for Criminal Law*. New York: Oxford University Press.
Moore, M. S. 1997. *Placing Blame*. New York: Oxford University Press.
Morris, S. 2018. The implications of rejecting free will: An empirical analysis. *Philosophical Psychology* 31(2): 299–321.
Morse, S. J. 2010. Lost in the translation? An essay on law and neuroscience. In *Law and Neuroscience: Current Legal Issues*, ed. M. Freeman, pp. 530–562. New York: Oxford University Press.
Morse, S. J. 2013. Common criminal law compatibilism. In *Neuroscience and Legal Responsibility*, ed. N. A. Vincent, pp. 27–52. New York: Oxford University Press.
Morse, S. J. 2018. The neuroscientific non-challenge to meaning, morals, and purpose. In *Neuroexistentialism: Meaning, Morals, and Purpose in the Age of Neuroscience*, eds. G. D. Caruso and O. Flanagan, pp. 333–358. New York: Oxford University Press.
Nadelhoffer, T. 2006. Bad acts, blameworthy agents, and intentional actions: Some problems for juror impartiality. *Philosophical Explorations* 9(2): 203–219.
Nadelhoffer, T. 2011. The threat of shrinking agency and free will disillusionism. In *Conscious Will and Responsibility: A Tribute to Benjamin Libet*, eds. W. Sinnott-Armstrong and L. Nadel, pp. 173–188. New York: Oxford University Press.
Nadelhoffer, T. (ed.). 2013. *The Future of Punishment*. New York: Oxford University Press.
Nadelhoffer, T. and D. G. Tocchetto. 2013. The potential dark side of believing in free will (and related concepts): Some preliminary findings. In *Exploring the Illusion of Free Will and Moral Responsibility*, ed. G. D. Caruso, pp. 121–140. Lanham, MD: Lexington Books.
Neimeth, C. and R. H. Sosis. 1973. A simulated jury: Characteristics of the defendant and the jurors. *Journal of Social Psychology* 90: 221–229.
Packer, H. L. 1968. *The Limits of the Criminal Sanction*. Stanford: Stanford University Press.
Pereboom, D. 1995. Determinism al dente. *Nous* 29: 21–45.
Pereboom, D. 2001. *Living without Free Will*. New York: Cambridge University Press.
Pereboom, D. 2013. Free will skepticism and criminal punishment. In *The Future of Punishment*, ed. T. Nadelhoffer, pp. 47–78. New York: Oxford University Press.
Pereboom, D. 2014. *Free Will, Agency, and Meaning in Life*. Oxford: Oxford University Press.
Pereboom, D. 2020. Incapacitation, reintegration, and limited general deterrence. *Neuroethics* 31(1): 87–97.
Pereboom, D. and G. D. Caruso. 2018. Hard-incompatibilism existentialism: Neuroscience, punishment, and meaning in life. In *Neuroexistentialism: Meaning, Morals, and Purpose in the Age of Neuroscience*, eds. G. D. Caruso and O. Flanagan, pp. 193–222. New York: Oxford University Press.
Pizarro, D., E. Ulhmann, and P. Salovey. 2003. Asymmetry in judgments of moral blame and praise: The role of perceived metadesires. *Psychological Science* 14: 267–272. https://journals.sagepub.com/doi/10.1111/1467-9280.03433
Powers, M. and R. Faden. 2006. *Social Justice: The Moral Foundations of Public Health and Health Policy*. New York: Oxford University Press.
Quinton, A. 1954. On punishment. *Analysis* 14: 1933–1942.

Roberts, J. V. and O. Gazal-Ayal. 2013. Statutory sentencing reform in Israel: Exploring the sentencing law of 2012. *Israel Law Review* 46(3): 455–479.
Robinson, P. H. 2008. *Distributive Principles of Criminal Law: Who Should Be Punished How Much*. New York: Oxford University Press.
Robinson, P. H. and M. T. Cahill. 2006. *Law Without Justice: Why Criminal Law Doesn't Give People What They Deserve*. New York: Cambridge University Press.
Rosen, G. 2004. Skepticism about moral responsibility. *Philosophical Perspectives* 18: 295–313.
Schlenker, B. R. 1980. *Impression Management: The Self-Concept, Social Identity, and Interpersonal Relations*. Brooks/Cole.
Sentencing Guidelines Council (England and Wales). 2004. *Overarching Principles: Seriousness*. London: Sentencing Guidelines Council. Available at: www.sentencingcouncil.org.uk/wp-content/uploads/Seriousness-guideline.pdf.
The Sentencing Project. 2017. *Still Life: America's Increasing Use of life and Long-Term Sentences*. Washington, DC. Report available at: www.sentencingproject.org/wp-content/uploads/2017/05/Still-Life.pdf.
Shariff, A. F., J. D. Greene, J. C. Karremans, J. Luguri, C. J. Clark, J. W. Schooler, R. F. Baumesiter, and K. D. Vohs. 2014. Free will and punishment: A mechanistic view of human nature reduces retribution. *Psychological Science* published online June 10: 1–8.
Shaw, E. 2014. *Free Will, Punishment, and Criminal Responsibility*. Dissertation Thesis. Edinburgh University. Available at: https://era.ed.ac.uk/bitstream/handle/1842/9590/Shaw2014.pdf?sequence=2&isAllowed=y.
Shaw, E. 2019a. Justice without more responsibility? *Journal of Information Ethics* 28(1): 95–114.
Shaw, E. 2019b. The implications of free will skepticism for establishing criminal liability. In *Free Will Skepticism in Law and Society: Challenging Retributive Justice*, eds. E. Shaw, D. Pereboom, and G. D. Caruso, pp. 192–206. Cambridge, UK: Cambridge University Press.
Shaw, E., D. Pereboom, and G. D. Caruso. 2019. *Free Will Skepticism in Law and Society: Challenging Retributive Justice*. New York: Cambridge University Press.
Sie, M. 2013. Free will, an illusion? An answer from a pragmatic sentimentalist point of view. In *Exploring the Illusion of Free Will and Moral Responsibility*, ed. G. D. Caruso, pp. 273–290. Lanham, MD: Lexington Books.
Smilansky, S. 2011. Free will, fundamental dualism, and the centrality of illusion. In *The Oxford Handbook of Free Will*, ed. R. Kane, pp. 425–441. New York: Oxford University Press.
Snyder, C. R., R. L. Higgins, and R. J. Stuckey. 1983. *Excuses: Masquerades in Search of Grace*. Eliot Werner Publications. www.amazon.com/Excuses-Masquerades-Search-Foundations-Psychology/dp/0975273817
Sommers, T. 2007. The objective attitude. *The Philosophical Quarterly* 57(28): 321–342.
Sosis, R. H. 1974. Internal-external control and the perception of responsibility of another for an accident. *Journal of Personality and Social Psychology* 30: 393–399.
Strawson, G. 1986. *Freedom and Belief*. Oxford: Oxford University Press.
Strawson, G. 1994. The impossibility of moral responsibility. *Philosophical Studies* 75 (1–2): 5–24.
Strawson, P. F. 1962. Freedom and resentment. *Proceedings of the British Academy* 36. Reprinted in *Free Will*, ed. G. Watson, pp. 59–80. New York: Oxford University Press.
Tadros, V. 2011. *The Ends of Harm: The Moral Foundations of Criminal Law*. New York: Oxford University Press.
Tasioulas, J. 2006. Punishment and repentance. *Philosophy* 81: 279–322.

Tonry, M. 2004. US sentencing systems fragmenting. In *Panel Reform in Overcrowded Times*, ed. M. Tonry, pp. 21–28. New York: Oxford.
Vargas, M. 2013a. *Building Better Beings: A Theory of Moral Responsibility*. New York: Oxford University Press.
Vargas, M. 2013b. If free will doesn't exist, neither does water. In *Exploring the Illusion of Free Will and Moral Responsibility*, ed. G. D. Caruso, pp. 177–202. Lanham, MD: Lexington Books.
Vilhauer, B. 2009a. Free will and reasonable doubt. *American Philosophical Quarterly* 46(2): 131–140.
Vilhaeur, B. 2009b. Free will skepticism and personhood as a desert base. *Canadian Journal of Philosophy* 39(3): 489–511.
Vilhaeur, B. 2012. Taking free will skepticism seriously. *The Philosophical Quarterly* 62(249): 833–852.
Vilhaeur, B. 2013a. The people problem. In *Exploring the Illusion of Free Will and Moral Responsibility*, ed. G. D. Caruso, pp. 141–160. Lexington Books.
Vilhauer, B. 2013b. Persons, punishment, and free will skepticism. *Philosophical Studies* 162 (2): 143–163.
Vilhauer, B. 2015. Free will and the asymmetrical justification of holding morally responsible. *The Philosophical Quarterly* 65(261): 772–789.
Von Hirsch, A. 1976. *Doing Justice: The Choice of Punishment*. Boston: Northeastern University Press.
Von Hirsch, A. 1981. Desert and previous convictions in sentencing. *Minnesota Law Review* 56 (841): 591–634.
Von Hirsch, A. 2007. The "desert" model for sentencing: Its influence, prospects, and alternatives. *Social Research* 74(2): 413–434.
Von Hirsch, A. 2017. *Deserved Criminal Sentences: An Overview*. Portland, Oregon: Hart Publishing.
Walen, A. 2014. Retributive justice. *Stanford Encyclopedia of Philosophy*. Available at: https://plato.stanford.edu/entries/justice-retributive/.
Waller, B. 1989. Denying responsibility: The difference it makes. *Analysis* 49(1): 44–47.
Waller, B. 1990. *Freedom Without Responsibility*. New York: Temple University Press.
Waller, B. 2006. Denying responsibility without making excuses. *American Philosophical Quarterly* 43(1): 81–90.
Waller, B. 2007. Sincere apology without moral responsibility. *Social Theory and Practice* 33 (3): 441–465.
Waller, B. 2011. *Against Moral Responsibility*. Cambridge, MA: MIT Press.
Waller, B. 2015. *The Stubborn System of Moral Responsibility*. Cambridge, MA: MIT Press.
Wittgenstein, L. 1961. *Notebooks 1914–1916*. Edited and translated by G. H. von Wright and G. E. M. Anscombe. New York: Harper/Blackwell.
Zaibert, L. 2018. *Rethinking Punishment*. New York: Cambridge University Press.
Zimmerman, M. J. 2011. *The Immorality of Punishment*. Peterborough: Broadview Press.

2 FREE WILL SKEPTICISM: HARD INCOMPATIBILISM AND HARD LUCK

Allen, R. F. 1995. Free will and indeterminism: Robert Kane's libertarianism. *Journal of Philosophical Research* 30: 341–355.
Almeida, M. and M. Berstein. 2003. Lucky libertarianism. *Philosophical Studies* 113(2): 93–119.
Arguilar, J. H. and A. A. Buckareff. (ed.). 2010. *Causing Human Actions: New Perspectives on the Causal Theory of Action*. MA: Bradford.

Audi, R. 1974. Moral responsibility, freedom and compulsion. *American Philosophical Quarterly* 19: 25–39.
Audi, R. 1991. Responsible action and virtuous character. *Ethics* 101: 304–321.
Audi, R. 1993. *Action, Intention and Reason*. Ithaca: Cornell University Press.
Austin, J. L. 1961.Ifs and cans. *Philosophical Papers*, pp. 205–232. New York: Oxford University Press.
Austin, J. L. 1966. Three ways of spilling ink. *Philosophical Review* 75(4): 427–440.
Avants, B., et al. 2012. Early childhood environment predicts frontal and temporal cortical thickness in the young adult brain. Presented at The Society for Neuroscience 2012 Meeting. http://archive.ismrm.org/2012/3159.html
Ayer, A. J. 1954. Freedom and necessity. In his *Philosophical Essays*, pp. 3–20. New York: St. Martin's Press.
Balaguer, M. 2009. *Free Will as an Open Scientific Problem*. Boston: MIT Press.
Berofsky, B. 1966. *Free Will and Determinism*. New York: Harper & Row.
Berofsky, B. 1971. *Determinism*. Princeton: Princeton University Press.
Berofsky, B. 1987. *Freedom from Necessity: The Metaphysical Basis of Responsibility*. London: Routledge & Kegan Paul.
Berofsky, B. 2002. If, cans, and free will: The issues. In *Oxford Handbook of Free Will*, ed. R. Kane, pp. 181–201. New York: Oxford University Press.
Bishop, J. 1989. *Natural Agency*. New York: Cambridge University Press.
Bohm, D. 1952. A suggested interpretation of the quantum theory in terms of "hidden" variables, I and II. *Physics Review* 85(2): 166–193.
Bohm, D. 1980. *Wholeness and the Implicate Order*. New York: Routledge.
Bok, H. 1998. *Freedom and Responsibility*. Princeton, NJ: Princeton University Press.
Broad, C. D. 1952. Determinism, indeterminism and libertarianism. In *Ethics and the History of Philosophy*, ed. C. D. Broad, pp. 195–217. London: Routledge & Kegan Paul.
Buckareff, A. A. *Can Agent-Causation Be Rendered Intelligible? An Essay on the Etiology of Free Action*. Dissertation: Texas A&M University.
Buckareff, A. A. 2001. Can the agency theory be salvaged? *Philosophia Christi* 3(1): 217–224.
Buckareff, A. A. 2011. How does agent-causal power work? *Modern Schoolman* 88(1–2): 105–121.
Buckareff, A. A. 2012. An action theoretic problem for intralevel mental causation. *Philosophical Studies* 22(1): 89–105.
Buckareff, A. A. 2017. A critique of substance causation. *Philosophia* 45(3): 1019–1026.
Bunge, M. 1980. *The Mind-Body Problem: A Psychobiological Approach*. Oxford: Pergamon Press.
Campbell, C. A. 1951. Is "free will" a pseudo-problem? *Mind* 60: 446–465.
Campbell, C. A. 1957. *On Selfhood and Godhood*. London: George Allen and Unwin.
Campbell, C. A. 1967. *In Defense of Free Will*. London: Allen and Unwin.
Capes, J. A. 2013. Mitigating soft compatibilism. *Philosophy and Phenomenological Research* 87(3): 640–663.
Capes, J. A. 2021. Manipulation and direct arguments. In *A Companion to Free Will*, ed. J. Campbell. New York: Wiley-Blackwell.
Caruso, G. D. 2012. *Consciousness and Free Will: A Determinist Account of the Illusion of Free Will*. Lanham, MD: Lexington Books.
Caruso, G. D. 2015a. Kane is not able: A reply to Vicens' "Self-forming actions and conflicts of intention." *Southwestern Philosophical Review* 31(2): 21–26.
Caruso, G. D. 2015b. Free will eliminativism: Reference, error, and phenomenology. *Philosophical Studies* 172(10): 2823–2833.
Caruso, G. D. 2015b. If consciousness is necessary condition for moral responsibility, then people are less responsible than we think. *Journal of Consciousness Studies* 22(7-8): 49–60.

Caruso, G. D. 2018. Consciousness, free will, and moral responsibility. In *Routledge Handbook of Consciousness*, ed. R. J. Gennaro, pp. 79–91. London: Routledge.
Caruso, G. D. 2019a. A defense of the luck pincer: Why luck (still) undermines moral responsibility. *Journal of Information Ethics* 28(1): 51–72.
Caruso, G. D. 2019b. Free will skepticism and its implications: An argument for optimism. In *Free Will Skepticism in Law and Society: Challenging Retributive Justice*, eds. E. Shaw, D. Pereboom, and G. D. Caruso, pp. 43–72. New York: Cambridge University Press.
Caruso, G. D. 2020. Why free will is not real: A reply to Christian List. *The Philosopher* 108(1): 67–71.
Caruso, G. D. and D. Pereboom. 2021. *Moral Responsibility Skepticism*. New York: Cambridge University Press.
Chisholm, R. M. 1964. Human freedom and the self. The Lindley Lecture, Department of Philosophy, University of Kansas; reprinted in *Free Will*, ed. G. Watson, pp. 24–35. New York: Oxford University Press.
Chisholm, R. M. 1966. Freedom and action. In *Freedom and Determinism*, ed. K. Lehrer, pp. 11–44. New York. Random House.
Chisholm, R. M. 1971. Reflections of human agency. *Idealistic Studies* 1: 33–46.
Chisholm, R. M. 1976. *Person and Object: A Metaphysic Study*. La Salle: Open Court.
Clarke, R. 1993. Toward a credible agent-causal account of free will. *Nous* 27: 191–203.
Clarke, R. 1996. Agent causation and event causation in the production of free action. *Philosophical Topics* 24(2): 19–48.
Clarke, R. 1999. Free choice, effort, and wanting more. *Philosophical Explorations* 2: 20–41.
Clarke, R. 2000. Modest libertarianism. *Philosophical Perspectives* 14: 21–45.
Clarke, R. 2002. Libertarian views: Critical survey of noncausal and event-causal accounts of free agency. In *The Oxford Handbook of Free Will*, ed. R. Kane, pp. 356–385. New York: Oxford University Press.
Clarke, R. 2003. *Libertarian Accounts of Free Will*. New York: Oxford University Press.
Clarke, R. and J. Capes. 2017. Incompatibilist (nondeterministic) theories of free will. *Stanford Encyclopedia of Philosophy*. Available at: https://plato.stanford.edu/entries/incompatibilism-theories/#3.1.
Coffman, E. J. 2007. Thinking about luck. *Synthese* 158: 385–398.
Cyr, T. W. 2016. The parallel manipulation argument. *Ethics* 126(4): 1075–1089.
Davidson, D. 1963. Actions, reasons and causes. *The Journal of Philosophy* 60: 685–700.
Davidson, D. 1973. Freedom to act. In *Essays on Freedom and Action*, ed. T. Honderich, pp. 67–86. London: Routledge and Kegan Paul.
Demetriou, K. (2010). The soft-line solution to Pereboom's four-case argument. *Australasian Journal of Philosophy* 88(4): 595–617.
Dennett, D. C. 1984. *Elbow Room*. Cambridge, MA: MIT Press.
Dennett, D. C. 1991. *Consciousness Explained*. Boston: Little Brown.
Dennett, D. C. 2003. *Freedom Evolves*. New York: Viking.
Deery, O. and E. Nahmias. 2017. Defeating manipulation arguments: Interventionist causation and compatibilist sourcehood. *Philosophical Studies* 174: 1255–1276.
Donagan, A. 1987. *Choice: The Essential Element in Human Action*. London: Routledge and Kegan Paul.
Dowell, J. 2006. The physical: Empirical, not metaphysical. *Philosophical Studies* 131: 25–60.
Driver, J. 2012. Luck and fortune in moral evaluation. In *Contrastivism in Philosophy: New Perspectives*, ed. M. Blaauw, pp. 154–72. New York: Routledge.
Dworkin, G. 1970a. Acting freely. *Nous* 4: 367–383.

Dworkin, G. 1970b. *Determinism, Free Will and Moral Responsibility*. Englewood Cliffs, NJ: Prentice-Hall.

Eccles, J. 1994. *How the Self Controls the Brain*. Berlin: Springer.

Eccles, J. and K. Popper. 1977. *The Self and Its Brain*. New York: Springer-Verlag.

Ekstrom, L. 2000. *Free Will: A Philosophical Study*. Boulder, CO: Westview Press.

Elzein, N. 2018. The demand for contrastive explanation. *Philosophical Studies*, DOI: 10.1007/s11098-018-1065-z.

Enc, B. 2003. *How We Act: Causes, Reasons, and Intentions*. New York: Oxford University Press.

Enoch, D. 2012. Being responsible, taking responsibility, and penumbral agency. In *Luck, Value, and Commitment: Themes from the Ethics of Bernard Williams*, eds. U. Heuer and G. Lang, pp. 95–132. New York: Oxford University Press.

Enoch, D. and A. Marmor. 2007. The case against moral luck. *Law and Philosophy* 26: 405–436.

Eshleman, A. 2019. Moral responsibility. *Stanford Encyclopedia of Philosophy*. Available at: https://plato.stanford.edu/entries/moral-responsibility/.

Farah, M. J. 2012. Neuroethics: The ethical, legal, and societal impact of neuroscience. *The Annual Review of Psychology* 63: 571–591.

Farah, M. J, D. M. Shera, J. H. Savage, L. Betancourt, J. M. Giannetta, N. L. Brodsky, E. K. Malmud, and H. Hurt. 2006. Childhood poverty: Specific associations with neurocognitive development. *Brain Research* 1110: 166–174.

Feldman, R. and A. A. Buckareff. 2003. Reasons explanation and pure agency. *Philosophical Studies* 112: 135–145.

Fischer, J. M. 1983. Incompatibilism. *Philosophical Studies* 43: 121–137.

Fischer, J. M. 1994. *The Metaphysics of Free Will: An Essay on Control*. Oxford: Blackwell.

Fischer, J. M. 2007. Compatibilism. In *Four Views on Free Will*, eds. J. M. Fischer, R. Kane, D. Pereboom, and M. Vargas. Malden, MA: Blackwell.

Fischer, J. M. 2011. The zygote argument remixed. *Analysis* 71(2): 267–272.

Fischer, J. M. 2014. Review of Free Will, Agency, and Meaning in Life. *Science, Religion, and Culture* 1(3): 202–208.

Fischer, J. M. and M. Ravizza. 1998. *Responsibility and Control: A Theory of Moral Responsibility*. New York: Cambridge University Press.

Foster, J. 1991. *The Immaterial Self: A Defense of the Cartesian Dualist Conception of Mind*. New York: Routledge.

Frankfurt, H. G. 1969. Alternative possibilities and moral responsibility. *Journal of Philosophy* 66: 828–839.

Frankfurt, H. G. 1971. Freedom of the will and the concept of a person. *Journal of Philosophy* 68(1): 5–20.

Frankfurt, H. G. 1988. *The Importance of What We Care About*. New York: Cambridge University Press.

Franklin, C. 2011a. The problem of enhanced control. *Australian Journal of Philosophy* 89: 687–706.

Franklin, C. 2011b. Farewell to the luck (or mind) argument. *Philosophical Studies* 156: 199–230.

Franklin, C. 2015. Agent-causation, explanation, and akrasia: A reply to Levy's hard luck. *Criminal Law and Philosophy* 9: 753–770.

Garret, B. J. 2013. Review of Levy's hard luck. *Philosophy in Review* 33: 212–214.

Gert, H. J. 2017. Awareness luck. *Philosophia*. DOI: 10.1007/s11406-017-9901-5.

Ginet, C. 1966. Might we have no choice? In *Freedom and Determinism*, ed. K. Lehrer, pp. 87–104. New York: Random House.

Ginet, C. 1980. The conditional analysis of freedom. In van Inwagen 1980, pp. 171–186.
Ginet, C. 1990. *On Action*. New York: Cambridge University Press.
Ginet, C. 1995. Reasons explanation of action: An incompatibilist account. In *Agents, Causes, and Events*, ed. T. O'Connor, pp. 69–93. New York: Oxford University Press.
Ginet, C. 1996. In defense of the principle of alternative possibilities: Why I don't find Frankfurt's argument convincing. *Philosophical Perspectives* 10: 403–417.
Ginet, C. 1997. Freedom, responsibility, and agency. *Journal of Ethics* 1: 85–98.
Ginet, C. 2002. Review of *living without free will*. *Journal of Ethics* 6: 305–309.
Ginet, C. 2007. An action can be both uncaused and up to the agent. In *Intentionality, Deliberation, and Autonomy*, eds. C. Lumer and S. Nannini, pp. 243–256. Farnhnam, UK: Ashgate.
Ginet, C. 2008. In defense of a non-causal account of reasons explanation. *Journal of Ethics* 12 (3–4): 229–237.
Gladwell, M. 2008. *Outliers: The Story of Success*. New York: Little Brown and Company.
Greco, J. 1995. A second paradox concerning responsibility and luck. *Metaphilosophy* 26: 81–96.
Griffith, M. 2010. Why agent-causal actions are not lucky. *American Philosophical Quarterly* 47: 43–56.
Haas, D. 2013. In defense of hard-line replies to the multiple-case manipulation argument. *Philosophical Studies* 163: 797–811.
Haji, I. 1999. Indeterminism and Frankfurt style examples. *Philosophical Explorations* 2: 42–58.
Haji, I. 2000. Indeterminism, explanation, and luck. *The Journal of Ethics* 4(3): 211–235.
Haji, I. 2002. *Deontic Morality and Control*. New York: Cambridge University Press.
Haji, I. 2004. Active control, agent-causation and free action. *Philosophical Explorations* 7(2): 131–148.
Haji, I. 2005. Libertarianism, luck, and action explanation. *Journal of Philosophical Research* 30: 321–340.
Haji, I. 2014. Event-causal libertarianism's control conundrum. *Grazer Philosophische Studien* 88: 227–246.
Haji, I. 2016. *Luck's Mischief*. New York: Oxford University Press.
Hales, S. 2016. Why every theory of luck is wrong. *Nous* 50: 490–508.
Harrison, G. K. 2010. A challenge for soft-line replies to manipulation cases. *Philosophia* 38(3): 555–568.
Hartman, R. J. 2017. *In Defense of Moral Luck: Why Luck Often Affects Praiseworthiness and Blameworthiness*. New York: Routledge.
Hasker, W. 1999. *The Emergent Self*. Ithaca: Cornell University Press.
Honderich, T. 2002. *How Free Are We?* New York: Oxford University Press.
Humbach, J. A. 2019. Do criminal minds cause crime? Neuroscience and the physicalism dilemma. *Washing University Jurisprudence Review* 12(1): 1–29.
Hume, D. 1739/1978. *A Treatise of Human Nature*. New York: Oxford University Press.
Hume, D. 1743/1960. *An Enquiry Concerning Human Understanding*. ed. L. A. Selby-Bigge. Oxford: Clarendon Press.
Jeppsson, S. 2016. Accountability, answerability, and freedom. *Social Theory and Practice* 42 (4): 681–705.
Kane, R. 1985. *Free Will and Values*. Albany: SUNY Press.
Kane, R. 1996. *The Significance of Free Will*. New York: Oxford University Press.
Kane, R. 1999. Responsibility, luck, and chance: Reflections on free will and indeterminism. *Journal of Philosophy* 96: 217–240.
Kane, R. 2002. Some neglected pathways in the free will labyrinth. In *The Oxford Handbook of Free Will*, ed. R. Kane, pp. 406–437. New York: Oxford University Press.

Kane, R. 2007. Libertarianism. In *Four Views on Free Will*, eds. J. M. Fischer, R. Kane, D. Pereboom, and M. Vargas, pp. 5–43. Malden: Blackwell.
Kane, R. 2011. Rethinking free will: New perspectives on an ancient problem. In *Oxford Handbook of Free Will*, ed. R. Kane, pp. 381–404. New York: Oxford University Press.
Kane, R. 2016. The complex tapestry of free will: Striving will, indeterminism, and volition streams. *Synthese* 196: 145–160.
Kant, I. 1781/1787/1987. *Critique of Pure Reason*, tr. P. Guyer and A. Wood. New York: Cambridge University Press.
Kant, I. 1785/1981. *Grounding for the Metaphysics of Morals*, tr. J. Ellington. Indianapolis: Hackett.
Kant, I. 1788/1996. *Critique of Practical Reasons*, tr. Mary Gregor. New York: Cambridge University Press.
Kim, J. 1990. Supervenience as a philosophical concept. *Metaphilosophy* 21: 1–27.
Kim, J. 1993. *Supervenience and Mind: Selected Philosophical Essays*. New York: Cambridge University Press.
Kim, J. 1999. Making sense of emergence. *Philosophical Studies* 95: 3–36.
King, M. 2013. The problem with manipulation. *Ethics* 124: 65–83.
Lamb, J. 1977. On a proof of incompatibilism. *The Philosophical Review* 86: 20–35.
Latus, A. 2000. Moral and epistemic luck. *Journal of Philosophical Research* 25: 149–172.
Latus, A. 2003. Constitutive luck. *Metaphilosophy* 34: 460–475.
Lehrer, K. 1964. "Could" and determinism. *Analysis* 24: 159–160.
Lehrer, K. 1966. An empirical disproof of determinism. In *Freedom and Determinism*, ed. K. Lehrer, pp. 175–202. New York: Random House.
Lehrer, K. 1968. Cans without ifs. *Analysis* 29(1): 29–32.
Lehrer, K. 1976. "Can" in theory and practice: A possible worlds analysis. In *Action Theory*, eds. M. Brand and D. Walton, pp. 67–97. Dordrecht: D. Reidel.
Lehrer, K. 1980. Preferences, conditionals and freedom. In *Time and Cause: Essays Presented to Richard Taylor*, ed. P. van Inwagen, pp. 76–96. Dordrecht: D. Reidel.
Lemos, J. 2018. *A Pragmatic Approach to Libertarian Free Will*. New York: Routledge.
Lemos, J. 2019. Kane, Pereboom, and event-causal libertarianism. *Philosophia*, doi.org/10.1007/s11406-019-0098-0.
Levin, M. 1979. *Metaphysics and the Mind-Body Problem*. New York: Oxford University Press.
Levy, N. 2008. Bad luck once again. *Philosophy and Phenomenological Research* 77(3): 749–754.
Levy, N. 2009a. Luck and history-sensitive compatibilism. *Philosophical Quarterly* 59(235): 237–251.
Levy, N. 2009b. Culpable ignorance and moral responsibility: A reply to Firtzpatrich. *Ethics* 119(4): 729–741.
Levy, N. 2011. *Hard Luck: How Luck Undermines Free Will and Moral Responsibility*. New York: Oxford University Press.
Levy, N. 2019. Putting the luck back in moral luck. *Midwest Studies in Philosophy* 43(1): 59–74.
Lewis, D. 1981. Are we free to break the laws? *Theoria* 47: 113–121.
Lewis, P. T. 2016. *Quantum Ontology: A Guide to the Metaphysics of Quantum Mechanics*. New York: Oxford University Press.
List, C. 2019. *Why Free Will is Real*. Cambridge, MA: Harvard University Press.
Lycan, W. G. 1997. *Consciousness*. Cambridge, MA: MIT Press.
Mariani, M. 2017. The neuroscience of inequality: Does poverty show up in children's brains? *The Guardian* (July 13). www.theguardian.com/inequality/2017/jul/13/neuroscience-inequality-does-poverty-show-up-in-childrens-brains

Matheson, B. (2016). In defense of the four-case argument. *Philosophical Studies* 173(7): 1963–1982.
McKenna, M. 2004. Responsibility and globally manipulation agents. *Philosophical Topics* 32: 169–192.
McKenna, M. 2005. Reasons reactivity and incompatibilist intuitions. *Philosophical Explorations* 8(2): 131–143.
McKenna, M. 2008. A hard-line reply to Pereboom's four-case manipulation argument. *Philosophy and Phenomenological Research* 77(1): 142–159.
McKenna, M. 2013. Reasons-responsiveness, agents, and mechanisms. In *Oxford Studies in Agency and Responsibility*, Vol. 1, ed. D. Shoemaker, pp.151–183. New York: Oxford University Press.
McKenna, M. 2014. Resisting the manipulation argument: A hard-liner takes it on the chin. *Philosophy and Phenomenological Research* 87(2): 467–487.
McKenna, M. and D. Pereboom. 2016. *Free Will: A Contemporary Introduction*. New York: Routledge.
Mele, A. R. 1992. *The Springs of Action*. New York: Oxford University Press.
Mele, A. R. 1995. *Autonomous Agents*. New York: Oxford University Press.
Mele, A. R. 1998. Review of Robert Kane's The Significance of Free Will. *Journal of Philosophy* 93: 581–584.
Mele, A. R. 1999. Ultimate responsibility and dumb luck. *Social Philosophy and Policy* 16(2): 274–293.
Mele, A. R. 2001. *Autonomous Agents*. New York: Oxford University Press.
Mele, A. R. 2005. Libertarianism, luck, and control. *Pacific Philosophical Quarterly* 86(3): 381–407.
Mele, A. R. 2006. *Free Will and Luck*. New York: Oxford University Press.
Mele, A. R. 2008. Manipulation, compatibilism, and moral responsibility. *The Journal of Ethics* 12: 263–286.
Mele, A. R. 2017. *Aspects of Agency: Decisions, Abilities, Explanations, and Free Will*. New York: Oxford University Press.
Mele, A. R. 2019. *Manipulated Agents: A Window to Moral Responsibility*. New York: Oxford University Press.
Mickelson, K. 2010. The soft-line solution to Pereboom's four-case argument. *Australasian Journal of Philosophy* 88(4): 595–617.
Mill, J. S. 1860/1947. *On Liberty*. Oxford: Blackwell.
Mill, J. S. 1865/1979. *An Examination of Sir William Hamilton's Philosophy*, ed. J. M. Robson. Toronto: Routledge & Kegan Paul.
Montesano Montessori, A. A. 2017. Can agents be causes? A critique of Timothy O'Connor's Theory of Free Action. Faculty of Humanities Thesis, Utrecht University. Available at: https://dspace.library.uu.nl/handle/1874/354579.
Moore, G. E. 1912. Free will. In *Ethics*, ed. G. E. Moore, pp. 84–95. New York: Oxford University Press.
Moore, M. 1997. *Placing Blame: A General Theory of Criminal Law*. New York: Oxford University Press.
Morse, S. J. 2008. Determinism and the death of folk psychology: Two challenges to responsibility from neuroscience. *Minnesota Journal of Law, Science, and Technology* 9(1): 1–36.
Morse, S. J. 2016. The inevitable mind in the age of neuroscience. In *Philosophical Foundations of Law and Neuroscience*, eds. D. Patterson and M. S. Pardo, pp. 29–50. New York: Oxford University Press.
Nagel, T. 1979. Moral luck. In *Mortal Questions*, pp. 24–38. New York: Cambridge University Press.

Neely, W. 1974. Freedom and desire. *Philosophical Review* 83: 32–54.
Nelkin, D. 2012. Replies in session on Making Sense of Freedom and Responsibility, Pacific Division Meeting of the American Philosophical Association, Seattle, Washington, April.
Nelkin, D. 2013. Moral luck. *Stanford Encyclopedia of Philosophy*. First published January 26, 2004, with substantive revision April 10, 2013.
Nielsen, K. 1971. *Reason and Practice: A Modern Introduction to Philosophy*. New York: Harper & Row.
Nietzsche, F. 1886/1992. *Beyond Good and Evil*. Trans. Walter Kaufmann. New York: Random House.
Novle, K., B. McCandiss, and M. Farah. 2007. Socioeconomic gradients predict individual differences in neurocognitive abilities. *Developmental Science* 10(4): 464–480.
Noble, K., M. F. Norman, and F. Farah. 2005. Neurocognitive correlates of socioeconomic status in kindergarten children. *Developmental Science* 8(1): 74–87.
O'Connor, T. 1995. Agent causation. In *Agents, Causes, and Events: Essays on Indeterminism and Free Will*, ed. T. O'Connor, pp. 173–200. New York: Oxford University Press.
O'Connor, T. 1996. Why agent causation? *Philosophical Topics* 24(2): 143–158.
O'Connor, T. 2000a. *Persons and Causes*. New York: Oxford University Press.
O'Connor, T. 2000b. Causality, mind, and free will. *Philosophical Perspectives* 14: 05–17.
O'Connor, T. 2002. Libertarian views: Dualist and agent-causal theories. In *The Oxford Handbook of Free Will*, ed. R. Kane, pp. 337–355. New York: Oxford University Press.
O'Connor, T. 2005. Freedom with a human face. *Midwest Studies in Philosophy* 29: 207–27.
O'Connor, T. 2009a. Agent-causal power. In *Dispositions and Causes*, ed. T. Handfield, pp. 189–214. New York: Oxford University Press.
O'Connor, T. 2009b. Degrees of freedom. *Philosophical Explorations* 12: 119–125.
O'Connor, T. 2011. Agent-causal theories of freedom. In *The Oxford Handbook of Free Will*, 2nd edition, ed. R. Kane, pp. 308–328. New York: Oxford University Press.
Papineau, D. 2002. *Thinking About Consciousness*. New York: Oxford University Press.
Paskell, M. R. 2014. Manipulation, Argument, and Experiment: Putting Folk Intuitions into Context. Honors Thesis. University of Arizona. Available at: http://hdl.handle.net/10150/321908.
Peels, R. 2015. The modal solution to the problem of moral luck. *American Philosophical Quarterly* 52: 73–87.
Pereboom, D. 1995. Determinism al dente. *Nous* 29: 21–45.
Pereboom, D. 2001. *Living without Free Will*. New York: Cambridge University Press.
Pereboom, D. 2004. Is our conception of agent causation incoherent? *Philosophical Topics* 29: 228–247.
Pereboom, D. 2007. Hard incompatibilism. In *Four Views on Free Will*, eds. J. M. Fischer, R. Kane, D. Pereboom, and M. Vargas, pp. 85–125. Oxford: Blackwell.
Pereboom, D. 2008. A hard-line reply to the multiple-case manipulation argument. *Philosophy and Phenomenological Research* 77(1): 160–170.
Pereboom, D. 2011. *Consciousness and the Prospects of Physicalism*. New York: Oxford University Press.
Pereboom, D. 2014a. *Free Will, Agency, and Meaning in Life*. New York: Oxford University Press.
Pereboom, D. 2014b. Responses to John Martin Fischer and Dana Nelkin. *Science, Religion and Culture* 1(3): 218.
Pereboom, D. 2017. Responsibility, agency, and the disappearing agent objection. In *Le Libre-Arbitre: Approaches Contemporaines*, ed. J-B Guillon, pp. 1–18. Paris, France: College de France.

Pereboom, D. 2018. Review of Alfred R. Mele's *Aspects of Agency: Decisions, Abilities, Explanations, and Free Will*. *Notre Dame Philosophical Reviews*, June 27. Available online: https://ndpr.nd.edu/news/aspects-of-agency-decisions-abilities-explanations-and-free-will/.

Pereboom, D. 2021. Lynne Baker on constitution, nonreductivism, and emergence. In *Common Sense Metaphysics: Themes from the Philosophy of Lynne Rudder Baker*, eds. L. R. Oliveira and K. Corcoran. New York: Routledge.

Pereboom, D. and G. D. Caruso. 2018. Hard-incompatibilism existentialism: Neuroscience, punishment, and meaning in life. In *Neuroexistentialism: Meaning, Morals, and Purpose in the Age of Neuroscience*, eds. G. D. Caruso and O. Flanagan, pp. 193–222. New York: Oxford University Press.

Pereboom, D and M. McKenna. 2021. Manipulation arguments against compatibilism. In *Oxford Handbook of Moral Responsibility*, eds. D. Kay Nelkin and D. Pereboom. New York: Oxford University Press.

Pritchard, D. 2005. *Epistemic Luck*. New York: Oxford University Press.

Pritchard, D. 2014. The modal account of luck. *Metaphilosophy* 45(4–5): 594–619.

Reid, T. 1788/1983. *Essays on the Active Powers of the Human Mind*. Cambridge, MA: MIT Press.

Reid, T. 1985. *The Works of Thomas Reid, D.D.*, Vols. 1 & 2, 8th ed., Sir William Hamilton, Edinburgh: James Thin. Reprinted with an introduction by H. M. Bracken. Hildeshein: George Olms Verlad, 1967.

Rivera-Lopez, E. 2016. How to reject resultant moral luck alone. *Journal of Value Inquiry* 50: 415–423.

Rosen, G. 2002. Culpability and ignorance. *Proceedings of the Aristotelian Society* 103(1): 61–84.

Rosen, G. 2004. Skepticism about moral responsibility. *Philosophical Perspectives* 18: 295–313.

Rosen, G. 2008. Kleinbart on the oblivious and other tales of ignorance and responsibility. *Journal of Philosophy* 105(10): 591–610.

Sartorio, C. 2016. *Causation and Free Will*. New York: Oxford University Press.

Scanlon, T. 1998. *What We Owe to Each Other*. Cambridge, MA: Harvard University Press.

Schlick, M. 1939. *The Problems of Ethics*. Authorized translation by David Rynin. New York: Prentice-Hall.

Schlick, M. 1966. When is a man responsible? In *Free Will and Determinism*, ed. B. Berofsky, pp. 54–62. New York: Harper and Row.

Sifferd, K. L. 2006. In defense of the use of commonsense psychology in the criminal law. *Law and Philosophy* 25(6): 571–612.

Sifferd, K. L. 2014. What does it mean to be a mechanism? Stephen Morse, non-reductivism, and mental causation. *Criminal Law and Philosophy* 11: 143–159.

Shoemaker, D. 2011. Attributability, answerability, and accountability: Toward a wider theory of moral responsibility. *Ethics* 121: 602–632.

Shoemaker, D. 2016. *Responsibility From the Margins*. New York: Oxford University Press.

Stace, W. T. 1952. *Religion and the Modern Mind*. New York: Lippincott. An excerpt of which is reprinted in *Introduction to Philosophy: Classical and Contemporary Readings*, 3rd ed. L. Pojman, pp. 382–387. New York: Oxford University Press.

Steward, H. 1997. *The Ontology of Mind: Events, Processes, and States*. New York: Oxford University Press.

Steward, H. 2012. *A Metaphysics for Freedom*. New York: Oxford University Press.

Stout, R. 1996. *Things That Happen Because They Should: A Teleological Approach to Action*. New York: Oxford University Press.

Strawson, G. 1986. *Freedom and Belief.* Oxford: Oxford University Press.
Strawson, G. 1994. The impossibility of moral responsibility. *Philosophical Studies* 75(1–2): 5–24.
Strawson, G. 2010. *Freedom and Belief, revised edition.* Oxford: Oxford University Press.
Strawson, P. F. 1962. Freedom and resentment. *Proceedings of the British Academy* 68: 187–211.
Swinburne, R. 1986. *The Evolution of the Soul.* Oxford: Clarendon Press.
Taylor, R. 1966. *Action and Purpose.* Englewood Cliffs, NJ: Prentice-Hall.
Taylor, R. 1974. *Metaphysic*, 4th ed. Englewood Cliffs, NJ: Prentice-Hall.
Tierney, H. 2013. A maneuver around the modified manipulation argument. *Philosophical Studies* 165(3): 753–763.
Tierney, H. 2014. Tackling it head one: How best to handle the modified manipulation argument. *Journal of Value Inquiry* 48(4): 663–675.
Tierney, H. and D. Glick. 2020. Desperately seeking sourcehood. *Philosophical Studies* 177: 953–970.
Todd, P. 2011. A new approach to manipulation arguments. *Philosophical Studies* 152: 127–133.
Todd, P. 2012. Manipulation and moral standing: An argument for incompatibilism. *Philosophical Imprint* 12: 1–18.
Todd, P. 2013. Defending (a modified version of) the zygote argument. *Philosophical Studies* 164: 189–203.
Todd, P. 2017. Manipulation arguments and the freedom to do otherwise. *Philosophy and Phenomenological Research* 95(2): 395–407.
Tognazzini, N. A. 2012. Review of *hard luck: How luck undermines free will and moral responsibility*. *Australasian Journal of Philosophy* 90: 809–812.
Tognazzini, N. A. 2014. The structure of a manipulation argument. *Ethics* 124(2): 358–369.
Vaidman, L. 2014. Quantum theory and determinism. *Quantum Studies: Mathematics and Foundations* 1: 5–38.
van Gulick, R. 2001. Reduction, emergence and other recent options on the mind/body problem: A philosophical overview. *Journal of Consciousness Studies* 8(9–10): 1–34.
van Inwagen, P. 1975. The incompatibility of free will and determinism. *Philosophical Studies* 25: 185–199.
van Inwagen, P. 1983. *An Essay on Free Will.* Oxford: Clarendon Press.
Van Miltenburg, N. 2015. *Freedom in Action.* Utrecht: Quaestiones Infinitae.
Vargas, M. 2007. Revisionism. In *Four Views on Free Will*, eds. J. M. Fischer, R. Kane, D. Pereboom, and M. Vargas, pp. 126–165. Malden, MA: Blackwell Publishing.
Vargas, M. 2009. Revisionism and free will: A statement and defense. *Philosophical Studies* 144(1): 45–62.
Vargas, M. 2011. Revisionist accounts of free will: Origins, varieties, and challenges. In *Oxford Handbook on Free Will*, 2nd edition, ed. R. Kane, pp. 457–484. New York: Oxford University Press.
Vargas, M. 2013. *Building Better Beings: A Theory of Moral Responsibility.* New York: Oxford University Press.
Vargas, M. 2019. Responsibility, methodology and desert. *The Journal of Information Ethics*: 131–147.
Vicens, L. 2015. Self-forming actions and conflicts of intention. *Southwest Philosophical Review* 31(1): 93–100.
Vicente, A. 2006. On the causal completeness of physics. *International Studies in the Philosophy of Science* 20(2): 149–171.
Vihvelin, K. 2007. Arguments for incompatibilism. *Stanford Encyclopedia of Philosophy*. Available at: https://stanford.library.sydney.edu.au/archives/spr2010/entries/incompatibilism-arguments/.

Wallace, R. J. 1994. *Responsibility and the Moral Sentiments*. Harvard: Harvard University Press.
Wallace, R. J. 1997. Review of John Martin Fischer's The Metaphysics of Free Will. *Journal of Philosophy* 94(3): 156–159.
Waller, B. 1988. Free will gone out of control. *Behaviorism* 16: 149–162.
Waller, B. N. 1989. Denying responsibility: The difference it makes. *Analysis* 49: 44–47.
Waller, B. 1990. *Freedom Without Responsibility*. New York: Temple University Press.
Waller, B. 2004. Virtue unrewarded: Morality without moral responsibility. *Philosophia* 31: 3–4.
Waller, B. 2011. *Against Moral Responsibility*. Cambridge, MA: MIT Press.
Waller, B. 2015. *The Stubborn System of Moral Responsibility*. Cambridge, MA: MIT Press.
Waller, R. 2014. The threat of effective intentions to moral responsibility in the zygote argument. *Philosophia* 42(1): 209–222.
Watson, G. 1975. Free agency. *Journal of Philosophy* 72: 205–220.
Watson, G. 1996. Two faces of responsibility. *Philosophical Topics* 24: 227–248.
Widerker, D. 1995. Libertarianism and Frankfurt's attack on the principle of alternative possibilities. *The Philosophical Review* 104: 247–261.
Widerker, D. 2005. Agent-causation and control. *Faith and Philosophy* 22: 87–98.
Widerker, D. 2006. Libertarianism and the philosophical significance of Frankfurt scenarios. *Journal of Philosophy* 103: 163–187.
Williams, B. 1981. *Moral Luck*. New York: Cambridge University Press.
Williams, B. 1993. Postscript. In *Moral Luck*, ed. D. Statman, pp. 251–258. Albany: State University of New York.
Wilson, D. L. 1976. On the nature of consciousness and physical reality. *Perspectives in Biology and Medicine* 19: 568–581.
Wilson, D. L. 1995. Seeking the neural correlate of consciousness. *American Scientist* 83: 269–270.
Wilson, D. L. 1999. Mind-brain interaction and violation of physical laws. *Journal of Consciousness Studies* 6(8–9): 185–200.
Woodward, J. (2003). *Making Things Happen: A Theory of Causal Explanation*. New York: Oxford University Press.
Zimmerman, M. 1987. Luck and moral responsibility. *Ethics* 97: 374–386.
Zimmerman, M. 1997. Moral responsibility and ignorance. *Ethics* 107(3): 410–426.
Zimmerman, M. 2002. Taking luck seriously. *The Journal of Philosophy* 99: 553–576.
Zimmerman, M. 2009. *Living with Uncertainty: The Moral Significance of Ignorance*. New York: Cambridge University Press.

3 THE EPISTEMIC ARGUMENT AGAINST RETRIBUTIVISM

Alexander, L., K. K. Ferzan, and S. Morse. 2009. *Crime and Culpability: A Theory of Criminal Law*. New York: Cambridge University Press.
Balaguer, M. 2009. *Free Will as an Open Scientific Problem*. Cambridge, MA: MIT Press.
Berman, M. 2008. Punishment and justification. *Ethics* 18: 258–290.
Boonin, D. 2008. *The Problem of Punishment*. Cambridge: Cambridge University Press.
Campbell, C. A. 1957. *On Selfhood and Godhood*. London: George Allen & Unwin.
Caruso, G. D. 2013. Introduction: Exploring the illusion of free will and moral responsibility. In *Exploring the Illusion of Free Will and Moral Responsibility*, ed. G. D. Caruso, pp. 1–16. Lanham, MD: Lexington Books.

Caruso, G. D. 2016. Free will skepticism and criminal behavior: A public health–quarantine model. *Southwest Philosophy Review* 32(1): 25–48.

Caruso, G. D. 2017a. *Public Health and Safety: The Social Determinants of Health and Criminal Behavior*. UK: ResearchLinks Books.

Caruso, G. D. 2017b. Free will skepticism and the question of creativity: Creativity, desert, and self-creation. *Ergo* 3(23): 23–39.

Caruso, G. D. 2018. Skepticism about moral responsibility. *Stanford Encyclopedia of Philosophy*. https://plato.stanford.edu/entries/skepticism-moral-responsibility/

Caruso, G. D. 2020. Justice without retribution: An epistemic argument against retributive criminal punishment. *Neuroethics* 13(1): 13–28.

Caruso, G. D. 2021. The public health–quarantine model. In *Oxford Handbook of Moral Responsibility*, eds. D. Nelkin and D. Pereboom. New York: Oxford University Press.

Chisholm, R. 1982. Human freedom and the self. In *Free Will*, ed. G. Watson, pp. 24–35. New York: Oxford University Press.

Clark, T. 2012. Clark comments on Dennett's review of Against Moral Responsibility. Naturalism.Org: www.naturalism.org/resources/book-reviews/exchange-on-wallers-against-moral-responsibility#toc-clark-comments-on-dennetts-review-of-against-moral-respo-UNoXiqrR.

Corrado, M. L. 2013a. Why do we resist hard incompatibilism? Thoughts on freedom and punishment. In *The Future of Punishment*, ed. T. Nadelhoffer, pp. 79–106. New York: Oxford University Press.

Corrado, M. L. 2013b. *Presumed Dangerous: Punishment, Responsibility, and Preventive Detention in American Jurisprudence*. Durham, NC: Carolina Academic Press.

Corrado, M. L. 2017. Punishment and the burden of proof. UNC Legal Studies Research Paper. Available at: https://ssrn.com/abstract=2997654 or http://dx.doi.org/10.2139/ssrn.2997654.

Corrado, M. L. 2019a. Criminal quarantine and the burden of proof. *Philosophia* 47(4): 1095–1110.

Corrado, M. L. 2019b. Fichte and the psychopath: Criminal justice turned upside down. In *Free Will Skepticism in Law and Society*, eds. E. Shaw, D. Pereboom, and G. Caruso, pp. 161–176. Cambridge: Cambridge University Press.

Dennett, D. C. 2012. Review of *Against Moral Responsibility* by Bruce Waller and Dennett's Rejoinder to Clark. Naturalism.org: www.naturalism.org/resources/book-reviews/dennett-review-of-against-moral-responsibility.

Dennett, D. C. and G. D. Caruso. 2021. *Just Deserts: Debating Free Will*. New York: Polity Books.

Double, R. 2002. The moral hardness of libertarianism. *Philo* 5: 226–234.

Double, R. 2017. The Hard-heartedness of some libertarians: A reply to John Lemos. *Journal of Philosophical Research* 42: 313–318.

Double, R. 2020. Review of John Lemos' A Pragmatic Approach to Libertarian Free Will. *Criminal Law and Philosophy*: doi.org/10.1007/s11572-020-09525-w.

Fischer, J. M. 1994. *The Metaphysics of Free Will: An Essay on Control*. Oxford: Blackwell.

James, W. 1884/1956. The dilemma of determinism. In *The Will to Believe: Human Immortality*, pp. 145–183. New York: Dover.

Jeppsson, S. M. I. 2020. Retributivism, justification and credence: The epistemic argument revisited. *Neuroethics*: doi.org/10.1007/s12152-020-09436-6.

Kane, R. 1996. *The Significance of Free Will*. New York: Oxford University Press.

Kant, I. 1790. *The Metaphysics of Morals*. Translated by W. Hastie. Radford, VA: A&D Books.

Lemos, J. 2018. *A Pragmatic Approach to Libertarian Free Will*. New York: Routledge.

Levy, N. 2011. *Hard Luck: How Luck Undermines Free Will and Moral Responsibility*. New York: Oxford University Press.

Mele, A. R. 2006. *Free Will and Luck*. New York: Oxford University Press.

Mele, A. R. 2017. *Aspects of Agency: Decisions, Abilities, Explanations, and Free Will*. New York: Oxford University Press.

Morse, S. J. 2013. Common criminal law compatibilism. In *Neuroscience and Legal Responsibility*, ed. N. A. Vincent. New York: Oxford University press.

Morse, S. J. 2015a. Criminal law and common sense: An essay on the perils and promise of neuroscience. *Marquette Law Review* 99: 39–72.

Morse, S. J. 2015b. Neuroscience, free will, and criminal responsibility. In *Free Will and the Brain: Neuroscientific, Philosophical, and Legal Perspectives*, ed. W. Glannon, pp. 251–286. Cambridge, MA: Cambridge University Press.

Morse, S. J. 2018. The neuroscientific non-challenge to meaning, morals, and purpose. In *Neuroexistentialism: Meaning, Morals, and Purpose in the Age of Neuroscience*, eds. G. D. Caruso and O. Flanagan, pp. 333–358. New York: Oxford University Press.

Nichols, S. 2007. After compatibilism: A naturalistic defense of the reactive attitudes. *Philosophical Perspectives* 21: 405–428.

Pereboom, D. 2001. *Living without Free Will*. New York: Cambridge University Press.

Pereboom, D. 2014. *Free Will, Agency, and Meaning in Life*. Oxford: Oxford University Press.

Pereboom, D. 2017. A defense of free will skepticism: Replies to commentaries by Victor Tadros, Saul Smilansky, Michael McKenna, and Alfred R. Mele on free will, agency, and meaning in life. *Criminal Law and Philosophy* 11(3): 617–636.

Pereboom, D. and G. D. Caruso. 2018. Hard-incompatibilist existentialism: Neuroscience, punishment, and meaning in life. In *Neuroexistentialism: Meaning, Morals, and Purpose in the Age of Neuroscience*, eds. G. D. Caruso and O. Flanagan, pp. 193–222. New York: Oxford University Press.

Pigliucci, M. and M. Boudry. 2014. Prove it! The burden of proof game in science vs. pseudoscience disputes. *Philosophia* 42: 487–502.

Shaw, E. 2014. *Free Will, Punishment, and Criminal Responsibility*. Dissertation Thesis. Edinburgh University. Available at: https://era.ed.ac.uk/bitstream/handle/1842/9590/Shaw2014.pdf?sequence=2&isAllowed=y.

Strawson, G. 1986. *Freedom and Belief*. Oxford: Oxford University Press.

Strawson, G. 1994. The impossibility of moral responsibility. *Philosophical Studies* 75(1): 5–24.

Strawson, P. F. 1982. Freedom and resentment. In *Free Will*, ed. G. Watson, pp. 59–80. New York: Oxford University Press. (Originally punished in *Proceedings of the British Academy* 36 [1962].)

Tadros, V. 2011. *The End of Harm: The Moral Foundations of Criminal Law*. New York: Oxford University Press.

Taylor, R. 1974. *Metaphysic*, 4th edition. Englewood Cliffs, NJ: Prentice-Hall.

van Inwagen, P. 1983. *An Essay on Free Will*. New York: Clarendon Press.

van Inwagen, P. 2000. Free will remains a mystery. *Philosophical Perspectives* 14: 1–19.

Vargas, M. 2007. Revisionism. In *Four Views on Free Will*, eds. J. M. Fischer, R. Kane, D. Pereboom, and M. Vargas, pp. 126–165. Oxford: Blackwell.

Vilhauer, B. 2009. Free will and reasonable doubt. *American Philosophical Quarterly* 46(2): 131–140.

Vilhaeur, B. 2012. Taking free will skepticism seriously. *The Philosophical Quarterly* 62(249): 833–852.

Vilhauer, B. 2013. Persons, punishment, and free will skepticism. *Philosophical Studies* 162(2): 143–163.

Vilhauer, B. 2015. Free will and the asymmetrical justification of holding morally responsible. *The Philosophical Quarterly* 65(261): 772–789.
Walen, A. 2014. Retributive justice. *The Stanford Encyclopedia of Philosophy*. Available at: https://plato.stanford.edu/entries/justice-retributive/.
Waller, B. 2011. *Against Moral Responsibility*. Cambridge, MA: MIT Press.
Waller, B. 2015. *The Stubborn System of Moral Responsibility*. Cambridge, MA: MIT Press.

4 ADDITIONAL REASONS FOR REJECTING RETRIBUTIVISM

ACLU. 2006. *Cracks in the System: Twenty Years of the Unjust Federal Crack Cocaine Law*. Washington, DC: American Civil Liberties Union. Available at: www.aclu.org/other/cracks-system-20-years-unjust-federal-crack-cocaine-law.
Alexander, L., K. Kessler Ferzan, and S. Morse. 2009. *Crime and Culpability: A Theory of Criminal Law*. New York: Cambridge University Press.
Alicke, M. D. 1994. Evidential and extra-evidential evaluations of social conduct. *Journal of Social Behavior and Personality* 9: 591–615.
Alicke, M. D. 2000. Culpable control and the psychology of blame. *Psychological Bulletin* 126: 556–574.
Alicke, M. D. 2008. Blaming badly. *Journal of Cognition and Culture* 8: 179–186.
Alicke, M. D., J. Buckingham, E. Zell, and T. Davis. 2008. Culpable control and counterfactual reasoning in the psychology of blame. *Personality and Social Psychology Bulletin* 34: 1371–1381.
American Psychological Association. 2014. Incarceration nation: The United States leads the world in incarceration. *Monitor on Psychology* 45(9). Available at: www.apa.org/monitor/2014/10/incarceration.
Ayres, I. and J. Waldfogel. 1994. A market test for race discrimination in bail setting. *Stanford Law Review* 987: 992.
Bada Math, S., C. N. Kumar, and S. Moirangthem. 2015. Insanity defense: Past, present, and future. *Indian Journal of Psychological Medicine* 37(4): 381–387.
Baird, A., J. Kennett, and E. Schier. 2020. Homicide and dementia: An investigation of legal, ethical, and clinical factors of Australian legal cases. *International Journal of Law and Psychiatry* 71: 1–13.
Banks, R. R., et al. 2006. Discrimination and implicit bias in a racially unequal society. *California Law Review* 1169(94): 1175.
Bartle, J. 2019. We know that prison doesn't work. So what are the alternatives? *The Guardian*, Friday, August 16, 2019. Available at: www.theguardian.com/commentisfree/2019/aug/16/we-know-that-prison-doesnt-work-so-what-are-the-alternatives.
Bazelon, D. L. 1976. The morality of the criminal law. *Southern California Law Review* 49: 385–405.
Berg, K. S. and N. Vidmar. 1975. Authoritarianism and recall of evidence about criminal behavior. *Journal of Research in Personality* 9: 147–157.
Binswanger, I. A., M. F. Stern, R. A. Deyo, et al. 2007. Release from prison: A high risk of death for former inmates. *New England Journal of Medicine* 356(2): 157–165.
Boonin, D. 2008. *The Problem of Punishment*. Cambridge: Cambridge University Press.
Boston Re-entry Study. 2015. *Lifetimes of Violence in a Sample of Released Prisoners*. Available at: https://scholar.harvard.edu/brucewestern/working-papers.
Brooks, T. 2012. *Punishment*. New York: Routledge.
Callender, J. 2010. *Free Will and Responsibility: A Guide for Practitioners*. New York: Oxford University Press.

Callender, J. 2019. Causality and responsibility in mentally disordered offenders. In *Free Will Skepticism in Law and Society: Challenging Retributive Justice*, eds. E. Shaw, D. Pereboom, and G. D. Caruso, pp. 177–191. New York: Cambridge University Press.

Caputo-Levine, D. D. 2013. The yard face: The contribution of inmate interpersonal violence to the carceral habitus. *Ethnography* 14: 165–185.

Chau, P. 2012. Duff on the legitimacy of punishment of socially deprived offenders. *Criminal Law and Philosophy* 6: 247–254.

Ciurria, M. 2014. Moral responsibility and mental health: Applying the standard of the reasonable person. *Philosophy, Psychiatry, and Psychology* 21(1): 1–12.

Ciurria, M. 2020. *An Intersectional Feminist Theory of Moral Responsibility*. New York: Routledge.

Clark, C. J., J. B. Luguri, P. H. Ditto, J. Knobe, A. F. Shariff, and R. F. Baumeister. 2014. Free to punish: A motivated account of free will. *Journal of Personal and Social Psychology* 106: 501–513.

Coogan, M. D. 2009. *A Brief Introduction to the Old Testament: The Hebrew Bible in Its Context*. New York: Oxford University Press.

Corrado, M. L. 2013a. Why do we resist hard incompatibilism? Thoughts on freedom and punishment. In *The Future of Punishment*, ed. T. Nadelhoffer, pp. 79–106. New York: Oxford University Press.

Corrado, M. L. 2013b. *Presumed Dangerous: Punishment, Responsibility, and Preventive Detention in American Jurisprudence*. Durham, NC: Carolina Academic Press.

Corrado, M. L. 2016a. Chapter one: Two models of criminal justice. UNC Legal Studies Research Paper, No. 2757078. Available at SSRN: https://ssrn.com/abstract=2757078 or http://dx.doi.org/10.2139/ssrn.2757078.

Corrado, M. L. 2016b. Chapter four: Quarantine and the problem of the third man. UNC Legal Studies Research Paper No. 2849473. Available at SSRN: https://ssrn.com/abstract=2849473.

Corrado, M. L. 2019a. Criminal quarantine and the burden of proof. *Philosophia* 47(4): 1095–1110.

Corrado, M. L. 2019b. Fichte and the psychopath: Criminal justice turned upside down. In *Free Will Skepticism in Law and Society*, eds. E. Shaw, D. Pereboom, and G. Caruso, pp. 161–176. Cambridge: Cambridge University Press.

Dart, T. 2015. American sniper' jurors: Defendant was using PTSD diagnosis as an excuse. *The Guardian*. Available at: www.theguardian.com/us-news/2015/feb/25/american-sniper-trial-jury-eddie-ray-routh-ptsd-excuse.

DeCaro, M. 2019. The indispensability of the manifest image. *Philosophy and Social Criticism*. DOI: 10.1177/0191453719826615.

Delgado, R. 1985. Rotten social background: Should the criminal law recognize a defense of severe environmental deprivation? *Law and Inequality* 3: 9–91.

Dobbie, W., J. Goldin, and C. S. Yang. 2018. The effect of pretrial detention on conviction, future crime, and employment: Evidence from randomly assigned judges. *American Economic Review* 108(2): 201–240.

Drug Policy Alliance. 1992. *Race and the Drug War*. www.drugpolicy.org/issues/race-and-drug-war.

Duff, A. 2001. *Punishment, Communication, and Community*. New York: Oxford University Press.

Dumont, D. M., B. Brockmann, S. Dickman, N. Alexander, and J. D. Rich. 2012. Public health and the epidemic of incarceration. *Annual Review of Public Health* 33: 325–339.

Eftan, M. G. 1974. The effect of physical appearance on the judgment of guilt, interpersonal attraction, and severity of recommended punishment in a simulated jury task. *Journal of Research and Personality* 8: 45–54.

Elliot, C. 1996. *The Rules of Insanity: Moral Responsibility and the Mentally Ill Offender*. Albany, NY: SUNY Press.

Enns, P. 2006. *Incarceration Nation: How the United States Became the Most Punitive Democracy in the World*. New York: Cambridge University Press.

Everett, J. A. C., C. J. Clark, J. B. Luguri, B. D. Earp, P. H. Ditto, and A. F. Shariff. 2018. *Political Differences in Free Will Beliefs are Driven by Differences in Moralization*. Available at: https://ssrn.com/abstract=3011597.

Feinberg, J. 1995. Equal punishment for failed attempts: Some bad but instructive arguments against it. *Arizona Law Review* 37: 117–133.

Fine, C. and J. Kennett. 2004. Mental impairment, moral understanding and criminal responsibility: Psychopathy and the purpose of punishment. *International Journal of Law and Psychiatry* 27(5): 425–443.

Fingarette, H. 1966. The concept of mental disease in criminal law insanity tests. *University of Chicago Law Review* 33(2): 229–248.

Fletcher, G. 2000. *Rethinking Criminal Law*. New York: Oxford University Press.

Garvey, S. P. 2014. Injustice, authority, and the criminal law. In *The Punitive Imagination: Law, Justice, and Responsibility*, ed. A. Sarat, pp. 42–81. Tuscaloosa: University of Alabama Press.

Glenn, A. L., A. Raine, and W. S. Laufer. 2011. Is it wrong to criminalize and punish psychopaths? *Emotion Review* 3: 302–304.

Godman, M. and A. Jefferson. 2017. On blaming and punishing psychopaths. *Criminal Law and Philosophy* 11(1): 127–142.

Granovetter, M. S. 1973. The strength of weak ties. *American Journal of Sociology* 78: 1360–1380.

Greenspan, P. 2016. Responsible psychopaths revisited. *Journal of Ethics* 20(1-3): 265–278.

Gruber, A. 2010. The false promise of retributive proportionality. *Jotwell Journal*, July 12. Available at: http://scholar.law.colorado.edu/cgi/viewcontent.cgi?article=1220&context=articles.

Gupta, A., C. Hansman, and E. Frenchman. 2016. The heavy costs of high bail: Evidence from judge randomization. *Journal of Legal Studies* 45(2): 471–505.

Haglund, A., D. Tidemalm, J. Jokinen, N. Langstrom, P. Lichtenstein, S. Fazel, and B. Runespn. 2014. Suicide after release from prison. *The Journal of Clinical Psychiatry* 85(10): 1047–1053.

Haji, I. 2010. Psychopathy, ethical perception, and moral culpability. *Neuroethics* 3(2): 135–150.

Harding, D. J. 2019. *On the Outside: Prisoner Reentry and Reintegration*. Chicago: University of Chicago Press.

Harding, D. J., J. D. Morenoff, A. P. Nguyen, S. D. Bushway, and I. A. Binswanger. 2019. A natural experiment study of the effects of imprisonment on violence in the community. *Nature Human Behavior* 3: 671–677.

Heffernan, W. C. and J. Kleinig (eds.). 2000. *From Social Justice to Criminal Justice: Poverty and the Administration of Criminal Law*. New York: Oxford University Press.

Hirstein, W., K. L. Sifferd, and T. K. Fagan. 2018. *Responsible Brain: Neuroscience, Law, and Human Culpability*. Cambridge, MA: MIT Press.

Holmes, O. W. 1881. *The Common Law*. Boston: Little, Brown.

Holmes, O. W. 1899. Law in science and science in law. *Harvard Law Review* 12: 443–463.

Howard, J. 2013. Punishment, socially deprived offenders, and democratic community. *Criminal Law and Philosophy* 7: 121–136.

Husak, D. 2016. *Ignorance of Law: A Philosophical Inquiry*. New York: Oxford University Press.

Jefferson, A. and K. Sifferd. 2018. Are psychopaths legally insane? *European Journal of Analytic Philosophy* 14(1): 79–96.

Johnson, R. 2009. Ever-increasing levels of parental incarceration and the consequences for children. In *Do Prisons Make Us Safer? The Benefits and Costs of the Prison Boom*, eds. S. Raphael and M. S. Stoll, pp. 1–24. New York: Russell Sage Foundation.

Justice Policy Institute. 2009. Cellblocks or Classrooms?: The Funding of Higher Education and Corrections and Its Impact on African American Men. www.justicepolicy.org/images/upload/02-09_REP_CellblocksClassrooms_BB-AC.pdf.

Kelly, E. 2018. *The Limits of Blame: Rethinking Punishment and Responsibility*. Cambridge, MA: Harvard University Press.

Kennett, J. 2001. *Agency and Responsibility: A Common-Sense Moral Psychology*. New York: Oxford University Press.

Kennett, J. 2007. Mental disorder, moral agency, and the self. In *Oxford Handbook of Bioethics*, ed. B. Steinbock, pp. 90–113. New York: Oxford University Press.

Kennett, J. 2010. Reasons, emotion, and moral judgment in the psychopath. In *Responsibility and Psychopathy: Interfacing Law, Psychiatry and Philosophy*, eds. L. Malatesti and J. McMillan, pp. 243–260. New York: Oxford University Press.

Kennett, J. and C. Fine. 2004. Mental impairment, moral understanding and criminal responsibility: Psychopathy and the purpose of punishment. *International Journal of Law and Psychiatry* 27(5): 425–443.

Kennett, J. and S. Matthews. 2002. Identity, control, and responsibility: The case of dissociative identity disorder. *Philosophical Psychology* 15(4): 509–526.

Kennett, J. and S. Matthews. 2009. Mental time travel, agency and responsibility. In *Psychiatry as Cognitive Neuroscience: Philosophical Perspectives*, eds. M. Broome and L. Bortolotti, pp. 327–350. New York: Oxford University Press.

King, M. and J. May. 2018. Moral responsibility and mental illness: A call for nuance. *Neuroethics* 11(1): 11–22.

Kling, J. R. 2006. Incarceration length, employment, and earnings. *Annuals of Economic Review* 96: 863–876.

Lamont, J. 1994. The concept of desert in distributive justice. *Philosophical Quarterly* 44(174): 45–64.

Langado, D. A. and S. Channon. 2008. Judgments of cause and blame: The effects of intentionality and foreseeability. *Cognition* 108: 754–770.

Lee, Y. 2009. Recidivism as omission: A relational account. *Texas Law Review* 87: 571–622.

Levy, K. 2005. The solution to the problem of outcome luck: Why harm is just as punishable as the wrongful action that causes it. *Law and Philosophy* 24: 264–303.

Levy, K. 2011. Dangerous psychopaths: Criminally responsible but not morally responsible, subject to criminal punishment and to preventive detention. *San Diego Law Review* 48: 1299–1395.

Levy, N. 2007. The responsibility of the psychopath revisited. *Philosophy, Psychiatry, and Psychology* 14: 129–138.

Levy, N. 2012. Skepticism and sanctions: The benefits of rejecting moral responsibility. *Law and Philosophy* 31: 477–493.

Levy, N. 2014. Psychopaths and blame: The argument from content. *Philosophical Psychology* 27(3): 351–367.

Loeffler, C. E. 2013. Does imprisonment alter the life course? Evidence on crime and employment from a natural experiment. *Criminology* 51: 137–166.

Moore, M. S. 1997. *Placing Blame*. New York: Oxford University Press.

Morris, N. 1968. Psychiatry and the dangerous criminal. *Southern California Law Review* 41: 514–547.

Morse, S. J. 2008. Psychopathy and criminal responsibility. *Neuroethics* 1: 205–212.
Murphey, D. and P. M. Cooper. 2015. *Parents Behind Bars: What Happens to Their Children?* Report by childtrends.org. Available at: www.childtrends.org/wp-content/uploads/2015/10/2015-42ParentsBehindBars.pdf.
Murphy, J. 1973. Marxism and retribution. *Philosophy and Public Affairs* 2: 217–243.
Mustard, D. B. 2001. Racial, ethnic, and gender disparities in sentencing: Evidence from the U.S. Federal Courts. *Jurisprudence, Law, and Economics* 285(44): 300.
National Research Council. 2014. *The Growth of Incarceration in the United States: Exploring Causes and Consequences.* www.nap.edu/read/18613/chapter/1
Nelkin, D. K. 2015. Psychopaths, incorrigible racists, and the face of responsibility. *Ethics* 125 (2): 357–390.
Nelkin, D. K. 2017. Fine cuts of moral agency: Dissociable deficits in psychopathy and autism. In *Current Controversies in Bioethics*, eds. S. M. Liao and C. O'Neil, pp. 47–66. New York: Routledge.
Nelkin, D. K. 2019. Frontotemporal dementia and the reactive attitudes: Two roles for the capacity to care? *Journal of Applied Philosophy* 36(5): 817–837.
Pager, D. 2007. *Marked: Race, Crime, and Finding Work in an Era of Mass Incarceration.* Chicago: University of Chicago Press.
Pilsbury, S. H. 2013. Why psychopaths are responsible. In *Handbook on Psychopathy and Law*, eds. K. A. Kiehl and W. Sinnott-Armstrong, pp. 297–213. New York: Oxford University Press.
Pratt, D., M. Piper, L. Appleby, R. Webb, and J. Shaw. 2006. Suicide in recently released prisoners: A population-based cohort study. *Lancet* 368(9530): 119–123.
Rachlinski, J., S. Johnson, A. J. Wistrich, and C. Guthrie. 2009. Does unconscious racial bias affect trial judges? *Notre Dame Law Review* 84(3): 1195–1246.
Raphael, S. and M. S. Stoll. 2009. Introduction. In *Do Prisons Make Us Safer? The Benefits and Costs of the Prison Boom*, eds. S. Raphael and M. S. Stoll, pp. 1–24. New York: Russell Sage Foundation.
Ristroph, A. 2006. Desert, democracy, and sentencing reform. *Journal of Criminal Law and Criminology* 96(4): 1293–1352.
Ristroph, A. 2009. How (not) to think like a punisher. *Florida Law Review* 61: 727–749.
Rudy-Hiller, F. 2018. The epistemic condition for moral responsibility. *Stanford Encyclopedia of Philosophy.* Available at: https://plato.stanford.edu/entries/moral-responsibility-epistemic/.
Schnittker, J. and A. John. 2007. Enduring stigma: The long-term effects of incarceration on health. *Journal of Health and Social Behavior* 48: 115–130.
Schnittker, J., M. Massoglia, and C. Uggen. 2012. Out and down: Incarceration and psychiatric disorders. *Journal of Health and Social Behavior* 53: 448–464.
Scholten, M. 2016. Schizophrenia and moral responsibility: A Kantian essay. *Philosophia* 44 (1): 205–225.
Shafer, L. R. 1996. The failure of retributivism. *Philosophical Studies* 82: 289–316.
Shoemaker, D. 2009. Responsibility and disability. *Metaphilosophy* 40(3-4): 438–461.
Shoemaker, D. 2010. Responsibility, agency, and cognitive disability. In *Cognitive Disability and Its Challenge to Moral Philosophy*, eds. E. F. Kittay and L. Carlson, pp. 201–223. New York: Wiley-Blackwell.
Shoemaker, D. 2011. Psychopathy, responsibility, and the moral/conventional distinction. *Southern Journal of Philosophy* 49: 99–124.
Shoemaker, D. 2015. *Responsibility from the Margins.* New York: Oxford University Press.
Sifferd, K. 2018. Review of Douglas Husak's ignorance of law: A philosophical inquiry. *Jurisprudence* 9(1): 186–191.

Sifferd, K. and W. Hirstein. 2013. On the criminal culpability of successful and unsuccessful psychopaths. *Neuroethics* 6: 129–140.
Singer, R. G. 1979. *Just Deserts: Sentencing Based on Equality and Desert*. Cambridge, MA: Ballinger.
Stråge, A. 2019. Minds, Brains, and Desert: On the Relevance of Neuroscience for Retributive Punishment. Dissertation. University of Gothenburg. https://philpapers.org/archive/STRMBA-3.pdf
Swanson, J. W., E. E. McGinty, S. Frazel, and V. M. Mays. 2015. Mental illness and reduction of gun violence and suicide: Bringing epidemiological research to policy. *Annual of Epidemiology* 25: 366–276.
Tadros, V. 2011. *The End of Harm: The Moral Foundations of Criminal Law*. New York: Oxford University Press.
Tonry, M. 1995. *Malign Neglect: Race, Crime, and Punishment in America*. New York: Oxford University Press.
Tonry, M. 2004. *Thinking About Crime: Sense and Sensibility in American Penal Culture*. New York: Oxford University Press.
Tonry, M. 2014. Can deserts be just in an unjust world? In *Liberal Criminal Theory: Essays for Andreas von Hirsch*, eds. A. P. Simester, U. Neumann, and A. Du. Bois-Pedain. Oxford: Hart.
Tonry, M. 2020. *Doing Justice, Preventing Crime*. New York: Oxford University Press.
Torrey, E. F., A. D. Kennard, D. Eslinger, R. Lamb, and J. Pavle. 2010. More mentally ill persons are in jails and prisons than hospitals: A survey of the states. Available at: www.treatmentadvocacycenter.org/storage/documents/final_jails_v_hospitals_study.pdf.
Tyler, J. H. and J. R. Kling. 2007. Prison-based education and reentry into the mainstream labor market. In *Barriers to Reentry? The Labor Market for Released Prisoners in the Post-Industrial America*, eds. S. Bushway, M. A. Stoll, and D. F. Welman, pp. 227–256.
United States Sentencing Commission. 1995. *Report to the Congress: Cocaine and Federal Sentencing Policy*. Available at: www.ussc.gov/research/congressional-reports/1995-report-congress-cocaine-and-federal-sentencing-policy.
United States Sentencing Commission. 2002. *Report to the Congress: Federal Cocaine Sentencing Policy*. Available at: www.ussc.gov/research/congressional-reports/2002-report-congress-federal-cocaine-sentencing-policy.
Vierra, A. 2016. Psychopathy, mental time travel, and legal responsibility. *Neuroethics* 9(2): 129–136.
Von Hirsch, A. and A. Ashworth. 2005. *Proportionate Sentencing: Exploring the Principles*. New York: Oxford University Press.
Wachs, T. D. and G. W. Evans. 2010. Chaos in context. In *Chaos and Its Influence on Children's Development: An Ecological Perspective*, eds. G. W. Evans and T. D. Wachs, pp. 3–13. Washington, DC: American Psychological Association.
Waldron, J. 1992. Lex Talionis. *Arizona Law Review* 34: 25–51.
Walen, A. 2010. Crime, culpability and moral luck: Comments on Alexander, Ferzan and Morse. *Law and Philosophy* 29: 373–384.
Walen, A. 2014. Retributive justice. *The Stanford Encyclopedia of Philosophy*. Available at: https://plato.stanford.edu/entries/justice-retributive/.
Wallace, R. J. 1994. *Responsibility and the Moral Sentiments*. Cambridge, MA: Harvard University Press.
Western, B. 2015. Lifetimes of violence in a sample of released prisoners. *The Russell Sage Foundation Journal of the Social Sciences* 1(2): 14–30.
Western, B., A. A. Braga, J. Davis, and C. Sirois. 2015. Stress and hardship after prison. *American Journal of Sociology* 120: 1512–1547.

Yaffe, G. 2018. *The Age of Culpability: Children and the Nature of Criminal Responsibility*. New York: Oxford University Press.
Yoffe, E. 2017. Innocence is irrelevant: This is the age of the plea bargain – and millions of Americans are suffering the consequences. *The Atlantic* (September Issue). Available at: www.theatlantic.com/magazine/archive/2017/09/innocence-is-irrelevant/534171/.
Zaibert, L. 2018. *Rethinking Punishment*. Cambridge: Cambridge University Press.
Zimmerman, M. 2006. Only a fool becomes a King: Buddhist stances on punishment. In *Buddhism and Violence*, ed. M. Zimmerman, pp. 213–242. Lumbini, Nepal: International Research Institute.
Zimmerman, M. 2011. *The Immorality of Punishment*. New York: Broadview Press.
Zlodre, J. and S. Fazel. 2012. All-cause and external mortality in released prisoners: A systemic view and meta-analysis. *American Journal of Public Health* 102(12): 67–75.

5 CONSEQUENTIALIST, EDUCATIONAL, AND MIXED THEORIES OF PUNISHMENT

Afifi, T. O., D. Ford, E. T. Gershoff, M. Merrick, A. Grogan-Kaylor, K. A. Ports, H. L. MacMillan, G. W. Holden, C. A. Taylor, S. J. Lee, and R. P. Bennett. 2017. Spanking and adult mental health impairment: The case for the designation of spanking as an adverse childhood experience. *Childhood Abuse and Negligence* 71: 24–31.
Bartle, J. 2019. We know that prison doesn't work. So what are the alternatives? *The Guardian*, Friday, August 16, 2019. Available at: www.theguardian.com/commentisfree/2019/aug/16/we-know-that-prison-doesnt-work-so-what-are-the-alternatives.
Bentham, J. 1823/1948. *An Introduction to the Principles of Morals and Legislation*. New York: Macmillan.
Boonin, D. 2008. *The Problem of Punishment*. New York: Cambridge University Press.
Bulow, W. 2018. Deserved delayed release? The communicative theory of punishment and indeterminate prison sentences. *Criminal Justice Ethics* 37(2): 164–181.
Cochrane, A. 2017. Prison on appeal: The idea of communicative incarceration. *Criminal Law and Philosophy* 11(2): 295–312.
Dagger, R. 2011. Jean Hampton's theory of punishment: A critical appreciation. *APA Newsletter on Philosophy of Law* 10(2): 6–11.
Dolinko, D. 1991. Some thoughts about retributivism. *Ethics* 101: 537–599.
Doob, A. and C. Webster. 2003. Sentencing severity and crime: Accepting the null hypothesis. *Crime and Justice* 30: 143–195.
Duff, R. A. 1986. *Trials and Punishment*. New York: Cambridge University Press.
Duff, R. A. 1996. Penal communications: Recent work in the philosophy of punishment. *Crime and Justice* 20: 1–97.
Duff, R. A. 1999. Penal communities. *Punishment and Society* 1(1): 27–43.
Duff, R. A. 2001. *Punishment, Communication, and Community*. New York: Oxford University Press.
Duff, R. A. 2003. Penance, punishment and the limits of community. *Punishment and Society* 5(3): 295–312.
Duff, R. A. 2009. Can we punish the perpetrators of atrocities? In *The Religious in Response to Mass Atrocity: Interdisciplinary Perspectives*, eds. T. Brudholm and T. Cushman, pp. 79–104. Cambridge: Cambridge University Press.

Duff, R. A. 2017. Legal punishment. *Stanford Encyclopedia of Philosophy*. Available at: https://plato.stanford.edu/entries/legal-punishment/.

Durrant, J. and R. Ensom. 2012. Physical punishment of children: Lessons from 20 years of research. *Canadian Medical Association Journal* 184(12): 1373–1377.

Engen, A. 2014. Communication, expression, and the justification of punishment. *Athens Journal of Humanities and Arts* 1(4): 299–307.

Feinberg, J. 1970. The expressive function of punishment. In *Doing and Deserving*, ed. J. Feinberg, pp. 95–118. Princeton: Princeton University Press.

Gendreau, P., C. Goggin, and F. T. Cullen. 1999. *The Effects of Prison Sentences on Recidivism*. Ottawa, Ontario, Canada: Public Works and Government Services Canada.

Gendreau, P., T. Little, and C. Goggin. 1996. A meta-analysis of adult offender recidivism: What works! *Criminology* 34(4): 575–607.

Gert, H., L. Radzik, and M. Hand. 2004. Hampton on the expressive power of punishment. *Journal of Social Philosophy* 35(1): 79–90.

Hampton, J. 1984. The moral education theory of punishment. *Philosophy and Public Affairs* 13: 208–238.

Hampton, J. 1991. A new theory of retribution. In *Liability and Responsibility: Essays in Law and Morals*, eds. R. G. Frey and C. W. Morris, pp. 377–414. New York: Cambridge University Press.

Hampton, J. 1992. Correcting harms versus righting wrongs: The goal of retribution. *UCLA Law Review* 39: 1659–1702.

Hampton, J. 1992. An expressive theory of retribution. In *Retributivism and Its Critics*, ed. W. Cragg, pp. 1–25. Stuttgart: Franz Steiner Verlag.

Hampton, J. 1994. Liberalism, retribution and criminality. In *In Harm's Way: Essays in Honor of Joel Feinberg*, eds. J. Coleman and A. Buchanan, pp. 159–182. New York: Cambridge University Press.

Hampton, J. 1998. Punishment, feminism, and political identity: A case study in the expressive meaning of the law. *Canadian Journal of Law and Jurisprudence* 11(1): 23–45.

Hampton, J. and J. G. Murphy. 1988. *Forgiveness and Mercy*. New York: Cambridge University Press.

Hanna, N. 2008. Say what? A critique of expressive retributivism. *Law and Philosophy* 27(2): 123–150.

Harding, D. J., J. D. Morenoff, A. P. Nguyen, S. D. Bushway, and I. A. Binswanger. 2019. A natural experiment study of the effect of imprisonment on violence in the community. *Nature Human Behavior* 3: 671–677.

Honderich, T. 2006. *Punishment: The Supposed Justification Revisited*. Ann Arbor, MI: Pluto Press.

Kazdin, A. E. and C. Benjet. 2003. Spanking children: Evidence and issues. *Current Directions in Psychological Science* 12(3): 99–103.

Lee, A. 2017. Defending a communicative theory of punishment: The relationship between hard treatment and amends. *Oxford Journal of Legal Studies* 37(1): 217–237.

Levin, M. A. 1971. Policy evaluations and recidivism. *Law and Society Review* 6(1): 17–46.

Marshall, M. J. 2002. *Why Spanking Doesn't Work: Stopping This Bad Habit and Getting the Upper Hand on Effective Discipline*. Springville, Utah: Bonneville Books.

Matravers, M. 2006. Who's still standing? A comment on Antony's Duff's preconditions of criminal liability. *Journal of Moral Philosophy* 3(3): 320–330.

Matravers, M. 2011. Duff on hard treatment. In *Crime, Punishment and Responsibility: The Jurisprudence of Antony Duff*, eds. R. Cruft, M. H. Kramer, and M. R. Reiff, pp. 68–86. New York: Oxford University Press.

McCloskey, H. J. 1972. A non-utilitarian approach to punishment. In *Philosophical Perspectives on Punishment*, ed. G. Ezorsky, pp. 119–134. Albany, NY: State University of New York Press.

Montague, P. 1995. *Punishment as Societal-Defense*. New York: Rowman & Littlefield.
Montague, P. 2009. Revisiting the censure theory of punishment. *Philosophia* 37(1): 125–131.
Mumola, C. 1999. Substance abuse and treatment, state and federal prisoners, 1997. *Bureau of Justice Statistics Report*. www.bjs.gov/content/pub/pdf/satsfp97.pdf
Murtagh, K. J. 2019. Free will skepticism, general deterrence, and the "use" objection. In *Free Will Skepticism in Law and Society: Challenging Retributive Justice*, eds. E. Shaw, D. Pereboom, and G. D. Caruso, pp. 139–158. New York: Cambridge University Press.
Nagin, D. S. 2013. Deterrence in the twenty-first century. In *Crime and Justice in America 1975–2025*, ed. M. Tonry, pp. 199–264. Chicago: University of Chicago Press.
Nagin, D. and G. Pogarsky. 2001. Integrating celerity, impulsivity, and extralegal sanction threats into a model of general deterrence: Theory and evidence. *Criminology* 39(4).
National Research Council. 2012. *Deterrence and the Death Penalty*. Washington, DC: The National Academies Press. https://doi.org/10.17226/13363.
Pereboom, D. 2001. *Living without Free Will*. New York: Cambridge University Press.
Pereboom, D. 2014. *Free Will, Agency, and Meaning in Life*. New York: Oxford University Press.
Pereboom, D. 2020. Incapacitation, reintegration, and limited general deterrence. *Neuroethics* 31(1): 87–97.
Radelet, M. L. and T. L. Lacock. 2009. Do executions lower homicide rates? The views of leading criminologists. *Criminal Law and Criminology* 99(2): 489–508.
Schinkel, M. 2014. Punishment as moral communication: The experiences of long-term prisoners. *Punishment and Society* 16(5): 578–597.
Sentencing Project. 2010. *Deterrence in Criminal Justice: Evaluating Certainty vs. Severity of Punishment*. Washington, DC: The Sentencing Project.
Shaw, E. 2019. Justice without moral responsibility? *Journal of Information Ethics* 28(1): 95–130.
Song, L. and R. Lieb. 1993. *Recidivism: The Effect of Incarceration and Length of Time Served*. Olympia, WA: Washington State Institute of Public Policy.
Sverdlik, S. 2014. Punishment and reform. *Criminal Law and Philosophy* 8(3): 619–633.
Tadros, V. 2011. *The Ends of Harm: The Moral Foundations of Criminal Law*. New York: Oxford University Press.
Ten, C. L. 1987. *Crime, Guilt, and Punishment*. Oxford: Clarendon Press.
Tunick, M. 1992. *Punishment Theory and Practice*. Los Angeles, CA: University of California Press.
Vitiello, M. 2002. Three strikes laws: A real or imagined deterrent to crime? *American Bar Association*. April 1, 2002. Available at: www.americanbar.org/groups/crsj/publications/human_rights_magazine_home/human_rights_vol29_2002/spring2002/hr_spring02_vitiello/.
Vitiello, M. 2004. Reforming three strikes' excesses. *Washington University Law Quarterly* 82 (1): 1–42.
Von Hirsch, A. 2003. Punishment, penance and the state: A reply to Duff. In *Debates in Contemporary Political Philosophy: An Anthology*, eds. D. Matravers and J. E. Pike, pp. 408–422. New York: Routledge.
Zaibert, L. 2018. *Rethinking Punishment*. New York: Cambridge University Press.
Zimmerman, M. J. 2011. *The Immorality of Punishment*. New York: Broadview Press.

6 PUBLIC HEALTH–QUARANTINE MODEL I: A NONRETRIBUTIVE APPROACH TO CRIMINAL BEHAVIOR

Anderson, E. 1999. What is the point of equality? *Ethics* 109(2): 287–337.
Baum, N. M., S. E. Gollust, and P. D. Jacobson. 2007. Looking ahead: Addressing ethical challenges in public health practice. *The Journal of Law, Medicine, and Ethics* 35(4): 657–667.

Beauchamp, T. and J. Childdress. 1989. *Principles of Biomedical Ethics*, 3rd edition. New York: Oxford University Press.

Bergelson, V. 2013. The duty to protect the victim – or the duty to suffer punishment? *Law and Philosophy* 32(2–3): 199–215.

Berlin, I. 1969. Two concepts of liberty. In *Four Essays on Liberty*, pp. 118–172. Oxford: Oxford University Press.

Caruso, G. D. and D. Pereboom. 2020. A non-punitive alternative to punishment. In *Routledge Handbook of the Philosophy and Science of Punishment*, eds. F. Focquaert, B. Waller, and E. Shaw, pp. 355–365. New York: Routledge.

Celello, P. 2014. Desert. *Internet Encyclopedia of Philosophy*. Available at: www.iep.utm.edu/desert/#H3.

Childress, J. F., R. R. Faden, R. D. Gaare, L. O. Gostin, J. Kahn, R. J. Bonnie, N. E. Kass, A. C. Mastroianni, J. D. Moreno, and P. Nieburg. 2002. Public health ethics: Mapping the terrain. *The Journal of Law, Medicine, and Ethics* 30(2): 170–178.

Claasen, R. 2016. An agent-based capability theory of justice. *European Journal of Philosophy* 24(3): 220–236.

Cohen, J. 1989. Democratic quality. *Ethics* 99: 727–751.

Cohen, Y. 2018. Deliberating in the presence of manipulation. *Canadian Journal of Philosophy* 48(1): 85–105.

Darwall, S. 1992. Internalism and agency. *Philosophical Perspectives* 6: 155–174.

Demetriou, K. 2010. The soft-line solution to Preboom's four-case argument. *Australasian Journal of Philosophy* 88(4): 595–617.

Dennett, D. C. 1984. *Elbow Room*. Cambridge: MIT Press.

Duff, R. A. 2013. Punishment and the duties of offenders. *Law and Philosophy* 32(1): 109–127.

Faden, R. and S. Shebaya. 2015. Public health ethics. *Stanford Encyclopedia of Philosophy*. http://plato.stanford.edu/entries/publichealth-ethics/.

Feldman, F. and B. Skow. 2015. Desert. *Stanford Encyclopedia of Philosophy*. Available at: https://plato.stanford.edu/entries/desert/#Justice.

Ferzan, K. K. 2005. Justifying self-defense. *Law and Philosophy* 24: 711–748.

Ferzan, K. K. 2013. Rethinking the end of harm. *Law and Philosophy* 32: 177–198.

Ferzan, K. K. and A. Grabczynska. 2009. Justifying killing in self-defence. *Journal of Criminal Law and Criminology* 99: 235–254.

Frowe, H. 2009. The justifiable infliction of unjust harm. *Proceedings of the Aristotelian Society* 109: 345–351.

Ginet, C. 1966. Might we have no choice? In *Freedom and Determinism*, ed. K. Lehrer, pp. 87–104. New York: Random House.

Gostin, L. O. 2012. A framework convention on global health: Health for all, justice for all. *Journal of the American Medical Association* 307(19): 2087–2092.

Haji, I. 2012. *Reason's Debt to Freedom*. New York: Oxford University Press.

Hume, D. 1983. *An Enquiry Concerning the Principles of Morals*. Edited by J. B. Schneewind. Indianapolis, IN: Hackett.

Institute of Medicine (USA). 2003. *The Future of the Public's Health in the 21st Century*. Washington: National Academies Press.

Jeppsson, S. 2016. Reasons, determinism and the ability to do otherwise. *Ethical Theory and Moral Practice* 19(5): 1225–1240.

Kant, I. 1785/1981. *Grounding for the Metaphysics of Morals*. Translated by J. Ellington. Indianapolis, IN: Hacket.

Kapitan, T. 1986. Deliberation and the presumption of open alternatives. *Philosophical Quarterly* 36: 230–251.

Kapitan, T. 1996. Modal principles in the metaphysics of free will. *Philosophical Perspective* 10: 419–445.
Kass, N. E. 2001. An ethical framework for public health. *American Journal of Public Health* 91 (11): 1776–1782.
Kelly, E. 2012. Desert and fairness in criminal justice. *Philosophical Topics* 40(1): 63–77.
Leverick, F. 2006. *Killing in Self-Defence*. New York: Oxford University Press.
Lippert-Rasmussen, K. 2015. "To serve and protect:" The ends of harm by Victor Tadros. *Criminal Law and Philosophy* 9: 49–71.
McCloskey, H. J. 1957. An examination of restricted utilitarianism. *Philosophical Review* 66 (4): 466–485.
Mele, A. 2006. *Free Will and Luck*. New York: Oxford University Press.
Mill, J. S. 1869. *On Liberty and Other Essays* (2nd edition). New York: Oxford University Press.
Moriarty, J. 2002. Desert and distributive justice in a theory of justice. *Journal of Social Philosophy* 33(1): 131–143.
Nelkin, D. 2004. Deliberative alternatives. *Philosophical Topics* 32(1): 215–240.
Nelkin, D. 2011. *Making Sense of Freedom and Responsibility*. New York: Oxford University Press.
Nelkin, D. 2019. Duties, desert, and the justification of punishment. *Criminal Law and Philosophy* 13(3): 425–438.
Nozick, R. 1974. *Anarchy, State, and Utopia*. New York: Basic Books.
Nuffield Council of Bioethics. 2007. *Public Health: Ethical Issues*. Cambridge: Cambridge Publishers.
Nussbaum, M. 1988. Nature, function, and capability: Aristotle on political distribution. In *Oxford Studies in Ancient Philosophy*, eds. J. Annas and R. Grimm, pp. 145–184. Oxford: Clarendon Press.
Nussbaum, M. 1992. Human functioning and social justice: In defense of Aristotelian essentialism. *Political Theory* 20(2): 202–246.
Nussbaum, M. 1997. Capabilities and human rights. *Fordham Law Review* 66: 273.
Nussbaum, M. 2000. *Women and Human Development*. Cambridge: Cambridge University Press.
Nussbaum, M. 2003. Capabilities as fundamental entitlements: Sen and social justice. *Feminist Economics* 9(2–3): 33–59.
Nussbaum, M. 2006. *Frontiers of Justice*. Cambridge, MA: The Belknap Press.
Nussbaum, M. 2011. *Creating Capabilities: The Human Development Approach*. Cambridge, MA: The Belknap Press of Harvard University Press.
Pereboom, D. 2001. *Living without Free Will*. New York: Cambridge University Press.
Pereboom, D. 2013. Free will skepticism and criminal punishment. In *The Future of Punishment*, ed. T. Nadelhoffer, pp. 49–78. New York: Oxford University Press.
Pereboom, D. 2014. *Free Will, Agency, and Meaning in Life*. Oxford: Oxford University Press.
Pereboom, D. and G. D. Caruso. 2018. Hard-incompatibilist existentialism: Neuroscience, punishment, and meaning in life. In *Neuroexistentialism: Meaning, Morals, and Purpose in the Age of Neuroscience*, eds. G. D. Caruso and O. Flanagan, pp. 193–222. New York: Oxford University Press.
Pettit, P. 1989. Determinism and deliberation. *Analysis* 49: 42–44.
Pettit, P. 2003. Agency-freedom and option-freedom. *Journal of Theoretical Politics* 15(4): 387–403.
Phua, K.-L. 2013. Ethical dilemmas in protecting individual rights versus public protection in the case of infectious diseases. *Infection Diseases: Research and Treatment* 6: 1–5.
Powers, M. and R. Faden. 2006. *Social Justice: The Moral Foundations of Public Health and Health Policy*. New York: Oxford University Press.

Rawls, J. 1971. *A Theory of Justice*. Cambridge, MA: Harvard University Press.
Robeyns, I. 2017. *Wellbeing, Freedom, and Social Justice: The Capabilities Approach Re-Examined*. Cambridge, UK: Open Books.
Schoeman, F. 1979. On incapacitating the dangerous. *American Philosophical Quarterly* 16: 27–35.
Sen, A. 1980. *The Tanner Lectures on Human Values*. ed. S. McMurrin. Salt Lake City: University of Utah Press.
Sen, A. 1984. *Resources, Values, and Development*. Oxford: Basil Blackwell.
Sen, A. 1985. *Commodities and Capabilities*. Oxford: Oxford University Press.
Sen, A. 1992. *Inequality Reexamined*. Cambridge, MA: Harvard University Press.
Sen, A. 1999. *Development as Freedom*. New York: Oxford University Press.
Sen, A. 2009. *The Idea of Justice*. New York: Penguin Books.
Shaw, E. 2019. Justice without moral responsibility? *Journal of Information Ethics* 28(1): 95–130.
Sher, G. 1987. *Desert*. Princeton: Princeton University Press.
Smilansky, S. 2019. Free will denial and deontological constraints. In *Free Will Skepticism in Law and Society: Challenging Retributive Justice*, eds. E. Shaw, D. Pereboom, and G. D. Caruso, pp. 29–42. New York: Cambridge University Press.
Stapleton, S. 2010. Hard Incompatibilist Challenges to Morality and Autonomy. Dissertation. Department of Philosophy, Cornell University, Ithaca NY. https://ecommons.cornell.edu/handle/1813/17665
Tabandeh, A., P. Gardoni, and C. Murphy. 2017. A reliability-based capability approach. *Risk Analysis* 38(2): 410–424.
Tadros, V. 2011. *The Ends of Harm: The Moral Foundations of Criminal Law*. New York: Oxford University Press.
Taylor, R. 1966. *Action and Purpose*. Englewood Cliffs, NJ: Prentice-Hall Inc.
Thomas, J. C., M. Sage, J. Dillenberg, and V. J. Guillory. 2002. A code of ethics for public health. *American Journal of Public Health* 92(7): 1057–1059.
Thomson, J. J. 1986. Self-defense and rights. In *Rights, Restitution, and Risk*, ed. W. Parent, 33–48. Cambridge, MA: Harvard University Press.
Thomson, J. J. 1991. Self-defense. *Philosophy and Public Affairs* 20: 283–310.
Uniacke, S. 1994. *Permissible Killing*. New York: Cambridge University Press.
Uniacke, S. 2015. Punishment as penalty. *Criminal Law and Philosophy* 9(1): 37–47.
Van Inwagen, P. 1983. *An Essay on Free Will*. New York: Oxford University Press.
Venkatapuram, S. 2011. *Health Justice: An Argument from the Capabilities Approach*. Cambridge: Polity Press.
Vilhaeur, B. 2009. Free will skepticism and personhood as a desert base. *Canadian Journal of Philosophy* 39(3): 489–511.
Vilhaeur, B. 2013a. The people problem. In *Exploring the Illusion of Free Will and Moral Responsibility*, ed. G. D. Caruso, pp. 141–160. Lanham, MD: Lexington Books.
Vilhauer, B. 2013b. Persons, punishment, and free will skepticism. *Philosophical Studies* 162 (2): 143–163.
Wallerstein, S. 2005. Justifying the right to self-defense: A theory of forced consequences. *Virginia Law Review* 91: 999–1035.
Wallerstein, S. 2009. Why causal responsibility matters. In *Criminal Law Conversations*, eds. P. Robinson, S. Garvey, and K. Kessler, pp. 396–397. New York: Oxford University Press.
Wasserman, D. 1987. Justifying self-defense. *Philosophy and Public Affairs* 16: 356–378.
Whitehouse, P., E. Juengst, M. Mehlman, and T. Murray. 1997. Enhancing cognition in the intellectually intact. *Hastings Center Report* 27: 14–22.

Wilkinson, T. M. 2007. Contagious disease and self-defence. *Res Publica* 13(4): 339–359.
Wolff, J. and A. de-Shalit. 2007. *Disadvantage*. New York: Oxford University Press.

7 PUBLIC HEALTH–QUARANTINE MODEL II: THE SOCIAL
DETERMINANTS OF HEALTH AND CRIMINAL BEHAVIOR

Acheson, D., D. Barkers, J. Chambers, H. Graham, M. Marmot, and M. Whitehead. 1998. *Independent Inquiry into Inequalities in Health Report*. London: Stationary Office.
American Civil Liberties Union. 2011. Prison Rape Elimination Act of 2002 (PREA). www.aclu.org/other/prison-rape-elimination-act-2003-prea.
Adams, A. E., R. M. Tolman, D. Bybee, C. M. Sullican, and A. C. Kennedy. 2013. The impact of intimate partner violence on low-income women's economic well-being: The mediating role of job stability. *Violence Against Women* 18: 1345–1367.
Adler, N. E., T. Boyce, M. A. Chesney, S. Cohen, S. Folk man, R. L. Kahn, and S. I. Syme. 1994. Socioeconomic status and health: The challenge of the gradient. *American Psychologist* 49: 15–24. www.semanticscholar.org/paper/Socioeconomic-status-and-health.-The-challenge-of-Adler-Boyce/db3ec5962ef688a1f0cc331bbd2f5a2496e424b3
Aizer, A. and J. Currie. 2017. Lead and juvenile delinquency: New evidence for linked birth, school and juvenile detention records. *National Bureau of Economic Research*, May 2017, no. 23392. www.nber.org/system/files/working_papers/w23392/w23392.pdf
Akil, L. and H. A. Ahmad. 2011. Effects of socioeconomic factors on obesity rates in four southern states and Colorado. *Ethnicity and Disease* 21(1): 58–62.
American Academy of Pediatrics Committee on Environmental Health. 2003. *Pediatric Environmental Health*, 2nd edition. Elk Grove Village, IL: American Academy of Pediatrics.
American Psychological Association. 2017. Violence and socioeconomic status fact sheet. Available at: www.apa.org/pi/ses/resources/publications/factsheet-violence.pdf.
American Public Health Association. 2017. Environmental health. Accessed on September 2, 2017: www.apha.org/topics-and-issues/environmental-health.
American Public Health Association. 2018. Violence is a public health issue: Public health is essential to understanding and treating violence in the U.S. Policy number: 20185. Available at: https://apha.org/policies-and-advocacy/public-health-policy-statements/policy-database/2019/01/28/violence-is-a-public-health-issue.
Anderson, J. M., M. Buenaventura, and P. Heaton. 2019. *Holistic Representation: An Innovative Approach to Defending Poor Clients Can Reduce Incarceration and Save Taxpayer Dollars– Without Harm to Public Safety*. RAND Corporation. Available at: www.rand.org/pubs/research_briefs/RB10050.html.
Anderson, N. E. and C. A. Armstead. 1995. Toward understanding the association of socioeconomic status and health: A new challenge for the biopsychosocial approach. *Psychosomatic Medicine* 57: 213–225.
Anderson, N. E. and K. A. Kiehl. 2014. Psychopathy: Developmental perspectives and their implications for treatment. *Restorative Neurology Neuroscience* 32(1): 103–117.
Andrews, D. A., J. Bonta, and I. Hoge. 1990. Classification for effective rehabilitation: Rediscovering psychology. *Criminal Justice and Behavior* 17(1): 19–52.
Bailey, K. 2012. Dying for coverage: The consequences of being uninsured. Families USA. http://familiesusa.org/product/dying-coverage-deadly-consequences-being-uninsured.
Bellinger, D. C., K. M. Stiles, and H. L. Needleman. 1992. Low-level lead exposure, intelligence, and academic achievement: A long-term follow-up study. *Pediatrics* 90(6): 855–861.

Berkman. L. and A. M. Epstein. 2008. Beyond health care: Socioeconomic status and health. *New England Journal of Medicine* 358(23): 2509–2510.
Billings, S. B. and K. T. Schnepel. 2015. *Life after Lead: Effects of Early Interventions for Children Exposed to Lead.* ARC Centre of Excellence for Children and Families over the Life Course. No. 2015-18. https://pubs.aeaweb.org/doi/pdfplus/10.1257/app.20160056
Binswanger, I. A., P. J. Blatchford, S. R. Mueller, and M. F. Stern. 2013. Mortality after prison release: Opioid overdose and other causes of death, risk factors, and time trends from 1999 to 2009. *Annuals of Internal Medicine* 159(9): 592–600.
Binswanger, I. A., M. F. Stern, R. A. Deyo, P. J. Heagerty, A. Cheadle, J. G. Elmore, and T. D. Koepsell. 2007. Release from prison – a high risk of death for former inmates. *New England Journal of Medicine* 256(2): 157–165.
Birbaumer, N., R. Veit, M. Lotze, M. Erb, C. Hermann, W. Grodd, and H. Flor. 2005. Deficient fear conditioning in psychopathy: A functional magnetic resonance imaging study. *Archives of General Psychiatry* 62(7): 799–805.
Blau, D. M. 1999. The effect of income on child development. *Review of Economic Statistics* 81: 261–276.
Bloom, B. 2004. The impact of California's parole policies on women. Testimony before the Little Hoover Commission, April 22, 2004. www.prisonlegalnews.org/news/publications/ca-women-on-parole-report/.
Blum, J., M. Ireland, and R. W. Blum. 2003. Gender differences in juvenile violence: A report from Add Health. *Journal of Adolescent Health* 32: 234–240.
Boccardi, M., G. B. Frisoni, R. D. Hare, E. Cavedo, P. Najt, and J. Tiihonen. 2011. Cortex and amygdala morphology in psychopaths. *Psychiatry Research: Neuroimaging* 193(2): 85–92.
Borofsky, L. A., I. Kellerman, B. Baucom, P. H. Oliver, and G. Margolin. 2013. Community violence exposure and adolescents' school engagement and academic achievement over time. *Psychology of Violence* 3: 1–15.
Bowker, L. 1980. *Prison Victimization.* New York: Elsevier.
Bradley, R. H. and R. F. Corwyn. 2002. Socioeconomic status and child development. *Annual Review of Psychology* 53: 371–399.
Bradley, R. H., R. F. Corwyn, M. Burchinal, H. P. McAdoo, and C. Garcia Coll. 2001. The home environments of children in the United States Part II: Relations and behavioral development through age thirteen. *Child Development* 72: 1868–1886.
Brito, N. H. and K. G. Noble. 2014. Socioeconomic status and structural brain development. *Frontiers in Neuroscience* 8: 276.
Brooks-Gunn, J. and G. J. Duncan. 1997. The effects of poverty on children. *Future Child* 7: 55–71.
Bullard, R. 1983. Solid waste sites and the black Houston community. *Sociological Inquiry* 53 (2–3): 273–288.
Bullard, R. 1987. *Invisible Houston: The Black Experience in Boom and Bust.* College Station, Tex.: Texas A&M University Press.
Bullard, R. 1990. *Dumping in Dixie: Race, Class, and Environmental Quality.* Boulder, Co.: Westview Press.
Bullard, R. 2010. Overcoming racism in environmental decision making. *Environment: Science and Policy for Sustainable Development* 36(4): 10–44. Reprinted in *Environmental Ethics: Readings in Theory and Application,* 5th edition, eds. L. P. Pojman and P. Pojman, pp. 644–659. Wadsworth, Cengage Learning.
Burns, J. M., P. A. Baghurst, M. G. Sawyer, A. J. McMichael, and S. L. Tong. 1999. Lifetime low-level exposure to environmental lead and children's emotional and behavioral development at ages 11–13 years. The Port Pirie Cohort study. *American Journal of Epidemiology* 149: 740–749.

Buss, C., C. Lord, M. Wadiwalla, D. H. Hellhammer, S. J. Lupiens, M. Meaney, and J. C. Pruessner. 2007. Maternal care modulates the relationship between prenatal risk and hippocampal volume in women but not in men. *Journal of Neuroscience* 27: 2592–2595.

Butts, J. A. and S. Delgado. 2017. *Repairing Trust: Young Men in Neighborhoods with Cure Violence Programs Report Growing Confidence in Police*. New York: John Jay College of Criminal Justice, Research and Evaluation Center.

Butts, J. A., C. G. Roman, L. Bostwick, and J. R. Porter. 2015. Cure violence: A public health model to reduce gun violence. *Annual Review of Public Health* 36: 39–53.

Buydens-Branchey, L., M. Branchey, and J. R. Hibbeln. 2008. Associations between increases in plasma n-3 polyunsaturated fatty acids following supplementation and decreases in anger and anxiety in substance abusers. *Progress in Neuro-Psychopharmacology and Biological Psychiatry* 32(2): 568–575.

Caldwell, M. F. and G. J. Van Rybroek. 2001. Efficacy of a decompression treatment model in the clinical management of violent juvenile offenders. *International Journal of Offender Therapy* 45(4): 469–477.

Caldwell, M. F. and G. J. Van Rybroek. 2005. Reducing violence in serious and violent juvenile offenders using intensive treatment. *International Journal Law. Psychiatry* 28(6): 622–636.

Carlen, P. 1988. *Women, Crime, and Poverty*. Philadelphia: Open University Press.

Carson, E. A. 2016. *Prisoners in 2015*. Washington, DC: US Department of Justice, Bureau of Justice Statistics.

Center for Climate and Security. 2016. *The Climate and Security Advisory Group: Briefing Book for New Administration*. https://climateandsecurity.files.wordpress.com/2016/09/climate-and-security-advisory-group_briefing-book-for-a-new-administration_2016_11.pdf.

Center for Nonviolence and Social Justice. 2019. *Healing Hurt People*. Available at: https://drexel.edu/cnvsj/healing-hurt-people/overview/.

Centers for Disease Control and Prevention. 2014. *Essentials for Childhood: Steps to Create Safe, Stable, Nurturing Relationships and Environments*. Available at: www.cdc.gov/violenceprevention/pdf/essentials_for_childhood_framework.pdf.

Centers for Disease Control and Prevention. 2016. Adverse childhood experiences (ACEs). Available at: www.cdc.gov/violenceprevention/acestudy/index.html.

Centers for Disease Control and Prevention. 2019. The public health approach to violence prevention. Downloaded on December 28, 2019: www.cdc.gov/violenceprevention/publichealthissue/publichealthapproach.html.

Cerdá, M., J. D. Morenoff, B. B. Hansen, K. J. Tessari Hicks, L. F. Duque, A. Restrepo, and A. V. Diez-Roux. 2012. Reducing violence by transforming neighborhoods: A natural experiment in Medellin, Colombia. *American Journal of Epidemiology* 175(10): 1045–1053.

Cerdá, M., M. Tracy, and K. M. Keyes. 2018. Reducing urban violence: A contrast of public health and criminal justice approaches. *Epidemiology* 29(1): 142–150.

Chen, E. 2004. Why socioeconomic status affects the health of children. *Current Directions in Psychological Science* 13(3): 112–115.

Chen, E., K. A. Matthews, and W. T. Boyce. 2002. Socioeconomic differences in children's health: How and why do these relationships change with age? *Psychological Bulletin* 126: 295–329.

Chung, J. 2016. *Felony Disenfranchisement: A Primer*. The Sentencing Project. www.sentencingproject.org/publications/felony-disenfranchisement-a-primer/.

Cloud, D. 2014. *On Life Support: Public Health in the Age of Mass Incarceration*. New York: Vera Institute of Justice. Available at: www.vera.org/publications/on-life-support-public-health-in-the-age-of-mass-incarceration.

Cohen, S., G. A. Kaplan, and J. T. Salonen. 1999. The role of psychological characteristics in the relation between socioeconomic status and perceived health. *Journal of Applied Social Psychology* 29: 445–468.

Conboy, B. T. and P. K. Kuhl. 2007. Early speech perception: Developing a culturally specific way of listening through social interaction. In *On Being Moved: From Mirror Neurons to Empathy*, ed. S. Braten, pp. 175–199. Amsterdam: John Benjamins.

Cooper, C., D. Eslinger, and P. Stolley. 2006. Hospital-based violence intervention programs work. *Journal of Trauma* 61: 534–540.

Cornell, D. G., J. Warren, G. Hawk, E. Staffoed, G. Oram, and D. Pine. 1996. Psychopathy in instrumental and reactive violent offenders. *Journal of Consulting and Clinical Psychology* 64(4): 783–790.

Corrigan, F., R. Gray, A. Strathdee, R. Skinner, A, Van Rhijn, and D. Horrobin. 1994. Fatty acid analysis of blood from violent offenders. *Journal of Forensic Psychiatry* 5(1): 83–92.

Costner, P. and J. Thornton. 1990. *Playing with Fire*. Washington, DC: Greenpeace.

Covey, H. C., S. Menard, and R. J. Franzese. 2013. Effects of adolescent physical abuse, exposure to neighborhood violence, and witnessing parental violence on adult socioeconomic status. *Child Maltreatment* 18: 85–97.

Crooks, D., N. E. Anderson, M. Widdows, N. Petseva, M. Koenigs, C. Pluto, and K. A. Kiehl. 2018. The relationship between cavum septum pellucidum and psychopathic traits in a large forensic sample. *Neuropsychologia* 112: 95–104.

Crowne, S. S., H. S. Juon, M. Ensminger, L. Burrell, E. McFarlane, and A. Duggan. 2011. Concurrent and long-term impact of intimate partner violence on employment stability. *Journal of Interpersonal Violence* 26: 1282–1304.

Dahlberg, L. L. and E. G. Krug. 2002. Violence: A global public health problem. In *World Report on Violence and Health*, eds. E. Krug, L. L. Dahlberg, J. A. Mercy, A. B. Zwi, and R. Lozano, pp. 1–56. World Health Organization.

Dahlberg, L. L. and J. A. Mercy. 2009. History of violence as a public health problem. *Virtual Mentor* 11: 167–172.

Daily Caller. 2014. Americans say "gun violence" is a criminal justice, not public-health issue, national poll finds. October 9, 2014. https://dailycaller.com/2014/10/09/americans-say-gun-violence-is-criminal-justice-not-public-health-issue-national-poll-finds/

Davis, K. 2003. *The Costs and Consequences of Being Uninsured*. New York, NY: The Commonwealth Fund.

Davis, M. 1997. Neurobiology of fear responses: The role of the amygdala. *Journal of Neuropsychiatry and Clinical Neuroscience* 9(3): 382–402.

Davis, M. and P. J. Whalen. 2001. The amygdala: Vigilance and emotion. *Molecular Psychiatry* 6(1): 13–34.

Davis, L. M., R. Bozick, J. L. Steele, J. Saunders, and J. N. V. Miles. 2013. *Evaluating the Effectiveness of Correctional Education: A Meta-Analysis of Programs That Provide Education to Incarcerated Adults*. Santa Monica, CA: RAND Corporation.

Deans, E. 2011. Diet and violence: Does diet affect our criminal behavior? *Psychology Today*, May 2, 2011. www.psychologytoday.com/blog/evolutionary-psychiatry/201105/diet-and-violence.

Delgado, S. A., L. Alsabahi, K. Wolff, N. Alexander, P. Cobar, and J. A. Butts. 2017. *The Effects of Cure Violence in the South Bronx and East New York, Brooklyn*. New York: John Jay College of Criminal Justice, Research and Evaluation Center.

De Oliveira-Souza, R., R. D. Hare, I. E. Bramati, G. J. Garrido, F. A. Ignácio, F. Tovar-Moll, and J. Moll. 2008. Psychopathy as a disorder of the moral brain: Fronto temporo-limbic grey matter reductions demonstrated by vox-based morphometry. *NeuroImage* 40(3): 1202–1213.

Department of Defense News. 2014. Hagel to address "threat multiplier" of climate change. DoD website: www.defense.gov/News/Article/Article/603440/.

Department of Defense, US 2015. *National Security Implications on Climate-Related Risks and Changing Climate.* http://archive.defense.gov/pubs/150724-congressional-report-on-national-implications-of-climate-change.pdf?source=govdelivery.

Diez-Roux, A. V., B. G. Link, and M. E. Northbridge. 2000. A multilevel analysis of income inequality and cardiovascular disease risk factors. *Social Science Medicine* 50: 673–687.

Doherty, M. 2015. Incarceration and Homelessness: Breaking the Cycle. E-*newsletter of the COPS Office* 8 (12). https://cops.usdoj.gov/html/dispatch/12-2015/incarceration_and_home lessness.asp.

Dolan, M. C. and R. S. Fullam. 2009. Psychopathy and functional magnetic resonance imaging blood oxygenation level-depend responses to emotional faces in violent patients with schizophrenia. *Biological Psychiatry* 66(6): 570–577.

D'Onofrio, B. M., J. A., Goodnight, C. A. Van Hulle, J. L. Rodgers, P. J. Rathouz, I. D. Waldman, and B. B. Lahey. 2009. A quasi-experimental analysis of the association between family income and offspring conduct problems. *Journal of Abnormal Child Psychology* 37: 415–429.

D'Onofrio, B. M., B. B. Lahey, E. Turkheimer, and P. Lichtenstein. 2013. Critical need for family-based, quasi-experimental designs in integrating genetic and social science research. *American Journal of Public Health* 103: 546–555.

Drum, K. 2016. Lead: American's real criminal element. *Mother Jones*, February 11, 2016. www.motherjones.com/environment/2016/02/lead-exposure-gasoline-crime-increase-children-health/.

Duncan, G. J. Brooks-Gunn, J. Yeung, and J. Smith. 1998. How much does childhood poverty affect the life chances of children? *American Sociological Review* 63: 406–423.

Durant, R. H., C. Cadenhead, R. A. Pendergrast, G. Slavens, and C. W. Linder. 1994. Factors associated with the use of violence among urban black adolescents. *American Journal of Public Health* 84: 612–617.

Eisman, A. B., S. A. Stoddard, J. Heinze. C. H. Caldwell, and M. A. Zimmerman. 2015. Depressive symptoms, social support, and violence exposure among urban youth: A longitudinal study of resilience. *Developmental Psychology* 51: 1307–1316.

Enamorado, T. and C. Rodriguez-Castelan. 2015. Income inequality and violent crime: Evidence from Mexico's drug war. *Journal of Developmental Economics* 120: 128–143.

Ermer, E., L. M. Cope, P. K. Nyalakanti, V. D. Calhoun, and K. A. Kiehl. 2011. Aberrant paralimbic gray matter in criminal psychopathy. *Journal of Abnormal Psychology* 121(3): 649–658.

Evans, G. W. 2006. Children development and the physical environment. *Annual review of Psychology* 57: 423–451.

Evans, J. R. 2006. *Forensic Applications of QEEG and Neurotherapy.* Informa Healthcare.

Fang, X., D. S. Brown, C. S. Florence, and J. A. Mercy. 2012. The economic burden of child maltreatment in the United States and implications for prevention. *Child Abuse and Neglect* 36: 156–165.

Feigenbaum, J. J. and C. Muller. 2016. Lead exposure and violent crime in the early twentieth century. *Explorations in Economic History* 62: 51–86.

Fergusson, D., N. Swain-Campbell, and J. Horwood. 2004. How does childhood economic disadvantage lead to crime? *Journal of Child Psychology and Psychiatry* 45(5): 956–966.

Finger, E. C., A. A. March, K. S. Blair, M. E. Reid, C. Sims, P. Ng, and J. R. Blair. 2011. Disruption reinforcement signaling in the orbitofrontal cortex and caudate in youth with conduct disorder or oppositional defiant disorder and high level of psychopathic traits. *American Journal of Psychiatry* 168(2): 152–162.

Flanagan, D. J., M. Singer, and K. Wester. 2001. Violence exposure, psychological trauma, and suicide risk in a community sample of dangerously violent adolescents. *Journal of the American Academy of Child and Adolescent Psychiatry* 40: 435–442.

Flanagan, D. J., M. Singer, L. Williams, and P. Castro. 1998. Adolescent violence exposure and victimization at home: Coping and psychological trauma symptoms. *International Review of Victimology* 6: 63–82.

Flannery, D. J., K. L. Wester, and M. Singer. 2004. Impact of exposure to violence in school on child and adolescent mental health and behavior. *Journal of Community Psychology* 32: 559–573.

Floud, J. E. and W. Young. 1981. *Dangerousness and Criminal Justice*. London: Heinemann.

Frank, J. W., C. M. Andrews, T. C. Green, A. M. Samuels, T. T. Trinh, and P. D. Friedmann. 2013. Emergency department utilization among recently released prisoners: A retrospective cohort study. *BMC Emergency Medicine* 13(1): 16.

Franks, P., P. C. Winters, D. J. Tancredi, and K. A. Fiscella. 2011. Do changes in traditional coronary heart disease risk factors over time explain the association between socio-economic status and coronary heart disease? *BMC Cardiovascular Disorders* 11: 28.

Frisell, T., P. Lichtenstein, and N. Langstrom. 2011. Violent crime runs in families: A total population study of 12.5 million individuals. *Psychological Medicine* 41: 97–105.

Galloway, T. A. and T. Skardhamar. 2010. Does parental income matter for onset of offending? *European Journal of Criminology* 7: 424–441.

Gesch, C. B., S. H. Hammond, S. E. Hampson, A. Eves, and M. J. Crowder. 2002. Influence of supplementary vitamins, minerals and essential fatty acids on the antisocial behavior of young adult prisoners. *The British Journal of Psychiatry* 181(1): 22–28.

Gilfus, M. 2002. Women's experiences of abuse as a risk factor for incarceration. *VAWnet Applied Research Forum, National Resource Center on Domestic Violence/Pennsylvania Coalition against Domestic Violence*. https://vawnet.org/sites/default/files/assets/files/2017-08/AR_Incarceration.pdf

Gkotsi, G.-M. and L. Benaroyo. 2012. Neuroscience and the treatment of mentally ill criminal offenders: Some ethics issues. *Journal of Ethics and Mental Health* 6: 1–7.

Glenn, A. L., A. Raine, P. S. Yaralian, and Y. Yang. 2010. Increased volume of the striatum in psychopathic individuals. *Biological Psychiatry* 67: 52–58.

Glenn, A. L., Y. Yang, and A. Raine. 2012. Neuroimaging in psychopathy and antisocial personality disorder: Functional significance and neurodevelopmental hypothesis. In *Neuroimaging in Forensic Psychiatry: From the Clinic to the Courtroom*, ed. J. R. Simpson, pp. 81–98. Oxford: Wiley-Blackwell.

Gordon, H. L., A. Baird, and A. End. 2004. Functional differences among those high and low on a trait measure of psychopathy. *Biological Psychiatry* 56(7): 516–521.

Gottfried, A. W., A. E. Gottfried, K. Bathrust, D. W. Guerin, and M. M. Parramore. 2003. Socioeconomic status in children's development and family environment: Infancy through adolescence. In *Socioeconomic Status, Parenting and Child Development*, eds. M. H. Bornstein and R. H. Bradley, pp. 189–207. Mahwah, NJ: Lawrence Erlbaum.

Gow, R. V., F. Vallee-Tourangeau, M. A. Crawford, E. Taylor, K. Ghebremeskl, A. A. Bueno, J. R. Hibbeln, A. Sumich, and K. Rubia. 2013. Omega-3 fatty acids are inversely related to callous and unemotional traits in adolescent boys with attention deficit hyperactivity disorder. *Prostaglandins Leukot Essent Fatty Acids* 88(6): 411–418.

Greenberg, G. A. and R. A. Rosenheck. 2008. Jail incarceration, homelessness, and mental health: A national study. *Psychiatry Service* 59(2): 170–177.

Gregory, S., R. J. Blair, D. Ffytche, A. Simmons, V. Kumari, S. Hodgins, and N. Blackwood. 2015. Punishment and psychopathy: A case-control functional MRI investigation of reinforcement learning in violent antisocial personality disorder men. *The Lancet* 2(2): 153–160.

Gregory, S., D. Ffytche, A. Simmons, V. Kumari, M. Howard, S. Hodgins, et al. 2012. The antisocial brain: Psychopathy matters. *Archives of General Psychiatry* 69: 962–972.

Gretemann, B. 2009. Improve mental health and neurofeedback. *Odewire Magazine*. March 1.

Hackman, D. A. and M. J. Farah. 2009. Socioeconomic status and the developing brain. *Trends in Cognitive Sciences* 13: 65–73.

Hackman, D. A., M. J. Farah, and M. J. Meaney. 2010. Socioeconomic status and the brain: Mechanistic insights from human and animal research. *National Review of Neuroscience* 11: 651–659.

Hager, E. 2018. The courts see a crime. These Lawyers see a whole life. *The Marshall Project*. November 12, 2018. Available at: www.themarshallproject.org/2018/11/12/the-courts-see-a-crime-these-lawyers-see-a-whole-life.

Hammond, C. D. 2011. What is neurofeedback; an update. *Journal of Neurotherapy* 15: 305–336.

Hao, L. and R. L. Matsueda. 2006. Family dynamics through childhood: A sibling model of behavior problems. *Social Science Research* 35: 500–524.

Hare, R. D. 1991. *The Hare Psychopathy Checklist-Revised*. Toronto, ON: Multi-Health Systems.

Hare, R. D. 2003. *The Hare Psychopathy Checklist-Revised, 2nd edition*. Toronto, ON: Multi-Health Systems.

Hare, R. D., D. Clark, and M. Grann. 2000. Psychopathy and the predictive validity of the PCL-R: An international perspective. *Behavioral Science and Law* 18: 623–645.

Hare, R. D. and C. S. Neumann. 2008. Psychopathy as a clinical and empirical construct. *Annual Review of Clinical Psychology* 4: 217–246.

Harenski, C. L., S. H. Kim, and S. Hamann. 2009. Neuroticism and psychopathy predict brain activation during moral and nonmoral emotion regulation. *Cognitive, Affective, and Behavioral Neuroscience* 9(1): 1–15.

Harlow, C. W. 2003. *Education and Correctional Populations*. Washington, DC: Department of Justice, Bureau of Justice Statistics. Available at: bjs.ojp.usdoj.gov/content/pub/pdf/ecp.pdf.

Hariss, G. T., M. E. Rice, and C. A. Cormier. 1991. Psychopathy and violent recidivism. *Law and Human Behavior* 15(6): 625–637.

Hart, B. and T. R. Risley. 1995. *Meaningful Differences in the Everyday Experience of Young American Children*. Baltimore, MD: Paul H. Brookes Publishing.

Hart, S. D., P. R. Kripp, and R. D. Hare. 1988. Performance of male psychopaths following conditional release from prison. *Journal of Consulting and Clinical Psychology* 56(2): 227–232.

Haviland, M., V. Frye, V. Rajah, J. Thukral, and M. Trinity. 2001. *The Family Protection and Domestic Violence Intervention Act of 1995. Examining the Effects of Mandatory Arrest in New York City*. New York: Family Violence Project, Urban Justice Center.

Heller, J. 2016. A framework connecting criminal justice and public health. Human Impact Partners and the National Criminal Justice and Public Health Alliance. www.humanimpact.org/from-the-hip-blog/a-framework-connecting-criminal-justice-and-public-health/.

Heller, S., A. H. A. Pollack, R. Ander, and J. Ludwig. 2013. Preventing youth violence and dropout: A randomized field experiment. Working Paper 19014. National Bureau of Economic Research, Cambridge, MA.

Hemenway, D. and M. Miller. 2013. Public health approach to the prevention of gun violence. *New England Journal of Medicine* 368: 2033–2035.

Hemphill, J. F., R. D. Hare, and S. Wong. 1988. Psychopathy and recidivism: A review. *Legal Criminology and Psychology* 3(1): 139–170.

Hibbeln, J. R. 2001. Seafood consumption and homicide mortality: A cross-national ecological analysis. *World Review of Nutrition and Dietetics* 88: 41–46.

Holzer, H. J., S. Raphael, and M. A. Stoll. 2003. *Employment Barriers Facing Ex-Offenders.* Washington, DC: The Urban Institute.

Human Rights Watch. 2004. *No Second Chance: People with Criminal Records Denied Access to Public Housing.* www.hrw.org/report/2004/11/17/no-second-chance/people-criminal-records-denied-access-public-housing.

Hummelstein, D. U., E. Warren, D. Thorne, and S. Woolhandler. 2005. Market Watch: Illness and injury as contributors to bankruptcy. *Health Affairs.* Available at: http://content.healthaffairs.org/content/suppl/2005/01/28/hlthaff.w5.63.DC1.

Institute of Medicine. 2002. *Care without Coverage: Too Little, Too Late.* Washington, DC: National Academy Press.

Institute of Medicine. 2009. *American's Uninsured Crisis: Consequences for Health and Health Care.* Washington, DC: National Academy Press.

Intergovernmental Panel on Climate Change (IPCC). 2014a. *Climate Change 2014: Synthesis Report.* Contribution of Working Groups I, II and III to the Fifth Assessment Report of the Intergovernmental Panel on Climate Change. www.ipcc.ch/report/ar5/syr/.

Intergovernmental Panel on Climate Change (IPCC). 2014b. *Climate Change 2014: Impacts, Adaptions, and Vulnerability.* www.ipcc.ch/report/ar5/wg2/.

Intergovernmental Panel on Climate Change (IPCC). 2014c. *Climate Change 2014: Mitigation of Climate Change.* www.ipcc.ch/report/ar5/wg3/.

Irwin, A., N. Valentine, C. Brown, R. Loewenson, O. Solar, H. Brown, T. Koller, and J. Vega. 2006. The commission on social determinants of health: Tackling the social roots of health inequalities. *PLos Med* 3(6): e106.

Irwin, J. 1980. *Prison in Turmoil.* Boston: Little Brown.

Jaffee, S. R., L. B. Strait, and C. L. Odgers. 2012. From correlates to causes: Can quasi-experimental studies and statistical innovation bring us closer to identifying the causes of antisocial behavior? *Psychological Bulletin* 138: 272–295.

James, D. J. and L. E. Glaze. 2006. *Mental Health Problems of Prison and Jail Inmates.* Washington, DC: Bureau of Justice Statistics. Available at: bjs.gov/content/pub/pdf/mhppji.pdf.

Jenkins, E. J. and C. C. Bell. 1994. Adolescent violence: Can it be curbed? *Adolescent Medicine* 1: 71–86.

Johnson, S. L., E. Wibbels, and R. Wilkinson. 2015. Economic inequality is related to cross-national prevalence of psychotic symptoms. *Social Psychiatry Psychiatric Epidemiology* 50: 1799–1807.

Jones, A. P., K. R. Laurens, C. M. Herba, G. J. Barker, and E. Viding. 2009. Amygdala hypoactivity to fearful faces in boys with conduct problems and callous unemotional traits. *American Journal of Psychiatry* 166(1): 95–102.

Jones, O. D. 2013. Seven ways neuroscience aids law. In *Neuroscience and the Human Person: New Perspectives on Human Activities,* eds. A. Battro, S. Deheane, and W. Singer, pp. 181–194. Vatican City: The Pontifical Academy of Sciences.

Jones, O. D., R. Marois, M. J. Farah, and H. T. Greely. 2013a. Law and neuroscience. *Journal of Neuroscience* 33(45): 17624–17630.

Jones, O. D., A. D. Wagner, D. L. Faigman, and M. E. Raichle. 2013b. Neuroscientists in court. *National Review of Neuroscience* 14(10): 730–736.

Jones, Peter, and Emma De Zoete. 2018. What does a "public health" approach to violence really mean? *Catch 22*, October 02. Available at: www.catch-22.org.uk/news/public-health-approach-to-violence/.

Kahn, R. S., P. H. Wise, and I. Kawachi. 2000. State income inequality, household income, and maternal mental and physical health: Cross sectional national survey. *BMJ* 321(7272): 1311–1215.

Katsiyannis, A., J. B. Ryan, D. Zhang, and A. Spann. 2008. Juvenile delinquency and recidivism: The impact of academic achievement. *Reading and Writing Quarterly* 24(2): 177–196.

Kawachi, I., B. P. Kennedy, K. Lochner, and D. Prothrow-Stith. 1997. Social capital, income inequality, and mortality. *American Journal of Public Health* 87: 1491–1498.

Kearney, M. S., B. H. Harris, E. Jacome, and L. Parker. 2014. Ten economic facts about crime and incarceration in the United States. Policy memo for The Hamilton Project. Available at: www.brookings.edu/research/ten-economic-facts-about-crime-and-incarceration-in-the-united-states/.

Kelly, M. 2000. Inequality and crime. *Review of Economics and Statistics* 82(4): 530–539.

Kendler, K. S., K. Sunquist, H. Ohisson, K. Palmer, H. Maes. M. A. Winkleby, and J. Sundquist. 2012. Genetic and family environmental influences on the risk for drug abuse: A national Swedish adoption study. *Archives of General Psychiatry* 69: 690–697.

Kennedy, B. O., I. Kawachi, and D. Prothrow-Stith. 1996. Income distribution and mortality: Cross sectional ecological study of the Robin Hood index in the United States. *BMJ* 312: 1004–1007.

Kiehl, K. A. and M. B. Hoffman. 2011. The criminal psychopath: History, neuroscience, treatment, and economics. *Jurimetrics* 51(4): 355–397.

Keihl, K. A., A. M. Smoth, R. D. Hare, A. Mendrek, B. B. Forster, J. Brink, and P. F. Liddle. 2001. Limbic abnormalities in affective processing by criminal psychopaths as revealed by functional magnetic resonance imaging. *Biological Psychiatry* 50(9): 677–684.

Kinney, P. L. 2008. Climate change, air quality, and human health. *American Journal of Preventive Medicine* 35(5): 459–467.

Koop, C. E. 1985. Surgeon General's workshop on violence and public health. Available at: www.nlm.nih.gov/exhibition/confrontingviolence/materials/OB10998.pdf.

Kuhl, P. K. 2007. Is speech learning "gated" by the social brain? *Developmental Science* 10: 110–120.

Kuhl, P. K., F. M. Tsao, and H. M. Liu. 2003. Foreign-language experience in infancy: Effects of short-term exposure and social interaction of phonetic learning. *Proceedings of the National Academy of Science, U.S.A.* 100: 9096–9101.

Lambert, S. F., K. Nylund-Gibson, N. Copeland-Linder, and N. S. Lalongo. 2010. Patterns of community violence exposure during adolescence. *American Journal of Community Psychology* 46(3–4): 289–302.

Lavelle, M. and M. Coyle. 1992. Unequal protection. *National Law Review* 21: 1–2.

Lawson, G. M., J. T. Duda, B. B. Avants, J. Wu, and M. J. Farah. 2013. Associations between children's socioeconomic status and prefrontal cortical thickness. *Developmental Science* 16: 641–652.

Lee, J. W. 2005. Public health is a social issue. *Lancet* 365: 1005–1006.

Leutgeb, V., M. Leitner, A. Wabnegger, D. Klug, W. Scharmuller, T. Zussner, and A. Schienie. 2015. Brain abnormalities in high-risk violent offenders and their association with psychopathic traits and criminal recidivism. *Neuroscience* 12(308): 194–201.

Leventhal, T. and J. Brooks-Gunn. 2000. The neighborhoods they live in: The effects of neighborhood residence on child and adolescent outcomes. *Psychological Bulletin* 126: 309–337.

Lewontin, R. 2000. *The Triple Helix: Gene, Organism and Environment*. Cambridge: Harvard University Press.
Liston, C., B. S. McEwen, and B. J. Casey. 2009. Psychosocial stress reversibly disrupts prefrontal processing and attentional control. *Proceedings of the National Academy of Science, U.S.A.* 106: 912–917.
Loring, M. T. and P. Beaudoin. 2000. Battered women as coerced victim-perpetrators. *Emotional Abuse* 3: 13.
Love, M. 2016. *50-State Comparison Loss and Restoration of Civil Rights and Firearms Privileges*. Washington, DC: National Association of Criminal Defense Lawyers.
Love, M., J. Roberts, and C. Klingele. 2013. *Collateral Consequences of Criminal Convictions: Law, Policy and Practice*. New York: Thomson West.
Lutham, R. and L. Klippan. 2016. From expected reoffender to trusted neighbor: Why we should rethink prisons. *The Conversation*, August 14. http://theconversation.com/from-expected-reoffender-to-trusted-neighbour-why-we-should-rethink-our-prisons-60114.
Mackey, A. P., A. S. Finn, J. A. Leonard, D. S. Jacoby-Senghor, M. R. West, C. F. Gabrieli, and J. D. Gabrieli. 2015. Neuroanatomical correlates of the income-achievement gap. *Psychological Science* 26: 925–933.
Martin, G. and C. L. Johnson. 2005. The boys totem town neurofeedback project: A pilot study of EEG biofeedback with incarcerated juvenile felons. *Journal of Neurotherapy* 9(3): 71–86.
Martinez, R. 1996. Latinos and lethal violence: The impact of poverty and inequality. *Social Problems* 43(2): 131–146.
McEwen, B. S. and P. J. Gianaros. 2010. Central role of the brain in stress and adaption: Links to socioeconomic status, health, and disease. *Annals of the N.Y. Academy of Science* 1186: 190–222.
McLoyd, V. C. 1998. Socioeconomic disadvantage and child development. *American Psychology* 53: 185.
McManus, J. 2018. What exactly is a public health approach to crime and disorder reduction? *The Commonplace Book*. Available at: https://jimmcmanus.wordpress.com/2018/10/03/what-exactly-is-a-public-health-approach-to-crime-and-disorder-reduction/.
McMillan, K. A., M. W. Enns, G. J. Asmundson, and J. Sareen. 2010. The association between income and distress, mental disorders, and suicide ideation and attempts: Findings from the collaborative psychiatric epidemiology surveys. *Journal of Clinical Psychiatry* 71: 1168–1175.
McWilliams, J. M. 2009. Health consequences of uninsurance among adults in the United States: Recent evidence and implications. *Milbank Quarterly* 87(2): 443–494.
Meixner, J. B. 2014. Applications of neuroscience in criminal law: Legal and methodological issues. *Current Neurology Neuroscience Reports* 15: 513.
Mercy, J. A, M. L. Rosenberg, K. E. Powell, C. V. Broome, and W. L. Roper. 1993. Public health policy for preventing violence. *Health Affairs*, Winter: 7–29.
Milam, A. J., C. D. M. Furr-Holden, and P. J. Leaf. 2010. Perceived school and neighborhood safety, neighborhood violence and academic achievement in urban school children. *The Urban Review* 42: 458–467.
Ministry of Justice. 2016. Safety in custody statistics bulletin: England and Wales. www.gov.uk/government/statistics/safety-in-custody-quarterly-update-to-june-2016.
Montague, B. T., D. L. Rosen, L. Solomon, A. Nunn, T. Green, M. Costa, et al. 2012. Tracking linkage to HIV care for former prisoners: A public health priority. *Virulence* 3 (3): 319–324.
Moore, M. H. 1993. Violence prevention: Criminal justice or public health? *Health Affairs* 12 (4): 34–45.

Muller, J. L., M. Sommers, K. Dohnel, T. Weber. M. D. Schmidt-Wilcke, and G. Hajak. 2008. Disturbed prefrontal and temporal brain function during emotion and cognitive interaction in criminal psychopathy. *Behavioral Science and Law* 26(1): 131–150.

National Coalition for the Homeless. 2009. Why are people homeless? Available at: www.nationalhomeless.org/factsheets/why.html.

National Commission on Correctional Health Care. 2002. *The Health Status of Soon-to-Be-Released Prisoners: A Report to Congress*. Chicago: National Commission on Correctional Health. www.ncchc.org/health-status-of-soon-to-be-released-inmates

National Immigration Law Center. 2014. Issue brief: The consequences of being uninsured. Available at: www.nilc.org/wp-content/uploads/2015/11/consequences-of-being-uninsured-2014-08.pdf.

Needleman, H. L., A. Schell, D. Bellinger, A. Leviton, and E. N. Allred. 1990. The long-term effects of exposure to low doses of lead in childhood: An 11-year follow-up report. *New England Journal of Medicine* 322(2): 83–88.

Noble, K. G., L. E. Engelhardt, N. H. Brito, L. Mack, E. Nail, R. F. Barr, W. P. Fifer, and A. Elliot. 2015a. Socioeconomic disparities in neurocognitive development in the first two years of life. *Developmental Psycholobiology*: DOI: 10.1002/dev.21303. www.ncbi.nlm.nih.gov/pmc/articles/PMC4821066/

Noble, K. G., S. M. Grieve, M. S. Korgaonkar, L. E. Engelhardt, E. Griffith, L. M. Williams, and A. M. Brickman. 2012b. Hippocampal volume varies with educational attainment across the life-span. *Frontiers in Human Neuroscience* 6: 307.

Noble, K. G., S. H. Houston, N. H. Brito, H. Bartsch, E. Kan, J. M. Kuperman, N. Akshoomoff, D. G. Amaral, C. S. Bloss, O. Libiger, and N. J. Schork. 2015b. Family income, parental education and brain structure in children and adolescents. *Nature Neuroscience* 18: 773–778.

Nobel, K. G., S. M. Houston, E. Kan, and E. R. Sowell. 2012a. Neural correlates of socioeconomic status in the development human brain. *Developmental Science* 15: 516–527.

Nussbaum, M. 2011. *Creating Capabilities: The Human Development Approach*. Cambridge, MA: Harvard University Press.

Office of the Surgeon General. 2001. *Youth Violence: A Report of the Surgeon General*. Washington, DC: US Department of Health and Human Services.

Ouimet, M. A. 2010. A world of homicides: The effect of economic development. Income inequality, and excess infant mortality on the homicide rate for 165 countries in 2010. *Homicide Studies* 16: 238–258.

Parker, R. N. 1989. Poverty subculture of violence, and type of homicide. *Social Forces* 67(4): 983–1007.

Parker, N., A. Pui-Yee Wong, G. Leonard, M. Perron, B. Pike, L. Richer, S. Veillette, Z. Pausova, and T. Paus. 2017. Income inequality, gene expression, and brain maturation during adolescence. *Scientific Reports* 7: DOI:10.1038/s41598-017-07735-2.

Patz, J., D. Campbell-Lendrum, T. Holloway, and J. A. Foley. 2005. Impact of regional climate change on human health. *Nature* 438(7066): 310–317.

Pew Charitable Trust. 2010. *Collateral Costs: Incarceration's Effect on Economic Mobility*. Washington, DC: Pew Charitable Trust.

Pereboom, D. 2001. *Living Without Free Will*. New York: Cambridge University Press.

Picard-Fritsche, S. and L. Cerniglia. 2013. *Testing a Public Health Approach to Gun Violence: An Evaluation of Crown Heights Save Our Streets, a Replication of the Cure Violence Model*. New York: Center for Court Innovation.

Piccolo, L. R., E. C. Merz, X. He, E. R. Sowell, and K. G. Noble. 2016. Age-related differences in cortical thickness vary by socioeconomic status. *PLos One* 11: 1–18.

Pickett, K., S. Kelly, E. Brunner, T. Lobstein, and R. Wilkinson. 2005. Wider income gaps, wider waistbands? An ecological study of obesity and income inequality. *Journal of Epidemiological Community Health* 59: 670–674.

Pickett, K. E. and R. G. Wilkinson. 2010. Inequality: An underacknowledged source of mental illness and distress. *British Journal of Psychiatry* 197: 426–428.

Poehlmann, J. 2003. New study shows children of incarcerated mothers experience multiple challenges. *Policy Institute for Family Impact Seminars*. Available at: www.purdue.edu/hhs/hdfs/fii/wp-content/uploads/2015/06/fia_nlarticle_v3i2.pdf.

Porter, S., A. Birt, and D. P. Boer. 2001. Investigation of the criminal and conditional release profiles of Canadian federal offenders as a function of psychopathy and age. *Law and Human Behavior* 25(6): 647–661.

Porter, S., L. Brinke, and K. Wilson. 2009. Profiles and conditional release performance of psychopathic and non-psychopathic sexual offenders. *Legal Criminology and Psychology* 14 (1): 109–111.

Powers, M. and R. Faden. 2006. *Social Justice: The Moral Foundations of Public Health and Health Policy*. New York: Oxford University Press.

Pridemore, W. A. 2011. Poverty matters: A reassessment of the inequality-homicide relationship in cross-national studies. *British Journal of Criminology* 51(5): 739–772.

Pruss-Ustun, A., D. Kay, L. Fewtell, and J. Bartram. 2004. Unsafe water, sanitation and hygiene. In *Comparative Quantification of Health Risks: Global and Regional Burden of Disease Attributable to Selected Major Risk Factors*, eds. M. Ezzati, A. D. Lopez, A. Rodgers, and C. J. L. Murray, pp. 1321–1352. Geneva: World Health Organization.

Public Health England & College of Policing. 2019. *Public Health Approaches in Policing: A Discussion Paper*. Available at: www.college.police.uk/What-we-do/Support/uniformed-policing-faculty/Documents/Public%20Health%20Approaches.pdf.

Quirk, D. A. 1995. Composite biofeedback conditioning and dangerous offenders: III. *Journal of Neurotherapy* 1(2): 44–54.

Raine, A. 2014. *The Anatomy of Violence: The Biological Roots of Crime*. New York: Vintage.

Raine, A., T. Lencz, S. Bihrle, L. LaCasse, and P. Colletti. 2000. Reduced prefrontal gray matter volume and reduced autonomic activity in antisocial personality disorder. *Archives of General Psychiatry* 57: 119–127.

Raine, A., R. A. Cheney, R. Ho, J. Portnoy, J. Liu, L. Soyfer, J. Hibbeln, and T. S. Richmond. 2016. Nutritional supplementation to reduce children aggression: A randomized stratified, single-blind, factorial trial. *The Journal of Child Psychology and Psychiatry* 57(9): 1038–1046.

Raine, A., J. Portnoy, J. Liu, T. Mahoomed, and J. Hibbeln. 2014. Reduction in behavior problems with omega-3 supplementation in children aged 8–16 years: A randomized, double-blind, placebo-controlled, stratified, parallel-group trial. *The Journal of Child Psychology and Psychiatry* 56(6): 509–520.

Rich, J. D., R. Chandler, B. A. Williams, D. Dumont, E. A. Wang, F. S. Taxman, S. A. Allen, J. G. Clarke, R. B. Greifinger, C. Wildeman, and F. C. Osher. 2014. How health care reform can transform the health of criminal justice-involved individuals. *Health Affairs* 33 (3): 462–467.

Rich, J. D., D. A. Wohl, C. G. Beckwith, A. C. Spaulding, N. E. Lepp, J. Baillargeon, et al. 2011. HIV-related research in correctional populations: Now is the time. *Current HIV/AIDS Reports*. 8(4): 288–296.

Richie, B. E. 2000. Challenges incarcerated women face as they return to their communities: Findings from life history interviews. *Crime and Delinquency* 47(3): 368–389.

Richie, B. E. and C. Johnsen. 1996. Abuse histories among newly incarcerated women in a New York City jail. *Journal of the American Medical Women's Association* 51(3): 111–117.

Rilling, J. K., A. L. Glenn, M. R. Jairam, G. Pagnoni, D. R. Goldsmith, H. A. Elfenbein, and S. O. Lilienfeld. 2007. Neural correlates of social cooperation and non-cooperation as function of psychopathy. *Biological Psychiatry* 67(6): 1260–1271.

Rise, M. E. and G. T. Harris. 1997. Cross-validation and extension of the violent risk-appraisal guide for child molesters and rapists. *Law and Human Behavior* 21(2): 231–238.

Rogan, W. J., et al. 2001. The effect of chelation therapy with succimer on neuropsychological development in children exposed to lead. *New England Journal of Medicine* 344(19): 1421–1426.

Rowe, M. L. and S. Goldin-Meadow. 2009. Early gesture selectively predicts later language learning. *Developmental Science* 12: 182–187.

Salekin, R. T., R. Rogers, and K. W. Sewell. 1996. A review and meta-analysis of the psychopathy checklist and psychopathy checklist-revised: Predictive validity of dangerousness. *Clinical Psychological Science* 3(3): 203–215.

Sampson, R. J. and J. H. Laub. 2003. Life-course disasters? Trajectories of crime among delinquent boys followed to age 70. *Criminology* 40: 319–339.

San Francisco Violence Prevention Services. 2019. Coordination. Available at: https://violenceprevention.sfgov.org/coordination.html.

Sareen, J., T. O. Afifi, K. A. McMillian, and G. J. Asmundson. 2011. Relationship between household income and mental disorders: Findings from a population-based longitudinal study. *Archives of General Psychiatry* 68: 419.

Sariasian, A., N. Langstrom, B. D'Onofrio, J. Hallqvist, J. Franck, and P. Lichtenstein. 2013. The impact of neighborhood deprivation on adolescent violent criminality and substance misuse: A longitudinal quasi-experimental study of the total Swedish population. *International Journal of Epidemiology* 42: 1057–1066.

Sariasian, A., H. Larsson, B. D'Onofrio, N. Langstrom, and P. Lichtenstein. 2014. Childhood family income, adolescent violent criminality and substance misuse: Quasi-experimental total population study. *British Journal of Psychiatry* 205: 286–290.

Schoenthaler, S. J. 1983a. The Alabama diet-behavior program: An evaluation at the Coosa Valley Regional Detention Center. *International Journal of Biosocial Research* 5(2): 79–87.

Schoenthaler, S. J. 1983b. Diet and crime: An empirical examination of the value of nutrition in the control and treatment of incarcerated juvenile offenders. *International Journal of Biosocial Research* 12(4): 25–39.

Schoenthaler, S. J. and I. D. Bier. 2000. The effect of vitamin-mineral supplementation on juvenile delinquency among American schoolchildren: A randomized, double-blind placebo-controlled trial. *Journal of Alternative and Complementary Medicine* 6(1): 7–17.

Shackle, S. 2018. These cities are beginning to treat violent crime as a public health issue. *Vice*, June 24, 2018. Available at: www.vice.com/en_us/article/3kydg5/these-cities-are-beginning-to-treat-violent-crime-as-a-public-health-issue.

Shen, F. X. 2010. The law and neuroscience bibliography: Navigating the emerging field of neurolaw. *Internal Journal of Legal Information*. 38: 352–399.

Siddons, E. 2018. Treating violence like a disease helped cut Colombia's murder rate by 82%. *Apolitical*, May 15. Available at: https://apolitical.co/solution_article/treating-violence-like-a-disease-helped-cut-colombias-murder-rate-by-82/.

Skogan, W. G. 2008. Evaluation of CeaseFire, a Chicago-based violence prevention program, 1991–2007. Available at: www.ncjrs.gov/pdffiles1/nij/grants/227181.pdf.

Skowyra, K. R. and J. J. Cocozza. 2006. *Blueprint for Change: A Comprehensive Model for the Identification and Treatment of Youth with Mental Health Needs in Contact with the Juvenile Justice System*. Washington, DC: National Center for Mental Health and

Juvenile Justice, PRA Associates, Inc. Available at: ncmhjj.com/wp-content/uploads/2013/12/Blueprint.pdf.

Smith, J. R., J. Brooks-Gunn, and P. Klebanov. 1997. The consequences of living in poverty for young children's cognitive and verbal ability and early school achievement. In *Consequences of Growing Up Poor*, eds. G. J. Duncan and J. Brooks-Gunn, pp. 132–189. New York: Russell Sage Foundation.

Smith, P. N. and M. W. Sams. 2005. Neurofeedback with juvenile offenders: A pilot study in the use of QEEG-based and analog-based remedial neurofeedback training. *Journal of Neurotherapy* 9(3): 87–99.

Social Metrics Commission. 2019. *Measuring Poverty 2019: A Report of the Social Metrics Commission*. Available at: https://socialmetricscommission.org.uk/wp-content/uploads/2019/07/SMC_measuring-poverty-201908_full-report.pdf.

Solitary Watch. 2012. How many prisoners are in solitary confinement in the United States? http://solitarywatch.com/2012/02/01/how-many-prisoners-are-in-solitary-confinement-in-the-united-states/.

Steadman, H. J., F. Osher, P. C. Robbins, B. Case, and S. Samuels. 2009. Prevalence of serious mental illness among jail inmates. *Psychiatric Services* 60: 761–765.

Steenland. 2011. Prisoner survival inside and outside of the institution: Implications for health-care planning. *American Journal of Epidemiology* 173(5): 479–487.

Storm, I. F., S. Thoresen, T. Wentzel-Larsen, and G. Dyb. 2013. Violence, bullying, and academic achievement: A study of 15-year-old adolescents and their school environment. *Child Abuse and Neglect* 37: 243–251.

Stouthamer-Loeber, M., E. H. Wei, D. L. Homish, and R. Loeber. 2002. Which family and demographic factors are related to both maltreatment and persistent serious juvenile delinquency? *Children's Services: Social Policy, Research, and Practice* 5: 261–272.

Stringhini, S., C. Carmeli, M. Jokela, M. Avendano, P. Muenning, F. Guida, F. Ricceri, A. D'Errico, H. Barros, M. Bochud, and M. Chadeau-Hyam. 2016. Socioeconomic status and the 25 x 25 risk factors as determinants of premature mortality: A multicohort study and meta-analysis of 1.7 million men and women. *Lancet* 389 (10075): 1229–1237.

Tiihonen, J., R. Rossi, M. Laakso, S. Hidgins, C. Testa, and G. B. Frisoni. 2008. Brain anatomy of persistent violent offenders: More rather than less. *Psychiatric Research and Neuroimaging* 163(3): 201–212.

Tottenham, N. and M. Sheridan. 2010. A review of adversity, the amygdala, and the hippocampus: A consideration of developmental timing. *Frontier of Human Neuroscience* 3: 68.

Uggen, C., R. Larson, and S. Shannon. 2016. *6 Million Lost Voters: State-Level Estimates of Felony Disenfranchisement*. Washington, DC: The Sentencing Project.

United Nations Press Release. 2017. Calling climate change direct threat, multiplier of many others at General Assembly Event, Secretary-General stresses need for urgent, decisive action. www.un.org/press/en/2017/sgsm18470.doc.htm.

United States Census Bureau. 2019. Income and Poverty in the United States: 2019. Available at: www.census.gov/library/publications/2019/demo/p60-266.html.

United States Conference of Mayors. 2015. *Hunger and Homelessness Survey: A Status Report on Hunger and Homelessness in American Cities*. http://mazon.org/assets/Uploads/Hunger-and-Homelessness-Survey.pdf

United States Environmental Protection Agency. 2010. *Our Nation's Air: Status and Trend through 2008*. Washington, DC: EPA.

Veit, R., H. Flor, M. Erb, C. Hermann, M. Lotze, W. Grodd, and N. Birbaumer. 2002. Brain circuits involved in emotional learning in antisocial behavior and social phobia in humans. *Neuroscience Letters* 328(3): 233–236.
Viding, E., E. McCroy, and A. Seara-Cardoso. 2014. Psychopathy. *Current Biology* 24(18): R871–R874.
Visher, C., S. Debus, and J. Yahner. 2008. *Employment after Prison: A Longitudinal Study of Releases in Three States*. Washington, DC: Urban Institute.
Viswanath, K. and K. Bond. 2007. Social determinants and nutrition: Reflections on the role of communication. *Journal of Nutrition Education and Behavior* 2: 20–24.
Vives-cases, C., L. Otero-Garcia, and J. Torrubiano. 2015. Intimate partner violence among women in Spain: The impact of regional-level male employment and income inequality. *European Journal of Public Health* 25: 1–7.
Waller, B. 2011. *Against Moral Responsibility*. Cambridge, MA: MIT Press.
Waller, B. 2014. *The Stubborn System of Moral Responsibility*. Cambridge, MA: MIT Press.
Wang, E. A., Y. Wang, and H. M. Krumholz. 2013. A high risk of hospitalization following release from correctional facilities in Medicare beneficiaries: A retrospective matched cohort study, 2002 to 2010. *JAMA Internal Medicine* 173(17): 1621–1628.
Weaver, C. M., J. G. Borkowski, and T. L. Whitman. 2008. Violence breeds violence: Childhood exposure and adolescent conduct problems. *Journal of Community Psychology* 36(1): 96–112.
Weaver, C. P., R. H. Moss, K. L. Ebi, P. H. Gleick, P. C. Stern, C. Telbaldi, R. S. Wilson, and J. L. Arvai. 2017. Reframing climate change assessments around risk: Recommendations for the US National Climate Assessment. *Environmental Research Letters* 12: http://iopscience.iop.org/article/10.1088/1748-9326/aa7494/pdf.
Webster, C. and S. Kingston. 2014. Anti-poverty strategies for the UK: Poverty and crime review. Project report. Joseph Rowntree Foundation. Available at: http://eprints.lancs.ac.uk/71188/1/JRF_Final_Poverty_and_Crime_Review_May_2014.pdf.
Webster, D. W., J. M. Whitehill, J. S. Vernick, and F. C. Curriero. 2013. Effects of Baltimore's safe streets program on gun violence: A replication of Chicago's CeaseFire program. *Journal of Urban Health* 90: 27–40.
Wilkinson, R. G. 1999. Health, hierarchy, and social anxiety. *Annuals of the N.Y. Academy of Science* 896: 48–63.
Williams, F. P. and M. D. McShane. 1998. *Criminological Theory: Selected Classic Readings*. Cincinnati, Ohio: Anderson Publishing.
World Bank. 2015. *Global Monitoring Report*. Available at: http://pubdocs.worldbank.org/en/503001444058224597/Global-Monitoring-Report-2015.pdf.
World Health Organization. 2002a. *World Health Report 2002*. Geneva, Switzerland: WHO.
World Health Organization. 2002b. *World Report on Violence and Health*. Geneva, Switzerland: WHO. Available at: www.who.int/violence_injury_prevention/violence/world_report/en/full_en.pdf?ua=1.
World Health Organization. 2004. *World Health Report 2004*. Geneva, Switzerland: WHO.
World Health Organization. 2005. *Air Quality Guidelines: Global Update 2005*. www.who.int/phe/health_topics/outdoorair/outdoorair_aqg/en/.
World Health Organization. 2006a. *Preventing Disease through Healthy Environments*. Geneva, Switzerland: WHO.
World Health Organization. 2006b. *Protecting Groundwater for Health: Managing the Quality of Drinking-water Sources*. London: IWA. www.who.int/water_sanitation_health/publications/PGWsection1.pdf.

World Health Organization. 2008. *Closing the Gap in a Generation: Health Equity through Action on the Social Determinants of Health. Final Report of the Commission on Social Determinants of Health.* Geneva, Switzerland: WHO.

World Health Organization. 2010. *Childhood Lead Poisoning.* Geneva, Switzerland: WHO.

World Health Organization. 2013. IARC: Outdoor air pollution a leading environmental cause of cancer deaths. International Agency for Research on Cancer, WHO. www.iarc.fr/en/media-centre/iarcnews/pdf/pr221_E.pdf.

World Health Organization. 2016a. Ambient (outdoor) air quality and health: Fact sheet. www.who.int/mediacentre/factsheets/fs313/en/.

World Health Organization. 2016b. Lead poising and health: Fact sheet. www.who.int/mediacentre/factsheets/fs379/en/.

World Health Organization. 2019. Definition of violence. Available at: www.who.int/violenceprevention/approach/definition/en/. Accessed on January 8, 2019.

World Health Organization (WHO) and Food and Agriculture Organization (FAO). 2003. *Joint WHO/FAO Expert Report on Diet, Nutrition and the Prevention of Chronic Disease.* Geneva, Switzerland: WHO.

World Health Organization and UNICEF. 2000. *Global Water Supply and Sanitation Assessment 2000 Report.* Geneva and New York: WHO and UNICEF.

Wortley, R. 2005. *Situational Prison Control.* New York: Cambridge University Press.

Wright, B. R. E, A. Caspi, T. E. Moffitt, R. A. Miech, and P. A Silva. 1999. Reconsidering the relationship between SES and delinquency: Causation but not correlation. *Criminology* 37: 175–194.

Wright, J. P., K. N. Dietrich, M. D. Ris, R. W. Hornung, S. D. Wessel, B. P. Lanphear, M. Ho, and M. N. Rae. 2008. Association of prenatal and childhood blood lead concentrations with criminal arrests in early adulthood. *PLoS Medicine* 5(5): e101.

Yang, Y., A. Raine, P. Colletti, A. W. Toga, and K. L. Narr. 2010. Morphological alterations in prefrontal cortex and amygdala in unsuccessful psychopaths. *Journal of Abnormal Psychology* 119(3): 546–554.

Yu, R., M. Aaltonen, S. Branje, T. Ristikari, W. Meeus, K. Salmela-Aro, G. M. Goodwin, and S. Fazel. 2017. Depression and violence in adolescence and young adults: Findings from three longitudinal cohorts. *Journal of American Academy of Adolescent Psychiatry* 56(8): 652–658.

Zaalberg, A., H. Nijman, E. Bulten, L. Stoosma, and C. Van der Staak. 2010. Effects of nutritional supplements on aggression, rule-breaking, and psychopathology among young adult prisoners. *Aggressive Behavior* 36(2): 117–126.

Zanarini, M. C. and F. R. Frankenburg. 2003. Omega-3 fatty acid treatment of women with borderline personality disorder: A double-blind, placebo-controlled pilot study. *American Journal of Psychiatry* 160(1): 167–169.

Zhang, X., X. Chen, and X. Zhang. 2018. The impact of exposure to air pollution on cognitive performance. *Proceedings of the National Academy of Sciences of the United States of America* 115(37): 9193–9197.

8 PUBLIC HEALTH–QUARANTINE MODEL III: HUMAN DIGNITY, VICTIMS' RIGHTS, REHABILITATION, AND PREEMPTIVE INCAPACITATION

Aagaard, L. 2014. Chemical castration of Danish sex offenders. *Journal of Bioethical Inquiry* 11 (2): 117–118.

Alexander, L., K. K. Ferzan, and S. Morse. 2009. *Crime and Culpability: A Theory of Criminal Law*. New York: Cambridge University Press.

Alliance for Safety and Justice. 2016. Crime survivors: The first-ever national survey of victims' views on safety and justice. Report available at: www.allianceforsafetyandjustice.org/wp-content/uploads/documents/Crime%20Survivors%20Speak%20Report.pdf.

Amnesty International. 2012. *Death Sentences and Executions 2011*. London: Amnesty International Publications.

Barryessa, C., J. A. Chandler, and P. Reiner. 2016. Public attitudes towards legally coerced biological treatments of criminals. *Journal of Law and the Biosciences* 3(3): 447–467.

Blumstein, A., M. Tonry, and A. Van Ness. 2005. Cross-national measure of punitiveness. *Crime and Justice* 33(1): 347–376.

Braithwaite, J. 1989. *Crime, Shame and Reintegration*. New York: Cambridge University Press.

Braithwaite, J. 2002. *Restorative Justice and Responsive Regulation*. New York: Oxford University Press.

Camp, V. and J. A. Wemmers. 2013. Victim satisfaction with restorative justice: More than simply procedural justice. *International Review of Victimology* 19(2): 117–143.

Carey, J. M. and D. L. Paulhus. 2013. Worldview implication of believing in free will and/or determinism: Politics, morality, and punitiveness. *Journal of Personality* 81(2): 130–141.

Center for Science and Law. 2012. Deep brain stimulation in rehabilitating criminal psychopaths. www.neulaw.org/blog/1034-class-blog/3972-deep-brain-stimulation-in-rehabilitating-criminal-psychopaths

Clark, C. J., P. H. Ditto, A. F. Shariff, J. B. Luguri, J. Knobe, and R. F. Baumeister. 2014. Free to punish: A motivated account of free will belief. *Journal of Personality and Social Psychology* 105(4): 501–513.

Corrado, M. L. 2001. The abolition of punishment. *Suffolk Law Review* 257.

Corrado, M. L. 2013. Why do we resist hard incompatibilism? Thoughts on freedom and punishment. In *The Future of Punishment*, ed. T. Nadelhoffer, pp. 49–78. New York: Oxford University Press.

Corrado, M. L. 2016. Chapter four: Quarantine and the problem of the third man. *UNC Legal Studies Research Paper No. 2849473*. Available at SSRN: https://papers.ssrn.com/sol3/papers.cfm?abstract_id=2849473.

Corrado, M. L. 2017. Insanity and free will: The humanitarian argument for abolition. In *The Insanity Defense: Multidisciplinary Views on Its History, Trends, and Controversies*, ed. Mark D. White, pp. 243–270. Praeger.

Corrado, M. L. 2018. Criminal quarantine and the burden of proof. *Philosophia*. Available at: https://doi-org.libproxy.lib.unc.edu/10.1007/s11406-018-0026-2.

Corrado, M. L. 2019a. Fitche and the psychopath: Criminal justice turned upside down. In *Free Will Skepticism in Law and Society: Challenging Retributive Justice*, eds. E. Shaw, D. Pereboom, and G. D. Caruso, pp. 161–176. New York: Cambridge University Press.

Corrado, M. L. 2019b. Free will fallibilism and the "two-standpoints" account of freedom. *Synthese*. Available at: https://doi.org/10.1007/s11229-019-02181-1.

Corrado, M. L. 2019c. Doing without desert. In *Free Will and Law: New Perspectives*, eds. A. McCay and M. Sevel, pp. 144–163. New York: Routledge.

Cowen, N. 2010. *Comparison of Crime in OECD Countries*. London: CIVITAS Institute for the Study of Civil Society.

Crick, F. 1994. *The Astonishing: The Scientific Search for the Soul*. New York: Touchstone.

Darwall, S. 1992. Internalism and agency. *Philosophical Perspectives* 6: 155–174.

Douglas, T. 2014. Criminal rehabilitation through medical intervention: Moral liability and the right to bodily integrity. *The Journal of Ethics* 18(2): 101–122.

Douglas, T. 2019. Nonconsensual neurocorrectives and bodily integrity: A reply to Shaw and Barn. *Neuroethics* 12(1): 107–118.

Douglas, T., P. Bonte, F. Focquaert, K. Devolder, and S. Sterckx. 2013. *Journal of Bioethical Inquiry* 10(3): 393–405.

Enns, P. 2006. *Incarceration Nation: How the United States Became the Most Punitive Democracy in the World.* New York: Cambridge University Press.

Everett, J. A., C. J. Clark, P. Meindl, J. B. Luguri, B. D. Earp, J. Graham, P. H. Ditto, and A. F. Shariff. 2019. Political differences in free will belief are driven by differences in moralization. Available at: www.researchgate.net/publication/318842505_Political_differences_in_free_will_belief_are_driven_by_differences_in_moralization.

Farrell, G. and K. Clarke. 2004. What does the world spend on criminal justice? The European Institute for Crime Prevention and Control, affiliated with the United Nations. NEUNI Paper No. 20. www.heuni.fi/material/attachments/heuni/papers/6KtlkZMtL/HEUNI_papers_20.pdf

Fischer, J. M. and M. Ravizza. 1998. *Responsibility and Control: A Theory of Moral Responsibility.* New York: Cambridge University Press.

Fletcher, G. 2000. *Rethinking Criminal Law.* New York: Oxford University Press.

Floud, J. E. and W. Young. 1981. *Dangerousness and Criminal Justice.* London: Heinemann.

Gross, H. 1979. *A Theory of Criminal Justice.* New York: Oxford University Press.

Henning, K. R. and B. Christopher Frueh. 1996. Cognitive-behavioral treatment of incarcerated offenders. *Criminal Justice and Behavior* 23: 523–541.

Huff Post. 2016. Norway proves that treating prison inmates as human beings actually works. August 3, 2016: www.huffingtonpost.com/entry/norway-prison_us_578418b6e4b0e05f05232cb7.

James, E. 2013. The Norwegian prison where inmates are treated like people. *The Guardian*, Monday, February 25: www.theguardian.com/society/2013/feb/25/norwegian-prison-inmates-treated-like-people.

Kant, I. 1785/1981. *Grounding for the Metaphysics of Morals*, trans. J. Ellington. Indianapolis: Hackett.

Kristoffersen, R. 2010. Relapse study in the correctional services of the Nordic countries. *EuroVista* 2(3): 168–176.

Lemos, J. 2013. *Freedom, Responsibility, and Determinism: A Philosophical Dialogue.* Indianapolis, IN: Hackett.

Lemos, J. 2016. Moral concerns about responsibility denial and the quarantine of violent criminals. *Law and Philosophy*. DOI: 10.1007/s10982-016-9266-0.

Lemos, J. 2018. *A Pragmatic Approach to Libertarian Free Will.* New York: Routledge.

Lewis, C. S. 1953. The humanitarian theory of punishment. *Twentieth Century: An Australian Quarterly Review* 3. Reprinted in C. S. Lewis, *God in the Dock*, ed. Walter Hooper, pp. 224–230. Grand Rapids: Willian B. Eerdmans.

Losen, D., C. Hodson, M. A. Keith II, K. Morrison, and S. Belway. 2015. Are we closing the school discipline gap? *The Center for Civil Rights Remedies*, February 23. https://civilrightsproject.ucla.edu/resources/projects/center-for-civil-rights-remedies/school-to-prison-folder/federal-reports/are-we-closing-the-school-discipline-gap

Losen, D., T. Martinez, and V. Okelola. 2014. Keeping California's kids in school: Fewer Students of color missing school for minor misbehavior. *The Center for Civil Rights Remedies*, June 10. https://escholarship.org/uc/item/3687h8gz

Matthews, R. 2006. Reintegrative shaming and restorative justice: Reconciliation or divorce? In *Institutionalizing Restorative Justice*, eds. I. Aertson, T. Daems, and L. Robert, pp. 237–260. Cullompton, Devon UK: Willan Publishing.
Morris, A. 2001. Revisiting reintegrative shaming. *Criminology Aotearoa/New Zealand* 16: 10–12.
Morris, A. 2002. Critiquing the critics: A brief response to critics of restorative justice. *British Journal of Criminology* 42: 596–615.
Morris, H. 1968. Persons and punishment. *Monist* 52: 475–501.
Morse, S. J. 1999. Neither desert nor disease. *Legal Theory* 5: 265–309.
Morse, S. J. 2018. The neuroscientific non-challenge to meaning, morals, and purpose. In *Neuroexistentialism: Meaning, Morals, and Purpose in the Age of Neuroscience*, eds. G. D. Caruso and O. Flanagan, pp. 333–358. New York: Oxford University Press.
Nadelhoffer, T., S. Bibas, S. Grafton, K. A. Kiehl, A. Mansfield, W. Sinnott-Armstrong, and M. Gazzaniga. 2012. Neuroprediction, violence, and the law: Setting the stage. *Neuroethics* 5: 67–99.
Nussbaum, M. 2011. *Creating Capabilities: The Human Development Approach*. Cambridge, MA: The Belknap Press of Harvard University Press.
Oldenquist, A. 1988. An explanation of retribution. *Journal of Philosophy* 85: 464–478.
Patterson, G. R., P. Chamberlain, and J. Reid. 1982. A comparative evaluation of a parent training program. *Behavior Therapy* 13: 638–650.
Paulhus, D. L. and J. M. Carey. 2011. The FAD-Plus: Measuring lay beliefs regarding free will and related constructs. *Journal of Personality Assessment* 93: 96–104.
Pereboom, D. 2001. *Living without Free Will*. New York: Cambridge University Press.
Pereboom, D. 2013. Free will skepticism and criminal punishment. In *The Future of Punishment*, ed. T. Nadelhoffer, pp. 49–78. New York: Oxford University Press.
Pereboom, D. 2014. *Free Will, Agency, and Meaning in Life*. Oxford: Oxford University Press.
Pereboom, D. 2016. Replies to Victor Tadros, Saul Smilansky, Michael McKenna, and
Pereboom, D. 2019. Free will skepticism and preventions of crime. In *Free Will Skepticism in Law and Society: Challenging Retributive Justice*, eds. E. Shaw, D. Pereboom, and G. D. Caruso, pp. 99–115. New York: Cambridge University Press.
Pereboom, D. and G. D. Caruso. 2018. Hard-incompatibilist existentialism: Neuroscience, punishment, and meaning in life. In *Neuroexistentialism: Meaning, Morals, and Purpose in the Age of Neuroscience*, eds. G. D. Caruso and O. Flanagan, pp. 193–222. New York: Oxford University Press.
Quirk, D. A. 1995. Composite biofeedback conditioning and dangerous offenders: III. *Journal of Neurotherapy* 1(2): 44–54.
Retzinger, S. M. and T. J. Scheff. 1996. Strategy for community conferences. In *Restorative Justice*, eds. B. Galaway and J. Ryan, pp. 315–336. Monsey, NY: Criminal Justice Books.
Richmond, E. 2015. When restorative justice in schools works. *The Atlantic*. December 29. www.theatlantic.com/education/archive/2015/12/when-restorative-justice-works/422088/
Robinson, P. H. 2008. Competing conceptions of modern desert: Vengeful, deontological, and empirical. *Cambridge Law Journal* 67(1): 145–175.
Schoeman, F. 1979. On incapacitating the dangerous. *American Philosophical Quarterly* 16: 27–35.
Scott, C. L. and T. Holmberg. 2003. Castration of sex offenders: Prisoners' rights versus public safety. *The Journal of the American Academy of Psychiatry and the Law* 31(4): 502–509.
Sentencing Project. 2017. *Still Life: America's Increasing Use of Life and Long-Term Sentences*. Washington, DC. Report available at: www.sentencingproject.org/wp-content/uploads/2017/05/Still-Life.pdf.

Shafer-Landau, R. 1996. The failure of retributivism. *Philosophical Studies* 82: 289–316.

Shariff, A. F., J. D. Greene, J. C. Karremans, J. Luguri, C. J. Clark, J. W. Schooler, R. F. Baumesiter and K. D. Vohs. 2014. Free will and punishment: A mechanistic view of human nature reduces retribution. *Psychological Science* published online June 10 1–8.

Shaw, E. 2018. Against the mandatory use of neurointerventions in criminal sentencing. In *Treatment for Crime: Philosophical Essays on Neurointerventions in Criminal Justice*, eds. D. Birks and T. Douglas, pp. 321–337. New York: Oxford University Press.

Shaw, E. 2019a. Justice without more responsibility? *Journal of Information Ethics* 28(1): 95–114.

Shaw, E. 2019b. The implications of free will skepticism for establishing criminal liability. In *Free Will Skepticism in Law and Society: Challenging Retributive Justice*, eds. E. Shaw, D. Pereboom, and G. D. Caruso, pp. 192–206. Cambridge, UK: Cambridge University Press.

Shaw, E. 2019c. The right to bodily integrity and the rehabilitation of offenders through medical interventions: A reply to Thomas Douglas. *Neuroethics* 12(1): 97–106.

Sommers, T. 2016. The three r's: Retribution, revenge, and reparation. *Philosophia* 44: 327–342.

Vilhaeur, B. 2009. Free will skepticism and personhood as a desert base. *Canadian Journal of Philosophy* 39(3): 489–511.

Vilhaeur, B. 2013a. The people problem. In *Exploring the Illusion of Free Will and Moral Responsibility*, ed. G. D. Caruso, pp. 141–160. Lanham, MD: Lexington Books.

Vilhauer, B. 2013b. Persons, punishment, and free will skepticism. *Philosophical Studies* 162 (2): 143–163.

Von Hirsch, A. and A. Ashworth. 2005. *Proportionate Sentencing: Exploring the Principles*. New York: Oxford University Press.

United States Department of Education Office for Civil Rights. 2014. Civil rights data collection: Data snapshot: School Discipline. Issue Brief No. 1, March 2014. https://files.eric.ed.gov/fulltext/ED577231.pdf

Walen, A. 2010. Crime, culpability and moral luck: Comment on Alexander, Ferzan and Morse. *Law and Philosophy* 29: 373–384.

Walen, A. 2014. Retributive justice. *Stanford Encyclopedia of Philosophy*. http://plato.stanford.edu/entries/justice-retributive/#Pro.

Walgrave, L. (ed.) 2002. *Restorative Justice and the Law*. Devon, UK: Willan Publishing.

Waller, B. 2011. *Against Moral Responsibility*. Cambridge, MA: MIT Press.

Waller, B. 2014. The culture of moral responsibility. *Southwest Philosophical Review* 30 (1): 3–17.

Waller, B. 2015. *The Stubborn System of Moral Responsibility*. Cambridge, MA: MIT Press.

Weatherburn, D. 2010. The effects of prison on adult re-offending. *Crime and Justice Bulletin NSW Bureau of Crime Statistics and Research: Contemporary Issues in Crime and Justice* 143: 1–12.

White, R. 1994. Shame and reintegration strategies: Individuals, state power and social interests. In *Family Conferencing and Juvenile Justice: The Way Forward or Misplaced Optimism?* eds. C. Alder and J. Wundersitz, pp. 181–196. Canberra ACT: Australian Institute of Criminology.

Whitman, J. Q. 1998. What is wrong with inflicting shame sanctions? *Yale Law Journal* 107: 1055–1092.

Yochelson, S. and S. Samenow. 1976. *The Criminal Personality: A Profile for Change*. New York: Aronson.

Yochelson, S. and S. Samenow. 1977. *The Criminal Personality: A Change Process*. New York: Aronson.

9 THE PUBLIC HEALTH–QUARANTINE MODEL IV FUNISHMENT, DETERRENCE, EVIDENTIARY STANDARDS, AND INDEFINITE DETENTION

Austin, J., L. B. Eisen, J. Cullen, and J. Frank. 2016. *How Many Americans Are Unnecessarily Incarcerated?* Brennan Center for Justice at New York University School of Law. Available at: www.brennancenter.org/sites/default/files/publications/Unnecessarily_Incarcerated_0.pdf.

Barber, G., R. Stone, S. Deck, V. Morris, S. Seelye, and A. Clark. 2008. *Cost of Homelessness in Metropolitan Louisville*. Louisville, KY: Coalition for the Homeless.

Boonin, D. 2008. *The Problem of Punishment*. New York: Cambridge University Press.

Bowker, L. 1980. *Prison Victimization*. New York: Elsevier.

Corrado, M. L. 2018. Criminal quarantine and the burden of proof. *Philosophia*. Available at: https://doi-org.libproxy.lib.unc.edu/10.1007/s11406-018-0026-2.

Corrado, M. L. 2019a. Fitche and the psychopath: Criminal justice turned upside down. In *Free Will Skepticism in Law and Society: Challenging Retributive Justice*, eds. E. Shaw, D. Pereboom, and G. D. Caruso, pp. 161–176. New York: Cambridge University Press.

Corrado, M. L. 2019b. Free will fallibilism and the "two-standpoints" account of freedom. *Synthese*. Available at: https://doi.org/10.1007/s11229-019-02181-1.

Donovan, S. and E. K. Shinseki. 2013. Homelessness is a public health issue. *American Journal of Public Health* 103(Supplement 2): S180.

Double, R. 2002. The moral hardness of libertarianism. *Philo* 5(2): 226–234.

Economic Roundtable. 2009. Where we sleep: Costs when homeless and housed in Los Angeles. www.economicrt.org.

Greenberg, G. A. and R. A. Rosenheck. 2008. Jail incarceration, homelessness, and mental health: A national study. *Psychiatry Service* 59(2): 170–177.

Gulcur, L., A. Stefancic, M. Shinn, S. Tsemberis, and S. Fischer. 2003. Housing, hospitalization and cost outcomes for homeless individuals with psychiatric disabilities participating in continuum of care housing first programmes. *Journal of Community and Applied Social Psychology* 13:171–186.

Huff Post. 2016. Norway proves that treating prison inmates as human beings actually works. August 3, 2016: www.huffingtonpost.com/entry/norway-prison_us_578418b6e4b0e05f05232cb7.

Irwin, J. 1980. *Prison in Turmoil*. Boston: Little Brown.

James, E. 2013. The Norwegian prison where inmates are treated like people. *The Guardian*, Monday, February 25: www.theguardian.com/society/2013/feb/25/norwegian-prison-inmates-treated-like-people.

Justice Policy Institute. 2011. Finding direction: Expanding criminal justice options by considering policies of other nations. Available at: www.justicepolicy.org/uploads/justicepolicy/documents/sentencing.pdf.

Kay, C. 2019. Short prison sentences as a last resort won't work unless the probation service is fixed. *The Conversation*, January 29. Available at: https://theconversation.com/short-prison-sentences-as-a-last-resort-wont-work-unless-the-probation-service-is-fixed-110480.

Kim, K. and B. Peterson. 2014. *Aging Behind Bars: Trends and Implication of Graying Prisoners in the Federal Prison System*. Urban Institute. Available at: www.urban.org/sites/default/

files/publication/33801/413222-Aging-Behind-Bars-Trends-and-Implications-of-Graying-Prisoners-in-the-Federal-Prison-System.PDF.

Lemos, J. 2016. Moral concerns about responsibility denial and the quarantine of violent criminals. *Law and Philosophy*. DOI: 10.1007/s10982-016-9266-0.

Lemos, J. 2018. *A Pragmatic Approach to Libertarian Free Will*. New York: Routledge.

Lutham, R. and L. Klippan. 2016. From expected reoffender to trusted neighbour: Why we should rethink our prisons. *The Conversation*, August 14: https://theconversation.com/from-expected-reoffender-to-trusted-neighbour-why-we-should-rethink-our-prisons-60114.

Mauer, M. 2016. A 20-year maximum for prison sentences. *Democracy: A Journal of Idea*. No. 39. Available at: https://democracyjournal.org/magazine/39/a-20-year-maximum-for-prison-sentences/.

Metraux, S. and D. P. Culhane. 2006. Recent incarceration history among a sheltered homeless population. *Crime and Delinquency* 52(3): 504–517.

Ministry of Justice. 2013. Compendium of re-offending statistics and analysis. Available at: https://assets.publishing.service.gov.uk/government/uploads/system/uploads/attachment_data/file/278133/compendium-reoffending-stats-2013.pdf.

Ministry of Justice. 2016. Safety in custody statistics bulletin: England and Wales. Available at: www.gov.uk/government/uploads/system/uploads/attachment_data/file/562897/safety-in-custody-bulletin.pdf.

Ministry of Justice. 2018. Offender management statistics quarterly: April to June 2018. Available at: www.gov.uk/government/statistics/offender-management-statistics-quarterly-april-to-june-2018.

Morisson, D. S. 2009. Homelessness as an independent risk factor for mortality: Results from a retrospective cohort study. *International Journal of Epidemiology* 38(3): 977–983.

Morse, S. S. J. 2018. The neuroscientific non-challenge, to meaning, morals and purpose. In *Neuroexistentialism: Meaning, Morals, and Purpose in the Age of Neuroscience*, eds. G. D. Caruso and O. Flanagan, pp. 333–358. New York: Oxford University Press.

National Health Care for the Homeless Council. 2011. Homelessness and health: What's the connection. Available at: www.nhchc.org/wp-content/uploads/2011/09/Hln_health_factsheet_Jan10.pdf.

Nazworth, S. 2014. Ability housing of northeast Florida. *Cost Benefit Analysis of Permanent Supportive Housing*. https://shnny.org/uploads/Florida-Homelessness-Report-2014.pdf

Nelkin, D. 2019. Duties, desert, and the justification of punishment. *Criminal Law and Philosophy* 13(3): 425–438.

O'Connell, J. J. (ed.) 2004. The health care of homeless persons: A manual of communicable diseases and common problems in shelters and on the streets. The Boston Health Care for the Homeless Program.

Patterson, G. R., P. Chamberlain, and J. Reid. 1982. A comparative evaluation of a parent training program. *Behavior Therapy* 13: 638–650.

Pereboom, D. 2017. A defense of free will skepticism: Replies to commentaries by Victor Tadros, Saul Smilansky, Michael McKenna, and Alfred R. Mele. *Criminal Law and Philosophy* 11(3): 617–636.

Mele, A. R. 2017. On Pereboom's disappearing agent argument. *Criminal Law and Philosophy* 11(3): 561–574.

McKenna, M. 2017. Manipulation arguments, basic desert, and moral responsibility: Assessing Derk Pereboom's *Free Will, Agency, and Meaning in Life*. *Criminal Law and Philosophy* 11(3): 575–589.

Tadros, V. 2017. Doing without desert. *Criminal Law and Philosophy* 11(3): 605–616.

Pereboom, D. 2019. Free will skepticism and preventions of crime. In *Free Will Skepticism in Law and Society: Challenging Retributive Justice*, eds. E. Shaw, D. Pereboom, and G. D. Caruso, pp. 99–115. New York: Cambridge University Press.

Pereboom, D. 2020. Incapacitation, reintegration, and limited general deterrence. *Neuroethics* 31(1): 87–97.

Prison Reform Trust. 2018. *Bromley Briefings Prison Factfile*. Autumn 2018. Available at: www.prisonreformtrust.org.uk/Portals/0/Documents/Bromley%20Briefings/Autumn%202018%20Factfile.pdf.

Robert Wood Johnson Foundation. 2009. *Housing for Homeless Alcoholics Can Reduce Costs to Taxpayers*, March 31, 2009, JAMA. www.rwjf.org/en/library/articles-and-news/2009/03/housing-for-homeless-alcoholics-can-reduce-costs-to-taxpayers.html

Robinson, P. H. 2008. Competing conceptions of modern desert: Vengeful, deontological, and empirical. *Cambridge Law Journal* 67(1): 145–175.

Scottish Government. 2019. *Criminal Proceedings in Scotland 2017-18*. Available at: www.gov.scot/publications/criminal-proceedings-scotland-2017-18/.

Singer, J. 2003. Taking it to the streets: Homelessness, health, and health care in the United States. *Journal of General Internal Medicine* 18(11): 964–965.

Smilansky, S. 1990. Utilitarianism and the "punishment" of the innocent: The general problem. *Analysis* 50: 256–261.

Smilansky, S. 2000. *Free Will and Illusion*. New York: Oxford University Press.

Smilansky, S. 2011. Hard determinism and punishment: A practical reduction. *Law and Philosophy* 30: 353–367.

Smilansky, S. 2016. Pereboom on punishment: Funishment, innocence, motivation, and other difficulties. *Criminal Law and Philosophy*. DOI:10.1007/s11572-016-9396-3.

Song, J., E. R. Ratner, D. M. Bartels, L. Alderton, B. Hudson, and J. S. Ahluwalia. 2007. Experiences with and attitudes toward death and dying among homeless persons. *Journal of General Internal Medicine* 22: 427–434.

Stewart, R. 2019. Reducing the use of short prison sentences in favour of a smarter approach. Revolving Door Agency. Available at: www.revolving-doors.org.uk/file/2347/download?token=e9wtT4iq.

Stromberg, P., et al. 2007. *The Relative Cost of Supportive Housing Services for Chronically Homeless Populations in Tulsa, Oklahoma*. Q2 Consulting, www.Q2consulting.com.

Tadros, V. 2011. *The End of Harm: The Moral Foundations of Criminal Law*. New York: Oxford University Press.

Tadros, V. 2016. *Wrongs and Crimes*. Oxford: Oxford University Press.

Tadros, V. 2017. Doing without desert. *Criminal Law and Philosophy* 11: 605–616.

Tejani, N., R. Rosenheck, J. Tsai, W. Kasprow, and J. F. McGuire. 2014. Incarceration histories of homeless veterans and progression through a national support housing program. *Community Mental Health Journal* 50: 514–519.

Tsai, J., A. S. Mares, R. A Rosenheck. 2012. Does housing chronically homeless adults lead to social integration? *Psychiatric Services* 63(5): 427–434.

Tsai, J., R. A. Rosenhack, W. J. Kasprow, and J. F. McGuire. 2013. Risk of incarceration and other characteristics of Iraq and Afghanistan era veterans in state and federal prisons. *Psychiatric Services* 64(1): 36–43.

Tsemberis, S. 2014. Housing First defined on Pathways to Housing.org, www.pathwaystohousingx.org.

United States Department of Education Office for Civil Rights. 2014. Civil rights data collection: Data snapshot: School Discipline. Issue Brief No. 1, March 2014. http://ocrdata.ed.gov/Downloads/CRDC-School-Discipline-Snapshot.pdf.

United States Sentencing Commission. 2017. *The Effects of Aging on Recidivism among Federal Offenders*. Washington, DC: United States Sentencing Commission.

Weatherburn, D. 2010. The effects of prison on adult re-offending. *Crime and Justice Bulletin NSW Bureau of Crime Statistics and Research: Contemporary Issues in Crime and Justice* 143: 1–12.

Wortley, R. 2005. *Situational Prison Control*. New York: Cambridge University Press.

Wrezel, O. 2009. Respiratory infections in the homeless. *UWO Medical Journal* 78(2): 61–65.

Zimmerman, M. J. 2011. *The Immorality of Punishment*. Buffalo, NY: Broadview Press.

Index

ability to do otherwise, 36, 40, 41, 42, 71–74
abuse, 22, 134, 135, 138, 141, 221, 222, 233–235, 236, 248, 249, 257, 268, 276, 280
  See also domestic violence
actus reus, 34, 297
Aguilar, Jesus, 67–70
Alexander, Larry, 113–117, 146
Alicke, Mark, 30
Anderson, Elizabeth, 202
Anderson, James, 262
Anderson, Nathan, 244–245, 246, 247, 248, 266
Andrade, Leandro, 25, 163
answerability, 30, 38, 286
Aristotle, 210, 218
attributability, 30, 37, 204, 286
autonomy, principle of, 187, 190–196
Ayres, Ian, 140

Baird, Amee, 132
Balaguer, Mark, 42, 54, 119
Bartle, Jarryd, 151, 166
basic desert, 2, 5, 14, 16, 21, 35, 36, 37, 38, 42, 45, 54, 70, 100, 107, 109, 110, 115, 118, 121, 122, 126, 127, 128, 134, 136, 137, 154, 171, 176, 180, 185, 191, 204, 205, 211, 212, 217, 224, 256, 271, 280, 286, 290, 297, 310
  and free will skepticism, 35–108
  and the Epistemic Argument, 109–127
  definition of, 1–3
Benaroyo, Lazare, 267
beneficence, 187, 196–198, 323
Benjamin, Georges, 238
Bentham, Jeremy, 157–158
Berlin, Isaah, 205
Berman, Mitchell, 5, 10, 11
Berofsky, Bernard, 72
big data, 267, 268
Blumstein, Alfred, 324

Bok, Hilary, 38
Boonin, David, 11, 110, 156, 178–179, 182, 313
Borkowski, John, 234
Boudry, Maarten, 112
Brahmanic jurisprudence, 143
Braithwaite, John, 290
Breivik, Andres, 326
Brito, N.H, 232
Buckareff, Andrei, 65, 67–70
Buenaventura, Maya, 262
Buggery Act of 1533, 142
Bullard, Robert, 264–266
Burgess, Anthony, 287

Campbell, C.A., 55, 118
capabilities, 29, 184, 188, 202–203, 204, 205, 206, 227, 233, 249, 271, 280
  and attachment, 202, 207, 219–221, 257
  and functionings, 202–204
  and health, 202, 207, 209–210, 257
  and opportunity freedoms, 205–206
  and personal security, 202, 207, 221–222, 257
  and reasoning, 202, 207, 210–217
  and respect, 202, 207, 222–227, 278
  and self-determination, 202, 207, 217–219, 257
  approach to justice, 29, 184, 188, 202–228, 249, 257, 278, 279
  basic, 204
  combined, 204
  internal, 204, 205, 206
cardinal proportionality, 147
Carey, Jasmine, 275, 276
causa sui, 37
causal closure, 62–65
causal exclusion problem, 65
Celello, Peter, 200, 201, 202
Cerdá, Magdalena, 254
Chisholm, Roderick, 55, 56, 67, 118

Clark, Cory, 2, 30, 31, 273
Clark, Tom, 122, 123
Clarke, Andy, 40, 66
Clarke, Randolph, 46, 55, 56
climate change, 241, 242, 264
Cochrane, Alasdair, 174, 175
Cohen, Yishai, 211, 215
compatibilism, 14, 35–39, 70–91, 109, 113, 115, 116, 117, 120, 121, 122, 127
 and hard luck, 91–106
 argument against, 70–91
 manipulation argument against, 74–91
conflict resolution principle, 29, 184, 192–196, 276, 277, 280
consequence argument, 118, 122
Corrado, Michael, 111, 112, 124–127, 286–287, 290, 292, 293, 294, 322–327
Crick, Francis, 275
culpable control model of blame, 30–31
Cure Violence Program, 254, 255, 256, 258

Dagger, Richard, 167
Darwall, Stephen, 29, 224, 226, 279
Davidson, Donald, 68
death penalty, 6, 10, 20, 29, 140, 142, 143, 148, 165, 182, 186, 271, 281
DeCaro, Mario, 149
Deery, Oisin, 85–91
dementia, 132, 133
Dennett, Daniel, 14, 26, 63, 73, 92, 93, 118, 121, 122–124, 213
Descartes, Rene, 63
desert. *See* basic desert; retributivism
 action-based, 225–226, 279
 negative, 9, 10, 149, 150
 personhood-based, 225–226, 279
 positive, 9
determinism, 4, 15, 28, 35, 36, 39, 70–91, 105, 106, 107, 113, 114, 118, 121
 and rational deliberation, 210–217
deterrence, 1, 21, 110, 137, 151, 156, 157–166, 167, 192, 270, 281, 297, 299, 303, 310–317
 general, 158, 162, 310, 311, 312
 specific (or special), 158, 311
disappearing agent objection, 45, 50, 51, 52, 53, 55, 67
Dolinko, David, 172
domestic violence, 34, 221, 222, 231, 233–235, 248, 257
Donovan, Shaun, 307
Double, Patrick, 111, 120
Double, Richard, 120, 309
downward causation, 65
drug courts, 153

dual efforts, 42, 44, 46, 47–50, 51
Duff, Antony, 135, 147, 174–182
Dunlea, James, 33

Einstein, Albert, 38
emergence, 57, 58, 61, 62, 63–67
emergent dualism, 58
Enns, Peter, 18, 25, 274
environmental discrimination, 264–266
environmental health, 238–244, 264–266, 268
epidemiology, 239, 250, 251
Epistemic Argument, 15–16, 17, 108, 109–127, 128, 129, 137, 154, 155, 176, 183, 256
Ermer, Elsa, 245
excuse-extensionism, 28

Faden, Ruth, 187–190, 191, 199–200, 202, 208, 209–211, 216, 217, 218, 219–220, 221, 222, 223, 227, 260
Fagan, Tyler, 134
Feinberg, Joel, 146, 168–170, 176, 182
Feldman, Richard, 69
Ferzan, Kimberly Kessler, 113–117, 146
Fischer, John Martin, 71, 75, 122, 223, 295
Flannery, Daniel, 234
Floud, Jean, 293
Focquaert, Farah, 29
Frankfurt, Harry, 71, 73, 75
free will
 and determinism, 36–37, 39, 70–91
 and indeterminism, 39, 40–70
 and mental causation, 60–65
 and rational deliberation, 210–217
 and the Epistemic Argument, 109–127
 arguments against, 35–108
 definition of, 1–3
 illusionism, 308–309
 implications of belief in, 30–34, 273, 275–276
 positions on, 35–39
 relevance to the criminal law, 3–9, 35, 106–108, 109–127, 168
 See also basic desert; compatibilism; free will skepticism; hard determinism; hard incompatibilism; hard luck; incompatibilism; libertarianism
free will skepticism, 8, 14–15, 20, 27, 35–108, 109–127, 128, 129, 154, 158, 167, 176, 183, 184, 185, 188, 191, 200–228, 256
 and funishment, 297–310
 and justice, 200–228
 and rational deliberation, 210–217
 and respect for persons, 222–227, 270–280
 and self-determination, 217–219

free will skepticism (cont.)
  arguments for, 35–108
  See also hard determinism; hard incompatibilism; hard luck
Frueh, Christopher, 288
funishment, 297–310

Gardoni, Paolo, 203
Gauke, David, 313
Gert, Heather, 94, 169, 170, 172–174
Gesch, Bernard, 243
Ginet, Carl, 40, 213
Gkotsi, Georgia, 267
Gladwell, Malcolm, 92
Glenn, Andrea, 133
Glick, David, 89–91
Gow, Rachel, 243
Green, Thomas Andrew, 4
Gregory, Sarah, 248
Greteman, Blaine, 267
Gruber, Aya, 148
guidance control, 71

Haas, Daniel, 83
Haji, Ishtiyaque, 57
Hampton, Jean, 166–168, 170–174, 177
Hand, Michael, 169, 170, 172–174
hard determinism, 36, 37, 39, 297
hard incompatibilism, 15, 35, 39, 106, 108, 224, 310
  argument for, 39–91
hard luck, 35, 39, 91–106, 108
Harding, David, 164
Harm Principle, 187, 191, 192, 195, 196
Hart, H. L. A., 13
Hartman, Robert, 94, 96, 100–106
Hasker, William, 58
Heaton, Paul, 262
Heiphetz, Larisa, 33
Heller, Jonathan, 249
Henning, Kris, 288
Hirstein, William, 134
Hobbes, Thomas, 71, 157
Hohensinn, Joseph, 261
holistic legal defense, 262
Holmes, Oliver Wendell, 61
homelessness, 235–237, 249, 257, 259, 306, 307, 308
Honderich, Ted, 177
human dignity, 29, 124, 125, 222–227, 258, 261, 270–280, 323
Hume, David, 75, 201
Husak, Douglas, 136

incapacitation, 1, 5, 7, 20, 21, 22, 23, 24, 25, 26, 27, 29, 126, 152, 159, 164, 166, 180, 184, 185, 189, 191, 192, 195, 197, 260, 270, 277, 292, 293, 296, 312, 323
incompatibilism, 40, 70–91, 106, 118
  leeway, 36, 71, 74
  source, 36, 71, 73, 74–91
Indeterminacy in Judgment Argument, 17, 108, 141–150, 155
indeterminism, 37, 39, 41, 42, 43, 44, 45, 46, 54, 106, 114
inequality, 23, 130, 198, 199, 204, 205, 219, 231, 232, 252, 302
informed consent, 190
insanity defense, 131, 132, 136
interventionist theories of causation, 85–91

James, William, 120
Jeppson, Sofia, 111, 212
Jones, Matthew, 4
just deserts, 15, 29, 33, 38, 91, 109, 122, 123, 125, 168, 174, 263, 270, 271, 272, 274

Kahn, Robert, 231
Kane, Robert, 41–55, 59, 119, 120
Kant, Immanuel, 10, 65, 120, 142, 147, 223, 224, 271, 272, 281
Kapitan, Tomis, 212, 213, 215
Kay, Christopher, 313
Kegan, Elena, 135
Kelly, Erin, 16, 128, 129–137, 138, 200
Kennett, Jeanette, 132
Khan, Sadiq, 253
Kiehl, Kent, 244–245, 246, 247, 248, 266
Kim, Jaegwon, 64
King, Matt, 78
Klippan, Lucy, 260, 261, 300
Koop, C. Everett, 252
Kubrick, Stanley, 287
Kyle, Chris, 132

Lamont, Julian, 146
Laufer, William, 133
Lee, Ambrose, 179–180
legal punishment, 17, 109, 110, 111, 112, 114, 115, 117, 121, 122, 127, 128, 150, 154, 156, 157, 158, 174, 256, 311
  definition of, 12–13
  See also punishment
Leibniz, Gottfried Wilhelm, 63
Lemos, John, 42, 44, 47–49, 54, 55, 120, 271, 317–322
Levin, Michael, 62
Levy, Ken, 146
Levy, Neil, 29, 37, 39, 57, 74, 94–106, 107, 122
Lewis, C.S., 26, 271
Lex Talionis, 147

libertarianism, 35–39, 40–70, 109, 114, 115, 117, 118, 120, 127, 308, 309
　agent-causal, 14, 39, 40, 55–70, 127
　argument against, 40–70
　event-causal, 14, 39, 40, 41–55, 119, 127
　negative constraint, 40
　positive constraint, 41
Limited Effectiveness Argument, 17, 108, 129, 150–154, 155
List, Christian, 40
luck, 15, 35, 37, 39, 45, 46, 47, 50, 53–54, 57, 74, 91–106
　awareness, 94
　causal, 93, 94
　circumstantial, 93
　constitutive, 15, 91, 94, 98, 99, 101, 104, 106
　present, 15, 94, 97, 99, 101, 104, 106
　resultant, 93
luck pincer, 94–106, 122
Lulham, Rohan, 260, 261, 300
Lycan, William, 84

Madoff, Bernie, 148
manipulation argument, 74–91, 122
　brain-implant malfunction case, 84–85, 88
　hard-line reply, 78–83
　soft-line reply, 78, 83–91
　Zygote example, 87–88, 89
manipulative use, 27, 29, 162, 163, 194, 195, 313
　prohibition on, 162, 164, 194, 313, 323
Marcus, Michael H., 8
Marshall, Thurgood, 19
mass incarceration, 8, 17, 25, 139, 148, 273, 281, 282
Mauer, Marc, 325
McKenna, Michael, 36, 73, 80–83, 84, 88
Meixner, John, 246
Mele, Al, 41, 42, 50–55, 57, 85, 87, 89, 97, 119
mens rea, 34, 297, 319
mental causation, 60–65
mental illness, 131, 132, 133, 153, 235–237, 258, 295
Mill, John Stuart, 191
Misalignment Argument, 17, 108, 129–137, 155
Model Penal Code, 6, 7–9, 148
Montessori, Alesander, 68
Moore, Mark, 255
Moore, Michael S., 5, 10, 150, 152
Morris, Herbert, 271, 287
Morse, Stephen, 26, 29, 61, 113–117, 146, 292, 318
Murphy, Colleen, 203
Murphy, Jeffrie, 135
Murtagh, Kevin, 159
Mustard, David, 140

Nadelhoffer, Thomas, 29, 30, 31, 32, 292
Nagel, Thomas, 91, 93
Nahmias, Eddy, 85–91
Nakamura, Kiminori, 324
naturalism, 60, 65, 121
Nelkin, Dana, 83, 94, 212, 213, 214, 215, 310
neurolaw, 246
Nichols, Shaun, 114
Nichols, Terry, 324
Nietzsche, Friedrich, 37
Noble, K.G., 232
nonmaleficence, 187, 196–198, 323
Nozick, Robert, 201
Nussbaum, Martha, 202, 203–205, 206, 207, 208, 209, 211, 217, 219, 221, 226, 280

O'Connor, Timothy, 40, 47, 55, 56, 57–59, 66, 68–70, 97
Offences Against the Person Act of 1861, 143
Oldenquist, Andrew, 271
ordinal proportionality, 147

Packer, Herbert, 4
Paulhus, Delroy, 275, 276
Pereboom, Derk, 2, 15, 20, 21, 26, 28, 29, 36, 38, 39, 40, 42, 45–46, 47, 51, 52, 57, 64, 65–67, 73, 74–78, 80–83, 85, 87, 88, 89, 111, 121, 122, 158–159, 162, 167, 184–186, 194, 195, 211, 212, 213, 214, 217, 224, 225, 256, 270, 279, 285, 286–291, 293, 297, 310–317, 321
Pettit, Philip, 205, 206, 212, 213
physical causal closure, 60
physicalism, 60, 62, 63, 65
Pickett, K.E., 231
Pigliucci, Massimo, 112
Poor Epistemic Position Argument, 17, 108, 129, 137–141, 155
poverty, 230–233, 248, 257, 258, 268, 302, 305
Powers, Madison, 187, 188, 199, 202, 208, 209–211, 216, 217, 218, 219–220, 221, 222, 223, 227, 260
precautionary principle, 116, 117, 126
presumption of harmlessness, 247, 293, 295, 296
presumption of innocence, 247, 293
principle of least infringement, 21, 26, 29, 150, 164, 185, 192, 195, 276, 277, 280, 292, 295, 323, 325
principle of normality, 29, 220, 261, 279, 301, 323
prisons
　and deterrence, 164–166
　and mental illness, 133, 258
　Bastoy Island, 260, 300, 301
　effects of, 33, 151–154, 221, 305–306
　Halden Prison, 260, 261, 300, 301
　hidden costs of, 303–310

prisons (cont.)
    Justice Center at Leoben, 260, 261, 262, 300
    Mark Prison, 260, 300
    number of people in U.S., 17–19, 273
    physical design of, 152, 221, 260–262, 300–303
    statistics, 17–19, 24, 133, 144, 145, 274
problem of evil, 163
psychopathy, 133, 134, 244–248, 266–267
    neuroscience of, 244–248
public health ethics, 20, 22, 184, 186–202, 208, 227, 248–257, 320
    and the social determinants of health, 229–248
public health–quarantine model, 1, 20–29, 124–127, 129, 150, 156, 163, 164, 166, 167, 168, 184–202, 227, 229
    and cost, 303–310
    and deterrence, 310–317
    and evidentiary standards, 317–322
    and funishment, 297–310
    and human dignity, 270–280
    and incapacitation, 20–23, 184–186, 189, 191, 192–196, 197, 257, 277, 293, 317, 320
    and indefinite detention, 270, 297, 322–327
    and innocent people, 150, 192–196, 271, 277, 280, 292, 321
    and preemptive incapacitation, 247, 267, 268, 270, 292–296
    and prevention, 248–268, 285
    and proportionality, 195, 270–280
    and public policy proposals, 257–268
    and reasons responsiveness, 286–291
    and rehabilitation, 9, 21, 24, 29, 30, 184, 186, 197, 286–291, 300–303, 304
    and social justice, 1, 20, 22, 29, 130, 187–190, 199–227, 229, 248–257, 268, 278, 279
    and victims' rights, 270, 280–286
    implications of, 23–25
    misconceptions of, 25–29, 286–291
    primary statement of, 20–23, 184–202
    See also conflict resolution principle; principle of least infringement; principle of normality;
punishment
    "use" objection, 158, 162–164, 182, 318
    and hard treatment, 169, 174, 178, 180, 181
    and innocent people, 150, 158, 160–162, 192–196, 270, 277
    communicative theories of, 1, 156, 168–182, 183
    consequentialist theories of, 1, 21, 27, 137, 156, 157–166, 182, 185, 192, 277, 318
    expressive theories of, 156, 166, 168–182, 183
    mixed theories of, 129, 156, 174–182
    moral education theories of, 1, 156, 166–168, 182
    See also legal punishment; retributivism

quarantine, 13, 20, 21, 22, 185, 186, 187, 189, 190, 191, 192, 194, 197, 198, 319, 320
Quirk, Douglas, 267

Rachlinski, Jeffrey, 140
racism, 23, 33, 131, 138, 144, 199, 200, 265
radical emergentism. See emergence
Radzik, Linda, 169, 170, 172–174
Raine, Adrian, 133, 243
Ravizza, Mark, 71, 75
Rawls, John, 200, 201, 226
reactive attitudes, 26, 113, 114, 121, 122
Reagan, Ronald, 33
reasons responsiveness, 27, 36, 71, 122, 125, 286–291
recidivism, 18, 27, 151, 153, 155, 165, 198, 229, 238, 244, 250, 274, 302, 305, 325
Reid, Thomas, 41, 55
respect for persons, 29, 125, 222–227, 270–280 See human dignity
responsibility. See basic desert; answerability; attributability; take charge responsibility
restorative justice, 285, 289
retributivism
    and desert, 1, 5–9, 11, 35, 106–108, 110, 125, 128, 129–141, 174, 175, 176, 177, 198, 270, 272
    and judging gravity, 141–150, 271, 323
    and proportionality, 5–8, 17, 124, 125, 128, 137, 141–150, 154, 270–280, 322, 326
    and respect for persons, 270–280
    definition of, 1, 4–5
    expressive, 170–174
    limited, 8
    weak, moderate, and strong, 9–12
    See also Epistemic Argument; Indeterminacy in Judgment Argument; Limited Effectiveness Argument; Poor Epistemic Position Argument; Skeptical Argument
retributivist tracking dilemma, 141
Rich, J.D., 238, 259
right of self-defense. See self-defense
Ristroph, Alice, 146, 148, 149, 150
Robeyns, Ingrid, 202, 205–206
Robinson, Paul, 283
Routh, Eddie Ray, 131

Samenow, Stanton, 288
Satcher, David, 252
Scanlon, Thomas, 38
Schier, Elizabeth, 132
Schinkel, Marguerite, 177
schizophrenia, 132
Schoeman, Ferdinand, 194, 292
Scholten, Matthé, 132
Schopenhauer, Arthur, 38

self-defense, 20, 21, 23, 26, 27, 126, 127, 136, 150, 159, 162, 164, 166, 178, 179, 185, 186, 192, 193, 194, 195, 196, 228, 277, 296, 310, 311, 316, 317, 326
self-forming actions, 42–44, 51, 53
Sen, Amartya, 202, 203, 204, 205, 207
Shackle, Samira, 252, 253, 254, 257
Shariff, Azim, 2, 3, 30, 31, 32, 275, 276, 277
Shaw, Elizabeth, 29, 111, 162, 194, 278, 279, 280
Shebaya, Sirine, 187–190, 191, 199–200
Shinseki, Eric, 307
Shoemaker, David, 37, 132, 133
Sie, Maureen, 31
Sifferd, Katrina, 61, 134, 136
Skeptical Argument against retributivism, 17, 35–108, 128, 129, 154
Smilansky, Saul, 26, 200, 297–310, 317, 320
social adversity defense, 134–135, 139
social determinants of criminal behavior, 20, 22, 23, 30, 229–248, 249, 257, 268
social determinants of health, 20, 22, 23, 229–248, 257, 268
social justice, 22, 186, 187, 188, 190, 199–227, 249, 264, 268, 278, 279
socioeconomic status. *See* poverty
solitary confinement, 18, 197, 274
Sommers, Tamler, 286
source incompatibilism, 74–91
sourcehood, 36, 71, 73, 78–79, 85–91
Stewart, Rory, 314
Stråge, Alva, 107
Strawson, Galen, 121, 122
Strawson, P.F., 26, 28, 114, 118, 121, 122

Tabandeh, Armin, 203
Tadros, Victor, 27, 111, 162–164, 194, 310
take charge responsibility, 30, 38
Taylor, Richard, 56, 59, 118, 211, 213
Ten, C.L., 159

Tierney, Hannah, 89–91
Todd, Patrick, 74, 83
Tognazzini, Neal, 78–80
Tonry, Michael, 134–135, 138
Typhoid Mary, 326

utilitarianism, 157, 158, 161, 185

Van Gulick, Robert, 63, 64
van Inwagen, Peter, 36, 97, 118, 120, 212, 214, 215
Vargas, Manuel, 2, 14, 54, 119
Vicens, Leigh, 50
victims' rights, 168, 270, 280–286
Vilhauer, Benjamin, 15, 29, 111, 112–113, 223, 225–226, 279
von Hirsh, Andreas, 135
voter disenfranchisement, 19, 24, 263

Waldfogel, Joel, 140
Walen, Alec, 9, 11, 13, 146, 147, 149, 270, 283
Wallace, Jay, 75
Waller, Bruce, 28, 29, 38, 39, 92, 118, 121, 122, 256, 272, 273, 275
Weaver, Chelsea, 234
Western, Bruce, 138
Whitman, Thomas, 234
Wilkinson, R.G., 231
Wittgenstein, Ludwig, 13
Wortley, Richard, 260

Yaffe, Gideon, 134
Yang, Yaling, 245
Yochelson, Samuel, 288
Yoffe, Emily, 139
Young, Warren, 293

Zaibert, Leo, 9, 12
Zimmerman, Michael, 12, 13, 110, 143, 313
Zohny, Hazem, 193